O9-AID-718

CASEWORK
A PSYCHOSOCIAL THERAPY

CASEWORK
A PSYCHOSOCIAL THERAPY
FOURTH EDITION

Mary E. Woods

and

Florence Hollis

McGRAW-HILL PUBLISHING COMPANY

New York St. Louis San Francisco Auckland Bogotá Caracas
Hamburg Lisbon London Madrid Mexico Milan Montreal New Delhi
Oklahoma City Paris San Juan São Paulo Singapore Sydney Tokyo Toronto

This book was set in Palatino by the College Composition Unit
in cooperation with Monotype Composition Company.
The editors were Phillip A. Butcher and Laura D. Warner.
The production supervisor was Stacey B. Alexander.
The cover was designed by Carla Bauer.
R. R. Donnelley & Sons Company was printer and binder.

CASEWORK

A Psychosocial Therapy

Copyright © 1990, 1981, 1972, 1964 by Florence Hollis and Mary E. Woods. All rights reserved. Printed in the United
States of America. Except as permitted under the United States Copyright Act of 1976, no part of this publication may be
reproduced or distributed in any form or by any means, or stored in a data base or retrieval system, without the prior
written permission of the publisher.

1 2 3 4 5 6 7 8 9 0   DOC   DOC   9 5 4 3 2 1 0

ISBN 0-07-557294-X

Library of Congress Cataloging-in-Publication Data

Woods, Mary E., (date).
    Casework, a psychosocial therapy / Mary E. Woods and Florence Hollis.—4th ed.
        p.   cm.
    Hollis' name appears first on the earlier edition.
    Includes bibliographical references.
    ISBN 0-07-557294-X
    1. Social casework.   2. Psychotherapy—Social aspects.
I. Hollis, Florence.   II. Title.
HV43.W64   1990
    361.3'2—dc20   89-13962

Contents

FOREWORD   vii
PREFACE   ix
TRIBUTE TO FLORENCE HOLLIS   xiii

Part One   THE THEORETICAL FRAMEWORK

1   **Casework Today**   3

2   **The Psychosocial Frame of Reference: An Overview**   25

3   **Examples of Clinical Social Work Practice**   61

4   **Classifications of Casework Treatment**   85

Part Two   TREATMENT: AN ANALYSIS OF PROCEDURES

5   **Sustainment, Direct Influence, and Exploration-Description-Ventilation**   105

6   **Reflective Discussion of the Person-Situation Configuration**   124

7   **Reflective Consideration of Pattern-Dynamic and Developmental Factors**   135

8   **Psychosocial Therapy and the Environment**   147

9   **Studying and Working with the Typology**   180

Part Three   DIAGNOSTIC UNDERSTANDING AND
              THE TREATMENT PROCESS

10   The Client-Worker Relationship   201

11   Initial Interviews and the Psychosocial Study   230

12   Assessment and Diagnostic Understanding   246

13   Diagnostic Understanding and Choice of
      Treatment Objectives   271

14   Diagnostic Understanding and Choice of
      Treatment Procedures   288

15   Family Therapy and Psychosocial Casework:
      A Theoretical Synthesis   305

16   The Clinical Practice of Family Therapy   335

17   Couple Treatment: Problems in Relationships   374

18   Couple Treatment: Clinical Issues and Techniques   404

19   Crisis Intervention and Brief Treatment   426

20   Termination   443

21   The Psychosocial Approach: Clinical Case Examples   453

      IN CONCLUSION   485
      APPENDIX   492
      BIBLIOGRAPHY   495
      INDEX   525

Foreword

When Mary Woods invited me to write a foreword to this important book—a further contribution by the Hollis-Woods team—I accepted with profound appreciation. Few, if any, books in social work have gone to a fourth edition. This indeed speaks to its importance. What has impressed me most about this book is its continuance of a theme so important in the three earlier editions: the quest for excellence. The first edition of *Psychosocial Therapy* by Florence Hollis was published in 1964; the current revision was completed by Woods after Hollis's death in 1987. As the times, knowledge, and practice have changed, this quest for excellence has provided new and up-to-date perspectives in each edition.

Psychosocial theory and the therapy emerging from it constitute an open, reaching, developing system. The theory does not here present itself in a dogmatic fashion, nor has it ever done so. Rather, the authors clearly take the position that this theory is the result of careful analysis of practice as it has evolved over the last three decades. It does not reject the past and our rich tradition, as some would, but builds on what has gone before and, by acknowledging and identifying change, develops new concepts for contemporary practice exigencies. In a note to me shortly before her death, Hollis referred to herself as an "explorer"; indeed, she was just that over her entire career. We can see the qualities of the explorer once again in this new edition by Woods and Hollis.

What is of particular importance in this revision is a growing comfort with diversity. Our profession has for too long sought a unitary, all-encompassing understanding of the highly complex realities with which we are faced in practice. This is not possible in a field such as ours; nor will it be possible in the foreseeable future, if ever.

This is a system that applies "across the board." Since across-the-board application may be differentially effective, it is our task to accept this variability, study it, seek to understand it, and—as indicated by the authors over the course of the book—modify the theory to make it even more effective across the board.

As in earlier editions, the book begins with an identification of changes in practice that need to be addressed to ensure that the content is contemporary.

Within the text, Woods and Hollis choose to continue use of the term "casework," among others, to describe the activities of a practitioner. However, they make it clear that a plurality of interventive methods is included in the practitioner's armamentarium. In this regard, the two new chapters (17 and 18) on couple treatment are a most important addition. This modality of clinical interviewing has too long appeared to be the "forgotten" method, and it deserves more attention. We continue to find additional uses for this method in work with other important dyads; Woods and Hollis mention some of these.

Of particular interest is the manner in which the material addresses cultural differences and the necessity for practice to be ethnically and culturally sensitive and aware. As the theory and practice of psychosocial therapy are becoming effectively used in an ever-broadening, worldwide context, this book and its earlier editions have been well received and useful in the international community. Writing like this helps us move away from the stereotypical perception that all social work theory has been developed from a North American perspective and inappropriately applied, or at times imposed, in other parts of the world.

Once again, Woods and Hollis stress the responsibility of our profession and all who practice therein to continue the process of building knowledge. I suggest that we are now past the day of the dramatic breakthrough of new knowledge. We are becoming more and more aware of the complexities of our practice and of the stages involved in the difficult task of doing solid evaluation research. We must be more humble about our expectations of research and accept that our knowledge will advance slowly as it does in other fields. But advance it will and must, as this volume demonstrates.

As before, Mary Woods and Florence Hollis have written a text that should be considered essential reading for practitioners at all levels, teachers and students alike. It is a book with import for social workers in many countries.

This fourth edition of *Casework: A Psychosocial Therapy* marks the end of an important phase in the history of social work clinical practice. It is not my task to write a eulogy of Florence Hollis here. Mary Woods has done so, beautifully and accurately, in her Tribute; others have done and will do the same at other times and places. But I do want to comment on how sad it is that this book includes the final writings of Florence Hollis for the profession, the last chapter of a long, rich, diverse, and powerfully effective series of contributions to social workers the world over. This is the end of an era. We have lost a pioneer. But, generously and thoughtfully, she left us with a foundation upon which to build. We must see this book as a new beginning, as a significant step in the development of knowledge in the theory and practice of the psychosocial tradition in social work.

We accept the challenge of these two colleagues and move forward.

Francis J. Turner

Mandel School of Applied Social Science
Case Western Reserve University
Cleveland

Preface

Casework: A Psychosocial Therapy is designed to give a clear presentation of the psychosocial approach. It deals with the "hows" and "whys" of clinical social work practice in the treatment of psychological, interpersonal, and social problems. The early chapters of the book describe the development of the approach, its roots in casework practice. The personality theory on which it operates—ego psychology, developmental and object relations concepts in a psychoanalytic context—is outlined in Chapter 2. Also in this chapter are discussions of the many concepts from other social and psychological theories upon which the psychosocial approach draws, including ecological and systems theories, family therapy, communication and role theories, plus other pertinent social science concepts and data. Throughout the text, theory is closely related to practice. Detailed illustrations are presented to demonstrate long-term and brief treatment cases; individual, couple, and family theory; and environmental interventions. Case materials describe work with voluntary and involuntary clients, with clients of various socioeconomic and cultural backgrounds, ages, and lifestyles.

Florence Hollis's research in identifying and classifying treatment procedures continues to be at the heart of this text. The evolution of her typology of worker-client communications and environmental procedures is outlined in Chapters 4 and 9, and its ongoing value for research and theory building is discussed. In Chapters 5 through 8 the procedures—the treatment techniques—are analyzed in detail and further explained by means of case examples. The applicability of the typology to clinical practice with individuals, couples, families, and collaterals is illustrated throughout the book.

This new edition has been revised and expanded to include many developments of recent years, demonstrating how they can be assimilated by the psychosocial approach. Requests from students, colleagues, and reviewers have resulted in four new chapters. Chapters 17 and 18 address special diagnostic and treatment issues involved in marital therapy; they also include sections on premarital counseling, cross-cultural relationships, gay and lesbian couples, special concerns of women, and extramarital affairs. Chapter 19 on crisis intervention and brief treatment and

Chapter 20 on termination are added to fill a need not met by earlier editions.

In greater detail and with deeper understanding than previously, we have endeavored to demonstrate that in both theory and practice, in every phase of clinical work, ecological and systems concepts can and must be integrated with psychodynamic theory; whether the immediate case or focus involves individual, conjoint, or environmental treatment, this synthesis is emphasized throughout the text. Some of the benefits and hazards of clinical diagnosis are addressed in this edition. The client-worker relationship chapter and other chapters have been expanded, with additional attention given to transference, countertransference, worker burnout, and mutuality. Other matters, including resistance, differences between worker and client, single-parent families and stepfamilies, adult children of alcoholics, and ethnicity, have been discussed in greater detail. More has been added to include current thinking on diagnosis and treatment of personality disorders. Discussions about unconscious phenomena have been commented upon in various parts of the book rather than relegated to a single chapter. Case materials are from recent clinical work and reflect some of the new kinds of treatment approaches used in various settings. Again, in response to requests, the chapter order has been changed slightly, with the hope that the new sequence will seem more logical to readers and instructors.

This fourth edition documents one more step in the growth of an approach to casework practice that has been developing for many years. We continue to be impressed by the soundness of psychosocial casework as a theoretical system. It is obviously an open system, constantly incorporating new ideas as well as corrections of old ideas, constantly expanding. While the system has a "skin" permeable enough to take in some of the new, it is resistant to ideas that have not been tested in practice or that are incompatible with its theoretical principles or value base. Change is therefore gradual, through assimilation rather than through assault. Comparison of the four editions of this book will clearly demonstrate this process. Chapter notes and the bibliography include references spanning more than fifty years, further attesting to both the continuity and the changes in direct casework practice, a practice that now serves more people than ever.

In our first chapter we have included a discussion of recent social trends and modifications in practice, a brief history of the development of the psychosocial approach from the "diagnostic" or "differential" approach, comments on education for clinical social work specialization, and a section on the empirical base of psychosocial casework, including some remarks on current research issues.

The principles on which diagnostic-differential casework was founded continue to be basic to psychosocial casework, but their interpretation and application in practice have changed in many ways and have been greatly expanded.

ACKNOWLEDGMENTS

My most profound appreciation goes to Florence Hollis for inviting me to share in the writing of the third edition and entrusting me with the fourth. Fortunately, before she died, I was able to tell her how much this opportunity has meant to me. In spite of her modest ways, I think she believed me.

My part in this book, started by Florence Hollis, in 1964, is the culmination of many influences in my life, professional and personal. It is not possible to acknowledge—or even to identify in my own mind—each person who has touched me or helped to shape my ideas. However, apart from my family, the hundreds of clients I have seen over the years—the many courageous people through whom I learned so much about painful human conditions and about the imaginative ways that can be found to struggle against personal miseries and environmental assaults—have taught me the most. Above all, my clients taught me the value of true listening, of mutuality, of self-direction, of tailoring each piece of work to the uniqueness of the person and his or her circumstances, and of humility. The very "demanding" or "recalcitrant" clients still often teach me the most.

I am also indebted to those students and supervisees whose fresh ideas, optimism, deep concern for people's suffering, and eagerness to find ever better ways to help challenge me to explore further, to look at old and new problems in new ways. I have been most fortunate to have had the opportunity to learn along with them.

Colleagues at Hunter College School of Social Work may be surprised to read here how important their support, confidence, and suggestions—even those offered in passing—have been to me and to this revision. Particular thanks go to Florence Vigilante. Harold Lewis, Mildred Mailick, Eileen Marshack, Maria Rosenbloom, and Robert Salmon have been most generous in their own special ways. Rebecca Donovan kindly provided some last-minute help.

My good friend and colleague, Dorothy Kitchell, carefully went over every chapter and offered important suggestions and invaluable encouragement; I am grateful beyond words for the hours she spent reading and reacting. Again with extraordinary generosity, Juliene Berk brought her editorial talents to several sections of the manuscript, and again her advice led to tighter, clearer text. Still another dear friend, Elmeta Phillips, organized many scraps of paper and miraculously produced the Bibliography, working uncomplainingly against the tight time frame I imposed. Words cannot adequately express my gratitude to these friends.

Others who freely gave support and help and/or were instrumental in directing me to case materials include Jane Bloomer, Linda Kurtz, Avra Mark, Carolyn Neuman, Julie Patton, Nina Shilling, and Susan Solomon. Anonymous reviewers also deserve thanks for very useful suggestions, many of which led to improvements and additions to the new revision. And I am grateful to Laura Warner, my Editing Supervisor at McGraw-Hill, for her patience, interest, and helpful suggestions.

I want to mention again a few of the many people who significantly influenced me in one way or another over the course of my professional development: the late Lucille Austin, Andre Ferber, Thelma Samson, and Maurice Shilling. The impressions they made endure and continue to influence my work and my writings.

Last, but far from least, I am very pleased that Francis J. Turner—an esteemed colleague and friend, and a person very dear to Florence Hollis—agreed to write the Foreword. Flo knew he would be doing this and was delighted. Thank you, Frank.

Mary E. Woods

Tribute to Florence Hollis

A native of Philadelphia, Florence Hollis did her undergraduate work at Wellesley College and received her master's degree from Smith College School of Social Work in 1931 and her doctorate from Bryn Mawr School of Social Work and Social Research in 1947. Her social work career began while she was an undergraduate and, after her graduation from Smith, she was immediately assigned to a leadership position at the Family Society in Philadelphia. Through the depression years, she worked at family agencies in Philadelphia and also in Cleveland, where she taught part time at Western Reserve University. For five years during the 1940s, Dr. Hollis was editor of the *Journal of Social Casework*. In 1947, she joined the faculty at the Columbia University School of Social Work, where she was a highly esteemed professor of casework in the master's and doctoral programs until her retirement in 1972. While at Columbia, she developed her typology of casework procedures, which became the basis for ongoing and rigorous research into worker-client communica-

tion and the casework process; her classification and the research based upon it have been at the core of all editions of this widely used text, which has been translated into several languages. During her years on the faculty of Columbia, she also taught many summer sessions at Smith and frequently conducted seminars and institutes in this country and abroad. She was active on academic committees and professional councils, including the Council on Social Work Education. Over the course of her career, she published three books and over forty articles on casework. As part of her very busy life, Florence Hollis saw clients on a regular basis; she considered this essential to the successful performance of her other professional roles.

I first met Florence Hollis when I was a student, in the early 1960s. Because she was interested, as I was, in an exchange of our sometimes divergent points of view, we had lunch and good conversations from time to time over the next several years. It was not until

1977, however, when she invited me to collaborate on the third edition of this book, that I spent extended amounts of time with her. From then on, until a few weeks before her death, I visited her several times a year at her lovely retirement home, Crosslands, at Kennett Square, Pennsylvania, and was in frequent contact with her by telephone. As her student, colleague, and coauthor, and as a friend to Flo Hollis, I feel most privileged to have known her.

When I was a student, Flo's interest in studying the relationship between casework and social class led her to urge her students—perhaps especially those of us with outlooks that were somewhat different from her own—to bring their thinking and casework experiences to the subject. She absorbed our suggestions and included many of them in her important paper published in *Social Casework* in October 1965, making sure to credit us with our contributions. As all who were taught by her know, she regularly sought and took serious students' ideas and reactions to her thinking.

As colleagues and coauthors of the third edition, we worked together closely for over two intense years. Always challenged, often exhilarated, occasionally frustrated, we hammered out our perspective and shared our ideas—surprised and pleased at how a meeting of the minds or new realizations often emerged from initially different slants on a particular question. We worked together also on the plans for revisions and additions to the fourth edition until her illness made this impossible.

Flo brought a spirit of mutuality and openness to our joint endeavors. In spite of her revered position in the field, she was modest, always eager to search for and consider new ideas and strategies that might enhance casework practice, *if these were grounded in real experience.* The accumulation of abstract knowledge had little meaning to her if it could not be used on behalf of distressed people who turn to caseworkers for help. With Immanuel Kant, she firmly believed "Experience without theory is blind, but theory without experience is mere intellectual play."

In fact, Flo chose me to help to revise her text because of my strong background in clinical work in general, and also because of my special interest, training, and experience in family and marital treatment—in conjoint therapy—a modality with which she herself had little involvement. Just a few months before her death, as we discussed the fourth edition and our plans to include two new chapters on couple treatment, she said that she wanted me to remark on the changes that had evolved in her thinking since the publication of her well-known *Women in Marital Conflict* in 1949. It was important to her that students and others who would be reading the new book recognize the need to be ever open to consonant new ideas, data, and theory as these emerge. Thus, while Florence Hollis strongly urged us to preserve and protect the years of knowledge derived from day-in, day-out casework experiences with clients—knowledge that has proved its value—for fifty years she was also in the forefront of those who had developed the psychosocial approach that was *specifically designed* to assimilate new information.

To the end, Florence Hollis took a serious interest in social and political matters. She was very disturbed by the cutbacks in federal funding of social programs that occurred during the Reagan administration. She was deeply concerned about what she saw as the deterioration of standards and values in the country and the world, particularly when people's health and well-being were directly affected. She abhorred poverty, war, and injustice of all kinds. From her sickbed she spoke often of the hideous conditions endured by growing numbers of homeless individuals and families. As all who knew her well can attest, she never hesitated to stand up and be counted for her strong convictions, even when these were unpopular. In her personal relationships, in her pioneering role in the development of casework, and in her worldview, she was uncompromisingly ethical. She was dedicated to seeking means to bring out the best in people and their situations, and to right the wrongs when she could.

For eight years she knew that she had lymphoma; she was indignant when the doctors told her—at age seventy-two—that she would be lucky to have ten more years. She wanted to reach the nineties, hers and the twentieth century's. Her mother had lived to ninety-one. When it became apparent in the last year that she would succumb sooner than she had hoped, she faced the facts squarely, complained very little, and made the best of the time she had left, letting go of life only after the price was too high and the rewards too few. Flo had an extraordinary religious faith that not only guided her through life but comforted her in her final years and days. From close friends who tended her daily in the Crosslands infirmary where she lived for several months, we learned that she died peacefully and willingly.

As a practitioner, educator, researcher, and author and, equally important, as a woman of integrity and caring, Florence Hollis made a contribution to modern-day clinical social work that is beyond measure. I am among hundreds who are grateful to her. She will endure in the memories of those who knew her; her wisdom will be passed on to many others through her writings.

I did not know just how much I would miss her. The revision of the book has been far lonelier without her. But I am fortunate to have gotten to know the many facets of Florence Hollis over her final decade. It means a lot to me to tell the readers of the fourth edition even these few things about her. I hope to have conveyed how much she deserves to be remembered.

Mary E. Woods

CASEWORK
A PSYCHOSOCIAL THERAPY

PART ONE

The Theoretical Framework

CHAPTER 1

Casework Today

The concern of this book is the description and analysis of the psychosocial approach to casework. Its ultimate purpose is to contribute to the improvement of the quality of casework or clinical social work treatment offered to individuals and families facing personal and social dilemmas with which they are not fully able to cope. These dilemmas have to do with the situations in which they live, their interpersonal relationships, their physical health, their individual functioning, or some combination of these elements. We will endeavor to analyze the dynamics of treatment procedures in such a way that the essential principles underlying them are sufficiently clear to enable readers to enhance their own treatment skills.

The psychosocial framework described in this book is an open system of thought. It has been able to assimilate many extensions of the knowledge and practices of earlier years. The increase of the range of knowledge creates a large learning task for all casework practitioners, those with experience and those just entering the field. Relatively little that the worker knew and used forty years ago has become obsolete. Instead, the knowledge base has been expanded, built upon, and enriched, so that today there is much more to learn than in earlier years and a wide range of approaches to study before the worker finds his or her own treatment emphases and preferences for specialization in practice.

The psychosocial approach includes in its methodology and in its applicability help with concrete practical problems and with interpersonal and intrapersonal difficulties. Naturally, different types of difficulty call for different emphases and techniques, *but the central principles apply across the board.* The typology of treatment procedures described in this book is appropriate to *any* clientele, even if it is applied in different ways to suit various client situations. The psychosocial approach was developed primarily in work with clients who voluntarily sought help or who, if reached out to or referred by others, became clients when they recognized that the caseworker was offering a service that might be helpful. In recent years, more and more efforts are being made to provide services to involuntary clients or to others who do not recognize a need for help as perceived by others or who do not trust the caseworker as a potential helper.

We will endeavor throughout to demonstrate the operational meanings of concepts by references to actual cases and clients (who have been disguised, of course) ranging from brief illustrations to fairly detailed case summaries. A broad range of voluntary and involuntary clients has been included. We believe that such concrete illustrations have the value of enhancing understanding of how principles and concepts are applied and of suggesting ways in which casework can be skillfully practiced.

We will begin this chapter with a discussion of recent developments in psychosocial casework knowledge and practice. This will be followed by a brief presentation of relevant historical background, designed to give the reader an understanding of some of casework's roots, and specifically of the context from which the psychosocial approach emerged and evolved. We will then offer a few comments on education for specialization in clinical social work. A final section will be devoted to considering the empirical base of casework on which theory is built and treatment processes and results may be studied; some problems in research are described.

RECENT DEVELOPMENTS

In the period between the original publication of this book (1964) and its present fourth edition there have been social trends and client requirements that have significantly affected every aspect of casework. Problems that come to the attention of social and health agencies have expanded. Large numbers of individuals and families are increasingly affected by teenage pregnancy, drug and alcohol problems, teenage suicide, the AIDS epidemic, the crisis of homelessness exacerbated by housing shortages and the deinstitutionalization of the mentally ill, the severe economic problems facing farmers and rural communities, widespread substandard education, chronic poverty, family violence, and child neglect.

Veterans of war and victims of rape and other crimes have brought attention to the phenomenon of posttraumatic stress. Tensions between various racial and ethnic groups have increased in some areas of the country. Many legal and illegal immigrants and refugees experience a broad range of difficulties. Only in recent years have the extent of incest and sexual abuse of children and the toll these take on personality development and on future relationships been so widely recognized. Casework practice has been stimulated—sometimes challenged and prodded—by the women's, gay and lesbian, and civil rights movements, that continue to mature and to shape our attitudes and thought. The high divorce rate, the increase in single-parent households and stepfamilies, the large number of women in the work force, and the need for day care planning have all influenced recent approaches to casework practice. In all walks of life the importance of clear communication has increased; value is placed on the open expression of feelings and ideas among people who are living or working closely together. Far more often than even a few years ago, the realities of terminal illness and death are frankly discussed; the dying patient and those who survive are freer to share grief with each other.[1]

More people than ever are seeking some kind of therapy for predictable life crises and transitions. While large numbers of clients have deep-seated family or emotional troubles or have to cope with noxious social conditions or catastrophic events, many other individuals and families view treatment as a means of prevention or as an opportunity for personal growth. Decreased support from family, church, and stable neighborhoods has given impetus to a search for "self-realization." With growing social acceptance of a wide range of lifestyles, casework help is frequently sought in order to consider new kinds of choices. Some clients want to learn how to be more effectively "assertive." Probably more than ever, caseworkers concern themselves with the development of conditions and capacities for health rather than only with the ameliorization of pathology. As this book will illustrate over and over again, more often than not, casework interventions are not directed at "sickness," but are fashioned to promote strengths and growth.[2] Practice continues to evolve to meet constantly changing needs and attitudes. Many, but of course not all, of these areas will be discussed to one degree or another over the course of this text.

Recent years have also seen positive shifts in general attitudes toward family and mental health services. Some people and groups who avoided treatment now seek it more readily; more men, more poor people, more individuals and families from certain ethnic backgrounds who in the past tended to shy away from any kind of social or psychological services are now voluntarily on the caseloads of social workers and other mental health professionals. It was estimated in 1981 that *34 million people in the United States were receiving professional psychotherapy or counseling.* This figure probably does not include those clients of social workers in some institutional settings, such as hospitals, nursing homes, schools, and day care centers. It is also probable that the number has steadily increased.

The division of labor among helping professionals has shifted remarkably over the course of a single decade. In 1975 there were 26,000 psychiatrists and 25,000 social workers providing psychotherapy in the United States. By 1985 *clinical social workers outnumbered psychiatrists almost two to one, with 60,000 social workers and 38,000 psychiatrists offering psychotherapy.* Of all mental health practitioners, clinical social workers, many of whom are in part- or full-time private practice, provide most psychotherapeutic services.[3] Many states now license social workers, making them eligible for third-party reimbursement; this development has also contributed to the setting of standards for advanced or independent practice.

Many treatment methods that were more or less experimental twenty-five years ago have matured and are now widely used. Some of these have developed into approaches that are alternatives or adjuncts to psychosocial casework. Others are expansions of the approach itself. Together, they provide workers with many new tools with which to assist individuals and families to cope with their concerns and dilemmas and move forward toward their goals.

Terminology and Overlapping Concepts

A few comments about some of the terminology used in this text are necessary. Because of its long history as the designation for service to individuals and families by social workers, we have chosen to keep "casework" as part of the title of this book and to use it in the course of our writing. We also use the more recently developed term "clinical social work." At present, the field defines "clinical social workers" in various ways. The writers prefer to use this designation to refer to workers who have had a concentration in the study of direct treatment of individuals and families in graduate school, including substantial work in emotional and interpersonal problems, and who have subsequently had some years of professionally supervised practice in direct service, and often some kind of postgraduate training. These workers differ from so-called generalists or generic social work practitioners who have opted for broader training and who have not had sufficient time to acquire a high degree of skill in direct or clinical treatment. Similarly, those with only undergraduate professional training have just started to study casework and cannot yet have mastered the complexities of clinical knowledge and practice. In this book, we are using the term *clinical social work* to refer to that more complicated part of casework for which "generic" and undergraduate training can only begin to prepare.[4]

The psychosocial approach represents a particular set of principles that can be followed by caseworkers at various levels of competence. In clinical social work practice, full use can be made of the entire system. Naturally, advanced skill and knowledge can be reached only by years of both practice and study. All aspects of the approach cannot be mastered at once. Fundamentals of psychosocial practice are being taught in many schools at the undergraduate level, and also in the preparation of generalists at the graduate level.

Different terms are also used in referring to the casework and clinical social work processes: "treatment," "the helping process," "intervention," "therapy," and "service." Each has its own claim to particular appropriateness, although they are often used interchangeably. We are using the word "treatment" in its general dictionary sense of "dealing with" or "acting or behaving toward another person in some specified way." The word has a sufficiently broad meaning to cover most casework activities. Some social workers object to this term because it implies an emphasis on "sickness" rather than on health, or because it seems to put the blame for any distress or dilemma upon the client rather than on dynamic interactions and systemic processes. When the term "treatment" is used in this book, it distinctly is not intended to carry any such connotations. "Helping" or the "helping process" or "service" is used even more broadly than "treatment" to cover all forms of casework practice, including specific acts of practical help. We have used "therapy" in this book and in its title to refer to work in which social and psychological means are used to enable individuals (singly or in family or in formed groups) to cope with environmental, interpersonal, and/or intrapsychic dilemmas—and the interactions among these—that are causing personal distress. The term "intervention" is preferred by some as a rather general term. It is commonly, but far from exclusively, used by family therapists, in work with formed groups, in the behavior modifica-

tion approach, and often in research. It is also preferred by others to whom the terms "treatment" and "therapy" seem to imply disease in the client or the idea that in some way clients are mainly responsible for their own unhappiness. The term "intervention" may seem to suggest a somewhat mechanistic or intrusive process, but nevertheless we have employed it as an alternative general term because of its wide use in the field.

The term "client" is used in this book to refer to an individual, a couple, or a family. In fact, in parent-child situations, dilemmas about aging people, or cases of catastrophic illnesses or severe physical or mental disabilities, "client" may actually refer to the relatives who must make decisions for others as well as to the individual with the obvious or presenting problem. Although the terms "collateral" (a person in a client's environment or network who affects or can be enlisted to affect the situation) and "collateral sources" (case histories, documents, reports, psychological tests, for example) may strike some people as old-fashioned, we see no need to coin a new word when the old one can convey the idea. Similarly, we have not discarded terms such as "environmental work" or "environmental modification." When interventions or procedures used by caseworkers focus on people or social or physical conditions *outside the client* (individual or family) these activities can be referred to by these terms.

We want to emphasize that divisions or chapter headings in this book are artificial and imply boundaries that exist only in theory. Yet, in order to describe and manage the material we present, we have to break it down into separate parts; in actual practice this is also necessary for assessment and intervention purposes. For example, as we will repeatedly stress, environmental influences are always part of the assessment of *any* situation addressed by caseworkers. In a given case, decisions about where to intervene—*which is often different from the location of the problem or dysfunction*—may require information about an individual's health or personality system, a family system, a social service system, or some aspect of the larger environmental system. If a person is mentally disabled, for example, the caseworker's efforts may be directed to location of resources rather than to intrapsychic explorations; inner anxiety may be relieved by finding a job; individuals who through no fault of their own have repeatedly been victimized by crime in their neighborhood may choose to seek better protection of their home, a new place to live, or a course in karate. Whether the problem seems to stem from inner, outer, or interactional forces, all aspects require consideration. In work with individuals, various systems and ecological concepts may be central to effective treatment. In family therapy, knowledge about personality may be as important as interactional theory.

Along the same lines, although there are four separate chapters on family and couple treatment, systems concepts and conjoint interviewing are discussed throughout the book. The treatment procedures we describe apply to individual and to conjoint treatment. We include a chapter on the psychosocial study and initial interviews; however, it goes without saying that treatment (the subject of other chapters) begins with the very first contact. Thus, material presented in each chapter interpenetrates all of the others; divisions and headings are for convenience and manageability only.

New Practice Trends in Changing Times

There have been many new trends in theories and practices in clinical social work in recent years. The psychosocial approach has been expanded by the addition of concepts from these new developments. Chief among these is family and couple treatment. Social workers have made substantial contributions to the family therapy movement. However, in the early 1960s, when the first edition of this book was being written, casework with clients was primarily limited to individual interviews.

At that time, we referred to joint interviews of married couples and family interviewing as "promising new trends" not covered by the data on which the book was based. Increasingly over the years it has become clear that conjoint treatment is a powerful tool for developing understanding of intrafamilial relationships and for bringing about change in these relationships which, in turn, often leads to intrapsychic change in individuals. Sometimes an entire contact consists of family interviews. Often, on the other hand, both individual and group interviewing are used in the same family, each form of work having its own purpose and value. Two expanded chapters include discussion of psychosocial family therapy, and of how family concepts and concepts derived from the psychodynamic study of the individual can be integrated in theory and in practice.

Marital problems continue to be a major focus of treatment, with gender roles changing in various degrees, depending on many factors, including ethnicity, geography, family tradition. As has been true for many years, improvement in the marriage is not the only acceptable goal; couples seek help to explore whether to try to improve the relationship or to separate. When divorce or separation is decided upon, often individuals seek help in recovering from the loss and in rearranging their lives. Cross-cultural couples are frequently seen by caseworkers. Second marriages often require complex adjustments, especially when children are involved. Gay couples, with and without children in their households, are bringing their relationship problems to treatment. Unmarried pairs ask for help in living together and sometimes in deciding to live together. Premarital counseling has become increasingly popular. Two new chapters on couple treatment are included in this edition.

Crisis treatment and task-centered, planned time-limited, and agency-limited services have been used extensively by social workers in recent years. Historically, brief services have constituted a large portion of casework practice. Budget problems, rising costs, increased concern with accountability, and preference of some clients have given added impetus to interest in setting time limits on services and clearly defining goals of treatment that can be achieved quickly. Although it is our view that the short-term treatment approach is not the best choice for many clients, for large numbers of others it has helped to keep treatment focused, eliminating aimless "drifting" or unnecessarily exhaustive interviews with clients. Similarly, the "contract," which makes explicit the mutual working agreement between client and worker, when flexibly implemented is helpful in maintaining a clear direction in treatment. These issues are discussed in the new chapter on brief treatment and elsewhere in the text.

In spite of frustrating and unpredictable problems involving funding, greater attention than ever is being paid to the need to link people with institutional resources, services, and opportunities. Systems and ecological theory has directed attention to the complexity of agency and other institutional operations, the interlocking of policy, administration, and staff personalities, and it has helped caseworkers in carrying out their responsibility for modifying and humanizing institutional functioning and services to clients. There is increased recognition of the importance of locating caseworkers in institutions and agencies where they can make themselves available in imaginative ways—in prenatal clinics, day care centers, communities of older people, hospitals and hospices, and so on—thus becoming enablers in the client's immediate "life space." Employee assistance programs often employ and/or refer to clinical social workers, offering convenient and confidential opportunities for workers to seek help with personal, job-related, or family problems.

Worker "burnout" has become a matter of increasing concern. Obviously when workers are overworked, underpaid, handling large caseloads of clients with recalcitrant problems and seemingly few solutions, given little recognition and support, or are exhausted and have poor morale for various other reasons, their effectiveness is seriously impaired. The identification and alleviation of systemic and other problems that contribute to burnout in social service professionals should be a prime concern of workers, supervisors, and administrators of social agencies. This subject is addressed for the first time in this fourth edition.

The use of the small group as a means of treatment by clinical social workers continues to grow steadily in importance. Discussion of work with groups has not been included in this text simply because—as much as we might like it to be—this cannot be an "everything" book! Work with groups is an extremely effective modality and, from our point of view, should be part of every caseworker's experience and training. The theory and practice of group treatment vary just as widely as does work with individuals and families. Clinical social workers seeking an approach to group therapy compatible with psychosocial theory can find it in writings of others who are experts in practice with formed groups.[5]

Caseworkers, along with other social workers, continue to be outspoken advocates of the poor, the elderly, blacks, Hispanics, American Indians, Asian Americans, and many others who are discriminated against and deprived of rights and power. The aspirations and needs of people trapped and debilitated by ghetto and slum life are more widely understood than formerly, although most caseworkers learned long ago how destructive it is to "blame the victim" of social injustice. Oversimplified concepts about the "culture of poverty" or the "underclass" have all but been discarded by social work thinkers. The great variations in both personality and circumstance among people who have in common the experience of poverty are being stressed. The possibility of individualizing service to persons and families in this heterogeneous group is thereby increased.

Knowledge from Other Disciplines

In many disciplines, the approach to knowledge known as *systems theory* has proved a useful tool for helping the mind to deal with the complexities of modern knowledge. Increasingly over the years, psychosocial casework has found this mode of thought most congenial for dealing conceptually with the multiplicity of psychological, familial, and social forces at work in the human situation. As early as 1941, Gordon Hamilton,[6] in a major paper, used the term *organismic* to characterize the psychosocial approach and referred to its use in 1938 by Henry A. Murray in *Explorations in Personality*. Murray, in describing an organism, said: "The organism is from the beginning a whole, from which the parts are derived by self-differentiation. The whole and its parts are mutually related; the whole being as essential to an understanding of the parts as the parts are to an understanding of the whole."[7] He also referred to human beings as adapting, integrating, and differentiating "within a changing environmental matrix." Systems theory adds to Murray's early conception the transactional concept of the interlocking relationships between individuals and their environments. When viewed from a systems perspective, the "case" of an individual or family includes the situation and is seen as a system of interrelated, reciprocal forces that dovetail and reinforce one another. Systems concepts, which will be discussed in greater detail in chapters that follow and are interwoven throughout the text, have been found extremely useful in clarifying aspects of the person-situation gestalt so central to the psychosocial approach.

Closely related to concepts from general systems theory are concepts derived from the ecological perspective in sociology which deals especially with the interdependence of men and their institutions. The ecological approach introduced into casework by Germain and Gitterman has focused attention on the complex intertwining of the person, family, and environments.[8] This aspect of ecology both parallels and contributes to the increased understanding of the nature of person-situation interactions and to the place of the environment in treatment, as these have been developing from the psychosocial point of view. This text attempts to demonstrate that in both theory and practice, systems and ecological concepts can and should be integrated with theories about personality and individual functioning. It is our hope that the day is past when a caseworker is torn between two perspectives that together, in our view, provide greater understanding and more opportunities for helping than have ever before been available to us. *In our psychosocial approach, ecological systems and psychodynamic perspectives have become inseparable.*

Communication theory continues to be of great interest to clinicians working with individuals, groups, families, and collaterals. The attention this theory attracts to the importance of nonverbal and paraverbal communication and to the "slippage" in communication that occurs when symbols are not given the same meaning by individuals who are attempting to communicate is of particular value to any caseworker. In many ways, as this book emphasizes, it contributes to understanding of barriers that often prevent effective discussion between individuals.

Understanding of cultural differences, among clients and between clients and workers, continues to be recognized as critically important to assessment and treatment. Wider and more sophisticated use is now being made of the knowledge contributed by the social sciences on ethnic, class, and regional factors in personality and social functioning. Study of values, traditions, role behavior, social interaction, family structure, and other related matters continues to deepen understanding of variations in both personality and life experience. Each population brings special strengths and vulnerabilities. It has become clear how careful we must be in our assessments to differentiate pathology from culturally determined attitudes and behavior. Equally important, we have learned that we must be sensitively attuned to stresses experienced by members of various groups; certain people experience repeated and traumatic events in their daily lives *only because* they are members of a particular ethnic or other identifiable group. As deeply committed as we are to incorporating cultural content, however, we are equally committed to avoiding the misuse of information; we must be cautious not to rely on partial theories and incomplete data. Abuses similar to those that accompany a narrow view of clinical diagnosis can occur. Oversimplification and stereotyping have led to *mistreatment* of clients and poor program planning.

New understanding also continually comes into the field from psychology, psychiatry, and other branches of medicine. Recent studies and clinical observations of individuals have led to new understandings of the diagnosis and treatment of clients with borderline and other personality disorders. "Self-psychology," a term and theory developed by Heinz Kohut, adds to other advances in personality theory; these will be commented upon in Chapter 2. New approaches to schizophrenia, spurred on in part by advances in psychopharmacology and by deinstitutionalization and the return to the community of many mentally ill patients, have affected casework treatment over the past twenty years. The psychoeducational approach, used more and more by caseworkers over the past decade, has incorporated educational and behavioral techniques to help the mentally ill and their families.

There is increasing evidence that many personality problems, clinical symptoms, and mood disorders have a physiological base that can be, or at some point in the future will be, modifiable with medications. Depression, bipolar disorders, and obsessive-compulsive conditions,

as well as schizophrenia, are now responsive to drug therapies; not long ago these were considered responsive primarily to psycotherapeutic procedures. In one study, even teenage suicide has been linked to abnormalities in the brain.[9] Of great importance to prevention, the experience of being touched, which is said to release certain chemicals in the brain of infants, has been demonstrated as being critical to healthy development of mind and body.[10]

The third edition of the *Diagnostic and Statistical Manual of Mental Disorders* (DSM-III and DSM-III-R) of the American Psychiatric Association has had a significant impact on caseworkers' approach to clinical diagnosis; among other changes, terms are better standardized, making it possible for colleagues from different disciplines or schools of thought to communicate with one another more effectively. These changes will be reflected in our new edition.

Fundamental to an understanding of all these new developments and changing needs, with their many variations, is a solid foundation in the basic knowledge and theory of casework practice. The task of evaluating the new emphases and enlarging the knowledge and understanding of caseworkers so that they can use them in practice, when appropriate, may seem formidable. It is made somewhat easier, however, because many new trends represent additions to already well established casework treatment methods, not anything diametrically opposed to them. Rather than tearing down an erroneous or grossly inadequate frame of reference, in the main the task is one of expanding the framework, sometimes with new methods and procedures, at other times with methods and procedures that have been underemphasized, although they were theoretically provided for in the overall scheme.

A clear understanding of fundamental principles is never more needed than when theory is being expanded and choices must be made between what is to be retained and what discarded of both the new and the old. It is, therefore, perhaps especially timely for caseworkers to formulate as clearly as possible the nature of their basic frame of reference. Treatment will become more effective only when what is potentially sound and useful in the new is admitted to the main body of principles whose value has already been demonstrated. Knowledge building should be a cooperative enterprise in which one reformulates, refines, and adds to existing knowledge and theory, accrediting the value of what has gone before in the certain realization that in due time others will have their turn at reshaping what now seems clear to us.

A BRIEF HISTORICAL BACKGROUND

During the great depression of the thirties, social casework was just beginning to outgrow its technical school, apprenticeship phase. In increasing numbers, schools of social work were moving toward affiliation with universities, and graduate schools were becoming the preferred method of education for entry into the emerging profession of social work. During that same period, the literature grew rapidly as the field became increasingly conscious of its methodology and of differences in point of view among practitioners. Prior to 1930 the writings of Mary Richmond, whose first book, *Friendly Visiting among the Poor: A Handbook for Charity Workers,*[11] appeared in 1899, provided the major basis for casework practice theory. For many years, beginning in 1905, Richmond was associated with the production of teaching materials, including many case histories printed by the Field Department of *Charities and Commons,* and from 1909 on by the Charities Organization Department of the Russell Sage Foundation. From 1910 through 1922, the one-month summer institutes, led by Richmond, for secretaries (as workers were then called) and other paid workers were a principal source of leadership in casework practice. Richmond's 1917 book, *Social Diagnosis,*[12] was based on cases drawn from children's agencies, medical settings, and the

family field. It also reflected her many years of study, discussion, and teaching. This volume was very widely used in schools and agencies throughout the country during the 1920s.

As is well known, Richmond's great contribution—in an age when poverty was thought to be predominantly the result of innate character defects—was to stress the effect of social relationships on the individual and his or her problems. In *Social Diagnosis,* she emphasized the need to study thoroughly the client's immediate social environment, present and past, to understand a case. Intervention in the client's environment was one of her two treatment methods and was later called "the indirect treatment method." *Social Diagnosis* presented and discussed many resourceful and imaginative illustrations of work in the environment designed to lessen pressure on the family or individual, to increase opportunities, and in various ways to favor the positive or healthy development of the client. In this respect, her point of view directly reflected the new developments in sociology of her period, which saw personality as shaped primarily by the social experiences of the individual.

Richmond added to this, however, a second category: direct treatment, the influence of "mind upon mind."[13] Under this category, Richmond stressed the development of a strong, trusting relationship through which a worker could influence a client toward activities and decisions that would be in his or her best interest. Suggestion and persuasion were predominant techniques, but there was also discussion of the need for frankness and honesty in the relationship and on the client's participation in decision making, which seems to suggest rational discussion, though this term was not used.

The decade following the publication of *Social Diagnosis* was one in which psychology was flourishing. The major impetus to social work's turn to psychological theories came from the association of social workers with psychiatrists during World War I, followed by the establishment of the specialty in psychiatric social work at the Smith College School of Social Work, the special department of mental hygiene at the New York School of Social Work, and the course in social psychiatry at the Pennsylvania School of Social Work.[14] During most of the twenties, various psychologies of that period were introduced into social work at different times and in different places. Robinson, in her chapter, "Working Psychologies in Social Case Work, 1920–1930," in *A Changing Psychology in Social Casework*, referred to the influence of John Dewey, H. A. Overstreet, William A. White, William Healy, Bernard Glueck, Marion Kenworthy, Jessie Taft, Ernest Groves, and others.[15] She wrote that Healy, in his influential *Reconstructing Behavior in Youth*, listed five sources of the "new psychology": (1) the Behavioristic School, (2) Thomas's View, (3) the Adlerian School, (4) the Freudian School, (5) the Jung [sic] School.[16] Of this period, Robinson wrote: "But these various and often conflicting viewpoints are frequently used indiscriminately, and nowhere has there been any attempt by a caseworker to organize or originate any psychological principles of interpretation."[17] In other words, social work was in a period of examination and ferment, seeking greater understanding of the personality than Richmond had been able to provide when social influences, heredity, physical makeup, and variations in intelligence were the main explanatory variables offered by psychology and psychiatry.

In 1930, with the publication of Robinson's book, a strong new influence entered the field, that of Otto Rank. Three years later, under the leadership of Taft and Robinson and their associates at the Pennsylvania School of Social Work, "functionalism" became a focused, distinctive approach to social casework. Functionalism not only brought Rankian psychology into the field but also found itself in strong disagreement with the Richmond approach and its successors. For the functionalist, treatment revolved around agency services and the client's

responses to these services. Rank's concept concerning the will took a central position. Past history was considered irrelevant. Diagnosis was deemphasized. Time limitations were used as a means of stimulating the client to act upon his or her problem. The terms "functional," "Rankian," and "Pennsylvania School" were used to refer to this point of view.

Meanwhile other schools, especially the other leading eastern schools—Smith, Simmons, New York, and Cleveland—and practitioners in agencies affiliated with them, were moving toward Freudian theory as the psychology yielding the most convincing explanations of the human personality as well as contributions to treatment methodology.[18] This approach, like Richmond's, required careful history taking, including information about the relevant past. This continued to be called a social study, although it had already become distinctly psychosocial, an effort to arrive at facts upon which a diagnosis could be based and a tentative treatment plan could be formulated. The terms "diagnostic," "differential," and "Freudian" were used to refer to this point of view.

Concurrently, the social climate was becoming less authoritarian, the concept of self-determination was widely discussed, and Dewey's theories of education were receiving increased acceptance. On the issue of self-determination, the two schools of the thirties in actuality were not far apart. The functional school, under the leadership of Robinson and Taft, put great emphasis on this concept and there was much ferment, as though a real difference on this principle were at issue.

Hamilton, for many years the leading exponent of the differential approach, stressed in her writings the individual's "right to be himself," the uniqueness of the client's goals and objectives, and the movement away from authority and manipulation, as early as 1937.[19] In her 1940 book, *Theory and Practice of Case Work*,[20] widely used as a text in all parts of the country, she reiterated these points. Hollis, another early representative of the differential school, wrote in 1939, "The final choice of the pattern he (the client) wants his life to take in matters large and small is his and not the worker's to make. . . . This principle is one of the most widely held in the field of casework. Its acceptance was greatly accelerated by its defense in Virginia P. Robinson's *A Changing Psychology in Social Case Work;* under the name of the client's right of 'self-determination' it was also discussed by Bertha C. Reynolds in *Between Client and Community;* it is either stated explicitly or implied in almost all the writings by caseworkers listed in the Bibliography."[21] This bibliography included writings of about forty of the leading nonfunctionalist caseworkers of the day. Actually, both functional and diagnostic schools had departed from the earlier directiveness or advice giving, and from the assumption that the worker would know what was best for the client in managing his or her own life.

It is not necessary here to go into all the differences between the two points of view. Gradually, the differential or diagnostic point of view developed far beyond its Richmond predecessor. The social part of the history became less extensive but continued to put great emphasis on family influences. As the newer psychology with emphasis on ego functioning developed, more effort was made to observe the client's functioning both directly within the interview and indirectly, as he or she described encounters with others. The old directive techniques still common in the twenties gave way to efforts to help individuals think for themselves and base decisions on their own judgment. The nature of history taking changed markedly with recognition of the fact that treatment begins immediately and that facts are gathered and observed more selectively and less formally than Richmond had advised.

While diagnostic thinking changed radically in response to increased understanding of personality, the idea that one must try to understand a person whom one is trying to help and

that current functioning is influenced by past as well as by present events continued to be regarded as basic to differential, individualizing treatment. Richmond's two major treatment modes—treatment through change or use of the environment and treatment through direct work with the client—were also carried over into the differential point of view. They were considered, as Richmond considered them, interlocking components in treatment.

By the end of the thirties, except for the functional school, Freudian psychology was widely accepted by caseworkers as the most useful basis for understanding personality. The major theoretical task of the forties was to define the ways in which psychoanalytic understanding could be used by caseworkers, what factors distinguished casework treatment from psychoanalysis, and what different kinds of work with clients existed within the broad methodology of differential casework. As answers to these questions began to take form, the further problem of developing guiding principles for the relationship of diagnosis to treatment emerged. These issues will be explored further in later chapters.

Until the mid-fifties, the functional and the diagnostic or differential approaches were the only generally recognized points of view in casework. Functionalism continued to be sponsored chiefly by the Pennsylvania School, the University of North Carolina School, and a few other schools. Its influence was felt strongly in a number of agencies in the east. The diagnostic school was more widely accepted as the main body of casework thought.

At about this time, a sudden spurt occurred in the growth of theory and practice within the diagnostic group. Most important of all was the increasing assimilation by caseworkers of the new understanding of the ego developing in the psychoanalytic field. Several efforts were also made in the late fifties to bridge diagnostic and functional thinking.[22] Out of one of these, Perlman's "problem-solving" approach developed. Experimentation also began with seeing both partners jointly in problems of marriage relationships. Then, beginning in the early sixties came family group treatment, crisis treatment, planned short-term treatment, and task-oriented treatment. The usefulness for our field of a number of other theoretical approaches has been, or is being, explored: Horney and Sullivan have been influential, the Rogerian approach (later called the client-centered system) is favored by some, behavior modification has many adherents, and others under study in recent years include cognitive theory, transactional analysis, the existential approach, and, most recently, the "life model," or ecological, approach.

In 1964, when the first edition of this book went to press, a number of these new approaches had been introduced. Many of these seemed, for the most part, to be variations in emphasis and areas of growth within the diagnostic-differential approach, with little or no basic incompatibility with that approach. When the term "psychosocial" was first used by Hollis in the subtitle of this book, it was a descriptive term, chosen to emphasize the fact that the diagnostic-differential approach was characterized by concern for both social and psychological aspects of life. Hamilton had used the term as early as 1941 in stressing the fact that all problems are to a degree both emotional and social.[23] The term was originally suggested in 1930 by Hankins, a sociologist, then teaching at the Smith School for Social Work.[24]

In 1969, a symposium was held in Chicago in memory of Charlotte Towle for the purpose of securing clear statements about the approaches then in operation in the casework field. Functional, problem-solving, behavioral modification, and "psychosocial" were chosen as four "general" approaches; family group treatment, crisis-oriented brief treatment, and adult socialization were seen as "middle-range approaches" addressed to specific groups in the general client population but having utility for wider application. In the publication of *Theories of Social Casework*, based on this series of discussions, the term "psychosocial casework" was used to designate the approach represented by the diagnostic-differential point of view.[25] Since then, "psychosocial" has been widely used as the designation for an approach described in publications by many writers as well as in this book. In both theory and practice, this point of view has now expanded considerably beyond the diagnostic-differential approach on which it was originally based. It is important to recognize that many elements now included in the psychosocial approach are by no means exclusive to it. When likenesses and differences between points of view are examined, it becomes apparent that there is indeed a considerable degree of agreement among most approaches on certain fundamental points which, as we see it, comprise a common core of casework practice.[26]

In this book, then, we are including both this common core of casework practice and concepts that are specifically components of the psychosocial approach.

EDUCATION FOR CLINICAL SOCIAL WORK SPECIALIZATION

Space does not allow for an in-depth discussion of educational issues. The authors' point of view on these matters is discussed in detail elsewhere.[27] However, a few comments are called for here. We have already mentioned the fact that many millions of people are receiving some form of professional psychotherapy or counseling and that, in terms of numbers, clinical social workers are the chief providers of these services. It is also true that a majority of social work students seem to be interested in careers in direct or clinical practice.[28] At some point, many of these will go into independent or private practice. Yet, to one degree or another in recent years, a significant number of graduate schools of social work have not provided master's students with adequate training for specialization in clinical work, preferring a more "generic" curriculum instead. Generally speaking, the curricula of doctoral programs have focused on administration, social policy, theory building, and research. In order to acquire advanced training and competence as clinicians, therefore, social workers have had to seek further education in institutes and Ph.D. programs directed by professions other than social work. In our view, a great contribution can be made to the quality of casework practice by the clinical doctorate. At last, a few clinical social work doctoral programs have emerged.[29]

Whether everyone likes it or not, we repeat: a large proportion of social workers choose to work with individuals, families, and small groups; in agencies and private practice, they provide the bulk of direct therapeutic services available. It is also probably true that some prospective social workers apply to graduate schools looking for "passports" to clinical careers, oblivious to the complex range of knowledge, heritage, visions, foundation of humanistic values, experience, creativity, and artistry that have combined to make social work—and clinical social work as a specialization   the profession that it is and all that we perennially strive to make it become. In our view, it is as counterproductive to criticize the students who want to become direct practitioners as it is to ignore the trend toward clinical specialization. Rather, we should be more committed than ever to providing our master's and doctoral students with the theory, the tools, and the experience that adequately prepare them for effective "on-line" clinical careers.

We must, first of all, teach both the psychodynamic and the social content that social work history has repeatedly demonstrated are necessary to work with individuals, families, and groups. There is an enormous amount of relevant theory, knowledge, and technical skill to be absorbed by students going into direct services; a "generic" education is too broad to do

the material justice. Equally important, caseworkers must be firmly grounded in social work's *unique* base of knowledge, its traditions and ethics.[30] Although there are overlaps, there are important issues that distinguish social work practitioners from other clinicians. Historically, caseworkers have served every group in society, always with special concern for the problems of the poor and the dislocated; they have demanded social reforms for the benefit of forgotten people whom no other helping profession has so consistently championed. Social work practitioners have been in the forefront of human services; as mentioned earlier, the populations served and the settings in which social workers can be found have expanded dramatically over recent decades. Shirley Cooper writes, "We have worked at the interface between the inner and outer world, which is what gives us our unique values about social justice and human rights."[31] Our vehement stands for self-determination and decent opportunities for every person and family, and our identification with all who struggle for betterment and self-fulfillment, derive from direct experience, not just from lofty ideals. Because of their familiarity with the needs of a broad range of people in a variety of situations and dilemmas, social workers have always been innovators of programs, of approaches, of techniques. More than members of any other profession, over many years social workers have put to valuable use their first-hand knowledge about environmental influences on human suffering; the provision of concrete services and the creative development and utilization of resources have been part of the caseworker's special stock in trade from the beginning. Psychosocial clinicians have not just borrowed a little of this and a little of that from other disciplines; over and over again they have broken new ground in hopes of better serving individuals and families from all walks of life. Knowledge about the history of casework, and all of the practice approaches that have derived directly from it, must be an important part of the education of the clinical social work specialist.

THE EMPIRICAL BASE

Psychosocial casework is, as we have already said, a blend of concepts derived from psychiatry, psychology, and the social sciences with a substantial body of empirical knowledge developed within the casework field itself. The direct empirical basis of the approach rests on the continued systematic study of treatment, focusing upon client response to the procedures employed.

Fortunately, the major outlines of the diagnostic-differential type of practice developed during a period when detailed process recording was common, especially in the family agency and psychiatric social work settings in which this approach developed. Supervision and consultation were also customary, with weekly conferences of several hours held regularly for discussion of complicated and baffling cases. Agency seminars for group study of cases recorded in detail were common, as were also regional seminars, reports at state and national conferences, and published papers based upon case studies.

The term "practice wisdom," sometimes used to describe this empirical basis, does not sufficiently convey the continuous study process through which practice was observed and examined, both case by case and in groups of cases. As in any other healthy profession, practice theory was built upon widely debated premises derived from *scrutiny by practicing social workers of actual experience.* Practice concepts were constantly modified, as well as expanded, as new evidence appeared. In later chapters, reference will be made to some of these changes in both practice and theory.

The first step in the development of any body of knowledge or theory is that of close accurate observation of the phenomena under study. This usually begins informally and proceeds to the collection of data based on increasingly systematic study. Formulation of concepts and hypotheses and experimental testing of these in small-scale studies are usually the next steps in the development of theory. Such experimental testing can be only as informative as the accuracy of the observed data on which it rests.

This is essentially the way in which the psychosocial approach has been built. Many of the early reports analyzed a single case. A number of others were based on study of a few cases, and a few were derived from systematic study of 50 to 100 or more cases.[32] For the most part, they were studies and articles based on practice designed to build, confirm, or demonstrate theory. They described, examined, and experimented but did not test or attempt to prove either theory or practice. Control groups were almost never used.

In "How It *Really* Was," Hollis describes how, in the early days of casework, "practice wisdom" was built through the study of detailed process recordings, collegial group thinking and exchange, open discussion of perplexing problems, and ongoing efforts to identify and test out approaches, procedures, and principles.[33]

Beginning in the 1960s and continuing into the 1970s, casework went through a period of experimentation and adaptation of a type of research methodology derived largely from the social sciences. As it turned out, the field was not ready for this type of research. But during this period there were a number of evaluative studies that attempted to measure the successfulness of programs and practice methods. Caseworkers were naively optimistic and researchers were equally naive about the fallacies inherent in applying certain methodologies, then in wide use in academic sociology, to a field in a relatively early stage of both knowledge and research development. Control and comparative group designs were emphasized with high reliance on probability statistics for relatively small samples. Emphasis was not on theory building but on outcome testing. These evaluative studies depended upon the ability to prove that a particular form of treatment is either better than no treatment at all or better than a second form of treatment.

To the dismay of caseworkers, many of the studies of this period failed to demonstrate good results. Even into the early 1980s, grave questions were therefore being raised about casework effectiveness. Controversy raged in the literature, with some researchers vehemently challenging traditional theories and methods of helping.[34] Some social workers began to doubt whether what they were doing with clients really helped after all, even when their own observations and their clients' informal evaluations led them to believe that it often did. But, because the control group statistical analysis type of research was so popular and highly respected during this time, the value of studies more suitable to clinical work was greatly underestimated, and the notion grew that there was no empirical basis for the casework practice of the day.

It is beyond the scope of this book to review the debates about the research that shook confidence in casework results during those years. Suffice it to say that even then, and also as time went on, new studies—and a reexamination of studies that presumably discredited casework effectiveness—produced different, more encouraging conclusions. Many weaknesses in the research designs of the control group type of studies were located. Statistical errors were uncovered, indicating the strong probability that even when results in the treatment group were better than in the control group, this difference was falsely attributed to chance and not favorably reported. Another important weakness was that, in a number of the studies, safeguards were not taken against coding in the "treated group" many cases in which the problem under consideration *was never treated and in all probability did not even exist.* In other words, even if particular clients in a study did not want or need help with an employment or marital problem,

for example, they would nevertheless be rated as showing "no improvement" in these areas unless safeguards were included. It makes little sense to assess casework outcome results when the problems being studied are not defined as problems by the clients and changes in these areas are therefore not viewed by either clients or workers as the purpose or goal of the casework contact. It is obvious that the failure to recognize this issue meant that such studies unintentionally loaded against the possibility of positive findings.

Many other important lessons were learned from the research of this earlier period about research methodology itself: the importance of specifying goals that theory would lead one to expect were attainable and the need to monitor treatment procedures to ascertain that the procedures under study were actually used, guarding against the use of measuring scales and other procedures that are only marginally appropriate for the cases under study, among others. Perhaps most important of all, writers began to warn, as caseworkers had for many years, against the *dangers of overgeneralizing* from a specific experiment or demonstration to casework as a whole. It was pointed out that lack of standardization of outcome measures among studies made cumulative results difficult to evaluate. Furthermore, it was realized that differences in findings and degrees of improvement could often be expected between voluntary and involuntary casework clients, between those who are motivated and see a need to change and those who are not. The competence of the workers also had to be taken into account. These points have been elaborated upon elsewhere.[35]

This is not to say that the findings of all early control group statistical analysis research were without value. On the contrary, some studies were very well designed and executed and brought important changes in psychosocial practice. A good illustration of a study of major significance to the field is reported in *Brief and Extended Casework* by Reid and Shyne.[36] This study demonstrated the value of shorter treatment combined with certain new techniques. It also demonstrated enormous variability in the work of different practitioners who were presumably following the same basic approach. Another excellent example of the control group statistical design is that of Weissman et al.,[37] who studied casework treatment of 106 depressed women. Favorable changes were reported in five areas: improved work performance, reduced interpersonal friction, freer communication, reduced anxiety, and better overall adjustment. It was further found that although medication alone reduced anxiety, it did not affect social adjustment. On the other hand, casework treatment did not reduce symptomatology. The researchers pointed out that this demonstrates that if studies do not distinguish between social adjustment and symptomatology in measuring the effects of psychotherapy, but wrap them up in the same measuring bundle, the results may be inconclusive, obliterating the favorable outcome on social adjustment alone.

As the fallibility of tests and constructed scales for measuring behavior became more apparent, researchers showed more willingness to add the views of clients themselves (whose satisfaction with treatment, after all, is of paramount importance) and of caseworkers, also, to the sources of evidence. The extraordinarily comprehensive and, in our view, very important Beck and Jones study, *Progress on Family Problems*,[38] using such data, produced many significant findings.

It seems safe to say that we have emerged from the period when the value of casework and clinical services was so seriously questioned. That casework can be effective is not now in grave doubt.[39] Positive findings from outcome studies in related disciplines as well as social work itself have bolstered confidence in the effectiveness of psychotherapy; family, marital, and brief therapies; behavioral treatments; and more.[40]

We are also wiser than we were. Most caseworkers, concerned about delivering ethical and accountable services, see some kind of systematic research as being more important than ever. They are attuned to becoming more focused and purposeful, more realistic and precise in trying to determine what they do and do not accomplish. Although the profession is always concerned with evaluating effectiveness and with theory building, greater attention is being given to the improvement of research approaches. However, problems persist. It should be no surprise that the route to *the* satisfactory research approach continues to elude us and new debates have taken over where the old ones left off. As is true about practice approaches, differences of opinion and emphasis involving research abound.

The single-case or single-subject design, which attempts to measure change at several points over the course of treatment, has been advocated by many as the research model most appropriate for evaluation of clinical practice. Introduced by the fields of behaviorism and behavior modification, this type of research has been adapted to the study of various casework approaches. Some people see it as a refinement of the case evaluation method, mentioned above, that was developed in the early days of social work. It is more methodical, however, and has the potential of being far more exact. In contrast to some of the group comparison experimental designs, it avoids the danger of reliance on scales that are only tangentially related to the phenomena under study and to the purposes of treatment. In the single-case method, researchers try to determine what treatment procedures have actually been used and then examine observed or directly reported changes that can be attributed to the use of these procedures. Thus, this type of research strategy is intended to make possible the analysis of a direct connection between the treatment step and hypothesized effect. Specific and real goals acceptable to the client and deemed feasible by the worker can be identified for each case, with results examined in relation to these goals. It is hoped that cumulative individual case study data will provide evidence upon which generalizations can be convincingly made. This approach to research has been viewed by some as casework's best answer to demands by public and private funding sources, by third-party payors, by clients, and by the profession itself to demonstrate effectiveness.[41]

According to many critics, however, the single-case design and other quantitative means of measuring change and outcome are only narrowly applicable to the study of casework and are not very useful for understanding the intricate process of worker interactions and communications. Many practitioners, and some researchers also, contend that the treatment process is too complex for quantitative study—that the phenomenon of caring or of attachment, for example, cannot be broken down into identifiable components. Some say that operational definitions of client problems cannot be accurately formulated; the wholeness of the person-situation gestalt cannot be understood by the observation of concrete, separate parts. The study of detailed process recordings, made more accurate by also employing audio- or videotapes, is believed by many to be as informative as quantitative studies, if not more so. Siporin writes: "Measurement is truly an essential aspect of practice, but the qualitative measures can be as valid and objective as quantitative ones, and quite a number of things exist and work in this world that we cannot measure."[42] Many believe that it is difficult to apply quantitative research to casework approaches other than behavior modification. In the review of a book written by an esteemed researcher (Tony Tripodi, who advocates the widespread use of single-case evaluations by social work practitioners), David Pharis points out:

Our graduate programs have long taught that some sort of disciplined case review is an abso-

lute necessity in responsible social work practice. The careful, intense, tutorial process of case supervision, historically utilized in graduate education and in the social work profession, has been the vehicle through which social workers learned to do systematic evaluative thinking about their work. Most case "evaluation" in the context of supervision, however, uses the framework of some theoretical perspective on human behavior....As a result, most practitioners may be more apt to use their preferred theoretical framework, rather than a research model, to evaluate client progress. Such evaluations, conducted within a theoretical framework, need not be any less rigorous, disciplined, or systematic than those based on the methods discussed in this book....

[P]erhaps most direct practice social workers just do not believe that such evaluations have a greater "payoff" in terms of improved work with clients. I suspect that most social workers still rely on their preferred theoretical framework and "common sense" to tell them when they are succeeding or failing. Until they are more dissatisfied with such criteria for evaluation at the single case level, Tripodi's research-based designs are likely to gather dust on the caseworker's desk, no matter how scientifically sound they may be.[43]

Practitioners also complain that the introduction of instruments (by practitioners or researchers) for measuring change during the course of treatment can be an intrusion on the process and, in fact, may even distort the therapy and the outcome; for practical and ethical reasons they admonish against this approach.

The quantitative model is also criticized because of what is viewed as an overdetermined need to justify casework theory and practice, to "prove" effectiveness, rather than to advance knowledge and theory. The results may be limiting and misleading. We quote Siporin again: "[T]he pressures for quantitative, logical, linear, overt behavioral approaches; for the pervasive, standardized computerized report forms; and for immediate, short-term, reportable, and therefore accountable results, all impose severe limitations and distortions.

These features have become oppressively restrictive, mechanistic, and reductionistic, and they have brought about an expectable counter-rebellion."[44]

Carol Meyer reminds us that many problems social workers deal with are actually impervious to interventions and, for that reason, effectiveness is an unreal expectation. Physicians, she adds, "know something about the difference between effectiveness and accountability in the treatment of cancer. When a problem is intractable, we social workers may not be effective, but we always must be accountable for carrying out the charge we have been given."[45]

To compound the problems, there is—as there always has been to some degree—tension between researchers and clinical workers. Practitioners often feel criticized or patronized by researchers, especially when it is implied that the workers, even if well-meaning, are misguided or ineffective in what they do. Some caseworkers are convinced that scientists cannot appreciate the artistry essential to the delivery of helpful services to clients; they say they are interested in *people*, not in abstractions, generalizations, or numbers. Researchers, on the other hand, often complain that practitioners are not scientifically oriented and are resistant to logical and systematic ways of looking at problems. Needless to say, the growth of knowledge, the status of our profession, and the improvement of casework treatment require a spirit of cooperation between clinicians and researchers. Each has much to learn from the knowledge, perspectives, and skills of the other; together they can contribute to improved methods of clinical experimentation and increased clinical competence.

No doubt the debates about research methodology will go on. We, the authors, believe that we need not make an either-or choice between quantitative and qualitative methods. Rather, as clinicians and researchers learn to collaborate more comfortably, we expect that they will begin to be able to determine which research approaches are most useful and informative under what particular circumstances. Depending on the kinds of clients, problems, treatment objectives, theoretical orientations of the practitioners, and many other variables, intelligent decisions can be made. With increased sophistication, it should become possible to select research strategies on the basis of the kinds of knowledge we are seeking, rather than on the basis of rigid adherence to one approach over another.[46]

In Chapter 2 we will turn to detailed discussion of some elements of the theoretical framework of psychosocial practice. We shall begin by attempting to clarify and elaborate on the nature of the continuous interaction between inner psychological processes and outer social systems in the development and functioning of individuals and families.

NOTES

1. A review of professional journals of the last decade, especially *Social Casework, Social Work,* and *Clinical Social Work Journal,* will reveal many references and articles related to these issues.

2. For elaboration on this important emphasis, see Ann Weick, "The Philosophical Context of a Health Model of Social Work," *Social Casework,* 67 (November 1986), 551–559; and Joy R. Powles Smith, "Social Health Concepts for Family Practice," *Social Casework,* 63 (June 1982), 363–369.

3. See the following issues of *The New York Times:* October 28, 1981, p. C8; March 1, 1983, pp. C1 and C6; and April 30, 1985, pp. C2 and C9.

4. For further discussion see an excellent article by Shirley Cooper, "The Master's and Beyond," in Judith Mishne, ed., *Psychotherapy and Training in Clinical Social Work* (New York: Gardner Press, 1980), pp. 19–35. See also Patricia L. Ewalt, ed., "Toward a Definition of Clinical Social Work," *The National Association of Social Work Conference Proceedings* (Washington, D.C.: The National Association of Social Workers, 1980).

5. See especially Helen Northen, *Social Work with Groups* (New York: Columbia University Press, 1969); and Helen Northen, "Psychosocial Practice in Small Groups," in Robert W. Roberts and Helen Northen, eds., *Theories of Social Work with Groups* (New York: Columbia University Press, 1976), pp. 116–152. See also Lawrence Shulman, *The Skills of Helping Individuals and Groups* (Itasca, Ill.: F. E. Peacock Publishers, 1984); Irving D. Yalom, *The Theory and Practice of Group Psychotherapy* (New York: Basic Books, 1985); and Mary McClure Goulding and Robert L. Goulding, *Changing Lives Through Redecision Therapy* (New York: Brunner/Mazel, 1979).

6. Gordon Hamilton, "The Underlying Philosophy of Social Case Work," *The Family*, 18 (July 1941), 139–148.

7. Henry A. Murray, *Explorations in Personality* (New York: Oxford University Press, 1938), pp. 38–39.

8. Carel B. Germain and Alex Gitterman, "The Life Model of Social Work Practice," *Social Service Review* (December 1976), 601–610; Carel B. Germain and Alex Gitterman, *The Life Model of Social Work Practice* (New York: Columbia University Press, 1980); and Carel B. Germain and Alex Gitterman, "The Life Model Approach to Social Work Practice Revisited," in Francis J. Turner, ed., *Social Work Treatment*, 3d ed. (New York: Free Press, 1986), pp. 618–643.

9. *The New York Times*, May 13, 1988, p. A12.

10. *The New York Times*, February 2, 1988, pp. C1 and C4.

11. Mary E. Richmond, *Friendly Visiting among the Poor: A Handbook for Charity Workers* (New York: Macmillan, 1899).

12. Mary E. Richmond, *Social Diagnosis* (New York: Russell Sage Foundation, 1917).

13. Mary E. Richmond, *What Is Social Casework?* (New York: Russell Sage Foundation, 1922), pp. 101–102.

14. Virginia Robinson, *A Changing Psychology in Social Case Work* (Chapel Hill: University of North Carolina Press, 1930), p. 54.

15. Ibid., pp. 81–93.

16. Ibid., p. 83.

17. Ibid., p. 81.

18. Contrary to popular opinion, psychoanalysis was not a major force in casework in the 1920s. Shirley Hellenbrand, in her careful study of this period, "Main Currents in Social Casework, 1918–36" (doctoral dissertation, Columbia University School of Social Work, New York, 1965), found very little mention of Freudian thinking in the literature or teaching materials of that period. Rather, it was gradually assimilated during the thirties and by the end of that decade was a major component of the diagnostic or differential position.

19. Gordon Hamilton, "Basic Concepts upon Which Case Work Practice Is Formulated," *Proceedings of the National Conference of Social Work* (Chicago: University of Chicago Press, 1937).

20. Gordon Hamilton, *Theory and Practice of Case Work* (New York: Columbia University Press, 1940), pp. 29 and 32.

21. Florence Hillis, *Social Casework in Practice: Six Case Studies* (New York: Family Welfare Association of America, 1939), p. 5.

22. See Herbert H. Aptekar, *The Dynamics of Casework and Counseling* (Boston: Houghton Mifflin, 1955); and Helen Harris Perlman, *Social Casework: A Problem-Solving Process* (Chicago: University of Chicago Press, 1957).

23. Hamilton, "Underlying Philosophy of Social Case Work," p. 141.

24. Frank Hankins, "Contributions of Sociology to Social Work," *Proceedings of the National Conference of Social Work* (Chicago: University of Chicago Press, 1930), p. 534.

25. Robert W. Roberts and Robert H. Nee, eds., *Theories of Social Casework* (Chicago: University of Chicago Press, 1970).

26. Turner deals well with the question in his chapter, "A Multitheory Perspective for Practice," in Turner, *Social Work Treatment*, pp. 645–658. Additional readings on casework's roots and evolution include Katherine A. Kendall, "A Sixty-Year Perspective of Social Work," *Social Casework*, 63 (September 1982), 424–428; and Florence Hollis, "How It *Really*

Was," *Smith College School for Social Work Journal*, 10 (Fall 1983), 3–9.

27. See Mary E. Woods, "The Implications of Psychosocial Practice for Clinical Social Work Education," in Louise S. Bandler, ed., *Education for Clinical Social Work Practice: Continuity and Change* (New York: Pergamon Press, 1983), pp. 55–75; and Florence Hollis, "On Revisiting Social Work," *Social Casework*, 61 (January 1980), 3–10.

Three relevant—now historic—papers expressing concern about the quality of education for clinical social work practice appear in *Clinical Social Work Journal*, 5 (Winter 1977): Helen Pinkus et al., "Education for the Practice of Clinical Social Work at the Master's Level: A Position Paper," 253–273; Shirley Cooper, "Reflections on Clinical Social Work," 303–315; and John D. Minor, "An Assessment of Social Work Education and Family Agency Practice," 336–341.

28. Richard M. Grinnell, Jr., and Nancy S. Kyte, in "The Future of Clinical Practice: A Study," *Clinical Social Work Journal*, 5 (Summer 1977), 132–138, conclude that their findings "appear to provide a strong measure of support for recent predictions of a swing in social work toward clinical practice." Of 1,582 graduate and undergraduate social work students studied, 53.2 percent designated casework, psychotherapy, or private practice (31.9 percent, 15.9 percent, and 5.4 percent, respectively) as their ideal employment choice.

29. See Rosemary Creed Lukton and Ruth Ehrlich Bro, "An Alternative Model for Curriculum Building in Clinical Social Work Education: The California Institute for Clinical Social Work," *Clinical Social Work Journal*, 16 (Spring 1988), 8–21. The authors discuss the fact that master's degree programs do not provide adequate training for clinical practice and describe an innovative clinical doctoral program.

30. See Harold Lewis's excellent book, *The Intellectual Base of Social Work Practice: Tools for Thought in a Helping Profession* (New York: The Haworth Press, 1982); Harold Lewis, "Teaching Ethics Through Ethical Teaching," *Journal of Teaching in Social Work* (Spring/Summer 1987), 3–14; and Charles S. Levy, *Social Work Ethics* (New York: Human Services Press, 1976).

31. Shirley Cooper, "The Master's and Beyond," p. 25.

32. It may be useful to cite a few illustrations. Among the small studies, ranging from nine to twelve cases, in chronological order are Marian F. Lewis, "Alcoholism and Family Casework," *The Family*, 18 (April 1937), 39–44; Rosemary Reynolds and Else Siegle, "A Study of Casework with Sado-Masochistic Marriage Partners," *Social Casework*, 40 (December 1959), 545–551; Joanne Geist and Norman Gerber, "Joint Interviewing: A Treatment Technique with Marriage Partners," *Social Casework*, 41 (February 1960), 76–83; Miriam Jolesch, "Casework Treatment of Young Married Couples," *Social Casework*, 43 (May 1962), 245–251; Richard D. Prodie, Betty L. Singer, and Marian Winterbottom, "Integration of Research Findings and Casework Techniques," *Social Casework*, 48 (June 1967), 360–366.

Among the larger studies, ranging from seventy-five to several hundred cases, in chronological order are Gordon Hamilton, *Psychotherapy in Child Guidance* (New York: Columbia University Press, 1947); Florence Hollis, *Women in Marital Conflict* (New York: Family Welfare Association of America, 1949); Lillian Ripple, Ernestina Alexander, and Bernice Polemis, *Motivation, Capacity, and Opportunity* (Chicago: University of Chicago Press, 1964); Leontine R. Young, *Wednesday's Children: A Study of Child Neglect and Abuse* (New York: McGraw-Hill, 1964); Margaret Bailey, "Casework Treatment of the Alcoholic and His Family," in *Alcoholism and Family Casework* (New York: Community Council of Greater New York, 1968), pp. 67–108; Catherine M. Bitterman, "The Multimarriage Family," *Social Casework*, 49 (April 1968), 218–221; Pauline C. Cohen and Merton S. Krause, *Casework with Wives of Alcoholics* (New York: Family Service Association of America, 1969).

33. Hollis, "How It *Really* Was," p. 8.

34. Joel Fischer, "Is Casework Effective? A Review," *Social Casework*, 18 (January 1973), 5–20; and Katharine M. Wood, "Casework Effectiveness: A New Look at the Research Evidence," *Social Work*, 23 (November 1978), 437–458. See also Fischer's review of Wood's article and Wood's rejoinder in *Social Work*, 24 (May 1979), 245–249. Although differing in emphasis and intensity of criticism of casework practice, both reviewed studies of casework (Fischer reviewed eleven, Wood reviewed twenty-two) and claimed that many showed negative outcomes.

35. See Florence Hollis, "Evaluation: Clinical Results and Research Methodology," *Clinical Social Work Journal,* 4 (Fall 1976), 204–222; and Ludwig L. Geismer, "Thirteen Evaluative Studies," in Edward J. Mullen et al., eds., *Evaluation of Social Intervention* (San Francisco: Jossey-Bass, 1972); Mullen himself examined thirteen studies and disagreed with Fischer's and Wood's claims. See also John A. Crane, "The Power of Social Intervention Experiments to Discriminate Differences Between Experimental and Control Groups," *Social Service Review,* 50 (June 1976), 224–242; in a statistically astute and persuasive article, Crane examined many of the control or contrast group studies reviewed by Fischer and Wood and argued, "Research evidence as to the effectiveness of case services in social work is much less clearcut than has often been assumed."

36. William J. Reid and Ann W. Shyne, *Brief and Extended Casework* (New York: Columbia University Press, 1969).

37. Myrna M. Weissman et al., "Treatment Effect on the Social Adjustment of Depressed Patients," *Archives of General Psychiatry,* 30 (June 1974), 771–778.

38. Dorothy Fahs Beck and Mary Ann Jones, *Progress on Family Problems* (New York: Family Service Association of America, 1973). The generally positive findings of this study were challenged by John R. Schuerman in a critical essay review, "Do Family Services Help?" *Social Service Review,* 49 (September 1975), 363–375. Interested readers will want to study the Beck response and Schuerman's further comments in *Social Service Review,* 50 (June 1976), 312–331.

39. See, for example, William J. Reid and Patricia Hanrahan, "Recent Evaluations of Social Work: Grounds for Optimism," *Social Work,* 27 (July 1982), 328–340; and Allen Rubin, "More Grounds for Optimism," *Social Work,* 30 (November–December 1985), 469–476. See also "Comments on Reid and Hanrahan," *Social Work,* 28 (January–February 1983), 74–79.

40. See Ray J. Thomlison, "Something Works: Evidence from Practice Effectiveness Studies," *Social Work,* 29 (January–February 1984), 51–56. Readers interested in research studies of outcomes and process of a broad range of treatments will want to look over

Sol L. Garfield and Allen E. Bergin, eds., *Handbook of Psychotherapy and Behavior Change* (New York: John Wiley & Sons, 1986); and Alan S. Gurman and David P. Kniskern, "Family Therapy Outcome Research: Knowns and Unknowns," in Gurman and Kniskern, eds., *Handbook of Family Therapy* (New York: Brunner/Mazel, 1981), pp. 742–775.

41. See Elane M. Nuehring and Anne B. Pascone, "Single-Subject Evaluation: A Tool for Quality Assurance, *Social Work,* 31 (September–October 1986), 359–365; Michael W. Howe, "Casework Self-Evaluation: A Single Subject Approach," *Social Service Review,* 48 (March 1974), 1–23; Rona L. Levy, "Overview of Single-Case Experiments," in Aaron Rosenblatt and Diana Waldfogel, eds., *Handbook of Clinical Social Work* (San Francisco: Jossey-Bass, 1983), pp. 583–602; Elizabeth Mutschler, "Evaluating Practice: A Study of Research Utilization by Practitioners," *Social Work,* 29 (July–August 1984), 332–337; and Kevin Corcoran and Joel Fischer, *Measures for Clinical Practice: A Sourcebook* (New York: The Free Press, 1987).

42. Max Siporin, "Current Social Work Perspectives on Clinical Practice," *Clinical Social Work Journal,* 13 (Fall 1985), 207.

See also Roy A. Ruckdeschel and Buford E. Farris, "Assessing Practice: A Critical Look at the Single-Case Design," *Social Casework,* 62 (September 1981), 413–419. In this important and persuasive paper the authors suggest a qualitative case-analysis model because, in their view (p. 419): "The single-case design has a very narrow range of applicability for social work practice. For most practical modalities, other than a behavioral framework, the data collected and presented are not able to answer questions of effectiveness."

43. David B. Pharis in a book review of Tony Tripodi's *Evaluative Research for Social Workers* (Englewood Cliffs, N.J.: Prentice Hall, 1983), in *Clinical Social Work Journal,* 15 (Summer 1987), 202.

44. Siporin, "Current Social Work Perspectives on Clinical Practice," 205.

45. Carol H. Meyer, "Editorial," *Social Work,* 29 (July–August 1984), 323.

46. Readers interested in the debate and differences regarding social work research should read especially Ludwig L. Geismar and Katherine M. Wood, "Evaluating Practice: Science as Faith," *Social Casework*, 63 (May 1982), 266–275; and André Ivanoff, Betty J. Blythe, and Scott Briar, "The Empirical Practice Debate," *Social Casework*, 68 (May 1987), 290–298.

Other recommended readings on research from various perspectives include Sharon Berlin, "Single Case Evaluation: Another Version," *Social Work Research and Abstracts*, 19 (Spring 1983), 3–11; Neal Broxmeyer, "Practitioner-Research in Treating a Borderline Child," *Social Work Research and Abstracts*, 14 (Winter 1978), 5–10; Richard K. Caputo, "The Role of Research in the Family Service Agency," *Social Casework*, 66 (April 1985), 205–212; Mary M. Dolan and Betsy S. Vourlekis, "A Field Project: Single-Subject Design in a Public Social Service Agency," *Journal of Social Service Research*, 6 (Spring–Summer 1983), 29–43; Irwin Epstein, "Pedagogy of the Perturbed: Teaching Research to the Reluctants," *Journal of Teaching in Social Work*, 1 (Spring/Summer 1987), 71–89; Martha Heineman-Peiper, "The Future of Social Work Research," *Social Work Research and Abstracts*, 21 (Winter 1985), 3–11; Randolph L. Lucente, "N = 1: Intensive Case Study Methodology Reconsidered," *Journal of Teaching in Social Work*, 1 (Fall/Winter 1987), 49–64; Jeanne C. Marsh, "Research Innovation in Social Work Practice: Avoiding the Headless Machine," *Social Service Review*, 57 (December 1983), 582–598; Judith Nelsen, "Issues in Single Subject Research for Non-Behaviorists," *Social Work Research and Abstracts*, 17 (Summer 1981), 31–37; Aaron Rosen, "Barriers to Utilization of Research by Social Work Practitioners," *Journal of Social Service Research*, 6 (Spring–Summer 1983), 1–15; Dennis Saleebey, "The Tension Between Research and Practice: Assumptions of the Experimental Paradigm," *Clinical Social Work Journal*, 7 (Winter 1979), 267–284; Deborah H. Siegel, "Defining Empirically Based Practice," *Social Work*, 29 (July–August 1984), 325–331.

There are also several useful articles in Section IV, Rosenblatt and Waldfogel, *Handbook of Clinical Social Work*.

CHAPTER 2

The Psychosocial Frame of Reference: An Overview

BASIC VALUES

In this chapter we are seeking to sketch the frame of reference upon which psychosocial casework rests. Certain basic values of casework form the first component of that framework. Psychosocial casework is characterized by its direct concern for the *well-being* of the individual. It is not its purpose to bring the individual into conformity with society and thus rid society of the social hazard presented by the discontented, unsatisfied, rebellious individual. On the contrary, casework came into being as a response to the needs of human beings for protection against social and natural deprivations and catastrophes. Historically, it represents a turning away from the laissez-faire doctrines that followed the unhappy combination of Malthusian thinking with Darwin's emphasis on the development of strength through the survival of the fittest. From its inception casework has stressed the value of the individual, and for the past sixty years it has consistently advocated the right of each person to live in a unique way, provided he or she does not infringe unduly upon the rights of others. Traditionally, caseworkers have been committed to doing all they can to help people to gain access to opportunities that promote maximum realization of their potentials and aspirations, and to reduce obstacles to self-fulfillment.[1]

This emphasis upon the innate worth of the individual is an extremely important, fundamental characteristic of casework. It is the ingredient that makes it possible to establish the relationship of trust that is so essential for effective treatment. From it grow the two essential characteristics of the caseworker's attitude toward a person coming for help: first, *acceptance,* and second, respect for the client's right to make his or her own decisions, often referred to as *self-determination.*

By *acceptance* we mean the maintaining of an attitude of warm goodwill toward the client, whether or not his or her way of behaving is socially acceptable and whether or not it is to the worker's personal liking. This is without doubt the main ingredient in the development of a therapeutic or helping relationship. At the beginning of treatment, the client is often distrustful of the worker's interest and desire to help and may also have feelings of helplessness,

25

lack of self-esteem, or fear of criticism. Uncritical acceptance by the worker lessens these fears and begins the building of a client-worker relationship in which the client feels support and can talk freely. In actual practice, of course, we may have to confront our own negative reactions to clients whose behavior is hostile, cold, destructive, or otherwise distasteful; achieving the ideal of warm goodwill sometimes takes deliberate effort. When meeting with families—especially if one is caught in the cross fire between angry, blaming family members—it can be difficult to maintain an attitude of acceptance and impartiality.

Acceptance goes beyond objectivity. It requires more than intellectual understanding of a person's behavior and plight. Mere tolerance is not enough. Acceptance of our clients—liking and feeling warmly toward them whether or not we like how they appear or what they do—requires an additional and essential element: *empathy.*[2] For our purposes, we define *empathy* as *the capacity to enter into and grasp the inner feelings or subjective state of another person.*

Perhaps even more than many others in the helping professions, caseworkers encounter people who are severely disabled, physically, emotionally, and mentally. Many of our clients have literally or figuratively been battered by life circumstances, by economic deprivation, by bigotry. Some have answered violence with violence. Others have learned to cope with life passively, unable or unwilling to seek alternatives to present circumstances. Still others respond to misfortune by deteriorating, emotionally or physically. Acceptance and understanding require caseworkers to *feel with* a broad range of excruciatingly painful experiences of others. We need to recognize the desperation that lies behind reactions to these experiences. Obviously, the more accurately we are able to empathize, the greater the likelihood that we can use our understanding in constructive interactions with our clients.

Acceptance is not to be confused with refraining from *evaluating* the appropriateness or usefulness of the client's ways of functioning. But even accurate and perceptive evaluation is of little value if it is accompanied by feelings of condemnation, hostility, or revulsion toward the client. Empathy is often the critical ingredient to maintaining a constant caring feeling.

Self-determination[3] is perhaps not a felicitous term; it is too absolute in its implications. What is really meant by this concept from the psychosocial perspective is that self-direction, the right to make one's own choices, is a highly valued attribute of the individual. The more that clients exercise autonomy, making decisions and directing their own lives, the better; and the less the caseworker tries to take over these responsibilities, the better.

It goes without saying, however, that the value of self-determination or self-realization is a relative concept in reality; it is subject to many conditions, constraints, and moral dilemmas. Many clients of social workers are so physically, socially, or economically handicapped that they have very few choices indeed.[4] It is our responsibility, as individual workers and as members of our profession, to do all we can to maximize opportunities for everybody, but in many cases the options of disadvantaged clients are extremely limited. Furthermore, people are constantly having to weigh their own preferences or desires against conflicting needs or wishes of others. A woman client, for example, may want very much to work full time but decide against it because of the lack of high-quality child-care resources for her preschool child. For career reasons, a man may want to relocate to another state but choose not to because his aging mother and father who live nearby are becoming increasingly dependent and isolated; he forfeits his opportunity because of feelings of duty and love for his parents.[5]

In order to make sound decisions, the client sometimes simply needs better information; often, help is needed from the caseworker in exploring and understanding various aspects of a dilemma. In some cases, the client's ego is to varying degrees impaired in its capacity for accurate perception or judgment, or its functioning is distorted by the operation of mechanisms of defense, so that the problem becomes one of helping the person to develop greater capacity for decision making. The objective of such work is to increase the *ability* to make decisions, not to make them for the client. In extreme situations, where there is danger of real harm to self or to others, or where the client or client's family is incapable of carrying this responsibility, the caseworker may have to take over and make decisions for the client. But this is done *only* where the necessity for such action is absolutely clear.

A belief in the value of self-determination does not mean that the caseworker plays a passive role with clients. On the contrary, change is promoted in clients' functioning when it is believed that this will enable them to meet their needs more effectively. A worker may actively encourage a client to take a high school equivalency test in order to be eligible for a better job *the client wants.* But whatever the means a worker chooses to bring about change must ever be consistent with the goal of increasing the client's capacity for self-direction: his or her autonomy. On an ongoing basis, the goals of the treatment must be shared and reviewed by worker and client together; self-direction by the client requires a casework relationship that fosters *mutuality.* Thus the relationship is consistently an honest one, the worker's showing respect for the wishes and goals of the client and sometimes offering suggestions or advice—not, however, as directives but as opinions that the client is free to accept or reject. Over and over again, workers may raise questions such as: "Would it help if...?" "Does it make sense to you to consider...?" "Do you think that idea will work out in practice?" Even these inquiries are designed to help clients become experts on making decisions that seem best to *them;* they are not intended to persuade them of a particular course of action.

A worker sometimes offers suggestions about *how* to reach a goal that a client or family desires. Obviously, this is entirely different from becoming directive about *what* goal or decision is to be chosen. In reaching decisions and moving toward the realization of an objective, the worker's role is to help clients clarify thinking. In other words, whenever possible—and this is most of the time—clients are helped to reason things through for themselves, to correct their own misconceptions, and to accept the maximum responsibility of which they are capable for formulating their own ideas. Where more active guidance is needed, because of lack of knowledge, as is sometimes true in child-rearing problems, or of limitations in education or intellectual capacity, more active guidance may be needed. But even in these circumstances, every effort is made to promote the client's self-directive ability. Strong emphasis is therefore placed on techniques for drawing out the client's own reasoning and decision-making capacities.

THE PERSON-IN-SITUATION

Psychosocial casework has always been concerned with the improvement of interpersonal relationships and life situations. In spite of shifting emphases over the years, it has consistently recognized the importance of internal psychological processes, external social and physical conditions, and the interplay among them. Throughout its history, in its endeavor to enable individuals to meet their needs and function adequately in their lives and social relationships, psychosocial thought has drawn continuously from other scientific fields as they uncovered data and developed theory that promised to throw light on the psychological, social, and interactional aspects of human problems. Psychology and psychiatry; cultural anthropology and studies in ethnicity; sociology, including theories on role and gender, communication, family and group dynamics; and systems and ecological theories all have contributed, and continue to contribute, essential knowledge to the field of psychosocial casework.

Gordon Hamilton's concept, "the person-in-his-situation," is central to casework theory and refers to the threefold configuration consisting of the person, the situation, and the interaction between them.[6] The terms *internal pressure* and *external pressure* have often been used to describe forces within the individual and forces within the environment as they impinge upon or interact with each other. External pressure is sometimes referred to as *press* and internal pressure as *stress.*

The person-situation interaction is highly complex. External press is immediately modified by the way in which the individual perceives it. Depending upon their individual natures, upon their needs or internal stress, individuals will react to their perceptions of press in their own particular ways. Furthermore, since the term "situation" often implies a human situation—family, friends, employer, teacher, and so on—or intricate social and physical environmental forces, the situation is at least as complicated as the "person" who confronts it. The individual's family is usually seen as a fundamental component of the "situation," and the interactions occurring in the family system in both past and present are of high salience. When a person overtly reacts to an external press, this reaction in turn becomes a press upon some other human being, who then responds with his or her own perceptions and needs. Hence, the individual and the environment can only be understood within the framework of their inextricable interdependence on one another.

Fundamental purposes of casework, and social work as a whole, include resolution or reduction of problems *arising out of disequilibrium between people and their environments.* Sometimes personalities or families are truly "pathological," "dysfunctional," or "inadequate." At other times, these same assessments can be applied to aspects of the world around the client. In addition to relatives and friends, these environments include other people, physical surroundings, cultural attitudes, organizations or institutions, even communities and larger social systems. When one or more of these are unhealthy or substandard (an ill spouse, lack of housing, discrimination, a tight job market, etc.), the client is, of course, directly affected. Problems may also be created by dysfunctional transactions *among* various systems in a client's milieu (take, for example, the stress for a child whose foster parents, natural parents, and child welfare worker are experiencing conflict or are pulling in different directions). Certainly many client difficulties are the consequence of dysfunctional interactions *between* a client and one or more aspects of the environment (spouse, in-laws, employer, neighbors, for example).

Often, an understanding of the person-in-situation requires an understanding of the psychology of the people involved in the *gestalt.** Equally often, it requires an analysis of environmental forces impinging on the person or family with whom one is working. There are also many instances, as this text will illustrate, when a worker's focus is actually on the interactions or reciprocal influences between people and their situations, rather than on the individual or the environment as such. As caseworkers, we aim to promote positive adaptations by correcting or preventing maladaptive interactions.[7]

SYSTEMS THEORY AND THE ECOLOGICAL PERSPECTIVE

The person-situation gestalt can well be regarded as a system, and many concepts derived from general systems theory and the ecological

---

*A term we use to describe a configuration of phenomena that is so well integrated that the *sum cannot be defined by its parts alone.*

point of view are extremely useful in describing and evaluating the various systems involved in the gestalt.[8] From these assessments, interventive approaches are then designed. Individuals are in constant interaction, or *transaction*, with members of their immediate family; with other relatives; with networks of friends and acquaintances; with employment, health, welfare, and a multitude of other systems, including value systems that are shaped by the interactions, past and present, with one's family, culture, and society. Through a spouse or a child there may be either direct or indirect interaction with other systems, such as the school or hospital system. In casework, the focus of attention, for assessment and intervention, goes beyond the individual or family to include those systems that appear to be of salient importance to the resolution of problems for which help is sought.

A primary characteristic of any system is that all its parts are in transaction, so that whatever affects one part of the system to some degree affects all parts. Change in one aspect *requires* changes in the others. *Adaptation* is defined as a transactional process in which people influence and shape their environments and, in turn, are influenced and shaped by them. People and their environments are constantly changing. As Germain writes: "People must adapt to changes in the self and in the environment in a continuing effort to fit the ever-changing conditions of existence to ever-changing human needs and aspirations. As a transactional concept, *adaptation* calls our attention simultaneously to qualities of the person and qualities of the environment."[9]

Recently, caseworkers have been more attuned than ever to the need to assess the "match" or "fit" between individuals and their environments. Rather than placing blame on a mother for an imperfect bond with a child, it is understood that characteristics of youngsters as well as those of parents can have profound implications for the parent-child relationship: the

quality of the "fit." Opportunities for resolution can be examined less defensively when it is clear that the problem is defined in terms of *difference* rather than inadequacy. Without ascribing pathology to an individual or to a workplace, assessing the "fit" between the worker and the job can provide guidelines for casework intervention. Vigilante gives examples: "The workplace that requires privacy may be experienced by some workers as isolation. On the other hand, the workplace that requires personal interaction may be experienced by a worker as invasion. . . . An authoritarian administration may make some workers feel controlled and powerless and make others secure and certain about expectations and performance."[10] An individual's temperament, needs, and preferences and the available opportunities can be evaluated and, whenever possible, matched to better suit both sides. This perspective contributes to a "no-fault" approach to reducing person-situation disequilibrium.

The interdependence of systems and their components of the person and the environment—becomes apparent in every situation that comes to the attention of social workers. If a young daughter in a family becomes seriously ill, for example, this is certain to affect both father and mother in some manner: worry over the child, direct involvement in the child's care, time and attention required by the child's condition. These changes then may influence many other systems in which each member is involved, such as the extended family, the employment situation, and the educational system. For instance, if the mother is now unable to make customary weekly visits to her elderly father, she may not only disappoint him but also interfere with plans made by her sister, with whom the father lives, to enjoy time freed by the expected visit. If the mother's value system requires her to give attention to elderly relatives, guilt at being unable to do so may create additional strain on her and those around her. The child's illness may worry her father so much that he becomes irritable or distracted at work, potentially contributing to tensions with fellow workers or superiors. Feeling harassed at the job, this man may then begin to place demands on his already overburdened wife, creating problems in the marital system that had previously been a source of comfort to both spouses. The sick girl may learn that, because of her absence, a classmate is being given a role in the school play that had originally been assigned to her. This disappointment may retard her recovery; this, in turn, reverberates in all of the other interdependent systems just mentioned.

As this example illustrates, when two systems are in interaction because they have a common member, occurrences in one system will, to some degree, affect the other system. This is sometimes referred to as *input* from one system to another, or as *transactions* between systems. If the illness of the child described above continues, there may well be repetitions of that input from the nuclear family system to the other systems and various additional *feedback* processes that occur among them. The mother's sister may put pressure on her to resume regular visits, ultimately adding to the already considerable tensions between husband and wife. The father's supervisor may be increasingly annoyed with him and cause worry about whether the job and security are in jeopardy. Mounting pressures and marital distress may then trigger angry interactions between parents and the other children in the family. These children may subsequently develop problems in school, in turn adding further to the strain between husband and wife.

Obviously, the possible cycle of events is endless, and the individuals being influenced by many forces at the same time undoubtedly will have to arrive at some resolution. Decisions may be made to effect some positive change in the environment: by the family's locating a babysitter for the child or a home health worker for the aging father to reduce pressures on the care-takers, by the mother's talking problems over with her sister, by the father's taking vacation time or explaining his unusual behavior to his supervisor, and so on. The couple, concerned about any or all of the escalating negative events in their lives, may agree to seek help in problem solving from a social worker. Even if only one parent evaluates his or her own behavior toward the other and takes steps to improve the quality of the marital interactions, very possibly all of the impinging relationships will improve. Just as one event—in this illustration, the child's illness—can precipitate many mounting negative transactions, so *one positive change* can be the beginning of a reversal of the downward spiral. Not only are all aspects of the system involved in the problem, the actions of *any* member can contribute to the solution.

When individuals attempt to cope with or modify their situations or their relationships to others, they have to make some changes within themselves. *The personality is itself a system* with various and sometimes conflicting forces within. Every action, every response, is shaped by these internal forces as well as by the presses and gratifications (either experienced or anticipated) from others with whom the individual is in interaction. As we shall see later on in this chapter, sometimes a small shift in the balance of the personality system can trigger significant changes in the individual and, subsequently, in the quality of transactions with other people or systems.

This realization that human beings are themselves systems of a very complicated and subtle nature radically modifies the application of systems theory to human transactions. If this fact is overlooked, in our view, the use of systems and ecological concepts becomes simplistic. From the psychosocial perspective, only by combining these extremely useful concepts with adequate knowledge of the nature of human personality can we productively understand the person-situation gestalt.

PERSONALITY AND SOCIAL FUNCTIONING

The emphasis of this book is upon psychosocial procedures used by clinical social workers to bring about change in the social functioning of individuals and families, particularly in interpersonal relationships. This is not the whole of casework, but it is an extremely important part of the whole and is carried on by all clinical social workers under whatever auspices they work. The data on which this book is based are derived primarily—but not totally—from family, medical, mental health, and child welfare agencies. Nevertheless, the principles hold for casework in any setting in which interpersonal relationships are a treatment concern.

Before we can comprehend the dynamics of psychosocial treatment, we must have a clear picture of what the caseworker understands by personality and its social functioning. Social functioning represents the interplay between the two major variables, the social environment and the individual, each of which, in turn, is a composite of various forces. The environment offers opportunities and gratifications, frustrations, and deprivations. As we have said, it consists not only of concrete realities—such as the availability of food, clothing, shelter, medical care, employment opportunities, physical safety, educational and recreational opportunities—but also of sociopsychological realities expressed through interpersonal relationships. For human beings need social relationships as much as they need food and shelter.[11] Studies of young chimpanzees have demonstrated that even they are profoundly affected by the absence of warm care by the mother chimp.[12] An individual must rely on the environment to provide opportunities for social relationships of all sorts: with parents, brothers and sisters, extended family relationships, marriage partners, lovers, friends, acquaintances. The quality of these relationships is to no small degree deter-

mined by forces independent of the individual's own efforts and choices.

Socially determined psychological realities also exert profound pressures, particularly in the areas of values and perceptions. Ethnic, class, race, regional, and role factors influence standards of behavior, aspirations, and perceptions of others and of self. At first these influences are transmitted primarily through the parents, later through other social institutions and relationships. The total environment, then, as experienced by any individual, is a complex set of interacting forces *impinging upon* the person simultaneously from many different directions and interacting with an equally complex set of forces *within* his or her own personality.[13]

THE PERSONALITY SYSTEM

Although Freud himself did not use modern systems theory, recent thinkers in our field have applied this framework to his concepts about personality. For years, of course, psychosocial workers have found the ideas developed by Freud and his followers extremely valuable.[14] Anna Freud, Hartman, Kris, Loewenstein, Rapaport, Jacobson, White, and many others made significant contributions to what is now referred to as "ego theory." Erikson, another ego psychologist, gave special attention to environmental and cultural influences, further increasing our understanding of the critical importance of the ego to individual adaptation and functioning; his thinking was therefore particularly appealing to psychosocial caseworkers. A number of other psychoanalytically oriented writers and practitioners have also built on Freud's basic tenets. Writers known as developmental and object relations theorists, including Spitz, Mahler, Fairbairn, Winnicott, and Guntrip, who were also grounded in psychoanalytic theory, added considerably to our understanding of psychological and social development. More recently, Kohut, who is known for his theory of self-psychology, and others, Kernberg among them, contributed to our knowledge of the origins and treatment of severe personality disorders resulting from developmental deficits and deprivations.[15] We will not attempt a detailed review of the accumulated, evolving knowledge incorporated by our psychosocial framework, but we will summarize certain features that have been particularly useful to the practice of casework.

The Id

Freud postulated a tripartite personality or psychic structure composed of the *id*, the *ego,* and the *superego.* The *id* can be thought of as a set of drives: drives that are present from birth, in various degrees of strength, in all individuals. "Pure" Freudians would describe these drives as libidinal and aggressive in nature. In short, Freud believed that the individual's behavior is guided by the drives of the id to seek pleasure and avoid "unpleasure"; this idea is referred to as the *pleasure principle.* Modification of the pleasure principle is achieved as the individual matures and the ego begins to operate on the *reality principle.* More modern thinkers, who have focused on object relations and self-psychology, teach that the infant's needs and strivings are for affirmation, admiration, stimulation, and dependence on or merger with the caretaker, followed by an equally important need for "optimal frustration" and the development of a sense of self. The goal of the early ego is to seek "objects"—other people—and, with maturity, to strive for a feeling of well-being, for *autonomy* and *satisfying interpersonal relations.*[16] The differences between Freud and the later thinkers are mostly a matter of emphasis, but the expanded ego theory and other newer theories have been extremely important to psychosocial casework because of the light they throw on social functioning; they have also provided an important conceptual link between intrapsychic

and family treatment, as later chapters of this book will illustrate.

In any event, the id can be conceptualized as the agency of the psychological structure that contains raw, chaotic, undifferentiated energies that are largely unconscious. The term *primary process* describes an unconscious process, a primitive way of thinking and being, that originates in early childhood, before the development of logical, rational thinking. Wishes are imbued with magical power. Hence, when a child has wished that a parent or sibling would get hurt, and some mishap subsequently occurs, the child may feel that he or she has actually caused it and therefore fear retaliation. When someone close has died, the child may regard this as an act of purposeful abandonment and resent it accordingly. Children cannot always distinguish their own thoughts and feelings from those of others; when angry, a child may believe others are angry at *him.* Contradictory ideas exist side by side in the mind, and no need is felt to reconcile them. When crossed, a young child may feel anger that is not tempered by the good things experienced from the same source that is now frustrating. The child generalizes indiscriminately, often experiencing all grown-up men to be like Father, all women like Mother. Certain individuals with developmental deficits or personality disorders can be inordinately ruled by primary process. In relatively mature adults, primary process usually becomes most apparent in dreams or in the compelling urge to take action *without thinking*; it refers to the primitive level of organization of innate drives or needs and the tendency of individuals to seek immediate and free discharge of excitation.[17]

The Ego

From birth onward the personality also includes a set of adaptive and growth-producing qualities, known in composite as the *ego.* As the ego develops, so does the *secondary process,* the function of which is to begin to bring order, memory, and reason to the drives and demands placed upon the individual by the id. The components of the ego, some of which are conscious and others which are unconscious, like the energies of the id, vary in strength and quality in different individuals and are subject to hereditary as well as environmental influences. In early Freudian theory, the ego was thought to develop out of the id and to be in a sense dependent on the development of the drives. Later theory sees the ego as independent and potentially much stronger than was formerly believed in its ability to deal with and move toward goals of its own selection. As will be better understood as we go along, the development of ego psychology gave a better theoretical underpinning for the positive results that could be achieved by those caseworkers who stressed working with the "strengths" of the personality rather than focusing primarily on "pathology" or on understanding of early causative factors. Combined with crisis theory (to be discussed in Chapter 19), modern ego theory led to the development of shorter treatment methods for certain types of difficulties. It also threw light upon various forms of personality disorders, to be discussed later on in this text.

While the ego system organizes, controls, and regulates the energies of the id, it also mediates stimuli and pressures placed upon it by the physical and social environment, and by the superego-ego ideal, to be described shortly. Commencing at birth, then, the ego increasingly finds means for dealing with chaotic emotion, internalized expectations, external dangers, and opportunities. At early ages we can see children begin to remember and think about positive and negative consequences of previous actions (a smile brought an adoring hug; a finger on the hot stove resulted in a burn or a spanking). As time goes on, youngsters use the capacity of reason to anticipate events that they have not yet experienced and learn to solve increasingly complicated problems. The totally dependent newborn becomes more and more autonomous: a process of development that we shall briefly discuss later in this chapter.

Specific Ego Functions   Bellak and his collaborators described and studied twelve functions of the ego as they are assessed "in schizophrenics, neurotics and normals." These are discussed in detail in their comprehensive report and elsewhere.[18] Some of those that are very important in casework assessment and treatment will be mentioned now.

Reality testing, when it is intact, refers to the ability to distinguish between—and accurately perceive and interpret—internal and external stimuli or events. *Judgment* allows an individual to anticipate probable consequences of behaviors and to act accordingly and appropriately on the basis of awareness of the probable consequences.

An important function of the ego is *regulation and control of drives, affects, and impulses*. This function includes the ability—under relatively normal circumstances and when required—to postpone expressing emotion or acting on impulse and the general capacity to endure strong feelings without becoming overwhelmed or flooded. *Under*control sometimes leads to serious interpersonal problems. *Over*control, on the other hand, may result in turning negative feelings against oneself or may prevent expression of softer or passionate feelings that enhance intimate relationships. The quality of one's *object relations* depends on the degree and kind of relatedness to others, including the capacity for autonomy, mutuality and reciprocity, empathy, intimacy, trust, and ability to maintain a sense of being related to others even in their absence.

Well-developed *thought processes* include the ability to remember, concentrate, and conceptualize, using either concrete or abstract thinking, depending on which is most appropriate to a particular situation. These functions of thought reflect the shift from primary to secondary process. *Synthetic-integrative functioning* refers to the capacity of the ego to organize and synthesize all aspects of one's personality (cognitive and affective), including behavior, even those that are contradictory or in conflict; without this capacity, the personality and behavior can be chaotic or fragmented. *Mastery* and *competence* are extremely important to casework assessment and refer to how competent a person feels and is in mastering, affecting, and interacting with essential aspects of his or her environment. Needless to say, a person's performance and efforts at mastering his or her surroundings have to be evaluated in conjunction with the responsiveness or recalcitrance of the environment, including other people in it. It also stands to reason that if the *actual* competence is significantly greater or less than the individual's *sense* of competence, disabling underachievement or grandiosity may follow.

All ego functioning must be evaluated in terms of the life circumstances of the person in question. Assessment of performance and capacity also has to take into account the level of functioning that is considered age-appropriate.

Ego Defenses The important *defensive functions* of the ego require special attention. Mechanisms of defense start to evolve in the very young child as a way of protecting the fragile, budding personality from being overwhelmed. Certain defenses normally begin to arise in infancy; others develop as the youngster grows older. Defenses, which are often but not always unconscious, have adaptive and protective functions. Broadly speaking, by means of defenses, the ego attempts to ward off anxiety or fear stemming from internal impulses and from the individual's reactions to real situational occurrences. Unacceptable urges or painful emotions are held at bay. A woman who has been taught that angry thoughts and feelings are "bad," for example, may protect herself against becoming aware of them. People sometimes restrain themselves from crying, for fear that their sadness

will overwhelm them. A man who has been told that he has a fatal illness may—at first or throughout the illness—ignore or twist the facts to avoid the terror and sadness of the truth. Adult personality traits are strongly influenced by which combinations of defenses characteristically predominate when the individual experiences inner or outer pressures.

By definition, defenses distort the actual situation to one degree or another. *They can serve healthy or pathological ends.* Defenses that operate on a temporary basis and yet are flexible may give the ego a chance to assimilate an overload of information or internal energy; the man mentioned above may need a little time to take in the full implications of his catastrophic illness. In an emergency, defenses allow us to take necessary action before fully registering the danger of the situation. These defensive functions are essential to maintaining a sense of balance and well-being.

On the other hand, the woman who persistently cannot permit herself to feel anger may remain aloof from other people in order to avoid the dreaded feelings and by doing so never enjoy close personal relationships. A person may develop somatic responses or symptoms that derive from diverting or choking off from awareness conflicts or emotions—jealousy, sadness, affection, anger, etc. If a man cannot risk the anxiety of confronting his wife with negative feelings, he may direct his anger at his son, thereby adding to rather than alleviating family distress. A person who lost a parent as a child may defend against tender feelings for fear of being bereaved again with the result that his or her relationships lack intimacy.

Unaware that they are using defenses that originated in childhood, adults may erroneously feel as vulnerable as they were when they were totally dependent on others and too immature to protect themselves adequately against real or feared threats, such as abandonment, rejection, and humiliation. Recognition that some of their predominant defense mechanisms are now "out of date" and dysfunctional, and no longer essential to survival, can be an important milestone for some people in casework treatment, especially treatment in which individuals seek to make changes within themselves in order to improve their social functioning.

In many cases, for people to feel and function better, or to make the changes they want to make in therapy, defenses need to be relaxed. In other cases, however, defenses need to be bolstered rather than mollified; for example, defenses required to fend off chaotic drives of the id may be too weak to prevent primitive affects from flooding a person's thought processes.

Common defenses   There are a number of defenses frequently and usefully employed by adults and, increasingly as they mature, by children from the beginnings of latency (age five or six) on. *Sublimation,* for example, is a process whereby instinctual impulses are altered and directed toward socially productive or creative activities; unacceptable aggressive drives are often converted into enthusiasm for sports or into advocacy for social change. Frightening impulses or feelings can be sublimated into acceptable endeavors. Feared or unwelcome sexual desires may be transformed into religious fervor. Or an individual who is fascinated by fire may actually reverse a drive to commit arson and become a firefighter! Tender feelings for others also are often sublimated and converted into loving attachments to animals or interest in romantic literature; of course, if *all* of a person's desires for relationships are channeled elsewhere, the result may be loneliness and disappointment.

Altruism is another often valuable defense; by recognizing the emotional gratifications of serving the needs of others, one's instinctual energies may then be channeled into generous, even self-sacrificing, activities. This defense becomes problematic, of course, when the urge to give is compulsive (say, when one insists on giving to others who do not require or want the gifts or services) or when one consistently repudiates one's *own* needs or aspirations and totally focuses on those of others. *Humor,* too, can serve a very constructive defensive function; when selectively employed, humor allows us to put personal shortcomings or stressful circumstances into a perspective that makes them more tolerable and more easily confronted or accepted.

Probably the most pervasive defense of all is *repression.* By this, anxiety-producing thoughts, feelings, memories are forgotten or else never experienced in the first place; they are pushed or drawn into the unconscious. It is this unconscious content, especially of early childhood, that is the center of attention in psychoanalysis; when aggressive, sexual, or relational drives are extensively repressed, personality conflicts and distortions arise. Although repressed material is a major pivot of neurotic distress, it is also true that everyone has repressed matter that will not and need not ever surface and does not appreciably interfere with functioning. Primitive primary process functioning is necessarily repressed in order to make way for the development of a more orderly secondary process, thereby enhancing the individual's growth to a higher level of functioning.

Suppressed material is more likely than repressed material to be accessible through procedures used by clinical social workers. In this mechanism, the anxiety-arousing mental content is pushed, at times consciously, only partly below the surface of the mind to the preconscious rather than to the unconscious. It is a commonly used and sometimes useful mechanism whereby a painful matter is put aside: "After a good night's sleep I'll forget all about it." Or, "I'll worry about that later, when I can do something about it."

Avoidance is a common—sometimes socially useful, sometimes self-destructive—defense. Simply stated, efforts are made by the individual to avoid a situation that is potentially disturbing. Like the other defenses already mentioned, depending on its pervasiveness and purpose, avoidance can be helpful or harmful to the person who uses it. When *isolation* is used as a defense, different parts of one's experience, especially events or memories and the feelings associated with them, are separated from each other so that matters that are actually interrelated appear not to affect one another. For example, an adult may be aware of general feelings of anger but may not relate these in any way to clearly remembered experiences of childhood abuse.

Intellectualization is frequently employed to fend off unacceptable affects, as is the case when one talks or thinks about potentially highly charged or disturbing issues in one's life without allowing the accompanying emotions to be fully experienced. Sometimes this defense is used constructively to enable people to "make sense" out of difficult situations or distressing feelings or to get through a crisis, but overuse can cramp one's capacity for experiencing and expressing emotion, including positive or pleasurable emotion. *Rationalization,* closely related to intellectualization, is used by everyone at times. Often people explain unhappy events with "It's all for the best." A woman who cannot give herself permission to have a vacation may justify doing so by persuading herself that her husband and children need a holiday. Excessive use of intellectualization and rationalization is often associated with obsessive-compulsive personality characteristics, but it is important not to generalize without sufficient data about the individual and his or her internal and external pressures.

Reaction formation is another common defense of the ego. It involves the substitution of one emotion or attitude for another, more or less opposite feeling. In order to try to endure intolerable oppression, rather than becoming enraged, people sometimes become detached, passive, or placating in their manner. Or one may defensively claim, "Of course I don't love him; in fact, I hate him." Sometimes an unwanted emotion is *turned against the self.* This is particularly true of anger, where the person becomes angry at the self when the logic of the situation would seem to require anger at another. If realization of this outwardly turned anger would cause too much anxiety, or if its expression would result in frightening reactions from others, the emotion may be experienced as feelings of self-criticism or depression: that is, as anger turned against the self.

Projection is a mechanism that can be observed in all people from time to time, but when it is pervasive and not accessible to correction by the facts, it becomes extremely dysfunctional. Briefly stated, in projection, the individual's unacknowledged thoughts and feelings are attributed to others. We may, for example, falsely see our own unacceptable motives, anger, loving feelings, or any number of fears or wishes in someone else. In severe cases, when negative projective mechanisms are used extensively, people sometimes see rejection or danger all around them, with the effect that they become overly suspicious, combative, or withdrawn, even though these responses are not warranted by the actual circumstances.

Displacement is another common defense which may or may not be problematic depending on the extent to which it is used. In displacement, feelings and thoughts that refer to one person are transferred to another. Sometimes this occurs because it seems less threatening to express feelings to the substituted person; it may feel safer to show anger to a child than to a spouse, for example. Displacement may result from superficial similarities between two people, or because both occupy the same role in relation to the person doing the displacing. Fear one has for one's father, for instance, may be displaced onto other men in authority. In *denial,* another frequently used defense, a person refuses to recognize the existence of an anxiety-provoking emotion, thought, internal conflict, or event. Denial, like avoidance, projection, and some of the other defenses already mentioned, can be adaptive under some circumstances, but most problematic when the person's perceptions are permanently distorted. A seven-year-old child replied, "He's not dead," when told his beloved older brother had been killed in an accident. In the short run, the defense helped the boy's young ego to pace the assimilation of the tragic event. Had he continued to deny the facts, however, the result would have had serious psychological implications.

Regression refers to the process of returning to an earlier stage of development in order to avoid an anxiety-producing situation. In the face of illness, loss, or unhappy relationships, adults may revert to childlike demanding or dependent behaviors. Regression sometimes occurs in response to anxieties about the approach of a new life cycle stage, such as going away to college or retiring. A child who has become appropriately independent may go back to clinging or whining after learning his parents are planning to divorce. Often the regressive reactions are temporary and adaptive, but sometimes the person then becomes dysfunctionally "fixated" or "stuck" at a particular level of maturity.

Additional defenses that have recently been emphasized have been of particular importance in the treatment of individuals with certain developmental deficits or borderline personality disorders. These defenses are believed to originate in very early childhood. One such mechanism is known as *splitting*. To ward off anxiety, the person divides his or her self-concept and image of others into all "good" and all "bad," with no balance or middle ground; self and others are alternately viewed as all-powerful or as needing to be devalued. To illustrate: A person, who has a sense of being magically omnipotent, "flips"—for little or no apparent reason—into a feeling of total helplessness and despair. A man who is angry at his wife over a minor matter is so consumed by negativity that he is virtually unable to remember that only moments before he had idolized

her. Because of the split, there can be no synthesis of the opposite experiences. Presumably, by avoiding the integration of contradictory feelings and thoughts—from the unconscious point of view of the person using the defense—the "good" is saved from being contaminated or overwhelmed by the "bad." *Primitive idealization*, the tendency to see others as totally "good," also protects positive attitudes from being spoiled by the negative. *Devaluation* refers to the pervasive inclination to attribute exaggerated "bad" qualities to self or others.

Projective identification, a term with several meanings, is sometimes used to describe a defense—similar to projection as described above—in which a person projects onto others aspects of his or her own unacceptable impulses or self-image. Once externalized, these feared attitudes or feelings that originated from within are seen in others, especially others with whom one is closely related; then, for reasons of self-preservation, the individual believes that the other people and their attributes need to be controlled or attacked. For example, a man who is consciously or unconsciously frightened by his own homosexual impulses may project these onto his son and then castigate the boy and restrict his associations with male friends. In projective identification, there is often a true inability to distinguish self from other. Some definitions of this concept further expand on the usual notions about projection by including the idea that the individual using the defense invokes behaviors in others that serve to confirm his or her distortions. For instance, a mother who has pervasive feelings of inferiority may project her sense of inadequacy, her image of herself, onto her daughter and then, unconsciously, find means to induce the child to fail.[19]

Classification of defense mechanisms Defenses are classified by some writers according to the developmental phases in which they originated. As we said earlier, some defenses arise in very young childhood, and others are erected as the youngster grows older. *Very* roughly speaking, the above listing of some of the common defenses begins with the most "mature" and ends with the most "primitive."[20]

As already indicated, in adults, many of the more "mature" defenses (such as sublimation, altruism, and humor) serve healthy, adaptive psychological purposes; they can also be utilized in a very socially productive manner. At the other end of the continuum, sometimes an adult person's *predominant* and *pervasive* defenses (such as splitting and projective identification) are those that originated at a very immature stage and have not been replaced by more mature defenses. Or some individuals habitually and severely regress in the face of internal or external demands. When defensive patterns are extremely immature, we often find that general functioning is—at least to some degree, in some areas of the person's life—impaired and dysfunctional. Of course, it is not uncommon for a particular individual to manifest defenses deriving from various developmental phases, not just from one; the level of maturity will depend in part on which level of defensive functioning dominates.

In the view of the authors, a classification of defenses based on levels of maturity has its shortcomings and can be misleading. For example, denial is sometimes seen as a "low-level" or "immature" defense. However, as previously noted, sometimes denial serves very healthy purposes and enables people to maintain equilibrium under threatening circumstances. At the other extreme, suppression is considered by some to be among the most "mature" defenses. Yet we know that if it is used excessively it may impede a person from taking necessary action. Repression is a defense that is often classified as "neurotic," and yet it is also essential to mature development. It is important, then, not to jump to conclusions about a person's pathology or level of devel-

opment on the basis of the manifestation of a particular defense; misuse of a classification may lead us to assume lesser (or greater) overall maturity than is actually the case and lead us to generalizations that cannot be substantiated. Furthermore, we repeat: *the pervasiveness, chronicity, and rigidity of a defense—not its mere presence—are critical in the assessment of a person's level of "maturity."* The constructive or destructive effect of a particular defensive style can also be appraised by determining whether it promotes healthy coping with life's pressures or whether it impedes rational behavior and decisions. Caseworkers and clients together frequently evaluate whether defenses are enhancing or interfering with gratifying interpersonal relationships. Finally, one cannot accurately evaluate how functional or dysfunctional defenses are without an overall understanding of the external circumstances that triggered the protective mechanisms.

To summarize this discussion of ego defenses: the individual's whole perception of the external world is a combination in varying degrees of what is actually there and what is perceived or expected to be there. We often do not see what we do not look for, but we create for ourselves what we seek to find. People who anticipate hostility may read belligerence into others' behavior whether or not it exists and by their own responses may very well give rise to hostility in the others. In so doing, to a high degree people create their own environments, a form of *self-fulfilling prophecy.*

Because defenses are employed by all people in varying degrees, caseworkers need to recognize and understand them. Defenses allow individuals to manage anxiety and to adjust to developmental, interpersonal, and environmental demands. But defenses that served us well in childhood often have outlived their usefulness and interfere with current functioning. Whether defenses are adaptive or maladaptive, it is important to remember that they have been developed as protection and, hence, should not be casually or impetuously challenged. Especially when defenses are rigid, special attention is required. Even if a client's goals point to the need to modify defenses, or even if disabling symptoms seem to derive from defensive patterns, care and accurate assessment of the individual's tolerance for change must guide the worker's interventions. Fortunately, as we shall see in later chapters, clients can often be helped to become aware of maladaptive ways of ego functioning, sometimes in individual instances and sometimes as patterns of behavior. Such awareness can then lead to positive changes.

The Superego–Ego Ideal

The concepts of superego and ego ideal, like that of ego, refer to both conscious and unconscious functions. They represent the individual's *conscience* and are composed of internalized parental prohibitions and values, as well as ideals and social and moral standards derived from the world around the individual. The superego-ego ideal contains the "do's and don'ts," the ethical views and aspirations of the individual's personality. It can be destructively self-critical and guilt-inducing; it can be idealistic and self-approving. Generally speaking, the *superego* represents that part of the conscience that is absorbed primarily from the parents by parental dictate or by identification with parents in early childhood. When it is overly severe it is not always functional because the harshness can lead to intense self-hate, self-punishment, and even virtual immobilization of various ego functions. When it is underdeveloped in an individual, the result can be antisocial behavior and a lack of feeling for others. The *ego ideal* is generally thought of as a later development, representing identifications with nonparental figures as well as with later perceptions of parents. It contains goals and ideals of later childhood, adolescence, and maturity. In contrast to some aspects of the superego, it is more likely to be

consciously acquired and subject to ego evaluation.

Personality Development

The advances made over recent decades in ego psychology and object relations theory, among others, have added to our understanding of child development and have been extremely valuable to casework practice. In particular, on the basis of observation of and clinical experience with parents and children, attention has been paid to concepts relevant to the development of the relatively *autonomous, self-reliant, well-related personality*. Briefly stated, optimal circumstances—including "good enough" parenting[21] and environmental conditions—for the child include the following:

1. Fairly consistent parental availability, responsiveness, and support, *and* the child's ability to bond with the parent and receive the attentions
2. Parental encouragement of the child's independence and self-direction, appropriately timed to the child's age, *and* the child's ability to assimilate that encouragement
3. Parents who take some sense of pleasure or delight in the child and in the child's accomplishments, *and* the child's ability to absorb the approval
4. Environmental conditions that are secure and supportive enough for the child's caretakers so that they are free to provide the child with the stability required for "good enough" parenting

Ideally, as the child proceeds through the separation-individuation process described by Mahler,[22] he or she begins to internalize an integrated sense of self and other; "good" and "bad" images that were "split" from one another in early infancy become consolidated around the age of two or even earlier. By the time children reach about three years of age, they have become able to maintain a stable, independent concept of significant people even in their absence (referred to as *object constancy*) and a realistic sense of ability and capacity for taking care of themselves at age-appropriate levels. A balanced but essentially positive memory of the parent (which earlier had been split into "good" or "bad" images) provides the youngster with a sense of continuity: there is the realization that even when he or she is alone, a parent will eventually return and it will be possible to manage until then. When the child's capacity for object constancy and some sense of his or her own identity have been attained, unless external changes reverse or retard growth, the child has the ego foundation on which to continue to mature.

On the other hand, problems may ensue when family and environmental conditions do not provide these fundamentals. Developmental failures may result when:

1. Parents overprotect their children and therefore do not foster individuality. Children who are not expected to take care of their own needs in age-appropriate ways and are not challenged by conditions providing "optimal frustration" often fail to master essential developmental tasks. Children who are always the center of attention in their families or can "do no wrong" in their parents' eyes often do not develop inner resources and self-assurance.

2. Parents prematurely and too frequently leave their children to their own devices. Deprived of the minimal guidance, support, and encouragement required for healthy growth, many children become depressed or "pseudo-independent" or develop some type of personality disturbance.

3. Parents are grossly inconsistent in their caretaking. Children who cannot count on fairly regular positive attention to their needs may not develop object constancy, self-esteem, mastery, and an adequate sense of competence. Dysfunctional personality traits and severe emotional disabilities may be the outcome.

4. As a result of constitutional factors or some incompatibility with their caretakers, children cannot get the benefit of even "good enough" nurturance.

5. Environmental conditions are inhumane, unpredictable, or assaultive. Many families try to raise children under impossible circumstances of poverty, homelessness, or extreme racial or ethnic discrimination. Inadequate resources, inconsistency, and violence in the larger world can render it almost impossible for parents to provide children with the minimal or basic conditions required for healthy development.

As the individual grows and matures, the importance of age-appropriate "good enough" conditions for personality development continues. Erik Erikson's seminal contributions to theory include his view of the growth of the healthy personality as it moves through developmental stages and crises and masters life's outer and inner challenges and dangers. If circumstances have allowed it, by adolescence the child has achieved, in successive steps, trust (versus distrust), autonomy (versus shame and doubt), initiative (versus guilt), industry (versus inferiority).[23] It stands to reason that each stage of development depends on the quality of the resolution of the one before it. Failure to master one essential challenge impairs successful handling of the next.

INTERACTIONS BETWEEN INDIVIDUALS AND THEIR ENVIRONMENTS

Because Freud and some of his followers elaborated more upon the needs and responses of the individual than upon the impact of the environment, it is sometimes assumed that psychoanalytic theory disregards environmental influences. In actuality, Freud strongly emphasized the influences of both intra- and extrafamilial life experiences. His theory definitely rests upon social interaction as well as upon intrapsychic factors. One of Freud's major departures from predecessors such as Janet and Charcot, who regarded neurosis as a manifestation of constitutional weakness, was to see neurosis in terms of human relationships. The person with a hysterical paralysis, for example, in psychoanalytic theory is believed to be using this symptom as protection from something feared in relationships with other people. Although Freudian theory sees neurosis as a way of resolving conflicts among inner drives, the superego, and the ego, it also recognizes that such conflicts themselves emerge from the interactions between the child and parents or other caretaking figures. The later thinkers, some of whom we have mentioned in this chapter, both corrected and enriched many of Freud's concepts and gave even more attention to the interactive aspects of personality development and functioning. These theories are harmonious with the psychosocial orientation of casework and are part of a total frame of reference that includes whatever data the social sciences can provide to illuminate the nature of the environment and the social forces with which the individual interacts.

This dual orientation lends itself very well to systematizing casework findings. Since the social worker's laboratory is the common everyday world, there is ample opportunity to observe the interplay between inner and outer forces. Social workers have repeatedly seen people change for the better and for the worse under the impact of beneficent and traumatic environments. In observing people of diverse classes, ethnic origins, and regions we become aware that adult behavior varies not only from group to group according to group norms but also within each group in accordance with the individual personality differences and life experiences of its members. Because traditionally social workers have dealt with family units, we are particularly aware of the interplay among family members, of the ongoing impact of outer events on each individual's "inner space," and

of the profound influence of parents as well as other members of the family upon the development of the child's personality.

It must be emphasized that psychosocial casework theory stoutly maintains that human beings are not merely products of their environments, clay upon which social influences leave their print. It insists, and rightly, that individuals make their own demands upon their surroundings. They not only are affected by their environment; they participate in creating it. Ego psychology underscores the capacity of the individual's ego to make changes in the environment, rather than just passively adapting to it.

The foregoing may seem highly theoretical, but it has major practical implications. It puts emphasis on *interaction*, particularly, although not exclusively, upon the individual's part in that interaction. In cases of marital unhappiness, it guards the worker against seeing the partner with whom the interview is being held as merely the victim in the relationship. In parent child disorders, it leads to a balanced examination of both what the parent is "doing to" and expecting of the child and what the child is "doing to" and demanding of the parent. In general, it leads to the assumption that the individual can almost always do *something* about a problem and that the worker's task is to enable the client to develop greater capacity to do so. Concurrently, recognition is given to the pressures stemming from the client's environment and to the problems of "fit" discussed earlier. It is always the responsibility of the caseworker to work with and for the client to try to ameliorate noxious conditions as well as to try to find ways to shape aspects of the environment so that they better suit the needs of the particular individual or family affected.

Contributions of Sociology and Anthropology

Casework's understanding of the interactions between the individual and the environment came not only from observation and case-by-case direct experience but also from the fields of sociology and cultural anthropology. These have been drawn upon extensively over the years to describe and explain the nature of the influences of one upon the other. Beginning with the work of Benedict and Mead,[24] the field was alerted in the thirties to the great differences between cultures and to the extent to which even such central matters as child rearing, marriage, and sexual behavior not only differ among cultures but are regulated by customs that are themselves a form of social agreement. Kardiner's work studying cultural influences on behavior was a "bridging" contribution between culture and personality theory.[25] Casework writers such as Boie and de la Fontaine[26] demonstrated the use of these concepts in the understanding of family and personality problems.

During and following the depression of the thirties, studies of the social effects of unemployment on individuals and families gave social workers new understanding of the pressures created by this periodically widespread social condition.[27] As marriage counseling developed in family agencies in the forties, studies of marriage and divorce from a social and psychological standpoint became important.[28]

The fifties and sixties saw the burgeoning of the family therapy movement, which, as the chapters on family treatment will discuss, was influenced by several of the social sciences. This period also advanced our understanding of the strong effects on personality and behavior of the lack of opportunities for education, employment, and recreation; these lacks, as we now know well, often combine with opportunities that are available for various kinds of deviant behavior, such as the use of hard drugs, participation in drug traffic, prostitution, and delinquent or antisocial behavior of various sorts.[29] Sociological facts and theories about poverty and political powerlessness, deterioration of the inner city, broken homes, child neglect, unmarried parenthood, racial discrimination, and

many other social issues were widely read in the fifties and sixties by social workers who were thinking more deeply than ever about integrating knowledge of the person and the environment in order to improve services and opportunities for clients.[30]

During the same period, studies of differentials in the treatment of psychiatric patients in both hospitals and clinics demonstrated the neglect and discrimination suffered by the poor in general, and by blacks and other minorities in particular. We learned the extent to which mental health practitioners brought a negative bias to the diagnosis and treatment of patients from minority and lower socioeconomic groups. Most disturbing of all were some subsequent research findings that pointed to vulnerable areas of social work itself, a profession that has prided itself on its advocacy of social justice and equal opportunity for all. Clinical judgments by caseworkers, too, could be adversely affected by sociocultural factors; idealistic caseworkers discovered that differences between worker and client were important variables in treatment and needed to be addressed.[31]

The concept of social role, expanded upon in the sixties, became an important link between social influences and personality development. Its contribution to casework practice will be discussed in the next section of this chapter, and also in the chapters on family and couple treatment. As the years went on, the influences of ethnicity on personality, family patterns, and casework treatment itself were more fully understood. While focus on the damaging effects of racism and prejudice continued, emphasis was also being placed on the positive traditions, belief systems, and influences of ethnic background on individual and family pride and on identity formation. Information and clinical experiences related to black, Hispanic, Mexican American, and American Indian cultures were more frequently included in social work curricula and journals.[32]

In recent years, increasing knowledge about

single-parent families, stepfamilies, unmarried mothers, homosexuality, alcoholism and substance abuse, child and spouse abuse, incest, and many other social phenomena has been incorporated by casework, influencing its approaches to treatment. The women's movement has stimulated studies on the traditional and unevenly changing roles of women and the positions of men and women in marriage, in family life, and in the workplace. The social effects of recent changes in marriage and divorce have been of particular interest to caseworkers. Many of these matters will be referred to over the course of this text.

We, the authors, applaud the abounding knowledge related to the diversity found among people of various ethnic and socioeconomic backgrounds. Data and clinical theories about "special groups" of all kinds have increased our awareness and improved our practice. Each group brings its special *strengths* and *vulnerabilities*. Members of various groups may be subject to very different *stresses*. For example, black, Greek, and Vietnamese teenagers may each have entirely different experiences with teachers, doctors, employers, and others whom they encounter. Certain people, as we know, have experienced repeated and traumatic events only because they are members of a certain group or have adopted a particular lifestyle. Some common experiences are shared by those who have been violated in some way within their own families. Obviously, no caseworker can become an expert on every group, but we should all become familiar with general information available about the people with whom we work most closely. It is also our responsibility as caseworkers to understand how our own backgrounds may affect our perceptions, our clinical strengths, and our prejudices.

Yet we wish to add a note of caution here. As committed as we are to the addition of new information, we are equally committed to avoiding the misuse of information. Relying on partial data about differences among people or generalizations about groups can be misleading at best, seriously countertherapeutic at worst. We must not fall into the trap of treating statistics: ("single parents are...," "incest survivors need...," "adult children of alcoholics require..."). When a client comes for help, he or she must be viewed not as a "culture carrier" ("black men feel...," "Italian mothers think...") but as an individual with particular idiosyncratic characteristics who may or may not evidence qualities often found in his or her particular category. In our wish to help those who seek our services, we must be sure that we are not replacing old stereotypes with new ones. Not only is each individual unique but ethnic and other group values and traditions are not static but ever-evolving; even generalizations that may have been valid at one point are constantly changing.

Social Components in Perceptions and Expectations

As noted above, the individual does not react to the environment as it exists but rather as he or she sees it, and a host of internal factors influence these perceptions. But misperceptions are certainly not a matter of individual psychology alone. A child learns that a stove is hot not only by direct experience but also by being told so by a person whose words are trusted. Unfortunately, when trust exists, a false statement will be believed as readily as a true one. If, on the basis of irrational prejudices, parents disapprove of neighbors with certain characteristics, the child learns to judge or shun them. Indeed, if it is "everybody" who holds something true, it becomes extremely difficult for even the good adult mind to have a contrary opinion. How many generations saw sails disappearing over the horizon and continued to believe the world was flat? A government's political enemies of one decade may become allies in the next, and perceptions of the general population often adapt accordingly.

Belief can be so strong that the believer is cut off from the opportunity of even testing it. Racial stereotypes are a cardinal example. Not only do many whites have misperceptions about blacks but blacks also may have misperceptions about whites. Similarly, the "generation gap" is based to no small degree on stereotypes that often cause people on both sides of the contrived dividing line to react according to distorted beliefs rather than realities. Conflict caused by clashing interests among various economic or cultural groups is often compounded by misinformation and distortions, sometimes newly created, and sometimes handed down from one generation to another; for many decades slave owners in this country purported that blacks were "happy" as slaves and would be incompetent or miserable as free people.

Attitudes and expectations that are part of one's perception of the environment, then, are a composite product of actual experience. Individual distortion grows out of ideals or prejudices incorporated from the idiosyncrasies of close associates and ideas assimilated through personal contact but actually the product of group opinion: class, ethnic, racial, regional, occupational, religious, political, and so on. Certain ideas are commonly held in the west but not in the east, in the north but not in the south, in cities but not in rural areas, in the Soviet Union but not in the United States, among white-collar but not among blue-collar workers, among whites but not among blacks, among women but not among men, in poverty-stricken city areas but not in suburbia, and so on. Some of these ideas are deliberately promoted and perpetuated by vested, self-serving interests for economic, political, or other advantage.

Role Theory

Especially helpful in understanding the interplay of person and situation is role theory.[33] A number of role concepts are particularly useful in understanding how the superego and ego ideal are shaped by social influences and the part played by such influences in the judgment and decisions of the ego. Role theory points out that the individuals and groups surrounding the child from birth onward hold certain behavioral expectations. Specific ways of behaving are commonly accepted as appropriate or necessary for individuals in certain areas of functioning—as parents, as husbands or wives, as employees—and they are perceived in terms of the way role performances conform, or fail to conform, to the norms held by the group. For instance, a man's perception of whether or not his wife loves him depends upon quite different cues in different groups. In some cultures, the wife's housekeeping tasks are deemed so important that the husband would see her subordination of them to interest in a job as personal neglect and evidence of lack of love. This perception might be reinforced by the opinions of his friends, before whom he could be disgraced. Similarly, a parent's view of a child usually depends greatly upon the extent to which the child behaves according to group-influenced expectations. The ways in which an adult is expected to fulfill obligations to elderly parents, teacher-pupil relationships, interracial relationships, the roles of priest, rabbi, or pastor and congregational member—all of these are in part culturally defined.

Status, or one's position in life, influences social expectations of behavior. Status may be ascribed by age, gender, ethnic or socioeconomic group into which one is born, or it may be achieved by getting married, by learning a trade or profession, and so on. In any culture a child is expected to act in many specific respects quite differently from an adult, an employer from an employee, a member of the upper classes from a poor farmer, and so on. The same person is also expected to act differently under different circumstances. Ways of behaving acceptable at a political rally or a football game are usually considered highly inappropriate in the course of professional functioning. In many respects, the behavior of the individual is shaped by society in general; other role expectations are a function of the particular ethnic group or class with which one identifies; still others are more specific to a particular family or individual. The importance of role designation in families is discussed in the chapters on family therapy.

Roles may be *complementary or noncomplementary.* Successful role performance of one person may require reciprocal performance by another. If one fails, the other is frustrated. A priest cannot act as a confessor if the parishioner does not come to confession. A wife who defines her role behavior as including management of the budget is frustrated in carrying out this role if her husband, disagreeing with this definition, independently makes important financial decisions.

Recent years have witnessed rapid changes in many culturally determined role expectations, in all types of interpersonal relations. Conflict in marriage may derive in part from changing roles of men and women. This can be particularly true when definitions differ about decision making in general or child care and distribution of household tasks, especially when a woman is working outside the home. In some cases it may be easier for a woman to claim her own expanded role than to be comfortable with a man's equally logical desire to be freed of some of the responsibilities he had accepted when he saw himself as head of the family and sole wage earner. Changing role definitions can cause inner turmoil for a young person. Many young women, for example, are torn between marrying early and raising a family immediately or taking many years first to establish themselves in a career. A young man, too, may be conflicted between becoming a "family man" or an independent single person. Even a generation ago these and many other role behaviors were more specifically defined.

Many role expectations, even those that are widespread, are by no means held identically by everyone. Sometimes this fact provides the basis for interpersonal tension or misunderstanding. A particular individual may expect another to behave in a certain way because of his or her status, although the second person defines the role behavior required in a different way. One elderly man is gratified when a young woman offers him a seat in a crowded bus; another man of the same age with different expectations of roles feels humiliated and angered by the offer.

Clients' expectations of how they should behave or how the caseworker will act will vary according to personal and social experience. Some casework clients assume that they must agree with and be directed by the worker, even though the worker is ethically and professionally bound to a process of mutuality and exchange between them. A man who has been trained to view women in very particular ways may have difficulty being comfortable with or taking seriously a female social worker.

If the worker is to convey the same impression of goodwill, objectivity, and competence to clients of varying life experience, he or she will need to become as aware as possible of their preconceptions and of the different interpretations they may make of his or her actions. Divergent expectations may be brought out in the open and a common ground for working agreed upon. A worker learns that in order to be effective one needs to be more "friendly," outgoing, or casual with some clients, more "professional" or formal with others. With involuntary or "hard-to-reach" clients, much generous and active help may be necessary to overcome the stereotype of the caseworker as an interfering or hostile "do-gooder" or as an indifferent bureaucrat. Role theory is not only important in assessing clients' life situations but in understanding what is required to establish a successful working relationship.

Communication

Recent years have seen great advances in our understanding of the processes of communication and of the various ways in which misunderstandings can arise.[34] Some of the findings especially pertinent to clinical social work will be discussed in later chapters, but brief reference to the communication factor is needed at this point.

Faulty perceptions or distortions by the ego—processes described earlier in this chapter—are viewed as major components in faulty communication among different members of a family or members of any other social system. Assumptions and preconceptions can cause people not to listen to each other at all or to hear something different from what has been said. Ego defenses such as projection and displacement interfere with many efforts to communicate. If a son-in-law expects the same negative reaction from a father-in-law that he got from his own father, his comment to the father-in-law may be aggressively asserted and then viewed by the latter as an expression of dislike rather than the fear it actually is. Of course, the father-in-law's provoked response may then sound angry or sarcastic and belie his underlying warm feelings for his son-in-law. Two men who want to be close nevertheless become increasingly alienated by and wary of one another.

As seen in this illustration, distortions of the ego's perceptions resulting from earlier experiences and from the ego's patterned defenses against anxiety are among the *internal factors* accounting for inaccurate assessments of others and failures in realistic reception of communications. Internal elaborations and attributions of intent by the receiver can cause endless misunderstandings. Distortions in the way intonation is heard also can make great differences in interpretation of meaning.

When working with clients we frequently find that communications are transmitted unclearly because people are afraid of being direct about what they mean. Some people do not communicate complaints or negative feelings lucidly for fear of "rocking the boat"; some are reluctant to state beliefs and preferences because they feel unentitled or assume that their assertions will not be accepted; others share tender feelings tentatively or not at all for fear of being rejected. It is often possible to assist people to express their thoughts and feelings clearly and without attacking others. To minimize misinterpretations and to allow problems to be resolved and relationships to thrive straightforward communication is usually essential.

There are equally important factors that are related to other aspects of the communication process. Most communication takes place through symbols, both verbal and nonverbal. For accurate communication, these symbols must be commonly understood by sender and receiver. The meaning of gestures, posture, intonation, and even words of the same language differs markedly among people of different educational backgrounds, social classes, and ethnic groups. Symbols of courtesy and discourtesy that are so basic to interpersonal relationships are particularly vulnerable to misperceptions.

INTERACTING SOURCES OF DISTRESS

When clients come to a clinical social worker for assistance because there has been a breakdown in social adjustment, this breakdown has three possible *interacting* factors:

1. Current life situations that exert excessive pressure or that fail to provide essential opportunities for satisfactory personal and social functioning.

2. Immature or faulty ego and superego functioning that derives from hereditary factors and/or developmental deficits and flaws. When these functions are underdeveloped, the individual often makes excessive demands on others to gratify infantile needs.

3. Overly restrictive or rigid ego defense mechanisms and/or superego functions.

The degree to which each of these is present varies with different people at different times. Sometimes all three substantially contribute to a client's dilemma.

Common among *current life pressures* are those of economic deprivation, lack of opportunities for employment, marginal working conditions, poor housing, dangerous neighborhoods, homelessness, substandard educational opportunities, racial and ethnic hostility, illness, and loss of love by death and separation. To these must be added innumerable individual life experiences that arouse frustration, anger, feelings of inadequacy, guilt, and so on. Pressures may occur, for example, in family relationships when the needs of one individual conflict in a major way with those of another.

The need to care for a retarded child or chronically ill family member, for example, may conflict with the vocational aspirations of a woman who is tied to the home by these circumstances. Such frustrations also exist when employment and living conditions are in fact very irritating and demanding, even though not substandard. And they certainly occur when general social conditions, such as racial discrimination or bias against a homosexual or any other lifestyle, create constant environmental pressure of overshadowing proportions.

Frustration with other people and situations is frequently a major component in a circle of deteriorating interaction. It can set up circular responses both in the situational interaction and within the personality. Externally, expression of the individual's anger and other behavior often further alienate sources of satisfaction in a reverberating pattern. Internally, the deprivation may increase the need for love or appreciation or self-expression and may increase feelings of lack of worth. These, in turn, increase the need for reassurance and gratification in the external world where these are already lacking or where antagonism has developed in reaction to the individual's negative attitudes or behavior.

Immature or inadequate ego and superego functioning can lead people to have exaggerated narcissistic needs, make excessive childlike demands upon the world, and feel inordinately dependent on or hostile toward others. Fear of separation, with resulting anxiety or timidity, often causes individuals to require excessive protection and prevents then from assuming adult responsibilities, from operating independently, or from engaging in reciprocal and loving adult relationships. Although it is sometimes possible for people with immature needs and retarded ego development to find social situations in which their needs are gratified, for the most part this does not occur. Rather, they are usually left with a constant sense of frustration and characteristically behave in ways that create antagonism in the social environment, thereby cutting off the very gratifications they crave and that might otherwise be available.

Faulty ego functioning also can include distorted perception of either the outside world or the self, poor judgment, excessive anxiety, difficulty managing impulses or behavior, poor reality testing, and immature uses of ego defenses. When superego and ego ideal functioning is extremely inadequate, it can mean that the individual has not incorporated much in the way of standards of "right and wrong" and has very few ethical views or personal aspirations. The conscience can be primitively harsh and literal. Usually when functioning is faulty, standards and self-requirements are unevenly developed rather than altogether absent.

Sometimes, because of cultural or idiosyncratic factors that existed in a person's background, standards of conduct that may seem flawed to others are actually out of harmony in the context of the current environment rather than underdeveloped as such. A pair of twins, for example, who were raised to do and share almost everything as a unit were discovered talking together during an examination at college; both young men, who actually had very firm ethical beliefs and would not have "cheated" in other ways, were amazed by the consternation their behavior provoked. In any case, of course, dissension with the outside world can be the result.

Faulty ego and superego functioning almost always adds substantially to environmental pressures felt by the individual. If the ego misperceives pressures, stress experienced in response to the distorted version of reality may be more severe than is appropriate to the actual life events. Faulty perceptions and judgments can also lead to actions that are self-defeating or unnecessarily deprive the person of satisfactions that might otherwise be within reach. In turn, the person then may seek associates who confirm his childlike distortions of the world, thus reinforcing the tendency to faulty general functioning.

Restrictive or rigid ego defenses and superego functions can lie behind difficulties clients bring to caseworkers. When the experience and/or expression of feelings, thoughts, conflicts, and behavior has been severely restrained, or when standards for self and others are impossibly unbending and perfectionistic, individuals may become symptomatic. When important aspects of one's emotional or intellectual life have been cast outside awareness, a person can experience considerable tension and distress. If individuals have buried their feelings or opinions, they often feel at the mercy of other people's ideas or behaviors toward them yet do not know how to define their own positions. In contrast to those with immature functioning, for whom help often takes the form of encouragement to *build* on their capacities, those with overly restrictive egos and superegos usually get relief from *uncovering* and *expressing* disowned feelings and thoughts or from *relaxing* and *softening* inner demands. It often happens that some aspects of a person are underdeveloped and other functions are overly restrained or demand-

ing, in which case a combination of these approaches may be considered. Cases discussed in the next chapter will demonstrate the interplay of all three elements in personal difficulties.

AMELIORATING THE INTERACTING SOURCES OF CLIENT DISTRESS
Person-in-Situation Stresses

When a major cause of a client's discomfort is in reaction to the *environment*, it is sometimes possible for the caseworker to modify the pressure or deficiency directly; location of an apartment, job, or medical services may be all that is required. In some instances, a referral by the caseworker to a resource may be more effective than the client's self-referral. Sometimes attitudes of individuals who are creating difficulties for the client can be altered through casework contact; when such modification is required, so-called environmental intervention actually becomes *psychological* in nature. Some services—child placement is a prime example—can be extremely complicated in the treatment required. Chapter 8 deals in greater detail with environmental procedures.

Environmental services rarely stand alone. They are often accompanied by work directly with the client, in which his or her reactions become a focus of attention. The public assistance client may (perhaps understandably) resent the eligibility process yet need the help that can be obtained only from the welfare agency. Out of fear or misunderstanding, the hospital patient may be unwilling to undergo recommended medical procedures. The child may not be ready to use educational or recreational services that have become available. Much preparation involving *both* the resource and the client, and the assessment of the "fit" between them, may be required before presenting difficulties can be resolved.

Instead of relieving environmental pressures directly, often the worker helps clients to bring about the necessary changes themselves, thereby reinforcing their feelings of competence. Obviously, environmental changes brought about solely for the purpose of removing unusual pressures or deficiencies need not involve an individual's effort to make changes. At times, however, improvement requires that client and worker address themselves to an ego problem, such as misinterpretations of events in the environment, dysfunctional reactions to pressures that do exist, or lack of confidence in the ability to initiate external changes.

A person may function more comfortably as a result of external change; in fact, outer changes actually can produce permanent shifts in the inner balance. If a person previously deprived is less frustrated and more gratified, energies may be released for psychological development that had previously been stunted; *at all stages of an individual's life, the ego has amazing innate powers of maturation.*

Sometimes it can be very difficult indeed to differentiate between an individual's inner life and the world outside, particularly when aspects of the environment impinge directly on a person's situation. As Loewenstein points out in her important article, "impulse-ridden youth with 'weak superegos' are quite able to obey rigid rules established by the gang to which they belong."[35] In practice, over and over again, we find that modifications of a client's external situation can result in emotional or behavioral changes, just as emotional growth can often give the individual the strength required to fully utilize or make changes in the environment. *The caseworker may concentrate, therefore, on that system or those systems that seem most accessible to change—not necessarily the most dysfunctional ones.*

It may be necessary to help a client to find personal alternatives to an unjust external condition; even serious economic or political injustice may require individual initiative to find new adaptations. At other times, internalized emotional disturbance may best be treated by altering the environment. For example, it may be more efficient and caring to help a man, victimized by unemployment, to retrain or relocate than it would be to wait until pressure can bring about changes in the unhealthy economic situation. As unfair as it may seem, individuals are constantly having to make new adaptations to counteract external assaults. On the other hand, a person with a severe or chronic psychiatric disorder may respond better to a supportive milieu than to therapy aimed directly at the intrapsychic disturbance or deficit. A symptomatic child may be quickly relieved by improvement in marital relations of the parents. Paradoxically, then, the caseworker's focus for intervention may be the seemingly healthiest aspect of the person-situation configuration, when this is the one most amenable to influence and change. The psychosocial approach to problems in or with the environment, therefore, requires an understanding of the people involved, the impinging environments, and the interactions among these, in order to evaluate which of them are likely to be modifiable.

As just mentioned, radical modification of the environment can bring about *lasting personality change.* Sometimes a change of jobs will bring about a better "fit" between work and personality, leading to greater personal comfort, improved functioning, and enhanced self-esteem. A woman may become less tense, less hostile, and more able to give love to her children when she is working outside the home and having others care for her children during the day than when she devotes her full time to their care. If the caseworker helps her to recognize this and to arrange her life so that she can take a job, there may be marked improvements in her feelings of well-being, her functioning, and her relationships, all of which may endure even if at some point she gives up her outside work. Lasting personality change can result when a particularly fortunate choice of a marriage partner leads to a long period of satisfying living that seems to undo the effects of earlier misfortune and brings about a real reorientation to life. A good marriage can be one of the best therapies! Women labeled as "dependent personalities" have often become autonomous and self-directed when exposed to the women's movement or to other influences in their lives. The phenomenon of religious conversion also can effect major personality change.

With children, enduring changes often occur readily in response to shifts in the environment, and this is the predominant method of casework treatment used with children. Major personality changes in the child, particularly the young child, can often be brought about by various forms of substitute parental care: adoption, foster care, or day care centers. Less extensive changes may be promoted by modifications in the school environment or by provision of recreational and other group experiences such as camping or bringing a "big brother" or other interested person into the situation. Because children's personalities are still so fluid, environmental changes profoundly affect their views of the world, their ego, and their emotional development; even when "good enough parenting" was not available earlier on, corrections can occur quite rapidly when youngsters are exposed to healing situations.

Often, we try to bring about changes in parents' attitudes and behavior. Family treatment (see Chapters 15 and 16) can be one of the most effective means of altering a child's environment and also of promoting personality changes. In a case where a mother may be encouraging her son's babyishness and excessive dependence on her, in family therapy it may be revealed that her overinvolvement in her son's life is a compensation for her husband's remoteness; the boy's development may also be retarded by the fact that the father has been displacing his unexpressed anger at his wife onto his son. If changes in the marriage that result in greater satisfactions in the relationships between husband and wife can be effected, the family environment will more likely support the boy's age-appropriate independence. When environ-

mental changes are impossible or are not sufficiently effective, direct casework with the child may either accompany environmental modification or become the major form of treatment.[36]

Direct Work with the Individual

To whatever extent the three factors described above contribute to the client's problem, change in the *person* frequently becomes an important goal of treatment. Such treatment may range from attempts to bring about lasting changes in the client's personality or way of functioning to temporary adjustments of behavior during a period of stress. These changes, as we have said, may be made by direct or indirect interventions. When *direct* work is decided upon, casework uses the client's current reactions and behavior and sometimes memories that are either immediately accessible to consciousness or for one reason or another suppressed, unverbalized, or uncomprehended. Truly repressed material that is so remote from consciousness that only such means as free association, hypnosis, or therapy under drugs can bring it to the surface is obviously not material that is available for use in most casework practice.

Psychosocial casework is a form of treatment that relies heavily upon reflective, cognitive procedures embodied in the matrix of a sound helping or therapeutic relationship. Whether the emphasis is on thinking things through, uncovering suppressed material, modifying rigidities in personality, building ego strengths, or planning action that will bring about environmental changes, the client is helped to define his or her own goals and needs. Casework seeks to engage the client's ego—the capacity to think, to reflect, to understand—in a reevaluation of internal and interactional issues. By engaging clients as fully as possible in their own treatment, caseworkers endeavor not only to preserve but also to enhance reliance upon the self to make decisions about themselves and their lives. In some cases the treatment process is extremely intense; sometimes it can take many months or more to achieve the desired results. At the other extreme are instances when just having a caseworker truly interested in understanding, someone to whom one can safely get things "off one's chest," can provide sufficient relief and clarity for the person to go on without help from there.

As indicated earlier, casework does make use of directive techniques such as suggestion, advice, and persuasion when diagnosis indicates that the client is unlikely to respond to measures that rely upon his or her own active thinking. This may be the case when one is so overwhelmed by pressing happenings in life—sickness, death, desertion—that one is unable to use one's usual reflective powers or when one is severely handicapped in doing so by the severity of ego impairment or deterioration. Advice sometimes is given about such matters as child rearing, job hunting, or achieving a goal, but it is almost always accompanied by explanations that supply understanding of the advice given. Directive procedures are *never* used in isolation from cognitive measures and are employed *only* when the client is not ready or able to use reflective procedures. Psychosocial casework therefore differs markedly from truly directive therapies in which the therapist takes a very active part in advising the client, relying primarily upon the weight of "professional authority" and upon the positive relationship to modify the client's, or patient's, responses. Chapters 4 through 7 describe psychosocial treatment procedures in detail.

THE BALANCE OF FORCES

Understanding the Balance

To understand how work that does not reach the "deeper" (repressed) layers of personality or does not substantially modify environmental influences can be effective, we must appreciate the various ways in which the personality system and its interactions with the environment constitute a balance, sometimes a very delicate balance, of forces.

We have already referred to the Freudian concept of the personality as consisting of id, ego, and superego-ego ideal. It is also useful to consider the balance of forces *within* each of these components, as seen from the vantage point of social functioning. For example, the primary process of the id—the raw, chaotic, undifferentiated emotion—can be counterbalanced by needs and drives that have been organized and regulated by the ego. Thus, immature energies can be counterpoised by drives that are more harmonious with the needs of others. For the individual, then, impulses can be postponed or the capacity for giving and receiving love can be accentuated without actually relating to the unconscious material of the id.

The ego and superego are also a balance of socially functional and dysfunctional tendencies. The ego does not always perceive and understand realistically. Certain defenses may obscure or distort the events of life. Self-confidence may be weak, guilt may be overbearing, general lack of ego integration may impede constructive action. An individual may function satisfactorily until some even minor external event provokes ill-considered and damaging action. The early and restrictive superego may still be so harsh that certain actions or feelings are inhibited in unnecessary and harmful ways. On the other hand, any of these weaknesses may be offset by other tendencies in the personality that promote personal growth and socially realistic, gratifying functioning. These include the capacity to function autonomously rather than only reactively, to feel competent, to make accurate appraisals of others, of the self, and of the external world; these and other ego functions are likely to result in responses that bring gratifications for the individual, contribute to meeting the needs of associates, and enhance the harmonious functioning of the social systems of which the individual is a part.

In a sense, opposing tendencies (whether within or between personality components) struggle with each other at any given moment, and the resultant action often depends on *whether strengths or weaknesses predominate.* When certain reactions or inner drives push the individual toward self-destructive behavior or into actions that hurt others, the healthy parts of the personality say no. When the ego distorts reality by projection or magical beliefs, or when other unconscious or primitive processes cause distortions, the healthy parts of the ego correct these and keep the irrational tendencies in check. It is often nip and tuck as to which side will win, depending upon the relative power the two sets of forces bring to bear in any particular situation. "If my wife had said just one more thing, I would have thrown the hammer at her." That is, "If I had been just a little more angry, nothing my ego was telling me would have been enough to keep me in control."

An important aspect of this balance of forces is that although the decision to act may hang upon a hair's weight of difference—either in the opposing intrapsychic forces or in the nature and force of external pressures—the action that this slight difference triggers may be of major proportions and have extensive consequences. If the wife just mentioned had in fact said "just one more thing," and the man did not call upon his judgment to regulate his reaction, he might have seriously hurt the woman and ended up in jail.

Anger left over from the family fight might then tip the scales in this man's decision to respond to criticism from his employer by throwing down his tools and walking off his job. The reverberations of this action in his personal and family life obviously could exacerbate the already desperate situation, but the action itself resulted from only slight changes in the man's ego capacity to manage his anger. A series of such transactions can combine and interact to make a pattern of considerable strength and significance.

Modifying the Balance of Forces

It is, as we have just illustrated, not the strength of a drive or the degree of a tendency toward distortion alone that determines whether a person takes action. These may be opposed by an equally strong counterforce, in the form of capacity for reality testing and ability to control impulses. When the opposing strengths are almost equally balanced, a relatively small amount of improvement in ego functioning may be enough to enable the individual to make significant changes in social functioning, which in turn may increase the sense of confidence and self-esteem, which can then promote enduring change in the person's behavior and feelings of well-being. This is one of the answers to the oft-repeated question: When the infantile demands and distortions are not directly modified, how can there be any real change? Although the demands and distortions may not be addressed directly by casework treatment, the person may handle them differently. If certain ego functions are strengthened or external pressure is alleviated, sometimes infantile qualities may even be permanently modified. Indeed, it is the belief in the positive capacities of the human being for change and growth that provides the main incentive for the treatment process.

Furthermore, all formative influences do not occur in early childhood, nor are they all unconscious. If, for example, unresolved oedipal rivalries have made a daughter see her mother as hostile, the daughter's feeling may be reinforced by experiencing actual hostility from her mother in the later years of growth. Or, conversely, it may be lessened somewhat by experiences of an opposite nature. In the latter instance, not only is the original tendency not reinforced but the ego is given a means by which to counteract the effect of the original distortion. In the former instance, when the mother's later behavior reinforces the daughter's belief that enmity must exist between them—a belief that may affect her attitude toward other women—there are several possible modes of treatment that need not involve an effort to uncover and correct the *original* oedipal material derived from early childhood.

In one approach, the client is encouraged to ventilate feelings about the events she spontaneously remembers or can recall. For a person who has not previously been able to express her anger toward her mother, eliciting it may have a useful cathartic effect, which in turn can reduce the amount of suppressed hostility pressing for displacement on current female figures in the client's life. If there has been guilt over the angry feelings, the worker's acceptance of them as natural may reduce the guilt and subsequent need to use defenses such as projection or turning against the self. If the anger has been displaced onto a female child or other adult women, it may be possible to enable the client through reflection to recognize and refrain from behavior that provokes counterhostility and causes her to experience constant repetitions of her original unhappy experience with a woman.

Another approach is to provide the client with an opportunity for a "corrective relationship."[37] For example, by allowing a relationship to develop in which the client regards a female worker in some respects as a maternal figure, it may be possible to counteract the earlier disappointing mother-daughter experience by enabling the client to see, through the new experience, that the characteristics of her relationship with her mother need not apply to all relationships with women. This may also tend to undo some of the attitudes about herself, men, marriage and sex, child raising, and so on, that she acquired in her early relationship with her parents.

Another alternative for the client and worker is to look carefully at current personal interactions in which the woman's unconscious attitudes have contributed to her unrealistic responses. Details of an interaction can be examined to see whether the responses were warranted by what the other person did, correcting unnecessary dysfunctional responses bit by bit using current realities. This can greatly strengthen the person's ability to correct misperceptions and restrain impulsive actions. Still another approach is to enable the client to review her conscious and preconscious or near-conscious early memories of experiences with her mother. By seeing their effects on her personality and on her current reactions to life, she may free herself from childhood and adolescent reinforcements of her oedipal distortions and, in turn, reduce the degree of distortion with which her adult ego must deal. Along with this reduction of the force of childhood experiences, she may be helped to recognize her tendency to carry over feelings from childhood to current relationships and may learn to improve these relationships by careful testing of her own reactions against the realities of other people's behavior. In actual practice, as will be discussed in later chapters, all of these approaches are used, sometimes even in the same interview. Characteristically, several are continuously used together.

Even when individual treatment is the treatment of choice, additional joint interviews can be effective. In the case just described, meetings with the woman and her mother or both of her parents might be arranged. By correcting distortions and improving *current* relationships with parents negative childhood influences can often be significantly dissipated. A "corrective relationship" with one's actual family can sometimes be more far-reaching than one provided by the caseworker. Even when the family relationships never become what the client might wish, family meetings can provide the opportunity for some sort of resolution that is often more difficult to achieve when clients simply talk about the people who have significantly influenced their lives.

Over and over we witness how small shifts in the balance of a family and the personalities within it can create significant and lasting changes. The following case illustrates this point.

Joan, a thirteen-year-old girl, was referred by her junior high school guidance counselor to a family agency because she appeared "morose" and recently had begun to underachieve. Family sessions which included Joan and her mother and stepfather, Mr. and Mrs. Smith, who had been married for six years, were arranged. Mrs. Smith had become critical of her daughter's blossoming interest in boys in part because she, the mother, had made a "mistake" and become pregnant many years ago and projected feelings that her daughter would do the same. Furthermore, the mother, who tended to be extremely anxious and compulsive, was particularly stressed for fear she would have to give up her job—upon which she depended for discharge of her high energies, approval, and a sense of competence—in order to supervise her daughter more closely. Her concern about not being able to work prompted even more anxiety and irritation with the girl. Joan, who had been afraid to challenge or reassure her mother, believing her mother would discount whatever she said, had become increasingly silent; this, in turn, further contributed to the mother's escalating apprehensions. Mrs. Smith reported that she was unable to sleep well or concentrate at work; she had always been nervous, she said, but now she feared that she was "going crazy."

Even though he had confidence in his stepdaughter and had a more comfortable relationship with Joan than his wife did, Mr. Smith had been reluctant to interfere or express his opinion, partly because he tended to be reserved and partly because he was not sure he had the "right" to be involved because he was not the girl's "real" father. With only a little encouragement from the caseworker, however, he did tell his wife that he did not think her anger and criticisms were helpful to Joan and, furthermore, that *he* trusted the child.

This single change by the stepfather triggered immediate and resounding shifts in the balance of the family system and the personalities of all of the members. Mrs. Smith's anxiety diminished almost immediately because "at last" her husband was willing to talk about and share the family burdens (which turned out to include more issues than concern about Joan). Feeling her stepfather's support and her mother's relaxation, Joan became more forthcoming; she was able to tell her mother convincingly that concerns about becoming sexually active were unwarranted; she also said that she wanted to become involved in some after-school art and drama programs which she had been afraid to discuss because she feared her mother would disapprove. Actually, Mrs. Smith was relieved because these were supervised activities of which she thoroughly approved. As a result of feeling less fearful, the mother's criticism of Joan abated. When she realized she need not quit her job, she began sleeping better and was no longer frightened about her mental state. Mr. and Mrs. Smith became more open with each other and, after a short time, felt closer. Joan, who had internalized feelings in reaction to her mother that she was somehow "bad," began to look better, smile more, and get good grades in school again.

Gently, the worker had encouraged Mr. Smith to assert himself with his wife. In turn, Mrs. Smith was comforted by his increased participation; her harsh superego, which had contributed to her anxiety about herself as well as to her criticisms of Joan, softened. Almost immediately, Joan appeared and said she felt more confident and cheerful; her interest in school improved. Four family sessions, two marital sessions, and one individual session with Joan were sufficient to shift the balance of forces and create positive changes. In a follow-up interview six months after termination, it was revealed that the improvements had endured: Joan had become more competent and independent; Mr. and Mrs. Smith were getting along and working together much better than before.

Experience in individual and family treatment has demonstrated that even in adulthood the ego is often readily open to influence and capable of growth and modification. In systems terms, we have learned that families and personalities are "open systems" that constantly shift in response to exchanges with the outside world, including situational changes and changes that can be brought about by interaction with the caseworker in the process of treatment.

In summary, when casework is employed to help clients achieve better social functioning, it can become a form of psychosocial therapy. In addition to improvements in the environment and external functioning, treatment can bring about such *internalized modifications* as improvement of the ego's perception and reality-testing ability; improved self-acceptance and self esteem; better integration of all aspects of the personality; shifts in the uses or rigidities of defenses; changes in the demands, or in the reactions to demands, of the superego; lasting reductions in the strength of destructive character traits such as chronic dependency or hostility; reduction of oppressive influences of parental ties; and maturation that not only consolidates capabilities but reduces self-defeating, driven behaviors. Such modifications are built into the personality and enable individuals to function better even when confronted by circumstances identical or essentially similar to those under which functioning was previously impaired. It is reasonable to expect that such changes will continue after treatment has ended.

Psychosocial treatment relies mainly on reflective procedures augmented by methods of direct influence and by direct efforts by the caseworker to bring about environmental changes when diagnosis indicates that these will be effective. Of paramount importance in such treat-ment is the relationship upon which it is based. The worker's acceptance of the client and wish to respond to the client's need are constant; this attitude is expressed in varying ways, depending upon the client's wishes and needs but always characterized by honesty and basic supportiveness. Often, when clients feel valued, they become better able to value themselves and others and thereby respond differently in relationships. Focus is always upon the person-situation gestalt, which is seen as an interacting balance of forces between the needs of the person and the influences upon him or her of the environment. Individual functioning is the end result of a complicated series of interactions between different parts of the personality highly susceptible to outside influences. In psychosocial therapy, influence is brought to bear on either the environment, including the family environment, or the personality or both. When it is directed toward the personality, it can reduce the force of destructive trends in the individual by decreasing the force of earlier life experiences and by increasing the capacities of the ego and superego to handle current life experiences more capably and realistically. Thus, the work strengthens clients in their ability to achieve goals they set for themselves. The remaining chapters in this book attempt to explain and illustrate the process of psychosocial therapy in greater detail.

NOTES

1. For fuller discussion of casework values and also of ethical issues, see Herbert Bisno, *The Philosophy of Social Work* (Washington, D.C.: Public Affairs Press, 1952). See also Harriet Bartlett, *The Common Base of Social Work Practice* (New York: National Association of Social Workers, 1970), pp. 63–69; William Gordon, "Knowledge and Value: Their Distinction and Relationship in Clarifying Social Work Practice," *Social Work*, 10 (July 1965), 32–35; Florence Hollis, "Principles and Assumptions Underlying Casework Practice," *Social Work* (London), 12 (1955), 41–55; Katherine Kendall, ed., *Social Work Values in an Age* *of Discontent* (New York: Council on Social Work Education, 1970); Charles S. Levy, *Social Work Ethics* (New York: Human Services Press, 1976); Harold Lewis, *The Intellectual Base of Social Work Practice* (New York: The Haworth Press, 1982); Harold Lewis, "Ethical Assessment," *Social Casework*, 65 (April 1984), 203–211; and Frederic B. Reamer, *Ethical Dilemmas in Social Service* (New York: Columbia University Press, 1982). See also *Code of Ethics of the National Association of Social Workers* (Silver Spring, Md.: National Association of Social Workers, 1980).

2. See especially Thomas Keefe, "Empathy: The Critical Skill," *Social Work*, 21 (January 1976), 10–14; and Thomas Keefe, "Empathy Skill and Critical Consciousness," *Social Casework*, 61 (September 1980), 387–393. See also David M. Berger, *Clinical Empathy* (Northvale, N.J.: Jason Aronson, 1987).

3. An excellent series of articles on this subject is to be found in F. E. McDermott, ed., *Self Determination in Social Work* (London: Routledge and Kegan Paul, 1975). See also a fine paper by Ann Weick and Loren Pope, "Knowing What's Best: A New Look at Self-Determination," *Social Casework*, 69 (January 1988), 10–16. In a small exploratory study it was found that there were enormous variations in the application of the principle of self-determination; see Suzanne D. Kassel and Rosalie A. Kane, "Self-Determination Dissected," *Clinical Social Work Journal*, 8 (Fall 1980), 161–178.

4. Raymond M. Berger makes this point in his article, "Social Work Practice Models: A Better Recipe," *Social Casework*, 67 (January 1986), 52. He takes a critical view of the psychosocial and other models of social work, claiming that they espouse abstract values that cannot be realized in practice. In our opinion, it is still our professional obligation to do all that we can to eliminate obstacles to self-realization, even though we often fall short of helping clients achieve their ideal goals.

5. See Howard Goldstein, "The Neglected Moral Link in Social Work Practice," *Social Work*, 32 (May–June 1987), 181–186; in this excellent article the author discusses complex personal and professional issues involved in helping clients deal with moral dilemmas.

6. Gordon Hamilton, *Theory and Practice of Social Case-*work, 2d ed. (New York: Columbia University Press, 1951).

7. See Harriet Bartlett, *The Common Base of Social Work Practice*, especially Chapter 11; and the "Introduction" to Carel B. Germain, ed., *Social Work Practice: People and Environments* (New York: Columbia University Press, 1979), pp. 1–22.

8. Ludwig von Bertalanffy, *General Systems Theory: Foundations, Development, Application* (New York: Braziller, 1968), is a basic reference on systems theory; William Gray, Frederick J. Duhl, and Nicholas D. Rizzo, eds., *General Systems Theory and Psychiatry* (Boston: Little Brown, 1969), is also useful as a general reference; Ervin Lazlo, ed., *The Relevance of General Systems Theory* (New York: Braziller, 1972), has excellent articles discussing the relevance of general systems theory to various disciplines.

Werner A. Lutz, in his *Concepts and Principles Underlying Social Casework Practice* (Washington, D.C.: National Association of Social Workers, 1956), first introduced the systems approach to casework. Articles from casework, psychiatry, and psychology increasingly recognized its usefulness; for example, see Gordon Allport, "The Open System in Personality Theory," *Journal of Abnormal and Social Psychology*, 61 (November 1960), 301–310; William Gordon, "Basic Constructs for an Integrative and Generative Conception of Social Work," in Gordon Hearn, ed., *The General Systems Approach: Contributions Toward a Holistic Conception of Social Work* (New York: Council on Social Work Education, 1969); and Florence Hollis, "'And What Shall We Teach?': The Social Work Educator and Knowledge," *Social Service Review*, 42 (June 1968), 184–196.

See also Mary Gorman Gyarfas, "A Systems Approach to Diagnosis," in Judith Mishne, ed., *Psychotherapy and Training in Clinical Social Work* (New York: Gardner Press, 1980), 49–63; and Margaret R. Rodway, "Systems Theory," in Francis J. Turner, ed., *Social Work Treatment*, 3d ed. (New York: The Free Press, 1986), 514–539. For references on the ecological approach, see Chapter 1, note 8. See also Paula Allen-Meares and Bruce A. Lane, "Grounding Social Work Practice in Theory: Ecosystems," *Social Casework*, 68 (November 1987), 515–521; and Carel B. Germain, "The Ecological Approach to People-Environmental Transactions," *Social Casework*, 62 (June 1981), 323–331.

9. Germain, "The Ecological Approach to People-Environmental Transactions," 326.

10. Florence Wexler Vigilante, "Use of Work in the Assessment and Intervention Process," *Social Casework*, 63 (May 1982), 297.

11. For a comprehensive review of the findings concerning the effects of maternal deprivation, see John Bowlby, *Maternal Care and Mental Health*, 2d ed. (Geneva: World Health Organization, 1952); and Mary D. Ainsworth, "The Effects of Maternal Deprivation: A Review of Findings and Controversy in the Context of Research Strategy," in *Deprivation of Maternal Care: A Reassessment of Its Effects* (Geneva: World Health Organization, 1962). See also Selma Fraiberg, *Every Child's Birthright: In Defense of Mothering* (New York: Basic Books, 1977); and John Bowlby, *Attachment and Loss*, vol. 3 (New York: Basic Books, 1980).

12. Jane van Lawick-Goodall, *In the Shadow of Man* (Boston: Houghton Mifflin, 1971).

13. There is a rich literature pertinent to the social worker's understanding of the nature of the social and ethnic components in the person-situation interaction. Many students and workers rely heavily on Monica McGoldrick et al., eds., *Ethnicity and Family Therapy* (New York: The Guilford Press, 1982). With this and other readings on the subject, it is, of course, necessary to beware of stereotyping; each individual and family assimilates cultural influences and experiences differently.

The following, in addition to those cited elsewhere, are a few of many useful references: Andrew Billingsley, *Black Families in White America* (Englewood Cliffs, N.J.: Prentice Hall, 1968); John A. Brown, "Clinical Social Work with Chicanos: Some Unwarranted Assumptions," *Clinical Social Work Journal*, 4 (Winter 1979), 256–266; Melvin Delgado, "Social Work and the Puerto Rican Community," *Social Casework*, 55 (February 1974), 117–123; Wynetta Devore, "The Life Model and Work with Black Families," *Social Casework*, 64 (November 1983), 525–531; Alejandro Garcia, "The Chicano and Social Work," *Social Casework*, 52 (May 1971), 274–278; Florence Hollis, "Casework and Social Class," *Social Casework*, 46 (October 1965), 463–471; Camille Jeffers, *Living Poor* (Ann Arbor, Mich.: Ann Arbor Publishers, 1967); Terry Jones, "Institutional Racism in the United States," *Social Work*, 19 (March 1974), 218–225; Norman Linzer, *The Jewish Family* (New York: Human Sciences Press, 1984); Sadye L. Logan, "Race, Identity, and Black Children: A Developmental Perspective," *Social Casework*, 61 (January 1981), 47–56; Doman Lum, "The Psychosocial Needs of the Chinese Elderly," *Social Casework*, 61 (February 1980), 100–106; Doman Lum, "Toward a Framework for Social Work Practice with Minorities," *Social Work*, 27 (May 1982), 244–249; Harriet Pipes McAdoo, *Black Families*, 2d ed. (Newbury Park, Calif.: Sage, 1988); Miguel Montiel and Paul Wong, "A Theoretical Critique of the Minority Perspective," *Social Casework*, 64 (February 1983), 112–117; Maria Rosenbloom, "Implications of the Holocaust for Social Work," *Social Casework*, 64 (April 1983), 205–213; Angela Shen Ryan, "Cultural Factors in Casework with Chinese-Americans," *Social Casework*, 66 (June 1985), 333–340; David D. Royce and Gladys T. Turner, "Strengths of Black Families: A Black Community's Perspective," *Social Work*, 25 (September 1980), 407–409; Ramon M. Salcido, "Problems of the Mexican-American Elderly in an Urban Setting," *Social Casework*, 60 (December 1979), 609–615; Beverly Sewell-Coker, Joyce Hamilton-Collins, and Edith Fein, "Social Work Practice with West Indian Immigrants," *Social Casework*, 66 (November 1985), 563–568; and Francis J. Turner, "Ethnic Difference and Client Performance," *Social Service Review*, 44 (March 1970), 1–10.

Social Casework, 51 (May 1970), devotes the entire issue to the black experience, with articles written by black authors; *Social Casework*, 55 (February 1974), is devoted to Puerto Rican culture; *Social Casework*, 57 (March 1976), is on Asian and Pacific Islander Americans; *Social Casework*, 61 (October 1980), is devoted to "The American Indian Today"; the entire issue of *Social Work*, 27 (January 1982), is on "Social Work and People of Color."

14. For comments on this, see Annette Garrett, "Modern Casework: The Contributions of Ego Psychology," in Howard J. Parad, ed., *Ego Psychology and Dynamic Casework* (New York: Family Service Association of America, 1958), 38–52; Gordon Hamilton, "A Theory of Personality: Freud's Contribution to Social Work," in Parad, *Ego Psychology and Dynamic Casework*, 11–37; Eleanor B. Weisberger, "The Current Usefulness of Psychoanalytic Theory to Casework," *Smith College Studies in Social Work*, 37

(February 1967), 106–118; Katherine Wood, "The Contribution of Psychoanalysis and Ego Psychology to Social Casework," in Herbert S. Strean, ed., *Social Casework* (Metuchen, N.J.: Scarecrow Press, 1971).

The first three chapters written by George Wiedeman in George Wiedeman, ed., *Personality Development and Deviation: A Textbook for Social Work* (New York: International Universities Press, 1975), 1–39, comprise an excellent review of psychoanalytic personality theory.

15. See Anna Freud, *The Ego and the Mechanisms of Defense* (New York: International Universities Press, 1946); Heinz Hartmann, *Ego Psychology and the Problem of Adaptation* (New York: International Universities Press, 1958); Heinz Hartmann, Ernst Kris, and R. Loewenstein, "Comments on the Formation of Psychic Structure," in Ruth S. Eissler et al., eds., *The Psychoanalytic Study of the Child*, vol. 2 (New York: International Universities Press, 1946), 11–38; Ernst Kris, "Notes on the Development and on Some Current Problems of Psychoanalytic Child Psychology," in Ruth S. Eissler et al., *The Psychoanalytic Study of the Child*, vol. 5 (New York: International Universities Press, 1950), 24–46; Erik Erikson, *Identity and the Life Cycle* (New York: International Universities Press, 1959); David Rapaport, *Organization and Pathology of Thought* (New York: Columbia University Press, 1951); Robert W. White, *Ego and Reality in Psychoanalytic Theory* (New York: International Universities Press, 1963).

For background on casework's integration of ego psychology, see Parad, *Ego Psychology and Dynamic Casework*; Howard J. Parad and Roger R. Miller, eds., *Ego-Oriented Casework: Problems and Perspectives* (New York: Family Service Association of America, 1963); and Isabel Stamm, "Ego Psychology in the Emerging Theoretical Base of Casework," in Alfred J. Kahn, ed., *Issues in American Social Work* (New York: Columbia University Press, 1959), 80–109.

Eda Goldstein's volume, *Ego Psychology and Social Work Practice* (New York: The Free Press, 1984), provides the most up-to-date and thorough discussion of concepts from ego psychology and their usefulness to social work practice. We also recommend three volumes by Gertrude and Rubin Blanck on ego, developmental, and object relations theories: *Ego Psychology: Theory and Practice* (New York: Columbia University Press, 1974); *Ego Psychology II: Psychoanalytic*

Developmental Psychology (New York: Columbia University Press, 1979); and *Beyond Ego Psychology: Developmental Object Relations Theory* (New York: Columbia University Press, 1986).

There are many other readings on developmental and object relations theories. We include here W. R. D. Fairbairn, *Object-Relations Theory of Personality* (New York: Basic Books, 1954); Harry Guntrip, *Personality Structure and Human Interaction* (London: Hogarth Press, 1961); Margaret S. Mahler et al., *The Psychological Birth of the Human Infant: Symbiosis and Individuation* (New York: Basic Books, 1975); Rene A. Spitz, "Anaclitic Depression," in *Psychoanalytic Study of the Child*, vol. 2 (New York: International Universities Press, 1946), 313–342; Donald W. Winnicott, *Collected Papers* (London: Tavistock, 1958); and Donald W. Winnicott, *Home Is Where We Start From* (New York: W. W. Norton, 1986), a collection of essays compiled after his death in 1972.

See also Otto Kernberg, *Borderline Conditions and Pathological Narcissism* (New York: Aronson, 1975); and Heinz Kohut, *The Restoration of the Self* (New York: International Universities Press, 1977).

16. See Miriam Elson's excellent and recommended book, *Self Psychology in Clinical Social Work* (New York: W. W. Norton, 1986), especially pp. 8–10.

17. Ways of thinking and feeling characteristic of the young child are vividly portrayed in the studies of Jean Piaget and Susan Isaacs. See especially Jean Piaget and Susan Isaacs, *Social Development in Young Children* (New York: Harcourt, Brace, 1937). For less detailed but useful descriptions, see Erik Erikson, *Childhood and Society* (New York: W. W. Norton, 1950); and Selma Fraiberg, *The Magic Years* (New York: Scribner's, 1959). John Flavell, *The Developmental Psychology of Jean Piaget* (Princeton, N.J.: Von Nostrand, 1963), deals with Piaget's work as a whole.

18. Leopold Bellak et al., *Ego Functions in Schizophrenics, Neurotics, and Normals* (New York: Wiley, 1973). See also Eda Goldstein, *Ego Psychology and Social Work Practice*.

19. Anna Freud's classic work, *Ego and the Mechanisms of Defense*, was the first comprehensive study of ego defenses. See also Eda Goldstein, *Ego Psychology and Social Work Practice*, chapter 4; Goldstein makes the important distinction between defense mechanisms and coping mechanisms (p. 69). See also

H. P. Laughlin, *The Ego and Its Defenses,* 2d ed. (New York: James Aronson, 1979), and George Wiedeman, *Personality Development and Deviation,* chapter 3.

For a discussion of some of the more "primitive" defenses, see Otto Kernberg, *Borderline Conditions and Pathological Narcissism;* and Otto Kernberg, "Borderline Personality Organization," in Michael H. Stone, ed., *Essential Papers on Borderline Disorders* (New York: New York University Press, 1986), especially pp. 299–307.

20. Discussions of classifications of defense mechanisms can be found in William W. Meissner, "Theories of Personality and Psychopathology: Classical Psychoanalysis," in Harold I. Kaplan and Benjamin J. Sadock, eds., *Comprehensive Textbook of Psychiatry* (Baltimore: Williams and Wilkins, 1985), especially pp. 388–390; and George Valliant, *Adaptation to Life* (Boston: Little, Brown, 1977).

21. The term "good enough mother" was introduced by Donald W. Winnicott to describe the part played by the mother (or substitute parent) in creating an environment that facilitates healthy psychological development of the infant. The good enough mother "starts off with an almost complete adaptation to her infant's needs, and as time proceeds she adapts less and less completely, gradually, according to the infant's growing ability to deal with her failure." See Donald W. Winnicott, "Transitional Objects and Transitional Phenomena: A Study of the First Not-Me Possession," in Peter Buckley, ed., *Essential Papers on Object Relations* (New York: New York University Press, 1986), p. 265.

22. See Margaret S. Mahler, *The Psychological Birth of the Human Infant.*

23. See Erik H. Erikson, *Childhood and Society,* chapter 8.

24. Ruth Benedict, *Patterns of Culture* (New York: Houghton Mifflin, 1934); Margaret Mead, *Sex and Temperament in Three Primitive Societies* (New York: Morrow, 1935).

25. Abram Kardiner, *The Individual and His Society* (New York: Columbia University Press, 1939).

26. Maurine Boie, "The Case Worker's Need for Orientation to the Culture of the Client," *Proceedings of the National Conference of Social Work* (Chicago: University of Chicago Press, 1937), 112–123; Ellse de la Fontaine, "Cultural and Psychological Implications in Case Work Treatment with Irish Clients," in *Cultural Problems in Social Case Work* (New York: Family Welfare Association of America, 1940), 21–37.

27. See especially Robert C. Angell, *The Family Encounters the Depression* (New York: Scribner's, 1936); Ruth Shonie Cavan and Katherine Howland Ranck, *The Family and the Depression* (Chicago: University of Chicago Press, 1938); and Mirra Komarovsky, *The Unemployed Man and His Family* (New York: Dryden Press, 1940).

28. Edmund Bergler, *Unhappy Marriage and Divorce* (New York: International Universities Press, 1946); Ernest W. Burgess and Leonard S. Cottrell, Jr., *Predicting Success or Failure in Marriage* (New York: Prentice Hall, 1939); Florence Hollis, *Women in Marital Conflict* (New York: Family Welfare Association of America, 1949); Lewis N. Terman, *Psychological Factors in Marital Happiness* (New York: McGraw-Hill, 1938); and Willard Waller, *The Old Love and the New* (New York: Liveright, 1930).

29. See, for example, two classic articles that influenced casework thought during this period: Richard A. Cloward, "Illegitimate Means, Anomie and Deviant Behavior," *American Sociological Review,* 24 (April 1959), 164–176; and Gregory Bateson, Don D. Jackson, Jay Haley, and John H. Weakland, "Toward a Theory of Schizophrenia," *Behavioral Science,* 1 (October 1956), 252–264.

30. See Nathan E. Cohen, ed., *Social Work and Social Problems* (New York: National Association of Social Workers, 1964); Louis A. Ferman, ed., *Poverty in America* (Ann Arbor: University of Michigan Press, 1965); Hylan Lewis, *Culture Class and Poverty* (Washington, D.C.: Cross Tell, 1967); and Henry S. Maas, "Socio-cultural Factors in Psychiatric Clinic Services for Children," *Smith College Studies,* 25 (February 1955), 1–90.

31. See August B. Hollingshead and Frederick C. Redlich, *Social Class and Mental Illness* (New York: Wiley, 1958). The Hollingshead-Redlich study on the greater prevalence of certain types of mental illness in lower socioeconomic classes aroused great interest and led to examination of the question of how prevalence was related to class-related differences in the formulation of diagnostic opinion and treatment.

32. See note 13.

33. See Liane Vida Davis, "Role Theory," in Francis J. Turner, *Social Work Treatment*, 541–563; and Bruce J. Biddle and Edwin Thomas, eds., *Role Theory: Concepts and Research* (New York: Wiley, 1966).

34. See Judith C. Nelsen, *Communication Theory and Social Work Practice* (Chicago: University of Chicago Press, 1980); and Judith C. Nelsen, "Communication Theory and Social Work Treatment," in Francis J. Turner, *Social Work Treatment*, 219–244. See also Mark Knapp, *Essentials of Nonverbal Communication* (New York: Holt, Rinehart and Winston, 1980); Virginia Satir, *Conjoint Family Therapy* (Palo Alto, Calif.: Science and Behavior Books, 1967, 1986); Paul Watzlawick, Janet Beavin, and Don D. Jackson, *Pragmatics of Human Communication: A Study of Interactional Patterns, Pathologies, and Paradoxes* (New York: W. W. Norton, 1967).

35 . Sophie Loewenstein, in a highly recommended article, "Inner and Outer Space in Social Casework," *Social Casework*, 60 (January 1979), 23–24.

36. Direct individual treatment of children is not a subject covered by this text. See Shirley Cooper and Leon Wanerman, *Children in Treatment* (New York: Brunner/Mazel, 1977); Margaret G. Frank, "Casework with Children: The Experience of Treatment," in Francis J. Turner, ed., *Differential Diagnosis and Treatment in Social Work*, 3d ed. (New York: The Free Press, 1983), pp. 5–14; Florence Lieberman, *Social Work with Children* (New York: Human Services Press, 1979); and Judith Mishne, *Clinical Work with Children* (New York: The Free Press, 1983).

37. For discussion of a "corrective relationship," see Lucille N. Austin, who introduced this term to casework, "Trends in Differential Treatment in Social Casework," *Journal of Social Casework*, 29 (June 1948), 203–211. Gertrude and Rubin Blanck, in *Ego Psychology II*, refer to the *reparative* experience: the therapist provides a therapeutic "climate" for the patient that fosters ego building and healthy development.

CHAPTER 3

Examples of Clinical Social Work Practice

Before we proceed with further discussion of the principles of psychosocial casework, some case illustrations may be of value in demonstrating the use in actual practice of the concepts presented in the previous chapter. By introducing real case situations, cases that will be referred to from time to time throughout the text, at this juncture we hope to provide the basis for a beginning understanding of how the theory guides treatment. All of the five case examples that follow illustrate situations in which serious breakdowns in social adjustment led the clients to seek or to be referred for clinical social work assistance. In each case, the problems in social functioning reflected, to one degree or another, the three types of causation described in Chapter 2. The dynamics of the treatment process by which the clients were enabled to achieve better functioning demonstrate clearly many of the points there.

These cases were selected to show competent casework practice and treatment that resulted in significant gains for the clients. Of course, even the most experienced worker sometimes must face the fact that a particular piece of work has not been as helpful as was

hoped. But these cases are representative of many in which workers and clients together are able to ameliorate person-situation disturbances.

Each case illustration will include a discussion of the three interacting factors that contributed to the clients' difficulties: (1) What current life or environmental situations were exerting excessive pressure or failing to provide opportunities necessary for satisfactory client functioning? (2) To what extent did immature or faulty ego-superego functioning and developmental deficits affect the clients' problems? (3) Which ego or superego functions were excessively restrictive or rigid and therefore maladaptive? Particular attention will be given to appraising the clients' personality strengths and environmental supports.

While studying the case material, it may be helpful for the reader to try to identify the ways in which these factors interacted to affect the clients and their problems: Specifically, how did casework intervention help to shift the balance of forces within the individual or family, or between the personality of the individual and the pressures from the environmental or interpersonal situation? Was the change in balance achieved by strengthening or modifying a specific aspect of the person-situation configuration, or did treatment address all three contributing factors? On the basis of the preliminary discussion in Chapter 2 of treatment procedures or techniques (further elaborated upon in Chapters 4 through 8), what interventions did the worker choose and why?

In general, the quality of the relationship between worker and client is seen by psychosocial caseworkers as crucial to the effectiveness of treatment. Basic to a good therapeutic alliance is the positive attitude of the worker toward the client. In these case presentations, attention will be given to the treatment relationship and how it varies according to the needs and personalities of the clients. Occasional mention will be made of the concept of *transference*. This phenomenon will be examined in greater detail in Chapter 10; suffice it to say for now that when we use this term here we are referring to feelings and attitudes (positive or negative) that the client brings to the worker from other (often early family) experiences in relationships. When the client develops a strong positive transference to the worker, trust and treatment are often enhanced, providing the client with temporary supports needed to mobilize resources sufficiently to cope with or resolve his or her difficulties. On the other hand, negative transference reactions, when discussed openly, can be important in helping a client develop self-understanding. As the reader will see, for some clients, transference reactions have little bearing on treatment; this is true when the worker is viewed realistically: primarily as an expert in treating problems of social functioning.

A MARITAL CRISIS

The case of Dick and Susan Jones* is of particular interest because it illustrates how clinical social work can sometimes help clients bring about substantial changes very quickly. The

worker's understanding of individual and interpersonal dynamics and the couple's motivation for change led to an improved marital relationship in eleven joint therapy sessions held over a period of three months.

Susan Jones, age thirty, telephoned a family service agency stating that her marriage of seven years was at the "crossroads." She was afraid of her husband, who, she said, had become an "angry man." They were arguing constantly. Although reluctantly, her husband Dick, age thirty-two, was willing to participate in marital counseling.

During the first meeting, the caseworker learned that the open conflict was precipitated a month earlier when Dick discovered that Susan was having an affair with her boss. Although the very short affair ended before marital therapy began, Dick was still enraged, distrustful, and frightened that he would lose Susan, in spite of Susan's reassurances that she wanted their marriage to work. They reported that they had considered terminating the marriage, but they wanted to keep the family together for the sake of their three "delightful" and "normal" children: Charles, age six, and twins Ann and Andy, age five.

Both Dick and Susan were from large, stable, two-parent working-class families. Dick's parents were characterized as more rigid and emotionally aloof than Susan's, whom they portrayed as warmer and more communicative. Although Dick was black and Protestant and Susan was white and Jewish, neither of their families had strongly disapproved of their courtship and marriage. Both sets of grandparents enjoyed their grandchildren and visited with the Joneses quite regularly; they were close but not intrusive and good in-law relationships had been established early in the marriage.

Since high school graduation, Dick had

*All case material in this book is disguised and fictitious names are used throughout.

worked for the electric company as a mechanic. Susan worked for several years before her marriage and, a year prior to her affair, had taken a secretarial job. Although the extra income was important, Susan's motivation to work again was in large part based on feeling trapped, bored, and isolated from adults when she was at home all day with the children. They lived in a rural area with very few opportunities for casual socializing, and Susan was afraid of becoming "nothing more than a housewife"; she spoke of needing to find her own "identity." Since Dick worked the evening shift, he had agreed to take on many of the child care and household functions. Although the division of roles was worked out comfortably between them, as treatment progressed, it became clear that he had been afraid from the beginning that Susan would find the outside world so attractive she would lose interest in him and in their home. He did not, however, resent sharing the duties (he even took pride in their vegetable garden and in doing canning and preserving), and he knew that she, like him, thoroughly enjoyed the children.

Neither Dick nor Susan evidenced severe personality difficulties. However, although Dick was conscientious in work, fond of his home, and caring in his relationships with the children, he tended to be passive and emotionally remote with Susan; generally, he let her take the lead. Susan, on the other hand, was a more expressive person who in many ways had been the pursuer of the relationship with her husband. Nevertheless, over the years she had not confronted Dick with her disappointment about the fact that he rarely initiated affectionate moments or sexual relations between them. By the same token, she had not encouraged him to share his dissatisfactions with her. Instead, she slowly but steadily began to withdraw. Although aware of the distance that was developing between them, Dick, too, took no steps to rekindle the intimacy they had enjoyed early in marriage. When Susan went back to work, she was flattered by her employer's attentions and briefly, albeit guiltily, yielded to them. Her remorse, she said, would not have allowed the affair to continue very long even if Dick had not discovered it.

Although it was Susan who initiated treatment, Dick joined the first session with more apparent motivation for self-understanding than she did. He was concerned about his inability to control his temper since discovering Susan's unfaithfulness to him; he found himself shouting at her on the slightest provocation. Furthermore, he disliked his distrust of Susan when his "reasonable mind" believed the affair was over. He said he wanted to make changes in himself and recognized that these would be important to the marriage. Susan, on the other hand, insisted that now that she was no longer involved with her boss, the rest of the problem was up to Dick. She had tried over the years to bring excitement to their life together, but nothing "set a fire under Dick." Contrary to Susan's expectations, however, Dick was quickly able to recognize the roots of the passivity about which she complained. As the youngest of seven children, with four older sisters who catered to him and yet dominated him, he had little chance to take the initiative in his relationship with them. He began to understand how he had carried this pattern of unassertiveness to his marriage.

By the third session, they were arguing less. Dick recognized that his anger had been in reaction to the blow to his self-respect and his feelings of helplessness in the face of Susan's betrayal. Tentatively, at first, he began to take the initiative in moving closer to Susan. Now it was Susan who maintained an aloof reserve; she was barely responsive to Dick. At first she explained this by saying that she was still afraid of his temper and felt safer at arm's length from him. As the worker pressed her to explore her feelings further, Susan acknowledged that because she had been angry with Dick for such a long time she now felt like "giving him a taste of his own medicine." Beyond that, and more to the point in the long run, she was keeping her tender feelings for him in check for fear that she would "fall" for his overtures, after which she expected he would revert to his remote and passive ways. Fortunately, Dick was not deterred and continued to risk being affectionate and open with Susan, with the result that Susan recognized the need to examine her own reactions.

As Susan developed greater awareness of the part she played in the problem, she explored some of the roots of her behavior. She was the second of four daughters and believed that her father preferred her older sister, Anita. As hard as Susan tried to please him, her father always seemed to find Anita smarter, prettier, and more talented than she. When she realized that much of her current resignation and anger at Dick were displaced feelings about her father, she began to take the chance and accept the changes Dick was making. Within a few weeks, their relationship grew warmer and more trusting, more like it used to be, they both said.

When treatment began, the caseworker and the couple had "contracted" for ten sessions with the understanding that the therapy could be extended, if necessary, after an evaluation at that time. During the tenth session they reported that they were feeling much more hopeful about their marriage, and both Dick and Susan had maintained an awareness of how each had participated in bringing about the crisis that had developed between them. They rarely resorted to blaming each other, but each took responsibility for working to make the relationship better. They decided to come for a final, eleventh meeting in which they were able to summarize and reinforce the good work they had done. Almost a year later they sent a Christmas card to the caseworker on which Susan wrote: "We are recommending marriage counseling to all our friends! We learned a lot and everything is going well."

What were the factors that contributed to threatening this marriage? In most respects, Dick and Susan were psychologically healthy.

Yet both brought to their relationship some unresolved emotional issues and personality features that played into the difficulties. Dick's lack of assertiveness in personal relationships was, in part, derived from his childhood experiences with his older sisters who were managerial and indulgent. Since they had expected little in return for their love—except compliance—Dick did not learn well enough how to take the initiative to get what he wanted when it was not naturally forthcoming. Also, he was not used to expressing openly his deeper feelings about anything. Therefore, when faced with the threat of losing Susan, he withdrew, feeling helpless and angry. Susan, for different reasons, also tended to despair in the face of withdrawn affection; since she felt she had never been fully appreciated and loved by her father, in spite of the fact that she came from a warm, essentially nurturing family, she could easily lose hope about ever having a man who truly treasured her.

In this case, then, some unfulfilled childhood needs and ego weaknesses interfered with adult adjustment. However, for both Dick and Susan, the damage was not pervasive and the deficiencies were less disabling than they are for many clients. In this marriage, each partner was able to bring good reality testing and an "observing ego" to the situation; both had the capacity to reflect on the aspects of their own personalities that led to the difficulties. They both functioned well in most areas, were able to take pride in their accomplishments, and were capable of enjoying life. Each was able to be empathic. Dick had the capacity to understand how his passivity had contributed to Susan's sense of isolation and subsequent willingness to engage in an extramarital affair. Because he was determined to save the marriage, he quickly learned to take initiative. Susan's sense of values (ego ideal and superego) helped her to recognize that her sexual relationship with her boss was no solution to her problems; her capacity for reality testing enabled her to understand that unless they worked on their marriage it would continue to deteriorate. She realized that by withdrawing from Dick she, too, had taken a passive role in the marital interaction.

The marital problems that the Jones couple experienced were not simply a product of the weaknesses of each. In interaction with one another, their separate vulnerabilities were aggravated and reinforced, resulting—as often occurs in marital and family relationships—in a sort of negative complementarity. As discussed in Chapter 2, one of the primary characteristics of a system is that the parts transact: acting and reacting one upon the other. The marital treatment, therefore, focused not only on the personalities of each partner, but also on the reciprocal dynamics, the circular interactions, between Dick and Susan. As their actions and reactions changed, the climate of the relationship improved and the unhappiness each was experiencing was alleviated. Because each brought many strengths, and because the marriage had been gratifying at an earlier point, it took relatively little work or time to resume a positive balance and achieve renewed satisfaction.

The therapeutic relationship was important in that the worker's competence, objectivity, and wish to help enabled Dick and Susan to trust her and reveal themselves. But, in contrast to many clinical cases, the worker did not need to make extensive use of sustaining procedures. Relatively little time was required for ventilation of feeling. The transference aspects of the treatment were negligible; primarily, the worker helped Dick and Susan to reflect on their situation, on their patterns of interaction, and on some aspects of their past lives that contributed to their marital problems. Once they understood the dynamics, between sessions they were able to bring about many improvements in their situation.

Although of relatively minor importance, it is worth noting that environmental influences, beyond those of the marital system itself, played a part in this couple's situation. In a general at-

mosphere in which the women's movement was advocating greater assertiveness, Susan's eagerness to have a life outside her home was supported. Unlike many marital pairs, Dick and Susan had the flexibility to redefine "male" and "female" roles in order to accommodate Susan's wish. Also, again in contrast to many other couples, the Joneses had a supportive extended family network in which the in-laws showed interest but did not interfere or take sides. This was especially impressive since the marriage was interracial. With a minimum of outside pressure, efforts to resolve the marital difficulties were enhanced.

SOME PROBLEMS OF AGING[1]

Clients often come to social workers at a time of crisis: when there has been an illness, the loss of a loved one, a change in employment or financial circumstances, or when new living arrangements are needed. Sometimes, as in the Jones case, a crisis occurs in reaction to a problem that has erupted in a family relationship. Any of these events can affect a person's self-esteem or sense of well-being. For the aged, who constitute a greater proportion of our population than ever before, disruptions in their lives are practically inevitable. It is often at these times that casework intervention is sought.

It should go without saying that the needs of older people have much in common with those of every age group. For the elderly as well as for the young, certain essentials are required in order to live with full dignity: an acceptable home, economic security, social status and recognition, a meaningful purpose in life. As difficult as it is for many people of all ages to fulfill the conditions necessary for optimum adjustment, the aged often have the hardest time of all.

Sometimes, when working with aged clients, there is a tendency to think in terms of "limited goals." Indeed, in some cases where there has been extreme physical or mental deterioration, the caseworker's efforts may have to be circumscribed. But there are large numbers of older people, starting with those in their sixties, who may have ten, twenty, or even thirty fulfilling years ahead of them. For clients in this group, substantial gains are often possible. The case illustration that follows is one in which the aim of therapy was to help the client, Mr. Kennedy, to reduce the impact of changes in his circumstances and to aid him to find satisfactory replacements for several losses he had endured. Had the young caseworker viewed Mr. Kennedy solely as an old man whose best years were behind him, she would have overlooked the possibilities for helping him as she did, in which case her client might well have rapidly declined into a state of hopelessness, poor health, and dependency.

Miss Kennedy, age twenty-seven, was referred by her psychiatrist to the geriatric service of an outpatient mental health clinic; she was seeking help for her sixty-seven-year-old father. An elementary school teacher, she had lived with her father until recently. Her mother had died of alcoholism thirteen years before. Mr. Kennedy, a construction worker, had been retired for two years and was maintaining himself with social security benefits and odd jobs as a handyman. His daughter portrayed him as a man who had always been active and an independent thinker; for many years he was an officer in his union local. He had lived in his neighborhood for thirty years, was well known, and was considered something of a "street-corner politician," devoting much time to agitating for social causes.

Six months previously, Miss Kennedy had moved to an apartment of her own, against her father's wishes. Since then Mr. Kennedy had become depressed and had given up his part-time work. He was blaming his daughter for leaving him alone in the apartment they had shared, with the entire rent to pay. He had two sons who lived at a distance and from whom, for all intents and purposes, he was estranged.

Miss Kennedy said he had always been domineering and possessive of her. Leaving him had not been easy, but she felt she had to take this step for the sake of her own "sanity." She knew that if she stayed, her father would interfere in her relationship with a man in whom she was interested. She felt guilty when he accused her of betraying him; she confided that sometimes she wet her bed after an explosive argument with him.

The worker explored the possibility of joint meetings between father and daughter, but Miss Kennedy adamantly refused. She further indicated that her psychiatrist, with whom she was in intensive treatment, had encouraged her to minimize her contacts with her father at this time. Since Miss Kennedy's therapy was expensive, she was not in a position to offer her father much financial help, even though she had recently given him a little money after he angrily demanded it. Miss Kennedy had spoken with her father about the clinic and believed he would be willing to meet with the worker, but she herself preferred no further involvement.

Even before contacting him, the worker began thinking about Mr. Kennedy. With the incomplete information she had, she made some tentative efforts to understand and "feel with" her new client and to get a sense of his current predicament.[2] Assumptions and predictions based on anticipatory preparation are always subject to revision. Nevertheless, she considered possible aspects of his objective and subjective situation: He is probably worried about money, she thought. Apparently he had been very dependent on his daughter for emotional as well as financial support, so it seemed likely that he would now feel profoundly bereft. She anticipated meeting a man who was not only lonely, but very frightened, angry, and depressed. He might have little motivation at this point to help or take care of himself; if this turned out to be true, the worker imagined that he might require considerable support and encouragement. Yet, he was described as a man who always did things "his way," so Mr. Kennedy would probably need reassurance that he would be in charge of whatever decisions were made. She also wondered how he would respond to a woman worker about the same age as his daughter. Would he transfer his anger onto the worker? Would he want to cling? Or would it be comforting for him to work with a young woman? Finally, the worker reflected on some of her own reactions that might be provoked by Mr. Kennedy and his situation. She had a recently widowered father who was finding it difficult to adjust; she realized she would have to guard against identifying too closely with Miss Kennedy and against becoming countertherapeutically reactive to Mr. Kennedy's possible dependency.

When the worker telephoned Mr. Kennedy, he readily agreed to come in to speak with her. He spent much of the first session berating his mother (who had left his father when he was a child); his wife, who had been a heavy drinker for many years; the Catholic Church, toward which he felt very bitter for various reasons; and, above all, his daughter. They had all mistreated him—"a good man"—and, in his view, the result would be an "early grave" for him. He had loved and cherished his daughter, he said, and now she was treating him like this: leaving him sick and penniless. He did not care whether he ate or worked. Actually his physical health was good, but he felt ill and listless. If only his daughter could come back to share the rent and keep him company, he was sure he would be all right again. Nothing else would help.

Without exploring alternatives at first, the worker recognized his loneliness and made evident her interest in helping. She expressed understanding of how difficult the recent changes had been for him. She voiced her confidence that, together, they might be able to find some answers. Fortunately, Mr. Kennedy took to the worker quickly, and there were several long interviews within a period of a month. They be-

gan to talk over steps he might take to improve his situation. Usually the worker followed the client's lead, but occasionally she offered some suggestions of her own. Gradually but consistently, Mr. Kennedy's feelings of hopelessness diffused and he began taking on new or renewed interests: He became attached to a puppy a neighbor gave him and took it with him everywhere he went. He solved a complex oil burner problem for his landlord for which he was paid. He began visiting with friends again. He resumed his interest in political affairs. Sometimes between meetings he would call the worker and tell her about the things he was doing.

It is important to note that in an early session with Mr. Kennedy, the worker (who was placed as a graduate student at the clinic) informed him that they would be working together for only a three-month period, after which she would be leaving the service. In view of Mr. Kennedy's strong reaction to losing the companionship of his daughter, it was especially important for the worker to give him as much advance notice of her plans as possible. She also reassured him that, if necessary, another worker (her supervisor) would be available to him after she left. Initially annoyed and unsettled by the worker's impending departure, he nevertheless was able to talk about his feelings easily; he asked about her plans, some of which she explained to him. He said he thought it was good that she was "bettering herself" by getting more training and added that he was proud his daughter had gotten a better education than either he or his wife had had.

Often an important indicator of a client's strengths (or weaknesses) can be found in the quality of the therapeutic relationship he or she is able to establish. The basic soundness of the personalities of Dick and Susan Jones was evidenced by the way they realistically related to their caseworker and quickly utilized her expertise to help them resolve their difficulties. Mr. Kennedy, who was feeling so bereft, needed the worker temporarily to fill a place that his daughter had left by moving out. By keeping in close touch with the worker, he was able to find the help his daughter no longer provided; he could become dependent (although certainly not blindly compliant!) until he was able to remobilize his own inner resources. Another area of strength was perceived immediately by the worker: although he was clearly depressed and shaken, in the first meeting he had come in fighting; he was neither withdrawn nor totally dispirited. With the worker's help, Mr. Kennedy was able to redirect his belligerent energies and utilize them in the service of more satisfying ends.

In their next-to-last session, the worker asked her supervisor, who would be the new worker available to Mr. Kennedy, to join them. While talking over his situation, the supervisor offered information about a nearby apartment building in need of a superintendent. He applied immediately and was accepted; in return for services, he was given a rent-free apartment. On several counts, it was fortunate indeed that the agency could direct him to this opportunity. Since it was the supervisor who gave him the information, the transition to the new worker was facilitated. Furthermore, since one of the most profound but frequent insults to the aged is the loss of feelings of usefulness and respect, the job served to reestablish these. Also highly important was the financial relief the job provided.

In the final meeting with the worker, Mr. Kennedy reported that his daughter was planning marriage, adding, "It's about time!" He was able to say that it had meant a lot to have someone to talk to, but that he was doing much better now. He wasn't sure he would need frequent appointments any more, but he liked the supervisor and would keep in touch with her. He concluded by wishing the worker good luck in her career and, interestingly, advised her to get married and have children because he was sure she would make a good mother! Before the worker left, Miss Kennedy telephoned to thank her and say that, although she still felt guilty

about leaving her father, he was no longer blaming her. He seemed more like his "old self" again.

With older clients, as with every client, it is important to take an individualized approach. One cannot generalize about "good planning." In this case, the worker was optimally helpful because she assessed the family situation, Mr. Kennedy's many strengths, and the resources available to him. For example, by knowing even as little as she did about Miss Kennedy's complicated involvement with her father, it was evident that he (unlike some elderly clients) would not be able to solve his problem by living with her. Eventually, the worker realized, he would have to accept this. Also, it was clear that Mr. Kennedy was not a man for whom hobbies, or many of the activities provided by the local senior citizens center, would have sufficed; he would have seen them as "busy work," an indication of his loss of status. What he needed was the very personal interest of the worker and an opportunity to feel purposeful and economically secure.

The effect of the worker-client relationship was by no means the only dynamic in treatment but, temporarily, it played a large part. This worker was really "there" for Mr. Kennedy when he was feeling rejected and needed someone to understand. The fact that it was a warm, yet very professional, relationship permitted the remarkably easy shift to the new worker. There has been a tendency to belittle "transference cures." Some distrust of such cures is well based. When nothing more is done than to use suggestion as a way of directly removing symptomatic behavior, it is extremely likely that a new form of symptom will arise. Not infrequently, it will be a more harmful symptom than the one originally chosen by the client. If, however, the transference relationship is used to remove or lessen the effect of the factors contributing to the maladjustment, as it was for Mr. Kennedy, it is an entirely different situation. Had the worker used her influence directly to induce her client to make certain decisions, this would have been "symptomatic" treatment. Very likely the improvement would then have been only temporary; experience would lead us to believe that when the worker left the clinic, he might have reverted to looking to his daughter to provide emotional supplies, as he had for so many years, and fallen into despair when she refused him. Instead, the relationship provided Mr. Kennedy with the support he needed to mobilize his strengths and seek his own solutions. As it turned out, he visited the new worker only a few times over a period of months, and the gains he had made were maintained.

Finally, it is important to note that in the treatment of Mr. Kennedy, a principle of economy was followed. Although the worker surmised that many of the difficulties he was experiencing had their roots in the traumas of his childhood, or in past family relationships, practically no attention was paid to this material in the actual treatment. His relationship with his daughter, for example, may well have been a reflection of earlier unfilled needs or grief over his unhappy marriage. When viewed in the framework of psychoanalytic theory, it is conceivable that there were unresolved oedipal issues. But, wisely, the worker made no effort to explore these more remote matters when it became clear that positive results could be achieved in the context of the present.

The reader might well ask at this point what the outcome of casework treatment would have been if Mr. Kennedy had been too ill to work or had not had so many well-developed ego functions on which to build. Under such circumstances, would he have been able to regain his self-esteem? Suppose he was forced to accept financial aid or had to be moved to a health-related facility? Surely these are situations many elderly clients face. Sometimes, it is true, solutions are at best compromises. But the case of Mr. Kennedy illustrates the fact that older clients in crisis are not necessarily on an irrevers-

ible downhill road. Even caseworkers can sometimes lose sight of the fact that many aging clients, including some who evidence a degree of physical or mental deterioration, *can* make changes and enjoy a dignified style of life.

A THREE-GENERATION "MULTIPROBLEM" FAMILY

This case and the one to follow have been selected to illustrate the complexity of skills required for successful intervention in clients' environments. As discussed in Chapter 2, and as illustrated in the case of Mr. Kennedy, assessment of the client's milieu is as essential as evaluation of personality; the "fit" or interface between the two is often the focus of casework attention. Direct work with the environment—with people who are part of the client's world or with people who can be introduced as helpful resources—is part of the total treatment process in many cases. Often a complex blend of environmental activities and direct work with clients is crucial to the success of casework treatment. A worker who fails to apply basic understanding and skills to work in the environment is seriously handicapped in efforts to help clients with intra- or interpersonal problems, as well as with clients who are oppressed by noxious social conditions.

People of all circumstances and class, educational, and ethnic backgrounds can require work with various systems that impinge upon them. The family we will describe now, the Wests, lived in a middle-class suburban community; the parents and grandparents were college-educated and trained for professions; they were white, of English-Scotch origins; their religious affiliation was Episcopalian. As we shall see, the ethnic and socioeconomic circumstances of the next family to be presented, the Stones, were quite different. Yet both families had multiple problems. In this connection, we caution against the lumping together of "multiproblem," "hard-to-reach," and poverty families.[3] These terms do not connote diagnostic entities; valid generalizations cannot be made on the basis of labels about family structure, individual personalities, or sociological characteristics. Many multiproblem families are not poor, many poor are not hard to reach, and many well-to-do families tenaciously resist change.

A forty-four-year-old widower, living with his ailing mother of seventy-seven and his fourteen-year-old daughter, applied for help at a community mental health agency. He had been referred by a guidance counselor at the high school because his daughter Ellen was failing her major subjects, skipping school, and associating with a disruptive group of classmates. She had been suspended several times and the counselor's efforts to guide her had failed. Very early in the initial interview, Mr. West also discussed other problems: He himself had been depressed since the death of his wife three years before. He was concerned about his pattern of periodic heavy drinking. Employed as an inspector for a government agency where he had worked for twenty years, he was not in jeopardy of losing his job because he could take sick leave when his drinking became incapacitating. Every few months he would sign himself into the hospital to "dry out" and then function well until he started drinking again. A further concern was his mother's rapidly failing health. When his wife died, Mr. West decided to move with Ellen and his son John (at the time of intake living away from home with a friend) into his mother's comfortable home in order to provide supervision and companionship for the children. Since then, however, the elder Mrs. West had become almost blind and hard of hearing, and she had developed a serious heart condition; her arthritis had become so severe that sometimes she could not walk downstairs without help. She seemed dispirited and hopeless, Mr. West told the worker. For the most part, Ellen fended for herself, and she and her grandmother were more irritating than helpful to one another.

Home visits by the worker and several meetings with all three family members resulted in a group decision to search for a live-in housekeeper. Although there were several reasons for arriving at this plan, the need seemed all the more pressing because Mr. West's work required him to be out many evenings, leaving Ellen and his infirm mother alone. The family income was limited, but as they talked it over with the worker, they realized that by cutting down on certain expenses they could afford a modest wage.

Fortunately, as it turned out, also on the worker's caseload was Mrs. Wilson, a seventy-two-year-old retired domestic worker and food caterer who had recently become depressed after the death of her sister, with whom she had lived for many years. She had considered doing day work but considered this too grueling for her at her age. Yet she was lonely and disliked being idle. When it occurred to the worker that this client also might be helped by taking a job with the West family, she assessed the entire situation carefully. It was important that she consider any aspects that might cause the arrangement to fail. Mrs. Wilson was a capable, dependable person who was interested in other people. At various times she had been active on church service committees and she had taken care of her ill sister at home for many months before the latter died. She had a sense of humor and seemed to get along with young people, as evidenced by the fact that two teenage great-nieces visited her often. And she had housekeeping skills; she had earned her living in related areas for most of her life. There were no apparent reasons why the West family would not find Mrs. Wilson a very pleasant and suitable housekeeper. The worker's major concern was that Mrs. Wilson, who tended at times to be overaccommodating to others, might feel obliged to take the job even if she did not really want to, either to please the worker or because she would consider it a duty to help people in trouble. Therefore, without any pressure, the worker fully explained the West family situation to her, adding that she might not be interested since the family had many problems. The worker urged Mrs. Wilson not to consider it unless she thought it would be of benefit to her. She assured her that the Wests could find a solution if she was not interested. The worker watched closely for any signs that might betray a negative reaction to the idea. But Mrs. Wilson seemed genuinely enthusiastic and said she wanted to meet the Wests. When introduced, she liked them all immediately. Afterward, Ellen, at that time not given to expressing positive feelings about anything, exclaimed: "What a lady!" Mr. West and his mother concurred. Mrs. Wilson agreed to the wage offered since, because of her age, her social security benefits would not be jeopardized.

Within a short period of time, this motherly, very competent woman was able to bring both warmth and organization to the West home. The family was eating regular meals together instead of haphazardly grabbing snacks as they had; Mrs. Wilson was able to enlist Ellen's help with many household tasks too difficult for both older women. Ellen told the worker that she enjoyed coming home from school to the aroma of Mrs. Wilson's cakes and cookies baking in the oven.

The adults, too, seemed heartened to have a home life again. When Mrs. Wilson went home for two days each week, both Ellen and her grandmother were impatient for her return. Mrs. Wilson herself reported that she had gained a "new lease on life" now that she felt needed and her days had a sense of purpose. John, who had moved out of the home a year before, after an angry argument with his father, returned to live in the household. A few family group meetings, which often included Mrs. Wilson, were held with the caseworker, in which the discussions ranged from practical housekeeping matters, to difficulties that arose among them, to sharing of some intense feelings of grief over the loss of the younger Mrs.

West, which had deeply affected all the family members.

The caseworker arranged for a public health nurse to visit Mr. West's mother twice weekly to give her baths and nursing care. Ellen stopped the truancy and, slowly, her academic work improved. The caseworker and Ellen met with the high school guidance counselor to make changes Ellen wanted in her course program. Learning that Ellen had an interest in the theater (her mother had been an actress), the caseworker located a drama class at the YWCA that the girl enjoyed and where she made friends. By the time Mrs. Wilson had been in the home for a year, no significant school problems remained for Ellen; Mrs. West, in spite of her infirmities, was more cheerful and comfortable; and the sullen, irritable relationships that had characterized the Wests' family life were replaced by greater affection and cooperation among them. Mr. West, however, continued his pattern of excessive, periodic drinking. In between bouts with alcohol, which were a little less frequent but just as intense, he felt better than he had. The family physician, to whom Mr. West turned for hospitalization when his drinking became incapacitating, warned him of the damage he was doing to his body. The caseworker explored his willingness to join Alcoholics Anonymous, but Mr. West staunchly refused. He disliked the organization's religious emphasis and, even more to the point, he could not bear the humiliation of sharing his private "weakness" with strangers.

Mr. West, who, after the first few months, was the only family member who still had regular weekly treatment sessions, began to realize that the onset of a period of drinking usually followed a disappointment in a relationship with a woman. For many reasons he had repeatedly failed in his attempts to find a loving sexual companion, and after each letdown he would become depressed and take "one drink," which would start the cycle all over again. A case that had begun with the need for considerable environmental intervention now became one in which direct treatment of Mr. West was the primary focus. At the time this case summary is being written, Mr. West is still in individual treatment, exploring the emotional aspects of his drinking and the problems that interfere with his developing a satisfying love relationship.

As this family's case illustrates, environmental intervention requires skilled and intricate work, coupled with sensitive understanding of individual and family dynamics. An unusual aspect of the case was that while Mrs. Wilson served as a resource for the family, the Wests were an equally important resource for Mrs. Wilson, who no longer required individual treatment after she began to work again. Relatively small adjustments of external conditions triggered significant shifts in the inner lives for all of the individuals involved. In addition to relieving some of the acute distress each person had been suffering, treatment in this case certainly served a preventive function. There was substantial evidence that, as the quality of life improved for the clients, feelings of well-being, relatedness, and self-esteem were nurtured. Without intervention, it is likely that these would have continued declining for each individual, as they had prior to referral to the caseworker.

A FAMILY IN CRISIS: CASEWORK IN PUBLIC WELFARE

In contrast to the West family, the family we present now was black, originally from the rural south, and had moved to a northern urban ghetto neighborhood six years previously; none of the adults had completed high school; the family was receiving public welfare; by tradition, the family members were Baptists. A crucial factor that the two case situations had in common, however, was the caseworker's focus on external conditions and opportunities; once again, the assessment of the environment was as important as the understanding of individual and family dynamics.

Mrs. Stone, a thirty-year-old woman receiving public assistance for herself and five children, ranging in age from fourteen to two years, was reported by a neighbor to the child protective services of the public welfare department. It was alleged that she was severely beating one of the children with a belt. Although the worker investigating the case determined that the report was unfounded, because of the many problems the family was facing, he referred Mrs. Stone to the family services division of the welfare agency. The oldest child, Doreen, was staying out late at night, was truant from school, and did not help around the house. Of even greater concern to the worker were his observations of Brian, age nine, who appeared withdrawn and depressed; the worker heard this child talk only when he muttered to himself. And, most pressing of all, the protective worker learned that the family was to be evicted because the landlord intended to use their apartment for a member of his own family—his right, according to city law.

In the heavily populated metropolitan area in which Mrs. Stone lived, the welfare department's income maintenance functions were separated from other services, two of which were the child protective service that had investigated the complaint against Mrs. Stone and the family services division, to which she was referred when it was ascertained that she had so many pressing problems. Many of the supervisors in the specialized services were MSWs; only a few of the caseworkers had master's degrees. As is often the case, the commissioner of welfare did not have a social work background but was trained in public administration.

The family services worker made a home visit and found Mrs. Stone to be an attractive, intelligent woman who seemed depressed, almost listless. When the worker told Mrs. Stone she knew of the impending eviction and wanted to help, Mrs. Stone hardly responded. She had asked the landlord for time but he was adamant; the city marshal would put the Stones out if they did not move within the next month. Mrs. Stone agreed to allow the worker to speak with the landlord, although neither she nor the worker felt hopeful about influencing him. Mrs. Stone said she felt sure nobody would want to rent to a "welfare family" with five children. Knowing of the acute housing shortage and widespread discrimination in the city, the worker agreed that finding another apartment would be very difficult indeed.

On this first visit, three of the five children were in school. The youngest, Michael, age two, an apparently placid baby, seemed well cared for and healthy. Brian, age nine, was lying in the bedroom staring (vacantly, the worker thought) at the ceiling with his thumb in his mouth. When the worker asked whether Brian was ill, she learned that he was not but that his teacher said he was not learning, even though he was smart. He was not to return to school until he was tested. Describing Brian as a good boy, "quiet and very deep," Mrs. Stone said she did not understand why the teacher was having trouble with him. She was more worried about her oldest child, Doreen, who had a "loud mouth," did not mind, and was always in trouble. As much as she yelled at Doreen, nothing helped.

Most of Mrs. Stone's relatives lived in the south. She had one brother, Robert, age twenty-one, who lived in another part of the city and attended a government training program in carpentry. She and Robert were close. Mrs. Stone married when she was fifteen and Mr. Stone, the father of the four oldest children, had left the household permanently three years before, after several previous separations. He was a heavy drinker, a sometimes violent man who did not keep in touch with the children or send money to the family. On the other hand, Michael's father visited often and voluntarily contributed to his child's support.

The worker later telephoned the landlord,

who maintained he had been more than patient because Mrs. Stone was a "nice woman." But with so many children, she could hardly be called an ideal tenant. Although not totally unsympathetic to the difficulty the family would have finding other housing, he planned to give the apartment to his son and nothing would change his mind. The worker then called Mr. Beck of the Legal Aid Society, who said that perhaps action could be stalled but, eventually, the landlord would be allowed to evict. The lawyer agreed to meet with Mrs. Stone.

The next home visit was scheduled when all of the children would be at home. When the worker arrived, Doreen was just leaving after a screaming exchange with her mother. Quietly, but angrily, Mrs. Stone said, "Sometimes I could kill her." Raymond, age twelve, and Cynthia, age six, were playing good-humoredly. Pointing to Raymond, Mrs. Stone said bitterly, "That's the one I was accused of beating." The worker said she could understand how upsetting it was to have been investigated. Mrs. Stone did not know who to be madder at, the person who had lied about her or the man who came to the house to "snoop." As she listened, the worker realized that it might take time for this client to trust her too.

Mr. Beck, the lawyer, was able to get a forty-five-day extension from the court to give the family time to find housing. Mrs. Stone spoke to her minister, who headed the Housing Action Council, a grass-roots group that worked for tenants' rights, but he was unable to find a suitable apartment. Those that were available were in deplorable condition. The worker met with the welfare housing consultant, who had little to offer but his pessimism. After exerting considerable pressure on the welfare commissioner's office, the supervisor got "broker's approval," which meant that Mrs. Stone was authorized to pay a realtor fee to locate an apartment.

Appearing unexpectedly at the welfare office late one afternoon, Mrs. Stone, close to tears, told the worker that the psychologist from the Board of Education thought Brian should go into the hospital. The more she talked, the angrier she became. She asked whether anything could be done. The worker, who had immediately sensed that Brian was emotionally disturbed, realized that Mrs. Stone was still determined to believe her child was not in trouble. While the mother was there the worker telephoned the psychologist, who told her that Brian's intelligence was above average, but that he was severely emotionally damaged; the boy was hallucinating and his fantasies were filled with violence. He had witnessed his father's brutally attacking his mother when he was six. The psychiatrist, who had also seen Brian, was strongly recommending hospitalization for observation; even long-term inpatient treatment might be necessary.

Mrs. Stone was furious, insisting, "He's *not* crazy." The supervisor, whom the worker had asked to sit in, pointed out that if, after observation, it was believed that Brian was not in danger of hurting himself or anyone else, by law he could not be kept in the hospital without Mrs. Stone's consent. Noting that the mother was listening now and not arguing, the supervisor added that since the psychologist seemed worried about Brian it might be best to have him checked and settle the matter one way or the other. When Mrs. Stone asked whether she had a choice, the supervisor admitted that she was not sure but told Mrs. Stone she could ask.

Reluctantly, Mrs. Stone allowed Brian to be admitted to the children's psychiatric unit of the city hospital. After three weeks, the doctor told her that the boy was definitely not suited for a regular classroom or even for a class for the emotionally disturbed within the school system. He was not likely, however, to be destructive to himself or others. Angrily, Mrs. Stone retorted that she could have told him that. Later, after talking with the hospital psychiatrist, the worker, at the suggestion of her supervisor, told Mrs. Stone about a new special day school pro-

gram for psychotic children, administered by the state hospital. Although the psychiatrist had recommended further hospitalization, he, too, was aware of how strongly Mrs. Stone opposed this. Also, Brian wanted to go home. The referral to the day school was made and, fortunately, Brian was accepted almost immediately.

Two days before the stay of eviction had expired, Mrs. Stone had not yet found an apartment. She pleaded with the worker to help. The supervisor had a good working relationship with the city marshal and was able to persuade him to delay the final action, but only for a few days. The following afternoon, Mrs. Stone, who had been following every lead, located a large, attractive apartment in a two-family brownstone. The rent, however, was sixty dollars over the amount allowed by the Welfare Department's regulations, and efforts by the supervisor to secure an "exception" from the commissioner's office met with failure. From the lawyer, Mr. Beck, Mrs. Stone learned that she had a right to a fair hearing from the state to determine whether the rent guidelines could be exceeded, and a petition was filed for a state review. The lawyer also filed for another stay of eviction. Mrs. Stone was aware, however, that these processes would take time, and that the particular apartment she had found surely would be rented before the decisions were handed down.

The next morning Mrs. Stone and her brother Robert, whom the worker had not met before, were waiting at the welfare office when the worker arrived. Robert, it turned out, had agreed to move with his sister to the new apartment if they could get approval for having his contribution cover the excess rent. After a series of calls to the commissioner's office, the worker was able to get this plan accepted. Robert said he was looking forward to living with his sister and helping to fix up the new apartment. Mrs. Stone learned that the landlord was slow to make repairs, and the worker offered information about a tenant education class on home maintenance given by the state university.

The worker praised Mrs. Stone, as she had throughout their work together, for taking the initiative, in spite of her understandable discouragement about the problems she faced. She had fought hard to hurdle what seemed to be almost impossible obstacles, and her work had paid off: now she had an apartment that she liked and Brian was adjusting very well to the day school. Before leaving, Mrs. Stone asked whether the worker would stop in and see her when she got settled. To herself, the worker wondered whether now that some of the crises were over, Mrs. Stone would want to work on her still contentious relationship with Doreen.

The complexity of environmental treatment, combined with direct work with clients, is well demonstrated by this case. In spite of the many factors mitigating against effective work (not the least of which was the fact that the worker was simultaneously carrying a hundred families on her caseload, some with comparable emergencies), the worker and her supervisor were in contact with over a dozen collaterals and agencies up to the point that this part of the summary of the Stone case ends. They were able to establish an excellent, mutually respectful relationship with the lawyer, one that would facilitate work for other clients in the future. This was particularly important because Mr. Beck had had less cooperative contacts with some members of the Welfare Department staff previously. Patience, tact, persistence, and optimism were all qualities the worker had—and needed to have—to gain Mrs. Stone's trust and to succeed as she did, with client and collaterals. On the other hand, cynicism, indifference, "burnout," and prejudice—characteristics often (sometimes unjustifiably) attributed to public welfare workers—might well have led to the demoralization of the Stone family. Clearly, Mrs. Stone became more hopeful and active when she had others who gave support and shared in her efforts. The worker and her supervisor

functioned in a broad range of roles in their endeavor to provide and locate resources and to interpret, mediate, and intervene in this family's environment. Together, they sought to bring about changes within the agency as well. Even when stymied by restrictive policies and laws, they, along with Mrs. Stone, found workable alternatives.

Given the commitment of worker and supervisor, this case illustrates that effective casework *is* possible in a public welfare agency, even in a dense urban area. Such commitment is most likely, we believe, where there is strong social work involvement. In this case, the supervisor had an MSW and years of experience and the caseworker had had one year of advanced training. We would add that, although similar work might have been possible in a private agency, the workers there probably would not have had the same access to or influence with public officials within and outside the welfare system; it is unlikely that they would have been able to bring about the modifications of rules and policies so important to the work with Mrs. Stone. On the other hand, of course, when caseloads are large, as they were in this agency, it follows that some clients will not get the services they need. When asked about caseload management, the supervisor interviewed about this case frankly admitted that often those clients and situations most accessible to change receive the most attention. There are many other clients whose emotional, physical, and situational difficulties are so recalcitrant and of such long standing that only small caseloads and, more likely, major social changes could begin to remedy them.

As we have said, it is sometimes difficult to assess where the effects of environmental pressures leave off and emotional relationship problems begin. As in the West case, once the critical issues facing the Stones were handled, the worker and family then could address other areas, including the angry relationship between Doreen and her mother; the need for special help for six-year-old Cynthia, who, it developed, had a learning disability; and the location of a day care program for Michael so that Mrs. Stone, who had long wanted a high school diploma, could attend a course to prepare for the equivalency examination. By remaining active with the family for six months after the Stones moved into the new apartment, the worker was then able to help with these and other matters. As the supervisor of this case pointed out, "When a family can't find a decent place to live, it hardly has the stamina to attend to much else, no matter how important."

EARLY DEPRIVATION

Some people need more extended and intensive treatment than was required by the clients thus far described in this chapter. Donna Zimmer, whose case we will now discuss, was in therapy for four years. In the view of the writers and the worker who treated her, a brief casework contact would have been, at best, of minimal value. Clinical experience has repeatedly demonstrated that when developmental deficits have been severe and healthy ego organization has been significantly interrupted, improved adjustment usually takes considerable time to achieve. This case is representative of many cases seen by clinical social workers for which such long-term treatment is necessary. It also illustrates the three types of causation mentioned on pages 46 and 47, and the complexity of the interactions among these factors. Treatment that addressed life history, early needs and deprivations, ego development, and current environmental pressures was vital to the successful outcome.[4]

Referred by her physician, Mrs. Zimmer, age thirty-three, applied to a family service agency. She had numerous somatic complaints that her doctor believed were primarily psychogenic. During her first appointment, she sobbed continually, said her stomach ached unbearably, and complained about being unfairly treated by

her mother, her ex-husband, and others. Over and over she said she might as well die, that she was "good for nothing." Although she was an attractive woman—petite, casually but tastefully dressed—her face was contorted, there were dark circles under her eyes, and during much of the interview she hugged her knees to her chest and rocked as she wept. In this initial meeting, and in many that followed, she evidenced intensive, pervasive anxiety and despair; she wanted help because she was afraid of "falling apart."

Mrs. Zimmer was seen at least once and often twice weekly during her four years of therapy. From time to time there were family meetings with her and her children. There were also several sessions held jointly with her mother. In early sessions with the worker, Mrs. Zimmer was able to provide relevant information freely about her current situation and background. In contrast to her chaotic emotional condition, her approach to factual material was thoughtful and well organized.

Mrs. Zimmer was clearly frightened about the extreme rage she often felt toward her children—Sonia, age eleven, and Michael, age eight—since her recent separation from her husband. Although she had ended her tempestuous marriage, she was reacting with strong feelings of anger and depression, as if she had been the one rejected and abandoned. Easily set off by even minor external pressures, she described herself as numb or empty when not in the grip of torment or rage. She characterized her husband as an angry man, otherwise emotionally remote, who could not fulfill his responsibilities. During their twelve years of marriage, he had worked only now and then and provided sporadic financial support for the children.

After her separation, Mrs. Zimmer had enrolled in a secretarial school. In spite of her emotional distress, she was able to concentrate enough to complete an accelerated course. But she was worried about finding a job during an economic recession and afraid she could not earn enough money to support herself and her children. Although her mother lived in the same city, she could not give financial help. Furthermore, Mrs. Zimmer felt her mother had little else to offer; frequently, she would make promises to drop by and then cancel at the last minute. No other relative lived within visiting distance.

The current situational pressures on Mrs. Zimmer were obvious. She was having to take full responsibility for the care of her children. She had few friends or people to whom she could turn. She was forced to try to enter a tight labor market with newly acquired skills and no previous work experience. Furthermore, the children were reacting negatively to the breakup of the marriage and were more likely to vent their anger at her than at their father for fear that even his occasional visits would end. Much of Mrs. Zimmer's distress, then, was realistically based.

But what unfulfilled infantile needs and flaws in ego development did Mrs. Zimmer bring to her already troubled circumstances? The oldest of five children in a Jewish lower-middle-class upwardly mobile family, she was placed at age three in a children's home for several weeks while her mother was hospitalized for postpartum depression. Mrs. Zimmer remembered this event vividly, and with intense fury; for her, it symbolized a general feeling of abandonment by her mother (a gentle, listless, guilt-ridden, self-effacing woman who seemed ineffectual and indecisive to her daughter). In addition to this separation from her family, when she was an infant Mrs. Zimmer herself was hospitalized several times for operations to correct a malformed eyelid. There were, then, many breaks in her early nurturing.

Furthermore, Mrs. Zimmer believed that by the age of seven or eight her mother had depended on her, the only girl, to be the "little mother" to her brothers. Her needs came last. As she saw it, any wish of hers was met with guilt-provoking responses that led her to feel undeserving. If she got what she wanted, other family members reacted with jealousy and anger. The worker surmised that Mrs. Zimmer's experience with early relationships had led her to believe that she would either be abandoned or "used" in the service of the needs of others. She never felt that she was loved freely for being herself.

Mrs. Zimmer still raged at her mother about the fact that on the same day she graduated from high school (at age sixteen with honors), one of her brothers was graduating from elementary school and her parents attended his ceremony and not hers. She recalled that when she complained, her father told her that education was much more important for boys than for girls. Like the man she married, her father was an angry, critical person who could not express loving feelings; her timid mother, she said, cowered and cringed in the face of his dominating personality. At the time her father died when she was seventeen, Mrs. Zimmer felt she had to take over as head of the household until she "escaped into marriage" at twenty-one.

During the first year of treatment, the extreme oscillations in her view of herself and others were striking. At times she railed at her parents and her husband, seeing them as "all bad" and herself as the "good" one who had been unappreciated and victimized by them. Then, abruptly, often within the same treatment session, she would shift to the opposite view and become convinced that she was the "bad" one, and she would see this as the reason for having been treated so "shabbily" by her family. When she experienced these negative feelings toward others or herself, her hostility and infantile aggressive feelings would consume her. She would often act impulsively. Angry feelings would then be displaced onto her children, particularly her son Michael, whom she came close to abusing physically, and whom she was afraid one day she would "kill in anger." Her longstanding rage, which the worker saw as deriving from early emotional deprivation, reinforced by later experiences, was often aimed at Michael, because she felt he ridiculed her as her father had. All of her personal relationships were fraught with conflict and vacillation; her behavior toward her mother and various men in her life was impulsive and erratic. On several occasions, Mrs. Zimmer had explosive encounters with friends when she felt that they were trying to take advantage of her or that they were unsympathetic to her problems. A flood of emotion would lead directly to uncontrolled action: rage led her to strike out aimlessly; when she felt lonely or despairing, she became clinging or demanding.

In considering the effects of Mrs. Zimmer's early experiences, it is important to avoid the simplistic view that her parents' inadequacies or the early separations had "caused" her adult difficulties. To do so would overlook the contributions of her innate endowments, of her experiences in interaction with her family and the wider world, and of the ways in which she used later events both to compound and to correct the effects of unfulfilled early needs. This point leads us to a discussion of the interplay of her drives, her ego development, and her current life circumstances.

Faulty ego functioning was apparent in her frequently distorted evaluation of herself and others: as "all good" or "all bad." Since anything less than "perfect" was judged by her to be "terrible," her "all bad" reactions predominated. Her ego's ability to regulate and control infantile impulses was seriously impaired, causing her to create more environmental pressures on herself. Her intellect, good judgment, and reality testing—evident in the less emotional aspects of her life—were very vulnerable when strong impulses were stimulated. Flawed ego organization was evident in her inability to balance positive and negative feelings. In effect, the memory of a pleasurable feeling could not be retained when negative ones (despair, rage, fear) arose; good and bad experiences could not be integrated; she often had difficulty differen-

tiating one feeling from another. Her defensive functioning—her heavy reliance on projection and denial and her "splitting"—provided evidence of the depth of her difficulties and also contributed to many of her interpersonal problems. During the early months of treatment, only rarely could she admit that her negativism and provocative behavior created difficulties for her.

Apparently, her parents had taken little delight in her accomplishments and therefore she, too, could not realistically appraise or enjoy them. Nor could she take pride in the achievements of her children. Superego development was apparent in her conscientiousness, ethical values, and consistent ability to deal honestly with others in practical matters; on the other hand, her superego was severe and, for the most part, unforgiving. When self-critical (for example, about her frequent anger at her son), she became overwhelmed with such remorse that she had little energy for self-understanding. To rid herself of these self-hating feelings, she would seek reasons to place blame on others.

Some ego functions were far better developed than others. On the positive side, she functioned competently (but rarely without anxiety) in the routine aspects of her life. She learned and could master new skills quickly. She consistently attended to the physical, educational, and even cultural development of her children. Her strengths and her good intelligence were of primary importance to her motivation for therapy and to its successful outcome. (It was not until the final months of therapy, however, that Mrs. Zimmer could say that she had kept coming to sessions because she had some hope that she could "get well." To have admitted that earlier, she said, would have made her feel vulnerable: afraid that the worker would try to "take away" her belief in herself, as she felt her parents had tried to do. But the regularity with which she kept appointments and participated in them gave evidence to the worker that there was a healthy part of Mrs. Zimmer that wanted change.)

The aim of treatment, then, was to help her to repair the damage while affirming her adaptive qualities. Specifically, the worker's treatment approach for the first year was in large measure supportive. During this time, Mrs. Zimmer poured out a great deal of rage, hopelessness, and despair. Alternately, she idolized and furiously distrusted her worker; on some occasions, she would try to cling to her physically and see her as her only "lifeboat"; at other times, often in an abrupt switch, she would accuse her of condemning her and wanting to be rid of her. Patiently and kindly, over and over again the worker conveyed her understanding of how deprived of genuine caring Mrs. Zimmer felt she had always been and acknowledged that, indeed, some early experiences had been hurtful to her. At the same time, she expressed confidence that now that Mrs. Zimmer was an adult—although it would probably take time—there was every reason to believe that she could grow to feel better and improve her life. When Mrs. Zimmer begged the worker to hold and rock her or to prolong the treatment hour, the worker assured her that she recognized that these requests stemmed from deep unhappiness but gently yet firmly explained the realities of what she could and could not do.

It would have been futile for the worker to make early efforts to help Mrs. Zimmer deal directly with her problems of impulse control, even though these were contributing to her many difficulties. For example, advice about how to handle her impulsivity would probably have been ineffective; in the worker's view, Mrs. Zimmer's ego controls were not yet sufficiently developed to change her reactions to stress. Efforts to persuade her to act differently when she could not might have reinforced her profound feelings of failure. On the other hand, when Mrs. Zimmer occasionally did complain about her inability to control her temper, the worker caringly agreed that her intense hostility *did* cre-

ate many problems for her, working against her own wish to be a good parent, to have friends, and to have a better relationship with her mother. False reassurance could have played into Mrs. Zimmer's tendency to blame others for her troubles. In general, however, the worker's approach at this stage was not to press Mrs. Zimmer to examine her behavior per se but rather to encourage her to try to understand the feelings that stimulated it.

After about a year of therapy, Mrs. Zimmer was feeling slightly better and realized, at least intellectually, that her caseworker would not abandon her. Her security about this was undoubtedly enhanced by the fact that the worker saw to it that the agency fee was adjusted during periods in which Mrs. Zimmer was financially pressed, and sometimes extra appointments and telephone reassurance were offered when Mrs. Zimmer was in acute distress. During the worker's summer vacation, she sent Mrs. Zimmer weekly postcards as a reminder of her ongoing interest, since separations to this client were synonymous with abandonment. All of this was indisputable proof of the worker's caring, difficult for Mrs. Zimmer to deny, even when she felt distrustful. Beyond this, the worker's ability to accept and remain unprovoked by Mrs. Zimmer's negative feelings, including those toward the worker herself, served to reduce them, relieve her anxiety, and foster greater trust. Negative responses the worker sometimes felt in the face of angry outbursts or of clinging, demanding behavior were tempered by her awareness of the depth of Mrs. Zimmer's pain and unhappiness.

From the onset, and throughout treatment, the worker avoided being drawn into debates with Mrs. Zimmer. The importance of this approach was demonstrated by an event that occurred after about eighteen months of therapy: Mrs. Zimmer telephoned to say she wanted to stop coming. The worker, although surprised by this sudden move, did not argue. Rather, she said that perhaps a vacation from therapy might have some value but suggested that they meet at least once again. Mrs. Zimmer agreed. As they discussed her wish to terminate, without pressure the worker asked whether Mrs. Zimmer thought she might not make further progress if she continued. On the other hand, the worker went on, perhaps Mrs. Zimmer's wish to conclude therapy was an indication of her wish to "try her wings on her own" for a while, an indication of how far she had come. Taken aback but apparently relieved, Mrs. Zimmer said that she really *did* want to continue her sessions. She explained that she had been afraid the worker would insist that she stay, and that expectation had made her feel "used," as she felt she had been used by her family, to whom she felt acceptable only if she did things the way they wanted her to.

As it developed, this session was a turning point for Mrs. Zimmer; she had asserted her independence: in and of itself a sign of growth. Furthermore, the worker supported her in this by not arguing or holding on to her, attitudes early experiences had led Mrs. Zimmer to anticipate from others. Rather than assuming that Mrs. Zimmer was just being hostile or resistant, the worker believed her move also reflected healthy strivings to grow up (self-assertion was replacing regressed anger and feelings of help-lessness). And, of utmost importance, this session firmly established for Mrs. Zimmer that it was *her* motivation that brought her to sessions, *not* the worker's need to possess or manipulate her. From this point on, Mrs. Zimmer became increasingly aware of the ways in which she distorted reality to conform to old expectations, thereby depriving herself of opportunities available to her in the present. Needless to say, the handling of Mrs. Zimmer's request to terminate required skill and delicacy, without which the client might have interpreted the worker's response as a rejection.

Now that a solid relationship had been established, the worker was able to confront Mrs. Zimmer and help her reflect on the contradic-tions between her feelings and her intellect and between her values and her behavior. To have done so earlier would probably have angered or frightened Mrs. Zimmer and might well have jeopardized the therapeutic relationship. But when it was possible, together they explored sudden reversals, such as when Mrs. Zimmer shifted from idealizing her children, her friends, and her caseworker to disparaging them. The worker challenged her unwillingness to entertain any other attitude than hatred toward her mother; Mrs. Zimmer was helped to tap other feelings, including sadness, longing, affection, and empathy. (Her mother's kindness as well as her blandness and dependency were apparent in joint therapy sessions, which gave the worker an opportunity to help Mrs. Zimmer take a more balanced and realistic view.) Similarly, when the client raged about how she wished her son had never been born, the worker expressed understanding of anger at his disobedience but wondered whether Mrs. Zimmer could remember that she had just spoken lovingly about him during the previous session. Asking her to think about this encouraged continuity of feeling and synthesis of "good" and "bad" feelings and experiences.

Mrs. Zimmer (and many clients with significant ego deficits and infantile residuals) often expressed her feelings in global terms: that is, it was hard for her to differentiate one feeling from another. Therefore, when she said she felt "awful," the worker urged her to get a better sense of what was wrong: was she feeling lonely, self-critical and guilty, hurt, abused, or just what? Often this was hard for her, but it was one of the important techniques employed by the worker that, over time, undoubtedly led to better ego functioning and self-awareness.

Similarly, it was necessary for Mrs. Zimmer to learn to distinguish feelings from thoughts. Sometimes when she was flooded by emotion—usually amorphous feelings of pain or rage—she did not use her intellect to bring reality or perspective to her reactions. If she had angry feelings toward a person, for example, she *believed* as well as *felt* that that person must be "bad." Increasingly, in no way discounting what she was feeling, the worker helped her to realize that her fury was often out of proportion to minor events that triggered it. Primary process functioning, described in Chapter 2, gradually yielded to rational review. Intellectual and emotional processes became much better integrated.

By the time Mrs. Zimmer had been in treatment for two years, improvement in all of her relationships could be noticed. Most of the time she was able to relate civilly to her ex-husband about the children and financial support. To her surprise, Mr. Zimmer became somewhat more consistent in sending payments and in visiting the children, and she could recognize that some of his hostile attitudes had been provoked by hers. Although at times she was still impulsive, her verbal abuse of the children was less extreme and less frequent; she no longer felt in danger of physically attacking her son Michael. More often than before, she began to take what she called "the middle road" in regard to her feelings and behavior; her emotions were no longer "all-or-nothing." When she was angry with someone, she was also able to maintain some awareness of her warm feelings. She was less likely either to idolize or to denigrate her worker; more frequently, she saw her as a helpful person who was also human.

During the third year of treatment, Mrs. Zimmer worked to achieve further stability within herself and in her relationships. Her improvement was strongly tested by Sonia, who by this time was fourteen and in angry rebellion most of the time. (During this period, Sonia was seen by another clinical social worker for about six months.) In spite of repeated fluctuations and regressions, Mrs. Zimmer was able to maintain a balance of feeling and behavior toward her daughter, recognizing that she, too, was having "growing pains." In other relationships she was able to react more appropriately,

tactfully, and warmly than she had. She saw it as a milestone in her therapy when, during a session with her mother, she was able to hug her and tell her that she very much wanted them to become closer than they had been; with occasional backsliding, their relationship improved substantially because Mrs. Zimmer had grown to accept her love for her mother, even though she disliked certain of her mother's qualities. Opposite feelings could now coexist.

But she was still having difficulty reaching out for new friends, even though she very much wanted them. She was afraid of rebuff and of her own volatility. During this period of loneliness, the worker's constant interest and confidence in the changes that had occurred and in the possibilities for more were very supportive. Mrs. Zimmer was afraid that the worker (like her mother, who tended to be suspicious of outsiders) would try to discourage her from friendships. Instead, without pressure, the worker shared some ideas about how Mrs. Zimmer might meet new people and was helpful to her by talking over the ways she was handling new relationships. By the end of this third year of work, Mrs. Zimmer had made several woman friends on her job and at her temple.

With little direct help from the worker, Mrs. Zimmer established herself vocationally. Once she completed her secretarial course, she located a job with a small firm, where she was immediately successful; she then returned to school part time to take bookkeeping, for which she had a natural aptitude. Within six months of completing her course, she was given a promotion and, by the time treatment ended, she had advanced to the position of full-charge bookkeeper. She was now better able than before to value her abilities and, by doing so, to bolster her self-esteem.

The final year of treatment focused intensively on her relationships with men. She had always been afraid of her sexual feelings (which, as she recalled, her father had directly discouraged); she realized she had married her husband partly because she was not attracted to him. Her sexuality was as frightening to her as her angry and tender feelings had been. After separation from her husband, her only sexual encounters were those she called "vindictive"; she would have relations once with a man for whom she had contempt and then refuse to see him again, delighting in the fantasy that she had punished him for "taking advantage" of her. Here again, the worker helped Mrs. Zimmer examine contradictions. For example, the worker asked whether expending so much energy "getting back"—through these men—at the people who had deprived her so long ago served her present wish to have positive relationships. The worker's attitude toward sex, as a natural and potentially rewarding adult experience, undoubtedly also gave Mrs. Zimmer "permission" to be less frightened and guilty about the possibility of enjoying it.

As she used defenses of "splitting," projection, and denial less persistently, good feelings became more available to her; slowly and tentatively, she reached the point of wanting "a person of my own to love." She began to date men she respected. She delayed becoming sexually involved until she grew to care deeply for one man whom she dated for several months during this phase of treatment. Before terminating therapy, she brought him to a session for the worker's "approval"; they were discussing marriage but neither she nor he wanted to rush into it.

The termination phase required careful handling by the worker.[5] The thought of leaving treatment excited Mrs. Zimmer but also stimulated old feelings of fear and anger. On the one hand, she was able to take justifiable pride in her hard-earned attainment of greater maturity and stability; on the other hand, she would sometimes feel outraged by the fact that she had had to work so hard to overcome the deprivations of her early years while, as she saw it, "normal" people could simply "sail" through life. Thoughts that perhaps the worker had wanted to get rid of her all along were activated as they talked about ending their work together. Separation fears were profound as Mrs. Zimmer began to say goodbye to her worker, who had, indeed, nurtured her through tumultuous times. Never before had Mrs. Zimmer experienced an intimate relationship in which her growth toward independence and adulthood was unambivalently encouraged. Although she was realistically grateful for this, the final phase of therapy also stirred a sense of loss associated with her childhood. When the worker helped her to examine and sort out her reactions, Mrs. Zimmer was able to distinguish which were projections or old feelings about herself as a "bad" person and which were genuine feelings of sadness aroused by termination. In the final session, Mrs. Zimmer presented the worker with a Hummel figurine of a smiling, robust child that symbolized for her the "second chance" she had been given to grow up "the right way."

In analyzing the case of Mrs. Zimmer, we see that treatment was slow, turbulent, marked by periods of stalemate and regression. Mrs. Zimmer's conflicted, vacillating relationship with her worker tended to replicate old relationships, reflecting inner turmoil and ego deficiencies. The worker's acceptance, patience, consistency, caring, and optimism were important dynamics of treatment. Fortunately, she neither retaliated when Mrs. Zimmer denounced her nor was countertransferentially seduced by excessive praise. Instead, Mrs. Zimmer was provided with a sustained experience of closeness without being hurt, "used," or abandoned.

However, it is important to note that the relationship was more than "corrective" (in the sense of providing parental support that she had not had). When the timing was right—always gently, sometimes firmly—the worker prodded her to reflect on distortions, contradictions, and oscillations; repeated discussions of current realities and of her feelings and behavior helped to strengthen ego functions of perception, judgment, synthetic functioning, and impulse control.

Previously dissociated feeling states became better integrated as ego functions consolidated and healed. For some clients who have excessively suppressed emotions, relaxation of restrictive defenses may be required. In Mrs. Zimmer's case, on the other hand, treatment was designed to provide the opportunity for her underdeveloped personality structure and defensive functioning to mature. Efforts to "uncover" feelings that were so raw and undifferentiated would have been counter-therapeutic.

When she attained success in one area of her life, her increased self-esteem served to help her make further gains. On the basis of the worker's diagnosis, little attempt was made to explore directly early life experiences that had contributed to this client's difficulties; many of these had occurred before there could be any memory of them. But treatment that worked with the residuals, later memories, and current issues—in the context of a positive relationship—resulted in significant personality change and improved functioning for Mrs. Zimmer.

In conclusion, we add that it was fortunate that Mrs. Zimmer was referred to an agency that had the flexibility to accommodate long-term, often twice-a-week therapy. We believe that efforts to abbreviate treatment would probably have failed, might have been experienced by Mrs. Zimmer as rejection, and perhaps would have discouraged her from seeking other therapy. Furthermore, when extended therapy is not made available, too often clients with severe personality deficits—in contrast to many others who *are* helped in brief treatment—only get "band-aid" assistance during crises. Each episode of treatment is too short to internalize lasting changes and to develop necessary self-awareness.

The five cases presented in this chapter illustrate clinical social work practice approached from the psychosocial point of view. In the chapters to follow, the theory and dynamics of the treatment process will be discussed in further detail. Additional case illustrations can be found in Chapter 21.

NOTES

1. For useful readings on problems and needs of the aging, see: Edith Freeman, "Multiple Losses in the Elderly: An Ecological Approach," *Social Casework*, 65 (May 1984), 287–296; John Goldmeier, "Helping the Elderly in Times of Stress," *Social Casework*, 66 (June 1985), 323–332; Robert J. Havinghurst, "Social and Psychological Needs of the Aging," *The Annals*, 279 (January 1952), 11–17; Margaret Milloy, "Casework with the Older Person in the Family," *Social Casework*, 45 (October 1964), 450–456; E. Palmore, ed., *Normal Aging and Normal Aging II* (Durham, N.C.: Duke University Press, 1970, 1974); Charlotte Towle, *Common Human Needs*, rev. ed. (New York: National Association of Social Workers, 1957), pp. 68–72; and the entire issue of *Journal of Social Welfare*, 5 (Spring 1978), in which several articles discuss various aspects of the aging process and problems encountered by the aging.

2. See Carel B. Germain and Alex Gitterman, *The Life Model of Social Work Practice* (New York: Columbia University Press, 1980), chapter 2; and Alfred Kadushin, *The Social Work Interview*, 2d ed. (New York: Columbia University Press, 1983), chapter 6. Both authors emphasize the value of "anticipatory empathy."

3. See Florence Hollis, "Casework and Social Class," *Social Casework*, 46 (October 1965), 463–471.

4. Mrs. Zimmer's clinical condition was diagnosed as "borderline personality organization" by the worker who treated her. For readings on this phenomenon, including theoretical discussions of faulty ego development and implications for practice, see the following writers, who share some common views but also have definite differences in emphasis: Gertrude and Rubin Blanck, *Ego Psychology II* (New York: Columbia University Press, 1979); Janet Bintzler, "Diagnosis and Treatment of Borderline Personality Organization," *Clinical Social Work Journal*, 6 (Summer 1978), 100–107; Sherry Eckrich, "Identification and Treatment of Borderline Personality Disorder," *Social Work*, 30 (March–April 1985), 166–171; Anne O. Freed, "The Borderline Personality," *Social Casework*, 61 (November 1980), 548–558; Anne O. Freed, "Differentiating Between Borderline and Narcissistic Personalities," *Social Casework*, 65 (September 1984), 395–404; Peter L. Giovacchini, *Developmental Disorders* (Northvale, N.J.: Jason Aronson, 1986); Eda G. Goldstein, "Clinical and Ecological Approaches to the Borderline Client," *Social Casework*, 64 (June 1983), 353–362; Roberta Graziano, "Making the Most of Your Time: Clinical Social Work with a Borderline Patient," *Clinical Social Work Journal*, 14 (Fall 1986), 262–275; Otto Kernberg, *Borderline Conditions and Pathological Narcissism* (New York: Aronson, 1975);

Otto Kernberg, *Severe Personality Disorders* (New York: Yale University Press, 1984); Heinz Kohut, *The Restoration of the Self* (New York: International Universities Press, 1977); James F. Masterson, *Psychology of the Borderline Adult* (New York: Brunner/Mazel, 1976); Joseph Palumbo, "Borderline Conditions: A Perspective from Self Psychology," *Clinical Social Work Journal*, 11 (Winter 1983), 323–338; and Mary E. Woods, "Personality Disorders," in Francis J. Turner, ed., *Adult Psychopathology: A Social Work Perspective* (New York: The Free Press, 1984), pp. 200–248.

5. The importance of careful and sensitive handling of the termination of treatment is discussed in Chapter 20 of this book.

CHAPTER 4

Classifications of Casework Treatment

Logic might dictate that we move into detailed discussion of the casework process by way of chapters first on initial interviews and psychosocial study, then on diagnosis and treatment planning, and finally on treatment procedures. But in order to understand what information we should seek in the psychosocial study and what type of diagnosis will be useful in treatment planning, we first need further understanding of the nature of treatment itself as it has evolved in psychosocial casework.

Treatment of whatever persuasion is a goal-directed process. Different means are used by various approaches to bring about an intended effect. There are many ways of classifying these means. We have found it useful to base classification on the dynamics a treatment step is intended to bring into play.

Suppose our client is a young widow who is afraid of an operation, partly because she is too sick to work out plans for the care of her children during her absence from home, partly because she is going to a strange doctor and is uncertain about the outcome of the operation, and partly because unconsciously she fears punishment for her hostile attitudes toward her mother, who had a similar illness and became permanently handicapped after an operation that the client erroneously assumes was similar to the one she is about to undergo. Many different dynamics can be employed to help this woman reduce her anxiety.

One alternative, among others, is the environmental one of providing for the care of the children during her absence. This can have a double effect: it will relieve her of that part of her anxiety caused by a realistic concern for the welfare of her children, and it will demonstrate to her that others care for her welfare and are ready to come to her assistance when she is weak and unable to manage her own affairs. We know that in serious illness regression may lead to a state of intense dependence. It is extremely important at such a time for the patient to feel that someone with strength will take care of her and her responsibilities. The way in which plans for children are made will also be of importance. If relatives or friends toward whom the patient has warm feelings can care for them, so much the better. When appropriate, family meetings may provide opportunities for making plans. If agency care for children must be sought, the degree of relief from anxiety will vary with the amount of confidence the mother and family members have in the goodwill and competence of the caseworker who makes this arrangement. Often, when trusted family members are involved and part of the planning process, there is less pressure felt by the patient—partly because others are taking over the responsibilities, and partly because the relatives feel they have some control over the process and do not then convey, intentionally or otherwise, doubts about the quality of the children's care to the mother.

A second possible mode of help consists of encouraging her and other family members, including the children, to express fears about the operation; the caseworker shows understanding of the anxiety, indicating that it is a natural reaction, not childish in the patient and perfectly normal in the family. Not infrequently it is possible to reassure a patient as well as her relatives that the doctors are interested and skillful. If the operation is not a dangerous one, this reality can also be used to allay fears in everyone *once they have been expressed*. Reduced anxiety in the patient can contribute to the success of the medical procedures. When family members feel reassured about what is happening, they are less likely inadvertently to reinforce undue apprehension in the patient.

A third way of reducing the anxiety would be to help the patient and family members understand more fully the facts about the operation itself. Arrangements can be made for them to talk in detail, together or separately, with the doctor. Sometimes they may need to go over the facts with the caseworker, clarifying their understanding of what the doctor said. Again, when family members feel informed, they are less likely to transfer their anxiety to the patient.

If it is needed, the patient and the worker can turn to a fourth alternative, that of the patient's seeking to gain understanding of the relationship between her hostility to her mother, her mother's illness, and the possibility that her present fears about her own illness are related in part to her guilt about this hostility. Naturally, the use of this alternative is dependent upon the patient's willingness to explore her feelings and her ability to make connections between these and current fears about the operation.

These procedures all have a common aim, to reduce anxiety, but the dynamics involved in each are different. In one instance, some of the stimuli for the anxiety are removed by environmental measures; in another reassurance is given, a procedure that depends for its effectiveness upon confidence in the worker; in the third, the patient and family members are encouraged to understand the situation more realistically; and in the fourth, the patient is helped to understand prior emotions involving interpersonal relationships and their consequences as these affect current reactions. In all of these, the worker must be keenly aware of how the patient's situation is significantly affected by environmental, family, and personality systems and how these interplay. The repertoire of treatment procedures used by the worker in this hypothetical example addressed each of these systems at one point or another; by doing so, the patient, her children, and other family members would more likely be relaxed during this stressful time than if the worker treated only the woman herself.

It was in an effort to seek a more orderly understanding of diagnostic-differential casework that Hollis developed the classification of treatment procedures used in the first edition of this book. As noted in Chapter 1, the approach, now called *psychosocial casework*, developed from the diagnostic-differential framework with some modifications and many additions and expansions of the original approach as new knowledge came into the field.

Before discussing this typology, we will review the general historical development of classifications in diagnostic-differential theory. Changes in classification reflect growth of knowledge. Each new typology was built upon former ones and attempted to define the scope of casework treatment, as well as to describe the procedures in use at different periods.

CLASSIFICATIONS REFLECTING GROWTH

There have been a number of classifications of casework treatment methods. In 1922 Mary Richmond, as noted earlier, made only the very simple distinction between "direct" and "indirect" treatment. By the former, she meant those processes that take place directly between the client and the worker—the "influence of mind upon mind"—and by the latter, changes the worker brings about in the client's human and physical environment.[1]

Despite the many changes that took place in casework in the thirties, it was not until 1947 that new classifications began to appear, reflecting the preceding years of growth in understanding of what Mary Richmond had called "direct treatment." By then, psychoanalytic concepts had not only been found useful in understanding psychological and emotional elements in personal problems but had also contributed to interviewing processes. It was clear, of course, that caseworkers were not conducting psychoanalyses and that there was a large part of casework only tangentially touched by psychoanalysis. However, since certain techniques had been borrowed from psychoanalytic methodology, it was important to define in what specific ways the two treatment methods did or did not overlap. The question of the extent to which caseworkers dealt with the unconscious was of special concern. A paper in 1947 by Grete Bibring,[2] a psychoanalyst who had worked closely with caseworkers for a number of years in Boston, mentioned five groups of technical procedures used by all types of therapists, including caseworkers. These were suggestion, emotional relief, immediate influence

(or manipulation), clarification, and interpretation. It was her impression that interpretation was used sparingly in casework, and chiefly in dealing with preconscious rather than unconscious material, but she did not altogether rule out interpretation of unconscious material. Her major distinction was between interpretation, which she characterized as having as its goal insight development (a principal objective of psychoanalysis), and the other techniques, for which insight development was not a goal.

Bibring's classification represented a distinct elaboration of the earlier direct treatment method and reflected the influence of psychoanalysis in enriching the caseworker's understanding of the ways in which psychological forces can be used in treatment. Suggestion, emotional relief, and manipulation, though not recognized in these terms, were undoubtedly a part of early casework methodology, as was also a technique not specifically designated by Bibring: that of helping the client to reason his way through to a favorable solution of his problems. Clarification, in the sense of helping the client to separate objective reality from distortions of the external world, was, like insight development, the result of the incorporation of analytic concepts and played little part in casework until the 1930s and 1940s.

Also in 1947, Hollis suggested another classification of treatment methods.[3] These were environmental modification (corresponding to the earlier indirect method) and psychological support, clarification, and insight development (representing subdivisions of direct treatment). This classification and Bibring's were similar in that both attempted to group techniques according to the psychological dynamics by which they operated. Bibring's suggestion, emotional relief, and manipulation corresponded to different aspects of the Hollis psychological support; insight development was similar in the two classifications. But Hollis was using the word "clarification" in a different sense than did Bibring, covering by that term the general encouragement of a reasoning approach to problems and to certain aspects of the separation of objective reality from distortions of external events. It was encouraging that there was so much basic similarity between the thinking of representatives of two different professions whose pertinent experience had been in completely different geographical locations: Cleveland and Boston.

The Austin Classification

In this same period, Lucille Austin also proposed her widely used classification.[4] She specified two main divisions: social therapy and psychotherapy, dividing the latter into (1) supportive therapy, having the aim of preventing a further breakdown; (2) insight therapy, having the aim of achieving a change in the ego and increasing its ability to deal with difficulties; and (3) experiential therapy, seen as intermediate in its goals between the first two. Social therapy involved environmental change, psychological support, and a rational approach to the solution of reality problems. Turning to the three forms of psychotherapy, supportive therapy relied heavily on psychological support and might often also include the techniques used in social therapy. In *insight* therapy, emphasis was placed on the emotional experience in the transference situation, interpretive techniques concerning feelings and unconscious motivations, and relevant childhood memories. In *experiential therapy*, the central focus was on the development and use of the relationship as a corrective emotional experience. In varying degrees, techniques used in the other two types of psychotherapy could be drawn upon, except that genetic interpretations concerning the relationship between developmental experiences and current behavior would not be emphasized.

Austin recognized that, although her supportive treatment was designed primarily to maintain present strengths, psychological improvement often occurred, as the ego gained strength to handle immediate situations, and the experience of more adequate functioning itself became a growth process. Similarly, in the experiential form of treatment, Austin wrote that "in certain cases maturation already under way is carried through to completion." She further maintained that the objectives of experiential treatment "are mainly loosening restrictive ties to figures in the past, redirecting emotional energies, and promoting growth through increased satisfactions in living."[5]

All three writers—Bibring, Hollis, and Austin—helped to clarify what caseworkers were doing in the forties and fifties. All established tentative boundaries between casework and psychoanalysis, holding that casework does not reach deeply unconscious material but may deal with content that, though not conscious, is relatively accessible. They also spelled out specific techniques distinguishing casework from psychoanalysis. Understanding of these issues set in motion a process of study to examine more closely the dynamics of the casework process.

The Issue of
Support versus Clarification

In 1953, a committee of the Family Service Association of America studied some of these issues and published a report based in part on reading a series of cases from family service agencies.[6] This report proposed a simple classification of casework into two types based on the *aim* of the treatment. It designated type A, or "supportive casework," as "treatment aimed at maintaining adaptive patterns," and type B, or "clarification," as "treatment aimed at modification of adaptive patterns." The first type of treatment was described as resting upon the use of such techniques as Bibring's "manipulation of the environment, reassurance, persuasion, direct advice and guidance, suggestion, logical discussion, exercise of professional authority and immediate influence."[7] The second was characterized mainly by its use of the technique of clarification (in the Bibring sense) in addition to the other techniques. The committee also reported that it had decided not to include a category corresponding to the insight development or insight therapy included in preceding classifications, because it found that this type of treatment was used in very few agencies.

Five years later, in 1958, this classification was further developed by a committee of the Community Service Society of New York in a document entitled *Method and Process in Social Casework*,[8] which described in more detail the techniques used in the "supportive treatment method" and the "modifying treatment methods," limiting the latter to modification of "selected ego mechanisms of defense."[9]

These two reports played an important part in illuminating several issues concerning casework treatment. Their specificity was a distinct improvement over earlier efforts. Three issues were identified and spelled out in a way that led to further study: (1) To what extent is "insight therapy" undertaken by caseworkers? (2) Are changes in adaptive patterns dependent upon the use of clarification as a predominant treatment technique? (3) Is casework correctly conceptualized as a dichotomous process having two distinct treatment modes, one in which clarification is the predominant technique and one in which this technique either is absent or plays a minor role?

PERSONALITY CHANGES AND TREATMENT TECHNIQUES

The first of these issues to be examined systematically was that of the relationship between changes in adaptive patterns and treatment method. Sidney Berkowitz,[10] in a paper given at the National Conference of Social Work in the spring of 1955, challenged the FSAA committee findings, taking the position that clarification is not the only way in which adaptive patterns can be modified. He maintained that, in his experience, such patterns could also be changed through a process of ego influence with little or no reference to, or clarification of, the relation of the past to the present.

This was an important question, because there was a tendency for caseworkers to put a sort of "halo" around "clarification" and to belittle all other work as "just" supportive. Berkowitz and many other practitioners believed the type of casework the committee named supportive to be of great value and not incapable of bringing changes in adaptive patterns. They feared that "nonclarifying" work was in danger of being used in a very oversimplified way because of this downgrading. Thus, much help that could be given without clarification would be lost.

To understand this question, we need to consider what is meant by a change in adaptive patterns.

A change in adaptive patterns is one that is internalized, built into the personality. It results in an improvement in functioning that cannot be fully accounted for by improved circumstances, passing of a crisis, or influence of the worker during the period of treatment; rather, it constitutes a change in the client's way of functioning that will enable him or her to respond differently even when the external situation has not changed and when the worker is not part of the client's current life. The individual will have learned to act differently and will respond to the same or similar life events more constructively than he or she did before treatment.

Improvement in functioning without a change in adaptive patterns might be said to occur in situations such as the following. A husband has been quarreling with his wife because of anxiety about his business. In discussions with the worker, he comes to understand the cause of his irritability, transfers to another position in which he is under less pressure, and subsequently is more even tempered at home. A widow, depressed because of the loss of her husband, is unable to care adequately for her children. She is helped during this period of grief, and, as the grief subsides, is able to function normally again in relation to the children. A construction worker loses a leg in an accident and is told he will no longer be able to continue in his line of work. He loses interest in life, does not try to obtain a prosthesis, and retreats to dependent, whining, childlike behavior, to the despair of his formerly dependent wife. After a good deal of skillful work, including some development of understanding of his current responses, he regains his former stability and finds a new work adjustment. In none of these cases have "new adaptive patterns" necessarily been established.

It was generally agreed that such improvements in *functioning* often occurred in response to supportive treatment methods and constituted a very important type of recovery from a period of strain or disaster that might otherwise result in permanent impairment of functioning. But could the other type of improved functioning, that which does rest upon modification of *habitual patterns* of behavior, be brought about without treatment in which clarification in the Bibring sense was a predominant technique?

A paper by Hollis[11] in 1956 described a small preliminary study of this question that supported Berkowitz's point of view. Hollis had asked workers in a family service agency in her community for illustrations simply of good supportive treatment. Ten cases were submitted, but one of these turned out to be a type B case and so could not be used. The nine remaining cases yielded six in which a change in adaptive patterns appeared to have taken place in response to supportive procedures. This, of course, was no indication of the *frequency* with which this ordinarily happens. Workers probably submitted their "best" supportive cases, though they did not know the purpose for which the cases were to be used. What these six cases did show, however, was that it is not at all *impossible* to bring about changes in adaptive patterns in supportive work, the point at issue. A brief description of a few of the cases in which this appeared to be so will illustrate the point.

Mrs. Knight, an exceedingly immature young woman still in her teens, was married to a man old enough to be her father. At first he thoroughly enjoyed her dependence, but soon he became irritated by her inability to manage his home and be an adequate mother to the two children of his former marriage. Mrs. Knight sought help "in growing up" from the caseworker. The approach was one of guidance and support, with reliance on elements in the relationship, on considerable logical discussion, on extensive use of a visiting housekeeper and of a nurse who educated the client in matters concerning her own and the children's health. With the ego strengthened by increased knowledge and skill, the maturation that had been arrested when Mrs. Knight was overwhelmed by demands beyond her ability to meet began again to take place, with marked improvement in her functioning as a wife and mother. There was every reason to believe that the improvement in adaptive patterns had been internalized and would be lasting.

Mrs. Landers, the mother of five children, was driven by a strong need to succeed, which showed itself in the form of perfectionistic demands upon the children and excessive self-criticism when difficulties arose in her own relationship with them. The worker became the "good mother" and on the basis of this relationship was able to help Mrs. Landers to handle the children more realistically and to reduce the severity of the demands of her superego upon the children and upon herself. Mrs. Landers became able to set up more lenient goals for her family and to see at a number of points that she was overreacting in holding herself so completely responsible for their behavior. Once again, a nurse was used for discussion of health problems; better housing plans were worked out; camp opportunities were provided for the children. Mrs. Landers learned new ways of handling her children and incorporated less demanding standards for herself and her family.

Mr. Ingersol, a married man of thirty-five, was repeatedly in trouble because of impulsive behavior at work and with his wife. Periodic drinking complicated the problem. The aim of treatment was to help him control his impulsiveness and his drinking. For a long time, Mr. Ingersol denied that his drinking was a problem and that his own behavior contributed to his quarrels with his wife. After treatment had advanced to a point where Mr. Ingersol trusted the caseworker, it was possible again and again to get him to go over the details of what happened between himself and his wife when he had been drinking excessively, to recall exactly how many drinks he had had and exactly what he did and said during the course of an evening. Gradually, he came to see that after a certain number of drinks he said things he would not otherwise have said, and that his behavior on such occasions precipitated certain responses from his wife that she would not otherwise have given. When he became able to admit to himself that his drinking really did cause trouble, he began to make a real effort to control it and succeeded in reducing it to a marked extent. A pattern of greater ego control was established, not by bringing suppressed material to consciousness or by seeking causative understanding of his drinking beyond current provocations, but by the effect of close examination of present realities.

Another factor at work in Mr. Ingersol's progress was the client-worker relationship itself. Mr. Ingersol was a dependent person who had greatly admired his father. He developed similar feelings toward his caseworker, whom he wanted to please as he had wanted to please his father. The worker did not interpret the transference but instead made use of it, giving Mr. Ingersol credit and appreciation when he showed understanding of the effects of his behavior and when he tried to modify it. His efforts to change were further fortified by the satisfaction he secured during periods of better relationship with his wife.

Logical discussion, advice, approval, and encouragement were all used in the effort to enable him to improve the quality and strength of his ego controls. At several points in this case clarification was very briefly used, but it was by no means the predominant technique. Considerable improvement in adaptive patterns seems to have occurred in this case, although one could not be wholly optimistic about the permanence of the new patterns.

In each of these cases, it appeared that changes in adaptive patterns occurred in response to techniques defined as "supportive." This gave further substance to the belief that the response to treatment was more fluid than the FSAA dichotomizing hypothesis maintained.

Diverse Approaches to Changes in Personality

Why are we so concerned about this question? Because a change in adaptive patterns makes it more possible that whatever improvement in functioning has occurred will continue not only in the immediate circumstances but in other vicissitudes which the individual may meet. A better method of functioning will have been learned and become part of the personality. What, then, are some of the ways in which changes in adaptive patterns can be achieved?

First, there is the basic personality change, often called "structural change" in psychoanalytic terminology. This includes and goes beyond changes in adaptive patterns. It occurs when some of the decisive formative experiences of life are reached and relived in treatment and undergo reevaluation. This is a psychoanalytic process involving the bringing to consciousness and understanding of material that was previously unconscious or repressed, such as memories, thoughts, or fantasies representing infantile destructive and sexual impulses and wishes, and reactions and distortions growing out of very early life experiences and deprivations. Many of the early feelings are revived in the transference in which the patient temporarily regresses to childhood. Structural change can be brought about by psychoanalysis and sometimes by less extensive psychotherapy carried on by therapists trained in psychoanalysis.

It was earlier pointed out, however, that irrational and inappropriate responses are also often based on *preconscious* influences, on events that at most have been *suppressed* rather than repressed and, hence, can be brought to the surface of the mind by the type of interviewing techniques used in casework. Indeed, many early influences are not even suppressed. Sometimes they are well remembered, but the client needs to recognize the connection between these childhood experiences and his or her current responses in order to see their irrationality. Experiences of adolescence and early adulthood may also be of great importance. The ego defenses, in particular, often operate on a preconscious level. Not infrequently, a person can become aware of and will modify defense patterns on seeing their irrationality or their harmfulness without needing to look back to factors that influenced the development of such patterns. That is, the dynamic may be understood independently of origins. Recognizing the influence of conscious and preconscious early life experiences and becoming aware of defenses are both forms of *clarification* in the FSAA use of the term and constitute a second way in which adaptational patterns can be modified.

A third way of bringing about changes in adaptive patterns consists of helping the individual to deal more effectively with current life relationships and problems. Better understanding of other people, thoughtfulness about the effects of one's ways of relating to others, fuller awareness of one's feelings and actions and of the effect of others on oneself will lead first to better functioning in the immediate current life, or at least a sector of current life. As individual incidents pile up, the adaptive patterns themselves may be modified, even though they have not been discussed as such. This form of change parallels natural life experience. Without the help of any type of therapy, the relatively healthy individual repeatedly learns from experiences as he or she seeks to develop more effective ways of mastering the vicissitudes of life. A similar process occurs in treatment, but the individual's efforts need to be augmented by professional help.

A fourth way in which change occurs in adaptive patterns is in the context of a strong positive relationship to another person who is accorded a leadership or pattern-setting role in some area of living. In such a relationship, the individual either identifies with and imitates the worker, or subscribes to the worker's values, or accepts his or her assessment, suggestions, and advice. The "corrective relationship" described by Austin as an important aspect of "experiential" treatment can bring change in this fourth way. Again, treatment parallels a process common in natural life experience.

A fifth way in which adaptive patterns can change is in response to more favorable life experiences. As noted earlier, these are relatively easy to arrange for children. Adults can often be helped to make such changes for themselves: a new marriage, a better or more suitable job, completion of educational plans, and so on. Again, similar processes occur in natural life.

A sixth way in which personality change comes about is through the positive reinforcement that results from more effective and satisfying functioning. Sometimes this reinforcement is in the form of verbal or nonverbal communications from the worker. More often, it arises in subsequent life experiences. When temporary change in functioning is rewarded by positive experiences in interpersonal relationships or in other important areas of functioning such as work, a powerful incentive is given to continue the new ways until they constitute a new adaptive pattern. This too commonly occurs in life.

Several of these ways of bringing about change usually take place together in work with one individual or family. It appears that treatment is actually a blend of many influences that in combination are designed to bring about more effective and satisfying functioning. In the opinions of many experienced practitioners, casework is not best conceptualized as a dichotomous process leading to two quite different outcomes. Rather, a more fluid model must be sought that would readily permit us to think in terms of a blend of procedures flexibly adapted to the complex set of needs brought by individuals and families.

DEVELOPING A TYPOLOGY

What sort of classification would be useful in relation to this revised understanding of the casework process? In 1958, Hollis began the process of devising a classification of treatment procedures in which the means by which treatment is carried out would be separated from treatment goals. This would permit workers and researchers to examine what procedures were actually used when changes occurred. It might also result in clearer thinking about the essential nature—the dynamics—of treatment procedures.

When work on such a classification, or typology, was begun, it was soon discovered that it is no simple matter to formulate a logical and useful classification of casework treatment, especially if this formulation was to be rich enough in its dimensions to make conceptually worthwhile distinctions, and yet not so elaborate as to be impractical.

It was important also to think about what purpose would be served by a treatment classification. Would it merely enable us to describe casework in a more orderly way in writing and teaching? This is one important use of classification; the very need for such clarity constitutes a strong impetus toward developing one. Would it provide agencies with a systematic way of grouping cases for reports of accountability, work distribution, evaluation, and the like?

Yes, but there was a more fundamental purpose: that of studying casework itself. Many questions needed to be answered in order to use casework effectively. For what configuration of personality tendencies and problems and what sorts of social problems is a particular treatment method or technique appropriate? What other factors—the client's wishes and responses, time available, worker skill, agency function, and so on—influence treatment choices? What is the result of using this or that technique under such and such circumstances? What alternative means are available to the end that client and worker have in mind? Under what circumstances is one means more likely to serve the purpose than another?

Before answers could be found to these questions, the numerous variables involved would have to be separated. In the end, ways would have to be found to identify and classify not only treatment procedures but also personality characteristics, types of problems and situational factors, outcomes, and relationships among these variables. Treatment procedures would be a good starting point.

It was particularly important that the *aim* of treatment and the *methods used* be examined as separate variables. Only by so doing could we hope to test the relationship of one to the other and examine the conditions under which specific techniques can lead to specific results.

A small preliminary study undertaken in 1958 was fruitful in pointing up the problems involved in classification and in providing material for experimentation with a series of classifications, each successively introducing modifications designed to fit the interview material more exactly and completely.

This was followed in 1959 by a study of 25 cases of not less than 12 interviews each, drawn from six agencies representing family service agencies, child guidance clinics, and psychiatric clinics in three different communities (Boston, Hartford, and New York). Interviews were examined line by line in an effort to characterize each recorded happening in each interview. Various groupings of techniques were tried in an effort to arrive at meaningful and essential distinctions between different processes. The tackling of each new case became a testing of the system worked out on previous cases and frequently involved modifications in the system to accommodate the new material. Further changes were made in the typology during this study, and as a result of two subsequent testings of the classifications by students at the Smith College School of Social Work in 1960 (15 interviews)[12] and at the New York School of Social Work (now Columbia University) in 1961 (50 interviews).[13] Later, Hollis and her colleagues [14] analyzed over 100 interviews from four family service agencies in three cities in different parts of the country (Cincinnati, Cleveland, Philadelphia). A reliability study was completed and some hypotheses tested (see Chapter 9).

Each agency participating in the 1959 study had been asked to submit examples both of supportive treatment and of treatment in which the technique of clarification was used, including an example of a case representing the greatest depth in treatment carried on in the agency. It was soon discovered that workers differed enormously in their interpretation of this request. Cases of a type considered clarification by one worker would actually involve less use of the technique of clarification than cases classified as supportive by another worker. Troublesome as this confusion was, it led to the very useful observation that there seemed to be *no sharp dividing line* between supportive and clarification cases. The subsequent study of 100 cases confirmed the fact that casework can best be described as a continuum, beginning with cases in which no clarification whatsoever was used, going on to those in which snatches of it were used from time to time, proceeding to others where it played a considerable part in treatment. Furthermore, it also became clear

that in most cases treatment moved through phases in which the balance between supportive work and clarification was constantly changing.

The typology that finally emerged dealt primarily with the interviewing process. It is essentially a classification of the communications that take place between client and worker, or collateral and worker. The typology has demonstrated its value in a number of research projects. Some of these will be described in Chapter 9. The typology has been particularly useful as a tool for clarifying what goes on in psychosocial casework and it will provide a framework for the discussion of treatment in this book. Obviously, it is not in any way the empirical base upon which psychosocial casework rests. Rather, it is a tool for studying this approach and for describing it. It allows us to follow the flow of each interview and can be used either in informal analysis or in more rigorous research. As had been hoped, it makes possible examination of the *dynamics* of treatment, and exploration of such questions as: In what way does a given procedure affect a client? What are the relationships of client personality factors to choice of treatment method? What is the relationship between problem and treatment steps? What factors in the client's response in a particular interview indicate the advisability of using a particular procedure? What procedures in early interviews are most likely to encourage the client to remain in treatment? And so on. As was pointed out earlier in illustration of the different ways in which anxiety can be reduced, a given result can be achieved by a variety of procedures, ranging from direct reassurance to full understanding of the intrapsychic cause of the anxiety. Under different circumstances and with different individuals, one approach will be more effective than another. This question of which means is most useful under different conditions is central to any study seeking to understand and improve casework methodology and is therefore a particularly useful central dimension for a classification of casework.

The classification also distinguishes sharply between the means employed and its actual effect. For example, the caseworker's expression of interest in and appreciation of a client's situation or feelings is a means generally thought to promote perception of the worker as someone who is interested and who is capable of understanding him or her. This strengthens the feeling that here is someone who will help or take care of the client. By this means, it is hoped, anxiety will be lessened and, consequently, functioning will be improved. A paranoid person, however, may interpret this same response by the caseworker as a kind of magic mind reading, an effort to bring the person under some obscure influence, and the technique will not have the desired effect. Nevertheless, in the typology proposed, if a worker, however unwisely, used this technique it would be classified as a "sustaining procedure," the term used for this type of *potentially* reassuring technique. Such a separation of the means employed from the outcome puts us in a position to examine the actual effect of a treatment step, to study the circumstances under which it does not have the desired effect, and thereafter to use it more appropriately; or, if by research we find it rarely has the effect we theoretically thought it should have, we are in a position to correct our theory.

A classification of this sort is not static: it can be modified as research and study constantly correct our theories and can also lend itself well to expansion as new techniques are developed.

THE MAIN DIVISIONS OF THE CLASSIFICATION

With these preliminaries, we may proceed to a brief description of the classification. Detailed discussion of the specific technical procedures included under the main divisions of the classification will be found in immediately following chapters. The major dimensions of the classification will be presented in this chapter, together with specific illustrations used only to clarify the meaning of the main categories; thus, we will be able to discuss certain general theoretical questions before going extensively into details of procedures.

Client–Worker Communications

For the moment, let us set aside the question of treatment through the environment, Richmond's indirect treatment, and deal only with those procedures that take place directly between worker and client, Richmond's direct treatment. When working directly with clients— whether singly or in pairs, or in family group treatment—it was found that the caseworkers' techniques can be placed in six major groupings. The first two of these derive their force or influence from the relationship that exists between client and worker, from the way in which the client regards the worker and the degree of influence the client accords the worker or permits in his or her life. The third draws its strength from ventilation, the description of stressful events and the expression of feelings that are causing distress. The fourth, fifth, and sixth groups rest primarily upon various kinds of reflective considerations promoted within the client.

The first group of procedures dealing with *sustainment* include such activities by the worker as demonstration of interest, desire to help, understanding, expressions of confidence in the client's abilities or competence, and reassurance concerning matters about which the client has anxiety and guilt.

Sustaining techniques are used in varying degrees in all cases. Much of this type of communication takes place through nonverbal or paraverbal means: nods, smiles, an attentive posture, murmurings. In the early interviews, no matter what else is done, the worker usually tries, by giving the client a sympathetic hearing and by using other sustaining techniques, to lessen anxiety and give the client the feeling that he or she is in a place where help will be forthcoming. Subsequently, cases vary in the extent to which sustaining techniques are needed, with fluctuations from time to time in the same case. Remarks such as "You are looking well today" or "I can understand how difficult that must have been" or "Such feelings are natural" are illustrative.

The second group of procedures dealing with *direct influence* include a range of techniques among which suggestion and advice are most frequently used. They involve in one form or another the expression of the worker's opinion about the kind of action a client should take, with such comments as "It might be better to do so-and-so," or "I think you ought to _____ ," or "No, I don't think that will work; you had better _____ ," and so on.

Procedures of direct influence are far less universally used than sustaining techniques, but, particularly in their more subtle forms, constitute a recognized part of casework treatment. One usually finds that where these procedures are being extensively used in the psychosocial approach there is also emphasis upon sustainment. Their effectiveness depends to a high degree upon the existence of a strong positive relationship between client and worker, which in turn is promoted by sustaining procedures.

The third group deals with *exploration, description,* and *ventilation.* It consists of communications designed to draw out descriptive and explanatory material from the client and to encourage the pouring out of pent-up feelings and description of emotionally charged events. This material, first of all, helps the worker to understand the person and his or her problems. In addition, considerable relief from tension is often felt by the client as a result of this outpouring. Quite frequently, this relief obtained by verbalization is supported by sustaining procedures that further reduce the accompanying anxiety or guilt. At other times, the content of

the ventilating process is picked up for the purpose of promoting reflective consideration of it: "Yes, tell me more about it" or "Yes, yes—go on," or "What about your job? How do things go there?"

The fourth grouping consists of communications designed to encourage reflective consideration of the person-situation configuration. It is designated *person-situation-reflection* and refers to reflection upon current and relatively recent events, exclusive of early life material. This broad category can be subdivided according to another dimension, that of the type of subject toward understanding of which the communication is directed. The areas of understanding may be (1) perception or understanding of others, of one's own health, or of any aspect of the outside world; (2) understanding of one's own behavior in terms of its actual or potential outcome or its effect on others or on the self; (3) awareness of the nature of one's own behavior; (4) awareness of causative aspects of one's own behavior when these lie in the interactions between the person and others; (5) evaluation of some aspect of the client's own behavior, in the sense of self-image, concepts of right and wrong, principles, values, or preferences; (6) awareness and understanding of feelings about the worker and the treatment process. In the first of these subdivisions attention is directed outward, in the second it is partly outward and partly inward, and in the last four it is directed inward to some aspect of the person's own feelings, thoughts, or actions: that is, toward a form of self-understanding that depends entirely upon reflection about specific interactions and reactions in the person-situation gestalt. To illustrate: (1) "Can you think of anything else that might be making your wife so nervous lately?" (2) "When you say things like that, how does it work? What happens?" (3) "You sound as though you were very angry." (4) "What actually happened that could have made you so angry? What do you think it was?" (5) "Somehow you sound as though you feel very uncomfortable about doing that.'' (6) ''Do you still think I am siding with John?''

It is impossible to imagine a case in which some of these types of person-situation reflection would not be used. The type of problem brought by the client is one of the important determinants of where the emphasis will be. The more realistic and external the problem, the greater the likelihood that interviews will emphasize procedures from the first two subdivisions; the greater the subjective involvement in the problem, the more likely it is that they will draw upon the third, fourth, and fifth subdivisions. These procedures of person-situation reflection are combined in varying degrees with sustaining techniques and may be accompanied to some degree also by direct influence. They are techniques that are also always an important part of the treatment process when other types of reflective consideration are in action.

The fifth main treatment category also relies upon reflective discussion. It consists of procedures for encouraging the client to think about the psychological patterns involved in his or her behavior and the dynamics of these patterns and tendencies. This category can be referred to as *pattern-dynamic reflection.* The client is helped to reflect upon some of the internal reasons for responses and actions, and encouraged to look at the dynamics of his or her behavior by studying the relationship between one aspect of this behavior and another. The client goes beyond thinking about a specific distortion of reality or inappropriate reaction toward consideration of the operations of the intrapsychic component itself: ''I wonder whether you don't often think other people dislike you when underneath you are critical of them''; ''Have you noticed how often that happens? You take it out on Mary when you're really mad at your wife.''

The sixth treatment category, also a type of reflective discussion, includes procedures for encouraging the client to think about the development of his or her psychological patterns or tendencies, again, a subjective area. This is des-

ignated *developmental reflection.* Here, the client is helped to deal with early life experiences that are important because, although they occurred in the past, they have been internalized to such a degree that they are now part of his or her responses to current situations. As in pattern-dynamic reflection, treatment revolves around consideration of the relationship of one facet of behavior, one reaction, to another; this time, however, in historical terms: ''You always talk about how wonderful your father was...sort of a superman. I should think that would be pretty hard to live up to....How was it?'' and later, ''Maybe that has something to do with your underrating yourself now.''

Person-in-Situation or Environmental Interventions

In the years following the great depression of the thirties until the development of poverty programs in the sixties, social work did not give the same quality of attention to ''indirect'' treatment of the environment as to ''direct'' treatment of individuals. Even family group treatment, one form of environmental intervention, was not common. This neglect tended to downgrade so-called environmental modification in the worker's mind, as though it were something one learned to do with one's left hand, something unworthy of serious analysis. Furthermore, we tended to think of direct work as psychological and indirect as nonpsychological or ''social.'' This is, of course, a false assumption. *In actuality, environmental work is extremely complex and takes place with people and through psychological means.* We cannot physically make a landlord, teacher, or anyone else—even the representative of a social agency—do something for the benefit of our clients. We have to talk with *people* about the clients' needs and desires, and in the process we must use psychological procedures of one sort or another. We also have to enlist our clients in reflections about what kinds of changes in their lives they are seeking.

Furthermore, in order to improve environmental conditions and opportunities, it is necessary to assess the particular needs, aspirations, and limitations of the clients we serve as well as the potential for change in the systems that surround them. It is casework's purpose to assist in providing the best possible "fit" or adaptation between person and situation. *The complexities of both sides of the match must therefore be evaluated.*

One can think in terms of treatment *through* the environment and modification *of* the environment. The former makes use of resources or opportunities that exist, are potentially available, or can be developed for the benefit of the client in the total situation. The latter deals with modifications that are needed in a situation in order to lessen pressures or increase opportunities and gratifications. A clear example of treatment through the environment would be a worker's enlisting the help of a warm, friendly relative to provide companionship and practical assistance for a woman experiencing postoperative depression. Work upon the environment is illustrated by a worker's intervening to bring change in a situation where a child is badly suited to a school placement or a landlord is failing to make necessary repairs. Examples of both kinds of treatment can be found in the Kennedy, West, and Stone cases described in Chapter 3.

Increased appreciation of the complexities involved in bringing about changes in the interactions between people and their environments led Hollis to suggest additional types of classification not developed in her original typology study. In the third edition of this book she introduced new categories of environmental procedures, giving recognition to the need to bring greater specificity to previously vague conceptualizations about "indirect" casework. She proposed the following three general ways of looking at and classifying environmental work, each having its values and uses.

First, it is sometimes useful to organize one's thinking about milieu work in terms of the *type of resource* one is trying to engage. A primary source of such help is the employing social agency itself. One thinks immediately of the child-placing agency where the workers are themselves responsible for making resources of the agency available, such as foster and adoptive homes. A second type closely related to the first is the employing agency or institution in which social work is not the sponsoring profession, but one of several services offered, for example, a hospital with a social service department. Here the worker is identified in the client's mind with the medical care and is in a good position to influence certain aspects of the medical service but, naturally, not to the same extent as would be true in the agency administered by social workers.

A third type of resource is the social agency of which the worker is *not* a staff member. A fourth type consists of non–social work organizations of which the worker is not a staff member.

Two additional types of environmental resource involve two sets of *individuals* in the milieu: (1) those who have an "instrumental" or task-oriented relationship to the client, such as employers and landlords, and (2) those who have an "expressive" or feeling-oriented relationship, such as relatives, friends, neighbors. Many differences exist in milieu work, depending upon which of these six types of situational contacts is involved. These will be discussed in Chapter 8.

One can also analyze environmental or milieu work from the viewpoint of the *type of communications* used. All milieu work takes place through some form of communication, regardless of whether it is verbal. Indeed, paraverbal and nonverbal communication is often of great importance. The type of classification presented in the preceding section on communications between worker and client is also of value in studying communications between worker and collateral. (*Collateral* is a term commonly used in casework to refer to contacts with individuals other than the client.) Environmental treatment makes use of the first four groups of procedures described for direct work with the client but does not use the fifth and sixth. One does not discuss with any collateral—be it a teacher, doctor, landlord, friend, or relative—the dynamics of his or her attitude or behavior or its development. It is only when a relative or sometimes a friend enters treatment that this type of reflection would become appropriate. On the other hand, each of the other four types of communication procedure *is* used in environmental work. There are times when the techniques of sustainment are important in building the relationship necessary to involve the collateral constructively, or less destructively, in the client's affairs. One does sometimes use direct influence-suggestion or advice. Exploration, description, and ventilation are of great importance. Indeed, encouragement of ventilation is often the key to a relationship that will permit cooperative work. The fourth group of procedures, person-situation reflection, almost always occurs in collateral work as the worker describes or explains a client and his or her needs. Through such discussion, the worker hopes to modify or enlarge the collateral's understanding of the client and his needs or to work with the collateral in seeking to understand the client and how to help him. These four categories can be very useful in analyzing samples of work with collaterals. Reasons for the success or failure of efforts to help the client through the milieu can often be located by so doing.

Environmental work can also be classified by *type of role:* that is, in terms of the role a worker may be assuming when working with a collateral individual or an agency. First, one may be the *provider* of a resource. This is true when one is the vehicle through which one's own agency's services are given. Second, one may be the *locator* of a resource, as when one seeks and finds

a resource that gives promise of meeting the client's need. Third, one's role may be that of *interpreter* of the client's need to a collateral. Fourth, in more difficult situations, one may become a *mediator* for the client with an unresponsive or poorly functioning collateral. Finally, in extreme situations, where an agency is clearly failing to carry its responsibilities or an individual is violating the client's rights, the worker may need to carry out a role characterized by *aggressive intervention.* The two latter roles are assumed when clients do not receive services for which they are eligible, especially public assistance, health care, housing, appropriate educational resources. The term *advocacy* describes activities through which the worker strives to secure for clients services to which they are entitled, but which they are unjustly denied or unable to secure by their own efforts.

In summary, then, this chapter offers a classification of treatment procedures that starts with the Richmond suggestion of separating casework into direct work with the client and indirect work with the environment on his or her behalf, and then goes on to pick up the component parts of more recent classifications, arriving at a new arrangement that uses as its logical foundation the major dynamics employed by clinical social work in its effort to enable the client to move toward his or her goals.

Accordingly, six categories of direct treatment and three types of classification of environmental treatment are delineated. The six categories of client-worker communications are:

A. Sustainment
B. Direct influence
C. Exploration, description, ventilation
D. Person-situation reflection concerning:
   1. Others, outside world in general, client's own health
   2. Effects of own behavior on self and others
   3. Nature of own behavior

4. Causative factors that lie in interactions of self with others or in situational provocation
5. Self-evaluation
6. Worker and treatment process
E. Pattern-dynamic reflection (discussion of dynamics of response patterns or tendencies)
F. Developmental reflection (discussion of developmental aspects of response patterns and tendencies)

The types of environmental procedures can be classified by:

A. Type of resource
  1. Worker's own social agency
  2. A non–social work organization in which worker is employed
  3. Another social work agency (i.e., not worker's own)
  4. A non–social work organization that:
    (a) Employs social workers but where worker is not employed
    (b) Does not employ social workers at all
  5. Individuals who are in:
    (a) An instrumental relationship with client
    (b) An expressive relationship to client
B. Type of communication (parallel to first four client-worker categories)
C. Type of role
  1. Provider of resources
  2. Locator of resources
  3. Interpreter of client to milieu person
  4. Mediator between client and milieu person
  5. Aggressive intervener between client and milieu person

According to this system, the treatment of any case as a whole is seen as a constantly changing blend of some or all of these treatment procedures. The nature of the blend will vary with the needs of the case and with the nature of the client's personality, his or her problem, and a number of other variables.

In Chapter 9 we will describe research that has been carried on subsequently concerning the first half of this typology, communications between client and worker. Before turning to this research, however, we will discuss in detail the use of the six sets of client-worker procedures and the three types of classification of environmental procedures in psychosocial casework.

NOTES

1. Mary E. Richmond, *What Is Social Casework? An Introductory Description* (New York: Russell Sage Foundation, 1922), p. 102. Other references of interest are Virginia P. Robinson, "An Analysis of Processes in the Records of Family Case Working Agencies," *The Family,* 2 (July 1921), 101–106; and *Social Casework, Generic and Specific: An Outline: A Report of the Milford Conference* (New York: American Association of Social Workers, 1929).

2. Grete L. Bibring, "Psychiatry and Social Work," *Journal of Social Casework,* 28 (June 1947), 203–211.

3. Florence Hollis, Casework in Marital Disharmony (doctoral dissertation, Bryn Mawr College, 1947); microfilmed (Ann Arbor, Mich.: University Microfilms, 1951). A similar classification is available in "The Techniques of Casework," *Journal of Social Casework,* 30 (June 1949), 235–244.

4. Lucille N. Austin, "Trends in Differential Treatment in Social Casework," *Journal of Social Casework,* 29 (June 1948), 203–211.

5. Ibid., p. 207. In a later article, "Qualifications for Psychotherapists, Social Caseworkers," *American Journal of Orthopsychiatry,* 26 (1956), 47–57, Austin suggests giving up the term "insight therapy" as an inaccurate designation, since insight is a quality or experience that may result from different procedures.

6. *Scope and Methods of the Family Service Agency,* Report of the Committee on Methods and Scope (New York: Family Service Association of America, 1953).

7. Ibid., p. 19.

8. See *Method and Process in Social Casework, Report of a Staff Committee, Community Service Society of New York* (New York: Family Service Association of America, 1958).

9. Ibid., p. 15.

10. Sidney Berkowitz was the first writer to raise questions about this issue. See his "Some Specific Techniques of Psychosocial Diagnosis and Treatment in Family Casework," *Social Casework*, 36 (November 1955), 399–406.

11. Florence Hollis, "Analysis of Two Casework Treatment Approaches," unpublished paper, read at Biennial Meeting of the Family Service Association of America, 1956.

12. Teresa P. Domanski, Marion M. Johns, and Margaret A. G. Manly, "An Investigation of a Scheme for the Classification of Casework Treatment Activities" (master's thesis, Smith College School for Social Work, Northampton, Mass., 1960).

13. Jacqueline Betz, Phyllis Hartmann, Arlene Jaroslaw, Sheila Levine, Dena Schein, Gordon Smith, and Barbara Zeiss, "A Study of the Usefulness and Reliability of the Hollis Treatment Classification Scheme: A Continuation of Previous Research in This Area" (master's thesis, Columbia University School of Social Work, New York, 1961).

14. Florence Hollis, *A Typology of Casework Treatment* (New York: Family Service Association of America, 1968). (A reprint of four articles published in 1967 and 1968 in *Social Casework*.)

PART TWO

Treatment: An Analysis of Procedures

Sustainment, Direct Influence, and Exploration– Description–Ventilation

Having discussed the skeletal outline of the Hollis classification of casework treatment, we shall try in this and the following chapters to put flesh on its bare bones.

Although in the reality of treatment there is a fluid mixture of procedures as interviews proceed, in order to understand their nature one has to pull them apart and examine them separately. From time to time, nevertheless, we will have to shift from discussion of one to another in order to see some of the relationships among them.

SUSTAINMENT

Sustaining procedures are those designed to reduce feelings of anxiety or lack of self-esteem or self-confidence by a direct expression of the worker's confidence or esteem for the client, or confidence that some external threat is not as dangerous as it seems, or—by demonstration of interest in the client—acceptance of the person and desire to help. In such work, the relief comes not from self-understanding but from the worker's implied assurance to the client who has placed confidence in him or her that it is not necessary to be so worried. The dynamic is not one of reasoning but of faith, dependent upon the client's confidence in the worker's knowledge and goodwill.

Sustaining procedures are perhaps the most basic and essential of all pyschosocial casework activities, for without them it would be extremely difficult even to explore the nature of the client's difficulties. When a person must seek help from someone else, discomfort and anxiety frequently arise. One is admitting to oneself as well as to others inability to handle one's own affairs. There is uncertainty about revealing oneself and intimate matters to another person. Have I come to the right place? What will the caseworker think of me? Will the worker try to get me to do something I don't want to do? Is the worker competent, truly interested, and ready to help? Will the worker be honest or insincere? Will this stranger criticize or judge me? Even when a person seeks help with practical problems only, some of these questions may occur. A number of people turn to clinical social workers wanting a sounding board in order to sort out issues related to important life decisions or to explore avenues for personal growth; these prospective clients, too, harbor apprehensions about what reactions they will encounter when they come for help. Experience has repeatedly shown that clients will be able to give more complete and less distorted information if initial tension is relieved and they feel safe enough to discuss their situations candidly.

In problems that involve interpersonal adjustment, some anxiety typically continues, although with variations in level, throughout the whole period of treatment. Often, the anxiety is itself one of the main problems in the individual's adjustment. Sometimes it is a general sense of incompetence or of inability to carry on life's activities adequately; sometimes it is acute concern about some external situation by which the client is confronted: an operation, a new and challenging job, a set of examinations. It may be a traumatic threat, such as an impending eviction or the possible breakup of a marriage; sometimes it is fear of inner impulses, aggressive or sexual, and sometimes it is fear of the superego or conscience, expressing itself as a sense of guilt.

In general, it can be said that the greater the client's anxiety or lack of self-confidence either initially or during the course of treatment, the more need there will be for the use of sustaining techniques. Chief among these is interested, sympathetic listening, which conveys to the client the worker's concern for his or her well-being. This skill comes naturally to most caseworkers, for it is usually an interest in people and their affairs that has brought them into social work in the first place. Nevertheless, workers do vary in their receptiveness and in their ways of showing it. Receptiveness can be indicated by a subtle set of techniques, often not adequately recorded, for the necessary attitude is often expressed more in the worker's bodily behavior than in words. Facial expression, tone of voice, even a way of sitting as one listens, convey the worker's interest as much as does choice of words. The client is not seeking avid curiosity or oversolicitude, but neither does he

or she want cold detachment.[1] An attitude of interest is essential throughout treatment. Special pains must be taken to communicate it to clients whenever their anxiety is high unless, as we shall see later, there is some special therapeutic reason for allowing tension to remain unrelieved.

Another component in the atmosphere between client and worker that can have sustaining value is the sense of mutuality, to be discussed in detail in Chapter 10. This is not an authoritative encounter in which a superior relates, however benevolently, to a weak inferior. It is an undertaking in which two people will work together on a problem. They have mutual respect and a mutual interest in improving the client's well-being. Frankness and openness contribute to a feeling of mutuality. Ideally, the worker brings this to the task. Sometimes for the client it cannot exist immediately, but grows as the work proceeds.

Some of the most powerful sustaining procedures are not conveyed by specific words so much as by the worker's total behavior and demeanor. These reveal certain underlying attitudes of the worker toward the client that tend to relieve anxiety and increase the client's self-respect and self-confidence.

Acceptance

A sustaining procedure that goes beyond expressing the basic attitude of interest, concern, and mutuality is that of conveying acceptance to a client.[2] This is a constant component of all treatment. It is particularly important that this positive, understanding attitude be conveyed to a person who is feeling guilt or shame or who is for some reason angry or afraid. It will be remembered from Chapter 2 that acceptance refers to the worker's continuing goodwill toward the client, whether or not the worker approves of the client's opinions and actions. A worker may be deeply disturbed by antisocial behavior that can be permanently damaging to its victims, such as physical assaultiveness or incest. Yet it is not only possible but necessary for the worker to communicate an attitude of acceptance even while stating clearly that the client's behavior indeed has been harmful to others.[3] Acceptance is not an expression of opinion about an act but an expression of goodwill toward the actor.

As difficult as it may seem to maintain an attitude of acceptance toward a client who has violently abused others, it can be equally challenging for a worker to maintain goodwill in the face of hostile or "demanding" behavior. Yet, acceptance is of utmost importance when working with individuals (such as Mrs. Zimmer, discussed in Chapter 3) who have severe developmental deficits. As we will examine more closely in Chapter 10, acceptance and empathy go hand in hand. When we realize that behavior sometimes pejoratively described as "manipulative," "guilt-provoking," or "self-centered" often derives from feelings of desperation, or from crucial needs that were left unattended during childhood, it becomes possible for us to function in a more understanding and healing manner.[4]

Reassurance

A further step in the sustaining process consists of reassurance about the client's feelings of guilt and anxiety. For instance, a mother who has great difficulty in recognizing feelings of hostility may in the course of treatment become aware of considerable anger toward her child. The worker may seek to reassure her by expressing understanding of the feeling and recognition of the provocation. This technique must be used with delicacy and discrimination. Yielding to the temptation to overuse reassurance in an attempt to build up a relationship or because the worker cannot endure the client's anxiety may merely leave the client with the feeling that the worker does not fully comprehend the reasons for guilt or anxiety or that the worker is

deficient in moral discrimination and therefore is not a person whose judgment matters. Moreover, when the client is ready to explore the reasons for actions, the worker needs to be particularly careful not to give reassurance so readily that the client is made completely comfortable and feels no need to seek understanding of troublesome behavior.

In the illustration in the previous paragraph, for example, it was important to reassure the mother at first because she had unusually high guilt and could acknowledge her feelings only with great reluctance. But after a period of the client's increased ability to talk about her angry feelings toward her child, the worker no longer needed to be reassuring; instead, she agreed that the feelings were unusually strong and, shifting to procedures for developing understanding, suggested seeking out some of the causes of this excessive irritation. Reassurance must be justified by reality, or the client will almost always sense falseness and at best get only temporary comfort. It certainly does no good to tell a man he need not fear an exploratory operation that he already knows may reveal the presence of cancer. Instead, one may want to go into procedures for reflective discussion of his fears in the light of the real situation. This too would lessen anxiety, but by a dynamic different from that of sustainment. If the client is panicky about the operation, the worker's calm consideration with him of its possible outcomes will in itself be a reassuring process. If the client is overreacting, either anticipating certain discovery of cancer when this possibility is not realistically justified or ignoring the possibility of medical help for the condition, even though it might be found to be malignant, reflective discussion combined with reassurance may clarify the realities of the patient's condition. His anxiety may be reduced by bringing to his attention the reality of a possible positive outcome of the operation and the fact that cure may be possible even if cancer is found. If the worker already has the client's confidence, further reassurance of the sustaining type could be offered by an expression of confidence in the doctors, when this is justified, to increase the client's trust in them.

If an individual is afraid of his or her own impulses, reassurance that he or she can control them is sometimes helpful, but only if the worker has a factual basis for believing that the client really is able to handle destructive feelings and wants to do so. Usually such reassurance must be accompanied by other procedures, especially forms of reflection where the dynamic is increased knowledge and understanding, thus giving the client reason to believe that greater control can be achieved and is worth achieving. The worker can refer to similar situations in which the client has been able to exercise control. Sometimes the worker goes into the dynamics of behavior, pointing out that an acknowledged impulse can be more easily held in check than a hidden one; or, the client may be helped to consider some of the unrealistic factors contributing to the urge to act on certain feelings. All these approaches can be strengthened by concurrent sustaining communications that convey the worker's understanding of the drive and acceptance of the individual even when the effort is to help the client reconsider unwise actions.

Obviously, except at the very beginning, sustaining procedures are usually preceded by exploration, description, and ventilation. One can scarcely react in a sustaining way until the client has talked about the matters that are causing feelings of inadequacy or anxiety. It is sometimes true, however, that a person is blocked from talking about these things. Then the worker's verbal and nonverbal indications of interest, concern, and desire to help are of value in overcoming the hesitation.

Encouragement

A similar process takes place when the worker expresses confidence in a client's abilities, recognizes achievements, shows pleasure in successes, and so on. Encouragement is especially important in work with children, and it is also effective with adults who lack self-confidence and are faced with especially difficult tasks or are going through a period of anxiety in which their normal self-confidence is weakened. There is a great difference, of course, between honest appreciation and false praise or flattery. The very fact that people are insecure often makes them extremely sensitive to hollow insincerity, and their confidence in the worker evaporates if they suspect encouraging comments are merely a technique meant to inject courage into their personalities.

When expressing confidence in the client's ability to handle some task or situation, it is important that the worker be realistic about the client's capacity but also sensitive to the client's own perception of his or her abilities. Too ready assurance, even when realistically justified, causes the client to bottle up anxiety, which may then reappear in full force at the very moment that whatever self-confidence he or she possesses is most needed. If the lack of self-confidence is very great, other procedures in addition to sustainment may be called for. Initial ventilation may be followed by whatever help the client is able to gain from reflective consideration of the situation that is causing so much fear.

One further caution concerning procedures of encouragement: they tend to arouse in the client a feeling that he or she should live up to the worker's expectations. Particularly if there is a possibility that the client will fail, it is important to deal in advance with the anxiety that this may create by making it clear—in words or in actions—that the worker will not be upset by failure, will continue to feel interest and confidence in the client, and will help the client to deal with disappointment and to find another solution. Other sustaining techniques of conveying acceptance and reassurance often need to accompany encouragement.[5]

Reaching Out

At times the client's need for sustainment is so strong and distrust or anxiety is so great that something more concrete than words is needed to demonstrate the worker's concern and wish to help. We are most familiar with the use of such techniques with children who, it has long been recognized by practitioners, need concrete evidence of the worker's goodwill. Small gifts have always been part of the worker's way of building up a positive relationship with children, especially young children. Snacks may help. It is also customary for the worker to express liking or fondness directly and, with small children, to convey it physically, by holding a child on one's lap, putting an arm protectively around an upset youngster, and the like.

A comparable process is sometimes needed with adults. The early literature on the "hard to reach" emphasized the importance of winning the client's confidence partly by doing concrete things for his or her benefit,[6] such as working out difficult situations with a landlord or with the department of welfare, arranging for camp for the children, taking the children to busy clinics when the mother cannot do this herself, or even providing money for various household needs. These are, of course, important services in their own right, but they also symbolize to the client the worker's interest and concern, and thus act as emotionally sustaining factors. It is important to recognize that the provision of such services is not only useful in work with the socioeconomically disadvantaged. The elderly, the physically or mentally disabled, those experiencing difficult life events, and many, many others who simply have not received a fair share of personal attention are often supported by the worker's special efforts to reach out and assist them.

Bandler[7] found that to persuade certain mothers to allow their children to go to nursery school, it was necessary to set up groups for the gratification of the mothers themselves because their own needs were so great. Sometimes when the contact has usually been in the office, the "reaching out" is a visit to the client at home in a period of stress; sometimes it is arranging for an extra interview or merely giving extra time in a regular interview. Sometimes it is securing information or making a phone call. Whenever the worker's action is designed *especially* to convey to the client concern and a desire to help, it represents this form of sustaining work. Again, it would not be the only procedure employed, but it might either accompany or be a necessary prelude to other techniques. In work with adults, such concrete demonstrations are not universally needed, and in any case they must be used with great discrimination based on sound diagnostic thinking. They should not, of course, grow out of the worker's enjoyment of the client's gratitude or need to encourage a dependent relationship.

Nonverbal Sustainment

As noted earlier, much sustainment is given by paraverbal and nonverbal means. Workers do not listen to clients impassively. Rather, there is often a series of sympathetic "umms," facial and bodily expressions of complete listening, facial changes and gestures that respond to, and sometimes mirror, what the client is saying or feeling. Brief verbal comments such as "yes," "I know," "I see," and repetition of the last word or two of a client's sentence are all used to show continuing attentiveness. As a matter of fact, the very way in which a client is received in an office can have either a reassuring effect or the opposite. Is the receptionist courteous? Is the waiting room pleasant? How does the worker greet the client? Interaction begins at once.

Workers differ in their nonverbal expressiveness. Through the use of one-way viewing screens, films, and videotapes, we are now in a position to study this elusive quality and its bearing upon successful work.

Secondary Sustainment

After some experience with the typology in both teaching and research, it became clear that there is both direct and indirect, or secondary, sustainment. Sustainment, that is, can be a by-product of procedures used primarily for the encouragement of reflection or even of exploration or direction. For instance, it not infrequently happens that we do not understand what a client is trying to say. One may then simply make comments such as "I don't quite know what you mean" and ask for further explanation until the communication is clear. This procedure is primarily a part of the process of exploration or ventilation, but it can also have the side effect of communicating to the client the worker's interest and constant attentiveness. In this sense, it is a secondary type of sustainment. A study by Boatman[8] of seventy-six tape-recorded interviews with thirty clients found that, in general, 10 percent of the communications that were classified as primarily something other than sustainment nevertheless carried this as a secondary probable effect.

It has been noted, in studying interviews, that workers differ greatly in the extent to which they insert sustaining words and phrases into their reflective communications when there is a possibility that these communications may arouse anxiety. Further research would be required to determine whether the smaller *quantity* of sustaining statements offered by some workers is compensated for by the *quality* of the overall support they provide, a matter that is difficult to measure directly. To study this question, client ratings of a worker's supportiveness and interest could be contrasted with the actual frequency of sustaining words and phrases.

A special problem arises with sustaining procedures in joint or family interviews. Comments that might easily be made in an individual interview have to be seen in the light of the effect they will have on other clients who will also hear them. If worker impartiality is not clearly established, sympathy with the hurt feelings of a wife, for example, may convey disapproval to the husband whom the wife is already blaming for "causing" the suffering. Or sustainment of one marital partner may arouse the jealousy of the other. This factor may account for the findings of a study by Ehrenkranz,[9] who in a content analysis comparing individual and joint interviews in marital counseling cases found significantly less sustainment when husband and wife were seen together than when they were seen separately. Some of these issues will be further discussed in the chapters on family and marital treatment.

DIRECT INFLUENCE

The second set of procedures, those designated direct influence, includes the various ways in which the worker tries by the force, in varying degrees, of his or her opinion to promote a specific kind of behavior by the client. For example, a worker may give advice or make suggestions about dealing more advantageously with an employer, consulting a doctor, going through with a medical recommendation, handling the children in a certain way, and so on.[10]

For many years, this type of activity has been suspect in casework. In the days of innocence, prior to the 1930s, when workers were universally thought to be wiser and better informed than clients, advice was one of the "visitor's" chief stocks in trade. Through bitter experience caseworkers gradually learned that the wife who took the worker's advice and separated from her alcoholic husband more often than not took him back again, despite her fear of the visitor's disapproval; that the mother who let herself be guided by the visitor's child-rearing theories somehow managed to demonstrate that they did not work with her Johnnie; and that the homemaker who let herself be taught how to make up a set of budget envelopes did not simultaneously learn how to keep her fingers out of the wrong envelope when the bill collector came to the door. Out of such experiences came considerable healthy reluctance about telling clients how to run their lives. Probably, the official position of casework on this matter has been more extreme than actual practice. Workers have probably intuitively recognized that there continues to be some need for guidance of some clients.

There is some evidence—and we would expect this to be so—that in parent-child problems workers are more likely to give advice than in marital work. Davis[11] reported a study of seventeen mothers and five fathers in which the general level of advice giving (less than 8 percent of all worker comments) was about twice as high as that found in studies of casework with marital problems. Upon follow-up, eleven months later, eleven of the seventeen mothers expressed satisfaction with the amount of advice given, none wanted less, and six would have liked more.

It is often said that clients with little education in lower-income groups come to agencies expecting to be given advice and are dissatisfied when the worker gives very little. A study by Reid and Shapiro[12] gave some support to this hypothesis. Using the Hollingshead and Redlich Class I to Class V scale of socioeconomic position, they found that only 1 of 31 clients in the two upper socioeconomic categories objected that too little advice had been given. Almost a fourth of the 151 clients in classes III to V did so object. Note, however, that three-fourths of the clients in these lower socioeconomic groups did *not* express such an objection.

This, of course, is only one aspect of the issue of how much advice is helpful. There are also questions such as: To what extent, when advice is given, is it used? To what extent has advice proved beneficial in the situation for which it was given? Then there is the hardest question of all to answer: In the long run, is it more helpful for the client to follow advice or to be helped to think things through without being given specific suggestions or opinions?

It is probably apparent to the reader by now that on ethical and practical grounds we, the authors, prefer to help clients—through reflective discussion—to make their own decisions about what steps they want to take and what changes they want to make. Certainly casework's commitment to the value of self-direction is better served thereby. In our experience, also, there is more positive carry-through into other aspects of their lives when clients participate in learning how to make their own choices than when they blindly follow the lead of the worker. Yet, it is also clear that under some circumstances direction from the worker not only is sought by clients but is useful to them. It becomes our responsibility to make the best determinations we can, on an ongoing basis, about when advice giving is indicated and when it may impede client self-reliance. The discussion that follows suggests some broad guidelines.

Degrees of Directiveness

Direct influence consists of a graduated set of techniques of varying degrees of directiveness. As one works with these procedures, one discovers that they constitute a range of processes that form a continuum. In the middle of the continuum, one may place the giving of advice: definitely *stating an opinion* or taking a stand concerning actions that the worker thinks the client should take. The worker may point out to a child's mother that Mary knows her way to school, is careful about crossing streets, and will have more chance to play with other children if her mother does not accompany her. Or the worker may comment to a man who is hesitating to ask for a seemingly deserved raise that several other people in his office have been given a raise, and that the only way to find out whether he can get one is to ask for it.

A less forceful way of presenting these same ideas might be for the worker to make a *suggestion.* One might comment to Mary's mother,

"It's only two blocks to the school. My guess is that Mary is old enough now to go that far with her friends." Or, one might comment to a second client, "Sometimes people just ask for a raise." The solution is raised in the client's mind in a way that conveys the worker's inclination toward it but leaves the client with the alternative of rejecting the idea without feeling that he or she is going contrary to the worker's definite opinion.

A still milder form of influence is that of simply *underlining*, giving emphasis to, a course of action the client is already contemplating. A mother thinks it might be a good idea to let six-year-old Mary walk to school alone; the worker agrees it would be worth trying. Or the client says he is thinking of asking the boss for a raise, and the worker nods approvingly. Even if this client eventually decides against the step, there is very little likelihood that he will feel he has opposed the worker's opinion, for it was his own idea in the first place. When the client does go ahead with an idea and it works, the client takes the credit; if it fails, the edge is taken off the failure, since the worker also made the mistake of thinking it would work.

Toward the other end of the continuum is *urging* or *insisting*, putting certain forcefulness behind the advice that is offered. The worker tells a mother that it is *essential* for her to take Janie to school, even though the child is frightened. Such pressure is sometimes necessary in treatment of a true school phobia, when the mother's own need to keep the child close to her may be contributing to the difficulty. Treatment of the child cannot wait upon a slow change in the mother's attitude, which might take months to bring about, for in the interim school problems may have been added to the initial phobia to such a degree that a permanent learning problem may ensue.[13] Also, Janie's fears may snowball dangerously if she does not return quickly to school.

Or the worker might tell the man he thinks it would be *very unwise* for him to ask for a raise when he is on such bad terms with his boss, that such an action might very well result in his being fired. When there is a possibility of severe consequences of an impulsive, ill-considered action, or when sufficient time is not available to help the client think a matter through rationally, such active persuasion may be worth trying. Sometimes it saves the client from unfortunate consequences. But if the client does not take the advice and suffers the predicted result, the worker must by all means avoid anything that can be construed as an "I told you so" attitude. Properly handled, with the client able to express disappointment and to feel that the worker, too, regrets this disappointment, the failure may open the way to reflective consideration of what was involved and possibly ward off its repetition.

Most extreme of all the directive techniques is *actual intervention in the client's life* by such measures as removing a child from a home in which the child is subjected to cruelty or to a high degree of neglect or taking a psychotic client to the receiving ward of a hospital. Such forceful interventions must rest on two conditions: first, one must be convinced that the step is fully justified and not motivated by some overreaction of one's own; second, one must have thorough knowledge of the community resources involved in the plan of action and of the extent to which they will support it. For if the effort fails, one may well have lost constructive contact with the client and made the situation worse. In the first illustration given, the worker must know the conditions under which a court would uphold the action in custody proceedings; in the second, the worker must have sound clinical knowledge of the probable nature of the client's illness and of the procedures of the hospital to which the patient is to be taken. In both instances, the action must be carried out with skill. Firmness and kindness are essential. The probability of the client's acceding to the action with a minimum of resistance and disturbance is enhanced if in the first instance the worker is devoid of punitive motivation, and in the second the worker's anxiety is sufficiently under control that the client does not sense it. In both instances, it is important for the worker to feel sufficiently confident of ability to carry through the action that the client will sense this strength and therefore reject the temptation to test it. Of course, the worker must also be convinced that the solution is preferable to the problem that inspired it.

Although in general it is best for a client to arrive at decisions by way of his or her own thinking, as understanding brings the individual to a possible solution, it is sometimes helpful for the caseworker to give support to the conclusions. In most situations, *preference should be given to the most gentle form of influence that can be employed successfully*, either putting ideas in the form of suggestions or reinforcing the client's own ideas.

There are many situations in which techniques of influence are appropriate. They are particularly useful in matters of child rearing, on which the worker, because of expert knowledge, is able to give the client good advice. Often the client is not yet ready to think things through, or strong cultural differences in expectations of the worker may lead the client to misinterpret the worker's refusal to give direction as a sign of indifference or incompetence. Although the worker does not need to comply with a client's expectations throughout the whole of treatment, it is often important to do so at the beginning.

The very anxious or depressed client is also sometimes in need of direction. It may be appropriate for the worker to provide it in the initial contact or throughout a period of crisis, gradually supplanting it, as the client's self-confidence grows, by methods that rest on understanding. Very dependent people, too, are often not capable of complete self-direction and need at least a measure of guidance from the worker,[14] as may also people whose sense of reality is weak, such as schizophrenics or se-

vere borderline personalities.[15] To reiterate: As long as the worker is philosophically committed to the value of self-direction, reasonably conscious of his or her own reactions to the client's need for dependence, and alert to every possibility of encouraging clients to think for themselves, wise use can be made of these procedures.

Risks in Advice Giving

Direct influence is, however, a treatment procedure in which there are several pitfalls. The most obvious is that one may give the wrong advice. Hence, the worker must be reasonably sure of knowing enough about what is best for the client to warrant advice. Especially on important decisions, the worker rarely knows enough to justify influencing another person. For instance, in a decision about whether or not to break up a marriage, a third person is not sufficiently aware of the subjective feelings and needs involved to weigh them adequately. This is true even when the objective realities seem, perhaps all too obviously, to point toward the wisdom of separation. As a safeguard against giving the wrong advice or preempting the client's decision-making abilities, the worker is best advised to use reflective discussion to try to help individuals arrive at awareness of both subjective and objective factors in their situations and to enable them to reach wise solutions for themselves. Only then may there be reason for the worker's reinforcing the client's decision by expressing agreement, but even this amount of influence is best used very sparingly.

A second safeguard is to be quite sure that the need for advice rests in the client and not in the worker. It is so tempting to tell people what to do; one feels so good to be called upon for professional advice! All the negative connotations of the word "authority" can be removed simply by putting "professional" in front of it, thereby transforming "authoritativeness" into "strength the client can lean on." That there is such a thing as professional expertise is not to be denied, and under certain circumstances it can be put to very good use.[16] However, the need to see oneself as an authority is not sufficient reason for invoking that role.

A third safeguard is to induce the client, whenever possible, to think things through independently, even when he is turning to the worker for answers. Clients sometimes seduce the worker into thinking advice is necessary when it is not. Some people like to be told what to do because passivity or dependence interferes with their ability to think things out for themselves and later, if things go wrong, they can always blame someone else. Anxious people, people with little self-confidence, and people who want very much to please others often ask for more direction than they really need.

In general, then, one can say that advice about decisions or goals is risky. Advice about *how to reach* a goal the *client* has set is more often appropriate, especially if it is unlikely that the client can think this through without help. For example, a worker might suggest that a client bring a tape recorder to treatment sessions; experience indicates that certain clients with extreme anxiety or those who have difficulty remembering for various reasons can benefit from reviewing material covered in meetings with their workers. Workers frequently make recommendations in individual and conjoint meetings about means for improving communication patterns. It is also common for workers to urge clients to bring in a spouse or other family members in order to address interpersonal problems or to discuss situations that affect other people who are close to them. In all of these instances, workers usually explain explicitly the connection between their suggestions and the clients' treatment goals.

Refusal to give advice, of course, should not be stated in an abrupt or withholding manner. Sometimes it is necessary to explain: "I'd give you advice if I thought it would help, but really *you* are the only one who can know what you

want to do. Let's work on it together and see whether you can come to your own decision." Or, with a different client, "It would be arrogant of me and insulting to you for me to assume I know better what is good for you than you do yourself."

Among the clients who typically seek a great deal of advice are obsessive-compulsive people.[17] Because they are usually very ambivalent, having a hard time making up their own minds, they tend to find an initial relief in being told what to do. Moreover, they are also usually dependent and have very strong superegos, so that they are very anxious to please people whom they regard as authorities. Asking for advice, in other words, is one way of playing out an inner wish to be a very good little boy or girl.

Because of the anxiety involved and the fact that the asked-for guidance becomes a gift (in the sustaining sense) that helps to build up a positive relationship, it sometimes is wise, especially in the early stages, to accede to the compulsive client's request. Direct advice, however, should be given tentatively, the worker offering it as something the client might like to try or as something that is often found helpful. Since the negativism of compulsive people sometimes leads them to ask for direction for the unconscious purpose of proving it will not work, this kind of qualifying comment will temper their need to show the advice is poor. If, on the other hand, they are truly trying to please the worker by following the advice, the tentative way in which it is offered will provide them with an anxiety-relieving excuse if they should fail.

Secondary Directiveness

Just as it has been found that there can be a secondary form of sustainment as a by-product of the use of other procedures, so direct influence is sometimes a secondary feature of other worker communications. This has not been systematically studied in the way Boatman examined sustainment. However, it seems obvious that in varying degrees workers word their communications, even in reflective discussion, in ways that suggest a course of action the worker thinks the client should take. For example, suppose a worker asks a woman who has said she wants to improve her relationship with her husband whether she thinks she will achieve her purpose by so consistently attacking or belittling him. In this instance, by implication, the worker is advising the client to change behavior toward her husband in order to achieve her goal of a better marriage relationship.

If one believes in the importance of self-direction, one needs to be very careful in reflective work about exerting a kind of secondary direct influence, by phrasing comments or questions in a manner that leads toward a certain answer. As already noted, it is especially important to avoid guiding clients toward *decisions* the worker favors. In other matters, one may sometimes want to lead a client to understand himself or herself or others in a particular way or, as in the above example, to help a person recognize how a particular mode of behavior may be self-defeating. But we need to be aware of the extent to which we are being directive, and clear about our purposes for being so.

A close relationship exists between sustaining techniques and direct influence. Procedures of direct influence, except for active intervention, are effective only in proportion to the client's trust in the worker. The client will come to the worker with certain preconceptions growing out of past experience with, or knowledge of, other social workers. Also, certain expectations are inherent in the worker's position: that is, they are *ascribed* to anyone functioning in this particular role. Immediately upon contact, the worker has to begin to *achieve* the reputation of a person to be trusted by virtue of his or her own ways of acting with the client. The client's trust in the worker will be made up mainly of

two components, respect for the worker's competence and belief in the worker's goodwill.[18] The latter is built up largely through sustaining processes.

Both direct influence and sustainment draw upon the client's dependence on the worker, a fact that must be kept in mind both in using these techniques and subsequently in helping the client regain or strengthen the ability to be self-reliant.

EXPLORATION–DESCRIPTION–VENTILATION

The third major division of the typology includes two related but different concepts: exploration-description and ventilation. To *describe* or explain is simply to give the facts as one sees them. To *ventilate* is to bring out feelings associated with the facts. Exploration-description is a part of psychosocial study, an effort to secure from clients descriptions of themselves and their situations and the interactions that are part of their dilemmas. It occurs not only in the beginning interviews when the initial picture is emerging but also in each subsequent interview, as the most recent events are gone over and bring to mind other connected events. It usually happens, however, that these factual descriptions are not neutral or emotionless. Clients frequently experience and sometimes express strong feelings on reviewing the facts as they see them. The distinction between experiencing and expressing feeling is an important one, and it is the chief reason that exploration-description and ventilation are placed together. Clients often experience feelings, even strongly, without showing them. Less strong feelings, especially, are often not overtly expressed. The worker, therefore, needs to be alert throughout the exploration-description process for feelings that would have been expected but may not have been revealed, responding in a way that will bring relief if these feelings do exist.

These procedures are also interlocked with those of reflection. In the latter, one often helps a client to become aware of feelings that have been suppressed. This is often followed by a great deal of ventilation concerning the events and feelings involved. This release or discharge can be an important way of reducing the intensity of feelings and of rechanneling emotional energies. Ventilation of suppressed feelings is altogether different from *abreaction*, the analytic term for the reliving in the treatment hours of life experiences, chiefly from the early years, that have been repressed and therefore are deeply unconscious.

Anger and Hatred

Feelings of anger and hatred are especially likely to lose some of their intensity if they can be given adequate verbal expression. This is particularly true for clients who have difficulty accepting negative or aggressive emotion. Very frequently, ventilation makes it possible later to move to reflective discussion of the circumstances and provocations under which anger is felt. Eventually, the client may be able to reach greater understanding of other people involved in the problem, faulty communication, ways of preventing anger-arousing situations, and so on. It is often important that such ventilation be accompanied by the sustaining process of acceptance.

Angry feelings are not always relieved through ventilation. As we shall describe shortly, sometimes expressions of anger are actually a defense against other, "softer" feelings which some clients find more difficult to face or admit. Also, anger is often a natural reaction to feeling helpless, trapped, or victimized. Although the feelings must be thoroughly understood and acknowledged by the worker, ultimately the anger is not likely to diffuse until the person no longer feels powerless and has gained some sense of control over his or her own life, even in the face of difficult life events.

Treatment, therefore, will often include reflective procedures aimed at finding ways to modify the constraining situation and/or the person's attitudes about it so that changes and new choices can be made.

Grief Reactions

The importance of enabling people to mourn has long been recognized in casework. Some individuals, either for cultural reasons or because they place an especially high value on being stoical or "strong," are embarrassed to show their grief. Ventilation plays an important role in bringing these feelings of grief to expression in a sympathetic atmosphere. With a person who is depressed after the loss of a loved one—whether through death or through separation of any other kind—it can be of special value to feel that here is a place where it is all right to cry and where the grief is understood.[19]

Similarly, expression of feeling can give relief to a person who has experienced a permanent disabling illness or injury or disfiguring surgery or who is facing death or the diagnosis of a fatal illness. Relatives, friends, and sometimes medical personnel may praise patients for their courage in maintaining a calm exterior when the person's greatest need is really to "let go."

As is true in the use of any treatment procedure, timing is important. When helping a client to bring out grief reactions, one must be ever sensitive to defenses holding back the discharge of feeling, and wait until the client is sufficiently comfortable to express his or her feelings.

Not infrequently, where we would expect grief, the underlying emotion is a different one: anger or fear. Reactions may occur in stages. Often, guilt or shame is also felt, for example, by a client who has lost a breast through surgery for cancer or one who has had a colostomy. For the terminally ill, there are often periods of denial or, occasionally, absolute refusal to believe that death is imminent. Such denial of the fact, of course, temporarily precludes the expression of feelings associated with it. In all of these instances, ventilation does not occur until after there has been a process of bringing the deeper emotions to awareness. Thus, a form of reflection will need to precede and make possible the actual ventilation of emotion.

Here, again, the worker must respect defenses and proceed with gentleness. Certainly, feelings about impending death should be approached when the client shows some sign of wanting to talk about them, not just when the worker thinks it would be good for the person to do so. In the case of Mrs. Stasio, to be presented in Chapter 21, denial was unusually mild and ventilation could be an ongoing emphasis in treatment.

Guilt Feelings

In the ventilation of guilt feelings, the interplay between ventilation and sustainment is particularly close.[20] Alleviation of feelings of guilt requires more than mere expression, although expression may be an important first step. It is the worker's attitude toward the guilt that is of primary importance. If the guilt is an appropriate response to events in the client's life, the worker's continued acceptance of the person after the guilt has been verbalized is of great value in reducing the intensity of these feelings. An accepting gesture is sometimes enough. Expressing sympathy with the feeling of guilt sometimes helps: "Yes, it is hard to find you have been wrong." "We all do things sometimes that we later wish we hadn't." "Yes, I know, it's awfully hard to face it." Guilt feelings are also often inappropriate: one may blame oneself too much, for too long, or for no reason. All too often, guilt that is derived from a harsh, punitive superego can be immobilizing and destructive to self-esteem. Ventilation should usually be followed by either sustainment or reflective discussion of these overreactions, or

both, in an effort to help the client assess these feelings more realistically.

This is not to say that it is always helpful for guilt to be relieved immediately. "Realistic" guilt can serve constructive purposes. Critical self-evaluation that helps individuals reflect on the disparity between their behavior and the ways they want to act or feel they should act or the kind of persons they wish to be can lead to productive changes. Constructive guilt can be preventive in that it helps people think before they take actions that may be hurtful to themselves or to others. For some clients with antisocial or some of the other personality disorders, the development of greater concern about the effects their actions have on others is a sign of growth. This may be accompanied by mild feelings of guilt when an interim stage has been reached, in which actions are still primarily at an immature, self-gratifying stage, but regret (sometimes a more useful emotion than guilt) is beginning to be felt about harm done to others.

Even when the problem is not real lack of concern for others, people often do not realize the extent to which they may be hurting others. When they become aware of the impact they do have—say, on husband, wife, or child—they may experience guilt or dismay over what they are doing. When this is so, it can be accepted as such. Such reactions may reinforce the building of self-awareness and sound ego controls. They can mark the growth of understanding of others and concern for them. They can provide incentive to acts of restitution that heal torn relationships as well as restore feelings of self-worth.

Often clinical social workers treat clients who have committed serious crimes or are batterers or sexual molesters. Even in these cases, guilt is not useful unless it guides people to reflect on their behavior and genuinely make amends. *Excessive and self-debasing guilt actually may only make matters worse.* Many destructive acts are perpetrated by people whose self-esteem is minimal and who have little confidence that they can change or that they can be valued by others. When one is working with such clients, many sustaining procedures may be required to help them gain enough self-acceptance to be able to reflect on themselves and the meanings of their actions. Too much attention given to the ventilation of guilt may actually defeat the purposes of the treatment.

Anxiety

Feelings of anxiety may be acute and primarily related to a particular event or situational stress, including that of coming to a professional for help. On the other hand, some clients experience chronic or repeated states of anxiety and have little knowledge of their causes. In both instances, such feelings can often be relieved in some measure during the exploratory phase. As the client relates the facts that precipitated the distress, or describes various aspects of present or past life, there is generally also a discharge of some of the emotion associated with these. The fact that the worker is not anxious can help the client find a way of dealing with the underlying issues contributing to the anxiety once it is expressed. Here, again, ventilation is followed by sustainment or reflection or both. Often, the worker's realistic confidence that the client has the strength to bear the anxiety, and can find ways of reducing it, is an important contributing factor to the client's being able to do so.

Sometimes anxiety is not directly expressed, but the worker can be alert to its signs. For example, a client may become restless or "block" when certain material is discussed, or may perspire or tremble. Under these circumstances, sometimes a sustaining word from the worker (e.g., "You seem to be having difficulty talking about this") can help the client ventilate the discomfort enough to allow further exploration of the trouble. Of course, there are times when anxiety is so keen that it is necessary for the worker to postpone exploration of a particular topic until the client can approach it without such apprehension.

Contraindications

Although a certain amount of emotional release is of value in all cases, there are some circumstances under which it should be held in check. Occasionally, so much anxiety, anger, or other emotion is ventilated that it seems to be "feeding on itself." Talking does not bring the client relief and a reduction of feeling, but instead deeper engrossment in it. If this seems to be occurring, the expression of emotion is not helpful, and the worker should not encourage it to continue, but should turn the client's attention either to less emotionally laden content or to the question of what can be done to modify the situation or the feelings about which the client has been talking. The worker may even say quite directly that it does not seem to help to keep going over these matters and that it might be better to try not to dwell on them so constantly. Adding to this, the worker might suggest that together they may be able to find other, more successful ways to gain relief and improve matters.

Moreover, sometimes the expression of one emotion serves to keep another hidden. For example, a client may defend against feelings of anger by excessively venting reactions of grief. Similarly, we often find that intense anger masks "softer" feelings such as sadness, fear, tenderness. Thus, when we put value on the "open" expression of feeling, it is important to be sure that the expression is of the basic emotion and not just of its "cover." A worker who is alert to this will listen for clues to the underlying feeling, and turn from ventilation to reflective discussion to promote the client's awareness of the tendency to use this form of protection against exposing a particular emotion, and of the reasons for feeling this is necessary.

Occasionally, especially with the psychotic

or near-psychotic person, ventilation may lead to the production of increasingly bizarre material, or it may become a stimulus to irrational actions. Accurate diagnostic assessment of the presence of psychotic trends alerts a worker to this possibility and to the fact that it may be more helpful to explore areas that will strengthen realistic thinking, rather than to encourage ventilation that may evoke material that in less seriously disturbed people would remain unconscious or would be better organized by synthesizing ego functions. This is not to say that all ventilation by disturbed people should be discouraged. For example, such clients can feel, sometimes very justifiably, that they are not taken seriously by others who have labeled them "crazy." In such situations, it can be extremely important for the worker to elicit and acknowledge feelings of hurt or anger about this, as was the case with Mrs. Barry (see Chapter 21).

Occasionally, a worker may observe that the client is deriving marked gratification from talking freely about himself or herself and seems to be making no effort to use the interviews to move toward any improvement either in dealing with inner problems or in coping with the situation. Sometimes this represents an effort to enlist the worker's sympathy. At other times, the client's complaints function only to postpone making essential changes; or they can be a way of putting all the blame for the troubles on others. Talking may provide sexual or masochistic satisfaction. Gratification of any of these kinds is of no value in helping clients to better their plight and should not be continued once it becomes clear that this is the prevailing mood. Sometimes, too, clients who seek gratification in these ways are people who cannot be helped by casework. Care must be taken, however, to move away from this type of communication in a constructive rather than a destructive way. Often the reason for discouraging it can be explained directly to the client, thus leading into a discussion of this aspect of the resistance. But

to do so successfully, the worker must be free of the hostile countertransference reactions that are so easily aroused by clients who make use of ventilation primarily for self-gratification.

Ventilation in Joint Interviews

As in sustainment, there is a difference in the extent to which ventilation of certain types can be used in joint and individual interviews. Ehrenkranz,[21] contrary to expectation, in a study comparing 58 joint interviews with 68 interviews with individuals, found "conspicuously" less ventilation in the joint interviews. She suggests that this may have been due to the workers' tendency to accentuate the positive when clients with marital problems were willing to have joint interviews. Hollis had a similar finding in comparing 20 joint interviews with 20 single-person interviews, reporting that this was especially true in ventilation of feelings about others.[22] There was probably some restraint in expressing hostile feelings in the presence of the other person. Actually, the expression of hostility in a joint interview can be a powerful therapeutic tool, and it is sometimes encouraged. This is particularly true if one partner has been unable to express such feelings to the other and is able to bring out the true feelings with the support of the worker. This expression can lead to more honest communication and prevent the bottling up of feelings that then either explode when the pressure becomes too great or find an outlet in devious and sometimes more harmful ways. Such expression can also have a profound influence on a partner who has been unwittingly hurtful because of lack of awareness of the spouse's feelings.

The extent to which such ventilation should be encouraged or discouraged in joint interviews depends upon its effect on both partners. Every effort should be made to discontinue it if it creates too much anxiety in either partner or leads to ever increasing hostility and counterhostility instead of greater understanding or the emergence of positive feelings. This need for caution is no doubt another cause of the finding that there is quantitatively less ventilation in joint than in individual interviews. It is also the authors' impression that if there were a measure of *intensity* of ventilation, in most cases it would be found to be much higher in joint interviews. When ventilation of hostility appears not to be helpful, this should be discussed with the clients. Sometimes it is best at such times to turn to individual interviews until a less destructive stage of the relationship has been reached. But, once again, the anger may in fact be a defense against risking "softer" feelings of disappointment, loneliness, and the longing for affection. Frequently, when these are elicited in joint interviews the destructive, hostile attacks subside. These matters will be discussed in detail in the chapters on family and couple treatment.

NOTES

1. For discussions of this see Clare Britton, "Casework Techniques in Child Care Services," *Social Casework*, 36 (January 1955), 3–13; Jerome Frank, "The Role of Hope in Psychotherapy," *International Journal of Psychiatry*, 5 (May 1967); Annette Garrett, *Interviewing: Its Principles and Methods*, 3d ed. (New York: Family Service Association of America, 1982); Alfred Kadushin, *The Social Work Interview*, 2d ed. (New York: Columbia University Press, 1983); Elizabeth Salomon, "Humanistic Values and Social Casework," *Social Casework*, 48 (January 1967), 26–32; and Charles B. Truax and Robert R. Carkuff, *Toward Effective Counseling and Psychotherapy: Training and Practice* (Chicago: Aldine, 1967). See Chapter 10 for additional references.

We also recommend three interesting papers in *Clinical Social Work Journal*, 14 (Spring 1986), that discuss issues around supportive treatment: Shirley Greenberg, "The Supportive Approach to Therapy," 6–13; Anna Ornstein, "'Supportive' Psychotherapy: A Contemporary View," 14–30; and Margaret Galdston Frank, "Discussion of Anna Ornstein's Paper," 31–38.

2. The importance of this concept has been emphasized in many articles beginning in the thirties. Examples of these early references include: Annette Garrett, *Interviewing: Its Principles and Methods* (New York: Family Service Association of America, 1942), pp. 22–24; Gordon Hamilton, "Basic Concepts in Social Casework," *The Family*, 18 (December 1937), 263–268; and Charlotte Towle, "Factors in Treatment," *Proceedings of the National Conference of Social Work, 1936* (Chicago:University of Chicago Press, 1936), 179–191. See Chapter 10 for current references.

3. See a classic paper by Alice W. Rue, "The Casework Approach to Protective Work," *The Family*, 18 (December 1937), 277–282. See also Deborah Bookin and Ruth E. Dunkle, "Elder Abuse: Issues for the Practitioner," *Social Casework*, 66 (January 1985), 3–12; Nora Dougherty, "The Holding Environment: Breaking the Cycle of Abuse," *Social Casework*, 64 (May 1983), 283–290; Dale Hardman, "The Matter of Trust," *Crime and Delinquency*, 15 (April 1969), 203–218; and Lois Lester, "The Special Needs of the Female Alcoholic," *Social Casework*, 63 (October 1982), 451–456. Many other references can be found in the notes of Chapter 8.

4. Note 4 of Chapter 3 provides several references on the treatment of borderline disorders which discuss the many ways in which these techniques are necessary to successful treatment. Case examples, with clients with various kinds of presenting difficulties, are to be found in Miriam Elson, *Self Psychology in Clinical Social Work* (New York: W. W. Norton, 1986); see also her discussion of this issue, pp. 5–7. Annette Garrett, *Interviewing: Its Principles and Methods*, 3d ed., also gives relevant case illustrations.

5. For illustrations and discussions of these sustaining techniques see, for example, Martha W. Chescheir, "Some Implications of Winnicott's Concepts for Clinical Practice," *Clinical Social Work Journal*, 13 (Fall 1985), 218–233; L. P. Laing, "The Use of Reassurance in Psychotherapy," *Smith College Studies in Social Work*, 22 (February 1952), 75–90; Grace K. Nicholls, "Treatment of a Disturbed Mother-Child Relationship: A Case Presentation," in Howard J. Parad, ed., *Ego Psychology and Dynamic Casework* (New York: Family Service Association of America, 1958), pp. 117–125.

6. For early discussions of work with the "hard to reach," see especially Alice Overton, "Serving Families Who Don't Want Help," *Social Casework*, 34 (July 1953), 304–309; and Walter Haas, "Reaching Out—A Dynamic Concept in Casework," *Social Work*, 4 (July 1959), 41–45. See also Charles King, "Family Therapy with the Deprived Family," *Social Casework*, 48 (April 1967), 203–208; and an interesting discussion by Allison D. Murdach, "Bargaining and Persuasion with Nonvoluntary Clients," *Social Work*, 25 (November 1980), 458–461. See also Chapter 11, note 4.

For examples of situations in which "feeding" (symbolic and concrete) is used to demonstrate worker interest see, for example, Blanca N. Rosenberg, "Planned Short-term Treatment in Developmental Crises," *Social Casework*, 56 (April 1975), 202–204; and James D. Troester and Joel A. Darby, "The Role of the Mini-Meal in Therapeutic Play Groups," *Social Casework*, 57 (February 1976), 97–103. Florence Lieberman also gives an interesting illllustration of this type of work in her discussion of work with emotionally deprived parents in *Social Work with Children* (New York: Human Services Press, 1979), pp. 264–268.

See also Mary Jane Greene and Betty Orman, "Nurturing the Unnurtured," *Social Casework*, 62 (September 1981), 398–404, for an interesting discussion of supportive and other techniques used with the emotionally and economically deprived client.

7. Louise S. Bandler, "Casework—A Process of Socialization," in Eleanor Pavenstedt, ed., *The Drifters* (Boston: Little, Brown, 1967), pp. 255–293. See also Lorraine Pokart Levy, "Services to Parents of Children in a Psychiatric Hospital," *Social Casework*, 58 (April 1977), 204–213.

8. Louise Boatman, "Caseworkers' Judgments of Clients' Hope: Some Correlates among Client-Situation Characteristics and among Workers' Communication Patterns" (doctoral dissertation, Columbia University School of Social Work, New York, 1974).

9. Shirley M. Ehrenkranz, "A Study of Joint Interviewing in the Treatment of Marital Problems," *Social Casework*, 48 (October 1967), 500.

10. For an interesting study of one of these procedures, see Ruth T. Koehler, "The Use of Advice in Casework," *Smith College Studies in Social Work*, 23 (February 1953), 151–165.

11. Inger P. Davis, "Advice-Giving in Parent Counseling," *Social Casework*, 56 (June 1975), 343–347. See also Levy, "Services to Parents," and Lieberman, *Social Work with Children*, pp. 268–270.

12. William Reid and Barbara Shapiro, "Client Reactions to Advice," *Social Service Review*, 43 (June 1969), 165–173. For further support of this view, see also findings by Patricia L. Ewalt and Janice Katz, in "An Examination of Advice Giving as a Therapeutic Intervention," *Smith College Studies in Social Work*, 47 (November 1976), 3–19.

A study by John E. Mayer and Noel Timms, *The Client Speaks: Working Class Impressions of Casework* (New York: Atherton, 1970), p. 93, suggested that satisfied clients received more guidance than less satisfied clients. A questionnaire devised by Marcia K. Goin et al. reported on in "Therapy Congruent with Class-Linked Expectations," *Archives of General Psychiatry*, 13 (August 1965), 133–137, was given to 250 applicants, mostly of lower socioeconomic status, seeking help at an outpatient psychiatric center; interestingly, only 34 percent indicated they wanted advice, in contrast to 52 percent who wanted to solve their problems by talking about feelings and past life. Of those seeking advice, one group received it and another did not, but no apparent differences in improvement rates were found. On the other hand, Geismer and his associates, after examining treatment outcomes, report: "The relatively more successful worker was found to have been supportive rather than directive . . . and to have elicited greater client participation in treatment." See Ludwig L. Geismer et al., *Early Supports for Family Life: A Social Work Experiment* (Metuchen, N.J.: Scarecrow Press, 1972). Clearly, further study of the question of directiveness in general is needed.

13. As suggested by Emanuel Klein in "The Reluctance to Go to School," in Ruth S. Eissler et al., eds., *The Psychoanalytic Study of the Child*, vol. 1 (New York: International Universities Press, 1945), pp. 263–279. See also Edwin Thomas, "Selected Sociobehavioral Techniques and Principles: An Approach to Interpersonal Helping," *Social Work*, 13 (January 1968), 12–26; and *The Sociobehavioral Approach and Application to Social Work* (New York: Council on Social Work Education, 1967). There is considerable evidence that conditioning, essentially a form of direct influence, can be effective in removing phobic symptoms. How-

ever, as Lieberman (*Social Work with Children*, pp. 173–176) points out, crisis intervention to remove school phobia is important, but the underlying anxiety and other symptoms are likely to persist or increase without additional treatment. For further readings on school phobia, see Elisabeth Lassers et al., "Steps in the Return to School of Children with School Phobia," *American Journal of Psychiatry*, 130 (March 1973), 265–268, reprinted in Francis J. Turner, ed., *Differential Diagnosis in Social Work*, 3d ed. (New York: The Free Press, 1983), pp. 819–828; Esther Marine, "School Refusal: Review of the Literature," *Social Service Review*, 42 (December 1968), 464–478; and "School Refusal: Who Should Intervene? (diagnostic and treatment categories)," *Journal of School Psychology*, 7 (1969), 63–70.

14. For illustrations and discussion, see Katherine Baldwin, "Crisis-Focused Casework in a Child Guidance Clinic," *Social Casework*, 49 (January 1968), 28–34; Ethel Panter, "Ego-Building Procedures that Foster Social Functioning," *Social Casework*, 48 (March 1967), 139–145; Eva Y. Deyken et al., "Treatment of Depressed Women," in Turner, *Differential Diagnosis*, 168–183; Sharon Wegscheider, *Another Chance: Hope and Health for the Alcoholic Family* (Palo Alto, Calif.: Science and Behavior Books, 1981), especially chapter 11; Irving Weisman, "Offender Status, Role Behavior and Treatment Considerations," *Social Casework*, 48 (July 1967), 422–425; Janice Wood Wetzel, *Clinical Handbook of Depression* (New York: Gardner Press, 1984); and Sheldon Zimberg et al., eds., *Practical Approaches to Alcoholism Psychotherapy* (New York: Plenum Press, 1978), especially pp. 3–18.

15. See, for example, Nathan W. Ackerman, *Treating the Troubled Family* (New York: Basic Books, 1966), especially pp. 237–288; Laura Farber, "Casework Treatment of Ambulatory Schizophrenics," in Turner, *Differential Diagnosis*, 325–336; Anne O. Freed, "The Borderline Personality," *Social Casework*, 61 (November 1980), 548–558; Margaret M. Heyman, "Some Methods in Direct Casework Treatment of the Schizophrenic," *Journal of Psychiatric Social Work*, 19 (Summer 1949), 18–24; and Judith C. Nelsen, "Treatment Issues in Schizophrenia," in Turner, *Differential Diagnosis*, 337–346.

16. Some general considerations involved in the use of authority of all degrees are well presented by Eliot

Studt. See her articles: "An Outline for Study of Social Authority Factors in Casework," *Social Casework*, 35 (June 1954), 231–238; and "Worker-Client Authority Relationships in Social Work," *Social Work*, 4 (January 1959), 18–28. See also Robert Foren and Bailey Royston, *Authority in Social Casework* (New York: Pergamon Press, 1968); Judith E. Gourse and Martha W. Chescheir, "Authority Issues in Treating Resistant Families," *Social Casework*, 62 (February 1981), 67–73; Elizabeth D. Hutchison, "Use of Authority in Direct Social Work Practice with Mandated Clients," *Social Service Review*, 61 (December 1987), 581–598; and Samuel Mencher, "The Concept of Authority and Social Casework," in *Casework Papers, 1960* (New York: Family Service Association of America, 1960), 126–138.

17. This is discussed by Sid Hirsohn in his "Casework with the Compulsive Mother," *Social Casework*, 32 (June 1951), 254–261. See also Catherine Bittermann, "Marital Adjustment Patterns of Clients with Compulsive Character Disorders: Implications for Treatment," *Social Casework*, 47 (November 1966), 575–582; and James F. Suess, "Short-Term Psychotherapy with the Compulsive Personality and the Obsessive-Compulsive Neurotic," *American Journal of Psychiatry*, 129 (1972), 270–275.

18. This question was studied in the 1950s by Norman A. Polansky and his associates. See Norman A. Polansky and Jacob Kounin, "Clients' Reactions to Initial Interviews: A Field Study," *Human Relations*, 9 (1956), 237–264; and Jacob Kounin et al., "Experimental Studies of Clients' Reactions to Initial Interviews," *Human Relations*, 9 (1956), 265–293. See also Chapter 10, note 2, for additional, more recent, references.

19. See Elizabeth Kubler-Ross, *On Death and Dying* (New York: Macmillan, 1969), especially chapter 9 on "The Patient's Family"; Eda LeShan, *Learning to Say Good-bye* (New York: Avon, 1976); Carleton Pilsecker, "Help for the Dying," in Turner, *Differential Diagnosis*; and Gwen Schwartz-Borden, "Grief Work: Prevention and Intervention," *Social Casework*, 67 (October 1986), 499–505. Dory Krongelb Beatrice, "Divorce: Problems, Goals, and Growth Facilitation," *Social Casework*, 60 (March 1979), 157–165, discusses the importance of "grief work" for divorcing people. In an excellent article by Lois I. Greenberg, "Therapeutic Grief Work with Children," *Social Casework,* 56 (July 1975), 396–403, case examples that demonstrate ways in which children are helped to ventilate grief reactions to parental deaths are given.

20. See Gary D. Anderson, "Enhancing Listening Skills for Work with Abusing Parents," *Social Casework,* 60 (December 1979), 602–608; Aaron Noah Hoorwitz, "Guidelines for Treating Father-Daughter Incest," *Social Casework,* 64 (November 1983), 515–524; and John W. Taylor, "Social Casework and the Multimodel Treatment of Incest," *Social Casework,* 67 (October 1986), 451–459. See also Fred K. Briard,

"Counseling Parents of Children with Learning Disabilities," *Social Casework,* 57 (November 1976), 581–585, for an excellent discussion of the need to help parents of learning-disabled children express guilt so they can respond constructively to their youngsters' needs.

21. See Ehrenkranz, "Study of Joint Interviewing," 498–502.

22. Florence Hollis, *A Typology of Casework Treatment* (New York: Family Service Association of America, 1968), p. 33.

CHAPTER 6

Reflective Discussion of the Person–Situation Configuration

As is evident from the preceding chapters, psychosocial casework places great emphasis on drawing clients into reflective consideration of their situations and of their functioning within them. In Chapter 4 we suggested the usefulness of three major divisions in work of this kind: person-situation reflection, in which consideration is given to the nature of the client's *situation,* his or her *responses* to it, and the interaction of situation and responses; pattern-dynamic reflection, in which response *patterns* or tendencies are considered; and developmental reflection, in which attention is centered on *developmental* factors in these patterns. The first category, the subject of this chapter, is a form of treatment universally used in casework. In the psychosocial approach, the worker characteristically tries to help the client arrive at some form of increased understanding, no matter how much the reflective discussion may need to be buttressed by sustaining, directive, or ventilating work.[1]

The procedures used in person-situation reflection are comments, questions, explanations, and paraverbal communications that promote the client's reflecting primarily upon current and recent events. Person-situation reflection is distinguished from developmental reflection by the fact that the latter is concerned with early life experiences, those that occur during the period when the individual would normally be living with parents, the years of growth to adulthood. Pertinent material located in time between the beginning of adulthood and the present is also considered as part of person-situation reflection.

As indicated earlier, it is possible to break this category into six subdivisions: the clients' consideration (1) of others, of the situation, or of their physical health; (2) of their own actions in terms of outcome, effects on self and others, or alternatives; (3) of the *nature* of their acts, thoughts, and feelings; (4) of the external provocations or stimuli or the immediate inner reasons for reactions and responses; (5) of their own acts, feelings, and thoughts from an evaluative stance; and (6) of their reactions to the worker and the treatment process.

OTHER PEOPLE, HEALTH, SITUATION

The first of these subdivisions has to do with the client's thinking about the *situation,* a form of reflection that might be called "extra-reflection." Here we are dealing partly with perception and partly with a question of knowledge. So often people see only a distorted or one-sided picture of the reality before them, either because they see or hear what they anticipate or because their feelings lead them to ignore or blot out important aspects of a situation. The father who is convinced that his son is retarded like his own older brother may remember or stress only those subjects or activities in which his son has failed, but may without noticing it reveal to the worker areas in which the son's learning has been unimpeded. The worker's first approach would usually be to call the father's attention to events that show the other side of the boy's capacities. In this sort of situation, workers often err by rushing into a discussion of the distortion itself—in this case, the displacement from brother to son—instead of seeing whether, when the client's attention is called to the reality picture, he or she is able by this procedure alone to modify earlier misconceptions. By testing the client's capacity to do this, one can measure the force of the need to distort.

There is a rule of parsimony in treatment as well as in science. If a person is able, with a little help, to perceive more realistically, it is not necessary to pursue the whys and wherefores of a previous failure to do so. If, on the other hand, the distortion does not yield to a look at the facts, the diagnostic information and material that this preliminary effort has provided can later be used to draw the client's attention to the discrepancy itself, between reality and his or her view of it. A perceptive client will often accept the cue and go on to talk about the matters that complicate feelings toward a child. Another will need more prompting from the worker in order for treatment to move on from person-situation reflection to pattern-dynamic or developmental reflection.

A person's lack of understanding of a situation may be due not so much to distortion of

the facts or blindness to them as to actual lack of knowledge about normal reactions. Parents, unaware of the universal turmoil of adolescence, the need to assert independence that so often shows itself in negativism, the seeking of peer approval—whether in clothes, hair, language, or relationships with the opposite sex—sometimes mistake normal and healthy reactions for alienation and revolt. In so doing, they may drive their children toward the very associations they fear. Of course, much of the turmoil of youth has to do with grave problems of our total society—racism, poverty, poor educational opportunities, and so on—problems beyond casework's direct reach, though we must all bear responsibility for trying to modify them. But nothing is gained by the parent's misconstruing normal development as complete loss of a child or by overreacting in a way that alienates the young person at the very moment when communication most needs to be kept open. More understanding can lead to more patience, which in turn furthers the chance of greater exchange of ideas between generations. This implies neither supine parental abnegation of adult thinking about wise and unwise activities nor evasion of parental guidance when reality demands it and the ability to influence the child effectively exists. But it does mean that the parent can be helped to see his child more realistically and in better perspective, thereby coming to understand more fully what the son or daughter is experiencing and to what inner needs and outer pressures he or she is responding. The parent then is certainly in a better position to help rather than hurt the child.

Harmful parental responses can also be due to commonly held prejudices and fears. A mother, for instance, may accept a child's report of being threatened by a child of another background—class, race, religion, or ethnicity—without inquiring for details of what actually happened to see whether the child might have misinterpreted or exaggerated the event or might have provoked the incident. The caseworker, first demonstrating appreciation of the mother's concern, can go on to ask about the details of what happened. This not only clarifies the reality for the mother but indirectly demonstrates the way in which the mother could have handled the situation. For the mother too needs first to comfort her son but then to help him to see whether his report of what happened was entirely accurate. If it was, then thought needs to be given to next steps: the second form of person-situation activity. What can the mother help the child to do? What can the mother herself do? If the report is not accurate, the mother can help her child not only because she enables him to see this particular episode more realistically but because this constitutes a step in the process of strengthening his ego's ability to assess reality.

Lack of imagination about another person's feelings or behavior or failure to identify with the feelings of another may also generate hostility between people. The husband intent on his own professional career fails to see that his wife is frustrated by a dead-end job that does not call on any of her college training. Nor does it occur to him that since she is really inexperienced in keeping house, and tired after eight hours at the office, she needs his help in caring for their home and children, even though they have bought expensive modern equipment. One man in such a situation had concluded that his wife was either incompetent or stubborn because he did not realize the extent to which her feelings of frustration with the circumstances of her life were interfering with functioning. As it turned out, he was not incapable of understanding his wife's reactions and needs when she explained herself in marital treatment sessions. Even before reflecting on his family of origin's attitudes toward women or his own "male chauvinism," he began to perceive her more accurately and fully. Without help, however, he was becoming constantly more irritated and more scornful of her—one of the very factors that drove her to distraction.

The very process of understanding another person more fully sets in motion a change in behavior. As we saw earlier, we do not respond to the actual situation, but to our *perception* of it. Thus, when a distorted perception is corrected, the response often corrects itself.

Joint and family interviews offer excellent opportunities for increased understanding of one person by another. People, such as the woman described above, often reveal aspects of themselves in the relative safety of the treatment situation that they have not had the courage to show in the hostile or anxiety-ridden home situation. A worker can draw out a client's thoughts and feelings for the specific purpose of enabling another family member who is listening to understand the one who is speaking.

The process of understanding the external world takes place not only in relation to people but also in respect to life events. Clients sometimes need help in understanding financial matters, a work situation, medical recommendations, or the implications of their own or someone else's physical condition. The psychoeducational approach to working with the mentally ill and their families has helped all involved to better comprehend the significance of diagnoses, symptoms, and treatment options; psychosis can be far less frightening when everyone—the psychiatric patient and those close to him or her—has an understanding of some of the expectations and requirements of the illness which, in turn, helps with inevitable day-to-day problems that arise.[2] The more fully clients can comprehend these points, the more appropriately will they handle them. Reflective consideration is a more tedious process than advice giving, but it increases the client's competence in a way that directive procedures do not.

Several choices of technique are open to the worker in helping clients to reflect upon their understanding of people and situations. Some workers like to explain things to their clients in a more or less didactic way; others are skillful in leading people to think things through for themselves. Some workers might immediately explain the universality of sibling jealousy to a mother who does not understand the irritability of her three-year-old after the birth of a new baby. In the psychosocial approach, we believe it is usually more effective to ask the mother whether she has herself thought of any explanation for the older child's peevishness. If she has not, there is still the possibility of inquiring whether she thinks the arrival of the new baby might be making Jane feel left out. Psychosocial theory holds that the more one can get clients to think for themselves, the more conviction they will have about the answers they find. Furthermore, their dependency on the worker will not be so greatly increased, and at the same time they will be helped to develop an ego skill that they can apply to other situations.

One form of reflective consideration of the situation is that of telling the client about ways in which changes can be brought through either legal or social action. For example, there are lawyers who are especially interested in problems of poverty and social injustice; in some areas resources are available for those seeking legal help to meet certain external problems, but clients often do not know of these possibilities. Straight information can increase the client's awareness of the resources within reach. Similarly, women's centers that have sprung up in recent years provide advice and activities relevant to various concerns of women. There are also organizations and neighborhood groups in which families can participate in effective group action to protest or improve adverse social conditions. It is just as important for workers to be well informed about these resources as about those of health, education, employment, and recreation.

DECISIONS, CONSEQUENCES, AND ALTERNATIVES

The second type of reflection concerning the person-situation gestalt lies between extra-

reflection and intrareflection and partakes of both. It involves decisions and activities of the client and their effects in interaction with the situation and the people with whom the client lives or associates. Over and over again, workers strive to help clients think about the effects of their own actions on others, or about their consequences for themselves.[3] An action may be a matter of practical decision, such as the advantages and disadvantages of moving into a housing project, the advisability of changing from one job to another, or the wisdom of training for a particular vocation. Or it may be a decision about a medical problem, such as whether or not to undergo recommended surgery.[4] Often, it involves a complicated emotional or interpersonal decision, such as whether or not to separate from husband or wife, to adopt a child, to place a child for adoption, or to have an abortion. In any of these instances, the client tries imaginatively to foresee what personal consequences a plan or decision may have and how it may affect other people whose lives are involved in the decision. The worker contributes to the reflective discussion by bringing the client's attention to aspects of the situation that may have been overlooked.

At other times, it is not a direct decision but an understanding of the effects of the client's own behavior on someone else that is involved in the reflection. A mother may not realize that when she hits her fourteen-year-old son in front of his friends, she is virtually compelling him to defy her in order to maintain the respect of his peers. A husband may not see that when he ridicules his wife about her weight, her angry reaction to him may actually increase her hunger for sweets.[5] A child may not realize that when he is a poor sport in losing games, his friends go to play with someone else.

Here as elsewhere, psychosocial workers hold that the best procedure for the worker is not to "explain" the relationship between behavior and consequences, but to lead the clients to see the sequence themselves: "What did

Mike do when you hit him in front of the other fellows?" "Does your wife eat less when you needle her about her weight?" "What happened just before Johnny left you to play with Bud?" Many times clients will draw the correct conclusions, once the effects of the behavior are brought to their attention. If more help is needed, the worker may go on with, "Do you suppose that...?" or "Have you noticed that...?" or "Often boys of this age...." When a full explanation is really needed, the worker should give it, but not until an effort has been made to see whether the client can arrive at conclusions independently, so that he or she will at least gain experience in thinking in terms of consequences in general as well as some understanding of the particular matter under consideration.

Discussion of decisions and future action is often linked with situational understanding. Greater knowledge of another person or of resources at one's command is naturally followed by consideration of what to do in the light of this knowledge. "How can I talk with Ted about this?" "What should I say to Jean?" The worker could respond with advice, but again it is usually more helpful to encourage clients to think the answer out for themselves, since this will increase their capacity to respond to future situations without help. Similarly, when the use of a resource is at issue, clients should be led step by step to consider the advantages and disadvantages rather than being advised to take one course or another.

A more subtle sort of misunderstanding about consequences is that of fearing reactions that in fact need not occur. A husband or wife may underestimate a spouse's ability to accept differences between them. A man may think that his wife will be angry if he takes a night to be with his friends when in actuality she might be glad for an evening alone, or vice versa. Fear that differences in lifestyles, tastes, feelings, pastimes will necessarily bring withdrawal of love is common and sometimes these do in fact be-

come a separating factor. But this is not a necessary consequence if thought is given to the effects of one person's behavior on another. Often, it is not the difference itself but the way in which the difference is asserted that makes the trouble. Close examination of this type of interaction is a very important type of reflection about consequences.

The worker can ask for details of the circumstances surrounding what appears to be a difference of this sort. "How did it come up?" "How did you put it?" "What did John really say or do?" "Have you talked it over?" "She doesn't sound so upset to me; are you sure...?" And so on. In this sort of situation, there is a close interweaving of thinking about consequences and trying to understand other persons and their needs. Again, family and couple sessions provide an excellent opportunity for discussions of differences and the meanings these have to the particular people involved.

INWARDLY DIRECTED AWARENESS

The third subdivision of this type of treatment, which parallels the procedure of helping the client look outward with greater perceptive accuracy, has to do with increasing the client's awareness of the nature of his or her own responses, thoughts, and feelings. These processes, which are forms of intrareflection, sometimes involve awareness of so-called hidden feelings or reactions. There are many degrees of "hiddenness." A client may be perfectly aware of reactions but may be afraid to speak of them because of shame or fears of ridicule or criticism. This may be the case, for example, with a mother who is fully aware of her anger toward one of her children but is ashamed to admit it, or with a woman who expects disapproval if she tells the worker about a recent abortion and her mixed feelings about it. Or the client may have refrained from talking about feelings because of a lack of recognition of their significance or importance: a man may know he is ashamed of having had a mental break-down but may never speak of it to the worker because he does not realize the way in which this shame is related to his employment failures. Or the client may be truly unaware of feelings because they are not part of conscious thought: a mother may not even be aware, for example, of the strong feelings of hostility she is harboring toward her child. We are talking here not of *early* memories but of reactions to current life. The uncovering of hidden *early* memories is part of the process of developmental reflection rather than of the *current* person-situation gestalt.

When workers believe they can "read" a client's thoughts or feelings, it is a great temptation to do so out loud. There are occasions when this is necessary, either because the client is unable to bring these into the open but will be relieved if the worker does so or because there is therapeutic justification for bringing them out even though this may produce discomfort. (Of course, when the worker *does* decide to speak for someone who has not yet spoken for herself or himself, it is essential to be open to corrections provided by the client; our educated or intuitive hunches can miss the mark to one degree or another.) Far more often, rather than articulating hidden material, skill lies in finding ways of enabling clients to bring it out themselves. In these instances, it becomes important for workers to manage their own curiosity or uneasiness about undisclosed matters.

Where full awareness is present, the client generally speaks about relevant material without any specific prompting, on becoming more secure with the worker in response to a sustaining approach. If, however, it is obvious to the worker that the client is struggling with the question of whether to speak of something or not, the worker may want to handle this hesitation directly by commenting that it is hard to speak freely but that perhaps, as the client becomes more comfortable, he or she will be able to do so. Or the worker may gently say, "I know

it is hard to talk sometimes, but I can only help you with the things you can bring yourself to talk about." Or, "Can you tell me what it is that makes it so hard for you to talk about this?" Or, "I have a feeling that you may be afraid I will criticize you. Is there anything I've said that makes you feel this way?" Or, "I'm not here to criticize you but to help you." Sustaining comments are particularly useful in putting the client more at ease.

At other times, when the worker is fairly sure of what a client is withholding, it may be possible to make comments that refer tangentially to the anticipated content, thus inviting the client to talk about it but still not facing him or her with it directly. One can, for instance, give reassurance of acceptance in advance of the client's communication: "It isn't always possible, you know, to feel love for a difficult child." Or, "Sometimes mothers, even though they try not to, do dislike a child." Or, "Sometimes a person is so unhappy about a pregnancy that they feel they have to do something about it." Often one can call the client's attention to discrepancies between fact and feeling, or overemphasis, or inconsistencies, as these may point toward important feelings. Sometimes this can be done merely by repeating the revealing statement in a questioning tone. For example, with an inflection of mild surprise, the worker might say to the uncomplaining but harried mother of a difficult child, "Are you saying that you *weren't* angry with Andy when he—once again—refused to go to bed?"

On the less frequent occasions when it is actually advisable to put the matter into words for the client, this can be done tentatively, making it possible for the client to maintain defenses if needed and also safeguarding the person from agreeing too readily to a possibly incorrect interpretation if the worker is not certain of the client's thinking. Occasionally, a direct, unqualified interpretation is helpful, but for this the worker should be very sure of the ground on which the comment is based.[6] As in the simpler process of spontaneous ventilation, when feelings are brought to expression, the worker has several choices as to the next step. It may be helpful to turn to sustaining procedures, trying immediately to allay the client's anxiety or guilt; one may seek to involve the client in further understanding of the dynamics or of developmental aspects of his or her reactions; at other times, it may be more advisable to concentrate on the immediate consequences of these reactions in the client's current life.

Closely related to the process of helping a person to become aware of feelings and thoughts is the process of encouraging the individual to recognize and consider unusual or problem activities or irrational reactions. The worker calls the client's attention to the fact that she has several times called Mary "Janet" or comments on the oddity that the client continuously works overtime without extra compensation for a boss he says he hates, despite the fact that he could easily get another job. This very important procedure is often neglected by inexperienced workers who lack the patience to wait for clients to do their own thinking. Again, the psychosocial position is that the more clients can think for themselves the better. When the client's attention is called to unproductive behavior or irrational reactions, if the individual is capable of so doing he or she is very likely to go on to consideration of either the consequences of the behavior or the reasons for it. The worker who omits this step and rushes on to an explanation or interpretation deprives the client of the chance to seek this out for himself. Furthermore, the risk of an inaccurate or inadequate explanation is always greater when trust is put in one's own insight instead of the client's.

RESPONSES TO SITUATIONAL PROVOCATIONS AND STIMULI

A fourth form of reflection consists of the effort to understand some of the reasons for reactions:

that is, the external provocations and internal thought processes that contribute to a reaction. A husband who is opposed to his wife's working looks at the possibility that he feels unloved because for him her managing their home symbolized love. Or he considers the possibility that her working seems to him to belittle his own place in the family. This type of causation lies in interactions with others, reasons for doing something that lie either in "the outer" or in a person's own feeling about "the outer." The worker might comment: "You have talked about how upset you were to lose the baby. Do you think this precipitated your present anger at Ben?" Or, "Does it seem to you that when you think your supervisor might criticize you, you become anxious and then start making mistakes?" Or, "Do you think you are actually most likely to withdraw from Lisa when she is especially affectionate?" Or, simply, "You seem tense today. Has anything happened?"

SELF-EVALUATION

Still another type of reflection, the fifth, has to do with self-evaluation. This may be in the superego sense of right or wrong or in the sense of thinking about the self-image, principles, values, preferences that have value implications. A worker may comment, "Don't you think you are really expecting too much of yourself?" Or, "Which means more to you, success in this competitive job or a closer relationship with Betty?"

Another facet of this process comes into play when the worker helps a client to use external realities to correct a distorted self-image. A boy who is excessively fearful of a school test is reminded of his successes in previous tests. A woman is helped to evaluate whether her image of herself as weak and helpless is justified by the facts. A girl who says she is not popular and has no one to invite to a party is encouraged to think over the several people she has previously said actually do like her. A man who feels unsure of his ability to perform on the job after absence due to serious illness is helped to reflect on capacities that remain intact in spite of current physical limitations. This type of reflection is closely related to reflection that develops a better understanding of external realities; indeed, the two processes often occur in rapid succession. But consideration of external reality here is the means by which clients are helped to become aware of misperceptions about themselves; it is not for the purpose of understanding another person. It is essentially *inwardly*, not *outwardly*, directed reflection.

REACTIONS TO THE WORKER AND TO TREATMENT

Psychosocial casework stresses the importance in person-situation reflection of a sixth form of reflection. This concerns the client's reactions to the worker, to treatment, or to agency rules and requirements. Just as the client may misperceive other aspects of the situation, so he or she may distort or fail to understand casework and the caseworker. Here, too, previous life experiences may lead the client to imagine hostility where it does not exist, to anticipate criticism, to fear domination, or to expect inappropriate gratification of dependency wishes. Or the client may simply lack knowledge of the nature of the casework "situation."

The probability of this type of reaction can be greatly lessened if there is adequate discussion, preferably in the first interview, of the purpose and nature of the contact—what the client wants, how the worker will try to help, the fact that these two people will be working together in an effort to lessen or resolve the dilemma— bringing out the mutuality of the effort.

There is a tendency to think that there is something mysterious about the casework relationship, something that makes it fragile and untouchable except by the very expert. In fact, it is no more complicated than—but just as complicated as—any other relationship. In the type of reflective discussion considered here, atti-

tudes and responses to the caseworker are handled in the same way as other attitudes and responses. Where distortions or misunderstandings exist, the clinical social worker tries to straighten them out by demonstrating the realities of his or her behavior toward the client and the actual nature of treatment.[7] If a dependent client accuses the worker of indifference because the worker is unwilling to prolong the interview, the worker may explain that time has to be scheduled, that it is not a matter of lack of interest, and that they can go on with the same discussion in their next interview. If, on the other hand, this represents a repeated attempt to control the worker, it is well to suggest that it seems to have become a problem, and that it is one that the client and the worker should look at in the next interview.

Understanding by the client of reactions to the worker can be a very fruitful source of understanding of similar reactions in other parts of his or her life. If the client thinks the worker is angry, it is well to find out what this conclusion is based on. If a remark has been misinterpreted, the worker can indicate what was really meant and reassure the client that there is no anger. (This assumes that the worker is truly not angry. When, as occasionally happens, one *is* angry, it is usually best to admit it and either explain why, or, when appropriate, apologize, or do both.) If the client expects advice and is disappointed at not getting it, a simple explanation of why the worker doesn't think it will help may clear the air. Clients do not need long and theoretical explanations of treatment processes, but when they ask for information or when misunderstandings arise, it is not only appropriate but essential to discuss the nature of casework in order for it to become a constructive participatory process. Participation in treatment is a role to which clients may be unaccustomed and it may need to be explicitly defined.

If a client is angry at being kept waiting, this annoyance should be aired or at least acknowledged. If clients are dissatisfied with treatment and think it is a waste of time to come for interviews, the dissatisfaction should be brought into the open so that the reasons for it can be discussed and misunderstandings straightened out. If they fantasize that the worker is interested in a personal relationship with them, this, too, must be brought into open expression.

Differences in background—education, nationality, color, religion, or minority status of any kind—may create a barrier to the development of a relationship of trust. This may be because of previous experience, prejudice, reluctance to turn to a representative of another race or ethnic group for help, or the worker's lack of knowledge that has led to misunderstanding or to actions that have unintentionally offended the client. The worker's first concern, of course, is to prevent such tension by being sufficiently sensitive to the likelihood of its occurrence as to guard against behavior that will either precipitate or aggravate it. This requires both knowledge of how a person of a different background may react and sensitivity to beginning reactions indicating that offense has been given or is anticipated. If hostility exists or offense results—or is thought to exist or to have resulted— it is best to try to bring it into the open so that it can be discussed. More frequently than not, honest discussion combined with sincere goodwill at least alleviates the tension. Obviously, it is important not to assume that hostility exists where it does not and not to assume it is due to race, ethnic, or class differences when in reality it has a quite different source.

When clients come to an agency because someone else—a school principal, marital partner, or concerned person in the community— insists, the worker can anticipate hostility and resistance. Although sustaining techniques are important, as noted earlier, reflective procedures cannot be dispensed with. Clients must know why the worker is there and for what initial purpose. They must know that they will not be judged, pushed around, or manipulated.

They must know that resentment is both understood and respected and that the worker asks primarily for a chance to demonstrate goodwill and potential helpfulness. The worker need not say this in so many words, but in one way or another the substance of these communications must get across to the client, along with an opportunity to express anger and fears about the intrusion.

It is sometimes held that caseworkers should not bring the client's thoughts about them to the surface, except in intensive psychological treatment. Experience has repeatedly shown the value of frank discussion of client's reactions to workers in the most matter-of-fact practical work. Psychosocial casework holds that all casework depends in part upon establishing and maintaining a sound relationship between client and worker. Obstacles to such a relationship can occur in any form of treatment and can best be removed by recognition and discussion. We discussed earlier the sustaining steps that must often be taken to convince the hard-to-reach or involuntary client of the worker's goodwill. It is equally important in such cases to bring the client's distrust into the open so that misconceptions can be explored and, when possible, corrected. Hard-to-reach clients have often had very bad experiences with other social workers or with people whom they mistakenly thought to be social workers, or their neighbors or friends have had such experiences. It is natural that they should expect and fear similar treatment from the current worker. Realistic discussion can be a first step in opening up the possibility of a more constructive casework relationship. This and other aspects of the client-worker relationship will be discussed in further detail in Chapter 10.

It has taken a good many pages to describe the treatment processes involved in reflective discussion of the person-situation configuration. This is not inappropriate, however, for, as we have seen, the type of understanding examined here is a central part of psychosocial casework treatment with all types of clients and problems.[8] In a great many cases, more extensive understanding is either unnecessary or inadvisable. Frequently, however, a certain amount of dynamic and developmental understanding is embedded in what is primarily person-situation understanding. Sometimes the worker sees an opportunity to deepen the client's understanding at crucial points. Interviews sometimes flow back and forth between the two types of understanding with person-situation reflection forming the base to which from time to time dynamic or developmental understanding is added. In situations in which dynamic and developmental reflection is a *major* part of treatment, preliminary discussion of current realities can provide important diagnostic information and serve as a base from which to proceed to thought about dynamic or developmental factors.

NOTES

1. Although the same term is not always used, the importance of "reflective discussion" has been referred to in the literature over the years. See, for example, Rosemary Reynolds and Else Siegle, "A Study of Casework with Sado-Masochistic Marriage Partners," *Social Casework,* 40 (December 1959), 545–551, for discussion of the use of reflective or "logical" discussion along with other techniques. Sidney Berkowitz also implies the use of such techniques in his article, "Some Specific Techniques of Psychosocial Diagnosis and Treatment in Family Casework," *Social Casework,* 36 (November 1955), 399–406, though it is not directly spelled out. Gordon Hamilton, in the revised edition of *Theory and Practice of Social Casework* (New York: Columbia University Press, 1951), p. 250, uses the term "counseling" to designate many of the techniques referred to in this chapter. William J. Reid and Ann Shyne refer to similar procedures in their terms "logical discussion," "identifying specific reactions," and "confrontation"; see *Brief and Extended Casework* (New York: Columbia University Press, 1969), pp. 70–72. The term "confrontation" is frequently found in casework literature and often refers to reflective procedures described in this chap-

ter; as one example of many, see Lois Lester, "The Special Needs of the Female Alcoholic," *Social Casework,* 63 (October 1982), 451–456. Some techniques referred to as "cognitive"—currently a popular term—are the same as reflective discussion; for example, see Terri D. Combs, "A Cognitive Therapy for Depression: Theory, Techniques, and Issues," *Social Casework,* 61 (June 1980), 361–366.

2. For use with parents faced with problems concerning their children, see Katherine Baldwin, "Crisis-Focused Casework in a Child Guidance Clinic," *Social Casework,* 49 (January 1968), 28–34; Harriette C. Johnson, "Working with Stepfamilies: Principles of Practice," in Francis J. Turner, ed., *Differential Diagnosis and Treatment in Social Work,* 3d ed. (New York: The Free Press, 1983), 829–839; Audrey T. McCullum, "Mothers' Preparation for Their Children's Hospitalization," *Social Casework,* 48 (July 1967), 407–415; and Ann Murphy et al., "Group Work with Parents of Children with Down's Syndrome," *Social Casework,* 53 (February 1972), 114–119. Donna M. Oradei and Nancy S. Waite, in "Admissions Conferences for Families of Stroke Patients," *Social Casework,* 56 (January 1975), 21–26, discuss a hospital program designed, in part, to provide families with information about the medical condition of the patients. Louise Bandler also gives many illustrations of this form of reflective discussion from her work with extremely deprived families in her chapter, "Casework—A Process of Socialization: Gains, Limitations, Conclusions," in Eleanor Pavenstedt, ed., *The Drifters: Children of Disorganized Lower-Class Families* (Boston: Little, Brown, 1967). See Rosemary Moynihan et al., "AIDS and Terminal Illness," *Social Casework,* 69 (June 1988), 380–387, for a discussion of issues that require reflection by AIDS victims. See Kayla F. Bernheim and Anthony F. Lehman, *Working with Families of the Mentally Ill* (New York: W. W. Norton, 1985), for a clear presentation of the psychoeducational approach. A useful article that describes this procedure in work with the mentally ill can be found in Mary Frances Libassi, "The Chronically Mentally Ill: A Practice Approach," *Social Casework,* 69 (February 1988), 88–96.

3. For illustrations and further discussion, see Margaret Ball, "Issues of Violence in Family Casework," *Social Casework,* 58 (January 1977), 3–12; Laura Farber, "Casework Treatment of Ambulatory Schizophrenics," in Turner, *Differential Diagnosis,* 325–

366; Aaron Noah Hoorwitz, "Guidelines for Treating Father-Daughter Incest," *Social Casework,* 64 (November 1983), 515–524; and Ronald H. Rooney, "Socialization Strategies for Involuntary Clients," *Social Casework,* 69 (March 1988), 131–140. Of value also is Reeva Lesoff's article, "What to Say When...," *Clinical Social Work Journal,* 5 (Spring 1977), 66–76, which discusses the writer's own interesting approach to helping parents recognize and reflect on the effects of their attitudes and actions on their children's behavior.

4. An excellent example of this is found in Barbara Bender, "Management of Acute Hospitalization Anxiety," *Social Casework* (January 1976), 19–26. Here the person-situation technique is combined with ventilation and developmental reflection, but the emphasis is on fuller understanding of the surgery.

5. Miriam Jolesch refers to this type of work in joint interviews with marital partners in her article, "Casework Treatment of Young Married Couples," *Social Casework,* 43 (May 1962), 245–251. See also Sally A. Holmes et al., "Working with the Parent in Child-Abuse Cases," *Social Casework,* 56 (January 1975), 3–12, who discuss and illustrate approaches to helping abusive parents become aware of when they have unrealistic expectations of their children.

6. A very interesting illustration of the use of this procedure is found in Pauline L. Scanlon, "Social Work with the Mentally Retarded Client," *Social Casework,* 59 (March 1978), 161–166.

7. See three excellent articles, Carl Hartman and Diane Reynolds, "Resistant Clients: Confrontation, Interpretation, and Alliance," *Social Casework,* 68 (April 1987), 205–213; Judith C. Nelsen, "Dealing with Resistance in Social Work Practice," *Social Casework,* 56 (December 1975), 587–592; and Sonya Rhodes, "The Personality of the Worker: An Unexplored Dimension in Treatment," *Social Casework,* 60 (May 1979), 259–264, for further discussions of this point.

In addition to references already given, good illustrations can be found especially in articles on work with people with schizophrenic disorders, with the "hard-to-reach," and with other clients who have high resistance to accepting help. See Celia Benny et al., "Clinical Complexities in Work Adjustment of Deprived Youth," *Social Casework,* 50 (June 1969), 330–336; Howard Goldstein, "A Cognitive-Humanistic Approach to the Hard-to-Reach Client," *Social Case-*

work, 67 (January 1986), 27–36; Dale E. Hardman, "The Matter of Trust," *Crime and Delinquency,* 15 (April 1969), 203–218; Margene M. Shea, "Establishing the Initial Relationships with Schizophrenic Patients," *Social Casework,* 37 (January 1956), 25–29; and Thomas J. Powell, "Negative Expectations of Treatment: Some Ideas About the Source and Management of Two Types," *Clinical Social Work Journal,* 1 (Fall 1973), 177–186. See Chapter 10 for additional references.

8. Additional illustrations and descriptions of approaches that use the kind of reflective procedures discussed in this chapter can be found in Janet Bintzler, "Diagnosis and Treatment of Borderline Personality Organization," *Clinical Social Work Journal,* 6 (Summer 1978), 100–107; Samuel P. Chiancola, "The Process of Separation and Divorce: A New Approach," *Social Casework,* 59 (October 1978), 494–499; Edith M. Freeman et al., "Clinical Practice with Employed Women," *Social Casework,* 68 (September 1987), 413–420; Larry Icard and Donald M. Traunstein, "Black, Gay, Alcoholic Men: Their Character and Treatment," *Social Casework,* 68 (May 1987), 267–272; Celia Leikin, "Identifying and Treating the Alcoholic," *Social Casework,* 67 (February 1986), 67–73; Salvador Minuchin and Braulio Montalvo, "Techniques for Working with the Disorganized Low Socio-Economic Families," *American Journal of Orthopsychiatry,* 37 (October 1967), 880–887; Jeanette Oppenheimer, "Use of Crisis Intervention in Casework with the Cancer Patient and His Family," *Social Work,* 12 (April 1967), 44–52; Sharon B. Shaw, "Parental Aging: Clinical Issues in Adult Psychotherapy," *Social Casework,* 68 (September 1987), 406–412; Ronald L. Taylor, "Marital Therapy in the Treatment of Incest," *Social Casework,* 65 (April 1984), 195–202; Philip W. Walker, "Premarital Counseling for the Developmentally Disabled," *Social Casework,* 58 (October 1977), 475–479; and Mary Warmbrod, "Counseling Bereaved Children: Stages in the Process," *Social Casework,* 67 (June 1986), 351–358.

In his interesting study of workers' and clients' perceptions of what helps, Anthony Maluccio found that both groups deemed reflective discussion between worker and client, in which workers are sensitive to clients' feelings, goals, etc., is *the* most important process of successful treatment. See Anthony Maluccio, *Learning from Clients* (New York: The Free Press, 1979).

CHAPTER 7

Reflective Consideration of Pattern-Dynamic and Developmental Factors

The two remaining forms of reflective communication are those that seek to promote dynamic and developmental understanding. Intrapsychic forces of which a person is not fully aware may so strongly influence behavior that it is not possible to perceive and act differently in response to person-situation reflection alone. It is sometimes helpful to turn such a person's attention briefly to the underlying dynamics of his or her personality or to early life experiences that are still unfavorably influencing current adjustment. Often, but not always, both types of understanding can be developed.

We are using here the word "understanding" rather than the term *insight* because the latter is used in psychoanalysis primarily to refer to understanding the workings of the *unconscious*.[1] Readers will recall that the terms *dynamic* and *developmental reflection* and the understanding to which these can lead refer in psychosocial theory primarily to *preconscious* rather than *unconscious* material. Some *preconscious* material, however, is not accessible merely by shifting attention to it. It has long been recognized that certain technical procedures can be and are employed by casework for the purpose of keeping the work for the most part on conscious and preconscious rather than unconscious verbalizations. Interviews are usually held with client and worker able to look directly at each other, they are spaced farther apart than in analysis proper—most often a week between interviews, though sometimes the client is seen several times a week—we use a permissive, eductive type of interviewing, distinctly not the same as free association.

Nevertheless, reflection on material that derives from the unconscious, such as in the discussion of some dreams or "slips," may be extremely valuable in achieving self-understanding. It is also true that unconscious or preconscious material may spontaneously rise to the surface under particular circumstances. An experience repressed or suppressed for years or even decades may suddenly be provoked into consciousness by a current, often powerful, event. Sometimes a client may be reminded of long-forgotten incidents when simply asked about early memories.

Readers will recall the discussion in Chapter 2 about the balance of forces within and between the various parts of the personality. Psychosocial theory supported by practice experience maintains that dynamic and developmental reflection, even though they may not lead to insight into the unconscious, can in many instances bring enough modification in the balance between functional and dysfunctional aspects of the personality system to strengthen the individual's ability to cope with the problems for which he or she seeks a clinical social worker's assistance.

REFLECTION CONCERNING DYNAMIC FACTORS

When we consider dynamic factors with the client, we are simply extending the process of intrareflection, using procedures—comments, questions, occasionally explanations—whose content and timing are designed to help the individual to pursue further some of the intrapsychic reasons for his or her feelings, attitudes, and ways of acting, to understand the influence of one personality characteristic upon another: in other words, the way in which thoughts and emotions work. Here we go beyond the understanding of single interactions or even a series of interactions, as was done in the person-situation gestalt, to consideration of the intrapsychic *pattern* or tendency that contributes to the interaction. Often, the client is aware, sometimes clearly and sometimes vaguely, of unrealistic or inappropriate behavior. The client may delve into the question of "why" without any prompting from the caseworker. At other times, the worker takes the first step by calling the inappropriateness or inconsistency to the client's attention—"Have you noticed that you don't have trouble in being firm with Paula but seem to be afraid to be firm with Ed?"—to a mother who does not realize that her difficulty in disciplining her son springs from her desperate fear of losing his love. At this point, the worker is moving beyond one interpersonal event to raise a question about a series of such events, a pattern. Presumably,

individual instances of difficulty in showing appropriate firmness had been considered before, but without enabling this mother to act more appropriately. The worker then suggests to the client that this may be part of a general tendency. Recognition of the pattern can turn the client's attention to the question of *why*. The answer may lie in displacement of feelings from husband to son, in underlying hostility to her son, in greater desire for this child's love, in specific early life events—to name a few of the possibilities—or in some combination of these.

Similarly, in another situation the worker says, "I wonder how it is that you can be so understanding of the children and yet seem unable to try to understand your husband" to a woman who is ordinarily very perceptive of other people's feelings but who only now begins to realize that she does not want to lessen the conflict with her husband because she fears intimacy and is uncomfortable with their sexual relationship; for many years she had felt "safer" not to be on good terms with him. Or, "What do you suppose makes you constantly insult people you say you want to be friends with?" to a man who defends himself against his fear of rejection by first antagonizing others. Often, the worker has already sensed what the underlying tendency is. Whenever possible, however, the worker encourages the client to seek the answer for himself rather than interpreting if for him.

Sometimes the client does not recognize problem behavior; in other words, it is *ego-syntonic*, acceptable to the ego, and must become *ego-alien*, unacceptable to the ego, if there is to be motivation to try to understand and modify it. A mother who continually got into tempestuous fights at the table with her son saw her reactions only in terms of his slow and sloppy eating habits, which she felt made such scenes inevitable. After a substantial period of patient listening, reflective discussion, and suggestions, the worker responded to the heated description of a stormy session with the comment

"You are like two children battling each other, aren't you?" Obviously, the remark carried a value judgment, for adults do not consider it a compliment to be told that they are behaving childishly. It carried force with this client because a strong relationship had been established between her and her worker, which made her value the worker's opinion. The fact that the worker rarely took a position of this sort gave it added significance. Sometimes the client, in response to such a stimulus, begins to think about reasons for his or her reactions; at other times, further comment is needed: "There seems to be something between you and George that we need to understand; what thoughts come to you about it?" In this situation, the client went on first to the realization that she prolonged the scenes at the table for the relief she derived from hitting her son and later to the discovery that she had identified her son with her husband and was taking out on him anger she did not dare to express directly to her husband.

Clients usually will seek understanding of thoughts or actions only when some dissatisfaction is felt with them, when they are recognized as unprofitable or in some way inappropriate or ego-alien. Until this attitude exists, dynamic interpretations will probably fall on deaf ears. When it does exist or has been brought into being, the client will often be able to arrive at understanding with relatively little use of interpretation by the worker.

Almost any aspect of the personality that is either conscious or preconscious may come under scrutiny in this type of procedure. Occasionally, unconscious matters may come through, but in general basic casework is not designed to uncover unconscious material.

Ego Defenses

A very common area in which understanding is sought is that of the ego defenses, such as avoidance, defensive hostility, and the various mechanisms of turning against the self: projec-

tion, intellectualization, rationalization, suppression, inhibition, and isolation. "Have you ever noticed that sometimes people get angry when they are scared? I wonder if you weren't pretty edgy about having that talk with your brother-in-law and in a way hit out at him before he had a chance to hit you." "Have you noticed how often you go off into this kind of theoretical discussion when I'm trying to get you to think about your own feelings toward Mary?" "You know, it's good that you try to learn so much about children, but sometimes I wonder whether it is a way of avoiding letting yourself realize what strong feelings you have when Johnny acts this way." "Do you think your wife was really mad, or were you so angry yourself that you kind of expected she would be? What did she actually say at the beginning?" "Do you think that you are feeling depressed because you are really so mad at Fred but feel you can't let it out? Sometimes, you know, you can turn those angry feelings against yourself and then you feel depressed." Questions and comments such as these can be as effective in family and marital sessions as they are in individual treatment, as Chapters 15 through 18 will illustrate.

Initially, defense mechanisms often have to be explained to clients because they may not be familiar with the way they work and cannot be expected to arrive at this kind of understanding entirely on their own. Subsequently, however, clients are frequently able to spot their own use of a particular defense. One of the goals of this type of treatment is to enable them to do this for themselves.

The greatest care is necessary in work with defenses, however, for they are self-protective mechanisms used by the personality to ward off anxiety. They should not be abruptly "broken through," but "worked through," when evaluation indicates that the individual is able to bear the anxiety involved. For the most part, interpretations should be made tentatively, and certainly in an atmosphere of acceptance, which often needs to be put into words.[2]

Superego

Important as defense mechanisms are, they are by no means the only part of the personality under scrutiny in the process of dynamic understanding. Often, certain superego characteristics need to be thought about, especially the oversensitivity of the severe conscience. A client who is too hard on herself may be helped by knowing that she is suffering from self-criticism rather than from the too-high requirements of others. The person who feels deeply hurt by the discovery of imperfections in himself or herself may be helped by recognizing that the demand for perfection is a function of his or her own personality. "Have you noticed how upset you get whenever anyone makes the slightest criticism of your work?" "You hold very high standards for yourself, don't you?" "I think you are harder on yourself than anyone else would be."[3]

One of the hazards of helping a person to become aware of superego severity is that the worker may appear to the client to be too lax in standards. It is extremely important to prevent this impression, and great care must be taken not to seem to be sponsoring antisocial behavior. If the client does, nevertheless, react in this way, the reaction must be brought into the open and discussed. "I have a feeling that you are worried that I may be too easygoing. Let's talk about it." It is important to clarify this question, making it clear that the worker is not opposed to maintaining standards but to experiencing unrealistic or harmful severity of conscience. When the client's feelings about this are brought out in the open and discussed, not only is the worker's position clarified but this may lead to a reflective discussion that reveals that it is the client's pattern to judge others in a similar manner.

A client who specifically illustrates this point is the mother of a child who had been sent to the agency for treatment because of school failures inconsistent with his intelligence. She was a very religious Protestant woman who set extremely high standards for herself and who initially found treatment difficult because the need to recognize that she might be contributing to her son's troubles shattered her faith in herself as a good mother. Every attempt at developing her understanding, no matter how carefully worded, was taken as a criticism from which she cringed. One of her underlying problems was her effort to suppress and inhibit all hostile impulses, and she felt extreme guilt over her failures to do so. When the worker tried to reduce her self-condemnation, she thought the worker was trying to undermine her faith and principles.

One day she brought a Bible to the interview and seemed quite agitated. When the worker asked her gently whether she had brought the Bible for a special reason, she opened it to the famous letter of Paul to the Corinthians on love, reading particularly the verse "When I was a child, I spoke as a child, I felt as a child, I thought as a child; now that I am a man I have put away childish things," and she cried as she finished it. The worker said it was a beautiful letter and asked whether she had ever thought of why it was written. Did she think perhaps Paul might have observed that many people brought into adulthood feelings and thoughts from childhood? Perhaps he wished to counsel people to put away these feelings and behave like adults. No one could quarrel with the ideals of love, charity, and understanding. Religion and psychiatry have the same goals; the only question is how to achieve them.

As the client seemed confused, the worker put her thoughts in terms of gardening, a known interest of this client. "If you had a garden and weeds were choking out the good plants, you could cut off the tops of the weeds and the garden would look good, but the roots would still be there. Wouldn't it be better to pull out the roots? It would be harder but the results would be better. The same thing is true for human emotions. Many of us try to hide our difficulties and stamp them down, but this takes energy that could be used for better things. It seems worthwhile to try to uproot the difficulties. The only method I know for uprooting them is to understand and face things that are painful and intolerable. I'm not arguing against the goals of religion, but sometimes I question the way it goes about attaining them." The client was silent for several minutes, and then said she was greatly relieved and that she had had no idea the caseworker had such deep understanding of her feelings.

A similar difficulty can occur under almost opposite circumstances. The client whose control of impulses is tenuous may have great anxiety about a sudden breakthrough of irrational behavior if strong, hidden desires are allowed to reach awareness. With such clients, it is extremely important for the worker to make clear the distinction between recognizing a desire or wish and carrying it out. One can state explicitly that this is not encouragement to act upon impulses but rather an expression of confidence that the client can be aware of them and yet effectively control them. If this type of approach is to be used, however, knowledge of the client must indicate that the ego is in fact able to control such impulses once they are recognized. When a danger of breakthrough does exist, obviously, it is better not to disturb the defenses against it. Careful diagnostic assessment, although always important, is essential to work in which greater understanding of one's own emotional patterns is involved.

Ego Functioning

Understanding can also be gained of various ego functions when they contribute to personal problems. It can be helpful for some individuals to become aware of excessively strong needs of the personality that, showing themselves in such traits as great dependence or a high degree of narcissism, can cause trouble for the individual. Persisting distortions in perception

and unrealistic ideas about one's own tendencies and capacities are also among the many ego areas in which help can be given. In the following case, for instance, part of the difficulty lay in the client's unrealistic fear of being unable to control impulses.

A retired man in his late sixties was extremely angry at his wife for pressuring him to relocate with her to another part of the country, a move he did not want to make. She had taken several trips to explore retirement homes, and he was becoming extremely anxious and frustrated by her persistence. At the same time, he had not been able to state his position on the matter firmly, nor did he initiate a discussion with her of possible alternatives or compromises. He felt victimized and defeated. The day his wife was to fly home from one of her trips, he called his caseworker in a severely frightened state. He confided that he had momentarily wished that the plane would crash. The worker, whom he trusted, was able to help him reduce his fear by pointing out that it often happens that when people feel angry and frustrated they have violent wishes and thoughts. Knowing the man as well as she did, the caseworker was able to reassure him that his impulse to see his wife dead in no way meant that he would therefore act on his wish in any way. The breakthrough of deeply hostile feelings led this very controlled and passive man to believe that he would either become ungovernably violent ("I feel like a murderer," he said) or break down emotionally. Once these suppressed feelings came to the surface, he was finally able to talk with his wife about his wishes for retirement. From this experience, he was able to reflect on his lifelong pattern of suppressing his own desires for fear he would lose the love of people close to him. Furthermore, he began to recognize how his pent-up anger was based on his feelings of helplessness in the face of his wife's tendency to dominate him.

An important step in the process of dynamic understanding is the client's bringing reason and judgment—cognitive awareness—to bear upon the personality characteristic and its functioning that has been brought to his or her attention. It was not enough for the religious mother to see that she was trying to handle her anger by suppressing it; she had to be able to think about what she was doing, to bring her own judgment to bear upon it. She had to become convinced that her way of handling her feelings was not helping her son before she was ready to try to give it up.

The client's reactions to the worker are also a fruitful source of dynamic understanding. As defense mechanisms or personality characteristics such as fear of criticism or excessive dependence come into play in the client-worker relationship, they can be used to enable the client to see the inner workings of his or her personality in action. The client can then use this understanding to recognize similar dynamics operating in other life experiences. These issues will be discussed in further detail in Chapter 10.

Pattern-dynamic reflection is usually built upon previous consideration of the current person-situation configuration. A few comments about the dynamics involved may enable the client to understand personality patterns more fully. This in turn may lessen the strength of some of the deterrents to realistic and appropriate perception and response. Discussion usually returns soon to the person-situation realm, where progress can be made in relating better to other people. Even in those cases where pattern-dynamic reflection is a major component in treatment, discussion never rests long in that realm exclusively. It is always accompanied by sustaining measures and may at times be supplemented by procedures of direct influence. Exploration, description, and ventilation, of course, remain essential ongoing processes. Dynamic understanding is frequently achieved without going into the development of the personality characteristic under discussion.

Personality Disorders

In earlier years, caseworkers, particularly those engaged in intensive or long-term treatment, worked mostly with clients who seemed to be handicapped by neurotic symptoms or conflicts. More recently, large numbers of people in the caseloads of clinical social workers are diagnosed as having personality disorders. For some time, it was generally believed that people in this group, in contrast to neurotic clients, were not capable of pattern-dynamic and developmental reflection. It was thought that their behavior was ego-syntonic—that is, acceptable to the ego—and the presence of underlying anxiety and pain was not recognized. Hence, it was believed that only person-situation reflection would be useful, helping such clients to see the ways in which they were really hurting or depriving themselves. However, clinical experience has since indicated that many such clients can be greatly helped by improved self-understanding and that they are capable of achieving this. Mrs. Zimmer in Chapter 3 is a clear example of this type of work.

Better understanding of the varieties of personality disorders and of their varying dynamics reveals great underlying discomfort, pain, and anxiety. The socially dysfunctional behavior is often only superficially ego-syntonic. The client's motivation for reflecting depends upon the degree to which his or her behavior can become "ego-alien" (i.e., unacceptable to his ego). If the client has the capacity for establishing a working relationship, and ego functions, especially reality testing and impulse control, are strong enough or can be strengthened sufficiently to work in these ways, tremendous benefit can come from intrareflection about personality dynamics or early life experiences. Since the difficulties in which people suffering from personality disorders find themselves tend to result from rigidly repetitive emotional, attitudinal, and behavioral patterns, understanding of these can be an important step toward change. Generally speaking, the more severe the character problem, the more sustainment is necessary before turning to reflective procedures; furthermore, during the course of exploring and understanding the intrapsychic bases for their troubles, these clients may need particular support to help them through the anxiety or depression that may accompany growing self-awareness. However, when given sufficient support as discomfort increases, these clients' motivation for treatment and change may increase dramatically.

DEVELOPMENTAL UNDERSTANDING

Encouragement of reflection upon developmental material is usually undertaken in an episodic way in psychosocial casework, certain themes being explored as it becomes apparent that factors in the client's development are blocking improvement in current social adjustment. The procedure is used to help the client become aware of the way in which certain present personality characteristics have been shaped by earlier life experiences, and sometimes to modify reactions to these experiences. It is sometimes necessary because certain dysfunctional characteristics cannot be overcome except by understanding of the experiences that contributed to their formation. The word "contributed" is used advisedly because casework never reaches all the determinants of a given phase of behavior. The ability to reach early causative factors is a relative matter, in any case. Analytic theory readily acknowledges that, in addition to constitutional factors, early preverbal experiences that cannot be reached even by analysis are potent in preparing an initial "personality set" that profoundly influences the way later infantile and childhood experiences are received by the individual. In fact, even though preverbal experiences are not remembered, individuals who were apparently neglected or treated inconsistently during infancy often benefit considerably from making inferences about early experiences

and how these influenced later difficulties, such as problems trusting others, pessimism, wide emotional swings, and confusion in distinguishing feelings from thoughts. It will be remembered that Mrs. Zimmer was relieved when she realized that some of her distressing personal problems derived from early deprivation.[4]

In Chapter 2, we pointed out that the factor of later reinforcement of earlier experiences is extremely important in personality development. Harmful infantile experiences are sometimes overcome by health-inducing later ones, but often, unfortunately, events serve to confirm and reinforce the child's misconceptions or distorted generalizations. Again, the concept of a balance of forces in the personality comes into play. Psychosocial casework theory holds that understanding of these later reinforcements can lessen the strength of damaging tendencies in the personality and may enable healthier components to take the ascendancy in controlling and directing personality functioning. The purpose of encouraging the client to reflect upon early life experiences is to bring about such a change in the personality system. In general, casework does not attempt to reach infantile experiences directly, but to examine later childhood and adolescent events, which can be considered genetic only in the sense that they are contributory developmental experiences.

Reflection versus Description–Ventilation

The worker cannot assume that every time clients talk about past life they are engaging in the process of developing understanding of it. Most of the time this is not the case. Often, the client is simply describing past experiences rather than reflecting upon them. At other times the client's talk about the past is for the purpose of catharsis. At such times a person may get considerable relief from telling the worker about painful life events and from expressing anger or grief about them. Again, the client very often brings in the past to justify present feelings, attitudes, or behavior. The individual is not then really trying to gain understanding but instead trying to explain to the worker why this or that reaction or feeling was appropriate or at least that he or she should not be blamed for so reacting; in other words, the past is used as a defense of a present position. A client may repeatedly say, for example, "Of course I'm sarcastic when I'm afraid I'll be criticized. When I was growing up, everyone in my family was like that." One woman told her therapy group over and over again that unless the members or leader asked her questions she would rarely speak, because her parents had never encouraged her to express herself; not until she was challenged over a period of many months did she indicate a wish to use this understanding of the past to change her behavior or to increase her opportunities for being listened to in the present. This type of defense is sometimes of great importance to the client, for it serves as protection against overly severe self-criticism. When this is so, care needs to be taken to ensure that it is not thoughtlessly or prematurely stripped away. Other clients talk about the past to evade thinking about the present. And, finally, clients sometimes have the impression that the past is what the worker is interested in, and talk about it in order to please the worker.

Movement into Developmental Reflection

There are many other times, however, when the client can be helped greatly in understanding unhealthy and unprofitable ways of acting by becoming aware of historical sources. Some clients quickly and spontaneously seek this kind of understanding. Others need help from the caseworker before they are ready and able to do so. Apparent readiness needs to be carefully distinguished from real readiness. Sophistica-

tion about Freudian ideas and other personality theories makes intellectualization about childhood events a particularly popular form of defense.

Sound movement into consideration of developmental factors follows much the same pattern as that just described for moving into the dynamics of psychological functioning. The client's attention is drawn to self-defeating or inconsistent behavior. Sometimes the client makes the choice of seeking further understanding, reacting in one way or the other to the worker's pointing up of the problem. At other times the worker takes the lead in steering thinking toward his or her earlier life. "Have you had feelings like this before?" "Does this make you think at all of similar things that have happened to you?" Or, more specifically, to a mother who is very upset by her son's barely average school report, "How was it for you in school?" Or to a man who is unduly upset in mentioning his brother's childhood failure in school, "You haven't told me much about your brother; what was he like?"[5] In these illustrations, the worker first explores the past and gives opportunities for ventilation about it in areas that would be expected to be related to the client's present feelings or actions. The client may then spontaneously move into developmental understanding by seeing connections, or the worker may promote thinking about this by suggesting them. "Yes, that must have been awfully hard to take. Are there times when Mary seems to be doing the same thing?" Or, "Did you notice that you used exactly those same words in telling me about Jim?" In the marital treatment of Dick and Susan Jones (see Chapter 3) both spouses reflected on some childhood experiences that had contributed to their current difficulties; this understanding, in turn, helped them both to consider behavior changes that were relevant to their present circumstances. In the couple sessions, not only was self-understanding achieved but Susan and Dick were also each able to realize that problematic reactions of the other often derived from early experiences and therefore need not be taken so personally.

Often, in previous general exploration of the client's earlier life, or as the client has talked about his or her childhood for other reasons, the worker will have obtained clues to areas in the client's life that may be of significance in understanding a particular reaction. These clues should certainly be used in guiding the client's association. A woman who was unreasonably resentful of what seemed to her neglect by her husband had earlier mentioned to the worker that her father had paid very little attention to her as a child. When she complained at length about her husband's neglect of her, the worker responded by asking her more about her father. The client, simply by thinking of the two parallel situations in juxtaposition, saw the similarity and asked whether she could be carrying some of her feeling toward her father over to her husband.

But sometimes the worker must make the connection. A mother was unreasonably angry with her adolescent daughter for borrowing her costume jewelry. The worker was already aware of this woman's deep hostility to her mother and suspected that it was being displaced onto her daughter. She also knew that as an adolescent and later, the client had been required to carry too much of the financial burden of the home, so that she had been deprived of many things she wanted. The worker ventured the comment, "I wonder if Joan's taking your things that way doesn't arouse the same feelings you had as a girl when your mother didn't let you get pretty things for yourself." This touched off an outburst of feeling about the client's deprived adolescence, followed by the realization that she had been taking out on her daughter the stored-up feelings of her own childhood. When subsequent family sessions were arranged, this mother was able to say that she thought she had been unfair in her reactions to Joan, that they stemmed from her own bitterness and had little to do with the jewelry incident. By sharing some of her own early experiences, the mother helped her daughter to understand her. Joan began to feel less guilty and angry and, in turn, could get closer to her mother than she had for some time. In this case, as so often happens, when one family member's developmental reflection resulted in changed behavior and more straightforward communication, the relationships and self-esteem of all involved—particularly Joan and her mother—improved as well.

Sometimes a client is fully aware of pertinent early experiences and little or no anxiety is involved in recalling them; the problem is simply to enable the individual to recognize the influence of past on present. At other times, the early feelings or experiences are to a degree hidden from view, for reasons that directly parallel the reasons for hiding current feelings and reactions: There may be fear of criticism of things that are perfectly well remembered; an event may not be regarded as significant or pertinent to the interview; or memories may have been suppressed or repressed because of their painfulness.

There are times when the recollection of an event and recognition of its influence in current life may not be enough. Rather, the past event itself may need to be thought about and *reevaluated* so that the feelings about it are modified. If a woman who is very resentful that her father did not provide adequately for his family can be helped to realize that his failure was due to a combination of illness and widespread national unemployment rather than to weakness of character or unwillingness to carry his family responsibilities, the amount of hostility she displaced upon her husband, a hardworking, conscientious individual who does not earn as much as she would like him to, may be substantially reduced. A woman who had felt that her parents discriminated against her by not letting her go to college was helped to recognize that she herself as a girl had not shown any interest in college. Thus, she saw that her parents might not have been discriminating against her but were perhaps unaware of her interest in further education. This recognition, in turn, not only led to a reduction of the client's hostility toward her parents and enabled her to have better current relationships with them; it also substantially reduced her feeling, which had carried over into all her adult relationships, that she was not loved and was somehow unworthy of love.

Before moving into this reevaluation process, it is often necessary to allow considerable ventilation of initial hostile feelings, partly because of the relief the client obtains from such an outpouring and from the worker's continued acceptance despite feelings about which the client may feel quite guilty, but also because there probably will not be readiness to reconsider earlier relationships until there has been an opportunity for catharsis. If the worker attempts the reevaluation process prematurely, the client is likely to resent it, thinking that the worker is unsympathetic, critical, or sympathetic to the person toward whom the client is hostile.

Obviously, reevaluation is useful only when the client has really misconstrued the earlier situation. Many times the early reality has in fact been extremely painful or even traumatic. Under such circumstances, ventilation, plus sympathetic acceptance by the worker and realization of the way in which early events are unnecessarily influencing current life, is appropriate.

Relationship with Worker

As we shall discuss further in Chapter 10, the relationship with the worker can also often be used as a source of developmental understanding. When the client is clearly reacting to the worker in terms of attitudes carried over from early life, the worker should, if consideration of these factors is deemed appropriate, help the person to recognize what he or she is doing. "Do you think that you fear criticism from me

as you did from your father?" "Do you see what you are doing? You are trying to get me to urge you to study just as your mother used to do. Then you will be angry at me for 'nagging,' just as you used to be angry at your mother." Interpretations like these would be appropriate only after a client has achieved some measure of understanding of feelings toward parents. Sometimes such transference interpretations are necessary to straighten out the relationship with the worker so that treatment can proceed. They are also of great value in helping the client to become aware of similar transferred reactions in other parts of current life. Because the worker is observing the client's reaction directly in a controlled situation, he or she is in an excellent position to make an accurate, convincing interpretation.[6] This is, of course, similar to the way in which transference reactions are sometimes handled in psychoanalysis. The difference lies in the type of relationship that each of the two approaches develops. In psychosocial casework, although in general we emphasize the reality relationship, a certain degree of transference nevertheless occurs. Our procedures are designed, however, to prevent *regression* in the transference. In other words, we do not seek to enable the client to go back to a reliving of infantile and very early childhood attitudes, needs, and reactions in the treatment relationship.

Again, the more the client can do independently, the better. If the client sees connections without help or questions the accuracy of his or her understanding of earlier events, fine. Otherwise, the more the worker can limit communications to starting the client on an appropriate train of thought by a question, suggestion, or tentative comment, the better. Interpretations, when they are necessary, should be made tentatively, unless the worker is absolutely sure of their accuracy. Here, as in every other form of understanding, the worker should endeavor to minimize the client's dependence, encouraging the ability to think for himself.[7] Periods of work on developmental patterns occur in many cases that are mainly focused on the person-situation configuration. Dynamic and developmental procedures often serve to push forward the process of person-situation understanding where such understanding is temporarily blocked by intrapsychic influences. And as with reflection upon dynamic factors, episodes of thinking about developmental factors are followed in treatment by a return to the person-situation configuration as soon as the new understanding has cleared the way for better perception and handling of current affairs. Sustaining comments often help to provide the client with the necessary confidence in the worker's goodwill and competence. When anxiety mounts as a result of some of the memories, feelings, and connections that are uncovered, sustaining communications can help to carry the client through a difficult period of work.

The procedures discussed in this and the preceding chapter are closely related. The intra-reflective procedures of the person-situation configuration can be skillfully used only when the worker has substantial psychological knowledge and understanding. A 1969 study reported by Mullen[8] and also by Reid and Shyne[9] found that some workers avoided using either pattern-dynamic or developmental reflection even when it would have been appropriate to do so. This would seem to represent a lack in either their training or their capacity for this kind of work. It is our experience that, when appropriate, these reflective procedures are more commonly used now than they were at the time of the study. In any event, from the psychosocial point of view, caseworkers engaged in treatment of disturbances in interpersonal relationships stand very much in need of the total repertory of casework procedures.

In order to promote consideration of dynamic or developmental matters as a major part of treatment, the worker must, in addition to being skilled in all the other casework processes, be thoroughly familiar with the workings of the personality—of unconscious as well as of con-

scious factors—and with the way in which the personality develops and early life events find continued expression in the adult personality. Workers must be particularly sensitive to the nuances of the clients' feelings, have considerable security when dealing with anxiety, and be aware of and able to control the flow of their own reactions. They must also be free of the need to probe into a client's life to secure vicarious satisfaction either of their own curiosity, of an appetite for power, or for other narcissistic gratifications.

NOTES

1. This matter is discussed in Greta Bibring's classic paper, "Psychiatry and Social Work," *Journal of Social Casework*, 28 (June 1947), 203–211.

2. Annette Garrett, in her article "The Worker-Client Relationship," in Howard J. Parad, ed., *Ego Psychology and Dynamic Casework* (New York: Family Service Association of America, 1958), pp. 53–54, 59–60, discusses this point in her section on transference and interpretation. See also Emanuel F. Hammer, "Interpretive Technique: A Primer," in Emanuel F. Hammer, ed., *Use of Interpretation in Treatment: Technique and Art* (New York: Grune & Stratton, 1968), 31–42; and Rudolph Lowenstein, "The Problem of Interpretation," *Psychoanalytic Quarterly*, 20 (January 1951), 1–14. Excellent illustrations and discussion of the need for some clients to defend against pervasive anxiety and depression through denial can be found in Alice H. Collins and James R. MacKey, "Delinquents Who Use the Primary Defense of Denial," in Francis J. Turner, ed., *Differential Diagnosis and Treatment in Social Work*, 2d ed. (New York: The Free Press, 1976), 64–75. Florence Lieberman, *Social Work with Children* (New York: Human Services Press, 1979), p. 282, also deals with the importance of respecting defenses in work with children.

3. In a still relevant paper, Lillian Kaplan and Jean B. Livermore discuss this issue in "Treatment of Two Patients with Punishing Super-Egos," *Journal of Social Casework*, 29 (October 1948), 310–316. For an interesting point of view and discussion of the super-ego, shame and guilt, and implications for treatment, see Helen Block Lewis, *Shame and Guilt in Neurosis*

(New York: International Universities Press, 1971). For useful readings on the current perspectives on the concept of shame, see Donald L. Nathanson, ed., *The Many Faces of Shame* (New York: The Guilford Press, 1987).

4. For elaboration of this point, see Gertrude Blanck and Rubin Blanck, *Ego Psychology, Theory and Practice* (New York: Columbia University Press, 1974); Miriam Elson, *Self Psychology in Clinical Social Work* (New York: W. W. Norton, 1986); and Phyllis Greenacre, ed., *Affective Disorders: A Psychoanalytic Contribution to Their Study* (New York: International Universities Press, 1953). For further readings on developmental psychology, see Chapter 3, note 4, and several of the notes in Chapter 2.

5. For illustrations, see Lucille N. Austin, "Diagnosis and Treatment of the Client with Anxiety Hysteria," in Parad, *Ego Psychology and Dynamic Casework*; and Hank Walzer, "Casework Treatment of the Depressed Parent," in Turner, *Differential Diagnosis*, 2d ed., 302–312. For an interesting approach to leading clients to developmental reflection in joint interviews, see Arlene S. Fontane, "Using Family of Origin Material in Short-Term Marriage Counseling," *Social Casework*, 60 (November 1979), 529–537. Chapters 16 and 18 provide illustrations of reflection on family of origin experiences in family and marital treatment.

6. See Andrew Watson, "Reality Testing and Transference in Psychotherapy," *Smith College Studies in Social Work*, 36 (June 1966), 191–209. Kenneth E. Reid, "Nonrational Dynamics of Client-Worker Interaction," *Social Casework*, 58 (December 1977), 600–606, deals very well with the nuances of the worker's own attitudes in transference situations. The matter of transference interpretations is discussed further in Chapter 10.

7. For very useful discussions of timing, methods, and purposes of interpretations, see Blanck and Blanck, *Ego Psychology: Theory and Practice*, especially pp. 314–337; and the still useful article by Ralph Ormsby, "Interpretations in Casework Therapy," *Journal of Social Casework*, 29 (April 1948), 135–141. Also of interest are several papers in Hammer, *Use of Interpretation*; and Jules Masserman, ed., *Depressions: Theories and Therapies* (New York: Grune & Stratton, 1970).

8. See Edward J. Mullen, "Differences in Worker Style in Casework," *Social Casework*, 50 (June 1969), 347–353.

9. William J. Reid and Ann W. Shyne, *Brief and Extended Casework* (New York: Columbia University Press, 1969), pp. 82–93.

CHAPTER 8

Psychosocial Therapy and the Environment

Psychosocial therapy, as the term implies, does not mean that every person-situation imbalance or disturbance requires that individuals must make changes from within. It is often the *situation* or *interactions* that must be treated, modified, changed. As discussed in Chapter 2, a vast number of problems experienced by the clients of clinical social workers do not stem from personality deficiencies; rather, they require analysis of *environmental deficits* or the *person-situation disequilibrium*. For instance, "deviance" of some sort may be an expected response to a closed or inadequate opportunity structure; myriad kinds of "pathology" may be the outcome of mystifying or double-binding communications; "acting out" may be the only alternative to resignation and hopelessness in the face of noxious social conditions.[1] As the psychosocial framework has incorporated systems and ecological perspectives, caseworkers following this approach have become increasingly sophisticated in their conceptualizations of the client-situation interplay, and this in turn has contributed to more precise assessments of what is wrong or what is needed to improve a given situation. Transactional concepts alert us to the

fact that the separation between person and environment is artificial and is made only for the purpose of evaluating interpenetrating components of the person-situation gestalt.

Similarly, "direct" and "indirect" work cannot actually be separated. Environmental interventions rarely stand alone. Caseworkers must engage their clients in making choices about changes they want to occur. Although we are always advocating the elimination of inhumane conditions and the enrichment of the general quality of people's lives, it is equally important to help our clients or potential clients determine what kinds of improvements or services they require. It serves no purpose to urge opportunities upon people who do not wish or feel free to use them. Without consistently consulting the presumed beneficiaries of change or of social services, we can err badly by making unilateral judgments based on what *we* have decided is best. Opportunities that suit one person may be uninteresting, frightening, or even repugnant to another. Again, the assessment of the "fit" between the person and environment is crucial to successful intervention. *Mutuality* between worker and client is at the bedrock of *all* casework activity, including efforts to enhance the quality of our clients' environments.

It is also true, of course, that in order to utilize whatever opportunities are made available, people can be helped to acquire new adaptive or coping skills; sometimes the casework relationship can be the medium through which people learn to develop or release capacities for change and growth. When clients' strengths and autonomy are supported, they are then in the best possible position to choose what kinds of environmental changes or resources will satisfy them.

People's inner and outer lives are, as described in Chapter 2 (see pages 48 to 50), inevitably intertwined, often making it difficult to differentiate between the two. Thus, sometimes environmental modifications result in enduring personality change. On the other hand, emotional growth may be required for the individual to maximize available opportunities, make changes that are desired, or find alternatives in the face of unjust but currently recalcitrant social conditions. It follows, then, that after assessing people, their environments, and the interactions among these, caseworkers usually focus their interventions on those systems most accessible to change, not necessarily the most "pathological" ones.

Some social workers think it is reactionary and/or futile to attempt to assist individuals in the face of societal evils and ills that can so profoundly grind them down. As the writers see it, however, one need not support or be satisfied with the status quo of a grossly imperfect social system in order to attempt to help people improve the quality of their lives *now*, before more basic changes become possible.

In this connection, it is important to remind ourselves of what casework can and cannot do. Some professional modesty is called for. While as *social workers*, individually and through professional organizations, our heritage compels us to advocate social change, to participate in movements and vigorously support legislation that challenges oppressive aspects of our social structure—our goals for change can far exceed our power. Yet we know what we, as *caseworkers, can* do. When working with victims of social injustice: We can be supportive. We can share with clients our distress with conditions and not (as we have sometimes been accused) try to "adjust" them to intolerable situations. We can develop techniques that are responsive to the needs of people living under miserable circumstances. We can assist people in their efforts to "negotiate the system." We can offer concrete help in changing or in opening up opportunities in the client's environment. We can promote policies and approaches in agencies and institutions where we have influence and thereby try to make service delivery more human and relevant. We can participate in reflecting on ways in which clients themselves, or in concert with others, can induce environmental changes. We can help to locate or create services or social networks for people who need or want them. Increasingly, social workers are providing resources *before* serious problems develop, by offering educational, therapeutic, facilitative services in clinics, schools, and day care centers, to populations "at risk," and so on, thereby helping to contribute to the *prevention* of future life problems or personality disturbances.[2] In this chapter we will be discussing some of the casework principles and skills required for such environmental work.

But the treatment we offer cannot "cure" the extraordinary problems that a large group of our clients face today. We readily acknowledge that casework does not and cannot eradicate poverty, homelessness, unemployment, discrimination, or the dehumanizing effects of a society that can place low priority on improving the quality of the lives of citizens increasingly beleaguered by the effects of urban conditions, political corruption, and impersonal bureaucracies. But casework should not be discredited because it does not do everything we wish it could.[3]

Sometimes students and caseworkers make the mistake of assuming that environmental work is needed only by the poor and the disadvantaged. The fact is that this kind of casework is of great importance to many clients: to children, the elderly, and the physically and mentally ill or disabled, and to many other individuals and families facing either "expectable" or extraordinary crises. Although those in poverty are particularly pressed by practical problems, people from all income groups benefit from environmental intervention to help them through difficulties or to improve their lives. Just as many poor or poorly educated clients with emotional problems have the capacity and motivation for introspection, so some well-to-do clients seek only "concrete" services. The tendency to assume that social action and environmental work are only relevant to the poor and that psychotherapy is useful only to the financially comfortable sells both groups short.[4]

It is sometimes thought that environmental work can be routinely delegated to paraprofessionals, or even to untrained volunteers. In some instances, such staff can be extremely helpful. They can become experts on resources, on clients' rights, on eligibility procedures. They can become forceful advocates. By demonstration they can teach clients to become more effective in the use of resources. But milieu work is not simple. In an important article, Germain discusses the intricacies of social work practice in the environment: "If . . . the complexity of environments can be conceptually delineated or specified, then it is possible to develop practice principles, skills, and techniques for work in environments and with transactions that will match in richness and diversity the principles and skills now available for work with individuals, families, groups, neighborhoods or communities."[5]

What is often required in environmental interventions, then, are caseworkers with the *most* experience and skill, workers who have knowledge about the inner and outer lives of people and about casework procedures and differential interviewing, workers who are interested in breaking new ground and developing increasingly sophisticated approaches. It is on the basis of direct practice that the most refined principles and skills will evolve. When we rely heavily on untrained personnel we imply that work with the environment does not have the same value as casework that focuses on psychological or family dynamics.

The complexity of environmental work was highlighted by one study that examined the use of concrete environmental modification by caseworkers employed in the family and children's services of one of the largest public welfare agencies in the midwest. Even in such an agency, where one would expect the need for concrete services to be high, concrete environmental intervention, compared to other intervention techniques, was found to be employed infrequently. The researchers suspected that its relatively low use, and its greater use by MSW than non-MSW caseworkers, might be accounted for by the intricacy of the interventive technique required to bring about environmental modification.[6]

ENVIRONMENTAL CHANGE BY CLIENT OR BY WORKER?

The general casework value of enabling the client to increase in competence has a direct bearing on the decision of how to deal with problems that either involve environmental etiology or in general depend upon the use of environmental resources for their solution. We are always confronted by the question of whether to intervene on the client's behalf or to encourage the client to attempt to tackle the milieu problem alone. By and large, the more one can do for oneself, the greater the increase in one's competence and in one's self-respect. But if this is to be the outcome, the change that is required must be one that the client is likely to be able to bring about. Some milieu, or environmental, factors are more responsive to the worker than to the client. Not infrequently the worker, because of status and role, has more "clout" and can influence the environment in a way that the client cannot. At other times, knowledge or skill in human relations may enable the worker to effect changes beyond the client's capacity to achieve by his or her own efforts.[7] For instance, although a patient could talk to a doctor about a medical problem, worker and client together might decide, on the basis of their knowledge of the particular doctor, that the client would not get the information needed for future planning if he or she asked for it initially.

The decision of when and when not to intervene in the environment rests upon the worker's assessment of the modifiability of the factors of the milieu, the client's capacity to handle them, and the agreement reached by worker and client about what approach would be most effective. There are occasional instances when the worker intervenes with collaterals (i.e., people in clients' environments who affect or can be enlisted to affect their situations) even though the clients could do this as effectively on their own. When carefully assessed, it may be decided that the meaning such a move would have to a particular client—such as a demonstration of worker interest to a person who is distrustful—temporarily outweighs the importance of supporting the client's efforts to seek the change independently. As we have discussed in earlier chapters, it has been demonstrated that in order to convince some "hard-to-reach" or involuntary clients that the worker is really well disposed toward them and interested in helping, it may be necessary to do practical things from which the clients derive benefit or pleasure.

Often, worker and client *together* may see a collateral person to explore opportunities or resources or work toward desired changes in the client's milieu. Such joint efforts have two advantages. First, the worker's knowledge and influence may contribute to a more successful result; second, the client has an opportunity to raise questions, express reactions, and perhaps learn through demonstration how to handle certain situations. But we would add a note of caution here: there are times when a worker's presence can be a liability rather than an asset, for example, if it seems to the worker or to the client that a collateral would interpret the worker's involvement as an intrusion or as a sign that the client is too weak or incapable to take care of his or her own affairs. Such interpretations, in some instances, might result in less willingness of the collateral to take an interest in the client than if the client made the contact independently.

In any event, in the view of the writers, whenever possible, clients should become *active* participants in bringing about the changes they seek, although, in some cases, extensive use of sustaining procedures and reflective discussion may be required before the client is prepared to take action. Even when caseworkers become advocates or "social brokers" for their clients and attempt to alleviate abhorrent environmental conditions or help them to "negotiate the system," the best results come when the worker carries out these functions *with* and not simply *for* individuals and families. Self-esteem and autonomy are better nurtured thereby. Treatment that reinforces the client's growth and competence will render the person better able to act on his or her own behalf when, inevitably, future difficulties arise. Furthermore, and this is important, direct involvement by clients can serve to allay suspicion about what others are saying about or planning for them.[8]

In previous chapters, we have considered forms of communication between worker and client. More often than not, this direct work with the client is accompanied by intervention in environmental systems of which the client is a part. In the preceding chapter, we saw that reflective discussion of dynamic and developmental factors is interwoven with all the other forms of client-worker communication. Cases vary: in some there is no work of this type; in others it occurs in a scattering of interviews; in still others it plays a major role. Similarly, some clients do not need environmental help, either because their problems do not involve the type of situational matters in which the worker can intervene directly or because the clients are able to act on their own behalf. At the other extreme are cases in which a major part of the work consists of bringing about environmental changes through communications between worker and collateral, through joint efforts with the client to modify some aspect of the milieu, or through the location of needed services and resources. Again, the concept of a blend is useful. Environmental work is intertwined with other procedures. It also involves subtleties and complexities that must be understood if it is to be carried on with skill.[9] The Kennedy, West, and Stone cases in Chapter 3 illustrate these points.

As outlined in Chapter 4, milieu work can be viewed in at least three ways: (1) in terms of the types of *communication* between worker and collateral; (2) in terms of the type of *resource* involved; and (3) in terms of the *role* or function that the worker is carrying. A discussion of each of these categories follows.

TYPES OF COMMUNICATION

In all communication with collaterals, the importance of *confidentiality* cannot be overemphasized. When the caseworker shares specific information about a client with another person or agency, it is essential that permission to release such information be obtained. Often this should be secured in writing (particularly when dealing with resources outside the family). Clients have a right to know with whom (within or outside the agency) information may be shared. Problems regarding legal liability of the worker or the employing agency are thereby minimized. Above all, straightforward discussion with clients about these matters, and conscientious attention to obtaining consent when re-

quired, also conveys respect for the client's ethical right to privacy and right to take charge of his or her own affairs.[10] The first four sets of communication procedures (sustainment, direct influence, exploration-description-ventilation, and person-situation reflection) are just as germane to environmental work as they are to direct work with the client. There is an unfortunate tendency to think of work directed toward the individual's environment as "manipulation" and therefore rather different in nature from actual contacts with the client. The contrary is true. As we have said, the skills needed for bringing about changes in the environment on the client's behalf are in many respects identical to those employed in direct work with the client.

Discussions with collaterals have many purposes. A worker may want to learn more about a client or about services or opportunities possibly available to the client. The worker may attempt to change or expand the collateral's understanding of the client and the circumstances, so that the collateral's attitude or actions will be tempered, or resources will be provided, or conditions over which the collateral has control will be modified and improved. But collaterals are often not free agents. They may be part of a system—school, business, court, police—with policies and regulations. Relatives may have heavy pressures of their own, or may be involved in disturbing interactions with the client, and therefore be reluctant to participate in a discussion or take steps to help. Therefore, many influences in addition to the client's needs may enter into a collateral's decisions.

As with the client, the worker has to assess—often very quickly, sometimes during a telephone conversation—the collateral's attitudes and feelings toward the client, the degree of interest, and the willingness to get involved in the client's concerns or situation. In an interview, the worker has to be attuned to the collateral's subtle responses, including the facial expression and other nonverbal behavior, to evaluate accurately the person's receptivity.

In work with collaterals, obviously contact has to be established, and *sustaining* procedures beyond common courtesy are often of great value. The client is not the only person who may be afraid of being blamed: so may the teacher, the public welfare worker, the nurse, the landlord, and, of course, the relative. They can be angry. They can be anxious. They have needs too. Their way of handling their feelings may be defensive hostility that leads them to attack either the worker or the client. Often, they too will respond better if the worker shows an understanding of the problem they are up against and has not come to criticize, if the worker is interested in their point of view and is willing to listen to the headaches the client has caused them. They, too, sometimes need encouragement concerning efforts they have already made to deal with the situation.

Procedures of *direct influence* have an important place in environmental work, particularly when the worker is trying to modify the way in which another person is acting toward the client. Reinforcement and suggestion play a large role in such activity, with advice sometimes of value, and insistence or even coercion occasionally necessary. The administrator of a nursing home, pressured by a long waiting list, may have to be strongly encouraged to admit an elderly client in urgent need of immediate care. A busy public welfare worker may have to be urged to cut through red tape quickly to give aid to a family burned out of its home by fire. Landlords who cannot be persuaded by other means may have to be told that violations in their buildings will be reported to the appropriate government agency unless immediate repairs are made.

Ventilation is sometimes useful when the person being interviewed has a great deal of emotion about the client or about the situation in which the person and the client are involved. The landlord resolved to evict an ill mother and her several active children may need to express a good deal of feeling about aggravations experienced with this family before being ready to reconsider such drastic action. So, too, may the nurse or the teacher who has had to put up with an "acting out" child or intrusive parent.

Sometimes collaterals vent feelings and express attitudes that are offensive to the worker. A landlord may complain that a building is being destroyed because the tenants are of a particular color or ethnic background. A white teacher may be prejudiced, incensed by actions of a black student that would be tolerated in others. More often than we would wish, welfare workers make denigrating remarks about "those people" on their caseloads. In such instances, it requires particular discipline and skill to listen, to continue to be supportive, to respond uncritically, and at the same time to avoid seeming to agree with the point of view being expressed or arguing for one's own view when this will do no good. It is obviously important not to alienate the very person from whom one is seeking help on behalf of a client; in many cases, direct confrontation would make matters worse rather than better. And often, once anger is expressed, the collateral may then be better prepared to listen to what the worker wants to say or ask. When this does not happen, certainly a more aggressive approach may be necessary. But such a decision should be made only by worker and client together, and only after full consideration has been given to the risks and possible repercussions involved. This point will be discussed more fully later in this chapter where worker roles are examined.

It goes without saying that when a worker attempts to persuade a collateral to adopt or change an attitude toward a client, careful evaluation of all pertinent aspects of the client-situation system is necessary. In every instance, the caseworker must have confidence that the client wants and will benefit from the changes being promoted; in order to know this, the worker must know the client. If, for example, a caseworker helps to reinstate a student suspended for truancy without understanding what this behavior means, or if a worker helps a man whose job performance has been erratic to locate a job he will not hold, does not want, or is not qualified for, the probability is great that the result will be frustration for the client and collateral alike. Past failures experienced by the client will only be reinforced by the caseworker's interventions based on faulty or inadequate assessment.

As in direct work, experience has shown that procedures for *reflective discussion* are of great value with collaterals wherever they can be used, particularly in the process of helping one person to understand another. Often, such understanding is brought about simply by telling the person about some aspects of the client and his or her life. At times the worker may enter into the reflective process with the interviewee in much the same way as with a client, although the scope of the contact is more limited, indeed frequently to a single interview. Often, worker and collateral—frequently with the participation of the client, too—are actually thinking together to arrive at a solution. Of course, care must be taken to estimate the ability as well as the willingness of the collateral person to listen or engage in reflective discussion.

The worker is less likely in such contacts to use reflective procedures that involve thinking about consequences to the *self*, although this, too, can occasionally take place. Sometimes, for example, collaterals will discover that the changes being sought will benefit them as well as the client. This kind of reflection may be extremely useful when the vested interests of the collaterals have made them resistant to understanding or responding to the needs of the client.

In one situation, Tom, a teenage boy employed after school in a restaurant to supplement his family's modest income, was fired for stealing food. "That's not my problem," the employer told the school social worker who had explained the difficult con-

ditions under which the boy and his widowed mother lived. The worker realized that efforts to expand the employer's view by giving information about the boy's background angered rather than appeased him; it was apparent that he needed to vent his feelings about Tom's actions. Therefore, the worker listened with understanding, making no attempts to deflect the anger. Then, only after the employer became calmer, Tom, who was present at the meeting, and the worker offered the idea that Tom could pay off his debt if he were allowed to work it off. Since Tom had been a good employee, the discussion of this suggestion led the employer to recognize the advantage to himself of giving the boy another chance.

In this example, it became clear that the employer was unwilling to be responsive to Tom's needs. Therefore, the worker used procedures of sustainment, encouraged ventilation, and only then made a direct suggestion. These procedures were followed by reflection in which the employer realized that his self-interest could be served by rehiring his youthful employee. The fact that Tom, who genuinely regretted what he had done, participated in the discussion—and offered a solution as well as apologies—may have supported the employer's confidence that the boy would not steal from him again. This case also illustrates that the *extent* of the communication procedures differs, but the greater part of the *range* is common to work with collaterals and clients alike.

Reflective procedures may also be necessary to straighten out the relationship between the caseworker and the collateral. The worker's intent or attitudes may need to be clarified before effective work can proceed. Sometimes a simple explanation will suffice. In other instances, the worker may try to elicit a collateral's negative reactions about the worker and the purpose of the interview, so that misinterpretations can be cleared up. Naturally, the details of achieving this kind of understanding depend on the context in which they are being applied, the need for such discussion, and the willingness of the collateral to engage in it. But, whether or not the interviewee's reactions are brought out into the open, the worker must be ever sensitive to them and skillful in finding tactful ways of conveying his or her own true attitudes and role. This is true whether the collateral is an employer, teacher, landlord, or member of the client's family.

Mrs. Davis, who was being seen by a clinical social worker, complained that her mother, who cared for Mrs. Davis's children during the day, was undermining Mrs. Davis's authority with the youngsters, with the result that they were becoming unmanageable. The grandmother disapproved of her daughter's treatment, yet reluctantly agreed to come to a joint interview with her. It was necessary for the worker to be accepting of the grandmother's view of her as an "interferer" and to realize that this woman was expecting to be criticized. Through demonstrating a supportive manner and telling her that her help was needed to better understand the children's problems, the worker conveyed her respect for the grandmother and the purpose for the meeting. Only then, and after giving a good deal of credit for her conscientious care of the children, was the worker able to discuss with her the apparent effects the conflicts between the adults were having on the youngsters. As it turned out, the grandmother agreed to come to subsequent meetings and, as the treatment evolved, Mrs. Davis and her mother were able to agree upon the latter's role as an experienced "consultant" to her daughter in the caretaking of the children. The tensions and competition between the two women were thereby virtually eliminated. The children's behavior improved in a short time in response to the changes made by the adults.

In summary, then, all that has been said about sustaining work, directive procedures, ventilation, and reflective discussion of the person-situation gestalt applies to work with people in the client's milieu as well as to contacts with the client: to indirect as well as direct treatment. On the other hand, it is extremely unlikely that collaterals will become involved in extensive intrapsychic reflection, especially dynamic or developmental aspects of their own reactions. When people in the client's milieu are sufficiently involved in the client's affairs to be willing to engage in the process of gaining self-understanding, the situation is one of interpersonal adjustment in which they, too, become clients. This can occur when a client's family becomes engaged in ongoing family treatment.

TYPES OF RESOURCES

Moving from types of communication to variations in the type of resource or collateral that the worker is using or attempting to use on behalf of clients, we arrive at a new set of considerations. In Chapter 4, five types of resources were distinguished: (1) the worker's own social agency; (2) the non–social work organization in which the worker is on staff or a member of its social work department; (3) the social agency where the worker is not employed; (4) the non–social work organization that (a) has social workers on staff but where the worker is not employed, or (b) does not employ social workers at all; (5) individuals in (a) an instrumental relationship with the client, or (b) an expressive relationship with the client.

Worker's Own Social Agency

The first type is the social agency in which the caseworker is employed. These are organizations that are under the leadership or direction of social workers. Here the worker has a twofold responsibility: first, to use these services appropriately and skillfully, whatever they may be, and second, to share responsibility for constant improvement in these resources. In a family service agency, for example, program changes and the addition of new agency services must often be approved by a lay board or by funding agencies. Becoming skilled at effectively presenting proposals to these bodies may be as important an aspect of the caseworker's function as is the skillful delivery of existing services.

For child welfare agencies, public and private, the foster home is an agency resource used on behalf of the client. No resource is more complicated and no resource requires more careful, thorough diagnostic assessment of the total child-parent-situation gestalt than that required in child placement. Certainly, the first four types of casework communication are continuously used in work with foster parents. As in work with other resource people, the expertise of the foster parent must be respected. Even the new foster parent usually has skill in child rearing, though he or she may be ignorant of the special complexities of caring for a *foster* child. The successful experienced foster parent has much to teach the caseworker new to the child placement field, just as the successful experienced teacher knows far more about the child as a learner in the classroom than the school social worker does.

There is a cooperative quality in work with other experts that calls for delicate sensitivity to considerations of status if a good working relationship is to be achieved. The fact that the foster parent receives money from the agency is an important component in the total picture. Worker and foster parent are both parts of the same agency system, both subject to agency policies; they are allies in caring for the child, but they have different places in the agency structure. The worker carries an authority that the foster parent does not have in that the worker's opinion carries great weight not only in the decision about the removal of particular children from the home but also in the decision of whether to use, or to continue using, the home at all. All that the worker says and does, then, has special meaning for the foster parent because it occurs within this context. A feeling that suggestions must be taken may lead to resentment and pretense. It is especially important that an atmosphere be created in which the foster parent is free both to express opinions different from the worker's and to ventilate feelings about the children in his or her care. Since the foster mother especially has not only the family income at stake but also her self-esteem, which may rest in large part upon her confidence in herself as a good mother, sustainment can be of vital importance.

Sometimes, it is true, work with foster parents moves close to the client-worker pattern found in parent-child adjustment problems in the natural family. Even then, however, the foster parent's status as an agency resource, and hence as a collateral, is still in existence. When the worker loses sight of this role, complications ensue. A particular type of complication can occur around visits between foster children and their own parents. Research suggests that visits by natural parents are of critical importance to the overall adjustment of foster children.[11] Yet there are many problems in working out such visits, not the least of which are the reactions of some foster parents who feel threatened by the children's feelings toward their natural parents. Skilled casework is required to handle these delicate issues, to help foster parents if they have feelings of competition and resentment toward the children's parents, but always without minimizing the role the foster parents are playing in the lives of the children for whom they are caring and their importance to the agency system. Similarly, often foster parents need sensitive understanding of the heartache they feel when a child, to whom they have become attached, has to be given up to another home or to be reunited with natural parents.

The child welfare agency is a particularly good example of the type of social agency in which the worker has a major responsibility for influencing agency policy. The worker is in a key position to observe the effects of policy on both clients and foster or adoptive parents, and should be thinking in terms of policy formulation as well as in terms of work with clients and substitute parents. Agencies can and sometimes do provide effective channels for passing on the worker's observations and ideas so that policy can be a fluid instrument with wide room for change and experimentation rather than a set of relatively fixed administrative rulings. Experimentation with new ideas is essential if service is to be pertinent and effective.

The public welfare agencies, which provide financial assistance and social services, are difficult to classify as to type of resource. Historically, they have been social agencies and as frustrated as its position often was, social work leadership unquestionably gave some measure of protection to public assistance clients, offering them services and representing their welfare as no other profession or interested group did. In recent years, however, there have been significant changes in the ways in which income assistance programs are being administered. More often than not, financial aid is dispensed on a standardized, impersonal basis with little direct connection with casework services that in the past, in the best agencies, were to a degree available when needed.

At present, some public agencies rendering various social services (child welfare and family services, preventive and protective services for children, protective and custodial services for adults who because of age or disability are unable to handle their affairs, homemaker services, etc.) have at least a small proportion of BSWs and MSWs on staff, particularly as supervisors. But many others have very few or no trained workers. Hence, although these agencies are technically social agencies, they are often staffed with workers not fully equipped with the knowledge, skills, or professional values required to render such difficult and demand-

ing services adequately. Furthermore, increasingly, control of programs is in the hands of administrators with no social work background, and basic policy is controlled to a high degree by law.

The trained caseworker employed by public welfare agencies (or, for that matter, other, especially large and bureaucratic, social service organizations) is often in the difficult position of being the representative of an agency but disagreeing with many of its policies. Sometimes workers can influence program or policy. Certainly, they have responsibility for doing everything possible to improve services and to use the resources available. Actually, in some agencies there is a degree of leeway in administrative policy and an opportunity for constructive change in response to pressure at the caseworker and supervisory level.[12]

But in many other agencies, where undesirable policies that are destructive to individuals or families in some way prevail, the workers face many complications in bringing the agency's resources to their clients. It is difficult enough when a policy that is necessary and fair creates hardship. Then the path is fairly clear: allow or even encourage the anger to be expressed, genuinely appreciate the hardship for the client, sometimes explain why the policy is necessary, and help the client to make the best possible adaptation to it. Under these circumstances, there is no basic conflict about carrying out the policy. But when the policy is either unfair, unwise, or unnecessary, it is even more important for the client to express anger and to know that the worker recognizes the hardship and genuinely regrets it.

Four alternative courses are open to workers. One is to express to clients personal disagreement with policy, and perhaps to tell of efforts that are being made to change it. At the same time workers may help clients to decide whether alternatives are available and, if they are not and if no legitimate way around it can be found, help them either to comply with agency policy or, if possible, to register their protests effectively.

The second course is for the workers to decide that they can no longer carry out policy with which they are in basic disagreement and leave the agency. There are situations in which this action is justified, but it is not a truly satisfactory solution. If all workers who disagree with a bad policy leave the agency, no one is left to fight for better ones. Workers who leave are all too easily replaced by workers without any social work education, who may not find it so difficult to carry out destructive agency policies. This is not to say that every worker needs to feel duty-bound to work forever under impossible conditions. Eventually, one may feel that one has fought long enough and that some one else should take up the cudgels. The subject of worker "burnout" is discussed in Chapter 10.

The third course is that taken by workers who stand strongly for better policy and stay within the system to work for it. In favorable situations, they are able to bring about improvements in policy and its administration. Sometimes they have the power, especially at the supervisory and higher administrative levels, through flexibility and intelligent application of policy, to modify its impact on the client considerably. (See the case of Mrs. Stone in Chapter 3 for an example of this kind of creative practice.) They may be able to give some protection to clients; at the very least, they can help prevent the situation from getting worse. Workers in public welfare services who choose either the second or third course can also work through channels external to the agency to bring about better legislation that can improve the whole system. The effort to bring such change has gone as far as court action by social work employees (sometimes joined by client activist groups) to challenge the legality of extreme policies.

The fourth course is the most precarious one: that of staying in the agency but circumventing its policies. It usually carries no particular danger to the workers, for if they lose their jobs they can generally find others and loss of the job is the worst that is likely to happen unless workers engage in criminal misconduct. But this course of action does introduce all sorts of complications into the client-worker relationship. Usually, it involves dishonesty in intrastaff relationships, often at several levels. And, aside from these hazards, the sidestepping of unjust policies can have the effect of postponing concerted efforts—by staff and clients alike—to work toward changing them.

Many people from all walks of life want and can use casework services. Individuals and families in poverty and those receiving income assistance often need the kind of help casework can give to deal with the many pressures in their lives.[13] They must have the same opportunity to receive first-rate services from professionally trained workers, from agencies with a social work orientation, as have those who can pay for them. Certainly, many of these services have to be operated under public auspices or, at least in part, to be publicly financed. As welfare policies change and keep changing, we believe it is incumbent on us all, whether we work in public departments of social services or not, to press for making sure these are available, readily accessible, and of high quality.

Non–Social Work Organization Where Worker Is Employed

The second type of resource is the organization with caseworkers on staff or with a department that employs them, but that is primarily controlled by another profession: for example, a hospital, school, or court. Included in this type would also be large government organizations (such as many of the public welfare agencies just described), some public mental health departments, and others where social workers are employed. In agencies of this type, caseworkers offer the client a resource with which they are associated but which is not their primary responsibility. Other factors being equal, the workers are in a less advantageous position than the predominant profession to bring change in the major agency service.

Nevertheless, in some such organizations social workers are hired (sometimes on a consultant basis) to share their expertise on human social behavior with school personnel, lawyers, medical professionals, public housing officials, and the like. In some school systems, for example, social workers run seminars for teachers and administrative personnel on such matters as family structure and dynamics, cultural influences on personality, and group dynamics. There are also hospitals with comparable programs run by social workers that have considerable influence on the services rendered by these facilities. In every case, the social workers are part of the service and therefore must do everything possible from their own observations of its effect on clients to contribute toward changes that will improve this service.

A social worker newly employed at an adult residential care facility for the frail elderly quickly noted that between meals most of the sixty-five residents either retreated to their small rooms or sat and slept or stared in the lounge area. Few participated in bingo games and other activities that were available. Social interaction was at a minimum. Deciding to explore residents' feelings about their leisure time, the worker developed a simple questionnaire, which she helped each person to fill out, inquiring about hobbies, recreations they used to enjoy, and activities they would like to have available at the residence. She wanted to find out whether their inactivity was a real choice or the result of a lack of appealing opportunities. In casual conversation, the residents made such comments as: "What's an old woman to do? Sit. What else is there?" But when they were questioned more closely, it turned out that many of the residents were eager for cultural

programs. As luck would have it, the social worker was a former English teacher and began a pilot poetry discussion group which, by the fourth meeting, had become so popular that it had to be divided into two sections! From this pilot project, an expanded recreational program developed. A multigenerational glee club which brought in members of high school choruses and church choirs was organized. With assistance from a volunteer journalist who lived in the community, a newspaper by and for the residents was developed. Residents were regularly canvassed for ideas about new projects.

In this example, even though there had been few innovations in programming for years prior to the worker's arrival, there was no resistance of the non–social work administration to the new approach to recreation. In fact, it was generally believed that the increased intellectual stimulation, socialization, and greater contact with the community at large would significantly promote the mental and emotional health of the elderly participants. Undoubtedly of importance to the success of the worker's approach was the fact that the residents were invited in on the planning phases of the new programs. There is persuasive evidence that when they feel they have some—even seemingly minor—control over their living situations, the elderly become significantly less depressed and their lives are actually prolonged.[14]

In every instance, social workers must have thorough knowledge of the system within which they are working, its lines of responsibility, and its power structure. They must understand the "culture" of the other profession or professions with which they are dealing. They must have infinite tact, a high degree of confidence in themselves and their profession, and the courage and zest to pursue aims in spite of exasperating discouragements.[15] The Stone case in Chapter 3 and the Barry case in Chapter 21 illustrate some of the complexities of interdisciplinary interaction. Usually, progress is cumulative. Once their competence and value have been established and recognized, the social workers are more likely to be listened to and, under the best circumstances, an attitude of mutual respect will permeate interrelationships.

In one hospital, the director of social service learned from an audit of drug overdose patients that a number of these patients had not been referred for casework attention. Therefore, she consulted with the nurses and discussed the importance of automatic notification of the social work department of all such cases at the time of admission. The nurses had not understood that casework services might be helpful to the families involved and had not made the referrals because frequently the patients were unconscious at the time of their arrival! Similarly, this same director persuaded the hospital administration to institute changes in the admitting procedures so that certain items of information could be elicited (such as whether or not a patient lives alone); by reviewing the screening data on every patient, the social work department could reach out to those who might be in need of casework services.

Systems theory observations concerning the importance of the *point of maximum reverberation** are fully confirmed in the role played by key persons in the medical and nursing hierarchy. It is extremely important that pressure for change be exercised only after sound diagnostic assessment of the system has been made. Usually, the most effective way for change to take place is for the department head to give

courageous leadership to the staff, following through in pressing for needed changes. At the same time, the staff needs to understand the complex forces within which change takes place in a large multiprofessional organization; sometimes an administrator cannot share with staff all that is going on, including all the efforts made, matters of timing, and sad, frustrating reasons for lack of progress. It is practically impossible to keep this sort of information confidential once it is shared, yet to divulge it may completely defeat the objectives in which all are interested. Change in a "host agency" calls for team play of the highest order, and nothing is more important in team play than mutual respect and trust.

Changes within the social work department itself have much in common with changes in the more autonomous social agency of the child welfare or family service type. Money is a factor in all agencies. Just as family agencies must often seek the approval of a lay board or a funding agency, so a department of an organization with a different primary function must secure approval of whatever intraagency authority it is responsible to.

When we turn from the worker-agency to the worker-client relationship in this second type of resource, we find that the worker is seen by the client not only as a caseworker but also as a representative of the major functions of the hospital, school, or court. Therefore, client reactions to these services, including their weaknesses, must be handled. The probation worker, for example, must try to find the common meeting ground between the function of the court and the aspirations of the client. The worker must be responsive to the client's often angry feelings about the policies of the agency that the worker represents. (In this respect, if the worker disagrees with important policies, the same considerations hold as discussed earlier concerning the worker in the social agency.)

Certainly, investigations of complaints received by courts and protective agencies may

---

* According to systems theory, change applied to part of a system will reverberate in a differential way throughout the system. A point of maximum reverberation is the point at which change will have the greatest effect on the total system.

result in client reactions ranging from un-yielding resistance to physical violence against the workers. Yet, in the experience of the writers, many involuntary clients *can* accept and do utilize casework services once it is established that the worker respects the client's wishes and goals.[16] (In the case of Mrs. Stone, described in Chapter 3, the mother accused of beating one of her children was able to accept a referral from the protective services worker to the family services division.) See also the Carter case, described in Chapter 21.

In addition to whatever practical or therapeutic services one may offer the client, it is also one of the important functions of a worker in an agency primarily under the auspices of another profession to facilitate the way in which the agency is being used as a resource by the client. The worker often interprets the agency services to the client and develops methods for inviting client feedback. Caseworkers in hospitals, for example, may arrange group meetings of patients or of patients' relatives not only to screen for those who need special services or to give them an opportunity to share their feelings about illness but also to express their reactions to the hospital services. Similarly, parent groups in day care centers are often organized to encourage parents to raise questions, to offer suggestions, and to get clarification of the operations of the program their children are attending.

The caseworker also helps the other professionals to understand the needs of the client better. Because the worker sees the client from a different vantage point and within a different professional frame of reference from the doctor, teacher, or judge, he or she can contribute greatly to the quality of the other service. At times the worker may need to act as mediator between the service and the client and sometimes even as active advocate on the client's behalf. Doctors may be reluctant to give adequate attention to certain patients because of their critical or hostile attitudes or their failure to un-

derstand or follow medical advice. The medical social worker can try to remedy this situation. A teacher may take a dislike to a child. By acquainting her with the facts of the child's background, the social worker in the school system may be able to modify the teacher's reactions. Here again thorough understanding of the organization as a system and of the ways of working, patterns of thought, and values of the other profession is essential if either mediation or active advocacy is to be successful.

Social Agency Where Worker Is Not Employed

The third type of resource is the social agency resource that employs social workers but where the worker who is helping the client is not a staff member. This type includes not only casework agencies but also community centers where there are opportunities for group experiences, hobby development, recreation, and social action through groups. Organizations such as homemaker services, day care centers, and employment counseling services also fall in this category when they are administered by social workers.

In general, social workers are familiar with what social agencies in most fields do. Entering a new community, the worker will usually want to become familiar as quickly as possible with a wide range of agencies. Caseworkers who have been in the community longer will be knowledgeable about such resources. It can be very valuable to meet with colleagues from other agencies over lunch and to plan exchange visits so workers can get to know one another's facilities firsthand.

Agencies often keep resource files. Common objectives, a common professional language and body of knowledge, and a common value system facilitate the use of such resources. But no profession is completely homogeneous. Within a range, values, objectives, language, and even knowledge differ. Idiosyncrasies and different points of view exist within as well as among professions. Here, too, one must be sensitive to the reaction of the other worker within the other agency and use communication skills. Social workers are people too. They can feel threatened or competitive; they also have their off days, days when they are under pressure or upset about work or personal affairs and not operating at their best.

A further factor in work with another social agency is, of course, the policies and resources of that agency. Some of these are fixed; others are flexible. In milieu work, it is often necessary for the caseworker to push toward the maximum extension of that flexibility. In so doing, if the worker has correctly assessed the client's need and interpreted it skillfully, a best ally should be a colleague in the other agency. Sometimes, too, the worker in the other agency is more familiar with other similar resources than is the first worker and therefore able to suggest alternatives when his or her own agency is unable to meet the need. There are times also when this worker's greater experience with the type of problem experienced by the client rightly leads to a different assessment of the client's need. Under these circumstances, conferences between workers are usually the best means for arriving at reassessment. It is extremely useful to develop friendly colleague relationships with workers in other agencies to facilitate this type of cooperative work.

Non–Social Work Agency Where Worker Is Not Employed

The fourth type of resource refers to the agency or organization not administered by social workers that either (1) has a social work department or social workers on staff, but where the worker helping the client is not a member, or (2) does not employ social workers at all.

In working with non–social work agencies that employ social workers, many of the considerations discussed in connection with social agencies, the third type of resource, can be applied. One difference, of course, is that workers in these non–social work agencies may be constrained by the profession or bureaucracy that administers them. We described this kind of problem in the discussion of the second type of resource: the non–social work agency where the worker is employed. Therefore, for example, if one is attempting to get certain services for a hospitalized client, the medical social worker may have to get clearance from the administrator or the doctors in order to see that they are provided. But again, the more one has established friendly working relationships with social workers in these settings, the more likely it is that efforts on a client's behalf will be given maximum consideration.

Various forms of group living for adults have become widespread. Halfway houses, under many different names and various auspices, offer protection to patients released from hospitals for the mentally ill, to rehabilitated drug addicts, and others. It is now well known that many mentally retarded adults can learn to function in the community when living in protected settings. Recreational and educational programs, including day care, are now offered to the above groups and to elderly people living in the general community. Usually these resources are not administered by social workers, although they may be employed there. Some of these facilities are part of large state departments, and therefore they are often subject to the many restraints and regulations associated with large bureaucracies.

The type of organization that does not employ social workers at all can include, among many others, legal aid organizations, public health and housing agencies, and tutoring and vocational or employment services, as well as schools, hospitals, and group and nursing homes that do not have social workers on staff.

The greater the worker's knowledge about the other organization or profession and the resources of the particular institution, the more likely he or she is to be able to help clients to make appropriate use of it. Much exploratory work may need to be done before the proper help can be secured. Not only will clients' time be wasted if they are sent to inappropriate places but some clients may also be discouraged from trying further. It may be ego-debilitating for some people. It may also reduce confidence in the worker's interest and competence, and it may have a negative effect on simultaneous direct work with clients. Both phone work and footwork may be necessary to prepare the way for a client's own first contact. Ingenuity in locating appropriate resources and skill in interesting other organizations in a client are particularly valuable in milieu work using resources not connected with social work.

A busy child welfare worker referred a woman client, with a marginal income, to the legal aid society to obtain advice about a custody suit that had been initiated by the client's divorced husband. After waiting weeks for an appointment, the client was then informed that she was not eligible on the basis of her income, as modest as it was. The worker then sought assistance from the bar association, which advised that there was a panel of low-fee attorneys who could assist the woman. Precious time and frustration could have been saved had the worker explored the available resources prior to making the referral.

Individual Collaterals

We have already seen in the section on types of communication a number of illustrations of contacts with *individuals* on the client's behalf. The fifth and last type of resource involves two categories of individuals: those in an *instrumental* (or *"task-oriented"*) relationship with the client and those in an *expressive* (or *"feeling-oriented"*) relationship with the person the worker is trying to help.

Instrumental Collaterals The subdivision instrumental collaterals includes, among others, employers or landlords. With these task-oriented individuals, the worker may be seeking such opportunities as jobs or better housing for the client or may be intervening on behalf of the client in a misunderstanding or clash that is creating hardship for the client. In each of these cases, the worker deals not with another profession or some type of service organization but with people who have their own interests at stake. They tend to be either indifferent to the client or hostile. In preparation for meeting with such collaterals, it is essential that the worker be sure of facts or else be aware of the possibility that he or she does not have all the facts. Overidentification with the client is a frequent cause of failure in this type of contact. There is no sense in persuading an employer to make special plans to hire a client by giving a false picture of the client's abilities or readiness for work. It will only end in embitterment on both sides. When liabilities are acknowledged and sympathetically interpreted, the collateral makes a decision realistically in the light of attitudes about the liabilities, willingness to take a risk, and assessment of how much damage may be done to the business if the liabilities cannot be overcome or contained. If the situation is such that the worker cannot be frank, it is better for the client to find his or her own job.

Similarly, when trying to modify the attitudes or actions of an instrumental collateral, the worker has to listen with an open mind to the collateral's side of the story. For example, a client may complain that the landlord has not painted his or her apartment. On speaking with the landlord, however, the worker may be told that the tenant-client has been neglectful or destructive of the property and for that reason the landlord feels justified in refusing to paint the apartment. The worker must then judge whether to press for greater understanding of the client's point of view, or perhaps to drain off some of the irritation and then work with the client to arrive at some mutual amelioration of the total situation.

Expressive Collaterals   The subdivision expressive collaterals includes those individuals who have an expressive, or feeling-oriented, relationship with the client. With these individuals the situation is quite different than that connected with instrumental collaterals, since an expressive relationship implies some investment in the client's welfare. This is true even when anger exists and the worker is intervening in the hope of improving their interaction. In such relationships, anger itself is a sign of caring, of involvement. With caring, a new component enters. The relative or even friend may feel that he or she knows the client better than the worker does, and indeed this may be true. Those collaterals who feel they have a stake in the situation may want the worker to change the client rather than to respond positively themselves to the worker's need for their help or to the worker's efforts to modify the collateral's relationships with the client. Some collaterals may even be opposed to the worker's efforts. As we shall discuss further in the chapters on family therapy, family members can be threatened by any change in the balance of the family system. They may, therefore, oppose change even though theoretically such change would benefit them as well as the client.

In work with these collaterals, we reach ground that is very close to work with the client. Sometimes, in fact, it turns into direct work in which the collateral becomes a second client, either through individual interviews or through a shift to family or joint interviewing. Short of this, however, relatives and friends can become powerful allies in treatment. Sometimes it is sufficient to let them know they are needed. At other times, work must be done to help them understand ways in which they can assist the client. Simply helping relatives and friends to see their importance to the client and the ways

in which they can help often motivates them to offer opportunities and psychological support. They may need assurance that a little involvement in the client's troubles will not result in their being left with greater responsibility than they are either obligated to assume or want to assume. This is particularly true when the client is elderly or disabled or when help with child care is required. Needless to say, the question of whether to intervene directly with friends or relatives or to help the individual to approach them is a delicate one calling for careful assessment and discussion with the client.

Family Sessions on Behalf of Individual Treatment   As the family therapy chapters will describe, often the problems of an individual are the impetus for exploratory family therapy. When a family is in treatment, each family member is in some way committed to the therapy. On the other hand, when an individual is in treatment and family members are invited for sessions, they are viewed as part of the individual's environment and related to as expressive collaterals. Besides providing the client with psychological support or practical help, the presence of family members in sessions can provide a powerful tool for freeing the client of internalized distortions that are interfering with functioning.

A twenty-two-year-old secretary, Sally, living with her divorced mother, sought treatment at a family agency during a crisis in her relationship with her fiancé with whom she was constantly arguing. She described her feelings toward her mother as "indifferent" or "mildly friendly." She was estranged from her father and had been angry with him since his separation from the family ten years earlier. A few weeks after she began treatment, her mother announced that she planned to remarry; after hearing this Sally became seriously depressed and had suicidal thoughts. Although reluctant at first, she accepted the caseworker's suggestion to bring her mother to a session with her. In the course of a total of three meetings, mother and daughter shared some old pains and achieved an intimacy and openness they had not enjoyed in many years. Sally recognized that her mother truly cared about her and she allowed herself to care in return. Later on in treatment, a joint meeting was arranged with Sally and her father, who made a special trip from another state to attend the session. Her father was able to clarify his reasons for leaving the family and reassured Sally that these had nothing to do with her. To Sally's amazement, he said he was very much interested in rebuilding his relationship with her. Sally's early parental introjects (her internalizations of an indifferent mother and a remote, punishing father) clearly had distorted her view of the current situation. As it turned out, she was able to share feelings and develop relationships with her parents that she never believed would be possible. Furthermore, she realized, she had been displacing and projecting some of these distortions onto her fiancé, and these had contributed heavily to the hostilities that had developed between them. During the latter part of the therapy, Sally's fiancé joined Sally for premarital counseling; in joint sessions, some of these issues became better understood by both.

Had the caseworker confined the treatment to individual meetings, Sally's myth about the hopelessness of deepening her relationships with her parents would have taken longer for her and the worker to recognize: either through talk about her parents or through transference with the worker. Since her distortions had a direct bearing on her difficulties with her fiancé, this relationship (which originally motivated her to seek help) might have deteriorated to the point that it could not have been saved, had she not resolved the long-standing problems with her mother and father. And, of course, the direct participation of her fiancé further facilitated the treatment.

Network Therapy[17] Sometimes the worker and client invite other people to help to accomplish psychological objectives identical in nature with those sought in direct treatment. Relatives, friends, teachers, and doctors are sometimes in a far better position than social workers to give sustaining help to a client. Often they do so spontaneously, but the caseworker can also motivate them to take this type of responsibility. Particularly with extremely anxious or depressed people, it is sometimes most helpful to enlist the interest of friends or relatives who like the client and have a warm nature, a good deal of common sense, and a capacity for equanimity. It is surprising how often such people can be found if the worker is alert to the possibility and not so tied to a desk that he or she never makes contact with them.

Simply stated, *network therapy* involves mobilizing feeling-oriented collaterals to provide a stable support group to a client in crisis and to prevent future difficulties. Some therapists have been known to organize "networks" of thirty or forty people; almost always a smaller group is sufficient.

Mrs. Antonini, a recently widowed fifty-eight-year-old housewife, whose children were grown and married, sought help at a community mental health clinic for depression. Her symptoms were so severe that it was feared that she could become suicidal and might have to be hospitalized, an idea Mrs. Antonini opposed. The clinical social worker was able to encourage her to join with her in calling a meeting of her children and a neighbor. Several of her in-laws, with whom there had been some friction over differences they had about decisions Mrs. Antonini had made about her husband's burial, were also invited. In a two-and-a-half-hour session, the worker introduced the problem of her client's depression and isolation and then turned to the assembled group for ideas about what could be done and how this "network" might be able to help. Mrs. Antonini's daughter, who took the most initiative during the meeting, suggested that a schedule could be worked out whereby family members and friends would alternate in being available for telephone or personal visits. Everyone agreed to this plan. Once the details of how each person in the network could be reached were worked out, it was decided that Mrs. Antonini would take the initiative for making the contacts when she needed or wanted them. It should be added that during this meeting the tensions with the in-laws were, in large part, relieved.

Slowly but surely, with the network as a consistent resource of support for Mrs. Antonini, combined with casework sessions and the location of some baby-sitting jobs, this client's depression lifted. Long after treatment ended, her network was available to her and, as it turned out, she was also able to provide support to other members when they faced difficulties in their own lives.

Similarly, in one family therapy case of a teenage boy, an only child in angry rebellion against his elderly parents, the therapist invited one of the boy's peers, a cousin, and a teacher to join a few sessions. The presence of network members was supportive to the entire family and helped to lend perspective to the boy and his parents, whose relationship had become so seriously polarized.

Artificial networks (in contrast to natural ones of relatives, friends, and others whom the client already knows) with mutual aid functions have long been utilized by Alcoholics Anonymous, weight-losers groups, and so on. More recently, various kinds of groups, organized formally and informally, provide support and a feeling of relatedness to single parents, homosexuals, members of a particular ethnic group,

and so on. When family and friends are not available, artificial networks may have to be created. Many social agencies and organizations provide groups for widows; for parents of mentally and physically disabled or ill children; for AIDS victims and their families; for children of alcoholics, incest survivors, and relatives of terminally ill patients. Indeed, group therapy itself can provide, among other things, a network of peer supports.

We conclude this section on resources by emphasizing the obvious: the clinical social worker is usually not the person who can *directly* provide the client with the major supports needed. Even when the worker-client relationship is a sustained and very important one, every client needs much more than that. If inadvertently a worker, out of enthusiasm to help or through possessiveness, in any manner implies he or she can meet most of a client's needs, this fosters an unhealthy dependency and holds out a promise that cannot possibly be delivered. Beyond that, as in the case of Sally, in many instances reassurance from family members is far more meaningful and bolstering to self-esteem than ongoing support from the most caring worker. All people require a sense of belonging and importance, and efforts to activate supportive people in the environment—for clients who do not have enough of them—can be among a caseworker's most helpful and rewarding functions.

Furthermore, it should also go without saying that the worker is often not in the best position to exercise direct influence in a client's life in ways the latter wants or needs it. Very often a friend or relative, "big brother," doctor, clergyman, lawyer, guidance counselor, or teacher carries more influence with the client, is better qualified to advise or aid in a particular area, and can be enlisted in the client's interest. A visiting nurse or homemaker can take on educational and supportive functions in their realms of expertise that the worker cannot. We do our clients a disservice if we neglect to provide easy access not only to essential agency services but to the many opportunities for nourishment and growth that can become available when we search hard enough to find them.

TYPES OF ROLES[18]

The aspect of environmental work that remains to be discussed is that of variations related to the role or function of the worker: (1) provider, (2) locater, or (3) creator of a resource; (4) interpreter; (5) mediator; and (6) aggressive intervener. Obviously, a worker often carries more than one role simultaneously when working with the client on various aspects of the milieu. The role may shift rapidly and conflict between roles can exist. Each role has its own characteristics.

One is a *provider* of a resource when one gives the resource through the agency in which one works. Many of the intricacies of this role have been discussed in the section on the worker's own social agency. Sometimes the worker's role as provider involves efforts to expand agency services. A caseworker in a mental health clinic, for example, may decide to organize a group for the relatives of recently discharged mental hospital patients or may plan a multiple family group for these patients and their families.

From the point of view of role, the worker represents the resource and the client reacts as though the worker were directly responsible for both the positive and negative features of the service given or withheld. A client may feel very appreciative of the caseworker who describes the agency's homemaker service that can be enlisted in the care of an elderly relative. On the other hand, a client may blame the caseworker or make accusations of discrimination if it is found that her income is too high to enroll her child in the agency's day care center funded to serve children of impoverished families. In the first case, there may be positive effects on concomitant direct work with the client; in the second, direct work may be impeded by the cli-

ent's anger. Thorough knowledge of agency policies, flexibility in their application, readiness to help clients decide whether they want the resource or want to qualify for it are all part of the administration of a resource. So also is working with clients' resentment and resistance when these occur. Direct and indirect work are here closely intertwined.

The role of *locater* of a resource is an extremely important one. Success in it depends not only on thorough knowledge of the local community, but also on imaginative assessment of the client's need. The worker must display ingenuity in finding the resource in unexpected places and skill in interesting particular individuals in making special provisions for the client's special needs. Assessing certain needs and locating some resources, such as the appropriate public welfare office or the state employment service, may be simple enough. But sometimes clients' needs are less routine: genetic counseling may be helpful to a newly married couple where one spouse has a family history of genetic problems; a clinic specializing in the treatment of headaches may be able to diagnose and bring relief to a suffering client; a teacher of braille may be helpful to a man who has recently lost his eyesight. Patience and much phone work and some footwork may be required to locate the resources that can be most helpful to the client. Especially in large urban areas, where there are so many agencies and services of all types, the caseworker may need to consult directories of social agencies and health facilities or else seek guidance from organizations that specialize in information and referral services.

Just beyond the locater role comes that of *creator* of a resource. The same qualities and activities are involved in this as in the more difficult aspects of the locater role. If, for example, the resources mentioned in the above paragraph cannot be located in or near the client's community, the worker, often with the help of a supervisor or department head, may attempt to influence a hospital to create specialty clinics for genetic counseling or for headache treatment; the worker may encourage a local school for blind children to offer classes for adults. Volunteers can often be interested in providing or arranging for various kinds of services when organized resources are not available or when those available do not offer quite what the client needs. Churches can sometimes be involved in such activity, as can "service-oriented" clubs of various types. For example, such organizations are frequently willing to sponsor Alcoholics Anonymous groups where there are none, children's camps, activities for single parents, special interest groups, and so on. The wider the worker's network of associations in the community, the more likely he or she is to be able to become a resource creator.

In the role of *interpreter*, the worker is helping someone else to understand or behave differently toward the client. The accuracy and completeness of the worker's own understanding of the client are the obvious baseline. As has been noted in the discussion of communication procedures with collaterals, it is essential also to be attuned to the attitudes and feelings of the person to whom one is trying to explain the client. Much of the time this is no simple fact-giving process, but an interactional one in which information and opinions are exchanged and feelings often come into play. Thus, the worker is often oriented to previously unknown aspects of the client's functioning that may be pertinent to direct work with the client.

Again, the worker must be absolutely sure that the client is willing to have the information shared. The information given should be only that which is pertinent to the objective of the contact. Particular care must be taken not to divulge inadvertently information that might create difficulty for the client. The nature of interpretive communications is strongly influenced by the type of collateral to whom information is being given. Other considerations being equal, the worker can share more freely with a fellow social worker or with a member of another helping profession. Beyond this, special care must be taken to be guided not only by the collateral's personality and attitude toward the client but also by knowledge of the role played in the client's life and of ways in which self-interest or other responsibilities may be involved. Occasionally, despite the greatest care, misuse is made of information. In one situation, which illustrates the need for extreme caution, a clinical social worker had seen a husband and wife for marital counseling. Several weeks after they terminated the couple separated. Family court had become involved and requested information about the agency contact. The worker obtained a written release from the wife and sent a summary of the treatment of the couple to the court, including some personal information about the husband, who later sued the agency and the worker for revealing confidential matters without consent. Sometimes, too, a client may think information has been misused even when it has not. The worker should be alert to the possibility of this in interviews with the client and should bring into the open any feelings on the client's part that the contact has misfired. Of course, as noted earlier, one way of minimizing suspicion is, when practical, for the client to be a participant in the conference with the collateral.

The next two roles to be discussed are those of *mediator* and *aggressive intervener*. They share some common features, since mediation and aggressive intervention are two aspects of case advocacy. Both go further than interpretation. Both assume some strain or conflict in the relationship between client and collateral. They differ, however, in method. Mediation relies on the force of greater understanding of the client and of his or her needs and rights by the collateral. Aggressive intervention calls for the use of some type of force.[19] Mediation involves both direct and indirect casework. In this type of work with the collateral, all that has been said about the role of interpreter holds for that of mediator, some of it with even greater force.

Since this role usually applies when there has already been tension between a client and another individual or representative of an institution, there is often anger or at best irritation or annoyance. When an institution or agency of some sort is involved, there is usually defensiveness about a decision already made or an action already taken. The possibility of client distortion or simply of misunderstanding or misinterpretation is high. The worker must be ready to listen to the other side and be able to withhold judgment. One must try to understand the collateral's point of view and sometimes must modify one's own. Mediation is a two-way street, and the interview with the collateral may lead the worker to expand a view of the client; the worker may feel that the client will have to make changes in behavior or viewpoint if improvement in the interpersonal situation is to occur. It is the worker's responsibility to share such impressions with the client, who, if in agreement and possessing the motivation, may then decide to try to alter his or her approach. Once worker and client are both convinced that their position is sufficiently persuasive, the right moment and the right words then need to be found to induce the collateral to reconsider actions or attitudes toward the client.

A sixteen-year-old boy, David, had been periodically suspended from school for cutting classes and for displaying a surly attitude toward teachers. David disliked the academic program and wanted to be transferred to a special vocational program to train in automobile mechanics, for which he had a special gift. The school authorities, however, who were clearly angry, were unwilling to refer him to this program, which would cost the school district money, because they assumed from his behavior that he would be a poor risk. After learning this, the worker was able to help David recognize that his attitude contributed to the school's unyielding position. Subsequently, a conference at the school was arranged by the worker. David participated and, with the worker's support, was able to speak for himself; he explained his unhappiness with his present program and apologized for his behavior. The worker's expression of confidence in David's seriousness about vocational training was instrumental in tipping the balance, and the transfer was approved. Months of direct work, in which the worker encouraged David's strengths, preceded mediation with the school. Had the worker intervened prematurely, before David was willing to share in the responsibility for the problem, the work undoubtedly would have backfired.

In terms of communication procedures, mediation requires ventilation and person-situation reflection, with timing and tact of the utmost importance.

In another situation, a landlord refused to rent an apartment to Mrs. Watson, who was receiving public assistance, stating that he had had bad luck with "welfare tenants." The worker from the welfare department, who knew this woman well, met with the landlord and assured him that Mrs. Watson's past record as a tenant was beyond reproach; the worker's willingness to vouch for Mrs. Watson persuaded him to rent to her after all. The worker's tact and appreciation of the landlord's concern for his property were crucial; had she discouraged him from revealing his strong feelings or argued with him about the injustice of stereotyping, the chances are that she would have alienated him and thereby unwittingly participated in preventing Mrs. Watson from getting the apartment she very much wanted.

The growth in the problem of destructive activities, especially by youths in their teens and young adults, has greatly complicated the question of intervention on the client's behalf. On the one hand, fear and hysteria lead to unjustified punitiveness, to hasty accusations founded on little evidence, and to exaggerated fears concerning what in other times would be considered a "normal" degree of "acting up." On the other hand, some of the forms that youth aggression now takes are often truly dangerous, and individuals have a right to protect themselves and others in legitimate ways. The social worker is not a lawyer for the client and does not have the legally recognized responsibility to plead the client's case, right or wrong. The social worker is just as deeply concerned about the client's rights and well-being as the lawyer, but the worker's orientation and responsibility are to the whole as well as to the part: to some degree to "the other" as well as to the client. Therefore, the decision about intervention calls for careful evaluations of long-run as well as short-run effects. In the role of mediator, the worker's *over-* or *underprotection* of the client can be unrealistic and lead to further aggressive activities that help neither client nor others. In any event, direct work with some clients may be needed to help them recognize their effects on others, as in the case of David, cited above.

There are times when it is clear that a client's rights are being ignored, denied, or abrogated and mediation has not been successful in attaining a correction of the injustice. Here the worker must turn to the second type of advocacy: aggressive intervention. The worker may argue forcefully for the client, often going beyond the collateral to a supervisor or a higher executive and enlisting the efforts of upper administrative levels of the agency. The worker may use other community resources, individual or organizational, to bring pressure to bear in the client's favor.

The staff of a family service agency had obtained repeated evidence that a large company in the city was refusing (sometimes bla-

tantly, sometimes more covertly) to hire qualified black workers except on the janitorial staff. For the agency members who wanted to protest, the situation was complicated by the fact that one of the lay board members of the agency held a management position with the company. For this reason, the board member was protective toward the firm and was also concerned—as were other board members—that the agency would alienate the company if it took a direct stand against it. Staff members, determined to take some kind of action, met with the board and persuasively argued that the local Commission on Human Rights should become involved. This public agency could assist several clients who had been discriminated against without revealing the agency's interest in the situation. A lengthy investigation by the commission resulted in an order to the company, backed up with the threat of penalty, to cease discriminating; as a result, the personnel practices of the firm were changed.

Furthermore, groups of lawyers and various activist organizations particularly interested in protecting the rights of clients who are in poverty or subject to discrimination have provided new and valuable resources upon which to call for case advocacy that go beyond what the social worker can do alone.

When the worker moves from persuasion to a form of pressure or exercise of power, new considerations come into focus. The use of power inevitably arouses hostility and resistance. If the worker uses it and loses, the client may be worse off than before because of the counterhostility that has been generated.

For instance, in the above example, had the agency itself taken direct aggressive action against the company that was discriminating against blacks, not only would it have lost an important board member but, of greater significance, the action might have antagonized this powerful firm enough to attempt to use its influence with the United Way, the funding body on which the agency heavily depended, to retaliate against the agency. If the agency's finances had thereby been jeopardized, the loss to many clients benefiting from its services would have been immeasurable. On the other hand, referral of the matter to a public agency with greater expertise and the authority to investigate eventually brought about the long overdue changes without causing any repercussions to the clients and without exposing the agency to attack.

Aggressive intervention is obviously a form of advocacy to be turned to only after other methods, including mediation, have failed; when one is quite sure that injustice is being done; and when the aggressive effort has some possibility of succeeding. When there is danger of backfire, clients should know this and decide themselves whether they want to take this risk, with the worker's helping to weigh the pros and cons realistically. The means that are taken will also affect the worker's total relationship with the clients and other objectives the worker may have with them, so these effects must also be taken into consideration.

Professional goals and ethics are also involved in the way in which aggressive intervention is carried on. The worker is still operating as a caseworker, and means that are in conflict with professional ethics are not justified by the ends they serve.[20] A caseworker should not, for example, wittingly misrepresent the facts, let alone lie under oath, or blindly advocate violent conduct against adversaries of the client, no matter how unjust their actions might be.

The interpreter and mediator roles stress the social worker's art of reconciliation, of bringing opposing interests into a cooperative relationship built on greater understanding. These are powerful tools. Aggressive intervention, on the other hand, is an approach of confrontation. It relies on force rather than on reconciliation. It,

too, is powerful, but it is a two-edged sword that should be used with caution and with an effort to anticipate unintended consequences.

When the worker is employed by an agency, the total system becomes pertinent to decisions about what means to use. Often, a higher level within the worker's own agency can bring pressure more effectively than the worker, possibly even succeeding through mediation so that aggressive intervention is not needed at all.

A distinction is commonly made between *case advocacy* and the more general *social action* or *social advocacy*. The former refers to the worker's efforts to remedy an immediate concrete injustice to which the individual client is being subjected. The latter refers to a more general attempt to bring about changes in policies or practices that adversely affect a whole group of clients or others in the community. In practice, the line between case advocacy and social action advocacy is sometimes blurred, as in the case of company discrimination described earlier.

It often happens that when clients gain self-confidence, some freedom from their own pressing concerns, and greater knowledge of the effect of community conditions, they join groups in the general community through which they can participate in social action. If clients show interest in this, one frequently can help locate appropriate groups to join just as one helps the clients locate other resources. We believe it is unwise to use the casework treatment relationship to *enlist* clients in causes, no matter how good those causes may be. To do so is similar in principle to steering clients into one's own church or political party and carries all the same hazards of clients feeling impelled to please their workers, upon whom they are dependent for social and psychological help. The caseworker's role differs in this respect from that of the community organizer, whose recognized role is often this very activity and is sometimes an acknowledged reason for contact with a client group.

With so much injustice and, often, widespread indifference to the needs and rights of others prevailing today, the need for social action and advocacy is great. Poverty, inadequate income assistance grants, discrimination, poor housing, homelessness, unemployment, and inferior educational facilities are conditions that have denied millions of citizens access to opportunities that many others take for granted. For some—particularly for many of the elderly, sick, and disabled—there are often no individual solutions. There must be massive reform even to touch upon the inhuman day-in-day-out realities of people trapped or neglected because of societal deficiencies.

Certainly, as we have said before, social work as a whole—let alone casework—cannot eradicate massive social problems. On the other hand, the caseworker does have avenues through which to participate in bringing about more modest but nevertheless significant social changes. Often, the agency of which the worker is a staff member is already engaged in social action within its area of competence and effectiveness. It may, then, be part of one's regular work to participate in this action. *The movement from case to cause is essential.* By collecting information about injustices and needed resources in individual cases, the worker can supply the data that can initiate the social advocacy, giving evidence through which change can be accomplished.[21] Agencies carry a definite responsibility for providing ways in which such information can be used. If the agency is not active in areas in which it could be effective the worker, as a staff member, can try to influence it to develop a social action program. The worker also has a personal political life, professional associations, and opportunities for common action with groups of colleagues.[22] Socially minded lawyers and social workers have also found recently that they have similar objectives, and they have worked collaboratively with great effectiveness. In fact, some social workers particularly interested in championing human rights have sought additional training in law. For psychosocial caseworkers, we see participation in social advocacy of one type or another as a clear professional responsibility.

ASSESSMENT OF THE PERSON–ENVIRONMENT GESTALT

It has taken many pages to describe some of the interactions that can occur between clients and their environments and to describe efforts caseworkers can try to facilitate improvements in these interactions. Yet, pervasive institutional changes come slowly. Major social reform is not a basic function or realistic goal of casework, even though we try to do all we can to ameliorate environmental deprivations. But there are times when, even within the framework of oppressive conditions and unresponsive systems, individuals and families *can* make changes to improve their lives rather than wait until their needs are met by hard-won social changes. In a particular situation, a worker and client may clearly see that the client's problems are induced by outer forces. But if the larger environment is not modifiable, it may still be possible to find some avenue of relief.

This is where *the caseworker's ability to assess the individual or family becomes crucial.* On the basis of the assessments, creative interventions may be devised. For example, a lonely elderly woman living on meager income assistance benefits may be healthy enough and emotionally suited to be employed as a foster grandmother for neglected children. A man who is demoralized because he can no longer find employment in his own craft may be versatile enough to train for another, more employable trade. Especially if support from his family can be elicited, an intelligent black student getting a second-rate education in an inferior segregated school system may have the courage and drive required to seek a transfer to a nearby all-white school that better suits his educational potential and aspirations. The worker must be able to evaluate each situation separately and determine whether a particular client has the capacity or motivation to circumvent, at least partially, the unhealthy social conditions that led to the difficulties.[23] What is important is that we not assume that *all* victims of a limited opportunity structure are totally trapped. Even though it would be our wish to help everyone so afflicted, there are some who can be helped, up to a point, in spite of great odds stacked against them. What is equally important is that caseworkers, feeling overwhelmed and helpless by the enormity of problems faced by some socioeconomically deprived and oppressed individuals and families, do not fall into the trap of blaming the victims for society's failures. When this happens, even concrete help that might be made available is not offered, or else it is rejected because clients sense the worker's lack of understanding.

We have said many times that the decision of who should intervene in the client's milieu is almost always a joint decision arrived at through discussions between worker and client. In the assessment, the worker also attempts to get a broad impression of the client's personality, evaluating the client's capacity *in relation to the particular task at hand*. Of course, the quality and responsiveness of the environment are simultaneously evaluated. Is the client intellectually able to deal with the system in question? Does he or she have the necessary language ability, or is an interpreter needed? Are perception, judgment, control, and self-directive capacities sufficiently strong that, with help in understanding the situation, the client will be able to handle it independently? If assistance is required, would involvement of a family member rather than or in addition to the worker be supportive? If a family as a whole is affected by a situation, are family members supportive of one another, or, as a result of feeling frustrated or demoralized, are they blaming and working against each other? Is the individual or family immediately ready to make agreed upon moves,

or are feelings so deeply involved in the situation that there is need for ventilation as a prelude to taking effective steps to improve the situation? When the pressure of underlying emotion is so great that it interferes with wise action or even consideration of action, ventilation may be required. When anxiety is high, or self-esteem low, or the defense of turning against the self is crippling the client's self-confidence or causing him or her to behave in self-damaging ways, a large measure of sustaining procedures may need to precede and accompany reflective discussion of the situation and ways in which it can be changed.

Note that the personality or family is not being assessed in the abstract here, but in relation to the task or situation that is being faced. People may be capable of rational consideration of one type of dilemma, but not of another; amenable to advice about matters on which the caseworker is regarded as an expert, but not amenable about others; overwhelmed by anxiety under some circumstances, cool and collected in others that to someone else might seem just as threatening.

Occasionally, the decision of who should intervene is influenced by a matter of timing. For the benefit of a child, it may be important for a teacher who has a negative attitude toward the youngster to be seen immediately, before the situation gets even worse. Though it might seem better for the child's parents to make the contact, for some reason it may take weeks before they can feel comfortable enough to do so. In this case, therefore, the parents and caseworker together may decide that it would be advisable for the worker to make the initial contact with the teacher.

Environmental work, then, depends not only on an assessment of the modifiability of environmental factors but on the client's and worker's view of the client's ability to bring about the necessary changes. Although the general direction is one in which the client is helped to achieve as much competence and independence as possible, intervening factors just discussed strongly influence the decision of whether the worker or the client takes a particular action in the environment.

A young, unmarried woman with two small children lived in an apartment with many violations, several of which were detrimental to health and even dangerous for the children. The woman's impulse control, her welfare worker knew, was poorly developed and her reality testing, especially under stress, could become distorted. Furthermore, the woman had already had screaming encounters with the landlord, who was known to be hostile and indifferent to the needs of his tenants. On the basis of her assessment of the woman's ego functioning and of her powerlessness in the face of this particular landlord, the caseworker agreed to intervene herself and—by threatening to report him to the city housing department—to force the landlord to make the urgently needed repairs. Had the worker insisted that the woman deal with the landlord herself, she might well have ended up hitting him and being taken to court by him. Needless to say, the repairs in the apartment so necessary to the health of this family might never have been accomplished.

In a contrasting situation, a depressed woman who had recently lost her job recognized that she was probably eligible for unemployment insurance benefits, but she felt unable to mobilize herself to go to the appropriate agency to apply for them. The caseworker considered accompanying her to the state insurance office. However, his assessment of her was that of a competent woman with no serious ego deficiencies and that "doing for" her in this way would only reinforce her seeming helplessness. Instead, he chose to encourage and support her capacity for autonomous functioning, in spite of her depression, which, in large part, was precipitated by her sense of helplessness upon losing her job.

The utility of environmental work is sometimes denigrated because it is too often seen vaguely as "only ego supportive," without further analysis of what part of the ego it is supporting or how the intrapsychic balance of the individual can be affected. In Chapter 2, we referred to the balance of forces in the personality system and pointed out that a small amount of change sometimes can tip the balance and result in considerable relief of distress or improvement of an individual's social functioning. For example, in the above illustration of the young woman for whom the caseworker intervened with the landlord, the caring evidenced by initiating the action could satisfy some of the client's longings for someone to minister to her needs; the worker further hoped that the support would quiet some of the woman's angry feelings. When they were less pressured by inner (id) drives, it was possible that some of her adaptive (ego) functions could be freed, strengthened, and mobilized. These, in turn, could help her to begin to gain better mastery over other aspects of her life. On the other hand, had the worker accompanied the depressed woman to apply for unemployment benefits, he might have unwittingly reinforced her depression by supporting her feelings of helplessness. It should be recognized, however, that although this woman actually was able to make the trip alone, many depressed clients could not have done so. Sometimes one must "test" a situation by observing a client's response when encouraged to act without help.

In another case, a man who was earning a marginal living became depressed and self-deprecating. His caseworker helped him to locate a better paying job and—with very little direct treatment—his mood lifted and his attitudes and relationships improved. His self-critical, punishing superego was less active and replaced by greater self-approval; his adaptive ego functions were no longer inhibited and immobilized. He was thereby freed to enjoy life more fully. In this situation, the worker correctly assumed that as this client's superego became less harsh there would be a shift in the balance of other aspects of his personality.

Here, again, the assessment of this client's personality structure, his abilities, and his motivation was essential to successful environmental treatment.

NOTES

1. See, for example, the following important, now classic papers: Richard A. Cloward, "Illegitimate Means, Anomie and Deviant Behavior," *American Sociological Review*, 24 (April 1959), 164–176; Gregory Bateson, Don D. Jackson, Jay Haley, and John Weakland, "Toward a Theory of Schizophrenia," *Behavioral Science*, 1 (October 1956), 252–264; Ronald D. Laing, "Mystification, Confusion, and Conflict," in Ivan Boszormenyi-Nagi and James L. Framo, eds., *Intensive Family Therapy* (New York: Harper & Row, 1965), 343–363.

See also two other excellent articles that deal brilliantly with issues pertinent to psychosocial therapy and the environment: Carel B. Germain, "The Ecological Approach to People-Environmental Transactions," *Social Casework*, 62 (June 1981), 323–331; and Sophie Freud Loewenstein, "Inner and Outer Space in Social Casework," *Social Casework*, 60 (January 1979), 19–29.

2. There are many good articles that discuss this approach and describe programs that provide preventive services of various kinds at the times and places they may be needed. See Stan Blazyk and Margaret M. Canavan, "Therapeutic Aspects of Discharge Planning," *Social Work*, 30 (November–December 1985), 489–496; Martin Bloom, "Social Prevention: An Ecological Approach," in Carel B. Germain, ed., *Social Work Practice* (New York: Columbia University Press, 1979), pp. 326–345; Anne Kurtzman Effron, "Children and Divorce: Help from an Elementary School," *Social Casework*, 61 (May 1980), 305–312;

Donna Haig Friedman and Steven Friedman, "Day Care as a Setting for Intervention in Family Systems," *Social Casework*, 63 (May 1982), 291–295; Sister M. Vincentia and Sister Ann Patrick Conrad, "A Parish Neighborhood Model for Social Work Practice," *Social Casework*, 61 (September 1980), 423–432; Carol Meyer, ed., *Preventive Intervention* (Washington, D.C.: National Association of Social Workers, 1975); Lydia Rapoport, "The Concept of Prevention in Social Work," *Social Work*, 6 (January 1961), 19–28; and Nancy Boyd Webb, "Crisis Consultation: Preventive Implications," *Social Casework*, 62 (October 1981), 465–471.

3. There have always been some social workers who have disparaged the casework approach, believing it puts the burden for change on the individual rather than on the society that deprives and oppresses. It is beyond the scope of this book to address this issue at length, but the reader may be interested in comments made on this subject by one social worker still well known for her years of dedication to advancing fundamental social changes. Writing during the depression of the 1930s, Bertha Reynolds responded to those who believed that casework should be put aside until "a just and healthy social order is achieved," by asking "is there not a place also for the development of personality, individual by individual?" If, she went on, casework can free people "from crippling accumulations of fear and hate so that they may have energy to use what intelligence they possess; if it educates in the best sense of the word for the use of freedom of choice and for healthier social relationships, it becomes not a luxury but a necessity in a time of social change. For, after all, do we not know, when we are most thoughtful about it, that we are held back from a better social order not by the absence of some lucky change to set in motion the wheels of normal living, but rather because we are not ready, as a people, to think freely and maturely? If social case work itself can grow up to a maturity which will create the conditions of more abundant and responsible life in the individuals with whom it enters into relationship, then indeed it has a place in the cooperative commonwealth which is our only hope for the future." Bertha Capen Reynolds, "A Study of Responsibility in Social Case Work," *Smith College Studies in Social Work*, 5 (September 1934), 126–127.

4. See, for example, Henry Wasserman, "Some Thoughts about Teaching Social Casework Today," *Smith College Studies in Social Work*, 43 (February 1973), 124–125, who comments that the general or ecological systems approach seems to appeal to students working in black or Chicano communities and that the psychological orientation is often seen as useful primarily in work with middle-class "neurotics." In our view such an unfortunate dichotomy, when put in practice, also sells graduate education short!

5. Germain, "The Ecological Approach to People-Environmental Transactions," p. 324.

For interesting discussions on the use of paraprofessionals, see Norman Epstein and Anne Shainline, "Paraprofessional Parent-Aides and Disadvantaged Families," *Social Casework*, 55 (April 1974), 230–236; Charles Grosser, "Local Residents as Mediators Between Middle Class Professional Workers and Lower-Class Clients," *Social Services Review*, 40 (March 1966), 56–63; David A. Hardcastle, "The Indigenous Nonprofessional in the Social Service Bureaucracy: A Critical Examination," *Social Work*, 16 (April 1971), 56–63; Harold M. Kase, "Purposeful Use of Indigenous Paraprofessionals," *Social Work*, 17 (March 1972), 109–110; Philip Kramer, "The Indigenous Worker: Hometowner, Striver, or Activist," *Social Work*, 17 (January 1972), 43–49; B. D. Rigby, ed., *Short-Term Training for Social Development: The Preparation of Front-Line Workers and Trainers* (New York: International Association of Schools of Social Work, 1978); and Francine Sobey, *The Non-Professional Revolution in Mental Health* (New York: Columbia University Press, 1970).

The reader will be interested in Dorothy Fahs Beck's study, *Counselor Characteristics: How They Affect Outcomes* (Milwaukee, Wisc.: Family Service America, 1988), especially pp. 35–48. To our surprise, with the possible exception of treatment of complicated family relationship problems, counselors *without* significant graduate-level education were found to be more effective in helping people with their difficulties than were those with professional education. These are some of the possible explanations offered by Beck for these unexpected findings: "Could it be that master's-level preparation for counseling concentrates to such a degree on training for therapy focused on family relationship problems that it does not prepare graduates adequately for work on other problems, particularly those requiring a heavy component of case management, information giving, referrals, home visits (with related travel requirements), case advocacy, or the coordination of support services? A further possibility is that some graduate programs may encourage students to value skill in family therapy more highly than corresponding skill in counseling focused on support and linkage functions, thus encouraging a greater investment in the former. Students looking toward a future in private practice may also push faculty in this direction. Some graduates may even attempt insight therapy or modification of basic family relationship patterns with clients who see their own needs solely in terms of concrete services and support, thus alienating them so that they drop out prematurely." As we will mention in our concluding section of this text, these findings may have implications for graduate education as well as for agency hiring and in-service training policies.

6. Richard M. Grinnell, Jr., and Nancy S. Kyte, "Environmental Modification: A Study," *Social Work*, 20 (July 1975), 313–318.

7. Bernard Neugeboren, "Opportunity Centered Social Services," *Social Work*, 15 (April 1970), 47–52, provides good examples.

8. For an excellent article on the importance of helping clients develop their own skills to modify the environment, see Joan Kay Hashimi, "Environmental Modification: Teaching Social Coping Skills," *Social Work*, 26 (July 1981), 323–326. See also Margaret H. Pearlman and Mildred G. Edwards, "Enabling in the Eighties: The Client Advocacy Group," *Social Casework*, 63 (November 1982), 532–539, in which the authors describe a method used for helping clients become their own advocates and become their own change agents.

9. Discussions of various aspects of the situational component of the person-situation gestalt can be found in the following readings: Salvatore Ambrosino, "Integrating Counseling, Family Life Education, and Family Advocacy," *Social Casework*, 60 (December 1979), 579–585; Gail K. Auslander and Howard Litwin, "Social Networks and the Poor: Toward Effective Policy and Practice," *Social Work*, 33 (May–June 1988), 234–238; Alice Q. Ayers, "Neighborhood Service: People Caring for People," *Social*

Casework, 54 (April 1973), 192–215; Louise Bandler, "Casework—A Process of Socialization: Gains, Limitations, Conclusions," in Eleanor Pavenstedt, ed., *The Drifters: Children of Disorganized Lower-Class Families* (Boston: Little, Brown, 1967), 255–296; Joyce O. Beckett, "Plant Closings: How Older Workers Are Affected," *Social Work,* 33 (January–February 1988), 29–33; Berta Fantl, "Preventive Intervention," *Social Work,* 7 (July 1962), 41–47; Carel B. Germain, "Social Context of Clinical Social Work," *Social Work,* 25 (November 1980), 483–488; Judith A. Lee and Carol R. Swenson, "Theory in Action: A Community Social Service Agency," *Social Casework,* 59 (June 1978), 359–370; Mildred D. Mailick, "A Situational Perspective in Casework Theory," *Social Casework,* 58 (July 1977), 401–411; Anthony N. Maluccio, "Promoting Competence Through Life Experiences," in Carel B. Germain, *Social Work Practice: People and Environments,* 282–302; Ben A. Orcutt, "Casework Intervention and the Problems of the Poor," *Social Casework,* 54 (February 1973), 85–95; Howard E. Prunty et al., "Confronting Racism in Inner-City Schools," *Social Work,* 22 (May 1977), 190–194; Beatrice Simcox Reiner, "The Feeling of Irrelevance: The Effects of a Nonsupportive Society," *Social Casework,* 60 (January 1979), 3–10; Max Siporin, "Social Treatment: A New-Old Helping Method," *Social Work,* 15 (July 1970), 13–25; Florence Wexler Vigilante and Mildred D. Mailick, "Needs-Resource Evaluation in the Assessment Process," *Social Work,* 33 (March–April 1988), 101–104; and James K. Whittaker et al., "The Ecological Paradigm in Child, Youth, and Family Services: Implications for Policy and Practice," *Social Service Review,* 60 (December 1986), 483–503.

See also Chapters 8 and 9 in Ann Hartman and Joan Laird's excellent book, *Family-Centered Social Work Practice* (New York: The Free Press, 1983).

10. For a book essential to all social work practitioners, see Suanna J. Wilson, *Confidentiality in Social Work: Issues and Principles* (New York: The Free Press, 1978). In addition to discussing ethical and practical principles of confidentiality, Wilson addresses many of the intricacies and ambiguities facing practitioners and agencies.

11. David Fanschel and Eugene B. Shinn, *Children in Foster Care: A Longitudinal Investigation* (New York: Columbia University Press, 1978), especially pp. 486–490. See also Joan Laird, "An Ecological Approach to

Child Welfare: Issues of Family Identity and Continuity," in Germain, ed., *Social Work Practice: People and Environments,* 174–209, for an intelligent and compassionate discussion of the importance of preserving ties between foster children and their biological families. Of interest also is Mary Ann Jones, Renee Neuman, and Ann W. Shyne, *A Second Chance for Families* (New York: Child Welfare League of America, 1976), a research report of a demonstration project in foster care designed to reduce or shorten placements away from home. See also Michael R. Sosin, "Delivering Services under Permanency Planning," *Social Service Review,* 61 (June 1987), 272–290.

12. The following readings deal with some of the roles and training needs of caseworkers in public welfare agencies, along with other issues relevant to public services: Leon H. Ginsberg, *The Practice of Social Work in Social Welfare* (New York: The Free Press, 1983); Jan L. Hagen, "Income Maintenance Workers: Technicians or Service Providers?" *Social Service Review,* 61 (June 1987), 261–273; Elizabeth W. Lindsey et al., "Evaluating Interpersonal Skills Training for Public Welfare Staff," *Social Service Review,* 61 (December 1987), 623–635; Anthony N. Maluccio et al., *Permanency Planning for Children: Concepts and Methods* (London: Tavistock, 1986); Diane Vinokur-Kaplan, "A National Survey of In-Service Training Experiences of Child Welfare Supervisors and Workers," *Social Service Review,* 61 (June 1987), 291–304; Thomas H. Walz and Harry J. Macy, "The MSW and the MPA: Confrontation of Two Professions in Public Welfare," *Journal of Sociology and Social Welfare,* 5 (January 1978), 100–117; and Elizabeth Wickenden, "A Perspective on Social Services," *Social Service Review,* 50 (December 1976), 570–585.

Also highly recommended: Joan Laird and Ann Hartman, eds., *A Handbook of Child Welfare: Context, Knowledge, and Practice* (New York: The Free Press, 1985), for excellent articles on child welfare practice in many of its aspects.

13. The contention that casework is ineffective with the poor is contradicted by the findings of Dorothy Fahs Beck and Mary Ann Jones, *Progress on Family Problems* (New York: Family Service Association of America, 1973). In this nationwide study of clients' and counselors' views on family agency services, based on 3,596 cases from 266 agencies, the researchers report (p. 116): "The socioeconomic status of clients proved to be a relatively minor factor in outcomes," adding, "minimum differentials in outcomes were achieved in spite of the greater handicaps faced by lower status clients—more problems, more difficult problems, less adequate environmental supports, and less knowledge of when and where to go for help." As they point out, some earlier research in casework and psychiatry had led to the opposite view: that the casework approach is not effective with such clients. "Perhaps," write Beck and Jones (p. 116), "the explanation [for their own findings] lies in the improved awareness of and accommodation to the needs and problems of the disadvantaged that are inherent in the current multiservice approach of many agencies and in their increasing use of planned, short-term, crisis-focused service." For a discussion of the background and research that led to the opinion that casework does not help the poor, see Ludwig L. Geismer et al., *Early Supports for Family Life: A Social Work Experiment* (Metuchen, N.J.: Scarecrow Press, 1972), especially pp. 72–77 and 108. It is interesting to note that Geismer's own study of a broad range of social services also does not support the view that casework is less successful with lower-status clients than with upper-status clients. See also Sol L. Garfield, "Research on Client Variables in Psychotherapy," in Garfield and Allen E. Bergin, *Handbook of Psychotherapy and Behavior Change*, 3d ed. (New York: John Wiley & Sons, 1986), whose review of relevant research suggests that social class is not related to treatment outcome (p. 233).

14. See *The New York Times*, October 7, 1986, pp. C1 and C9. See also Alicia S. Cook, "A Model for Working with the Elderly in Institutions," *Social Casework*, 61 (April 1980), 234–239; and Janice Wood Wetzel, "Interventions with the Depressed Elderly in Institutions," *Social Casework*, 61 (April 1980), 234–239.

15. For readings on some of the problems faced by social workers in various organizational settings and suggestions about how changes may be brought about, see Ralph L. Dolgoff, "Clinicians as Policymakers," *Social Casework*, 62 (May 1981), 284–292; George Brager and Stephen Holloway, *Changing Human Service Organizations* (New York: The Free Press, 1978); William Brennan and Shanti Khinduka, "Role Discrepancies and Professional Socialization: The Case of the Juvenile Probation Officer," *Social Work*, 15 (April 1970), 87–94; Wilbur A. Finch, Jr.,

"Social Workers versus Bureaucracy," *Social Work*, 21 (September 1976), 370–374; Bruce S. Jansson and June Simmons, "The Survival of Social Work Units in Host Organizations," *Social Work*, 31 (September–October 1986), 339–343; Laura J. Lee, "The Social Worker in the Political Environment of a School System," *Social Work*, 28 (July–August 1983), 302–306; Kathleen A. Olmstead, "The Influence of Minority Social Work Students on an Agency's Service Methods," *Social Work*, 28 (July–August 1983), 308–312; Rino J. Patti, "Limitations and Prospects of Internal Advocacy," *Social Casework*, 55 (November 1974), 537–545; Herman Resnick, "Effecting Internal Change in Human Service Organizations," *Social Casework*, 58 (November 1977), 546–553; and Harold H. Weissman, *Overcoming Mismanagement in the Human Services* (San Francisco: Jossey-Bass, 1973).

16. See especially the excellent article by Norman Ostbloom and Sedahlia Jasper Crase, "A Model for Conceptualizing Child Abuse Causation and Intervention," *Social Casework*, 61 (March 1980), 164–172. Using case examples of work with abusing parents, the writers discuss the importance of support, a meaningful worker-client relationship, and respect for client autonomy and decision making. Stephen Magura, "Clients View Outcomes of Child Protective Services," *Social Casework*, 63 (November 1982), 522–531, reports on a study in which a majority of clients surveyed—who were receiving public protective services for abuse, neglect, and parent-child conflict—reported an improvement in self-confidence and an increased capacity to cope with feelings and life stresses (pp. 529–531): "There was a high degree of correspondence in how clients rated case improvement and satisfaction with their caseworker"; the author concludes, "A good relationship is usually a necessary, though not a sufficient, condition for case improvement." In any event, empathy, genuineness, unconditional positive regard, and accessibility were the reasons given by clients for satisfaction with their caseworkers. "Dissatisfactions, which were infrequent, focused on unwanted advice, lack of skill, or inaccessibility." Confirming previous studies, the findings indicate that "training and competency in the conduct of relationships is essential to successful protective services casework."

See also David Ehline and Peggy O'Dea Tigue, "Alcoholism: Early Identification and Intervention in the Social Service Agency," *Child Welfare*, 56 (November 1977), 584–592; Gale Goldberg, "Breaking the Communication Barrier: The Initial Interview with an Abusing Parent," *Child Welfare*, 54 (April 1975), 274–282; Sally Ann Holmes, "A Holistic Approach to the Treatment of Violent Families," *Social Casework*, 62 (December 1981), 594–600; C. Henry Kempe and Ray E. Helfer, eds., *Helping the Battered Child and His Family* (Philadelphia: Lippincott, 1972); Genevieve B. Oxley, "Involuntary Clients' Responses to a Treatment Experience," *Social Casework*, 58 (December 1977), 607–614; and Frederick Roth, "A Practice Regimen for Diagnosis and Treatment of Child Abuse," *Child Welfare*, 54 (April 1975), 268–273.

One of the authors (Woods) worked for seven years (1956–1963) in a child protective agency's law enforcement division, located in a large metropolitan area, investigating complaints of serious child abuse. In Woods's experience, a large proportion of the clients of the protective agency *voluntarily* returned, requesting services and referrals, in spite of the fact that originally casework services had been imposed upon them.

17. See Carolyn L. Attneave, "Social Networks as the Unit of Intervention," in Philip J. Guerin, Jr., ed., *Family Therapy* (New York: Gardiner Press, 1976), pp. 220–232; Gail K. Auslander and Howard Litwin, "The Parameters of Network Intervention: A Social Work Application," *Social Service Review*, 61 (June 1987), 305–318; Alice H. Collins and Diane L. Pancoast, *Natural Helping Networks: A Strategy for Prevention* (Washington D.C.: National Association of Social Workers, 1976); Anne O. Freed, "The Family Agency and the Kinship System of the Elderly," *Social Casework*, 56 (December 1975), 579–586; Eilene L. G. McIntyre, "Social Networks: Potential for Practice," *Social Work*, 31 (November–December 1986), 421–426; Uri Rueveni, *Networking Families in Crisis* (New York: Human Services Press, 1979); Ross V. Speck and Carolyn L. Attneave, "Social Network Intervention," in Clifford J. Sager and Helen Singer Kaplan, eds., *Progress in Group and Family Therapy* (New York: Brunner/Mazel, 1972); Carol Swenson, "Social Networks, Mutual Aid, and the Life Model Practice," in Germain, *Social Work Practice*, 213–238; and James K. Whittaker and James Garbarino, eds., *Social Support Networks: Informal Helping in the Human Services* (Hawthorne, N.Y.: Aldine Publishing, 1983).

18. Lest we forget! The social worker's role in reducing environmental pressures has been recognized for many years. Wrote Mary Richmond: "Social casework may be defined as the art of doing different things for and with different people by cooperation with them to achieve at one and the same time their own and society's betterment." See Mary Richmond, *The Long View* (New York: Russell Sage Foundation, 1930), p. 174; Florence Hollis, "Environmental (Indirect) Treatment as Determined by Client's Needs," in *Differential Approach in Casework Treatment* (New York: Family Welfare Association of America, 1936); and Florence Hollis, *Social Case Work in Practice: Six Case Studies* (New York: Family Welfare Association of America, 1939), especially pp. 295–298.

In recent years, because of the increasing complexity of service delivery systems, case management has become a professional position often assumed by social workers; the case manager's functions are aimed at coordinating services for clients and ensuring that clients receive appropriate services when they need them. Many of the roles described in this chapter are carried out by case managers, but, of course, often clinical and case management functions are carried out by the same worker. See Gerald G. O'Connor, "Case Management: System and Practice," *Social Casework*, 69 (February 1988), 97–106; and Peter J. Johnson and Allen Rubin, "Case Management in Mental Health: A Social Work Domain?" *Social Work*, 28 (January–February 1983), 49–55.

19. For varying, sometimes controversial, viewpoints and approaches to advocacy, social action, and aggressive intervention, see George A. Brager, "Advocacy and Political Behavior," *Social Work*, 13 (April 1968), 5–15; Richard A. Cloward and Frances Fox Piven, "Notes Toward a Radical Social Work," in Roy Bailey and Mike Brake, eds., *Radical Social Work* (New York: Pantheon Books, 1975), pp. vii–xlviii; S. K. Khinduka and Bernard J. Coughlin, "A Conceptualization of Social Action," *Social Service Review*, 49 (March 1975), 1–14; and Michael Sousin and Sharon Caulum, "Advocacy: A Conceptualization for Social Work Practice," *Social Work*, 28 (January–February 1983), 12–17.

20. Gordon Hamilton discusses this in "The Role of Social Casework in Social Policy," *Social Casework*, 33 (October 1952), 315–324. See also Charles S. Levy, "Advocacy and the Injustice of Justice," *Social Ser-

vice Review, 48 (March 1974), 39–50; and Neil Gilbert and Harry Specht, "Advocacy and Professional Ethics," *Social Work,* 21 (July 1976), 288–293.

21. Alvin Schorr, "Editorial Page," *Social Work,* 11 (July 1966), 2; Robert Sunley, "Family Advocacy from Case to Cause," *Social Casework,* 51 (June 1970), 347–357; Charlotte Towle, "Social Work: Cause and Function," in Helen H. Perlman, ed., *Helping: Charlotte Towle on Social Work and Social Casework* (Chicago:University of Chicago Press, 1969), pp. 277–299.

22. National Association of Social Workers, Ad hoc Committee on Advocacy, "Champion of Social Victims," *Social Work,* 14 (April 1969), 16–22. See also several articles on social workers and political action in *Social Work,* 26 (July 1981).

23. On the need to understand the individual client, Bertha Reynolds wrote, "Since human beings need all sorts of things—ranging from food and shelter to recreation, education, friendship—and since attitudes play a part in their getting or not getting all of these, there can be no such a thing as social case work that does not take account of attitudes." She added: "But I am equally sure that no case work can succeed in isolating a person's attitudes and treating them apart from the conditions of his life in which they find expression." Reynolds, "A Study of Responsibility in Social Case Work," 12.

CHAPTER 9

Studying and Working with the Typology

It is not uncommon for clinical social workers to have an antipathy toward research. We say we are interested in *people*, not in abstractions and generalizations. But the time has come when research, highly sophisticated research, is necessary not only for further progress in improving our methods, but also for the very survival of our branch of social work. In Chapter 1 we referred to some evaluative research studies that have been interpreted to indicate that casework in general is ineffective, and we discussed some of the fallacies that exist in much of this research. One of the misfortunes of recent years has been the separation of research from practice. Only as skilled practitioners invest at least part of their time in research will we have sophisticated clinical studies.

The purpose of this chapter is to describe some clinical research that is not evaluative but seeks to throw light on the actual nature of the psychosocial form of treatment as practiced by clinical social workers. What do we really do? What processes do we use? Not until this is definitively clarified can we begin to study with precision such important questions as: What procedures are most useful in helping in one

kind of problem or another? With one type of personality or another? One socioeconomic group or another? Does a given procedure affect the client in the way we expect it to? What part does the client take in this process? We say this is a mutual undertaking. To what extent is it, and under what circumstances? To answer such questions convincingly, we need to make detailed analyses of what actually takes place in interviews, and we need research tools with which to do this.

It was in an effort to develop such a tool and to answer the initial question of what procedures the psychosocial caseworker uses that the research which is the subject of this chapter was undertaken.[1] The studies were made possible by a five-year grant from the National Institute of Mental Health (NIMH).* The first objective was to develop a typology or classification of casework processes that would describe all the procedures the worker uses in communicating with clients. In Chapter 4 we described the early

---

* Grant No. MH-00513, National Institute of Mental Health, U.S. Department of Health, Education and Welfare.

case studies, beginning in 1958, from which Hollis arrived at a classification that could be tested and experimented with in a larger, more rigorous study. In these studies, the researcher had set up the best classification she could devise on the basis of theory then current, and tried to use it to sort out the interview content in a preliminary series of cases. When it was found that certain activities of the worker did not fit this classification, corrections were made in the typology to achieve a better "fit." This occurred over and over again until the classification began to accommodate the data. Meanwhile, a logical organization began to emerge that made it possible to set up clear, mutually exclusive categories.

Concurrently with these studies, the classification was used in teaching, and thus exposed to the thinking and criticism of students in both master's and doctoral programs. As was noted earlier, students were also helpful in using the classification at its various stages in both master's theses and doctoral dissertations. Several of the most important features of the typology emerged from class discussion and student suggestions. One of these was the realization that the treatment process cannot be fully represented by classifying worker communications alone, since to varying degrees the client is self-propelling: that is, treats himself or herself. To catch the full dynamics of what is going on, one must include what the client is doing as well as the worker's activity. Interestingly enough, we were unable to find at that time any other classification for content analysis in any of the therapeutic fields that had attempted this type of study of client activity. It was found that most of the treatment categories developed for workers in our study could refer to client communications as well as to those of the worker. By including client communications in any study, one is giving full recognition to the fact that to a large degree treatment is something the client either does or fails to do for himself or herself. In the reflective categories, these codings also

serve to indicate to what extent the worker's intent of stimulating the client to reflection is followed by actual reflection by the client. A second major idea first suggested in class discussion was that work in the environment on the client's behalf basically involves many of the same forms of communication as those used in direct work with the client.

TESTING THE TYPOLOGY'S USABILITY

The next step taken by Hollis in the continuing study was to use the classification on new material to see to what degree independent coders could agree in classifying interview content. This was first undertaken by two groups of Smith College and New York School students in the studies referred to in Chapter 4. These studies located ambiguities in the typology and led to changes in several items. It was following this that the NIMH grant was obtained and larger studies undertaken with the help of doctoral students. Fortunately a number of students with good backgrounds in casework practice were studying for their doctorates when this project was in its early stages and it was possible to enlist their interest. Francis Turner and Yetta Appel were the principal coders in the early stages and contributed a great deal to the clarification and application of the typology. Appel searched the literature and organized it into comparative charts. Turner also used the typology in his dissertation and later in other studies. Shirley Ehrenkranz, in her dissertation, was the first to experiment with the typology in joint interviews. Others who worked with me from time to time included Trudy Bradley, Shirley Hellenbrand, Edward Mullen, Ben Avis Orcutt, William Reid, and Fil Verdiani. Many of these associates are now well known in education, research, and practice.

A total of 123 interviews from 63 cases were used in these subsequent studies. The cases were carried by workers in six family service agencies in Cleveland, Cincinnati, Detroit, New

York, and Philadelphia. The following criteria were set up:

1. The case be one in which at the end of the first interview the problem to be worked on was marital adjustment.

2. The case be new to the agency.

3. The case be the first of the above type assigned to the worker in the natural course of work, either after a given date or after completion of five interviews in a case previously assigned for study.

4. Participants be master's degree caseworkers.

5. The recording meet certain criteria discussed by the project director with the workers who volunteered to participate. Workers were asked to do very detailed "process recording," particularly indicating the interplay between client and worker in a way that would make clear which one initiated topics. Interviews were to be recorded not later than the second day after the interview was held. A minimum length was set at three single-spaced pages of typing.

Obviously, this was not verbatim reproduction but a detailed description of what transpired with considerable paraphrasing. Although studies using both tape recording and process recording indicate that some skewing of material occurs in process recording, on the whole there is great similarity in the findings derived from these two kinds of recording. Excerpts from three of the interviews reproduced in Figures 1, 2, and 3 (pages 184, 186, and 188),* illustrate the kind of detail secured. See pages 192 to 194 for comments on some further differences found between tapes and process recording.†

---

* Figures 1, 2, and 3 from Florence Hollis, *A Typology of Casework,* © 1967, 1968 by Family Service Association of America. Reprinted by permission of the publisher.

† Four students, Marianne Buchenhorner, Robert Howell, Minna Koenigsberg, and Helen Sloss, made an exploratory study of this question in their master's thesis, "The Use of Content Analysis to Compare Three Types of Case-

This material was initially used to develop operational definitions for each category of the classifications and to clear up ambiguities in the typology. Where necessary, modifications were made in the definitions and new categories were developed. Procedures were also worked out for coding in a way that would make it possible to handle the material quantitatively. This is not necessary for ordinary on-the-job use of the classification, but it is essential if it is to be used in research comparing groups of cases. For the purposes of the studies, it was decided to do line-by-line content analysis determining the proper coding by using the clause having its subject and predicate on the coded line.

The next step was a reliability study. A report of this is in the Appendix. The typology had by then reached the point that it appeared to accommodate over 95 percent of all casework communications between client and worker and could be used with reasonable reliability to make these communications accessible to quantitative research. The reliability study was followed first by a profile of the first five interviews, then by a study of continuers and discontinuers, and finally by studies of cases in which joint interviewing of married couples was the treatment mode.

The Coding

Three examples taken from interviews coded in the study show how case material was analyzed with this tool. See Figures 1, 2, and 3 and their accompanying codings in Charts 1, 2, and 3. The capital letters in the chart correspond to the major divisions of the classification discussed on pages 95 to 97 in Chapter 4. The numerals correspond to the subdivision of current person-situation reflective comments dis-

---

work Recording" (Columbia University School of Social Work, 1966). The principal difference found was a smaller proportion of sustaining communication on the tapes than in the process recordings.

cussed on pages 96 and 97. In these examples, the units coded were clauses. Each line
was coded according to the clause having its
subject and predicate on that line. When there
were two such clauses, two codings were given.
When there was no such communication, the
line was placed in the "U" column.

The symbols used in the chart are as follows:

X = Client communication
O = Worker communication
A = Sustainment
B = Direct influence
C = Exploration-description-ventilation
D = Person-situation reflection
E = Pattern-dynamic reflection
F = Developmental reflection
U = Unclassified

Subdivisions of D are as follows:

1. Concerning others or any aspect of the
outside world or of the client's physical health
2. Concerning the effect or outcome of the
client's own behavior
3. Concerning the nature of the client's own
behavior
4. Concerning the provocation or current
causation of his or her behavior
5. Concerning evaluative aspects of his or her
behavior
6. Concerning treatment and the client-
worker relationship

The coded chart makes it easy to follow the
flow of an interview. Did a worker's reflective
comment induce a period of reflection for the
client or did the client respond briefly and return to explanations and ventilation? To what
extent does the client initiate reflective comments without needing stimulation by the
worker? The charts give the answers. Note how
clearly the contrast among the three interview
samples shows up. Both client and worker in
the first case stick almost entirely to exploration-
description-ventilation. In the second sample,

communications are almost entirely in person-
situation reflection, with the worker taking an
active part in stimulating this and also offering
sustainment. In the third interview, the worker's comment initiates the switch from the
client's exploration-description-ventilation to
reflection, but thereafter the worker is considerably less active than in the second excerpt.

Informal Use of Typology

When using the typology informally for study
of one's own work or analysis of a single case,
one can simply indicate the categories in pencil
by code letter in the margins of the record. This
can give a quick picture of the type of intervention the worker is using and the nature of the
client's participation in the treatment process.
One can quickly spot, for instance, whether client or worker is entirely involved in description and ventilation or engaged in reflection.
Having made this objective observation, the
worker is then prompted to consider its significance: Has one perhaps not been sufficiently
active in stimulating the client to reflection? On
the other hand, perhaps at that particular stage
it is necessary and important for a great deal of
ventilation to take place.

It is possible to observe whether sustaining
comments seem to have enabled a client to talk
more freely or think more actively, or whether
they have instead merely induced complacency
or passivity. Or whether there has been an absence of sustainment where it could have been
helpful. Similarly, many different questions concerning the nature of the worker's activities and
the client's responses can be observed.

Analysis of a series of interviews of one's own
with a number of clients enables a worker to
spot personal idiosyncrasies. Do I tend toward
activity or toward passivity? Am I too reassuring? How directive am I? In reflective communications, do I tend to stimulate the client to
think or tend to give explanations or interpretations? To what extent are my procedures var-

15 but her husband would want to go home every other weekend. He would
16 leave her with his mother and then he would go out for the entire
17 weekend. Sometimes she would visit her mother on Sunday. If
18 they went there he would behave but if he stayed with his parents,
19 he didn't. With some anger in her voice she told me they
20 had bought furniture three times since they are here. Each time
21 he would want to go back home to live and actually they moved
22 back three times. However, when they went down there they wouldn't
23 have anything. In fact, she said there were times when they
24 didn't have enough to eat. I wondered how he always managed to
25 get jobs. She said one time he worked in a filling station;
26 another time he helped a man build a garage. I wondered what
27 he does up here and she said he works for the D. plant, and they
28 have taken him back each time that he returned. I said he must
29 be a good worker if they did this and she said he is and that is
30 the reason he has always gotten his job back. She said they
31 could have bought a home in the time they have been here if he
32 would only have stayed and acted like people should act. Now
33 he wants another baby. He told her when he came back last weekend
34 if she had another baby that would be all he wants. Their
35 youngest child is seven.
36   I asked how Mr. Z. was with the children. She said he is real
37 good with them. Makes over them and does like any normal father.
38 She feels the marital problem is hard on the children. The one
39 girl has dropped in her grades in school and while she isn't
40 certain it is because of the trouble at home, Mrs. Z feels
41 there must be some connection. The older girl can cry but the

FIGURE 1
Record No. 18: Excerpt from a First Interview

	A	B	C	D	E	F	1	2	3	4	5	6	U	
15			X											15
16			X											16
17			X											17
18			X											18
19			X											19
20			X											20
21			X											21
22			X											22
23			X											23
24				O			O							24
25			X											25
26			X											26
27			OX											27
28			X											28
29				O			O							29
30				X			X							30
31			X											31
32			X											32
33			X											33
34			X											34
35			X											35
36			O											36
37			X											37
38			X											38
39			X											39
40			X											40
41			X											41

CHART 1

13 man should. I asked if she thought it was possible to force him
14 to marry her if he really did not want to, that many men do not
15 and of course many women do not care to marry either regardless
16 of pregnancy, by her own statements earlier his relatives tried
17 to influence him against marrying her, but he did anyway, and
18 from my impression of Mr. R. from the one interview, he did not
19 indicate any regrets about marrying her and does seem to care about
20 her. She answered that it is true, his uncles tried to persuade
21 him against marriage, but he could not have gotten away with it
22 anyway, because she was the "apple of my daddy's eye" and
23 her daddy made Mr. R. marry her, and Mr. R. knew her daddy would
24 not take any foolishness from him. Breaking down completely she
25 continued that she loved her daddy so much, and he her, and yet
26 she disgraced him and her mother, she disgraced her whole family,
27 when they had so much confidence in her and such high hopes for
28 her. They were shocked when she got pregnant and it was weeks
29 before they even spoke to her, and they forgave her but they have
30 not forgotten. I said it was rather cruel of them to stop speaking
31 to her for getting pregnant, but more importantly, since she
32 feels there is something to forgive she has not forgiven herself,
33 when everyone else has, and I thought perhaps her feeling against
34 herself for getting pregnant before marriage is causing her much
35 too much grief and other emotional problems, which is causing
36 herself and her whole family trouble. She continued crying, saying
37 "I know it is, I know it is, but I can't help it," to which I said
38 that we would continue to talk more about it and perhaps after
39 she will be able to feel differently about it. Eventually she
40 calmed down and meekly asked, "Do you really think I will?" to
41 which I said I thought she would if she really wanted to.

FIGURE 2
Record No. 27: Excerpt from a Third Interview

	A	B	C	D	E	F	1	2	3	4	5	6	U	
13				O			O							13
14				O			O							14
15				O			O							15
16				O			O							16
17				O			O							17
18				O			O							18
19				O			O							19
20				X			X							20
21				X			X							21
22				X			X							22
23				X			X							23
24				X			X							24
25				X			X		X					25
26				X							X			26
27				X							X			27
28			X											28
29			X											29
30	O													30
31	O													31
32				O							O			32
33				O							O			33
34					O									34
35					O									35
36				O				O						36
37				X	X				X					37
38		O												38
39	O													39
40				X					X					40
41	O													41

CHART 2

1 I learned at this point that for five years during the marriage,
2 at the time when Mrs. Y. became involved with the other man, she had
3 worked as a doctor's assistant. Since then, she has on occasion done
4 fill in work for a doctor who has provided all kinds of free medical
5 services. This doctor recently called saying that one of his employees
6 was leaving, and asking if Mrs. Y. would work on Saturdays temporarily.
7 Her husband opposes this on the grounds that she should stay home
8 with the children. Mrs. Y. could not see this—he is at home on
9 Saturdays, can watch the children. Besides, they have their own
10 activities. She didn't see that it would hurt anyone for her to work
11 one day a week. I said perhaps her husband wants her to stay home
12 with him. She became a little thoughtful, saying that this might be
13 true, but when they are home together on Saturdays, he is out in the
14 barn working, she is running errands, etc., it is not that they are
15 sitting there kissing and holding hands.
16   At this, Mrs. Y. began to tell me that she is a very affectionate
17 person. But she can't show affection overtly to her children. This
18 sometimes bothers her—though she likes to cuddle "the baby in the
19 family." She guessed she felt this way about her oldest daughter
20 when she was born, but when the 2nd came along 2 years later she was
21 so overwhelmed with responsibility that she stopped being so affec-
22 tionate. She commented that neither of her parents had been people
23 who were affectionate with children. Maybe this explains the need she
24 has for affection. She commented here that her husband is not so af-
25 fectionate as she wished he was. When I asked about this, she said in
26 some ways they are very affectionate with each other, they always kiss
27 hello and goodby, she waves to him from the door, etc. Their friends
28 have commented on this. However, something is missing. I asked her
29 to think about what this was. She guessed she felt her husband's af-
30 fection was routine. She goes to him, hugs him, just on impulse,
31 but he never does this with her. I said this seemed to puzzle her,
32 and she believed it did. Went on to say that her husband doesn't like
33 her relationship with the children, her not being affectionate with
34 them. I said earlier she seemed to be connecting this with the fact
35 that her parents had not been affectionate with her. It might be
36 that because she hadn't received affection, it was hard to give it.
37 She couldn't understand this, though, because she can give it to her
38 husband. Maybe this seemed so important to him because his mother
39 was very affectionate with him. Even now, she kisses him when she
40 sees him. He has always been her favorite child. Perhaps he expects
41 that she be the same way with her children. She commented, as she

FIGURE 3
Record No. 34: Excerpt from a Second Interview

	A	B	C	D	E	F	1	2	3	4	5	6	U	
1													X	1
2			X											2
3			X											3
4			X											4
5			X											5
6			X											6
7			X											7
8			X											8
9			X											9
10			X											10
11				O			O							11
12				X			X							12
13				X			X							13
14				X			X							14
15													X	15
16				X					X					16
17				X					X					17
18				X					X					18
19				X					X					19
20				X						X				20
21				X						X				21
22						X								22
23						X								23
24				X					X					24
25				O					O					25
26				X					X					26
27				X					X					27
28				X					X					28
29				OX					OX					29
30				X					X					30
31				XO			XO							31
32		X		X			X							32
33		X												33
34						O								34
35						O								35
36						U								36
37						X								37
38				X			X							38
39				X			X							39
40				X			X							40
41				X			X							41
Total:														
X	0	0	11	21	0	3	9	0	10	2	0	0	2	X
O	0	0	0	4	0	3	2	0	2	0	0	0	0	O
T	0	0	11	25	0	6	11	0	12	2	0	0	2	T
	A	B	C	D	E	F	1	2	3	4	5	6	U	

CHART 3

ied in accordance with the needs of different clients?

Employed in this way, the typology can be a most useful tool for analyzing general tendencies in one's own work, and also in examining individual cases to determine exactly what both client and worker are doing. If one's main interest lies in self-study or in comparison of the treatment style of one worker with another, or even of one group of workers with another, it may be sufficient to analyze worker comments alone. This is far less time-consuming since, the study found, in psychosocial work the client usually talks at least three times as much as the worker.

Study of Distribution of Procedures

The first study in which the classification was used in hypothesis testing attempted to answer such questions as "What are caseworkers really doing? What procedures do we use? Where do we put our emphasis?" The researcher's thinking at that time, 1960, was expressed in a series of hypotheses. It was predicted that communications (of both client and worker) would appear in the following order of frequency: first, exploration-description-ventilation; second, person-situation reflection; third, sustainment; fourth, developmental reflection; fifth and sixth, either pattern-dynamic reflection or direct influence. It was also predicted, seventh, that person-situation reflection would reach a maximum in the third interview and, eighth, remain steady from then on and that, ninth, pattern-dynamic reflection would be rare in the first and second interviews but more frequent in the third, fourth, and fifth. It was predicted, tenth, that early life reflection would be similar to pattern-dynamic reflection, though somewhat more frequent, and eleventh, that direct influence would be rare throughout.

For this study, the first five interviews of fifteen individual interview cases of marriage counseling were used. Seventy-five interviews were coded by two independent judges. When there was disagreement between judges, the material was reviewed by a third judge, the principal researcher, who entered a final rating in each instance. These codings then became the basis for establishing a "profile" of the distribution of communications.

TABLE 1

MAJOR CATEGORY COMMUNICATIONS EXPRESSED AS PERCENTAGES OF TOTAL COMMUNICATIONS (15 CASES)

| | Client communications | | | | | Worker communications | | | | |
| | Interview | | | | | Interview | | | | |
Category	1	2	3	4	5	1	2	3	4	5
A*	—	—	—	—	—	02.0	01.7	01.5	01.6	01.6
B*	—	—	—	—	—	00.6	00.8	00.7	01.3	00.7
C	78.3	62.4	60.8	60.8	56.4	08.4	07.0	06.9	06.0	06.7
D	05.7	14.4	17.3	17.1	18.7	04.8	10.8	11.7	12.1	14.6
E	—	00.4	00.3	00.2	00.1	—	00.2	00.5	00.5	00.6
F	00.1	01.8	00.2	00.2	00.2	00.1	00.5	00.1	00.2	00.3
Total	84.1	79.0	78.6	78.3	75.4	15.9	21.0	21.4	21.7	24.5

*Not applicable to client communications.
Source: Florence Hollis, *A Typology of Casework*, © 1967, 1968 by Family Service Association of America. Reprinted by permission of the publisher.

Table 1 and Chart 4 show the results of this analysis. Table 1 gives the average percentage of all communications (i.e., client plus worker) in which each major type of procedure occurred in each of the five successive interviews. Chart 4 pictures this in graphic form for A, B, C, and D (E and F communications were so few they could not be charted).

One is at once struck by the extent to which client talk outweighs worker talk—three to five times as much—although the amount that the worker contributes increases as the interviews progress. This shift can be attributed to two major factors. First, the client's need for unburdening and the worker's need to learn as much as possible about the situation combine to put the emphasis on ventilation-description-exploration in the first interview. Usually, a brief inquiry from the worker suffices to touch off a fairly lengthy response from the client. Second, the worker's increased understanding of the situation, the client's desire for more definitive responses, and often the client's growing readiness for understanding lead to greater activity by the worker in subsequent interviews. Note that the proportion of both client and worker communications falling in reflective categories triples between the first and fifth interviews. Equally apparent is the important part played continuously by the client's descriptive communications and ventilation. A small part of this material relates to the client's early life, but pre-

CHART 4

Client and Worker Communications by Major Category:
Percentage of total interviews (15 cases)

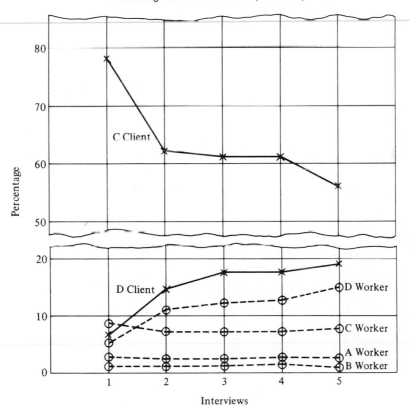

dominantly it is related to current and recent events. Current person-situation reflection is clearly the second most important treatment process. Sustainment, although quantitatively small, is remarkably steady throughout the five interviews. Direct influence, pattern-dynamic reflection, and developmental reflection are all rare, with pattern-dynamic reflection, contrary to prediction, slightly more frequent than developmental reflection except in the second interview, where exploration of the past occasionally seems to lead to reflection about it. The fact that direct influence, contrary to prediction, is somewhat more frequent than developmental or pattern-dynamic reflection is accounted for by the number of comments made by the worker concerning how to use the interviews themselves. That is, they pertain to the treatment process itself rather than to advice about the client's decisions or actions in outside life. Further analysis indicated that an average of only 0.3 percent of the total content was of the latter type over the five interviews. Both client and worker person-situation reflection take their main jump in the second interview and increase slowly thereafter. The amount of developmental and pattern-dynamic reflection is so small that changes from one interview to another cannot be considered sufficient to indicate trends. Of the original hypotheses, then, the first, second, and third were fully supported by the study; the seventh and ninth were partially supported. Direct influence was somewhat more frequent than predicted; developmental reflection and pattern-dynamic reflection were both of low frequency, as predicted. Contrary to expectation, however, pattern-dynamic reflection was slightly more frequent than developmental.

What about variations between individual cases within these groups? Do they tend to be very much alike, or is there considerable variation in the work done with different families and individuals even when they seek help for the same problem? Uniformity is not the rule.

On the contrary, there is great variation. Analysis revealed that over the first five interviews, total person-situation reflection varied from an average of 9 percent per interview in one case to 48 percent per interview in another. Over the third, fourth, and fifth interviews, one-third of the cases had less than 20 percent of their content in this category, one-third had between 20 and 39 percent, and one-third had 40 percent or over. Pattern-dynamic reflection varied from one case in which it did not appear in any interview to four cases in which it was touched on in three of the five interviews, although it never reached more than 4.2 percent of any one interview. Developmental reflection was absent in almost half the cases. Its maximum in a single interview was 9.4 percent.

This diversity is as we should expect it to be, for many factors influence the development of treatment: the nature of the problems the client is dealing with, the qualities and abilities of the client, the worker's preferences and skills, the time available, and other variables.

COMPARISON OF DATA FROM SEVERAL STUDIES

It is of value to compare these findings with those of three other researchers who have conducted similar studies. Mullen,[2] who used the Hollis instrument in a study of 87 taped interviews of marital and parent-child problems, included in his report a table combining four profiles: his own findings, the Hollis findings, the findings of a study of 121 taped interviews of marital and parent-child problems by Reid, and of one by Pinkus consisting of 111 taped interviews from psychiatric clinics and family agencies. The last two studies used the Reid-Shyne reformulation of the Community Service Society classification[3] (see Table 2). Mullen was thoroughly familiar with both classifications and was able to work out approximate equivalents between the two typologies.

In Table 2 worker communications only are

TABLE 2

A COMPARISON OF FOUR PROCESS STUDIES

Treatment procedure[a]	Proportion of worker communication			
	Mullen[b]	Hollis[c]	Reid-CSS[d]	Pinkus[e]
Sustainment (A)	.027	.081	.043	.050
Direct influence (B)	.052	.036	.040	.015
Exploration-description-ventilation (C)	.368	.398	.463	.508
Person-situation reflection (D)	.459	.457	.354	.313
Personality reflection (E)	.005	.013	.014	.050
Early life reflection (F)	.014	.015	.020	.016
Other[f]	.073	—	.066	.048
Total	.998	1.000	1.000	1.000

[a]Two classifications were used in these four studies, the Hollis and the Reid-CSS typologies. The figures are, therefore, approximations.
[b]Marital and parent-child problems. Hollis system. Continued-service client interviews one through fourteen, N = 87 taped interviews, 35 clients, 6 workers. See Edward J. Mullen, "Casework Treatment Procedures as a Function of Client Diagnostic Variables. A Study of Their Relationship in the Casework Interview" (doctoral dissertation, Columbia University School of Social Work, 1968), p. 119.
[c]Marital problems. Hollis system. Client interviews one through five. N = 75 process (written) interviews, 15 clients, 11 workers. See Florence Hollis, "A Profile of Early Interviews in Marital Counseling," *Social Casework,* 49 (January 1968), 39. (The figures are the means of the five groups of interviews reported by Hollis.)
[d]Marital and parent-child problems. Reid-CSS system. Short-term and continued-service client interviews one through five. N = 121 taped interviews, 30 cases, 7 workers. See William J. Reid, "Characteristics of Casework Intervention," *Welfare in Review,* 5 (October 1967), 13–14.
[e]Psychiatric and family problems. Reid-CSS system. Primarily beyond client interview fifteen. N = 111 taped interviews, 59 workers. See Helen Pinkus, "Casework Techniques Related to Selected Characteristics of Clients and Workers" (doctoral dissertation, Columbia University School of Social Work, 1968), p. 176.
[f]Technical and inaudible.
Source: Edward J. Mullen, "Casework Communication," *Social Casework,* 49 (November 1968), 551. Copyright © 1967, 1968 by Family Service Association of America. Reprinted by permission of the publisher.

used, and the percentages represent proportions of total worker communications rather than, as in the previous tables, percentages of the total of worker plus client communications.* Note that in all four studies more than 80 percent of the worker's part in the interview is devoted to exploration-description-ventilation and person-situation reflection. Pattern-dynamic reflection (which Mullen terms "personality reflection") is 5 percent or less, developmental (which Mullen terms "early life reflection") does not exceed 2 percent, direct influence is never more than 5.2 percent, and sustainment does

not exceed 8.1 percent. As noted above, direct influence in the sense of advice or suggestions about matters outside the treatment situation itself is very small.

It is probable that more sustainment actually occurs in interviews than these studies reveal. Sustaining communications are very often of a nonverbal or paraverbal nature. Tape recordings do not reveal nonverbal communications at all, and the coding unit used did not provide for paraverbal phenomena from the tapes. Use of the typology on interviews recorded on videotape would probably reveal a far larger component of sustainment than has been noted in the studies so far reported. In the process recording, such communications were coded if they were described in the recording. This may

---

* For instance, total directive communications, which in the Hollis study constituted approximately 0.8 percent of all worker plus client communications, are 3.6 percent of worker communications.

account for the higher figure in the Hollis study. It is doubtful, however, that more than a very small proportion of the nonverbal and para-verbal sustaining communications were actual-ly recorded even in the process material.

Note that in the relative proportion of C and D material, Mullen and Hollis find more D while Reid and Pinkus both find more C material. It is very likely that this is due to differences in the coding units used in the two systems. The units used by Reid and Pinkus did not give weighting to the length of a communication, whereas the Hollis system did. Since C-type comments by the worker tend to be shorter than D-type comments, which often include expla-nations and interpretations, this technical dif-ference might explain the lighter weighting given C and the heavier weighting given D by the Hollis system.

These, then, are the central tendencies, the picture one gets by averaging the work done over many cases. Exploration-description-venti-lation and person-situation reflection are clearly the central procedures, with the other four in a peripheral role.

Two important features of these studies must be kept in mind:

1. The first three studies used by Mullen in Table 2 consisted of cases in which *only* inter-personal adjustment problems were the focus of attention. The fourth study included was heavily weighted with such problems. In work with severely disorganized families, for in-stance, we should probably find more use of directive techniques and perhaps also more sustainment. Even so, the core treatment pro-cedures would probably still be exploration-description-ventilation and person-situation re-flection. Other types of problems might produce somewhat different profiles. Further studies are needed to test these assumptions.

2. None of these studies included an anal-ysis of environmental treatment. Undoubtedly, some direct work with factors in the environ-ment was going on in many of these cases, even though the type of dysfunction involved called mainly for direct work with the individual. In other types of cases, in which the problem lies more in the social system than in interpersonal relationships, environmental work might as-sume major proportions.

A further word about pattern-dynamic and developmental reflection. The extremely small number of communications in these categories might lead one to think that forms of treatment leading to understanding in these areas are of little importance. This is not true. It used to be supposed that there were only a few cases in which this type of understanding was sought, and that in those cases a considerable portion of time was spent in talking directly about the dynamics of behavior and its development. It is now apparent that bits of such reflection are, not infrequently, embedded in a much larger matrix of understanding of current life events and responses, and that moments of such in-sight are followed by further person-situation content, which benefits from the insight gained. Such moments of insight are found in a wide range of cases. In a few cases, pattern-dynamic and developmental reflection become an exten-sive part of treatment.

Self-understanding is, of course, much broader than pattern-dynamic and developmen-tal understanding. Readers will recall that the last four divisions of current person-situation understanding look at inward aspects of func-tioning. The second division looks both in-wardly to what a person has done and out-wardly to its effects or potential effects on others. So it can be said to be half inwardly di-rected and half outwardly. The first subdivision of person-situation reflection looks outward. By adding these communications to the outward-looking half of the second subdivision of person-situation reflection, one can arrive at an index of extrareflection. In contrast, by adding the in-ward facing D communications to E and F communications, one can secure an index of intrareflection. Examination of interviews 3, 4, and 5 of the profile study reveals that reflective comments are about evenly divided between intra- and extrareflection despite the very small amount of pattern-dynamic or developmental reflection.

A PROFILE OF THE CASEWORK PROCESS

Research inevitably deals in such abstractions that one tends to lose sight of the meaning and significance of the findings. What do these studies tell us about the nature of worker-client communications in psychosocial casework involving individual work with clients? Are they harmonious with the position set forth in earlier chapters?

The picture we get in these studies of clients having principally interpersonal relationship problems is of a reality-based treatment in which the individual is helped to learn about himself or herself primarily by learning to understand what is going on in the interactions—the transactions—of current life. On the one hand, it is a process of trying to understand other people with whom one has meaningful relationships, elements in one's practical life situation, sometimes one's physical condition and medical care. On the other hand, and intertwined with this, a person attempts to become more aware of reactions to specific people and, in specific circumstances, more aware of what touches off certain kinds of reactions. Sometimes one evaluates reactions; sometimes one looks at them in terms of their actual or possible consequences. In order to engage in these reflective processes, the client is encouraged to talk at length, descriptively, and often with emotion about the self, about associates, and about the situation, to a worker who listens with attention, understanding, and acceptance. The worker helps to focus the exploration-description-ventilation process

on pertinent content and through sustaining expressions encourages the formation of the relationship of trust necessary for one person to use another's help. Directive techniques are used sparingly. Understanding of intrapsychic patterns and their development is by no means unimportant, although procedures dealing with them are used much less frequently than person-situation reflection. Procedures of pattern-dynamic and developmental reflection are used in highly varying degree. In many cases they do not appear at all, in others occasionally, and in some with fair regularity over a period of treatment. They usually rely for much of their impact on substantial prior and subsequent work on understanding the current person-situation gestalt. The picture is distinctly one of a blend of procedures, with the admixture of those procedures leading to intrapsychic understanding following the pattern of a continuum.

FURTHER STUDIES

This typology has now been used as a research instrument in a number of other studies, as can be seen from the following partial list.

Boatman, Louise, "Caseworkers' Judgments of Clients' Hope."[4]

Chamberlain, Edna. "Testing with a Treatment Typology."[5]

Davis, Inger P. "Use of Influence Techniques in Casework with Parents."[6]

Ehrenkranz, Shirley, M. "A Study of the Techniques and Procedures Used in Joint Interviewing in the Treatment of Marital Problems."[7]

Hollis, Florence. "Continuance and Discontinuance in Marital Counseling and Some Observations on Joint Interviews."[8]

Montgomery, Mitzie I. R. "Feedback Systems, Interaction Analysis, and Counseling Models in Professional Programmes."[9]

Mullen, Edward J. "Casework Treatment Procedures as a Function of Client Diagnostic Variables."[10]

Orcutt, Ben Avis. "Process Analysis in the First Phase of Treatment"—a part of a larger study, *Casework with Wives of Alcoholics.*[11]

Turner, Francis J. "Ethnic Differences and Client Performance"[12] "Social Work Treatment and Value Differences."[13]

In most of these studies, groups of cases were compared in order to determine the extent to which procedures used in treatment vary in association with other variables. Each of the ten studies produced important findings. Some of these findings support aspects of currently accepted theory. Some throw other aspects into question. Others that are primarily descriptive have brought previously unnoted or at least undemonstrated tendencies to light. One study (Montgomery) used the typology successfully in analyzing three different treatment approaches using interviews conducted by Fritz Perls, Carl Rogers, and Virginia Satir.

Sustainment and Countersustainment

The study by Boatman is of special interest here because it deals with an important aspect of sustainment. As we began using the typology, it became apparent that workers varied a great deal in the ways in which they chose and expressed communications designed primarily for other than direct sustainment. One has the impression that some workers seem to maintain a sustaining "atmosphere" and others do not. Others even seem to come close to a "counter-sustaining" climate. Boatman studied this phenomenon as part of a doctoral dissertation investigating correlates of various factors with caseworkers' judgment of client hopefulness. She examined the possibility that sustainment is given not only by the directly sustaining communications coded A but also *indirectly* by the supportive quality of some

communications whose primary dynamic is either reflection, exploration-ventilation, or direct influence. Indirectly sustaining communications were designated as those B, C, D, E, and F communications expressing "encouragement, approval, agreement, reassurance or identification of the worker with the client's ideas, attitudes, feelings or behavior." In contrast, B, C, D, E, and F communications expressing "discouragement, disapproval, disagreement, stimulation of anxiety, or identification of the worker with attitudes, ideas, feelings or behavior contrary to those of the client were considered to be 'counter-sustaining.'" For instance:

Indirect sustainment: To a wife who overreacts to her husband's anger and fears that he no longer loves her: "Do you think Ted may express anger pretty easily? You told me his family is much more spontaneous than yours. Lots of people can be angry and love very much at the same time, you know."

Or, to a client with excessively high self-expectations: "Why are you so hard on yourself?"

Countersustainment: A client who has told her worker she has a hard time getting to work on time complains that her boss is "so irritable" in the mornings. Worker asks whether she thinks her late arrivals might have anything to do with it.

Boatman found that almost 8 percent of the "non-A" communications in her study were indirectly sustaining. This was more than two and a half times as much sustainment as was given in her sample by direct sustaining (A) comments. She also found that over 5 percent of the coded communications were *countersustaining*. The study went on to examine the extent to which workers differ from each other in their general supportiveness. Mullen had already shown that workers vary a great deal in the extent to which they use different procedures. Direct sustainment, however, he found to be an exception to this tendency. In contrast, Boatman's findings show that if one includes *indirect* sustainment, there is indeed very great variation among workers. The extremes ran from one worker whose interviews showed sustainment and countersustainment in almost equal degrees to another whose sustainment/countersustainment ratio was eight to one.

Obviously, this is an area needing much further study. One could, for instance, examine relationships between total sustainment-countersustainment and client progress in either problem solving or general functioning, by combining a measurement of progress such as that developed by Dorothy Beck of the Family Service Association of America,[14] with measurements of sustainment-countersustainment. With the Beck technique, one could easily locate a small group of workers with high outcomes and another with low outcomes; analysis of each group over even a small sample of interviews might reveal highly significant differences in approach. A similar phenomenon exists in the measurement of directiveness. Undoubtedly, workers differ in the extent to which their reflective comments contain directive elements. This has not yet been studied but would be a very useful area of exploration.

Need for Further Research

Much interesting research lies ahead for skilled practitioners who are intellectually curious, accurately discriminating, very patient, and seriously interested in helping strengthen the scientific foundation of clinical social work practice.

The typology itself needs further development. Work needs to be done on the unit to be coded. The small units used, although good from the point of view of precision, are expensive to use because the coding becomes very time-consuming. If a way can be found to code larger units reliably, the usefulness of the typology will be increased. It should be noted,

however, that it is not necessary to use the entire typology in every study. If one is interested in directiveness, for example, it could well be that only the B worker comments needed coding. Once located, each such unit could be studied for appropriateness, effect, differences between workers, and so on. It is also quite possible to add new categories, especially subcategories of the major six, when these are needed to study special questions. For instance, one might want to subdivide the C category by a time factor in order to see how much emphasis is placed on past history. Or one might look into the *content* of worker interpretations by devising suitable subcategories to the three reflective divisions.

The value of the typology in environmental or milieu treatment has not as yet been examined at all, and of course this should be done. As for substantive studies, the questions that need examination are myriad. To name a few: Are certain "worker styles" associated with higher effectiveness of treatment with certain types of problems or certain types of personality? What are the components of these styles? What are the emphases within them? How do such factors as socioeconomic class or education relate to treatment procedures? In another type of study, one could take a series of person-situation reflection episodes or a series of pattern-dynamic or developmental episodes to examine what evidence there is that these did or did not affect the client's subsequent responses.

Caseworkers have long and inconclusively debated, on the basis of observed data, many issues that would lend themselves to more rigorous study. To move ahead in such studies, we must state our hypotheses in accurate terms based on the realities of casework practice, we must define our objectives far more precisely than heretofore, and we must continue to develop research instruments specifically designed for the examination and measurement of the phenomena to which they are to be applied.

NOTES

1. Readers interested in the full report of the research should turn to Florence Hollis, *A Typology of Casework Treatment* (New York: Family Service Association of America, 1968).

2. Edward J. Mullen, "Casework Communication," *Social Casework*, 49 (November 1968), 546–551.

3. This classification is described in William J. Reid and Ann Shyne, *Brief and Extended Casework* (New York: Columbia University Press, 1969), pp. 70–72.

4. Louise Boatman, "Caseworkers' Judgments of Clients' Hope: Some Correlates among Client-Situation Characteristics and among Workers' Communication Patterns" (doctoral dissertation, Columbia University School of Social Work, New York, 1974).

5. Edna Chamberlain, "Testing with a Treatment Typology," *Australian Journal of Social Work*, 22 (December 1969), 3–8.

6. Inger P. Davis, "Use of Influence Techniques in Casework with Parents" (doctoral dissertation, University of Chicago, March 1969). See also her article "Advice-Giving in Parent Counseling," *Social Casework*, 56 (June 1975), 343–347.

7. Shirley Ehrenkranz, "A Study of the Techniques and Procedures Used in Joint Interviewing in the Treatment of Marital Problems" (doctoral dissertation, Columbia University School of Social Work, New York, 1967). Two articles based on the dissertation were published: "A Study of Joint Interviewing in the Treatment of Marital Problems," *Social Casework*, 48 (October and November 1967), 498–502, 570–574.

8. Florence Hollis, "Continuance and Discontinuance in Marital Counseling and Some Observations on Joint Interviews," in Hollis, *Typology of Casework Treatment*, pp. 27–34.

9. Mitzie I. R. Montgomery, "Feedback Systems, Interaction Analysis and Counseling Models in Professional Programs" (doctoral dissertation, University of Edinburgh, 1973).

10. Edward J. Mullen, "Casework Treatment Procedures as a Function of Client Diagnostic Variables" (doctoral dissertation, Columbia University School of Social Work, New York, 1968). Three articles based on the dissertation were published: "Casework Communication," *Social Casework*, 49 (November 1968), 546–551; "The Relation Between Diagnosis and Treatment in Casework," *Social Casework*, 50 (April 1969), 218–226; "Difference in Worker Style in Casework," *Social Casework*, 50 (June 1969), 347–353.

11. Ben Avis Orcutt, "Process Analysis in the First Phase of Treatment," in Pauline Cohen and Merton Krause, eds., *Casework with Wives of Alcoholics* (New York: Family Service Association of America, 1971), pp. 147–164.

12. Francis Turner, "Social Work Treatment and Value Differences" (doctoral dissertation, Columbia University School of Social Work, 1963). An article was based on the dissertation "A Comparison of Procedures in the Treatment of Clients with Two Different Value Orientations," *Social Casework*, 45 (May 1964), 273–277.

13. Francis Turner, "Ethnic Difference and Client Performance," *Social Service Review*, 44 (March 1970), 1–10.

14. Dorothy Fahs Beck and Mary Ann Jones, *Progress on Family Problems* (New York: Family Service Association of America, 1973).

PART THREE

Diagnostic
Understanding
and
the Treatment Process

CHAPTER 10

The Client–Worker Relationship

Basic to psychosocial casework treatment, and one of its most powerful tools, is the relationship between worker and client. Experience has demonstrated that successful treatment depends heavily on the quality of this relationship. The Beck and Jones follow-up study of over 3,500 cases from family agencies (in which, however, the theoretical approaches to treatment were not specified) found a very strong, highly significant association to exist between good worker-client relationships and positive treatment outcomes. Those relationships rated by clients and workers as "unsatisfactory" resulted in far less change in treatment than those rated "very satisfactory"; consistent and substantial increases in client gains were found as ratings of the relationship moved along the scale from negative to positive extremes. No other client or service characteristic analyzed in this study was found to be as important to good outcome as the worker-client relationship.[1]

Research and above all observation of practice have identified many of the components or underpinnings of the positive therapeutic relationship. Some of these will be discussed in detail over the course of this chapter. Broadly speaking, therapist characteristics of nonpossessive warmth and concern, genuineness, empathy, and nonjudgmental acceptance have been found by some studies—and are known by many clinicians—to appreciably enhance therapeutic interaction. The worker's optimism, objectivity, professional competence, and capacity to communicate these to the client play an important part in the quality of the treatment relationship.[2] Particularly in intensive therapy, but to some degree in every case, the worker's self-awareness is crucial to effective casework. The client, too, participates in establishing a favorable relationship: he or she must be able to muster the hope and courage necessary to engage in treatment, and, with the worker's help, the client must develop motivation for change; beyond that, the person must be able to achieve some measure of trust in the worker's desire to help and ability to do so. Furthermore, whether the treatment is centered around individual, interpersonal, or environmental problems, or some combination of these, and whether the contact is brief or long term, an effective relationship requires that the worker and client work together to arrive at some mutual agreement on the purpose of treatment and the objectives they jointly seek.

Four particularly significant aspects of the treatment relationship will be examined in this chapter. We will be viewing it as (1) a means of communication between client and worker; (2) a set of attitudes; (3) a set of responses, expressed in behavior; and (4) a mutual effort. We will then consider the part these elements play in the dynamics of treatment. Since attitudes and responses are basic ingredients in verbal and nonverbal communication and in mutuality, we will begin by discussing these two aspects first.

REALISTIC ATTITUDES AND RESPONSES

What attitudes and responses exist between worker and client? We customarily think of them as being of two kinds: realistic and unrealistic.[3] Unrealistic attitudes and responses include *transference* and *countertransference*.

Client Reactions

Realistic attitudes, appropriate to the situation, will differ among clients in accordance with variations in the significance the treatment situation has for them. It is common knowledge among clinicians that when people come for help with interpersonal problems, they almost always experience some anxiety. This is partly so because they usually have some awareness that their problems lie to some degree within themselves. Even when an individual has defended against recognizing this, it is still present underneath and a realistic cause of anxiety. Characteristically, people also experience discomfort about entering into relationships in which they expect to be dependent. Clients applying for casework service often express this uneasiness directly: "I wanted to solve it myself" or "I was ashamed to ask for help." Experience has shown us that, to the client, com-

ing for help can signify weakness, despite the fact that the recognition of the need for help and the decision to come for it require strength. To admit that one has been unable to solve difficulties without outside assistance can evoke childlike feelings, feelings of failure. It can be a blow to self-esteem. By seeking casework services, clients often feel they are acknowledging that another person is wiser or stronger. Taking the first step in allowing oneself to come under the influence of another unknown or little known person can be very frightening indeed.

Such feelings are widespread, but the intensity with which they are experienced will vary. Anxiety will be greater, for instance, when clients are consulting the worker about matters that are of vital interest or are emotionally laden than when the consultation is about peripheral matters; it will also vary with the degree to which clients consciously or unconsciously believe themselves to be at fault, and with the intrinsic nature of the matters about which they must talk.

Many other types of client reaction can be realistic responses to varying circumstances. If the client has been either overtly or subtly pressed to apply for treatment, there may be anger as well as anxiety. Clients may take referral for treatment as criticism of their abilities or as a reflection on their emotional balance. The involuntary client, on whom casework services have been imposed by an authoritative agency or court action, can be extremely resentful at being compelled to accept help. (See the Carter case in Chapter 21.) Adolescents, too, can be angry about being required by their parents or others to see a clinical social worker, particularly when—as is often the case—they see the problem as deriving from family or some kind of external difficulties which they cannot resolve on their own.

The desire to use casework treatment to bring about change, particularly internal change, will vary greatly, depending not only upon whether or not the client has come for help voluntarily but also on the nature of the changes that the client may anticipate, the degree of satisfaction the person has in present ways, and the fixity of ways of behaving that may have to be given up.

What the client knows about the agency or casework will also affect initial attitudes. If the client has heard favorable reports about the agency or an individual worker, a sympathetic, skillful reception will be anticipated. A previous bad experience or negative reports by others may lead the client to expect the worker to be critical or hostile or condescending. Community, ethnic, and class attitudes toward casework or toward a particular agency may affect one's feelings as to whether coming for help is respectable or degrading and will condition one's expectation of what treatment itself will be like. Some clients who have not previously experienced casework help may tend to expect advice and a somewhat authoritative approach, whereas others with some knowledge of modern dynamic psychology may anticipate a more sympathetic and thought-provoking approach. The latter group, however, may have even more doubts concerning the competence of the caseworker than the more naïve clients, particularly if they have the notion that casework treatment is "second best" to treatment with a clinical psychologist or psychiatrist and have come to a caseworker because they cannot afford any other resource or are not yet ready to commit themselves to it.

It is sometimes assumed that the economically disadvantaged or the poorly educated minority client will be less interested in casework treatment than the middle-class college graduate, black or white. This is by no means always the case. Furthermore, even when it is so, to label a particular client "resistant" or "unmotivated" may deny certain realities of American life. A client who has experienced prejudice, social oppression, and deprivation of many kinds understandably may approach the middle-class caseworker, the often "white agency," and the treatment process with apprehension. The client may fear that the actual differences between them—in terms of money, power, education, and life experience—are so great that there can be no meeting ground, no understanding by the worker of the client's situation. Trust itself is difficult enough to achieve, but it is all the more difficult to bridge the gap between people from vastly different backgrounds, particularly in the context of a society in which racism and class biases prevail. It is therefore not unusual for some clients to view their caseworkers with fear, suspicion, or anger. (Again, see the Carter case in Chapter 21.) Of course, although it is useful to anticipate a particular reaction, one has to be careful not to stereotype. But when distrust *is* evident, it may take a good deal of painstaking work to convince the client that the worker's intent is not to intrude, or to depreciate group pride or aspirations, but to assist. Shortly, we will discuss the worker's responsibility for promoting a climate of mutual respect and understanding, but the point here is that from the client's point of view these are all realistic responses, in the sense that they are either appropriate reactions to the actual situation, or else to reality as it is seen by the client's group.[4]

Similarly, as soon as a client meets a clinical social worker, the latter's physical appearance and manner set new reactions in motion. A young worker may find an older adult distrustful of his or her skill, particularly if this is not counterbalanced by obvious superiority in education. On the other hand, this worker may be more trusted than an older worker by an adolescent, who may expect greater understanding from peers and near-peers than from older people. Although class differences, including general education, may increase the confidence of a blue-collar worker in the professional ability of the caseworker, they may also make him or her fearful of being misunderstood and misjudged and may increase feelings of anxiety and resentment concerning a situation in which he or she feels inferior and dependent. In some instances, the less educated client may feel (sometimes realistically) that life experiences have been better teachers than the young worker's books. At another extreme, the professional or upper-class client may believe that the worker is not as "intellectual" or "cultivated," and this client may therefore be doubtful about the caseworker's ability to help.

Sex differences also arouse different realistic reactions. A man may find it initially difficult to turn to a woman for professional help, the extent of this attitude varying with people of different backgrounds. A particularly pretty, handsome, or vital worker may arouse feelings of sexual attraction, even though there is no seductiveness in his or her actual manner. A client may be skeptical about bringing marital or parent-child problems to an unmarried caseworker with no children. The appearance of the worker's office and experiences in the waiting room will add to the client's reactions. And all these responses can take place independently of what the worker actually *does!*

What the worker says and the way he or she acts when saying it are obviously the next set of reality factors affecting the client's realistic responses. Before jumping to the conclusion that a client is displaying either transference reactions or subjectively conditioned resistance, it is very important for the worker to make certain that he or she is not actually saying or doing something that is giving the client a realistic basis for certain responses. Workers *are* sometimes hostile, or at least critical or uninterested. Some workers, out of their own needs, act in a superior, overly impersonal way. Some enjoy a subtle type of domination that puts the client in an unnecessarily dependent or inferior position. Some reveal their desire to be loved or at least admired and appreciated. Some are unconsciously seductive. Some are late for appointments, forgetful about doing things they have promised, and so on. Even the best of caseworkers will exhibit occasional "untherapeutic" reactions, by which we mean attitudes or responses that are not helpful or healing. Caseworkers too are affected by mood changes, health, events in work or private life quite outside the particular treatment situation, and other factors. Who of us at some time—on a hot day or when short of sleep or under the influence of an antihistamine—has not yawned in a way that could not be entirely concealed from the client?

It is also true that some caseworkers do stereotype or react anxiously to clients of particular racial or cultural backgrounds. They may be biased against certain groups, or they may view some clients only as victims of oppression and thereby fail to see them also as people with unique experiences and personalities. There are also workers who have fixed attitudes toward clients of a particular sex, age, lifestyle, or physical condition, or toward those who have certain intellectual or emotional disabilities.[5] As we shall discuss more fully later on in this chapter, the development of self-awareness about countertherapeutic reactions can be among the most challenging tasks for the clinical social worker to achieve. But when these do occur and clients react to them, they are responding realistically.

Worker Reactions

This brings us to the realistic aspects of the *worker's* part in the treatment relationship. The well-trained, self-aware worker's responses are not the natural reactions of one person on the street to another. The worker entering the field begins with such natural responses, of course, but they are subject to other influences that are the product of purpose and training. The worker's perception of the client is not that of the average person; attitudinal response to the perception is different, and overt behavior is different. A person who is trained as a psychosocial therapist does not see a client's behavior as an isolated event. This worker has become attuned to the reasons for client responses, the kinds of life histories that lie behind different response tendencies, the defenses people use to cope with anxiety. The psychosocial therapist reacts not simply to the client's overt behavior but to a complex of stimuli that includes possible reasons for the behavior and the knowledge that, even if they are not apparent, reasons do exist, whether in life experience or in constitution. The stimulus, then, is different for the clinical worker than for the lay person. The perception—or, better, apperception—includes many elements that are the part of the worker's experience and education. To the well-trained clinician, the cue "anger" under some circumstances may read "defensive hostility" or "anxiety" or a defense against "softer" feelings; the cue "defensive" may sometimes read "overly severe superego" and may express the client's fear of criticism. If the client's response is thus read, the worker's response is automatically different from what it would otherwise be.

Diagnostic thinking about the client helps the worker to understand and respond realistically to the meaning of the client's defenses. For example, an obsessive-compulsive client may be fending off strong, frightening instinctual urges by intellectualization; a hysterical client may relate seductively to a worker; a dependent, emotionally deprived client may bring anger or unrealistic expectations, derived from past ungratifying relationships, to the caseworker; a man with a diagnosis of schizophrenia may talk evasively out of fear of exposing deeper thoughts and feelings that humiliate him or that he fears will repel the worker. Similarly, the homosexual client may underplay strong feelings about sexual preference for fear the worker will look down on or try to change him or her. Dislike of clients' qualities or behavior can be more easily overcome when they are understood as reactions to pain or fear. In some social work graduate schools and field placement agencies, students are helped through role playing to get

as close as possible to the inner feelings of the client. Putting oneself in the shoes of another, so to speak, can help to generate one's empathic responses.

Workers' reactions are further modified by the fact that in their training and experience they have been exposed to observation of a great deal of human suffering. They have lived with clients through disappointment, sorrow, physical suffering, death, crippling frustration, and hopelessness; they have been closely associated with the torture of mental illness; they have read and listened to life history after life history in which the distortions of the adult personality could be traced step by step to misfortunes, deprivations, mistreatment, mishandling, and misunderstandings in childhood. Unless they have remained untouched by these experiences, they cannot but respond with more spontaneous understanding and acceptance than would have been the case if they had not become caseworkers. Herein lies one of the answers to the question often put to therapists: "How can you be so unspontaneous? Don't you get worn out controlling, or concealing, your natural reaction?" The point is that the worker's natural, spontaneous reaction itself is different from that of the untrained person because both perception and judgment have been modified by training and experience. Of course, no worker ever reaches the perfection of understanding and acceptance just implied, but that fact does not modify our conviction that successful psychosocial caseworkers must always strive in that direction.

Although genuine responses of the caseworker to the client usually do have a predominantly positive flavor or sympathizing, accepting, liking, and wanting to help, *worker responses that are not therapeutically useful, even though they may be realistic, nevertheless occur in varying degree.* There may be irritation at the client who is hostile and attacking, or who is resistive and thwarts the worker's therapeutic intent (or aspirations). Workers may feel threatened by a client's anger or negative feelings toward them; they may be overly concerned about whether their clients like them. Despite training, there may be residues of dislike of or insensitivity to clients whose behavior runs counter to the customs or mores of the worker's own class or ethnic group. There may be particular resentment of the client who mistreats another person, child or adult. An especially attractive client may arouse erotic reactions. Very commonly, there is realistic anxiety about ability to help: the client may be confronted by almost insoluble problems and may sometimes be so seriously disturbed that the problem is beyond the worker's skill. Threats of suicide especially arouse the worker's anxiety. Occasionally, a desperately angry, psychotic, or near-psychotic person arouses realistic fear of bodily harm.

Even when workers fail to achieve understanding and acceptance and instead feel hostility, aversion, or some other antitherapeutic emotion, they usually try to avoid translating it into speech or action. This is for two reasons: because the worker knows it will hurt the client and does not want to do this, and because the purpose in being with the client is a therapeutic one and to show feelings impulsively will defeat that purpose. The fact that workers have been trained to become aware of their reactions makes it easier to control their expression than would otherwise be the case.

One sometimes hears the opinion that the worker should never refrain from spontaneous expression of reactions on the grounds that to refrain introduces insincerity into the relationship. In our view, this is at best a misleading half-truth. We are certainly in agreement with the need for genuineness, frankness, and simplicity in the relationship, but to refrain from showing an emotion is not insincerity. Whether the feeling is one of anger, boredom, sexual attraction, or intense like or dislike, the seasoned psychosocial worker makes every effort to guide the expression of personal feelings according to their value to the therapeutic work. As we

will soon point out, spontaneous or direct articulations of a worker's emotions, whether positive or negative, *can* sometimes benefit the client when they have a bearing on mutual goals. When this is so, the worker may choose to express them. But, as we see it, they are neither justified nor necessary when based on the worker's own need to be "open" or "natural." Objectivity and reserve about the expression of feelings do not preclude warmth and genuineness. The creative yet controlled "use of self" requires that the worker keep a constant and conscious balance between head and heart, distance and closeness. It is true that the therapeutic relationship can be intensely personal—indeed, it can be uniquely intimate—as the client lays bare inner feelings and dilemmas. But it is for this reason, above all, that it is critically important to take every precaution to protect clients from emotional reactions of the worker that are not truly in their behalf.

A man came resistantly with his wife to a second appointment with a clinical social worker to discuss his wife's wish to begin marital counseling. When he entered the interviewing room he protested loudly about the lingering fumes from the cigar smoked by the client who had preceded him. Impulsively, he emptied the ashtray that contained the butt into the wastebasket. A few minutes after the interview began, smoke started to rise from the basket and the worker had to douse the smoldering contents before proceeding. She felt angry in the face of this man's apparently controlling behavior and the inconvenience it had caused her. At the same time, she recognized that his actions derived from his fear and anger at being "dragged" by his wife into treatment (as well as his real dislike of cigar smoke); she knew that he expected to be blamed for the marital problems. Rather than sharing her immediate emotional response to the incident, the worker was able to connect with her empathy for this man's anxiety. Once she had given herself time to put her anger into perspective, with a light touch she simply said, "Sometimes the smoke has to clear before we can get down to work."

There are special circumstances, however, in which it is highly therapeutic to allow clients to become aware of negative (or positive) reactions as part of the process of helping them to understand themselves or the effects they sometimes have on other people. Worker feedback can stimulate reflection about habitual patterns of behavior and about the meaning of recurrent feelings or thoughts. But the timing of this type of intervention is important; it must be diagnostically sound and geared to the client's readiness, not to the worker's need for spontaneity.

Mrs. Glass, diagnosed as having a borderline personality, periodically accused her worker of not being interested in her; she bitterly attacked the worker for not always being instantly available by telephone. These complaints did not annoy the worker since she saw them as an expression of the client's rage, rooted in early parental deprivation. However, during one phase of treatment Mrs. Glass began to stall at the end of each session; sometimes she would cling to the worker, begging to be hugged. This behavior became increasingly irritating to the worker, who often had another client waiting; she was angered by Mrs. Glass's seeming lack of consideration. But whether the worker became firm or appealed to the client's reason, the latter persisted in trying to prolong the hour. After several weeks of this, the worker finally opened a session by sharing her feeling with Mrs. Glass. She told her that she had begun to resent being delayed; she pointed out that she was always prompt for Mrs. Glass's sessions and that she wanted to give the same courtesy to her other clients. When these reactions were shared with

Mrs. Glass, with whom the worker had a solid relationship, the client was then able to work on her intense and ever present feeling of "never getting enough"; discussions that followed gave the worker an opportunity to help Mrs. Glass see how she was alienating other people by so persistently concentrating on what was lacking in a relationship rather than on the benefits available to her.

In another situation, a charming and attractive man, whose wife had recently deserted him, had a gift for recounting amusing stories to his worker that the latter found she thoroughly enjoyed. She gave the client credit for his intelligence and humor; she found herself tempted to sit back and be entertained. However, sensing that his behavior was defensive, she shared with the client the difficulty she was having directing their discussions to the problems that had brought him into treatment; she found herself easily diverted by his wit, she told him. When these reactions were brought to the client's attention, he was able to recognize that he was avoiding painful material by being entertaining. He also realized that he had a long-standing pattern of attempting to curry favor from others by being the center of attention and by making them laugh. As it turned out, reflection on these issues was far more pertinent to the therapy than the worker's ongoing appreciation of this client's talents for showmanship.

Sometimes a worker's subjective reactions to a client can be useful as a diagnostic tool. For example, if a worker feels depleted after an interview with a client it may be a signal that the client is depressed, is dependent, or has passive-aggressive qualities. A client who is or feels helpless, deprived, or needy may prompt the worker to feel inordinately protective or to have the "urge to rescue." Irritation, frustration, or guilt may be the reaction to clients whose behavior is demanding, "manipulative," intrusive, or excessively ingratiating. Feelings of anxiety and loss of confidence in the worker may be the effect of overt or subtle criticism or devaluing of him or her by a client. Narcissistic, emotionally detached, or obsessive client styles may result in boredom or daydreaming by the worker. Obviously, *each worker's response is unique*, but, with experience, one becomes familiar with one's own particular reactions that may give clues to a client's personality qualities or inner state. It goes without saying that just as we have to substantiate theoretical hunches about our clients and their situations, speculations about diagnoses deriving from our own subjective responses must be *very* carefully verified on the basis of other data before they become part of our overall evaluations.

Inevitably, a worker, however experienced or self-aware, will on occasion inadvertently or impulsively disclose countertherapeutic reactions to a client. Whether these are based realistically on the client's behavior or are caused by something within the worker, they may be expressed in a way that is not in the client's best interests. Even so, when this happens such reactions can often be turned to therapeutic use. For example, if a client senses anger and asks about it the worker should not deny it (this would be insincerity) but handle the situation realistically, depending on whether the response was appropriate to the client's actions or an overreaction; the worker's honesty can help to strengthen the client's trust. By the same token, when it becomes clear that the worker and the client are interacting in a counterproductive pattern of any sort, usually the question is not whether to bring this up but how and when to do so. By taking responsibility for his or her part in the problem, the worker realistically acknowledges being "human" and capable of making mistakes. Of course, whenever a worker has acted in a countertherapeutic manner, it is important that the client be encouraged to express his or her reactions to the incident. The feedback is important for the worker

and can give the client a feeling of being listened to and understood. The worker is thus demonstrating that even though people and relationships are complex, *open exchanges about difficulties that arise can often lead to resolution and growth*. For many clients, fearful of sharing feelings or of being blamed, the worker-client relationship can serve as a model for handling problems that arise with other people in their lives.

In summary, then, despite workers' efforts to prevent negative responses from affecting the work with the client, they sometimes do show themselves in one form or another and, when they do, usually they can be dealt with openly; above all, they become part of the reality to which the client is reacting and must be taken into account before the worker judges that the client's responses are due to transference.

UNREALISTIC ATTITUDES AND RESPONSES: TRANSFERENCE AND COUNTERTRANSFERENCE

A client's unrealistic reactions spring from two sources so closely related that it is often impossible to separate them. When we speak of *transference* reactions, we usually mean that the client displaces onto the worker feelings or attitudes originally experienced in early childhood toward a family member—most often but not necessarily the father or mother—and responds to the worker as if he or she were this person. A similar phenomenon can occur with displacement from later important associates. These are clear and specific transference reactions. Less specific is the client's bringing into treatment any distorted way of relating to people that has become a part of his or her personality, whether or not the client identifies the worker in a direct way with early family figures. All these unrealistic reactions can be positive or negative (in the sense of warm or hostile), and they may represent id, ego, or superego aspects of the personality.

Generally speaking, transference is an unconscious or preconscious process. At the same time, however, the client may be well aware that the reaction to the therapist is inappropriately intense; the client may sense feeling unduly angry with, fearful of, or adoring of the therapist. Strong feelings of longing or dependency may be stimulated by the relationship with the worker. In some cases, particularly if clients are unable to maintain an "observing ego" when flooded with strong emotion (as occurred at times during the treatment of Mrs. Zimmer, described in Chapter 3), they are unaware that their reactions are at all unrealistic, based on earlier experiences and deprivations; they often assume that they are natural responses to the worker's actual personality or behavior.

As we have seen, it is usually therapeutic to encourage the client to express openly real feelings toward the worker. Similarly (as we shall explain more fully later in this chapter), discussion of the client's negative or positive displaced feelings can play an important role in the treatment process. There are times when they can complicate and even obstruct it; they can interfere with client-worker communication. They can bewilder worker and client alike. On the other hand, when they are brought out into the open, they often provide the client with one of the richest sources of dynamic and developmental understanding and therefore can be among the most useful components of the treatment relationship.

The worker is also sometimes unrealistic in reactions to the client.[6] Workers, too, may identify clients with early or later figures in their lives or may bring into the treatment relationships distorted ways of relating to people that are part of their own personalities. They displace feelings, attitudes, and fantasies onto some clients more than onto others, depending on their particular life experiences. Although a very important part of a worker's training consists in developing awareness of these tenden-

cies in order to keep them at a minimum, they are never completely overcome and may therefore be part of the reality to which the client is reacting. The term *countertransference* is rather broadly used to cover not only these unrealistic reactions of the worker but also realistic responses, such as those discussed earlier.

Sometimes beginning students have even greater difficulty becoming aware of countertransference of displaced feelings than they have mastering casework theory and skills. Yet irrational reactions can seriously interfere with the therapeutic relationship and the treatment process; when activated, the worker's responsiveness and understanding can be impaired. Personal therapy (which we, the writers, would encourage every clinical social worker to consider seriously) can be of great value in increasing understanding of one's own reactions, prejudices, and relationship patterns. It may significantly increase the worker's ability to be ever sensitive to inner feelings and attitudes catalyzed by clients. It also may enhance one's humility and empathy to have a firsthand experience at being "on the other side of the desk."

As one reflects on the work one does, one must continually ask oneself questions such as: What are my responses to the character or behavior of this particular client? What kinds of clients trigger intense reactions within me? Are these reactions realistic or derived from other life experiences or personality qualities of my own? If they are realistic, in what way (and when) can I therapeutically share these with the client? If unrealistic (in which case we rarely choose to burden the client with them), to whom or what in my own life am I reacting? For example, do I feel overly protective toward this woman because of my early experiences with a chronically ill sister? Does this man annoy me because he is in some ways like my husband, with whom I am having problems? Or is his managerial manner reminiscent of my father? Does this client's resistance threaten my sense of competence? Am I trying to elicit praise or gratitude from my clients to serve my own needs? Given the fact that I am a member of a society that fosters racist attitudes and class and ethnic biases, am I feeling superior (or inferior) to this client? On the other hand, is my compassion for the "underdog" so keen that I fail to understand truly the uniqueness of the particular victim of injustice to whom I am relating?

The chapters on family and couple treatment discuss transference and countertransference issues that relate specifically to these modalities.

Worker Burnout

"Burnout" has been a subject of deep concern among social workers in recent years.[7] When used to describe a condition experienced by direct service workers, the term generally includes such symptoms as emotional exhaustion; lack of interest in or detachment from the needs, pains, and aspirations of clients; cynical, punitive, or blaming attitudes toward clients; hopelessness. These responses, in turn, often lead to low morale, absenteeism, and job turnover. Burnout has been found among child welfare, community mental health, and family service workers, although contributing influences may vary. In fact, it has become evident that numerous factors, including agency procedures and policies, community attitudes, desperate and unyielding problems that afflict clients, interact to create the burnout phenomenon. In this connection, as others have pointed out, it is not the workers who should be held primarily responsible for burnout; this evaluation indeed has the effect of blaming the victim. As mentioned in Chapter 8, situations specifically contributing to stress in each setting have to be identified and confronted and, when possible, ameliorated.

In any event, clients often feel discouraged about problems that are even more overwhelming than the worker's, and they need reassurance that something can change. But it stands

to reason that when workers are feeling tired, hopeless, and angry, they are often unable to mobilize the energy or optimism to be of much help to others. In addition to doing everything they can to try to humanize their agencies, then, individual workers have to determine how they can best take care of themselves and their own lives. This is necessary in order to be professionally effective—to say nothing of personally content. Even when working under the most benign conditions, workers' intense daily involvement in other people's heartaches and despair requires that they take pains to bring positive balance into their own lives, that they take care of their personal relationships, and that on a regular basis they seek gratifying opportunities for recreation and renewal.

PROBLEMS OF COMMUNICATION BETWEEN CLIENT AND WORKER

It follows that the nature of the feelings and attitudes (realistic and unrealistic) that exist between worker and client profoundly affects communication between them. If the parent of a schizophrenic child is trying to describe the child's unreachableness to a worker who has negative countertransference attitudes to mothers and blames them for all their children's difficulties, the worker may fail to understand the mother's communication, interpret it as a rejection of the child, and fail to be alerted to this and other danger signals that point to the child's serious illness.[8] Compounding the problem, the mother may sense the worker's reaction (even if it has not been made explicit) and screen her communications in order to please the worker or evade her criticism.

If the client, on the other hand, has identified the worker with an insincere, manipulating mother, he or she may construe the worker's efforts to communicate acceptance and encouragement as flattery with an ulterior motive. This type of misinterpretation can sometimes be overcome by repeated demonstration of the worker's sincerity and lack of desire to manipulate, but the process can ordinarily be greatly accelerated by bringing the client's distrust out into the open. Then it can at least be recognized as a factor in the relationship and reacted to by the worker, and perhaps be understood by the client in dynamic or developmental terms.

Another source of distortion in communication is the assignment of different meanings to symbols. All communication, verbal and nonverbal, makes use of symbols, but if the two people trying to communicate do not assign the same meaning to the symbols, the communication will obviously be distorted. The most blatant example of such distortion is the misunderstanding that can easily occur when the client has only a partial understanding of English. More subtle are differences in choice of words, which may be dependent upon class, education, ethnic background, age, region, and other variables. Not only do workers need to understand the full significance of their clients' words but they must also be able to express their own ideas in words that will accurately communicate their meanings to the client. This does not require, however, that workers adopt their clients' vernacular: to do so introduces into the relationship an element of falseness that is antitherapeutic. The client whose background differs greatly from the worker's does not expect the worker to be like him or her and might not come for help if this were the case. But there is a middle ground in which, at key points, words can be introduced that particularly express the worker's meaning in the client's language. With most people, simple nontechnical language is the most likely to be clearly understood.[9]

In all cases, but particularly when there are differences in background or age between worker and client, it is usually helpful to bring concern about possible misunderstandings into the open. A worker might say: "Since you and I have been trained in different languages, let's

make extra sure that we understand each other. If you find that you have trouble with any words I use, please let me know. And suppose I ask you to explain if I find I do not quite understand what you are saying." Or an older worker might say to a teenage client: "The slang of my generation is somewhat different from yours. Would you mind if I asked you about an expression you may use if its meaning is not quite clear to me?" Not only is communication enhanced but a spirit of equality can be fostered by asking clients to share their expertise in areas in which the worker is not well informed.

Not only words but actions or nonverbal communications are symbolic of feelings and attitudes. Facial expression, tone of voice, inflection, posture, gestures all convey meaning.[10] When the worker and client are of different backgrounds, nonverbal messages sent and received require particular attention, as is true for the verbal exchanges between them. But even when people are of similar cultures, class, and education, nonverbal communications can be easily misunderstood. Often, workers will take it for granted that by their actions they have conveyed a particular feeling or attitude when they have not, or they may assume they understand the significance of a client's gesture or facial expression without exploring it further. Accurate communication requires that the worker be alert to any tendency to rely on suppositions about nonverbal messages; the fact is that they often need verbal clarification because they can be so open to divergent interpretations.

Clear communication of every kind is difficult to achieve.[11] Clarifying and qualifying statements we make and checking out the meaning of messages received require an understanding of the complexity of communication and of the many subtle ways in which communication can fail. The same word or phrase has different meanings for different people or in different contexts. A client may use the word "we" and mean himself, himself and his wife, his entire family, his social or cultural group. Similarly, people often say "you" when they mean "I" (e.g., "You get angry when your kids act up in public"). The phrase "Take it easy" can imply "Don't be so hard on me," "Take good care of yourself," or "I'll see you again." Furthermore, the subjective connotation of a particular word varies. Even simple but charged words such as "mothering," "discipline," and "responsibility" call upon the worker to make sure when these expressions are used that their full meanings are mutually understood. Also, many messages, particularly those that attempt to describe inner emotional experiences, are next to impossible to convey thoroughly with words. Even when clients say they are "heartbroken," "pained," or "in love," or use other words of equal intensity, the depth or particular quality of the feeling is not fully transmitted. Similarly, if the worker says, "I understand," the client can only begin to know the level on which the worker means this: Does the worker understand the facts or feelings? Is the worker recognizing the truth in what the client says? Is he or she expressing empathy and caring? Sometimes when words are accompanied by nonverbal expressions the communication becomes clearer. For example, a sympathetic nod or a facial expression signifying that the worker feels "with" a client's pain may help to clarify what is meant by "I understand." Of course, the possibility of misinterpretation must still be considered.

In everyday life, as well as in treatment sessions, people tend to fill in unknowns about what another person is saying with assumptions. Sometimes these assumptions can be very accurate. On the other hand, one of the primary failures in communication derives from incomplete messages: A sends only a partial message and B, rather than asking A to elaborate, inaccurately completes it and acts upon it. For example, a worker may end a session with "Shall we meet again at this time next week?" The client may assume that the worker is not really asking for an opinion, but that the worker wants

another meeting. Or a client may say something like "I always enjoy sex with my husband," and the worker may assume that the client enjoys orgasm. Unless the worker attempts to get further clarification, it may be much later before he or she learns that the client enjoys closeness and affection with her husband and gets pleasure from pleasing him, but that she is also disappointed that she has never achieved sexual climax.

It is incumbent upon the worker to attempt continually to get feedback from the client about his or her understanding of the worker's message, such as "What are your thoughts about getting together next week?" By the same token, when the client makes an incomplete statement, such as "I always enjoy sex," the worker can ask, "What do you find particularly satisfying about your sexual life?" By seeking clarification and feedback, the worker is more likely to elicit mixed feelings, disappointments, and other concerns. Along the same lines, when the worker has a hunch about a client's reaction, it is best to check it out: "You sound as though you were hurt by your husband's remarks. Am I right?" To this, the client can respond with, "Yes, that's right," or she can correct the worker's impression by saying, "No, it's not that I feel hurt; rather I feel inferior, like a child, when he speaks to me in that way."

To complicate the matter, unclear or incomplete communications are sometimes intended to evade certain issues. The worker who simply said, "Shall we meet again at this time next week?" may have hoped to avoid hearing that the client did not want to return. And the client who did not elaborate on her concerns about never achieving orgasm may have been embarrassed to bring it up, or she may have felt that exploring the problem would be too painful to face. This does not mean that the worker should insist that clients discuss issues before they are ready to do so. It does mean that if the communication gets precise enough, the worker can then be alerted to areas that may require further exploration in the future.

Problems in communication derive not only from misunderstood, incomplete, or evasive messages. People can also send ambiguous and contradictory messages: when a worker suggests an appointment change *he* wants but implies it would be better for the client; when he shows anger or boredom but denies it; or when he articulates warm interest in a client but keeps the client waiting for an appointment without explanation. When the client says, "I really love my wife" and stiffens or frowns, or when he says, "I am angry at my wife" and smiles, he is sending two opposing messages simultaneously. It is the worker's responsibility to enhance worker-client communication by persistently attempting to clarify conflicting communications. "The therapist," writes Satir, "must see himself as a model of communication ... he must take care to be aware of his own prejudices and unconscious assumptions so as not to fall into the trap he warns others about, that of suiting reality to himself. In addition the way he interprets and structures the action of therapy from the start is the first step in introducing ... new techniques of communication."[12]

Compton and Galaway[13] identify six worker barriers to effective communication with clients. As they point out, these barriers will seriously affect the validity and reliability of information received from clients, on which treatment plans and goals are based. Barriers are created:

1. When the worker *anticipates* what the client will say. This occurs when one is so sure (or wants to be so sure) of what the client means that one fails to listen to the actual communication; the worker may be threatened by what the client is really saying, or fear having to change a point of view if the full meaning of what the client says is grasped.

2. When the worker *assumes* to know the meaning of an unclear client message and acts on the assumption rather than checking out the client's actual intent.

3. When the worker *stereotypes* a member of a group—for example, the delinquent, the white Protestant, or the schizophrenic—and thereby fails to perceive an individual above and beyond (or atypical of) the category to which he or she belongs. Communication is impeded, therefore, because the worker will tend to erect barriers (1) and (2) above, and to anticipate or make assumptions about the client's message.

4. When the worker *fails to make the purpose of an interview (or treatment) explicit.* The effect can be that the worker and client have divergent or even conflicting views of the objectives of their work together. Obviously, worker-client communication will become problematical since each will operate on separate assumptions about their joint purpose.

5. When the worker *prematurely expects or urges the client to make particular changes.* The impatient worker may fail to elicit or hear important data on which to base a sound judgment about treatment decisions; the worker may have insufficient information or may disregard communications from the client that clarify what changes the client can and wants to make. Furthermore, the worker's effort to urge or advise change, particularly in the early stages of treatment, can create barriers to trust and therefore to communication. (Along the same lines, we would add, if one attempts to arrive at a diagnosis too soon, before the necessary facts are in, one may tend to listen only to material that supports the premature conclusion.

6. When the worker is *inattentive.* If the worker's mind wanders (or it excessively fatigued, restless, preoccupied, or given to daydreaming) it is impossible truly to listen and respond to the client.

MUTUAL AGREEMENT: CLIENT PARTICIPATION AND MOTIVATION

In recent years the trend in the client-worker relationship is one in which the worker tends to be more relaxed than formerly, with the result that the climate between the two is freer, less formal and distant. Among clinical social workers, there are differences in emphasis in the extent to which they follow this trend. There are also variations to be considered on the basis of diagnostic assessment, as we will point out later in this chapter. Nevertheless, generally the worker attempts to promote an environment of equality in which he or she and the client work together to search for answers to the problems at hand. Worker and client are both experts in their own right; they both share responsibility for how the treatment progresses. The worker is trained to assess people's difficulties and strengths, to understand "the-person-in-his-situation," and to use that knowledge and those treatment procedures that can help people make changes, function more effectively, and enjoy life more comfortably or fully. It is only our clients, however, who can know how dissatisfied they are, what their dreams and ambitions are made of, what changes in their situations or emotional reactions they are looking for, and whether they find treatment helpful.

There has been some controversy among clinical practitioners about the question of mutuality between worker and client. We have already discussed our views on this issue as it relates to worker spontaneity; we have stressed the importance, as we see it, of limiting worker openness to those instances when it is relevant to the treatment. However, disagreements also exist when it comes to defining the differential roles of worker and client in formulating treatment procedures and goals.

The idea of planning treatment and treatment goals raises serious value questions in the minds of some caseworkers.[14] If you truly believe in the importance of self-determination for a client, they say, how can you talk about *planning* treatment for this person? Isn't this something that is up to the client alone? Some solve the dilemma by seeing agencies as offering certain types of services that the client chooses either

to use or to reject. In our view, this does not really solve the problem, but only circumvents it, for it is the agencies that make the choices, deciding both what services to offer and what constitutes eligibility for them. A client is not given a foster home for a child just because he or she wants one, nor are clients allowed to choose the type of foster home their children are placed in, any more than they can decide to be given financial assistance. Clients are not likely to know whether the superego needs strengthening or liberalizing (although they may be aware of being too perfectionistic or self-critical and not know what to do about it). It is usually the worker and not the client who is best equipped to know whether a mother should be helped to see her children's needs more clearly or should work on the question of why, if she does see them clearly, she cannot put this understanding into constructive action.

The truth that lies at the opposite extreme, however, is that it is not only inadvisable but almost impossible to impose treatment or goals upon a client. Except in certain aspects of protective work, when a worker may be doing something against the client's will—taking a seriously psychotic woman to a hospital, placing a child who is being badly mistreated, reporting a delinquent's parole violations to the court—the use of treatment and goal setting always involves the exercise of choice by the client. Under almost all circumstances (including in public welfare agencies), the client does or should have every right to reject casework service as a whole or any particular goal of treatment a worker may espouse.

In actual fact, the client can and often does negate the worker's efforts. The worker can offer wholehearted reassurance, but it will not become reassurance to the client who is unwilling to accept it, to believe in it. The worker can suggest and advise, but it is the client who chooses whether or not to follow the advice. The worker may feel sure that it would be best for a client to end a marriage, to spend money more carefully, to change jobs, to deal with a drinking or weight problem, but only the client can decide, from his or her point of view, whether these plans are best and whether he or she wants to work toward them. Workers can try to stimulate clients to think about their situations or themselves; only the clients can *do* it. Interpretations are futile unless clients are willing to consider their validity. During the course of treatment, methods often have to be changed from one approach to another simply because a client is unwilling to make use of the kind of help the worker has first offered or shows that he or she wants (or can better use) something the worker has not yet offered. Similarly, goals are frequently modified or revised as treatment progresses, as worker and client reach an understanding about what the client wants and what will help.

Determining the direction and goals of treatment, then, is almost never the exclusive function of either the worker or the client. Rather, it is a mutual affair in which the worker is responsible for what is *offered* and for explanation of why it is being offered, but the client exercises control over what is *accepted*. Thus, except for certain techniques used in protective work, no treatment can be successful if the client lacks *motivation* to use it. The client must have some discomfort with life as it is and have some hope that change is possible. Sometimes motivation exists spontaneously. At other times, the creation of motivation is an early task of treatment.

Not only must client and worker participate in the treatment process, but caseworkers are more keenly aware than ever of the importance of making sure that there is *explicit* mutual agreement between them when it comes to the nature of treatment and its goals.[15] Client motivation and successful treatment can depend heavily on whether the expectations, methods, and objectives of the treatment process are mutually arrived at, whether they are shared and understood. Clinical observations and research indicate that, without such a common defini-

tion, or where there is a clash of perspectives between worker and client, the worker's therapeutic efforts often fail.[16] Disappointments, frustrations, unfocused treatment, and early terminations are among the dangers inherent when there are "hidden" or "double" agendas or when divergent assumptions are made by worker and client. Throughout treatment, expectations and goals must be openly communicated by the worker and regularly elicited from the client as, together, they formulate and reformulate or expand them. As clients learn new ways of exploring themselves and their situations, the worker accepts the value of clients' ideas about what they want. The "therapeutic alliance" develops as a result of a deepening understanding between both as they arrive at a shared approach to their work together.

Let us mention here that we must be ever careful not to label our clients "resistant" simply because their views of problems, goals, or solutions differ from ours. Rather, it is our job to facilitate an *open discussion* of the divergent ideas in the hope that through ongoing reflection an agreed upon approach, in which the client has fully participated, will evolve. (The concept of "resistance" will be elaborated upon in Chapter 13.)

Mutuality is as complex as it is necessary. For example, parents may apply for help for their seven-year-old son's behavior problem in school. The immediate goal for the parents is the improvement of the boy's conduct. However, during the exploratory phase, the worker may get the impression that the boy is acting out some of the marital strains between the parents. Although initially the worker and parents mutually agree on the latter's goals, if it seems clear that change for the boy is unlikely unless the parents address the marital difficulties, it is the worker's responsibility to share these views with the clients at an appropriate time. After doing so, it is still the parents' choice, first, *whether* and, second, *how* they want to resolve the marital conflict. Often, the worker has to assume leadership in advancing goals or new options, but it is still the client's prerogative to accept or reject these or to offer alternative proposals.

There are also times when the worker, for ethical or other reasons, cannot agree upon goals advanced by the client. An extreme example is that of the woman who asked a worker to tell her young son that he could be arrested if he continued to wet his bed, on the belief that this would frighten him and "teach him a lesson." The worker could not agree to participate in this plan, but it was the worker's responsibility to explain why she could not and then to suggest that they reflect on the situation further in order to arrive at an alternative on which both could agree.

It should be clear, then, that in no way do we imply that mutual agreement means that the worker's role is a passive one; in no sense is the worker abdicating authority—to the contrary, the worker is defining it. By explicitly stating that it is the client's task to learn to make choices and decide on what life plans are suitable, the worker is freed to offer expert help in the pursuit of mutually understood goals. This function is manifold: The worker can provide information the client does not have. The worker can give feedback about distortions or contradictions in the client's outlook or behavior (such as by asking a man to consider whether he thinks he will get the response he wants from his wife by berating her). The worker can lend active guidance to the client in the selection of treatment aims. He or she can recommend procedures within treatment sessions (such as suggesting that a marital couple discuss a problem with each other or that they make "I" statements rather than "you" observations). The worker can share ideas about means that experience demonstrates have been effective in solving problems or bringing issues into focus. The worker can explain, in terms the client can understand, that self-direction and a developing sense of mastery over one's life can be cru-

cial to resolving person-situation difficulties or emotional distress; in this way, the worker urges the client to take responsibility for participating actively in seeking solutions and in giving the worker feedback about the treatment. Workers who are secure in their skills can distinguish which areas of expertise are theirs, and which must be the client's, and take responsibility for holding both to their jobs.

It is not only ethical and important to client motivation to view the worker-client relationship as a collaborative partnership: implicit is the further point that mutuality provides an opportunity for the client to strengthen ego functions such as reality testing, judgment, competence, and autonomy. The treatment process itself can be an arena in which clients develop powers; locate resources, from within and without; and gain experience in effectively taking charge of their lives. (Even the "involuntary" clients, such as those seen by protective or probation workers, will be most successfully engaged and motivated if the worker makes it crystal clear that their needs, concerns, visions, and goals are the stuff on which successful treatment depends.) With clients who expect to be given advice about what to do or how to live, the worker must take a particularly active role in helping them to begin to think and function independently.

Miss Clay, a timid forty-four-year-old single woman who lived with her domineering mother, came to a clinical social worker because she had begun to cry frequently and uncontrollably. Her job as a switchboard operator was jeopardized because of her tearfulness. Her mother, her older brother, and her boss, she complained, tried to manage her every move; they often ridiculed her and treated her as though she were incompetent. She resented them but was afraid to take independent stands of her own. In the early phase of therapy, she continually asked the worker questions such as: "Do you think I should move?" "Would it help if I changed jobs?" "Should I learn to drive a car?" The worker warmly but clearly told her that she was not going to direct her in making these choices since she had too many people running her life already. She would, however, talk over various aspects of the options she was considering. At first, the worker had to keep reminding Miss Clay that their purpose together was to help her reach her own solutions. As time went on, however, this client not only began making decisions for herself but was able to recognize the important part she played in encouraging others to treat her like a child.

Perhaps a mention of the *contract* would be helpful here. When this term is used to describe the explicit, conscious agreement between worker and client concerning the nature and aims of treatment, we endorse the concept. Sometimes, however, the contract is viewed as a formal, rigid, or binding (sometimes written) agreement. In our opinion, particularly when problems are complicated, neither the client nor the worker can easily arrive at what treatment will entail, how their perceptions of the situation may change, or what new issues or goals may arise as treatment progresses. In fact, at the beginning of treatment, the contract may simply be a mutual recognition of the fact that it may take time to determine the length and objectives of therapy. In the case cited above, the worker and client agreed that only as they worked together would it become clear what steps Miss Clay would want to take to feel better about herself. On the other hand, there are times when a worker may offer a suggestion such as "Why don't we meet together for six sessions and then, together, evaluate where to go from there?" This kind of approach or proposed contract can be reassuring to resistant clients who fear they will be snared into an interminable treatment process; in other situations, it may mean that the worker believes

the problem can be resolved quickly. We, the writers, see little need for the written contract in psychosocial treatment (except, perhaps, around such concrete matters as fees). As long as there is open communication between worker and client and an understanding that client participation is highly valued and essential, too much literal dependence on a contract can be distracting and can seriously hamper the flexibility necessary to effective treatment.

THE CLIENT–WORKER RELATIONSHIP IN THE DYNAMICS OF TREATMENT

Thus far, we have been considering the elements that go into the relationship between client and worker. What part do these elements play in treatment?

We must first distinguish between the basic therapeutic relationship and special uses to which elements in the relationship can be put. On the worker's part, no matter what the form of treatment, the attitude must be a positive one, with concern for the client's well-being, liking, respect, and acceptance of the client as an individual, and a wish for that person to be happier, or at least more comfortable and better able to handle situations. For themselves, workers need to have confidence in their skills and in the possibility of their effectiveness in aiding clients. A study by Ripple, Alexander, and Polemis[17] found an attitude of positive encouragement in the worker the primary factor in both continuance of treatment and outcome. The initial work with those clients who continued in treatment was characterized "by warmly positive affect, efforts to relieve discomfort, assurance that the situation could at least be improved, and a plan to begin work on the problem." On the other hand, "a bland, seemingly uninvolved eliciting and appraisal of the client's situation, in which the worker appeared neutral in affect" was strongly associated with discontinuance and with an unfavorable outcome in those clients who did continue despite the worker's lack of encouragement.

Along similar lines, the research of Truax and Carkhuff found that positive outcomes in psychotherapy were associated with the quality of the patient-therapist relationship; three characteristics of the therapist were found to be strongly associated with patient improvement: accurate empathy, nonpossessive warmth, and genuineness. Although some other researchers did not obtain the same results, our experience strongly supports the importance of these "core conditions."[18] Frank has stressed the importance of the therapist's ability to convey hope and confidence to patients.[19] Of course, the worker's positive personality qualities and attitudes are not enough; knowledge of theory, technical competence, and experience can play an equally important part in treatment outcomes. Nevertheless, the more free the worker is of countertherapeutic communications of any sort, the more likely it is that the client will sense that it is safe to trust the worker and engage in treatment.

The client will need to have enough capacity to perceive the worker in these terms to keep coming for treatment, not only "bringing the body" but participating in the process. This means that no matter how great are the transference and other unrealistic components of a client's attitude toward the worker, he or she must be able at least part of the time to perceive the worker as a person to be trusted. Sometimes, in the early weeks of treatment, the client is kept coming only by external forces or by feelings of distrusting desperation. The first task of treatment, then, is to find a way of communicating cues to the real nature of the worker's attitudes so that the client will gain confidence in the worker as a therapist, counselor, or simply "helper." With many clients there are periods in treatment when the realistic view of the worker is obscured by unrealistic reactions, but these clients are usually carried over such periods by previous positive perception, of which some parts of them remain aware.

The worker's goodwill and warmth toward the client are demonstrated in large part by sustaining procedures. Variations in the use of these techniques with different clients should not depend upon the extent of the worker's actual positive feelings toward the clients: they should reflect the worker's assessment or diagnostic understanding of a particular client. Some clients consistently need to have the basic therapeutic attitude demonstrated to them more clearly than other clients do. A client seeking concrete services may need information primarily and require only a minimum of support; on the other hand, when a particular client is passing through a period of anxiety, he or she especially needs to be aware of the worker's goodwill. When the client has strong transference feelings toward the worker, sustaining procedures will usually promote the positive side of the transference and will take on added significance to the client, who will feel as if reassurance or love is being received from someone who was important in early life. Clients with personality or schizophrenic disorders, although often able to benefit from reflective procedures, nevertheless need more support than many other clients do, particularly—but not only—during the early phase of treatment. They need ongoing acceptance, comfort, admiration of positive qualities and achievements. But for most clients capable of change and growth, overemphasis on sustaining procedures can create excessive dependency in both its realistic and its transference components.[20] "Optimum frustration," discussed in Chapter 2, fosters self-reliant functioning. Therefore, sometimes we help by not being ever available to speak with clients on the telephone, by expecting certain courtesies or appropriate behaviors rather than indulging immature functioning, by not "doing for" people what they can do for themselves.

Techniques of direct influence depend for effectiveness in considerable part upon the client's confidence in the worker as an expert or, particularly in persuasion and active intervention, as a person of authority. Workers using these techniques must also have this self-image if clients are to take them seriously. One of the troubles young workers encounter in the field of child welfare, where they may have to advise foster mothers who are many years their senior and experienced with children although they themselves may have had mainly book learning, is that they quite rightly lack confidence in the extent of their competence and inadvertently communicate this fact to the foster mothers. As explained in Chapter 9, there is evidence that directive procedures are more often used to help the client learn how to utilize interviews and the therapeutic relationship than they are to give the client advice about personal decisions. Often, an emphasis on directive techniques is combined with stress on sustaining procedures. In combination, these techniques encourage and gratify a positive, dependent relationship of either the real or the transference type.

Exploration and ventilation often require support and acceptance that go beyond simple sustaining procedures. The worker's empathy, or ability to feel *as if* he or she were the client, to experience deeply the client's feelings (without, as Rogers and others caution, ever "losing the 'as if' condition"),[21] can be highly therapeutic. When, for example, a client is grieving the death of a loved one or is filled with anxiety, the worker's profound understanding of the pain or desperation involved can in itself bring relief.

In considering the person-situation type of reflective discussion, we turn to the possibility of modifying the relationship by bringing the relationship into discussion. In the types of treatment just considered, the worker's attitude is really *demonstrated*. Even though this takes place through words, it is not in itself discussed. But now the client's reactions to the worker are brought into the open and the client is invited to test them against what the worker presents as the reality of the situation between them. In the process, the worker becomes better in-

formed about the client's reactions and if they are unrealistic or inappropriate has an opportunity to judge whether they are due to misunderstandings or distortions of the client's. In either case, as discussed earlier, the worker has an opportunity to straighten the matter out and to establish a therapeutically positive relationship through which the clients can learn a great deal about themselves, their reactions, and their ways of relating to others.

The nature of the worker's activities in helping clients think about person-situation configurations often conveys to clients a picture of what the worker is like—at least, it shows what the worker is *not* like.[22] The fact that the worker refrains from excessive advice giving or from condemnation and encourages clients to think for themselves may establish the worker as different from parents who have had a destructive controlling influence on the clients. This may encourage strong positive feelings toward the worker based on the reality of the relationship. Sometimes this reflective discussion is buttressed by a demonstration of sustaining attitudes and by a mild form of direct influence that encourages pleasurable, psychologically healthy activities discouraged in the past by restrictive or hostile parents. This particular combination of procedures is sometimes known as a *corrective relationship* and is referred to by Austin as "experiential" treatment. Usually the client has at first regarded the worker as a parent substitute, anticipating, because of transference reactions, that the worker will respond to verbalizations and behavior as the client's parent would have done. When the worker reacts differently, the effect of the early parental situation is in a measure corrected.[23] The client, responding to the worker as to a parent, is now accepted as he or she was not by the true parent and given, so to speak, a liberal emotional education instead of the restrictive one originally experienced. Although the second experience does not efface the first, it can do much to counteract it.

This corrective relationship treatment, we want to emphasize, is to be distinguished from the type of corrective emotional experience in which the therapist plays a "role" artificially constructed to meet what are judged to be the corrective needs of their patients. It is rather the presentation of a consistently therapeutic attitude toward clients in which the worker is realistic in enlightened terms, represents adult reactions (in the sense of both privileges and responsibilities), and is continuously accepting of clients and their needs.

In present-day clinical practice, clients are more frequently diagnosed as having personality disorders than neuroses. In certain of these disorders, client difficulties may spring not so much from oversevere as from inconsistent, neglectful, or even overindulgent parents. These clients, who in their early years were deprived of reliable nurturance or well-timed encouragement of independent functioning, are likely to manifest borderline traits or some other type of developmental disorder. In all of these, the realistic and transference relationships to the worker can facilitate the closing of developmental gaps and the resumption of the growth process that had been interrupted or distorted at some point along the way.

When the problem is one of "acting out," the corrective feature in the relationship may be that the worker comes to represent a pattern of more realistic, in the sense of stronger, ego controls than the individual has previously experienced. Sometimes the main therapeutic task is helping clients to find ways to refrain from behavior that constantly causes them trouble and defeats their own purposes. In these corrective relationships, it is most important that clients see the therapist as someone who does not stand for an overly restrictive life and is not disapproving, but who is interested in helping the clients learn not to defeat their own ends by activities that inevitably boomerang. As discussed on pages 216 and 217, it was necessary for Miss Clay to experience a relationship in which her thoughts, feelings, and capacity for making her own decisions—in short, her independence—were valued rather than denigrated. For clients with borderline personality disorders, the corrective aspects of the relationship may involve the worker's demonstrating, often over and over again, consistent caring, optimism, and patience and the ability to handle hostility without either retaliating or withdrawing. The work with Mrs. Zimmer, discussed in Chapter 3, illustrates this kind of relationship.

An important facet of the corrective relationship is the effect it can have on the client's self-image. We know that children often see themselves as their parents see them. When clients themselves have unrealistically dismal pictures of themselves and the worker holds a more optimistic view, the worker can convey this attitude to the clients in many ways. In the context of a transference, the experiencing of such an attitude in the worker can powerfully affect the client's self-image. It can be even further strengthened if through developmental reflection the clients can become aware of the sources of some of their self-devaluations and can come to understand the dynamics of how certain experiences have given them unrealistic pictures of themselves. Once a person's self-esteem is strengthened, he or she is far more likely to manage life's ups and downs and to find and maintain nurturing relationships outside the treatment situation.

Sometimes, as the chapters on family therapy and environmental work explain, corrective work can be facilitated by bringing the client's parents into treatment sessions. When it is possible for a client to get realistic reactions, acceptance, and support from parents rather than indirectly through the positive transference relationship with the worker, the therapeutic work may be accelerated. One small sign of parental caring and encouragement can be as effective as many sessions with a supportive worker. This is not always possible, however, unless the parents themselves have a corrective experience.

The factor of the client's self-image is affected in a special way by the worker's "therapeutic optimism." This, in turn, is related to the worker's professional security and optimism. Although one can never know in advance the actual outcome of a phase of treatment, the worker does foresee the possibility that as a result of treatment the client will be more comfortable or more effective, or both; if there were not some hope of this, there would be no justification for continuing the contact. Such therapeutic optimism can be perceived by most clients and holds the meaning that someone believes in their possibilities, sees them as better than they see themselves. Even in the absence of the type of transference and life experience upon which corrective relationship treatment is based, the worker's optimism affects the client's self-image and is an important therapeutic element in treatment. The Jones marital case in Chapter 3 illustrates this point.

Another fairly universal factor in successful treatment springs from the client's tendency to identify with a worker with whom there is a positive relationship. Clients often say, in describing a difficult current happening in their lives, "I tried to think, 'What would _____ (the worker) do about that?' and then I said _____ .'" What they then say is often close to what the worker has said to them under similar circumstances. This phenomenon is sometimes described as the worker's "lending the strength of the ego" to the client. It is an imitative sort of learning, similar to a child's learning from imitation of the parent with whom he or she identifies, that can be incorporated in a lasting way into the client's personality. Such learning depends on the existence of positive reality feelings toward the worker, feelings often reinforced by a positive transference.

This type of identification is sometimes accelerated by assigning a worker who is of the same sex, a similar age, and sometimes the same race or ethnic background as the client. In this case, however, the worker has to guard against the possibility of overidentifying with the client and overusing the transference. Paraprofessional workers can sometimes be particularly useful as "role models," but careful supervision by a clinical social worker is especially important here because of both the possibility of overidentification and the tendency of some untrained or insufficiently trained workers to attempt to impose their own values and goals on the client.

Diagnosis affects the nature of transference. For example, an obsessive-compulsive man may be so eager to be a "perfect" client and please the worker that he takes on a deferential attitude. At the same time, his unconscious need to control may influence him to resist the strong positive involvement in the therapeutic relationship necessary for change to occur. Bringing these transference reactions out in discussions can be central to helping him to reflect on his ambivalence toward treatment and on the conflict between his strong need to win favor and his anxiety about intimacy. When the difficulty is a borderline disorder, the client may suddenly vacillate between seeing the worker as "all good" (i.e., the loving, perfect parent) and "all bad" (i.e., depriving and uncaring). The client may alternately cling to and distrust the worker. The quality of the transference not only helps in formulating the diagnosis but becomes a useful tool in treatment. With Mrs. Zimmer, the transference and subsequent reflection on the extreme reversals in the ways she experienced the worker were basic to her progress in integrating her "good" and "bad" feelings about herself and others.

From this discussion, it becomes clear that clinical social workers often use the treatment situation to help their clients increase dynamic or developmental reflection and self-understanding. However, the therapist-client relationship, particularly in its transference aspects, is different in casework and in psychoanalysis. Repressed (in contrast to suppressed, preconscious) emotion and conflicts, for example, are not usually brought into consciousness although their derivatives often are. The case of Jed Cooper in Chapter 21 illustrates this point.

Mrs. Zimmer's situation was somewhat different. The feelings she transferred to the worker were not repressed; rather they were raw, chaotic, undifferentiated emotion that emerged under stress or intensity because of flaws in early ego development. She was, of course, unaware of some of the specific sources of her emotional reactions, because many of the inconsistencies in her upbringing occurred before she could speak or remember. For some time she did not realize that she was displacing childhood feelings—such as rage, despair, terror—onto the worker. Ultimately, though, she became keenly aware of the vacillations of affect in all of her relationships, including the treatment relationship. In addition to the supportive, "ego-building" function of the relationship, it also provided her with the opportunity to reflect on the probable origins of the extremes within her and to work productively toward consolidating these.[24]

Since clinical social workers do not use free association under ordinary circumstances, the client is under no compulsion to verbalize all thoughts about the worker as in psychoanalysis. And, perhaps most important of all, the general way of conducting casework treatment does not encourage extensive regression in the transference. To put it more concretely, the casework client does not become as deeply immersed as the analysand in the unconscious fantasy that the worker is a parent. Although the client may react to a certain extent as though this were so, the cathexis of the idea is not nearly so strong as it would be in analysis. Likewise, since the client is not encouraged to regress—to feel and, within the treatment hour, to behave as a young child or even an infant—the client in a relationship with a worker reexperiences the phenomena of early childhood in only a very fragmentary way. The client is more likely to reexperience the reflections of these earliest reactions as they appeared later in childhood and adolescent relationships with parents. As Annette Garrett put it in her excellent paper on the transference in casework, the caseworker does not encourage the transference neurosis.[25]

Some caseworkers, fearful of going too deeply into the transference, have taken the position that transference reactions should not be interpreted for purposes of aiding the client's self-understanding but discussed only as necessary for the maintenance, or restoration, of a positive relationship. Such a position arises, perhaps, from lack of clarity about the various elements in the transference as it appears in clinical social work, particularly about the fact that there are ego-dystonic preconscious elements in the transference, just as there are in all other phenomena; irrational components affected by childhood experiences and even those originally based in infancy and very early life are often reflected to some degree in the client-worker relationship. There is in reality no more "danger" in touching these elements as they appear in the transference than there is in commenting on them as they emerge in other areas of clients' lives.

Among the procedures used in reflective consideration of pattern-dynamic and developmental content, then, are those that help the client to understand dynamically some of the transference and other unrealistic responses to the worker and the way in which these responses repeat earlier reactions to parents and other closely related people.[26] The client can then put this self-understanding to use in recognizing similar reactions as they occur in current life situations outside of treatment. The client is then in a position to correct distortions and to respond to people more realistically. We deprive the client of a potent source of help in the struggle toward realistic living if we neglect to use the vivid "here-and-now" experiences that occur between client and caseworker.[27]

A FURTHER WORD ON CLIENT–WORKER MUTUALITY

The tendency in recent years to move toward greater informality and mutuality in the treatment relationship is regarded by the writers as a sound one. It is appropriately responsive to widespread distaste for anything that approaches authoritarianism. It should be evident, of course, that we do not favor a climate so casual that the client assumes the worker is encouraging a social relationship, in which case very obvious and realistic difficulties can ensue; the limits should always be made clear. But, as we have said, we do endorse a caring, professional relationship that avoids aloofness and that fosters as much equality as possible, a working alliance in which the client participates actively in the treatment process and in the selection of treatment objectives.

Certain very real questions arise, however, concerning the degree of informality and expressed warmth that is useful under different circumstances. This is particularly so when self-understanding is an aspect of treatment and in certain types of corrective relationships. For the most part, there is agreement among psychosocial workers that neither a cold, intellectual approach, on the one hand, nor a "hail fellow well met" stance, on the other, is appropriate. But some tend to favor a fairly formal relationship, especially for those clients who have difficulty becoming aware of negative feelings. These practitioners point out that a worker can be so "relaxed" or "kind" that the client is thereby inhibited from expressing even those negatives of which he or she is keenly conscious. Similarly, they maintain, the client can see the informal worker as such a "real person" that transference fantasies or irrational feelings may not get a chance to come to the fore. The less giving, restrained relationship can help to intensify these, making it more possible for the client to become aware of them while attempting to develop self-understanding.

Other caseworkers lean toward a more relaxed relationship, out of concern for those clients who require strong support and an easygoing manner to feel safe enough to share their feelings and fantasies. They point out that in some cases, when the worker is too formal, clients can be inhibited from sharing personal reactions for fear they will be criticized or misunderstood. Clients have been known to terminate treatment prematurely because they felt "put on the spot" by a worker's reserve.

Actually, these differences may not be as great as they seem on the surface. A middle ground between the two positions can be found, even though a worker's emphasis may be influenced to some degree by his or her natural personality style. But, in our view, the approach should depend primarily on diagnostic assessment. For example, particularly in the first months, Mrs. Zimmer required a great deal of sustainment and open encouragement in order to trust the worker enough to engage in long-term treatment. A remote stance would probably have been so anxiety-producing that she would have discontinued therapy. Furthermore, she had no difficulty in becoming aware of strongly negative reactions to the worker, even in the face of the worker's warmly outgoing approach. In fact, an important aspect of the therapy involved helping Mrs. Zimmer to contrast her angry accusations about the worker's lack of interest with the worker's actual attitudes and behavior. Since this worker had been consistent in actively helping, in demonstrating that she cared, willing to be available by telephone in times of stress, and so on, it was possible to confront Mrs. Zimmer with her distorted reactions. A more withholding approach might well have confirmed her skewed view that the worker was indifferent or hostile to her. Effective work in the Kennedy, West, and Stone cases (also in Chapter 3) and the Carter case (Chapter 21) required a worker with a warm, active, flexible approach to reach out to the clients and their family members. A rigid, subdued, or humorless worker probably would not have been able to engage or help these clients. On the other hand, there are many people who feel so guilty about angry, competitive, or "unkind" feelings of any sort toward the worker that they have particular difficulty expressing these in a climate of relaxed friendliness; they feel more "justified" in sharing them when the therapeutic relationship is less giving than it was in Mrs. Zimmer's case. Certainly, research in this area would be useful to refine our knowledge and help us to distinguish the conditions under which one or the other emphasis is most effective. But lacking that, as we see it, the choice should depend more on the client's personality and circumstances than on the worker's need for reserve or for camaraderie.

The question also arises as to whether it is accurate to say that a "corrective" relationship, in which the worker is in some measure seen as a "good parent," is truly "mutual" or "equal." For example, Mr. Kennedy (again, see Chapter 3) turned to the worker for nurturance or "mothering" before he could mobilize himself to begin to take constructive action. The temporary positive transference relationship, in which he was indeed dependent, and in that sense unequal to the worker, gave him the support he needed in order to arrive at his own decisions. On the other hand, certainly mutuality was evidenced by the fact that at no time did the worker use the relationship to attempt to induce Mr. Kennedy to resolve his predicament in a particular way; the success of the treatment depended on the fact that he made his own choices and carved out his own directions. The objectives of treatment, to reduce his depression and to find satisfactory solutions to his situation, were mutually understood and agreed upon. In some instances, then, equality per se may be temporarily limited because of the client's need for dependence. The client may need to lean heavily on a worker, sometimes in an almost childlike manner. Yet even when this is

so, the overall goal of any treatment is to help the client become as self-reliant and autonomous as possible. As we see it, mutuality—in the sense that worker and client come to a shared agreement about the course and purposes of treatment—must be carefully preserved in every therapeutic relationship.

NOTES

1. Dorothy Fahs Beck and Mary Ann Jones, *Progress on Family Problems* (New York: Family Service Association of America, 1973), pp. 128–129.

2. For clinical discussions and reports of research findings from several disciplines on some of the ingredients believed to be important to a successful therapeutic relationship, see Fred E. Fiedler, "The Concept of the Ideal Therapeutic Relationship," *Journal of Consulting Psychology,* 14 (August 1950), 239–245; Jerome D. Frank, "The Dynamics of the Psychotherapeutic Relationship," *Psychiatry,* 22 (February 1959), 17–39; Jerome D. Frank, "The Role of Hope in Psychotherapy," *International Journal of Psychiatry,* 5 (May 1968), 383–395; Thomas Keefe, "Empathy: The Critical Skill," *Social Work,* 21 (January 1976), 10–14; Alan Keith-Lucas, *The Giving and Taking of Help* (Chapel Hill: University of North Carolina Press, 1971), especially pp. 47–65; Carl Rogers, "The Therapeutic Relationship: Recent Theory and Research," in Floyd Matson and Ashley Montagu, eds., *The Human Dialogue* (New York: The Free Press, 1967), pp. 246–259; Angelo Smaldino, "The Importance of Hope in the Casework Relationship," *Social Casework,* 56 (July 1975), 328–333; Charles B. Truax and Robert R. Carkuff, *Toward Effective Counseling and Psychotherapy: Training and Practice* (Chicago: Aldine, 1967), especially pp. 176–189; and Charles B. Truax and Kevin Mitchell, "Research on Certain Therapist Interpersonal Skills in Relation to Process and Outcome," in Allen E. Bergin and Sol L. Garfield, eds., *Handbook of Psychotherapy and Behavior Change: An Empirical Analysis* (New York: Wiley, 1971), pp. 299–344.

See also note 18 to this chapter for discussion related to research on worker characteristics of accurate empathy, genuineness, and nonpossessive warmth.

3. Annette Garrett points out the importance of this distinction in her paper "The Worker-Client Relationship," in Howard J. Parad, ed., *Ego Psychology in Dynamic Casework* (New York: Family Service Association of America, 1958), pp. 53–54, 59–60.

4. Variation among groups, especially among different classes in their attitudes toward and expectations of treatment agencies, has been a subject of interest over the years and is often touched on in articles on work with the poor, with blue-collar workers, and with ethnic minorities. For the most part, these articles are speculative and impressionistic rather than definitive, but they do serve to alert us to attitudes that may exist. For discussions from various perspectives, see H. Aronson and Betty Overall, "Treatment Expectations of Patients in Two Social Classes," *Social Work*, 11 (January 1966), 35–41; John A. Brown, "Clinical Social Work with Chicanos: Some Unwarranted Assumptions," *Clinical Social Work Journal*, 4 (Winter 1979), 256–265; Leopold Caligor and Miltiades Zaphiropoulos, "Blue-Collar Psychotherapy: Stereotype and Myth," in Earl G. Witenberg, ed., *Interpersonal Explorations in Psychoanalysis* (New York: Basic Books, 1973), pp. 218–234; Alejandro Garcia, "The Chicano and Social Work," *Social Casework*, 52 (May 1971), 274–278; Sonia Badillo Ghali, "Culture Sensitivity and the Puerto Rican Client," *Social Casework*, 58 (October 1977), 459–468; Robert Gould, "Dr. Strangeclass: Or How I Stopped Worrying about Theory and Began Treating the Blue-Collar Worker," *American Journal of Orthopsychiatry*, 37 (January 1967), 78–86; Man Keugh Ho, "Social Work with Asian Americans," *Social Casework*, 57 (March 1976), 195–201; Gordon N. Keller, "Bicultural Social Work and Anthropology," *Social Casework*, 53 (October 1972), 455–465; Faustina Ramirez Knoll; "Casework Services for Mexican Americans," *Social Casework*, 52 (May 1971), 279–284; Frederick C. Redlich, August B. Hollingshead, and Elizabeth Bellis, "Social Class Differences in Attitudes Toward Psychiatry," *American Journal of Orthopsychiatry*, 25 (January 1955), 60–70; "Social Work with the Wealthy," *Social Casework*, 57 (April 1976), 254–258; Olive Petro and Betty French, "The Black Client's View of Himself," *Social Casework*, 53 (October 1972), 466–474; and John Spiegel, "Some Cultural Aspects of Transference and Counter-Transference," in Jules Masserman, ed., *Individual and Familial Dynamics*

(New York: Grune & Stratton, 1959), 160–182.

It is most encouraging that recent research studies (which confirm our own practice experience) indicate that patients or clients of low socioeconomic status do not seem to be as negative or as unsophisticated about or as unable to use psychotherapy as reports and observational findings in the 1950s suggested that they were. See Chapter 8, note 13, for references on this topic.

In a very interesting and recommended paper by Raymond P. Lorion and Robert D. Felner, "Research on Mental Health Interventions with the Disadvantaged," in Sol L. Garfield and Allen E. Bergin, *Handbook of Psychotherapy and Behavior Change* (New York: John Wiley & Sons, 1986), 739–775, many aspects of treatment for the poor are discussed. One point, among many, that the authors make in their survey of the relevant research is that often time-limited therapies are the most effective. It is suggested that assisting low-income clients to cope with or resist environmental demands and helping in the location of resources and social networks may increase commitment to treatment. Fortunately, the authors emphasize that the poor are not in any way a homogeneous group; obviously, generalizations about treatment of low-income clients cannot be made.

In any event, as the following note will indicate, problems around treatment of clients different from their therapists may derive from bias among therapists as much as from reluctance of clients to engage in treatment.

5. There are many warnings against stereotyping in the literature, going back to the twenties, if not earlier. Mary Richmond dealt with it briefly in *Social Diagnosis* (New York: Russell Sage Foundation, 1917), pp. 97–98. The study by August B. Hollingshead and Frederick C. Redlich, *Social Class and Mental Illness* (New York: Wiley, 1958), found that psychiatrists' diagnoses, treatment recommendations, and subjective responses were significantly affected by the patient's social class. There are other, more recent, research reports that suggest that clients of low socioeconomic status are less likely than those in the middle or upper classes to be accepted or referred for psychotherapy; they are also more likely to be referred for inpatient and drug treatment, to less experienced therapists, and to less intense psychotherapy. See Garfield and Bergin, *Handbook of Psychotherapy and*

Behavior Change, pp. 214–215. See also Joel Fischer and Henry Miller, "The Effect of Client Race and Social Class on Clinical Judgments," *Clinical Social Work Journal,* 1 (Summer 1973), 100–109; and Donna L. Franklin, "Does Client Social Class Affect Clinical Judgment?" *Social Casework,* 67 (September 1986), 424–432. Their studies indicate that some clinical social workers, when reading case materials, can be biased solely by the social class variable. Recommendations about treatment differed according to socioeconomic status, even though case materials were identical except for social class. Another study suggests that mental health workers feel more competent when dealing with clients of their own ethnic group than with clients of any other group; see Susan Meyers Chandler, "Self-Perceived Competency in Cross-Cultural Counseling," *Social Casework,* 61 (June 1980), 347–353. Of interest also is a good article by Frank Pittman III, "Children of the Rich," *Family Process,* 24 (December 1985), 461–472, in which the author discusses, among other topics, therapist countertransference reactions to wealthy clients.

Scott M. Briar's carefully designed doctoral study, which was reported in his article "Use of Theory in Studying Effects of Client Social Class on Students' Judgments," *Social Work,* 6 (July 1961), 91–97, indicates that the judgments of social work students were influenced by knowledge of the client's class, but Briar did not find a consistent inverse relationship (as had been hypothesized) between the student's own responses versus his or her predictions of client's responses and the distance in social class background between worker and client. He did find a slight tendency for students to assume greater similarity between themselves and the client when middle- rather that lower-class status was attributed to the client. The study did not attempt to evaluate whether the judgments themselves were or were not justified in view of the client's ascribed class status. It is possible that the great emphasis in casework training over the past thirty years on acceptance of differences and on self-determination by the client has acted as a safeguard against at least the grosser forms of class bias entering the treatment process.

Nevertheless, social workers and others continue to be alert to the dangers of racism, sexism, class, and other culturally influenced biases among therapists; certainly, the need for awareness of the subtle and blatant adverse influences of such worker attitudes on the helping relationship cannot be overemphasized. Jeanette Alexander, in "Alternate Life Styles: Relationship Between New Realities and Practice," *Clinical Social Work Journal,* 4 (Winter 1976), 289–301, warns against resistance to accepting changing lifestyles; Caree Rozen Brown and Marilyn Levitt Hellinger, in "Therapists' Attitudes Toward Women," *Social Work,* 20 (July 1975), 266–270, found that many of the therapists in their study, particularly males, held "traditional" attitudes about women; Shirley Cooper, in "A Look at the Effect of Racism on Clinical Work," *Social Casework,* 54 (February 1973), 76–84, suggests that when therapists are influenced by "color blindness," "ethnocentricity," or "white guilt," they may fail to individualize their client; Esther Fibush and BeAlva Turnquest, in "A Black and White Approach to the Problem of Racism," *Social Casework,* 51 (October 1970), 459–466, describe an approach to the effects of racism on clients and workers; Alex Gitterman and Alice Schaeffer, in an excellent article, "The White Professional and the Black Client," *Social Casework,* 53 (May 1972), 280–291, optimistically discuss methods for overcoming barriers to the white-black helping relationship; James W. Grimm and James D. Orten, in "Student Attitudes Toward the Poor," *Social Work,* 18 (January 1973), 94–100, found in their interesting study that first-year graduate social work students held varying attitudes toward the poor associated with differences in background and experience; Charles Grosser's "Local Residents as Mediators Between Middle-Class Professional Workers and Lower-Class Clients," *Social Service Review,* 40 (March 1966), 56–63, deals with the question of bias in indigenous workers; David Hallowitz, in "Counseling and Treatment of the Poor Black Family," *Social Casework,* 56 (October 1975), 451–459, discusses the importance of the therapist's being aware of and dealing with his or her own prejudices and with the distrust and hostility that the black client may feel; Kenneth C. Hallum's "Social Class and Psychotherapy: A Sociolinguistic Approach," *Clinical Social Work Journal,* 6 (Fall 1978), 188–201, challenges some of the traditional psychotherapeutic approaches to work with "lower-status" clients; Man Keung Ho and Eunice McDowell, in "The Black Worker–White Client Relationship," *Clinical Social Work Journal,* 1 (Fall 1973), 161–167, discuss the need for the black worker to understand his or her own cross-racial feelings. Alfred

Kadushin's excellent review of several studies, "The Racial Factor in the Interview," *Social Work*, 17 (May 1972), 88–98, concludes that, despite difficulties, white workers can and do work effectively with nonwhite clients and that certain advantages may accrue from racially mixed worker-client relationships; Thomas Keefe, in "The Economic Context of Empathy," *Social Work*, 23 (November 1978), 460–465, discusses empathy as an important factor in work with clients beset by harsh economic realities; Helen A. Mendes, in "Countertransferences and Counter-Culture Clients," *Social Casework*, 58 (March 1977), 159–163, discusses the problems of therapist bias against alternative lifestyles; Salvador Minuchin and Braulio Montalvo, in "Techniques for Working with Disorganized Low Socio-Economic Families," *American Journal of Orthopsychiatry*, 37 (October 1967), 880–887, deal with the special approaches necessary for working with some poor families; Emelicia Mizio's "White Worker–Minority Client," *Social Work*, 17 (May 1972), 82–86, discusses the need for social workers to subject themselves to critical self-examination of their racial attitudes; Barbara Shannon, in "Implication of White Racism for Social Work Practice," *Social Casework*, 51 (May 1970), 270–276, warns against hidden antagonism due to racism; B. L. Stempler, "Effects of Aversive Racism on White Social Work Students," *Social Casework*, 56 (October 1975), 460–467, argues for the need to reeducate social work students against insidious racist attitudes; Evelyn Stiles et al., in "Hear It Like It Is," *Social Casework*, 53 (May 1972), 292–299, offer case material in which the value of sensitive discussions of racial matters is illustrated.

The reader is also referred to George P. Banks, "The Effects of Race on One-to-One Helping Interviews," *Social Science Review*, 45 (June 1971), 137–146; Julia Bloch, "The White Worker and the Negro Client in Psychotherapy," *Social Work*, 13 (April 1968), 36–42; Crawford E. Burns, "White Staff, Black Children: Is There a Problem?" *Child Welfare*, 50 (February 1971), 90–96; Roger R. Miller, "Student Research Perspectives on Race in Casework Practice," *Smith College Studies in Social Work*, 41 (November 1970), 10–23; and Clemmont Vontross, "Cultural Barriers in Counseling Relationships," *Journal of Counseling Psychology*, 18 (January 1971), 7–13. These articles, among many others, make strong statements about the issues associated with interracial or intergroup helping relationships.

For a review of research on the implications for outcome of the therapist's ethnicity, class, and sex, and the relevance of matching patients and therapists according to these, see Larry E. Beutler et al., "Therapist Variables in Psychotherapy Process and Outcome," in Garfield and Bergin, *Psychotherapy and Behavior Change*, 257–310. Studies have not consistently found substantial differences in treatment outcome as a function of patient and therapist ethnic matches. Few studies are available by which the relationship between therapists' socioeconomic status or background and treatment outcome can be adequately assessed. Of interest, however, is the conclusion (p. 265) that "current findings suggest that female therapists, first, and therapists of the patient's gender, second, facilitate treatment benefit, especially if these therapists present a nonstereotypic sexual viewpoint."

The reader is also referred to Elaine B. Pinderhughes, "Teaching Empathy in Cross-Cultural Social Work, " *Social Work*, 14 (July 1969), 312–316, for a useful discussion of the importance of empathy in mollifying clients' sense of powerlessness derived from racial and ethnic differences.

6. See, for example, Rubin Blanck, "Countertransference in Treatment of the Borderline Patient," *Clinical Social Work Journal*, 1 (Summer 1973), 110–117; Dean Briggs, "The Trainee and the Borderline Client: Countertransference Pitfalls," *Clinical Social Work Journal*, 7 (Summer 1979), 133–145; Joan Dunkel and Shellie Hatfield, "Countertransference Issues in Working with Persons with AIDS," *Social Work*, 31 (March–April 1986); Elinor Dunn Grayer and Patricia R. Sax, "A Model for the Diagnostic and Therapeutic Use of Countertransference," *Clinical Social Work Journal*, 14 (Winter 1986), 295–307; Mary L. Gottesfeld and Florence Lieberman, "The Pathological Therapist," *Social Casework*, 60 (July 1979), 387–393; Florence Lieberman and Mary L. Gottesfeld, "The Repulsive Client," *Clinical Social Work Journal*, 1 (Spring 1973), 22–31, in which the authors discuss therapeutic approaches to clients who are demanding, "schizophrenogenic," helpless, and hopeless; John Maltsberger and Dan Buie, "Countertransference Hate in the Treatment of Suicidal Patients," *Archives of General Psychiatry*, 30 (May 1974), 625–633; Kenneth E. Reid, "Nonrational Dynamics of Client-Worker Interaction," *Social Casework*, 58 (December 1977), 600–

606; Sonya Rhodes, "The Personality of the Worker: An Unexplored Dimension in Treatment," *Social Casework*, 60 (May 1979), 259–264, distinguishes countertransference reactions from worker personality traits; Gerald Schamess, "Boundary Issues in Countertransference: A Developmental Perspective," *Clinical Social Work Journal*, 9 (Winter 1981), 244–257; Mary C. Schwartz, "Helping the Worker with Countertransference," *Social Work*, 23 (May 1978), 204–209; and Donald W. Winnicott, "Hate in Countertransference," *International Journal of Psychoanalysis*, 30 (part 2, 1949), 69–74.

See also Miriam Elson, *Self Psychology in Clinical Social Work* (New York: W. W. Norton, 1986), chapter 6, "Transference and Countertransference."

7. For useful readings, see Dorothy Fahs Beck, "Counselor Burnout in Family Service Agencies," *Social Casework*, 68 (January 1987), 3–15; Srinika Jayaratne and Wayne A. Chess, "Job Satisfaction, Burnout, and Turnover: A National Study," *Social Work*, 29 (September–October 1984), 448–453; Anne Minahan, "Editorial Page: 'Burnout' and Organizational Change," *Social Work*, 25 (March 1980), 87; Nancy Ratliff, "Stress and Burnout in the Helping Professions," *Social Casework*, 69 (March 1988), 147–154; Joan Streepy, "Direct-Service Providers and Burnout," *Social Casework*, 62 (June 1981), 352–361; and Joseph A. Walsh, "Burnout and Values in the Social Service Profession," *Social Casework*, 68 (May 1987), 279–283.

8. For a discussion of this in work with foster parents, see Robert Nadel, "Interviewing Style and Foster Parents' Verbal Accessibility," *Child Welfare*, 46 (April 1967), 207–213.

9. Camille Jeffers is quite specific about this. See her *Living Poor* (Ann Arbor, Mich.: Ann Arbor Publishers, 1967), p. 122.

For further discussions of communication between worker and client, see John D. Cormican, "Linguistic Issues in Interviewing," *Social Casework*, 59 (March 1978), 145–151; Sheldon R. Gelman, "Esoterica: A Zero Sum Game in the Helping Professions," *Social Casework*, 61 (January 1980), 48–53; Nancy Mavogenes et al., "But Can the Client Understand It?" *Social Work*, 22 (March 1977), 110–112; Marilyn Austin Rumelhart, "When Understanding the Situation Is the Real Problem," *Social Casework*, 65 (January 1984), 27–33; and Brett Seabury, "Communication Problems in Social Work Practice," *Social Work*, 25 (January 1980), 40–44.

10. See Chapter 15, note 45.

11. For a clear summary of some of the difficulties involved in achieving functional communication, see Virginia Satir, *Conjoint Family Therapy*, rev. ed. (Palo Alto, Calif.: Science and Behavior Books, 1967), especially pp. 63–90. See also Paul Watzlawick, *The Language of Change: Elements of Therapeutic Communication* (New York: Basic Books, 1978). Refer also to Chapter 2, note 34.

12. Satir, *Conjoint Family Therapy*, p. 97.

13. Beulah Roberts Compton and Burt Galaway, *Social Work Processes*, 3d ed. (Chicago: Dorsey Press, 1984), pp. 275–281.

14. See Kenneth Pray, "A Restatement of the Generic Principles of Social Casework Practice," *Journal of Social Casework*, 28 (October 1947), 283–290, for a statement of this point of view.

15. See Werner Gottlieb and Joe. H. Stanley, "Mutual Goals and Goal-Setting in Casework," *Social Casework*, 48 (October 1967), 471–477; Anthony N. Maluccio and Wilma D. Marlow, "The Case for the Contract," *Social Work*, 19 (January 1974), 28–36, also reprinted in Compton and Galaway, *Social Work Processes*, 407–414; and Elizabeth A. Sirles, "Client-Counselor Agreement on Problem and Change," *Social Casework*, 63 (June 1982), 348–353.

16. See Anthony N. Maluccio, *Learning from Clients: Interpersonal Helping as Viewed by Clients and Social Workers* (New York: The Free Press, 1979); John E. Mayer and Noel Timms, "Clash in Perspective Between Worker and Client," *Social Casework*, 50 (January 1969), 32–40; and Phyllis R. Silverman, "A Reexamination of the Intake Procedure," *Social Casework*, 51 (December 1970), 625–634.

17. Lilian Ripple, Ernestina Alexander, and Bernice Polemis, *Motivation, Capacity and Opportunity*, Social Service Monographs (Chicago: University of Chicago Press, 1964).

18. Truax and Carkhuff, *Effective Counseling and Psychotherapy*, pp. 176–189, and Truax and Mitchell, "Therapist Interpersonal Skills." These studies and others suggested that therapists who are accurately empathic, genuine, and nonpossessively warm, regardless of training, modality used, or theoretical approach, are effective with a wide range of problems and client populations, in a variety of treatment settings. Clearly, as is true of every aspect of psychotherapy research, further work is needed to ascertain under what special conditions improvement occurs. However, our clinical experience and that of many of our colleagues persuade us of the therapeutic *and* humanistic value of these worker characteristics, although certainly they are explicitly expressed in varying degrees, depending on the needs of the client, the treatment situation, and the personality of the worker. Furthermore, as indicated in this chapter, we do not believe that these worker characteristics are *sufficient* conditions for successful treatment; competence of the worker and client motivation and perception of worker qualities and attitudes are among many other factors that must be considered.

For further discussion of therapist relationship attitudes, see Beutler et al., "Therapist Variables in Psychotherapy Process and Outcome," especially pp. 276–282.

19. Frank, "The Role of Hope in Psychotherapy."

20. For a still useful illustration see Leopold Bellak, "Psychiatric Aspects of Tuberculosis," *Social Casework,* 31 (May 1950), 183–189. See also Elson, *Self Psychology in Social Work,* especially p. 72.

21. Carl Rogers, "Client-Centered Therapy," in C. H. Patterson, ed., *Theories of Counseling and Psychotherapy* (New York: Harper & Row, 1966), p. 409. Rogers coined the familiar term "unconditional positive regard," a concept generally accepted by therapists as a necessary attitude toward clients.

22. John Spiegel puts this in the language of role theory in "The Social Roles of Doctor and Patient in Psychoanalysis and Psychotherapy," *Psychiatry,* 17 (November 1954), 369–376.

23. For discussion of this see Lucille N. Austin, "Trends in Differential Treatment in Social Casework," *Journal of Social Casework,* 29 (June 1948), 203–211; Gertrude and Rubin Blanck, *Ego Psychology II* (New York: Columbia University Press, 1979); and Otilda Krug, "The Dynamic Use of the Ego Functions in Casework Practice," *Social Casework,* 36 (December 1955), 443–450.

24. See Elson, *Self Psychology in Clinical Social Work,*

for further discussion of this treatment issue. See also Chapter 3, note 4, for additional references.

25. Garrett, "Worker-Client Relationship," pp. 56–58.

26. For discussion and illustrations, see Gerald Appel, "Some Aspects of Transference and Counter-Transference in Marital Counseling," *Social Casework,* 47 (May 1966), 307–312; Rubin Blanck, "The Case for Individual Treatment," *Social Casework,* 47 (February 1965), 70–74; and Andrew Watson, "Reality Testing and Transference in Psychotherapy," *Smith College Studies in Social Work,* 36 (June 1966), 191–209.

27. Additional special aspects of the casework relationship are discussed in the following: Marcia Abramson, "The Autonomy-Paternalism Dilemma in Social Work Practice," *Social Casework,* 66 (September 1985), 387–393; Pauline Cohen and Merton Krause, *Casework with Wives of Alcoholics* (New York: Family Service Association of America, 1971), p. 48; Martha W. Elliott, "Hospitality as a Professional Virtue," *Social Casework,* 65 (February 1984), 109–112; Marilyn Lammert, "Experience as Knowing: Utilizing Therapist Self-Awareness," *Social Casework,* 67 (June 1986), 369–376; Pauline Lide, "Dynamic Mental Representation: An Analysis of the Empathic Process," *Social Casework,* 47 (March 1966), 146–151; Pauline Lide, "An Experimental Study of Empathic Functioning," *Social Service Review,* 41 (March 1967), 23–30; Joseph Palumbo, "Spontaneous Self Disclosures in Psychotherapy," *Clinical Social Work Journal,* 15 (Summer 1987), 107–120; and Allyn Zanger, "A Study of Factors Related to Clinical Empathy," *Smith College Studies in Social Work,* 38 (February 1968), 116–131. See also Chapter 2, note 2, for more references on empathy.

For further readings relevant to the therapeutic relationship, the reader is referred to the following: Felix Biestek, *The Casework Relationship* (Chicago: Loyola University Press, 1957); Compton and Galaway, *Social Work Processes,* chapter 6; Alfred Kadushin, *The Social Work Interview,* 2d ed. (New York: Columbia University Press, 1983); Alice Overton, "Establishing the Relationship," *Crime and Delinquency,* 11 (July 1965), 229–238; Helen Harris Perlman, *Relationship: The Heart of Helping People* (Chicago: University of Chicago Press, 1979); and Enola Proctor, "Defining the Worker-Client Relationship," *Social Work,* 27 (September 1982), 430–435.

CHAPTER 11

Initial Interviews and the Psychosocial Study

Thus far we have considered the frame of reference upon which psychosocial casework treatment rests. We have discussed various means and procedures by which the worker endeavors to enable clients to bring improvement to their lives. We must now turn to the more specific question of how treatment is related to a particular individual, couple, or family confronted by the need to cope with practical, emotional, or interpersonal problems.

Of course, treatment begins from the moment of the first contact, even when client and worker initially speak over the telephone or when the agency receptionist greets an individual or family. The subjects of this and the next three chapters—social study, diagnosis, selection of treatment objectives, and choice of treatment procedures—are inevitably intertwined. They are also always going on at the same time. Nevertheless, we artificially try to separate them in order to analyze each of these aspects of the therapeutic process.

Strong emphasis is placed in psychosocial casework on the importance of trying to understand clearly what an individual's or family's dilemmas are, and what contributes to them,

as the basis upon which treatment can be tailored to the particular clients. This understanding rests first upon an accurate and adequate factual base that is obtained primarily, though not by any means entirely, in early interviews. It is called the *psychosocial study*.

It is extremely important to be clear about the difference between psychosocial study, a process of gathering facts, and diagnostic understanding. Psychosocial study involves observation and orderly arrangement of the *facts* about a client and his or her situation. Diagnostic understanding, on the other hand, represents *the thinking* of the worker *about* the facts: the inferences drawn from them. It will be strongly influenced by the frame of reference used for guidance in understanding the meaning of the facts. Mary Richmond quoted Dr. Richard Cabot: "In social study you open your eyes and look, in diagnosis you close them and think."[1] If these diverse processes are not kept separate in the worker's mind, there is great danger of skewing the facts to fit the theory, asking questions in such a way that answers fitting a priori assumptions are likely to emerge.

Both client and worker contribute to defining the course treatment will take. It depends first on the nature of the difficulties, what the clients see as the problem, and the kind of help that is being sought. In many instances, as the contact moves on, clients develop a different understanding of their troubles and become ready for a kind of help for which they did not at first have any motivation. Often clients' definitions of their concerns and salient issues evolve over time, simply by talking things out to someone or because the worker has enabled them to reflect on matters differently. The worker's contribution to the course treatment takes depends upon knowledge of the nature of the individuals seeking treatment, of the current situation, of interactions within the person-situation system, and of the variety of factors that are contributing or have contributed to the clients' predicaments. This seeking of understanding is actually a continuous process, although it is emphasized especially in early interviews. It goes hand in hand with the treatment process itself, and as treatment continues, new understandings emerge. At the very beginning, the understanding provides a basis upon which choices are made by client and worker about the duration and nature of treatment.

The ways in which clients handle their part in such choices, in turn, become an important part of the social study. Indeed, the first interview, in which social study begins and important decisions about treatment are made, is of central importance.

THE INITIAL INTERVIEW

Even before meeting a client or family, there is often some information, however minimal, available to help the worker prepare for the initial interview. This anticipatory preparation can be of two kinds, as discussed by Germain and Gitterman.[2] *Cognitive preparation* is based on thoughts the worker has about the clients and their situations. If, for example, it is known that the home of a family one expects to see for the first time has burned down, or a family had to move in with relatives because there was no heat or hot water, the worker might immediately consider possible resources for temporary housing. Or, if one is about to see a family in which the only child, described by the parents as "perfect" until now, has suddenly begun to underachieve and behave disruptively in school, one may consider the possibility that there has been some change in the status of the parents' marriage or relationships with the extended family. One may also wonder whether something happened in the school situation to precipitate the child's uncharacteristic actions. Similarly, if a couple recently emigrated from Pakistan has applied for help, the worker unfamiliar with cultural patterns and traditions of that country is likely to seek information about these in order to try to better understand the people who are coming for an interview.

Affective or *empathic preparation* involves the effort to put oneself in the other's shoes. What would it feel like suddenly to lose one's home or try to live in below-freezing temperatures without heat? How might a heretofore "model" child feel upon losing the status of being an excellent and well-behaved student? How pressured must that child have felt to give up such a positive position at home and at school? What might it be like to be new to this country and among the very few Pakistani people living in the particular area?

It goes without saying that *anticipatory hunches and empathic feelings of the worker are tentative and are immediately modified on the basis of information and attitudes presented by the clients when they are actually seen.*

Very frequently, it can be anticipated that clients will feel considerable anxiety when they come to a first meeting. Treatment issues relevant to clients' initial discomfort are discussed in Chapter 14.

Initial Decisions

In a first interview, two of the many questions to be answered are: (1) Is this the right place for the client to be helped? and (2) For how long shall we decide to work together? We usually begin with the first of these: "Can I help you?" or "Can you tell me what prompted your call to the agency?" or "Can you tell me what your concerns are?" Later in the first interview, perhaps: "Are there other troubles?" "Are there other things you are worrying about?" Or even, "I get the impression there are other things that may be worrying you. Is that right?" At some later point, one often asks: "How do you think we can help you?" or "Did you have something special in mind that you hoped we could do?" Whether the first meeting is with an individual, a couple, or a family group, in some form these questions must be asked. Specific issues related to interviewing families and couples are discussed in the chapters describing these modalities.

Sometimes the problem is not one with which the worker or the agency can help, and this has to be explained. Usually there is some other resource about which one can tell the client. When this is so, it has been demonstrated that "referral" is far more effective than simple "steering."[3] In referral, the worker does not stop with giving information about another resource but, if the client consents, contacts the other agency, sometimes arranging an appointment, but in any case preparing the way for an easy reception. One must be certain here that the clients *want* this assistance and that efforts to expedite matters are not seen as either rejection by the worker or railroading into an undesired contact. Sometimes there are questions to be answered about the other resource, and sometimes feelings need to be worked through about whether or not to pursue help at another place.

It is important to emphasize here that it often takes a lot of preparation and mobilization of courage for clients to decide to ask for help with problems, particularly when they relate to private or painful personal or family matters. Thus, extreme sensitivity is required of the

worker when explaining to clients that, after all that, they have come to the wrong agency and that if they still want assistance they must start over again.

Frequently caseworkers offer services to hospital patients and their families, students and their parents, and so on. In these cases, obviously, more initiative has to be taken by the worker. One must first explain in nonthreatening terms the reasons for the reachout. One might say to certain potential clients: "Sometimes family members have concerns about the patient's condition and progress or want to talk over plans for future care." Or, a school social worker might say to parents of a young child: "The teacher has noticed that Jennifer recently seems a little preoccupied, and we wondered whether you have noticed any changes yourselves. We thought we could be most helpful to her if we better understood what might be worrying her."

Some initial interviews take place with involuntary clients—those conducted by workers in court or protective settings, for example—or with clients who have been referred to other agencies by such services. (See the Carter case in Chapter 21.) Often adolescents are brought or referred to treatment against their will.[4] In these cases, the worker's questions take a somewhat different tack. It is essential to help clients express their negative or mixed feelings about the interview at the beginning. Once that is done, a worker may go on with, "Even though you did not want to have this meeting, do you think there are any matters that we might be able to help you with?" Or, "Are there some things that might be useful to you to talk over?" Sometimes an offer of practical assistance helps clients to feel more comfortable. Trust may be enhanced by assurances about the confidentiality of information that is shared, when these assurances are realistically given. Certainly, it is essential for the worker to show warm interest as well as understanding of the feelings of reluctance.

Deciding on Length of Treatment

If it appears that the client has "come to the right place" and is going to return, sometime during that first interview, usually toward the end, a preliminary estimate is made of how long the work will take. (Brief services will be discussed further in Chapter 19.) Sometimes, in the initial interview, client and worker both believe that the client has received all the help needed or available. "Thank you, that's what I needed to know," from a client who was seeking homemaking services to help with the care of an elderly relative and was given information about resources. "I guess if that's the way it is, I'd better not try to find a job," from a mother who has learned that there are no local day care facilities for her year-old baby while she works. "I see, I hadn't thought of it that way; I think I can handle it better now," from a man seeking ideas on how to handle a discussion about drugs and alcohol with his teenage son. "You really helped me to see how the kids might be reacting this way as a result of the separation," from a woman who was having trouble managing her children after her abrupt decision to leave her husband.

In some cases, the worker may think that further meetings might be helpful even though the client believes the single interview is all that is needed. It may be appropriate then to indicate that, in the worker's experience, such matters are sometimes more complicated than they seem and it might be better to go a little more slowly: "Would it make sense to you to come back and talk a little further about this?" Or, "Do you think another meeting might help to make it all a little clearer than it is right now?" Or, "Do you want to try out what we discussed and come back another time to talk over how or whether it worked?"

Sometimes the agreement at this point is only for another interview so that client and worker can understand the dilemma better before deciding whether or not to continue. At other times a definite commitment can be made for a longer period. The worker usually suggests a time span. It may be, "I think we may need two or three more meetings to think this through," or "I would suggest that we plan on weekly meetings for two (or some other number of) months and then evaluate the situation." Or: "It takes time to work these things through. As you said, it has been a long time that all of this has been building up. Why don't we plan to meet for six sessions and then decide whether you want to go further?"

The suggestion of an initial time span can be especially helpful with many reluctant clients or with others who fear that they will be snagged into an interminable treatment process. With others, we might want to say: "It's hard to know yet how long we may want to meet. Let's decide that as we go along and know more about what is involved." There is some evidence that many men tend to prefer a commitment to planned short-term service and that women may be comfortable with open-ended service, although this may not be as true as it used to be.[5]

The decision, of course, is always a mutual one. The client may refuse or suggest a different time period. The worker may simply assent or else pursue the matter further if this seems appropriate. Clarifying time arrangements and arriving at agreement about these as well as about appointment times and, where appropriate, fees, are part of what is sometimes called the *contract*.

Locating the Problem

A second area in which mutual understanding is needed is that of ascertaining "the problem to be worked on." Sometimes this is quite simply and directly the problem the client brings. It may be concrete—housing, complications in receiving financial benefits, arrangements for day care for children, planning for discharge of a patient from the hospital, and so on. Or it may be both practical and psychological—job difficulties, a child's school problem, a marital problem. Experience leads us to think, however, that one can never be sure of whether there are additional ramifications to the presenting problem without asking the client whether there are other troubles or exploring factors that may be contributing to the difficulties that may also require consideration. For instance, it may develop that the housing problem is acute because neighbors object to unruly children and a host of other contributing problems. The housing problem is still real and perhaps the most urgent part of the problem to be dealt with, but this problem is likely to repeat itself if this remains the sole focus of attention. Or it may be that a very elderly person has to move from a fourth-floor walkup. The question then may arise: Is moving to another apartment the best solution? This may require much broader discussion than the housing question alone. Or a client may appear depressed. This needs to be commented on and, if the client is willing, talked about in terms of how long, what precipitated the feelings, how deep the feelings of depression are (e.g., "How does it affect you? How is your appetite? Are you sleeping a lot? What do you do with your time? Do you see friends, relatives? What medicines are you taking?") A barrage of questions is not appropriate, of course, but such areas as these should be covered as they appear relevant.

With a child's school problems, in addition to getting specific details of the difficulties and prior school history, one would certainly inquire about the child's behavior with other children and in the home. One would ask, too, how other children in the home are getting along and, when the timing is right, about relations between the parents or with others involved in the child's care. The latter can be explored by asking the parent present in the interview how the other parent (or adults involved in caretaking) responds to the child or the problem. Obviously, joint meetings with the parents and family meetings give the worker the opportunity to ask and observe directly. To the parents one might say: "I imagine you sometimes find you are in disagreement about how to manage Billy's problems with homework. Is that so?" The answers may help to uncover the inevitable differences, the conflict between parents, or the notion held by some parents that they have to bury disagreements rather than work to resolve them.

In other words, *in psychosocial casework we explore outwardly from the problem to areas that one theoretically expects will be related to it.* For the child with the school problem, in addition to those areas just mentioned, the exploration will probably include questions about health, intellectual ability, learning problems, previous school history, sibling relationships, and so on. Other leads may come from the content of the interview itself. Sometimes, it is learned that illness in the family, work problems, substance abuse, parental or intergenerational conflicts, cultural frictions, and so on, are involved.

When the actual problems seem broader than or different from the presenting one, this needs to be commented on in a way that will bring possible complications to the client's attention. One must ascertain whether the clients are willing for these to become part of the casework process along with the presenting problem. Sometimes one can be quite specific about this, but at other times a more general "These things all seem related, don't they?" or "You do seem troubled about a lot of things; do you think we might look at them and try to sort them out?" is sufficient. The important thing is that—*when the timing is right*—these possible additions to the client's original request for help be brought to his or her attention and that the worker find out whether or not the client is willing to participate in consideration of them.

In some casework approaches, this defining of the problem is a very specific process ending in a contract that specifies just what facets of the problems or behavior will be modified. In the psychosocial approach, initially, while the problem or some aspects of it may be well defined, attention is broader, focusing on other potentially relevant parts of the gestalt, and the process is usually kept more open for greater understanding as the facts are revealed to both client and worker. Nevertheless, clients should become aware of what the focus or areas of work may be, insofar as these can be foreseen, and should either explicitly or tacitly agree to address these.

Sometimes, the problem of coming to a common understanding of the dimensions of a difficulty is so complicated that several interviews are needed to help clients arrive at decisions as to whether they want to continue and whether along broad or narrow lines. When the worker thinks it will be impossible to give help if discussion is limited to the restricted area of the presenting problem, this must be explained when the time is ripe. This might be the case, for example, if it appeared that a child's behavior problem was so directly related to serious strife between parents that it would be impossible to help the child without also working on the parents' conflict.

Precipitating Factors

Ascertaining the event or events that finally brought about the request for assistance and those that seem to have precipitated the emergence of the problem is important. To the extent possible, these should be inquired about in the first interview, although it may take many more meetings to uncover all such significant information. Facts about issues that may have triggered problems are often key to the diagnostic understanding of the dynamics of the dilemma. Frequently, the client will talk about these spontaneously. At other times one can ask: "What happened that you decided to come in just now?" Or, "Can you put your finger on just when you first became aware of this?" Or, "Did anything special happen at that time?"

Sometimes clients have no awareness of the precipitating events, but by asking questions the worker can pinpoint and bring to their attention possible contributing factors to the problem at hand. Information about events that occurred either at the same time or in close proximity to the presenting difficulty may be obtained by the worker asking questions such as: "Did you say that your mother died shortly before your daughter began to refuse to go to school?" "Did you find yourself feeling depressed about the same time you moved to the new apartment?" "Am I right that your headaches began soon after your husband changed jobs?" A genogram, a tool that will be mentioned in the chapters on couple treatment, sometimes reveals to worker and clients alike data about family incidents that may have influenced the present situation.

Differences between Worker and Client

When seeing clients for the first time, the worker gives consideration to dissimilarities between interviewer and interviewee in ethnic or class background, age, gender, lifestyle, and so on.[6] This issue was discussed in Chapter 10. Sometimes it is necessary to address the differences almost immediately: "Are you finding any problems feeling comfortable speaking with a white (black, older, younger, male, female, etc.) social worker?" Sometimes just this kind of recognition puts people at ease. Occasionally, worker and client together may decide to try to locate another worker who is more similar to the client and with whom he or she will feel more at ease. When clients are particularly distraught they may not be at all concerned about these matters, as long as they sense that the worker is interested and knowledgeable about the problems of concern. In some cases, because of differences in background and life experience, it may be necessary to give detailed explanations of agency functions and casework services, although other clients are more familiar with this information.

In any event, in the social study workers need to be alert to attitudes of personal reticence, distrust because of differences, marked dissimilarities in experience and values between client and worker, or difficulties in casting the worker in a therapeutic role. For these are all obstacles to treatment of any type, even the briefest type. It is, then, the worker's responsibility to make every effort to bridge the gap by becoming as familiar as possible with some of the generalizations about people at various stages of life or about a client's cultural traditions and patterns, class identifications, and so on. However, and even more important from our point of view, the worker must approach clients of different backgrounds—and all clients—with a great deal of humility. *Our most important information about clients comes from clients themselves.* They are the experts on what differences mean to them. They are also the most reliable resource of information on what aspects of ever-changing cultural influences bear on the problems they bring or the way they approach the worker and the treatment process.

There are many variations among people of similar origins or ages. It is therefore essential for the worker to seek specific data from clients themselves: "Is your distress over the abortion compounded by religious feelings?" "I am not very familiar with some of the traditions of the country in which you were raised. Can you tell me whether this matter has some special meaning to you?" "Are there experiences you have had in your particular upbringing that you think pertain to this situation or that you think I need to understand?" When asked courteously, these questions convey respect, interest, and the worker's willingness to learn; they contribute to a climate of mutuality. Furthermore, such inquiries sometimes can help clients feel better about themselves, because recognition is being given to what *they know* rather than to ways in which they may feel at fault or inadequate.

Who Is to Be Seen?

There is also the question of whether to proceed with an applicant alone or to suggest seeing others in the family. Sometimes this decision is made on the telephone, with the worker's saying something like: "Would it be possible for you and your husband to come in together since you are both so involved in this matter?" "Why don't you bring the entire family in so we can get everyone's point of view about what the problems are and what can be done about them?" It happens often that one family member has made the application for help and yet it appears to the worker in the first interview that it would be advisable to include others. In recent years there has been greater willingness, among clients and workers, to have conjoint meetings. Sometimes in the first interview with an individual client, help can be offered about how to tell other family members about the treatment and how to invite them to join in without putting them on the defensive. For example, when a client tells other family members that their help is needed it is far less threatening than announcing to them that "the social worker wants you to come because she thinks your behavior is causing the problem"!

Some therapists refuse to treat clients with family problems unless conjoint interviews can be arranged. Others (with whom the writers agree) would certainly favor interviewing all persons involved (usually together) but would not insist on it if the client were strongly opposed or if the others were unwilling to be involved. We do not push past defenses. Ordinarily, we explore the client's reluctance to having joint or family meetings. Sometimes clients have good reasons for their "resistance" and it is important to take these into consideration. On the other hand, if indicated, one might say something like: "Do you think we could get a better idea of John's real feelings about this if we asked him to join us?" Or, "Since John knows that you are disturbed about your marriage, is it possible that he will be even more upset wondering what you are saying here about him than he would be if he came to meetings? This could allow him the opportunity to know exactly what is on your mind and for him to discuss the situation from his point of view." If there is still reluctance, the worker may agree with or at least accede to the client's wishes; at other times, when circumstances seem to call for it, he or she presses further. Along these lines, in our opinion, it is important to let clients know that when one person makes changes in therapy, these changes can affect the quality of a relationship with someone who is closely involved but not participating; therefore, it may be wiser and fairer to include that person in the treatment or at least offer him or her the option of being involved.

If conjoint interviews are handled as a routine expectation rather than as a major issue, the individual applicant usually accepts these as a natural procedure, unless there are special reasons for the interview to be regarded with concern. If there are such reasons—such as lack of trust, fear of the consequences, a felt need for "something of my own"—it is important to understand them, for they often contribute important information to the social study and diagnostic understanding.

In some cases, of course, it is best to plan individual interviews; in others, joint treatment of two or more people may be agreed upon; in still others, the whole family may become involved. Chapter 16 suggests some indications and contraindications for family therapy. Over the course of treatment, one can move back and forth from one mode to another as each seems to be called for. In the first interview, however, one merely decides upon the immediate future. Yet it can be helpful to prepare clients for possibly including family members in the future. Whether or not ongoing conjoint interviews are decided upon, the social study of many problems

often can be greatly facilitated by multiple-person or family interviews; one has the opportunity to observe in vivo the interactions among family members as well as to learn directly from as many people as possible their views of the situation.

Observation and Deduction

While all this is going on, the worker is closely observing the ways in which the client handles this first interview and the way in which he or she relates to the worker. Is the client direct and open, relating naturally to the worker and explaining the situation in a fairly clear way? Or does the person appear anxious and fearful? confused? withdrawn? hostile? overly friendly? Are some ego defenses immediately apparent? What strengths emerge? Is affect appropriate to the material the client is discussing? Does he or she seem depressed? Is there reason to suspect any form of neurological illness? Such things are learned from observation and deduction within the interview as the client explains the problem and talks about the present situation, related past events, and his or her own efforts to deal with the relationships and the situation. It is particularly useful to ask clients what they have already tried to alleviate the troubles: what has worked, what has failed. Answers to such questions not only provide important information but also can tell us a great deal about the client's ego capacities, ability to "cope," and ways of doing so. Furthermore, such inquiries often serve to elicit the active participation of clients, helping them to recognize the importance of their input to solving the difficulties.

Gains in the First Interview

Progress can usually be made in the first interview, not only in defining the problem but also in securing information that will lead to understanding of the interlocking factors that may be contributing to it. This not only helps the worker but also turns the client's mind toward issues that he or she may later want to think about more fully. The process of mutuality, as described in Chapter 10, is also introduced by the worker in this first meeting, through words and action.

The worker's way of greeting the client and opening the interview conveys respect, interest, and desire to help. If the interview is unhurried, with time and privacy protected so that it will not be interrupted, the client benefits by feeling the full and undivided attention of the worker. Surroundings, insofar as possible, should be attractive and professional in style for this conveys respect for the client. Ideally, he or she will leave the first interview feeling some relief from pressure, some hope that here is someone who is competent to help, and, at best, some readiness to take the first steps toward understanding and alleviating the problem.

Where the problem concerns emotions, the client typically experiences relief in the first interview simply by talking about the situation and the feelings that go with it to a worker who is constantly attentive, appreciates the person's feelings, is accepting, and offers help. On the other hand, sometimes when the client is part of the problem, it is difficult for him or her to come to even a beginning realization of this fact. With care and tact, such difficulties can often be suggested by the worker and talked about together: "Do you think the time and concern involved in taking such good care of your ill mother may make your daughter (husband, wife) feel you have lost some interest in her (him)?" "Do you sometimes try to be a good sport and go along with what others want but then find you resent this and suddenly explode over some small matter?" Treatment thus begins immediately.

THE EXPLORATORY PERIOD AND THE FACT-GATHERING PROCESS

After the first interview, social study, diagnostic understanding, and treatment continue to go hand in hand. Each interview adds its increment as new aspects of the person and the person-situation gestalt emerge. The worker is dealing with a living, changing process. Feelings change, new events constantly occur, people reveal themselves more fully as trust grows. One needs to be sensitive to clients' feelings and responses and to the significance of new information throughout the contact, even though the main outlines of a psychosocial study are arrived at early on. The length of time this takes and the amount of information secured are proportionate to the time span agreed on for treatment. All of these are directly related to the complexity of the problem and the extent to which client and worker try to deal with these complexities. Obviously, if it is decided that a very brief contact is appropriate, one sticks close to the "problem to be solved" in seeking information. In more extended treatment, the original social study, leading to a fairly clear understanding of the client's needs and the main treatment themes, is usually completed within the first four to six interviews. During this early exploratory period, clients themselves also gain further understanding of the trouble, benefit from the ventilation that occurs, and experience support from the worker. Often considerable progress can be made in working on and resolving practical problems. Intrareflection is usually also encouraged, but with some cautiousness and tentativeness until the dimensions of the problem are clarified. Clients' responses to all forms of reflective communications are among the most important sources of information and of diagnostic understanding. The better clients are able to think clearly about themselves and their situations, and the more flexibility they demonstrate, the more likely it is that they will be able to make necessary changes.[7]

As we have indicated, during the study process the worker will indeed be reaching for diagnostic understanding. Preliminary formulations help in knowing what areas need further exploration. Nevertheless, it is essential to guard against "contamination" of one by the other, making a clear distinction between facts and opinions.

How does the worker know what lines of inquiry to follow in a psychosocial study, and how does one go about it? People come to a caseworker with a specific problem. "My child is irritable, mopes, and pays no attention to what I say." Or, "Since my husband died a year ago everything has gone wrong. Now the rent is going up. I don't want to be a burden to any of my children." Or, "We just can't understand each other anymore: every time I open my mouth she takes the other side." Always there is a person-person or a person-situation gestalt involved. Or, to put it another way, certain systems are involved: the parent-child system, the husband-wife system, the family system, the health, school, or work system. A set of interacting forces is at work, and what goes on in one system inevitably affects what happens in another. The worker listens to the client receptively but not passively. Knowledge of factors that often contribute to different kinds of dilemmas immediately suggests the various systems that may be pertinent. In a marital problem, for instance, the worker is concerned first with the interactions between the partners. Then the worker needs understanding of the major features of the two personalities. Children may also be part of the picture. Since marital problems are so often complicated by interactions and histories with relatives, the worker is alert to references to members of the extended family, either in the present or earlier in life, and uses these to inquire about major relationships. Factors in the husband's or wife's employment system are often of significance. Friendships may be important. Crowded housing or other crises in living can seriously contribute to marital tension. Worries about health can upset a relationship.

A parent-child problem would involve some of these same systems plus additional ones, especially at school. In the case of an older person facing a decision about living arrangements or discharge from a medical facility, not only are immediate family relationships important but also the families of the children (especially if living with them is at issue), friends and neighbors, the client's health, and resources for alternative living arrangements. In fact, in parent-child situations, or dilemmas about aging people, or situations involving catastrophic illnesses or severe physical or mental disabilities, the term "client" may actually refer to relatives who must make decisions for others as well as to the individual with the obvious problem. In any event, each type of difficulty that emerges in early interviews suggests avenues that may need to be explored.

The fact-gathering process receives its impetus and direction from two sources: the client's desire to tell about the difficulties and the worker's desire to understand what they are, how they came about, and what motivation, capacities, and opportunities exist for dealing with them. Psychosocial casework uses a fluid form of interviewing that combines these two sets of interests. By encouraging the client to follow trends of thought related to the problem as they come naturally to his or her mind and leading the client to develop them further, the worker gains access to the elaboration of significant matters with relative ease. At the same time, the worker often must fill the inevitable gaps in this type of exploration by directing the interview along lines that the client does not spontaneously introduce. The worker can do so easily when such matters are "adjacent" to subjects the client is discussing or flow logically from them, or they can be explored when the client has temporarily exhausted spontaneous productions and is ready to follow the therapist's lead. "You have never told me much about your father." "Set me straight on your schooling; where were you when you finished?" "You haven't said much about your work; what do you do and how do you like it?" The caseworker needs to take a fairly active part in the gathering of information, for, as we have said, it is not possible in casework to depend on free association to lead to significant material. Clients cannot be expected to know completely what information is needed, nor can they always free themselves, without help, from reluctance to discuss painful material that may be highly relevant to an understanding of their troubles. Sometimes, out of curiosity or overconscientiousness, a worker may inquire into areas of a client's life that are truly irrelevant to the difficulties at hand or so remote that the client may be offended or confused by the worker's probing. Before asking, then, one must question one's own motives for making the inquiries. Obviously, especially in regard to highly intimate or painful matters, it is important that the reasons for asking about anything be made clear so the client can understand the pertinence.

In areas in which a problem appears, it is necessary to inquire not only about the details of the problem but also about the client's participation in the difficulty. It is not enough for the client to say, "My wife is a spendthrift"; the worker needs to follow up with specific questions: "In what way?" "Can you help me to understand by giving me a recent example?" By getting detailed accounts of what happens in the client's household when there is conflict over money, one can begin to evaluate to what extent—if at all—overspending actually seems to be occurring, what sorts of situations either within the wife's personality or in the interaction between husband and wife touch it off, what purpose it may serve in the marital relationship, what part the husband's response to the overspending may play in its repetition, and so on. The event or circumstances that precipitated the client's decision to come for help are usually of considerable significance, although it may be a minor event in itself. Obviously, it is ideal to see husband and wife together to obtain the most accurate information about these issues.

The best way to secure a clear picture of interaction is not simply to ask direct questions but rather to encourage the client—or, if it is a joint or family interview, the clients—to describe things in detail. This tends to bring a good deal of ventilation and enables clients to relive the situation with details of what actually happened. This style of interviewing does not interrupt the natural flow of the clients' thoughts, yet allows the worker to observe the nature of the interplay and the degree of feeling about it.

If initial evidence indicates that there is little or no basis for the husband's accusations about his wife's spending, for instance, the worker looks for circumstances under which the client believes it to be true, what factor within the client or in the marital interaction might have touched it off, and what purpose his unrealistic reaction serves. Again, an important aspect of these explorations is their revelation of how the client tries to cope with whatever difficulty he is experiencing, knowledge that is especially useful in throwing light on ego functioning, dysfunctional interactional patterns, etc.

Throughout the initial phase, in individual or conjoint meetings, the worker continues to observe clients' reactions in response to the treatment situation carefully. What is being asked of the worker? Is there sensitivity to blame or criticism? Is there fear that the worker will take the "side" of one family member over another? How accurately are they perceiving the worker and the worker's reactions? To what extent is there warmth, hostility, or remoteness toward the worker? These observations throw light on the nature of the clients' demands and expectations of others, on ego and superego functioning, on their relationship styles, and other aspects of their life situations.

Physical and Emotional Illness

An important area of the social study that should not be neglected is the client's physical health. In fact, caseworkers often refer to a "biopsychosocial" study. In most cases, questions about health and recent medical examinations are routinely asked. The psychosocial worker is alert not only to what the client says but also to other signs that might point to the possibility of illness. Appearance, of course, tells a good deal. Other indications of ill health that the client may not fully appreciate appear in references to poor appetite, tiredness, or sleep problems as well as to mild symptomatology such as pain, swelling, rashes, indigestion, and dizziness. It is known that certain physical conditions have characteristic effects on personality functioning, and alertness to them will often help account for the client's reactions. Aside from these constant effects, any illness is likely to play a significant part in interpersonal difficulties. It frequently causes pain or anxiety.[8] It often increases self-centeredness and provokes regression to greater dependence. It can be used as an escape from unpleasant responsibilities or interactions. It can change the self-image and distort relationships in family life. The worker is also alert to the effect of bodily changes associated with different periods of life: the uneven growth rate and the genital and secondary sexual growth changes of adolescence, reactions to the climacteric and to physical changes of old age. Experiences around menstruation and pregnancy are often relevant. Unusual physical features or disabilities also have direct bearing on social and inner functioning.

When personal adjustment problems are involved, it is also well to inquire about the use of drugs that have psychological effects. Legal drugs of this type are often prescribed by physicians, and supplies can sometimes be secured for self-dosage. Even when addiction is not a problem, such medications often contribute to troublesome moods or side effects. "Are you under a doctor's care? What has been prescribed?" Or, "Has your doctor given you anything to calm your nerves or to help you sleep or to pep you up?" To the person who is not seeing a doctor: "Do you sometimes need to take something to keep your nerves quiet?" Routine questions about illegal drug use or alcohol habits are usually necessary. Having witnessed the tragic effects on emotional, physical, and family life deriving from substance abuse in clients from all walks of life, caseworkers are now more alert than ever to this possibility. Familiarity with physical changes and behavioral indicators associated with substance addiction is essential. The timing and way in which these inquiries are made are, of course, of crucial importance.[9]

The worker needs also to be alert for indications of mental or emotional illness or symptomatology. Clients often refer to these tangentially or even describe them without realizing their significance. References to periods of "nervousness," "tiredness," "depression," or extreme boredom warrant inquiry. One may pick up clues that there is delusional thinking or that there have been hallucinations. References to periods of hospitalization or long absences from work may mean mental illness or alcoholism as well as physical illness. If the client mentions loss of memory or periods of "blanking out," further questions about these should be asked. Data that might point toward depersonalization should be followed up. Flight of ideas and substitution of associative thinking for logical thought should be noted if they occur. Affect can be observed. Compulsions usually reveal themselves or are mentioned by the client.

Early History

So far we have been mainly considering data from the present or recent past. To what extent does the psychosocial worker go into earlier history? Certainly, one wants to learn the client's thoughts about when the present difficulty began. This may be in the recent past, some years earlier, or, in some instances, in early life. Sometimes, however, the client does not see childhood and adolescence as pertinent to the problem unless the worker somehow makes the connection. Exploration of early life, of course, is made only when the worker has specific reason to believe that this will throw light on the problem. Such exploration tends to be thematic rather than wide-ranging, pursuing certain relationships of certain time periods that seem to have relevance. As we said, sometimes the genogram can provide a useful means for getting perspective on the client's personal and family history.

Unexplained gaps in a history are sometimes due to a period of trouble: mental or emotional illness, difficulty with the law, substance abuse, or periods of mental conflict and pain. One needs to be alert to the sequence of events, especially important happenings that preceded or coincided with periods of symptomatology or poor functioning. For instance, a child's regression may have followed the severe illness or death of a parent or grandparent, especially if the child was kept in the dark about it and never helped to work through the grief. Changes in employment may bring a change in family patterns and perceptions and contribute to marked changes in family behavior and relationships. The same careful regard for details must attend the exploration of the client's past that accompanies the exploration of current events. It is not enough for the client to say, "My mother always preferred my older brother." The worker seeks out details, asking, "In what way?" "What makes you think so?" "Could you tell me more about that?"

Additional Sources of Information

As we have said, and as the chapters on family and couple treatment will further explain, it is now widely accepted that in cases of children's problems or marital difficulty conjoint interviews have significant advantages. Even individual meetings with family members of clients do not usually have the same value for social study as marital or family sessions. Conjoint ses-

sions are often more effective than individual meetings because a picture is worth a thousand words, not only to the worker who is trying to gather the facts but also to family members whose attention can be brought to interactional patterns *while they are in process*. Communication styles, relationship patterns, emotional responses, distortions and discrepancies in perceptions among family members become much more apparent in conjoint sessions.[10] Such interviews may include husband and wife, parent and child, or a whole family.

Another possible important source of information is the visit to the client's home.[11] Some clients for various reasons—health, transportation, unavailability of baby-sitters, etc.—actually cannot come to an agency office. There are people who are sensitive about home visits, however, fearing that the worker wants to "snoop" for information. Others may feel embarrassed about modest or inadequate homes. When there are such concerns, they must be taken seriously, of course. Sometimes the client can be reassured by an explanation of how a visit might add to the worker's understanding and ability to help. But such a plan should be pursued *only* if and when the client is clearly willing for the worker to come.

In some cases, the home visit makes possible important observations about family functioning, the family's pride in the home, many personality characteristics of its occupants, etc. Firsthand witnessing of parents' interactions with children in the natural setting of the home may provide especially significant data. At times, a worker can become more empathically attuned to housing or neighborhood conditions some families must endure. When certain types of situational problems are of importance, or there is a need to reach out to a family, home visits are often essential. One may grasp a natural opportunity that arises for an interview in the home as a means of widening the scope of the social study. It is not, however, necessary or even advisable in many cases.

In addition to interviews with the client and the immediate family, it is sometimes useful to consult, with the client's knowledge and consent—on a very selective basis—other people who may be in a position to add to the worker's understanding of the client. This issue was discussed in Chapter 8. When a child is involved it may be particularly useful to talk with the teacher. Often, a contact with a doctor yields valuable medical information. Occasionally a member of the clergy, employer, or friend can add to the understanding of a particular aspect of the client's problem. As we have said, it is always important in seeing collaterals to gauge the potential effect of the interview on the client and his or her relationship to the worker. Only under exceptional circumstances, principally of a protective nature, is it wise to seek information at the expense of arousing antitherapeutic reactions in the client. This is not to say that contacts with other people should never be made if the client is anxious about them. Anxiety frequently occurs, at least to a mild degree, but discussions with the client before and after meeting with the collateral provide opportunities to relieve uneasy feelings. As was suggested earlier, under some circumstances, one can lessen anxiety by suggesting that the client participate in contacts with collaterals if he or she wishes to do so. This can also encourage the client's active involvement in the entire treatment process.

Obviously, reports of medical or psychiatric diagnosis or treatment, of psychological tests, and of previous treatment may be pertinent to the social study. These and other types of written material should be secured selectively during the social study period as well as later in the contact.

Thus, the study starts with what the client sees as the problem and its antecedents, as well as what he or she has tried to do about it and has thought about how it can be resolved. If appropriate, the study can then move on to look for present and sometimes past factors that may be contributing to the current dilemma.

Throughout the exploration, one must be attuned to the anxieties of the client. One does not push through defenses. If a client is reluctant to talk about something that seems important, one may comment on this reluctance. Perhaps the client can tell you why. Perhaps he or she cannot or continues to resist. One can say, "Maybe later on it will be easier for you to talk about this. I think it may help you when you can bring yourself to it." Or, "When you are ready, it will probably help us better to understand what is happening." If the worker thinks the reluctance to talk may be due to distrust or to the worker's attitudes, this too can be explored. "I know it is hard to talk about such things. You don't know me very well yet. Perhaps later you will trust me to understand."

We see, then, that although psychosocial workers do not follow a set pattern for social study interviews, they do have in mind definite ideas concerning the type of information they want to obtain about clients and their situations. A great deal of ineffectual drifting and failure to formulate suitable treatment approaches results when the caseworker is too passive in seeking specific information, especially in early interviews.

As the caseworker learns about clients and their lives, he or she begins to form opinions about the nature of the difficulties. Often in trying to formulate diagnostic thinking, the worker recognizes gaps in a psychosocial study, areas of information about which further inquiry must be made in order to arrive at a clearer picture. It is important to guard against allowing speculation to substitute for facts. The best way to obtain an accurate picture is to enable clients to have sufficient confidence in the worker so that they can speak fully and frankly.[12]

NOTES

1. Mary Richmond, *Social Diagnosis* (New York: Russell Sage Foundation, 1917), p. 347.

2. Carel B. Germain and Alex Gitterman, *The Life*

Model of Social Work Practice (New York: Columbia University Press, 1980). See also Alfred Kadushin, *The Social Work Interview,* 2d ed. (New York: Columbia University Press, 1983), chapter 6.

3. In their broad study of family agency services, Dorothy Fahs Beck and Mary Ann Jones report, "Advance contact by the counselor with the resource to which a client is referred was found to increase significantly the proportion of clients who follow through on a referral." See *Progress on Family Problems* (New York: Family Service Association of America, 1973), pp. 6, 67. See also Leonard S. Kogan, "The Short-Term Case in a Family Agency," *Social Casework,* 38 (June 1957), 296–302.

4. For references relevant to working with involuntary clients, see Judith Cingolani, "Social Conflict Perspective on Work with Involuntary Clients," *Social Work,* 29 (September–October 1984), 442–446; Howard Goldstein, "A Cognitive-Humanistic Approach to the Hard-to-Reach Client," *Social Casework,* 67 (January 1986), 27–36; Judith Gourse and Martha W. Chescheir, "Authority Issues in Treating Resistant Families," *Social Casework,* 62 (February 1981), 67–73; Janet Moore-Kirkland, "Mobilizing Motivation: From Theory to Practice," in Anthony N. Maluccio, ed., *Promoting Competence in Clients: A New/Old Approach to Social Work Practice* (New York: Macmillan, 1981), 27–54; Allison D. Murdach, "Bargaining and Persuasion with Nonvoluntary Clients," *Social Work,* 25 (November 1980), 458–461; Genevieve Oxley, "Involuntary Clients' Response to a Treatment Experience," in Anthony N. Maluccio and Paula Sinanoglu, eds., *Parents of Children in Placement* (New York: Child Welfare League of America, 1981), 401–413; Ronald H. Rooney, "Socialization Strategies for Involuntary Clients," *Social Casework,* 69 (March 1988), 131–140; Shirley B. Schlosberg and Richard M. Kagan, "Practice Strategies for Engaging Chronic Multiproblem Families," *Social Casework,* 69 (January 1988), 3–9; and Jack Weitzman, "Engaging the Severely Dysfunctional Family in Treatment: Basic Considerations," *Family Process,* 24 (December 1985), 473–485. See also Chapter 5, note 6.

5. See notes to Chapter 19 for references on brief and crisis treatments.

6. See Chapter 10, notes 4 and 5.

7. For a valuable approach to initial interviews from the point of view of communication, see Judith C. Nelsen's chapter on the subject in her book, *Communication Theory and Social Work* (Chicago: University of Chicago Press), pp. 43–65. See also Wayne D. Duehn and Nazneed Mayadas, "Starting Where the Client Is: An Empirical Investigation," *Social Casework,* 60 (February 1979), 67–74, for an interesting study and discussion of the importance of empathically "hearing" the client's concerns and priorities in intake interviews; and Elsa Marziali, "The First Session: An Interpersonal Encounter," *Social Casework,* 69 (January 1988), 23–27. We also recommend Howard Goldstein's "Starting Where the Client Is," *Social Casework,* 64 (May 1983), 267–275, for a very helpful discussion of the need to try to grasp the reality—the perceptions and individuality—of clients, rather than making assumptions based on our own expectations.

8. For an interesting discussion of this, see Mark Zborowski, "Cultural Components in Response to Pain," *Journal of Social Issues,* 8 (1952), 16–30. For other readings relevant to this subject, see Norman Decker, "Anxiety in the General Hospital," in William E. Fann et al., eds., *Phenomenology and Treatment of Anxiety* (New York: Spectrum, 1979), pp. 287–298; Ursula Granite, "Foundations for Social Work on Open-Heart Surgery Service," *Social Casework,* 59 (February 1978), 101–105; and Alice Ullman, "Teaching Medical Students to Understand Stress in Illness," *Social Casework,* 57 (November 1976), 568–574.

9. See Julius Rubin, "Drug Addiction," chapter 22, in George Wiedeman, *Personality Development and Deviation* (New York: International Universities Press, 1975). For further references on substance abuse, see Chapter 21, note 4.

10. See notes to Chapters 15 and 16. An article examining family-oriented interviewing and treatment in social work suggests that caseworkers' lack of knowledge and training for family work has limited its use by them. On the basis of a survey designed to determine family, caseworker, and agency needs, specific training objectives are recommended to help caseworkers learn to understand family interaction and communication and become skilled at intervening. See Linda M. Anderson et al., "Training in Family Treatment: Needs and Objectives," *Social Case-*

work, 60 (June 1979), 323–329. Without adequate training, of course, the caseworker can be confounded by the vast amount of data derived from family interviews and thus be unable to use it meaningfully for social study purposes.

11. Although it has fallen into disrepute from time to time, over many years the home visit has been viewed as having value for reaching out to reluctant or home-bound clients and for social study, diagnosis, treatment, and research. For readings that discuss and illustrate its use for a wide variety of client populations and problems, see Marjorie Behrens and Nathan Ackerman, "The Home Visit as an Aid in Family Diagnosis and Therapy," *Social Casework*, 37 (January 1956), 11–19; Mary Larkin Bloom, "Usefulness of the Home Visit for Diagnosis and Treatment, *Social Casework*, 54 (February 1973), 67–73; Rachel A. Levine, "Treatment in the Home," *Social*

Work, 9 (January 1964), 19–28; Sharon K. Moynihan, "Home Visits for Family Treatment," *Social Casework*, 55 (December 1974), 612–617; Kadushin, *The Social Work Interview*, pp. 142–145; David Kantor and William Lehr, *Inside the Family* (San Francisco: Jossey-Bass, 1975); Jules Henry, *Pathways to Madness* (New York: Random House, 1971); and Frances H. Scherz, "Family Intaractions: Some Problems and Implications for Casework," in Howard J. Parad and Roger R. Miller, eds., *Ego-Oriented Casework: Problems and Perspectives* (New York: Family Service Association of America, 1963), especially pp. 139–141.

12. For historical background as well as their relevance to this chapter, the reader is referred to chapters 3, 4, and 5 in Richmond, *Social Diagnosis*, and chapters 6, 7, and 8 in Gordon Hamilton, *Theory and Practice of Social Casework*, 2d ed. (New York: Columbia University Press, 1951)

CHAPTER 12

Assessment and Diagnostic Understanding

Understanding is central to psychosocial treatment. Much understanding is intuitive. One immediately senses anxiety, anger, grief. Common knowledge of causative factors brings immediate explanations to mind. But one cannot rely upon intuition alone.[1] Common knowledge is notoriously undependable. These constitute only a first step in the process of understanding, providing *hypotheses* to be checked out against reality. Through the psychosocial study, the fact-gathering process, the worker seeks to come as close as possible to securing an accurate picture of the client's inner and outer situation. In assessment and diagnosis, the worker attempts to *understand*—to give meaning to—that picture in order to answer the question "How can this person be helped?"

The terms "diagnosis," "assessment," and "evaluation" are sometimes used interchangeably. For some social workers, the word "diagnosis" suggests adherence to a "medical model" of casework. The concern is that those who use the term are placing the responsibility for difficulty on the client rather than on the situation and are furthermore concentrating on the person's weaknesses—the "illness," the

"pathology"—rather than his or her strengths and abilities. This would be true if one sought diagnostic understanding of clients and their weaknesses alone. It is *not* true if one seeks also to understand situational components, to assess both strengths and weaknesses, and to understand the circular interactions that constantly recur between the various components of the system or gestalt of which the client is a part. Let it be said here that whatever terms are used, the point of view of this book is that both the client and the situation are usually involved in the problem, and that it is in their interactions and interrelationships that many explanations can be found, and that the recognition of strengths is of paramount importance to diagnostic assessment.

CLIENT–WORKER PARTICIPATION

Client and worker in psychosocial casework both participate in developing diagnostic understanding. Once the value of trying to understand the reasons for feelings and behavior is established—or, better still, experienced—clients themselves will often look for explanations and contributing factors. In individual or conjoint meetings, the worker also suggests lines of thought and often tests hypotheses by asking for clients' reactions to them. "From what you say, it seems as though Steve's bedwetting began shortly after Jane broke her leg. I expect you had to concentrate a lot on Jane for a while. Do you think there is a connection?" Or, "It sounds as if you were really furious at your mother for staying so long. Was it easier to take it out on Ann?" Or, "Have you asked Bill to put the kids to bed or do you just wait for him to offer?" Or, "Do you think it is easier in this family to express anger than other feelings?"

In each of these illustrations, the worker's thinking was ahead of the client's. This is not always the case. Many clients spontaneously seek explanations of behavior and express their own thinking, to which the worker in turn reacts. These explanations often show considerable insight. A woman who was considering leaving her recovering alcoholic husband said: "We are a bad match. I used to think everything would be all right after he quit drinking. But now I realize that his willingness to let me boss him around brings out the worst in me and makes it hard for me to respect him." At other times client explanations are rationalizations and intellectualizations (e.g., "He would be all right if he took his vitamins" or "I think he has an oedipal problem with his mother") to which the worker may listen in silence or, when the timing is right, indicate some doubt: "Perhaps, but I think there is more to it than that." Or, "Are you truly satisfied with that yourself?" Or, "Do you really think that John is the only one who needs to make changes?" Or, "You know, you've read a lot of psychology, and sometimes knowledge of that kind can get in the way of real understanding. Right now, it is your feelings that are important. Can you try to let them come and not bother so much about reasons and explanations?"

Even though the client is the best expert on what he thinks and feels and wants, ordinarily, and particularly at the beginning of treatment, the worker can be expected to understand some points more quickly and more fully than the client. This is so for several reasons:

1. In situations in which they are so closely involved, people are often blind to what they are doing and reveal by behavior many things of which they are not aware.

2. People tend to see other people's contributions to problems more clearly than their own, in part because they fear being blamed themselves.

3. Although every situation is unique and different in detail from all others, it is also true that, in general, human beings have a great deal in common, react in similar ways, develop in similar ways, and are exposed to similar life events. Working over and over again with clients caught in successive dilemmas, not identical but nevertheless similar, enables the clinical social worker to understand the new client's problem more quickly and more fully than would be possible without prior experience.

4. Knowledge has been accumulated by social work, psychiatry, and the social sciences that can illuminate human problems and that is part of the social worker's education. This consists of knowledge of the dynamics of human behavior and of human development, knowledge of family functioning and of the social and physical environment, and of the various ways in which interacting factors in both past and present can create problems of pressure, deprivation, or dysfunction.

The client's own assessment of the situation is nevertheless enormously important on many levels. This issue will be discussed in further detail in a later section of this chapter.

THE ASSESSMENT PROCESS AND DYNAMIC UNDERSTANDING

How, then, does the diagnostic assessment proceed? The total process consists of trying to understand (1) what the trouble is, (2) what factors seem to be contributing to the trouble, and (3) what can be changed and modified. *We evaluate motivation* and *capacities* within the *person* and *opportunities for change* in the social and physical *situation.*[2] Strengths as well as weaknesses in person, situation, and *interactions* are prime considerations.

Diagnostic assessment takes place in two different ways. First, as the worker listens in an interview to what clients are saying, he or she constantly tries to answer the three questions just posed, for what he or she does in the current interview will be determined by this understanding. Second, periodically during the total contact, the worker needs to look back over all that is known about the person-situation gestalt in order to answer these questions more fully in the light of this total knowledge. When treatment is expected to continue beyond a few interviews, the first of these more extensive assessments should occur after about four or six interviews, when the initial social study is usually completed. This generally provides sufficient information to arrive at a working basis for the major outlines of ongoing treatment, subject to modification by later diagnostic reassessment. The first diagnostic thinking is taken as a set of *working probabilities* to be constantly rechecked, extended, and modified, as additional information emerges during ongoing treatment and as the clients' feelings, attitudes, and circumstances change. *Treatment continually uncovers the diagnosis.*

In order to understand what the trouble is, the worker begins by a sort of scanning of the whole "field": all of the facts brought out in the psychosocial study. The diagnostic process moves from delineating *what* the realities of the client-situation gestalt are to *why* the problems exist. In *dynamic understanding,* we look at the data of the social study to see which of the observed features seem to be contributing to the client's difficulties.

Worker and client together seek to under-stand the dynamics of the client's dilemma in terms of both current interactions and the effect of prior events, recent or remote, on client functioning. Assessments of the individual and the situation here go hand in hand. We continually try to determine to what extent clients' problems lie within the situations, including family situations, that confront them and to what extent and in what way they are the product of unusual needs within the personality of the clients or of flawed ego or superego functioning. *One must understand the pressures people are under before one can have any opinion about the adequacy or inadequacy of individual or family functioning.*

We then try to establish interrelationships among the various factors that combine to create the client's discomfort or problems in social functioning. We are particularly interested in looking at the *ways in which these components interact.* In this process, a systems approach is again useful since the problem does not lie simply in a given weakness in the personality or in a specific lack or condition in the milieu but in the way that various weaknesses or idiosyncrasies in the total system interplay and affect each other. Since, as we have seen, every factor in a system affects every other factor in that system, the worker scans the field again, looking for interactions.

Suppose ten-year-old Steve is doing poorly in school despite normal intelligence, and we know that he and his teacher are in constant conflict. Is the teacher critical of Steve because he is disruptive, because he has been placed in a class for which he is not suited, or because his mother criticized her, or because Steve is black, has poor clothing, or is big for his age and looks as though he ought to behave in a more mature way than he does? Or is she critical because the principal is pressing her about the reading-grade average of her class or because she is embroiled in faculty disagreements about the wisdom of a strike and is irritable with all of her students even though Steve seems to be more affected by her moods than the other students? Only by talking with the teacher as well as with Steve can we get hints of what lies behind the strain existing between them. And only as we come to understand the interplay of pertinent factors in the situation will we know what steps can be realistically taken to ease Steve's dilemma.

In the end, we are concerned with the interactions and the "fit" between people and their situations and are looking for the points at which therapeutic interventions would be most effective. But in order to arrive at understanding of these we may have to examine many of the elements separately.

What Is Needed for Clients to Participate in Treatment

We have discussed in some detail in Chapters 2, 10, and 11 some of the general requirements of the worker and the treatment process for effective interviewing and engagement. However, our assessment must be finely tuned to the needs of the particular clients we are seeing. Some clients require very little sustainment (such as the Jones couple in Chapter 3); others (Jed Cooper in Chapter 21) require a great deal in order to feel comfortable and trusting. Some clients like lively and even intense interactions with the worker, and others prefer to maintain considerable "space" or even an aloof distance. Some clients, in individual and family sessions, find silences next to unbearable, yet others welcome quiet moments for reflecting or for getting "centered." *Assessment of the clients and their situations are of little value unless we simultaneously evaluate what clients require in the treatment process in order to carry on their most effective work.*

One must also assess whether the particular workers employed by an agency, the availability of treatment hours, the frequency of appointments possible, the agency's flexibility in terms of long-term treatment or home visits, the fee schedule, the location of the agency, and so on, all suit the clients' needs. If not, can changes be made to accommodate the clients or should they be referred elsewhere?

Symptoms

In individuals, families, and societies symptoms usually have a message value. They tell us that something is wrong somewhere. Usually the symptom is not the ultimate problem, and often it is not or cannot be treated directly. Rather, the symptom may serve as an SOS. Heart palpitations may indicate that one has heart disease or anxiety or that one has fallen in love! A child's behavior problem may signal a learning disability, marital conflict, family stress or dysfunction. Homelessness and drastic dips in the stock market point to serious social and economic problems.

Traditional psychoanalytic thinkers viewed symptoms primarily as evidence of internal unconscious conflict, such as between drives (the id) and the ego or superego. More recently, family and systems theories have added to our knowledge and alerted us to interpersonal aspects of symptomatology. Inner and outer phenomena are much more intertwined than was previously recognized.[3] Frequently, as will be discussed more fully in the family and couple chapters, "antisystem" symptoms (i.e., symptoms that a particular family or social system cannot tolerate) are required in order to force change. In some families, for example, a child's lie may be sufficient to upset the family balance and press the family into treatment; in other families, auto theft by an adolescent may be accepted with a "boys will be boys" attitude and, *if* there is internal pressure for change, the young man may have to "find" a symptom that will be more convincing to get across the message that something is wrong.

It has long been known that "symptomatic treatment," direct effort to "cure" a symptom, too often is followed by development of another, sometimes even more disabling, symptom. A woman successfully treated for chronic headaches may develop a spastic colon, for example, if no other changes are made in her situation. Similarly, in family treatment we have learned that if one symptomatic child improves, a sibling often begins to have difficulties. To the surprise of some people, it is not unusual for a spouse of an alcoholic to become depressed when the latter stops drinking. Along the same lines, a symptom often helps to maintain the balance of a relationship: a spouse may, consciously or unconsciously, "pretend" to be more dependent and helpless than he or she actually is in order to accommodate a partner's need to feel in control or superior and thereby protect the relationship, even at a price that compromises autonomy. In any event, when symptoms are present, further exploration is required to understand underlying meanings and issues.

The Situation

In evaluating the various features of the situational component, one can use the concept of *an average expectable environment,* where the term *average expectable* signifies "within the range of normally healthy experience."[4] It is where the actual experiences vary to a substantial degree from these expectable ones, especially where they vary in the negative direction, that worker and client look for external "press": factors that contribute to the client's problem. An income below the poverty line would constitute an external pressure; so would subjection to day-in-day-out prejudice because of race, sexual orientation, age, or gender; so would substandard housing, inferior schooling, inadequate medical care, poor health, lack of employment opportunity, extremely stressful or unpleasant working conditions, and so on. Many clients seen by social workers are subject to such extraordinarily noxious external conditions that it is remarkable that they survive as well as they often do.

On the positive side, one looks for *opportunities:* the availability of better schools, the prac-

tical possibility of moving to a better neighborhood, the strengths of a skillful teacher, the young adult in a family or friendship network who might help a disturbed adolescent, the relative or friend on whom a depressed adult or a disabled older person might depend, the availability of work, of retraining, of an understanding employer, and so on. Are there available self-help or therapeutic groups appropriate to the clients' needs and interests? If the family has church connections, is this a resource? Within the family, one also looks for strengths. Who is able to give what is needed? Who can take leadership in resolving problems?

In personal relationships, an "average expectable environment" assumes reasonably satisfying family relationships and opportunities for friendships. This does not mean that these relationships are necessarily conflict-free, any more than, in the area of income, "average" is equated with great wealth. These expectations vary, of course, according to ethnic, class, and other variables and must be viewed from the standpoint of both general expectations and those of particular clients. An extremely authoritative husband may be "expectable" in Turkish culture, but he may be experienced as a distinct "pressure" by a woman brought up in this country or even by a Turkish woman if she has lived here long enough to expect greater equality in marriage. The client's own view of these factors is of paramount importance. To what extent does he or she experience these as stress factors?

If parents are concerned about a child, whom they see as a problem, the worker can assess the quality of the parents' functioning only in the light of the realities of the child's behavior that confront the parents. What is living with this son or daughter like at the moment? Is the child so withdrawn that he or she is hard to reach? Is the youngster provocative in a hostile way, "expectably" arousing parental anger? Is the child's behavior publicly humiliating to the parents? If the child is ill, how much of a strain does caring for him or her cause? Are parents being deprived of sleep? Are there constant demands?

Obviously, in any sort of problem, the worker must assess the pressures to which the client is responding. An individual's problems actually never stand alone. It is also the exception rather than the rule to find pressure in one spot alone. As the chapters on family and couple treatment will describe, usually there are people in either the immediate or the wider family who are part of the difficulty. Some years ago, Otto Pollak[5] called our attention to pressures brought by grandparents, aunts and uncles, and other more distant relatives—directly or indirectly—on problems of children. These pressures also frequently influence marital difficulties, which, in turn, interact with the children's situations.

Even when they are not presented by the client as a major problem, employment, housing, and neighborhood conditions can be important contributing factors to parent-child or couple conflict. Certainly, the realities of the school environment—the opportunities for learning and for socialization, the respect for students, and so on—are of great significance for children. Social institutions such as the courts and police have negative as well as remedial impact on the problems that occur in many communities.

Whatever the situational problems are within or outside the family, one must assess not only whether the pressures are relatively ordinary or extraordinary but also whether they are transient or enduring. When assessing the many multidimensional processes in the external situation in interaction with individuals and families, the worker must try to determine which are the most salient influences and which are most accessible to intervention.

The Personality System

In individual, couple, or family treatment, we almost always make some assessment of personality dynamics and characteristics. The more complex the treatment, the more we usually need to understand about the workings of the personalities. Among the important factors to evaluate is client *motivation*. How much interest is there in making changes or working toward certain goals? Usually there is motivation for some changes and not for others. Motivation is closely linked to the degree of *hope* that change is possible. The worker's role in both eliciting motivation and supporting realistic optimism is discussed in other chapters, especially Chapters 10, 13, and 14. It is nevertheless important here to emphasize the significance of these in the overall assessment.

Capacity for "normal" or optimal functioning and for change must be evaluated. For example, is the person employable? retrainable if necessary? Does a high school student have the ability to apply for college? Can an elderly woman function alone at home after discharge from the hospital? Does a husband have sufficient role flexibility to take on or share child care functions when his wife becomes ill or gets a full-time job? Some fairly well functioning people want very much to make intrapsychic changes or modify their situations but cannot seem to do so because of extreme rigidity. Others with more severe personality deficiencies are sometimes able to make more substantial gains in treatment. The capacity for change is not entirely contingent on the seriousness of the clinical diagnosis.

In assessing the personality system, it is again helpful to use the concept of "average expectations." Flexible norms that exist within every cultural group set up in a general way expectations of how an individual with a "healthy" personality will act and react. These expectations create a theoretical frame of reference against which one can view the functioning of any individual. It is important to keep in mind the fact that this is *theoretical*. It does not imply a *stereotype* of expectations of how a "healthy individual" will function. Wilson Bentley, who spent a lifetime studying snow crystals, took over 6,000 photomicrographic pictures of snowflakes. Out of these 6,000 pictures, he was unable to discover any two that were identical. In his discussion of Bentley's research, John Stewart Collis[6] writes: "The variety is inexhaustible, but very often (though it would be rash to say always) the foundation of a hexagonal shape is adhered to, so that each is a little star with six rays crossing at an angle of sixty degrees." People are a bit more complicated than snowflakes, but they too have both infinite individuality and common patterns!

Personality is so complicated that one has to view its functioning in a systematic way in order to understand and to assess its strengths, its weaknesses, its potential. Just as one scans the field of the client's milieu, the various systems of the person-situation gestalt, so one can assess the data of the social study that concerns the person. Psychoanalytic, ego psychology, and object relationship theories provide a picture of the "patterns," the basic structures and functions of personalities, from which individual variations grow. To recognize the patterns quickly and carefully, the worker is helped by keeping in mind general knowledge of the major aspects of personality and its functioning. Rereading the overview of the personality system presented in Chapter 2 can be useful to the reader at this point.

The Tripartite Personality Structure When assessing the personality system, inferences made about the qualities and interactions of *id, ego,* and *superego/ego ideal* become important. We know that personality functioning must be evaluated in conjunction with situational circumstances because, as we have repeatedly said, *individual characteristics—strengths and deficits— cannot be accurately assessed without a full appreciation of the social context in which these are observed.* Of course, it is also always important to view personality in terms of developmental phases. Nevertheless, it is also true that many features of personality, particularly of adult personality, are enduring and have been with the person for many years, beginning in childhood.

Among the many questions one may ask when assessing personality are: Is there evidence of dysfunctional residues of primary process thinking, or have secondary process functions developed fairly successfully? Is the ego able to regulate and control impulses when necessary? Do emotions frequently "drown out" intellectual functioning? Does the person seem capable of mature, loving relationships in which there is tenderness and constancy? Is there the capacity for consideration and realistic trust of others? Is the person relatively consistent in his or her feelings, or is there an unusual amount of ambivalence or mood fluctuation? Are there unresolved hostilities or overly intense attachments to parents to the extent that these interfere with current family or other relationships? Is the person able to stand up to others when necessary and pursue goals with vigor, or is there extreme inhibition or destructive aggression?

An extremely important question is: Is the individual able to see things as they are, or is there constant distortion? Is the person generally able to test perceptions and plans for action against reality before coming to conclusions about them? Or is there a consistent tendency to distort or make untested assumptions? How sound is the person's judgment? Is self-image fairly accurate or does the person over- or underestimate actual abilities? Does the person have adequate self-respect? To what extent is the individual clear about his or her identity? Can his or her own opinions, values, feelings, and sense of purpose hold up even in the face of criticism? Or does the person stubbornly maintain a point of view even in the face of information that disproves it? Mastery and competence are extremely important in assessing how well people can cope and get things done. How able are they in affecting or interacting with other people or functioning within the various systems with which they are involved?

Is intelligence average? above? below? Is thinking overly concrete when abstract concepts are required? Are there gaps in the ways thoughts are processed? Are memory and concentration on par with expectations? One must be especially careful in assessing intelligence, for it is easy to confuse the results of educational level or cultural background with basic intelligence. Sometimes people with very limited education have been well schooled in life experience and demonstrate keen understanding of the world and human relationships. Functional intelligence is often diminished by depression, anxiety, distraction, and other emotional conditions. If assessing intelligence appears to be a problem, a more definitive evaluation can sometimes be made by psychological examinations as long as the well-known limitations and cultural biases of these are taken into consideration.

Assessing *ego defenses*, described in detail in Chapter 2, is *very* important. Which defenses does the person rely upon most? Are they functional or dysfunctional in terms of the person's relationships and life situation? Are they serving healthy or pathological psychological ends? Are they rigid and entrenched or flexible when circumstances require?

One sometimes hears the term *ego strength* used as if the ego were some kind of composite force that could be measured as a unit. Rather, as discussed in detail in Chapter 2, it is a series of functions and qualities of many different and interpenetrating dimensions. Perception is accurate or inaccurate, judgment is sound or unsound, self-image is appropriate or inappropriate. One may be highly competent or relatively incompetent, function more or less autonomously, have good or poor capacity for object relationships. Only the control functions of the ego may be strong or weak. One may say about the ego as a whole that it functions well or poorly, but this description is not as useful as a delineation of *which* aspects of the ego function well, which poorly, and when poorly in what way.

Superego-ego ideal qualities are also important. Is the person overridden with feelings of guilt or shame? Is the person overly critical and overly self-punishing for what most would think of as minor transgressions? Is there an extreme tendency toward embarrassment or humiliation? Are there lacunae, spots where standards would be expected but are absent? What is the quality of the person's self-standards? Are aspirations commensurate with background and life roles? Are they realistic and stable? Are there indications of inconsistencies, such as those sometimes characteristic of narcissistic or borderline personalities?

In evaluating the client's superego-ego ideal functioning, the worker considers both the general structure of the superego, its relative strength or weakness in the personality, and the quality of its demands, the level of its demands and the consistency of the standards it supports. Particularly in this aspect of the personality, assessment is made in the light of ethnic background, class, education, regional differences, sexual orientation, and variations in age. Clients sometimes have multiple reference groups from which ego ideal aspirations are derived: they are exposed to the general culture, which upholds one set of aspirations, and to family and peer cultures which may be quite different. Is there conflict among these demands?

The extent to which the worker needs to assess personality qualities and functioning varies a great deal with the predicament about which clients are seeking or willing to accept help. Assessments are arrived at by deductions from the picture described by clients about the problem, the situation, and themselves as well as from direct observations of the clients and their functioning in individual and conjoint interviews.

Variable Expectations Forming an opinion about whether or not a person's functioning is within the "average expectable" range or varies from it sufficiently to be problematic is not an easy task. As indicated in Chapter 2 in the discussion of role expectations, there is no single model of appropriate or realistic or healthy (or whatever term is chosen) functioning. This is influenced by many variables[7]: age, sex, class, ethnic background, religion, educational level, geographic location, social role, as well as idiosyncratic differences. Normal aggressiveness for a person of one background is defined as overaggressiveness for a person of another. People of different backgrounds normally emphasize different defenses and have different norms for expressing sexual feelings, tenderness, anger, and so on. Certainly, concepts of appropriate male and female ways of acting are very differently defined in different parts of the world. Even the level of psychosexual maturity expected of men and women varies among different cultures.[8]

Fortunately, in this country, recent years have seen some shifts in stereotyped expectations of male and female personality styles. Heretofore, in general, men were discouraged from the expression of many of the "softer" feelings: sadness, fear, and to some degree even tenderness. Strong, sometimes disabling defenses (repression, intellectualization, etc.) were often required in order to subdue normal emotion. This is still true, but less pervasively so. Women, on the other hand, were, to one degree or another, warned against the demonstration of assertiveness, to say nothing of aggression. Sometimes women were taught to seek their ends by devious behaviors, through manipulation or seduction; often, however, these were either unacceptable or ineffective, and women sometimes developed depressive symptoms because opportunities for healthy assertion and achievements were blocked by social expectations. Needless to say, cultural background still plays an important part in gender expectations.

The general atmosphere within which an individual is reacting and particular antecedent events are also significant to personality assessment. In periods of turmoil, such as when students and others are enraged by events such as unpopular wars, police brutality, prejudice against minorities and homosexuals, unbearable neighborhood conditions and the like, it would be a grave error to think that the passions unleashed indicated abnormal character traits of the participants. Campus and community rioting may sometimes attract people with poor impulse control or hitherto contained fury seeking release, but many normally well-balanced individuals also find themselves enraged beyond endurance or may determine that aggressive action is essential to foster change. As can be seen, assessment of personality factors is far from a simple process. It requires not only knowledge of the general nature of personality but also finely tuned judgments about the interacting influences of situational realities brought together in the social study.

Disentangling Interactions   How does one go about assessing complicated personality characteristics? It is a process of applying clinical judgment to knowledge of the ways in which clients interact with others, including the caseworker, and handle their own affairs. Again, it is impossible to evaluate components of the personality properly, except as they are seen in the context of an individual's situation. One must take into account the whole gestalt. For instance, one cannot judge whether a reaction of anger or anxiety is normal or excessive unless one knows the realities behind it. It is one thing to be plagued by the fear of losing a job in normal times when one's performance is adequate and quite another when there is a recession or one's performance is marginal. It is one thing for a client to accuse his wife of belittling him when in actuality she does constantly criticize and devalue him and quite another for him to distort her remarks, projecting onto them his own devalued self-image or experiences he has had with others in his life. Feelings of depression may be part of a particular physical illness syndrome, a reaction to the loss of a valued friend, a response to a dysfunctional marital relationship, or, in the absence of any such provocations in reality, evidence of a bipolar disorder.

This disentangling of the reverberating interactions between external realities and the individual is a most complicated task. Sometimes, however, the worker can bring general knowledge to bear on the situation. For instance, the worker often knows what a given neighborhood is like, or how a particular doctor reacts to patients, or what the eligibility procedures in the local public assistance agency are. General knowledge of this type, however, has to be used with caution. Sometimes the doctor, public assistance worker, or school principal has not acted in a specific instance in the way prior knowledge would lead one to expect. Direct observation is more certain. It is simplest when it has been possible in the social study to observe the interplay with the externals directly. Here lies the great advantage of the worker's having direct contact during the social study with the principals in any interpersonal problem, and of the home visit, and of couple and family interviews from which so much can be learned. But even insights thus gained are not infallible and sometimes give the worker a false sense of certainty.[9] Things that have been "seen with my own eyes" and "heard with my own ears" carry great weight, but they are also subject to misinterpretation by the worker because of countertransference and other subjective judgments.

Another method of disentangling the objective from the subjective is to evaluate the circumstantial detail that the client uses to support opinions and reactions. Does the situation described bring the worker to the same conclusion? Insofar as the worker's own perceptions and judgments are realistic, he or she can then evaluate the client's reactions. One reason for emphasizing the importance of self-awareness in worker training is to reduce biases, or at least

to bring them near enough to consciousness to alert one to possible sources of error in judgment.[10] As discussed in Chapter 10, a worker's own subjective responses to clients can sometimes provide useful information for personality assessment.

Repetitiveness provides another useful clue in assessing behavior, for if an individual has a tendency to over- or underreact, to distort, to deny, to intellectualize to excess, and so on, it will not occur in a single instance only but will show itself again and again. If the same type of seemingly unrealistic response arises several times, and particularly if in each instance it occurs in reaction to *different people*, the chance is very great that a dysfunctional personality factor is involved. This illustrates the special value of knowing the client's history when the nature of the problem requires particularly careful assessment of the personality. Since psychosocial workers believe that much of the personality structure is shaped in early life, it is expected that repetitive patterns will often show themselves clearly in the life history and in interactions with family of origin members. Specific symptoms or evidence of neurotic, personality, or psychotic disorders in the client's past are, of course, of great significance. Current or past substance abuse and experience with battering, incest, and so on, also are important leads to understanding present personality functioning.

Family Systems Theory, Complementarity, and Communication

In problems of interpersonal adjustment, such as marital or parent-child problems, one person is in a sense the other person's situation, and vice versa. The term "complementarity" is sometimes used to describe these characteristic patterns.[11] As noted earlier, the action of one person upon another takes effect only in the form in which it is perceived by the other. For example, Susan may use a complaining tone because of tiredness, but if her husband Joe perceives the tone as anger, he reacts to it as such. Susan's response, in turn, may be silence, or martyrlike murmurings, or explosive retaliation, depending upon her personality, the earlier experiences of the day that have set a mood, her perception of Joe, her notion of the requirement of the role in which she is functioning, the pressures she is under, and a variety of other factors. Joe's next response is subject to similarly complicated influences.

If one studies a series of such transactions, one finds that similar patterns in interaction can characterize the behavior of whole families. In most cases in which there are problems of social functioning or even severe individual stress and symptomatology, dynamic diagnosis must include evaluation of interactions with family members and other significant people. This involves understanding of the way in which one person's attitudes and behavior set off or provoke certain responses in the other, the extent to which this is consciously or unconsciously purposeful, and the extent to which unrecognized complementary needs or defenses are being expressed in the process. In family and marital conflict, the worker may make serious treatment errors if he or she is not aware of complementarity in various relationships in the family. Some so-called father-daughter marriages or mother-son marriages, relationships in which there is inequality based on gender or other factors, "sadomasochistic" couples, adult children who continue to live with their parents in very dependent or "symbiotic" relationships, alcoholic families, and many other complementary relationships are complex and delicately balanced, requiring careful assessment before treatment goals are determined. Sometimes a worker may find that serious trouble has emerged in a family where a previously existing complementarity has been disturbed.[12] In some such cases, where there is the possibility that the upset balance may result in emotional breakdown or suicide, for example,

serious consideration must be given to the possibility of helping to restore the previous balance. Family relationships are not infrequently the means by which individuals with rather serious handicaps in functioning are enabled through complementarity to function at a reasonable level of personal satisfaction, social effectiveness, and stability.

Just as individual behaviors and attitudes repeat themselves over and over again, so interactions among family members become patterned and entrenched. Particular behaviors are predictably followed by certain reactions which foster other repetitive responses, and so on, in circular transactions. When these represent persistent dysfunctional family styles, a family member may become symptomatic or problems may arise between the family and systems that surround it, thus bringing the family to the attention of clinical social workers.

In any social or interpersonal system the quality of communication determines and, in turn, is affected by the nature of the relationships among the people involved.[13] When communication is dysfunctional—when people *persistently* send confusing, contradictory, or incomplete messages, for example, or inaccurately receive messages from others—this can be viewed as both cause and effect of problematic relationships. Communication and interaction are intertwined. In most cases in which there are personal or family adjustment problems, one needs to assess communication patterns and, if they are dysfunctional, try to determine what interferes with clear communication and what these patterns tell us about the relationship. We ask ourselves such questions as: Are certain ego defenses interfering with full expression of attitudes, desires, and reactions? Are defenses interfering in reception of these by another? Are nonverbal behaviors contradicting verbal statements? Do poor communication patterns reflect realistic or unrealistic fear of retaliation or abandonment? Is lack of autonomous functioning revealed by unclear statements made by family members to one another? Are either words or gestures being misinterpreted because of variations of meaning related to sociocultural factors?

The four chapters in this book devoted to family and couple treatment discuss assessment of interactional and communication patterns in greater detail.

Use of the Past

Previous life history, as we have said, often reveals repetitive patterns. These can be immensely valuable in helping the worker to understand "causation" in the developmental sense of how the person came to be the way he or she is. Knowledge of early family relationships is particularly helpful in understanding the level of psychosexual development and autonomous functioning and the nature of parental attachments, sexual orientation, superego-ego ideal development, many qualities of the ego, and the basis for anxieties that give rise to ego defenses. Traumatic events in a child's early years—death of a parent, placement in an institution, and so on—or ongoing neglect or unavailability of "good enough" parenting sometimes adds to our understanding of certain developmental deficits and personality disorders. Family history can also help to explain intergenerational patterns of behavior and interaction; a genogram may reveal that alcoholism, depression and suicide, violence and abuse, incest or other problems have recurred throughout the family system down through the years. It is also important to evaluate sharp discrepancies in the way an individual functions at different times in life; these can provide excellent clues to the ways in which situational factors affect a particular person.

Psychosocial caseworkers always have thought in terms of *multiple* causation, recognizing the *circular effect* of interacting contributing factors in the present and those derived from the past. Transactions of the past are in-

corporated in present personalities and relationship patterns, thereby influencing the nature of the current interactions; the past thus lives on to modify the present. This systems point of view is in contrast to linear thinking, e.g.: "Jane is depressed because she was raised by a domineering mother." Rather, Jane's depression may be understood in part as her particular low-key personality's reactions to a controlling mother and alcoholic father from whom she felt little comfort and who discouraged independent development. Self-esteem was further influenced by the fact that she attended a small rural school with no girls her age to play with and received poor instruction from a teacher who lacked warmth or sensitivity to children. In order to get some relief, at age sixteen she married Henry and moved to an urban manufacturing area where she knew no one and felt very out of place. Henry, like her father, developed a drinking problem. Her father died and her mother discontinued any communication with her after Jane refused to leave her husband and go back to live with her mother and mentally handicapped brother. Jane had four children within five years. When the oldest child was seven, the factories in the area closed down and Jane's husband was out of work for almost a year. For a few months, Jane had an extramarital affair which she took few pains to conceal from her husband; when he discovered it, for the first time he beat her severely. Jane made several efforts to leave her increasingly destructive marital relationship; on one occasion she was able to find adequate housing and receive public assistance, but she returned to live with her husband because, she said, she felt sorry for him. A few months later her mother contacted her after many years of estrangement; Jane became clinically depressed and was briefly hospitalized.

This abbreviated case history can only be fully appreciated in "no-fault" systems terms, as a network of circular and evolving interactions over time in which the issues of cause and effect as such become irrelevant. All people in this tragic situation affected and were affected by past and present actions of others, which, in turn, were influenced by conditions in other impinging systems and every individual's reactions to these. As we shall discuss again in the two upcoming chapters on treatment, part of the assessment process requires a determination of where treatment interventions would be most effective. *Therapy, as we have said, is most successful when it addresses those aspects of the system that are most accessible to change, not necessarily those that seem to be the "sickest."* In the case just described, some short-term work with Jane's husband, who was quite shaken by his wife's depression and feared losing her, resulted in his making significant behavioral changes; Jane, in turn, became more optimistic about her marriage and after several months of couple treatment, the relationship improved. At the time this chapter is being written, Jane is working on finding more loving ways of relating to her mother. As these interactions improve, her relationships with her husband and children are positively affected, in part because her internalization of her mother's interactions with her had afflicted her self-esteem and present relationships.

Often, by acquiring a different understanding of past experiences or different attitudes toward them, people begin to interact differently in the present and thereby help not only themselves but others who are part of the same family or social system. Again, a change in one part of a system inevitably impacts on the other parts.

The Client's Own Assessments

We want to emphasize that although the worker is trained to understand human behavior and relationships, he or she alone cannot properly assess the dilemmas people bring to treatment. The clients' own evaluations of their troubles are of utmost importance for many reasons.

First, clients are the ones who know what they think and feel, what the circumstances are like for *them*, what has helped or has not helped in the past, and so on. Over and over again, we ask: "What have you tried?" "Does this explanation seem accurate to you?" "What are you hoping to change?" Understanding is based in large measure on the meaning of the situation to the client. A worker may not want to see an adult daughter continue to live with and care for her aging parents instead of becoming more independent, but the assessment of the situation as well as the treatment goals are contingent on the *client's* preferences and values, not the worker's. The worker's respect for the value of self-determination is basic to the assessment process. Second, client motivation and self-esteem are enhanced by the worker's confidence in clients' ideas and opinions: the expectation that understanding is within their reach, not something that is delivered from "on high" by the worker. Third, it is important that clients become *experts on themselves* because this helps them to develop the tools to make changes, to make new choices, to relate differently to others, to find solutions. Thus, for both ethical and practical reasons, the spirit of mutuality is essential not only to establishing goals but to achieving the fullest understanding of what is wrong and why. Too often in mental health circles assessments are made by the therapist or in case conferences without sufficient input from clients.

CLASSIFICATION

Another step in diagnosis is classification or categorization, recognizing that a characteristic or set of characteristics belongs to a known grouping about which generalized knowledge exists. Three types of classification or categorization have so far been found by psychosocial workers to have particular value for treatment: health, problem, and clinical diagnosis.

Health

The *medical classification,* or diagnosis, often has implications for personal and social consequences, which are guideposts to casework treatment.[14] For instance, a childhood diabetic may need help with feelings that he or she is defective and with resentment at the deprivations of foods or activities that friends can enjoy. An adolescent athlete whose knee is permanently injured may consequently lose status as "star" of the high school team or have to give up a dream of making the major leagues. After a diagnosis of heart dysfunction, a successful business man may have to limit his activities and give up strenuous interests and outlets, some of which he had engaged in to distance himself from his unsatisfying marriage. A person with multiple sclerosis is confronted with the certainty that physical functioning will become increasingly impaired over time, and this fact will have practical and emotional implications not only for the person but for all members of the family. The man who has had a serious stroke or certain kind of injury is placed in a regressive and dependent condition, requiring him to relearn previously automatic processes he had mastered as an infant, such as speaking and walking. Catastrophic illnesses—terminal cancer, kidney failure, AIDS, etc.—have tragic meanings to individuals and loved ones. Knowledge of the implications of various physical disorders and disabilities and the adjustments they require immediately provides the worker with information for the overall assessment once the medical diagnosis has been made.

Problem

A second type of classification refers to problems that include family dysfunction, marital conflict, parent-child problems, unwanted pregnancy, delinquency, substance abuse, unemployment, old age, premature births, incest survival, and situations involving children of alcoholics and terminal illness. These tell something about the difficulty and can become the focal point for assembling data about the disorder. They also suggest major dimensions of the treatment steps that may need to be taken.

Unwanted pregnancy, for instance, immediately suggests that prenatal care may be needed. Arrangements for confinement may have to be made. The worker will need to explore the mother's feelings toward the child and toward the child's father. If it is an intact family, with or without formal marriage, the mother and father together may need to be helped to come to a decision about whether to go through with the pregnancy. In many cases of unwanted pregnancy, attitudes toward abortion may be elicited.

If the parents are not living together, they, or sometimes the client alone, may want to come to decisions about the relationship and plans for the baby. The single-parent solution may be considered in terms both of its possibility and of the problems that would be involved for this particular parent. If the parents are making a home together, they may want to talk about the possibility of marriage. The reasons for the child's not being wanted will need to be explored. Sometimes problems interfering with acceptance of the child, by the expectant mother or her family, are worked through. If they are not, but abortion is also not possible or acceptable, alternative plans have to be made for the child's custody and care. Especially, but not exclusively, in teenage pregnancy, conjoint meetings with parental families may be required for purposes of assessment. One does not necessarily deal with each of these dimensions in every case of unwanted pregnancy, but each of them needs to be in the worker's mind as possible matters for consideration.

A similar type of tentative outline of dimensions for assessment can be made in relation to any problem category; in some situations, the outline for evaluation is even more complicated than the one just given, and in others it is far less complex. Obviously, a given client or family may have several types of problems, each with its own treatment requirements.[15]

Clinical Diagnosis

Third, the *clinical* classification, or clinical diagnosis, is a combination of terms derived from psychiatry and used to designate certain major personality configurations. In recent years, the revised editions of the *Diagnostic and Statistical Manual of Mental Disorders* (DSM), published by the American Psychiatric Association, have been used more widely by social workers than previously.[16] The DSM classifications reflect the "state of the art" as judged by respected clinicians and researchers. Although social workers have had broad experience with personality assessment and psychosocial evaluation, they have no typology that begins to compete with the DSM. Classifications in recent editions of the manual are based on more extensive field trials than those in the earlier editions were; the systematic descriptions of various disorders and inclusion of diagnostic criteria undoubtedly have improved reliability.

Social workers often have responsibility for making diagnostic decisions and formulating treatment plans based on these. It has become essential, therefore, that they be familiar with the typologies and standards of current practice. As members of multidisciplinary treatment teams, social workers need to be able to share in a common language about diagnosis so that they can communicate with colleagues. Increasingly, DSM has become the official manual in mental health facilities. Agreement on nomenclature is now far greater than before, resulting in less confusion about terms applied to patients.

Of course, the caseworker often does not have sufficiently extensive contacts with a client to make a clinical diagnosis with any degree of certainty. In many situations, especially in brief treatment, if there is no indication of psychosis, further delineation of the clinical diagnosis is not needed in order to help the client with the particular problem that has brought him or her to the worker. Problems with family or other social systems often are not the function of actual clinical disorders. But when difficulties in the personality itself are the object of treatment, such a diagnosis may be very useful in bringing clarity to the overall evaluation and treatment process.

For a number of reasons, clinical classification is far more complicated than problem classification. The client usually tells the worker what the problem is, but the clinical classification must be deduced from facts and observations of the social study and assessment. It depends in part upon the recognition of signs or symptoms that are generally recognized as characteristic of particular neurotic, psychotic, or personality disorders. Hallucinations, delusions, severe depression or anxiety, compulsions, phobias, for example, usually lead one to consider a category of mental disorder. The clinical diagnosis is an attempt to define or classify, or put into a category, one of the predominant ways in which the personality as a whole functions, when there is indication of substantial dysfunction or distress. Notice that it is the *functioning* or the *condition* that is categorized, *not the person.*

It is important to emphasize here that purposely and appropriately, DSM takes a generally atheoretical and descriptive approach to clinical diagnosis, thereby making the manual useful to clinicians of various theoretical orientations and to researchers. For psychosocial workers, however, its value is curtailed because psychodynamic and etiological theory is ignored. From our point of view, whenever possible, clinical diagnosis should be more than descriptive, based not only on behavior or symptoms but on understanding of the underlying structure or nature of the difficulty. For example, as illustrated in the case of Mrs.

Zimmer in Chapter 3, we view many personality disorders in part as the outgrowth of early deprivation and flaws in ego development.

When personality diagnosis is called for, the worker first attempts to arrive at the broadest discriminations. Is the person apparently functioning adequately without serious distress or impairment? Is there evidence of psychosis or some kind of neurosis or personality disorder? If the person does not fit clearly into any one of these classifications, between which major categories does the difficulty seem to lie?

Psychosis   The extent to which clinical workers are familiar with psychoses depends on the settings in which they practice. Obviously, in a psychiatric hospital or outpatient facility, workers will be familiar with many types of mental disorders. Although psychosis is in some respects a medical condition, all practitioners should learn to recognize the major symptoms of schizophrenia and other psychotic conditions. *Persistent* delusions—of persecution, of grandeur, of having one's thoughts controlled, of controlling thoughts of others, of being spoken to by the dead, of "thought broadcasting," (i.e., the notion that others can hear one's thoughts), of "thought insertion," (i.e., that thoughts of others are being inserted into one's mind), etc.—suggest the possibility of schizophrenia, although it is always necessary to take into consideration any cultural basis for seemingly "bizarre" thoughts. Auditory, visual, or olfactory hallucinations; "thought disorders," including loose associations, constant jumping from one idea to another, and incoherence; flat or "inappropriate" affect (e.g., laughter in the face of sad events or unprovoked outburst of anger); certain types of disturbed psychomotor activity, including extremely odd mannerisms and catatonia, are all characteristic of some schizophrenic disorders. For most individuals who are severely afflicted, there are confusions around identity, limited capacity to take reasonable care of oneself, and recurrent problems in interpersonal relationships. Often, but certainly not always, these disorders first appear in adolescence or early adulthood.

The bipolar (formally known as manic-depressive) disorders sometimes have and sometimes do not have psychotic features. Bipolar conditions are characterized by episodes of excited, often euphoric, sometimes grandiose thinking and behavior; at other times there may be episodes of depression, from mild to psychotic. These occurrences may alternate with periods of relatively "normal" moods, but clients are often either manic or depressed when they come to our attention. Actually, whether psychosis is involved or not, a bipolar disorder frequently responds well to medication. Therefore, when a worker suspects a person has this condition, psychiatric consultation is definitely in order.

There are people who have been diagnosed as having schizophrenia, yet they function quite well most of the time in many areas of life. Some people, probably relatively few, have an acute breakdown that never recurs. For others, episodes of severe psychotic symptomatology are years apart, with periods of remission, full or partial, in between. Often medication can prevent or minimize exacerbation of symptoms. Occasionally, remissions are spontaneous. Tragically, there are a substantial number of people who are chronically disabled by schizophrenia and whose functioning deteriorates over a period of years. Unfortunately there are no "cures." Even when severe episodes are alleviated by medication or various kinds of therapy (including family treatment) and other supportive services, many people with schizophrenia become increasingly disabled over the years. Sad to say, the long-term downhill course this disorder frequently follows is often compounded by the cumulative consequences of medications; although drugs certainly assist patients in their ability to function, they often do so at a price. In any event, accurate diagnosis of various forms of schizophrenia requires knowledge of the course the condition has taken; a full history from the patient and/or the family is therefore extremely important.

By being alert to any of the symptoms of psychosis and related disorders, it is then possible to determine which of one's clients should be referred for a psychiatric diagnosis and evaluation for possible medication or hospitalization. One need not arrive at a definitive diagnosis, of course, but when there is evidence enough to suspect psychosis a medical opinion should be sought. Where an organic factor is involved, caseworkers have very little diagnostic competence, but here too they need to have sufficient knowledge of symptomatology to recognize signs that can then be reported to a medical consultant.

Neuroses and Personality Disorders When psychosis is not indicated, but the cause of the problem seems to lie sufficiently within the client to indicate some type of personality disturbance, the next distinction to be made is most frequently between some type of personality disorder and neurosis. Neurosis and neurotic symptoms are basically responses to internalized or intrapsychic conflicts, stress between ego, id, and superego. The stress can be significantly augmented by life events. From the psychoanalytic point of view, in neurosis, the individual in childhood reached a fairly high level of psychosexual development in dealing with oedipal problems, although the personality may have regressed from this level under recent pressures. Repression, suppression, isolation, intellectualization, and rationalization (see Chapter 2) are common ego defenses. An extremely demanding superego, compulsive and perfectionistic tendencies, obsessions, excessive fears and worries, conversion symptoms (i.e., specific physical symptoms that derive solely from inner conflicts or needs) are among the indicators that *may* lead to a diagnosis of neuroses. Obviously, cultural factors and current life circumstances must be weighed in be-

fore a definitive determination is made. Many people with neurotic features function extremely well even though they may be painfully unhappy.[17]

In personality disorders, psychological development has not been as fully reached as in neuroses. The roots of the difficulties lie in large part in the early formation of the ego, the failure to develop a repertoire of ego functions and defenses that operate adequately; ego synthesis is not fully achieved. Anxiety in neurosis results from conflict between differentiated parts of the personality. In severe personality disorders, especially but not exclusively borderline and narcissistic conditions, anxiety may result from the unevenly developed ego's effort to avoid regression to a very early stage, a stage characterized by strong feelings of helplessness, and to stave off ego disorganization. Many of the more "primitive" or "immature" ego defenses described in Chapter 2—including pervasive denial, regression, "splitting," projective identification, primitive idealization, and devaluation—can be found in some people with serious personality disorders. Some degree of impulsivity and failures of judgment and reality testing are not uncommon. People whose intellectual functions are easily overwhelmed by emotion, who consistently have a very fragile sense of their own well-being or the goodwill of others, who are self-centered with little capacity for reciprocity, affectional attachment, or empathy in relationships, may be showing signs of personality disorder. As is true in all psychological conditions, personality disorders fall along a continuum from the relatively mild to the very severe. Most of us have some traits that are associated with these disorders, especially under stress. It is therefore important to get an overview of the person's overall patterns of functioning before arriving at a diagnosis.

In most cases in which long-term treatment of interpersonal maladjustment is undertaken, it is possible for the experienced clinical worker to make finer distinctions among the neuroses, such as those among obsessive-compulsive neurosis, hysterical neurosis, and depressive neurosis (dysthymia). Similarly, distinctions among personality disorders are important; avoidant and schizoid disorders have some similar features but very important differences. Borderline, dependent, and passive-aggressive personality disorders have some common but many distinctive features. Although space limitations prohibit us from including detailed descriptions of the many neurotic and personality disorders, clinical social workers dealing with intrapsychic and interpersonal problems need to be familiar with the literature that elaborates on the assessment and treatment of these conditions.[18]

Today, personality disorders seem to be diagnosed more often than neurotic disorders. Features of neuroses and personality disorders often appear together, however. Not uncommonly, several categories of neurosis or personality disorder can be observed in the same person. There are very few "pure" conditions or disorders. Clinical terms represent a cluster of focal points on several different continua. When individuals show features of more than one disorder, all possibilities should be kept in mind with indication of where the greater emphasis lies as it relates to the person's current concerns or treatment objectives.

When intensive work on interpersonal problems is being undertaken with individuals suffering from any type of severe clinical disturbance, there is often value in psychiatric consultation. The more severe the dysfunction appears to be, the more important such consultation is. Any sort of physical symptoms also call for medical evaluation, even when in the worker's judgment these appear to be of psychological origin. Psychological problems in clients with serious psychosomatic disorders should be treated under medical auspices or in close coordination with medical treatment. If depression is present to any significant degree, psychiatric consultation is often helpful, partly because the border between neurotic and psychotic depression is sometimes hard to distinguish, partly because medication may be indicated, and partly because it is useful to have medical opinion as to whether the severity of the depression or possibility of suicide makes medical supervision or even hospitalization advisable. Problems with drug and alcohol abuse also often require medical consultation.

One has to add that the helpfulness of psychiatric consultation depends upon the quality of psychiatry available. There is much variation in the training and experience of psychiatrists and in the hospital conditions under which they practice. Consequently, the advantages of consultation vary. If a patient interview is required, these advantages have to be weighed against the disadvantage of procedures that the client will be put through and the attitudes that may be faced in the medical diagnostic process. Communities and settings vary enormously in the quality of psychiatric consultation available.

Value of Clinical Diagnosis

The value of clinical diagnosis is sometimes questioned, in the belief that the dynamic diagnosis is sufficient and subject to fewer risks. But the clinical diagnosis has an additional value of designating a cluster of factors—traits, behaviors, thought and feeling patterns—characteristically found together. For instance, the term *obsessive-compulsive disorder or neurosis*, when correctly applied, immediately conveys certain information about a client. From the psychoanalytic point of view, it signifies that the individual has reached the oedipal stage of development in relationship to parents but has not resolved all of the conflicts of this period and has regressed to some degree to an earlier period of development. People with this diagnosis have severe superegos to which they may be overly submissive on the surface but which they are unconsciously fighting. They are often very sensitive to criticism and have strong dependency needs, even though these may be covered over. They sometimes very much want to please the worker and other "parent" figures but at other times can either be negative or subtly sabotage suggestions. Often perfectionism and ambivalence are present. Obsessions and/or compulsions can cause much distress, take up a great deal of time, and interfere with functioning. There is usually heavy use of such defenses as intellectualization, rationalization, isolation, and reaction formation. Parents with this condition may be strict in bringing up children, ambivalent in training them, or strict on the surface while unconsciously promoting them to act out. Of course, not all these characteristics will be true of every person with an obsessive-compulsive disorder, but the presence of a few of them in the absence of contrary evidence will alert the worker to the probable diagnosis and to avenues to explore that will either confirm the diagnosis or contradict it.

A clinical diagnosis, then, suggests many qualities the person with a particular disorder *may* have even if they have not yet been observed or described by the client. As another example, if an individual is accurately diagnosed as having an avoidant personality disorder, we know there has been a long-term maladaptive pattern of functioning. We can also expect that the client will have extraordinary sensitivity to real or anticipated criticism, frequent and extreme feelings of anguish and humiliation when sensing even the slightest disapproval, painful shyness, deeply felt loneliness, severe self-criticism and self-doubt, and yet a strong desire for social relationships and affection (in contrast to a person with a schizoid personality disorder). Again, although the individual may not have all of these characteristics, it is likely that many of them will be manifested to one degree or another.

Using the above example, there are immediate implications for treatment. For instance, we know we must work cautiously, respecting the client's need for gentleness and distance, avoiding strong interpretations or confronta-

tions. Even though the longing for social contact is strong, we would hesitate to make an early referral for any kind of group experience until it seemed likely that the client could tolerate the stress of intense social interaction without taking flight.

Thus, as it takes firm shape, the clinical diagnosis becomes a sort of index to many factors about the individual that have not yet become clear from what has been observed or said. It often enables the worker to anticipate reactions to contemplated treatment steps and to guide them accordingly. Such foreknowledge can also help greatly in the control of antitherapeutic countertransference reactions. Intellectualism that accompanies the obsessive-compulsive disorder, for example, can arouse feelings of frustration and dislike in the worker. If, however, the worker can recognize this trait as a defense against anxiety created by an oversevere conscience, knowing that the client feels in part like a child afraid of a harsh mother or father, negative feelings may well be displaced by the desire to help. In the borderline personality disorder, the worker will not be surprised by extreme oscillations of feeling about the self and others, including feelings about the worker. Splitting of others into "good" and "bad" often occurs. The use of projection and denial will be expected and understood as familiar components of the condition, making it easier to accept clients with this disorder and their sometimes provocative attitudes and behaviors.

An accurate diagnosis not only suggests some of the factors and patterns that may be present but usually tells us something about the durability of the problems associated with it: a personality disorder points to long-term dysfunctional traits; dysthymia in an adult means that the person has been in a depressed mood for at least two years, etc. Specific symptoms such as phobias, hysterical or conversion symptoms, obsessions, compulsions, evidences of depression, various defenses such as "splitting," delusional thinking, and so on, quickly alert the worker to *possible* diagnoses. Symptoms alone, however, do not establish a clinical diagnosis. There are always several possible explanations of any symptom. It is only when a specific form of behavior can be shown to be part of a larger configuration characteristic of the disorder in question that any certainty can be felt about the diagnosis.

One weakness of the *dynamic* diagnosis taken by itself is that it tends to see a little bit of this and a little bit of that in an individual without reaching a definite delineation. It is when one tries to say whether the difficulty is primarily a personality disorder or a neurosis; whether a borderline personality disorder, schizophrenia, or a major depressive episode; and so on, that incompleteness in the psychosocial study or lack of clear-cut evaluation of the facts often becomes apparent. This assumes, of course, that when a *clinical* diagnosis is arrived at, it is not a glib designation based on superficial impressions.[19]

Hazards and Misuse of Clinical Diagnosis

There are indeed several dangers involved in the use of diagnostic categories. One is that of stereotyping, assuming that all people with the same condition are exactly alike. As noted earlier, each person has many individual qualities that make him or her unlike anyone else, despite the fact that in the rough outlines of a personality disturbance an individual may have much in common with others suffering from the same disorder. Another danger is careless categorization, assuming a person belongs in a given group because of superficial qualities or overlooking other qualities that point in another direction. Again, it is essential to be clear that we are not diagnosing *people,* but *characteristics* of people and their situations that interfere with their coping and contentment.

The clinical diagnosis, by definition, focuses on pathology. Diagnosticians have not yet developed a systematic means for assessing pos-

itive qualities and traits that bear upon the way individuals handle themselves and their lives. For example, two individuals may be correctly diagnosed as having a schizoid personality disorder; some of the same etiological and psychodynamic factors may be similar, but the two people may lead very different lives. One may live marginally as a recluse or on the streets; the other may be a high-functioning forest ranger or researcher. Of course, the opportunity structure may play a crucial part in the very different lifestyles.

It also follows from this example that the second individual may have better developed thought processes, more useful defense mechanisms, a greater sense of mastery and competence, more capacity for autonomous functioning, and—as both cause and effect of these—greater self-esteem. The assessment of ego and superego-ego ideal functions may be more useful than the clinical diagnosis. Talents, sense of humor, values, flexibility, curiosity, capacity for empathy and altruism, all can have enormous significance for evaluation and treatment.

Diagnosis is admittedly a subjective process, despite the fact that it is an effort to increase the objectivity with which one views clients and their treatment needs. As a subjective process that often deals with impressionistic data, it is open to influence by suggestion. One form of suggestion that is prevalent is the currently popular diagnosis. Just as appendicitis was widely overdiagnosed in a recent period of medical history and before that tonsillectomies were far too widely performed, so in psychiatry schizophrenia has sometimes been too easily assumed to exist, and, especially today, borderline personality disorder may too often seem the appropriate designation. The subjectivity of diagnosis is illustrated by the fact that strong protest by gay rights and other concerned groups apparently was required to persuade the Board of Trustees of the American Psychiatric Association to vote in 1973 that homosexuality should not, after all, be classified as a mental disorder.

This was one instance when the biases of those being diagnosed won out over the traditional prejudices of the diagnosticians!

Along the same lines, the "normal" personality in one culture, place, family, or period of history may be considered "disordered" in another. Behavior or traits acceptable in New York City's Greenwich Village might be viewed as bizarre in a small town in the middle west or in a rural area of Canada. Hairstyles in the 1960s were often used as a measure of normality or disturbance!

Extremely disturbing are indications from research and from practical experience that lower-social-class clients tend to be diagnosed by mental health practitioners, including social work clinicians, more negatively than members of the upper socioeconomic classes.[20] To the extent that clinical judgments made about lower-class clients are more discouraging than those made about members of other classes, the likelihood is that poor people often will not be offered the best opportunities for treatment.

From the psychosocial perspective, the purely descriptive approach of DSM may be misleading. For example, it may be revealed after a period of treatment that hysterical features are a defense against a narcissistic personality structure; phobic symptoms may cover a borderline condition; compulsive traits may defend against a psychotic process; alcoholic problems may cover dependency, obsessional traits, physical pain, etc.

Another danger is that of premature diagnosis. When definitive data is not available to make a clinical diagnosis, it is better to admit that we have not been able to establish one than to fix a label superficially. The rate of agreement among clinical diagnosticians is not as high as we would wish, although reliability has improved in recent years. The fact that a high degree of accuracy has not been achieved is not an argument against an effort to improve diagnostic skill. It *is* an argument against snap judgments and against *overreliance* on the clinical diagnosis. The greatest safety lies in building our understanding on many sources of information—the assessment and dynamic diagnosis, the problem classification, health, and the clinical classification—using all of the knowledge that each of these can obtain for us.

Many generally well-functioning people seek social work help under stress. If a worker feels pressured to arrive at a clinical diagnosis, it may be a distorted one, only describing the client's reactions in the crisis state and not at other times. It is also imperative that we emphasize that even severe clinical conditions are *significantly* affected, positively or negatively, by external circumstances and by the range of options available, including opportunities for decent work, housing, and fulfillment of interpersonal relationships.

Some diagnoses, such as schizophrenia or borderline personality, can seem so discouraging that there is danger that they may in effect relegate the person to very superficial treatment or even to no treatment at all. Obviously, this should not happen. A clinical diagnosis is never a pejorative. The diagnosis tells the worker something about what may help and what probably will not help, but it certainly should not be used as an excuse for not *trying* to help. Realization of the great variation among individuals given the same diagnosis precludes such stereotyping in treatment. The fact is that *the degree to which a person is dissatisfied with his or her condition may be more important than the diagnosed disorder.* The capacity for optimism can be a critical factor. Motivation for change relies heavily on discomfort with the status quo and hope that things can be better.

The whole person-situation gestalt concept, then, puts the clinical diagnosis in perspective as only one of several aspects of the total diagnostic assessment. The reader will recall the work described in Chapter 3 with Mrs. Zimmer, who was diagnosed as having a borderline personality disorder. Over time this client made very significant changes in fundamental aspects of her personality. In Chapter 21, work with Mrs. Barry, who was suffering from paranoid schizophrenia, will be presented. Paranoid schizophrenia is often considered an especially discouraging diagnosis. Yet, Mrs. Barry was able to gain a good deal of understanding about herself and her relationship with her husband and was also able to recognize the importance of overcoming her reluctance to take medication. Subsequently, she was well enough to live fairly comfortably in the community, avoiding rehospitalization. In such cases, knowledge of the clinical diagnosis makes substantial difference in treatment, but the assessment of the client's individuality and strengths is of equal importance.[21]

THE TIME FACTOR

Naturally, the degree to which one can arrive at an understanding of the person-in-situation varies with the fullness of the social study on which it depends. Even in a short contact of one to four interviews, one must understand enough of the interplay of inner and outer dynamics to enhance the client's ability to cope with the main problem (often the presenting one) in a way that either resolves it or diminishes its severity. Pressures that can be modified, opportunities or resources that can be located within the limits of time available are assessed. Even in brief contacts, one can get an impression of certain features of a client's ego: perceptive ability, coping powers, ways of handling anxiety, and so on. One sometimes also observes major defenses such as projection, turning against the self, reaction formation, rationalization, and intellectualization. Aspects of the superego may show themselves if it is unusually severe, lax, or inconsistent. Impulsiveness or rigidity is often immediately apparent. Usually, however, it will be difficult to assess the *degree* to which any of these characteristics exist.

Turning to the dynamic diagnosis, one certainly has to understand something of the dynamics of both inner and outer forces and of the interplay between them in all clinical social work whether the contact is brief or extensive. Without this, very little help can be given. In crisis treatment (to be discussed in Chapter 19), where former conflicts and problems may have been brought to the surface because of the present trauma, quick recognition of dynamic elements is required.

A clinical diagnosis, on the other hand, can rarely be arrived at in the first interview and usually only when there is a very serious disorder: psychosis, severe neurotic symptomatology, or personality dysfunction. Usually the clinical diagnosis will be established only very tentatively if at all in the entire brief contact. So little time is available in which help can be given that treatment occupies center stage very quickly. Because the factual basis is therefore inevitably restricted, it is not only difficult but sometimes risky to try to determine a clinical diagnosis; often it is not at all clear whether any such diagnosis is even appropriate.

In general, diagnostic understanding in very brief treatment will be limited to components of the person-situation gestalt that are close to the matters to be dealt with and close to the immediate treatment process.

In summary, then, diagnostic assessment involves a many-faceted but orderly understanding of the client-situation configuration. The caseworker tries to understand the nature of the interaction of the multiple factors contributing to the client's difficulties—internal and external factors, past sources of present aspects of the difficulties, and internal dynamics within the personality or among the environmental forces. In preparing for the treatment planning, all that is known, strengths as well as weaknesses, is reviewed and evaluated for the purpose of learning how best to help.[22]

As the contact progresses, the fund of knowledge grows and the worker repeatedly refers to it in making the decisions that either modify or implement plans made at the outset of treatment. The more orderly the ongoing diagnostic process in which assessment is made and dynamic understanding grows, the more wisely will the worker decide what treatment to offer the client.

NOTES

1. *Intuition* is defined by Webster as "the act or process of coming to direct knowledge or certainty without reasoning or inferring; immediate cognizance or conviction without rational thought; revelation by insight or innate knowledge." The subject is rarely discussed in the literature on psychotherapy; in fact, a search led us to only one reference, which cautions against reliance upon it: Robert Cancro, "An Overview of the Schizophrenic Syndrome," in Cancro et al., eds., *Strategic Intervention in Schizophrenia* (New York: Behavioral Publications, 1974), p. 6. He writes, "We must be wary of the intuitive diagnosis in which we sense the presence of the thought disorder but cannot illustrate it with the patient's verbal productions." This admonition applies equally to the assessment of any client quality or condition; we must be able to back up our intuitive understanding with facts, knowledge, and reason. On the other hand, for discussions of empathy as a component in understanding, see references in Chapter 2, note 2.

2. Lillian Ripple, Ernestina Alexander, and Bernice Polemis, *Motivation, Capacity and Opportunity* (Chicago: University of Chicago Press, 1964).

3. Highly recommended readings on this subject include James L. Framo, "Symptoms from a Family Transactional Viewpoint," in *Explorations in Marital and Family Therapy: Selected Papers of James L. Framo* (New York: Springer, 1982), 11–57; and Sophie Freud Loewenstein, "Inner and Outer Space in Social Casework," *Social Casework*, 60 (January 1979), 19–29.

4. Heinz Hartmann, *Ego Psychology and the Problem of Adaptation* (New York: International Universities Press, 1958), p. 23.

5. Otto Pollak, *Social Science and Psychotherapy for Children* (New York: Russell Sage Foundation, 1952).

6. John Stewart Collis, *The Vision of Glory* (New York: Braziller, 1973), p. 81.

7. The sources of knowledge concerning these variations are myriad. Many useful references have been included in notes to several other chapters. The following are also of value: Urie Bronfenbrenner, "Socialization and Social Class Through Time and Space," in Eleanor E. Maccoby, Theodore M. Newcomb, and Eugene L. Hartley, eds., *Readings in Social Psychology* (New York: Holt, Rinehart & Winston, 1958); Shirley Hellenbrand, "Client Value Orientations: Implications for Diagnosis and Treatment," *Social Casework*, 42 (April 1961), 163–169; Charles H. Mindel and Robert W. Habenstein, *Ethnic Families in America* (New York: Elsevier, 1976); Emelicia Mizio, "Commentary," *Social Casework*, 58 (October 1977), 469–474; Arlene S. Skolnick and Jerome H. Skolnick, eds., *Family in Transition*, 2d ed. (Boston: Little, Brown, 1977). See also the first four articles on changing sex roles in *Social Casework*, 57 (February 1976), and the special issue on women in *Social Work*, 21 (November 1976).

8. See Margaret Mead, *Sex and Temperament in Three Primitive Societies* (New York: Morrow, 1935), and *Male and Female: A Study of the Sexes in a Changing World* (New York: Morrow, 1949).

9. For an excellent discussion of "evidence," see Mary E. Richmond, *Social Diagnosis* (New York: Russell Sage Foundation, 1917), chapter 4.

10. See discussions and many references cited in Chapter 10. See especially Marilyn Lammert, "Experience as Knowing: Utilizing Therapist Self-Awareness," *Social Casework*, 67 (June 1986), 369–376; and Mary C. Schwartz, "Helping the Worker with Countertransference," *Social Work*, 23 (May 1978), 204–209.

11. In addition to discussion and references on this in Chapters 15, 16, 17, and 18, see also some of the valuable writings that over the years have described and provided examples of this phenomenon: Nathan W. Ackerman, "The Diagnosis of Neurotic Marital Interaction," *Social Casework*, 35 (April 1954), 139–147; Florence Hollis, *Women in Marital Conflict* (New York: Family Service Association of America, 1949), pp. 90, 97, 209; Carol Meyer, "Complementarity and Marital Conflict: The Development of a Concept and Its

Application to the Casework Method" (doctoral dissertation, Columbia University School of Social Work, 1957); Bela Mittlemann, "Analysis of Reciprocal Neurotic Patterns in Family Relationships," in Victor W. Eisenstein, ed., *Neurotic Interaction in Marriage* (New York: Basic Books, 1956), 81–100; Otto Pollak, "Systems Theory and the Functions of Marriage," in Gertrude Einstein, ed., *Learning to Apply New Concepts to Casework Practice* (New York: Family Service Association of America, 1968), 75–95; and Rosemary Reynolds and Elsie Siegle, "A Study of Casework with Sado-Masochistic Marriage Partners," *Social Casework*, 40 (December 1959), 545–551.

12. See, for example, Marjorie Berlatsky, "Some Aspects of the Marital Problems of the Elderly," *Social Casework*, 43 (May 1962), 233–237; Frank S. Pittman III and Kalman Flomenhaft, "Treating the Doll's House Marriage," *Family Process*, 9 (June 1970), 143–155; and Sue Vesper, "Casework Aimed at Supporting Marital Role Reversal," *Social Casework*, 43 (June 1962), 303–307.

13. There are many references on the important subject of communication in Chapters 2, 10, 15, 16, 17, and 18. For now, see Judith C. Nelsen, *Communication Theory and Social Work Practice* (Chicago: University of Chicago Press, 1980); and Virginia Satir, *Conjoint Family Therapy*, rev. ed. (Palo Alto, Calif.: Science and Behavior Books, 1967), Part 2.

14. See Francis J. Turner, ed., *Differential Diagnosis and Treatment in Social Work*, 3d ed. (New York: The Free Press, 1983), Part 3, for several useful articles on physical disorders.

15. See Turner, *Differential Diagnosis*, Part 5, for articles discussing a variety of presenting problems.

16. The American Psychiatric Association, *Diagnostic and Statistical Manual of Mental Disorders*, 3d ed., rev. (Washington, D.C.: APA, 1987). This DSM-III-R and DSM-III, published in 1980, have been used far more widely by mental health professionals than any of the earlier diagnostic manuals. See Janet B. W. Williams, "DSM-III: A Comprehensive Approach to Diagnosis," *Social Work*, 26 (March 1981), 101–106, for a discussion of the importance of social workers' being familiar with the manual.

17. See John C. Nemiah, "Psychoneurotic Disorders," in Armando M. Nicholi, Jr., ed., *The Harvard Guide to Modern Psychiatry* (Cambridge, Mass: Harvard University Press, 1978), pp. 173–197; chapters 15, 16, 17 of George Wiedeman, ed., *Personality Development and Deviation* (New York: International Universities Press, 1975). Several chapters in Francis J. Turner, *Adult Psychopathology* (New York: The Free Press, 1984), are also pertinent.

18. In addition to references cited above, see Harold I. Kaplan and Benjamin J. Sadock, eds., *Comprehensive Textbook of Psychiatry*, 4th ed. (Baltimore, Md.: Williams & Wilkins, 1985), for several excellent chapters that discuss personality disorders and other psychiatric conditions; Theodore Millon, *Disorders of Personality* (New York: John Wiley & Sons, 1981); and Mary E. Woods, "Personality Disorders," in Turner, ed., *Adult Psychopathology*, 200–248. See also Miriam Elson, *Self Psychology in Clinical Social Work* (New York: W. W. Norton, 1986); and, for further references, Chapter 3, note 4.

19. Although necessarily we have had to be selective, in addition to those already cited we particularly recommend the following readings and compilations of papers relevant to clinical assessment and diagnosis, to personality development, and to treatment of psychiatric disturbances: Silvano Arieti, *Interpretation of Schizophrenia*, 2d ed. (New York: Basic Books, 1974); Leopold Bellak et al., *Ego Functions in Schizophrenics, Neurotics, and Normals* (New York: Wiley, 1973); William E. Fann et al., eds., *Phenomenology and Treatment of Anxiety* (New York: Spectrum, 1979); Sherman C. Feinstein and Peter L. Giovacchini, eds., *Adolescent Psychiatry: Developmental and Clinical Studies* (Chicago: University of Chicago Press, 1978); Theodore Lidz, *The Person: His Development Throughout the Life Cycle* (New York: Basic Books, 1968); Judith Marks Mishne, *Clinical Work with Adolescents* (New York: The Free Press, 1986); Judith C. Nelsen, "Treatment-Planning for Schizophrenia," *Social Casework*, 56 (February 1975), 67–73; Judith C. Nelsen, "Treatment Issues in Schizophrenia," *Social Casework*, 56 (March 1975), 145–151; Joseph Palumbo, "Theories of Narcissism and the Practice of Clinical Social Work," *Clinical Social Work Journal*, 4 (Fall 1976), 147–161; Norman A. Polansky et al., "Loneliness and Isolation in Child Neglect," *Social Casework*, 66 (January 1985), 38–47; Leon Salzman, *The Obsessive Personality* (New York: Science House, 1968); Janice Wood Wetzel, *Clinical Handbook of Depression* (New

York: Gardner Press, 1984); Ervin Zentner and Monna Zentner, "The Psychomechanic, Nonchemical Management of Depression," *Social Casework*, 66 (May 1985), 275–286; and Monna Zentner, "The Paranoid Client," *Social Casework*, 61 (March 1980), 138–145.

20. See Chapter 10, note 5.

21. The danger of misuse of clinical diagnoses is conveyed in articles by Herb Kutchins and Stuart A. Kirk, "DSM-III and Social Work Malpractice," *Social Work*, 32 (May–June 1987), 205–211; and Charles S. Levy, "Labeling: The Social Worker's Responsibility," *Social Casework*, 62 (June 1981), 332–342. See also Nancy Atwood, "Professional Prejudice and the Psychotic Client," *Social Work*, 27 (March 1982), 172–177, for a discussion of worker bias against the psychotic client; suggestions are offered to counteract this and to minimize diagnostic stereotyping.

22. We highly recommend Yolanda R. Scheunemann and Betty French, "Diagnosis as the Foundation of Professional Service," *Social Casework*, 55 (March 1974), 135–141, which provides guidelines for exploration and treatment planning; and Florence Wexler Vigilante and Mildred D. Mailick, "Needs-Resource Evaluation in the Assessment Process," *Social Work*, 33 (March–April 1988), 101–104, which provides a framework for understanding the dynamic relationship between intrapsychic and social needs and for assessing the availability of institutional resources.

CHAPTER 13

Diagnostic Understanding and Choice of Treatment Objectives

We now come to questions associated with treatment planning. This includes the clarification of the objectives of treatment, various subobjectives or subgoals to be sought as stations on the way to final goals, and the choice of means—treatment procedures—by which such objectives can be achieved. It is generally agreed by caseworkers that *the final word on objectives is said by clients*. It is their lives that are being changed and, for the most part, they who will make the changes. However, at the outset, they may or may not be clear about what they want or aware of what is needed or what can be done. The worker, on the other hand, on the basis of an understanding of the client-situation gestalt, is responsible for formulating the kinds of help that will be offered to clients. When, often after some amount of reflective discussion, clients become clear about what they want to work on or achieve, the worker in turn can begin formulating the various subobjectives that will constitute steps toward the achievement of the clients' objectives. Some are immediately apparent; others emerge gradually as treatment and further diagnostic understanding develop.

The knowledge made available by the psychosocial study and the diagnostic assessment is used in two ways. First, it provides both client and worker with a basis for major decisions concerning the objectives and general direction of treatment and for details of its early stages. Second, it provides a fund of information on which the worker will continue to draw throughout the whole association with the client. Knowledge attained in the initial stages gives perspective to what comes later and is often drawn on in helping clients to increase their own understanding. Throughout psychosocial treatment, diagnostic conclusions remain a backdrop against which necessary decisions about details of procedure can be made. In thinking about the best way to help clients in their efforts to cope with their difficulties, the worker first envisages tentative goals of treatment and then assesses the procedures by which the clients can be helped to reach them. Objectives are influenced not only by what types of changes might be desirable but also by whether or not means for bringing about such changes exist, both in the client-situation gestalt and in the casework process. In the present chapter we will consider objectives, moving on in the next to treatment methodology.

ULTIMATE OR LONG-RANGE OBJECTIVES

The ultimate, mutually accepted objective of treatment is always some type of improvement in living conditions or personal-social life. Residents of a geriatric facility may need some sort of melioration of their environment; even within the narrow limits of their circumstances, it may be possible to provide more choices or more contact with family members.[1] Many clients seek improvement in personal comfort or satisfaction in achievements or in their functioning as this affects people with whom they are associated. These types of improvements often go hand in hand, although the client may be primarily concerned with one more than with the other. There is so much interplay between an individual and family members (or sometimes other people in a person's environment) that change in one individual's functioning usually significantly affects the relationships. Sometimes improvement in an individual's functioning is welcomed by others. For example, the person may become easier to live with: more relaxed, freer, more giving in love and friendship, less hostile, more direct and clear in communications, able to be more responsible, able to avoid overuse of alcohol. As a result he or she may have more fulfilling relationships with others. However, as we have pointed out, sometimes when an individual makes changes, the relationship is negatively affected or other people close to that person become threatened. If, for example, a woman in individual treatment makes a decision to establish herself in a career or to be more assertive with her husband who has tended to dominate her, serious problems in the marriage may evolve. Or, if an alcoholic gives up drinking—often to his surprise since he has been blamed and has blamed himself for family dissension—his wife may still be dissatisfied with the marriage or other family members may manifest some new kind of symptomatology, which, in turn, affects family relationships. This is why we believe that, if at all possible, when individuals come into treatment, it is both ethical and effective to include spouses or other closely involved people at some point, if not in ongoing conjoint therapy, so that changes can be incorporated more smoothly by the relationship system. In this way, each member has some input into how changes can be accommodated, ideally to the benefit of all.

The long-range goal is, of course, often related to the problem that clients are aware of at the beginning of the contact. It may, however, differ from the initial objectives as the client comes to redefine problems and needs. Sometimes clients have a broad awareness of the nature of the problem at the outset of treatment. In the very first interview, a mother may say, "I know there is something wrong with the way I am handling Tommy." She does not know all that lies behind the trouble, but she sees that she herself is involved as well as Tommy and, either explicitly or implicitly, recognizes that the goal of treatment requires that changes be made by her as well as by her son. Very often, however, in interpersonal problems, the client sees the trouble as lying only in the other person: child, husband, wife. Parents may see the problems of their teenage son as unrelated to their unhappy marriage although, in fact, he is reacting strongly to his concern that they will divorce and is (often unconsciously) bringing attention to himself in hopes that they will unite in efforts to help him.[2]

Sometimes, the problem does seem to lie primarily in someone else, but even here interaction is involved and there is need for some change in the person seeking help along with whatever is occurring in other members of a family. If, for example, a husband works all of the time and is rarely home or is having extramarital affairs, the behavior may in some way reflect (but *not* be caused by!) problems in the marital relationship. In any event, if it is the wife who is coming for help, she will have to make decisions about what to do about her situation. Does she want to try to engage him with her in therapy? Does she still care about him and simply want to try to accommodate his behavior? Does she want to leave him? If so, is this realistic at this time? Frequently, too, the very location of a problem appears to be in one area of functioning at the outset of treatment but in another after a few interviews. The client may see the problem as difficulty with a child, while the worker, listening to the divergent ways in which he and his wife handle the child, may locate the trouble as being also, or even primarily, tension between husband and wife. The worker then will need to find ways of helping the client to make this connection so that he too will have the objective of improving the marriage, at least as it contributes to the child's problems. We are repeatedly struck by how often children's symptoms subside when parents begin to address their own difficulties.

In some cases where the problem is almost exclusively an external one, the goal is to promote changes in the outer situation, either directly or by helping the client to do this. In others, in order to get some relief, the client may have to develop new ways of circumventing or adapting to the disturbing problems. For example, if a work or school situation is entirely unsatisfactory or intolerable, client and worker together may search for new opportunities. If an elderly relative joins the household and is creating tension, new means of coping with the situation may be found. Rather than just being irritated with the relative's tendency to intrude on the handling of children or management of household matters, the parents may find ways to include the older person as a "consultant," thereby providing him or her with a role and some sense of effectiveness, and yet maintain their own authority as parents and managers of their home. Once creative approaches to dealing with external problems have proved successful, often when similar problems occur in the future clients are then better able to handle them without help. Thus, the achievement of specific objectives can lead to increased confidence and improved overall functioning.

In the process of dealing with the initial problem, others often emerge; clients raise these problems in their sessions for discussion, thus broadening the scope of treatment. Workers sometimes *prevent* this by keeping the focus narrow and by settling for brief treatment. In such cases, it is the worker who really decides on limited treatment by never letting the client know that more help is available and might be beneficial. It is the authors' point of view that if additional problems become apparent, and the worker or the setting is not prepared to provide extended treatment, opportunities for appropriate referral should be offered. In the case of Mrs. Barry (Chapter 21), the worker in the psychiatric hospital attempted to refer her and her husband for marital treatment when it became apparent that Mrs. Barry's psychosis was only one of the issues that could be beneficially addressed.

Ultimate goals are sometimes quite limited and specific and at other times quite broad. The goal may be to enable an older person to arrange more suitable living arrangements, to work through a patient's reluctance to consent to a necessary operation, to help parents decide whether or not to seek residential placement for a physically or mentally handicapped child. On the other hand, as we have seen, it may be to bring about a better marital or parent-child relationship, or to help a client with chronic schizophrenia to make a better work and social adjustment, or to enable a person with a personality disorder to function more realistically and with greater personal satisfaction. Occasionally, worker and client simply cannot agree. A case in point is that of a client who asked a worker to arrange for her seven-year-old son to be put in the local jail for a few days to impress him with the consequences of dis-obedience. Obviously, the worker could not comply. The only possible course was to accept the mother's desire to help her son behave dif-ferently and explain that the worker did not think jail would really help but that she would be glad to help her think about other ways of trying to influence the boy. If the client had in-sisted on her original goal (she did not!), help would necessarily have been refused.

MOTIVATION AND OBJECTIVES

No matter how accurate the worker's thinking about appropriate subgoals may be, the force creating movement toward these objectives is dependent on the client's motivation.[3] This mo-tivation, in turn, is dependent upon a variety of factors. One of these is the client's own de-gree of discomfort with things as they are. Have the clients come in on their own volition or have they been urged or even coerced into seeking help? In the latter instance, if the referral was pressed upon people by relatives, by school, or by a supervisor at work because of personality or substance abuse problems, much will depend on the therapist's skill in enabling the person to recognize the potential gain that may result from participating in treatment. Such clients may need to ventilate a good deal of feeling about the situation that precipitated the referral and about the person who urged it. Beyond that, they will need to be convinced of the worker's acceptance and interest in understanding and helping, for their own sake rather than to please others who are expressing dissatisfac-tion. And, except in certain protective or court-mandated treatment, the client will also need to know that the worker does not intend to impose help or change but is there as an enabler, and only with the client's consent. Guided by the client's goals and motivation, worker and client arrive at some sort of "con-tract" about the purposes and nature of their work together.[4]

The absence of motivation can make case-work with involuntary clients extremely diffi-cult. Nevertheless, with clients who do not have the freedom to decide against casework contact, the worker can often devise techniques to en-gage their interest in considering goals that suit their needs and purposes. The Carter case in Chapter 21 illustrates this point. Sometimes cli-ents are given "space" to choose to get help from the treatment process when the worker "joins the resistance" and says something like "It re-ally seems like you are not interested in making any changes right now." When the client is no longer in the position of feeling that he or she must defy or react against the worker's efforts, motivation may then emerge.[5]

Motivation is very much affected by *hope*. It is easier to pursue a goal if one has faith that it can be achieved. Hope is partly influenced by the dilemma itself, which may be either a stub-bornly intransigent one or one that can be rem-edied with relative ease. Most troubles, how-ever, fall between these extremes. The worker's attitude, both expressed and unexpressed, can then have considerable influence upon the de-gree of hope felt by the client. It is often helpful for the worker to put into words a belief that the client indeed can achieve greater comfort or satisfaction through treatment, when the worker is confident that this is so.[6]

Other Factors Affecting Motivation

We know that clients often enter treatment with a good deal of trepidation and often with un-derlying resentment at having to take what is in varying degrees a dependent position. This can be true even when clients come of their own volition, with favorable attitudes toward the agency and the nature of treatment. In a cul-ture that values independence as much as ours does, it is not easy to admit that one cannot handle one's own problems, although, as we have said, increasing numbers of people seek some sort of counseling or psychotherapy. Fear of criticism or blame and fear of changes to which treatment may lead are often present, too. The resulting anxiety and discomfort may decrease motivation and make participation difficult.

On the other hand, without some anxiety motivation may lag. For anxiety is often the mobilizing force behind the request for help. The ideal therapeutic situation is one in which clients are anxious enough about their difficulties to want help and to keep coming for it but not so afraid that fear interferes with the ability to use help. When the circumstances that concern clients are—or, during the process of treatment, become—like "a thorn in the side," motivation is often high, even when there is considerable anxiety about the nature or the difficulty of the process required to make changes. People who are ordinarily very private about personal matters often will tolerate the discomfort of revealing themselves to the worker or to other family members when the problems seem severe enough to them to require this. In our experience, when alcoholics are threatened with the loss of their spouse or their employment, they are more likely to seek help for a drinking problem than when marriage and job—or something else of value—are not at risk.

Along the same lines, motivation is affected by the client's appreciation of the nature of a problem and its ramifications. Most individuals tend, in one way or another, to minimize or to blind themselves to their difficulties. A husband may remember that he was irritable last night but does not fully appreciate the fact that last night was only one of many and that he is slowly becoming disgusted with his marriage, while his wife is becoming withdrawn and despondent. His motivation for treatment may be very low unless in the first few interviews he can come to realize that his marriage is really in trouble and that his wife, despite her defensive appearance of indifference, is deeply hurt because she still has a great deal of love for him. Not infrequently, when in joint interviews one

partner's caring for the other comes to light during the exploratory period, the other will exclaim, "But I thought you didn't care anymore. Why haven't you told me this before?" Or, "How could I have been so blind!" After such realizations, motivation may come to life. Their occurrence at any stage of treatment may mark the turning point from resistance to full participation and may make possible intermediate goals quite different from those thought feasible before.

Motivation and Values

Motivation is closely related to values. Only if parents believe that a child should do well in school will they become interested in improving the child's school adjustment. Only if parents believe that a child should be happy and spontaneous will they be disturbed by the child's excessive anxiety and inhibitions. Only if a wife believes in an egalitarian marriage will she complain if her husband is dominating. Clearly, class and ethnic factors, as well as more individualized family and personal norms, enter into these values.[7]

The fact that a certain way of functioning is the "mode" for a particular ethnic group or class is not in itself, however, sufficient to ensure that it is the most useful way of functioning if the client's goals appear to be impeded by it. Certainly workers must not try to impose on clients their own ways of doing things. But it is equally fallacious to give blind allegiance to cultural pluralism. The worker must steer carefully between these twin errors, neither introducing culturally foreign goals because of personal preference for them nor feeling inhibited from trying to motivate clients to alter culturally conditioned ways if there is reason to believe that their social functioning and personal well-being or that of other family members will be improved by such change.[8] When cultural customs interfere with goals that interest them, the worker may be able to offer a broader vision of choices in ways of being. Men in some cultures are raised with the slogan "Men do not cry"; women from many parts of the country and world were taught that they should be deferential to their husbands; some children are still expected to be "seen and not heard." Yet, when individuals or families seek treatment for some problem or tragedy that has befallen them, it is often necessary to question whether these particular traditions are serving them well *at this point*.

Here we can see the value of encouraging reflection. Similarly, in a family in which a teenage son may be angry at his father's "old world" expectations and demands, the worker can help the father see how hard it is for the son to make friends when he is so much more restricted than his peers are, possibly asking the father about his own teenage experiences and the importance of his friendships outside the family, if indeed these have been valued by him. Along with this, the son can be encouraged to understand the basis for his father's ideas and the differences in the old country and the new. The worker's major task here is to offer options and help both father and son reflect on whether and how they wish to resolve the conflict between them.

It has long been recognized that workers' values, including those deriving from class and ethnic background, often enter into judgments concerning treatment goals and that attention must be paid to the question of whether these are realistic in the client's terms. Certainly, the worker's *personal* values must not be translated into goals for the client. His or her *professional* norms and values, on the other hand, inevitably and quite appropriately become a factor in what are proposed as treatment objectives. When a mother complains about an adolescent daughter's behavior, the worker compares the mother's description with a general knowledge of the range of adolescent behavior that can be tolerated without bringing harm to the child or her associates and weighs the relationship of

the type of behavior shown by the child in terms of later adult adjustment. The worker's evaluation should include, as well, considerations of class and ethnic background that influence role expectations and constitute part of any evaluation of norms. Under some circumstances the worker's tentative objective may be to bring about a narrowing of the gap between the initial problem as presented by a client and the worker's professional conception of socially and personally healthy functioning. Of course, such an objective is realizable only if the client also comes to see its value.

Many clients are extremely self-critical and have been trained that it is "only right" to be very harsh with themselves about any real or imagined shortcomings or mistakes. In these cases, the worker may realize that their unyieldingly demanding superegos significantly impair ego functions that could enhance their lives and relationships. Workers often help clients realize that a more compassionate and balanced view of themselves may ultimately lead to greater personal comfort and freedom. This type of evaluation leading to client-worker reflection is a constant part of the development of treatment themes and objectives.

RESISTANCE

Resistance may be defined as anything that clients do or feel, consciously or unconsciously, that interferes with the mutually agreed upon work and goals of therapy. As Nelsen points out in her very good article: "Resistance is a most useful sign of something going awry, of a relationship or issue needing clarification."[9] In many respects, resistance and motivation are two sides of the same coin: to "reduce resistance" is often to "increase motivation." The term "resistance" is used pejoratively at times; it is occasionally implied that clients who evidence resistant behavior are doing so deliberately or out of stubbornness. Workers can talk about resistance in a way that implies that they have "caught" the client at something. Occasionally, groups are unfairly characterized as "resistant": the poor, the uneducated, the "hard-to-reach," or the adolescent may be stereotyped as such when, in fact, the worker simply may not have found ways to engage them or to determine what goals might interest them.

Yet, in most therapy situations, resistance is natural and should be expected to one degree or another. It can provide clients with opportunities for self-understanding. It can be a way of letting the worker know that something is amiss in the treatment relationship or process. In order to address resistance (which, with an eye on timing, we almost always should), we must first try to determine, *primarily through discussion with clients,* what clients are actually resisting. An individual client or family may start missing appointments, changing the subject, seeming worried or uneasy during sessions, heavily using defenses of intellectualization or denial, or refusing to bring in family members who are very much involved in the problems at hand. Treatment is usually being impeded by such attitudes or behavior. Clients' reactions to the therapy process must be explored. Is there resistance to the worker's approach or style? Or is the worker's agenda different from that of the clients? Are clients in disagreement with goals set forth by the worker but averse to saying so? Is the client worried about worker criticism? Is there (realistic or unrealistic) concern about the repercussions of inviting an angry spouse to join the sessions? Is there resistance to facing painful material? Or does it represent natural hesitation about changing ways of thinking and behaving, even when the client sees this as necessary? Is there reluctance to modify long-standing relationship patterns even though these are dysfunctional?

Generally speaking, it is the worker's responsibility to anticipate resistance and to become attuned to signs of it. One must then find ways to discuss it. The worker may inquire: "Are you finding it hard to understand why I am asking

questions about this?" Or, one might say: "As we go along, you may find yourself dissatisfied with the way we are working on this, or you may feel upset by or in disagreement with some things I say. It will be helpful if you will mention these as we go along." Or, "I sense that it is just too hard right now to ask your husband to join us." Or, "Some subjects are painful to discuss. Do let me know when you find it hard to talk about something." Or, "As much as one may want to make things better, it can still be hard to change old habits." These comments not only help to bring resistance out in the open but also protect the *mutuality* of the treatment, a critical issue discussed in detail in Chapter 10 on the client-worker relationship.

When a client is often late or is skipping sessions one might say, "Are you having some mixed feelings about our work together?" Or, when a client volunteers nothing about being appreciably late: "Did you have trouble getting here today?" This nonthreatening question leaves room for the client either to share information about something that caused a delay or to raise some other issues that suggest uneasiness about coming to the session. To a person who has the goal of "getting my life together" but is at the same time evading discussion of self-destructive behavior: "You have told me that you wish to get help to put your life in order, but I sense that some of the issues that relate to this goal are almost too painful for you to look at." Or, "Have you noticed that when I suggest looking at other ways of dealing with your feelings, you quickly change the subject?" Or, to a heavy drinker, "When you keep saying that you wouldn't drink so much if Susan behaved differently, do you think you are finding it hard to take a look at your part in what is happening?" To a couple: "Do you think it is easier for you both to focus on your son's mischief than on the tension in your own relationship?" When the worker's nonjudgmental interest in the client is accompanied by bringing resistance out in the open, the treatment process is usually significantly enhanced. Of course, there must be a willingness to listen to negative comments from clients, even when they are about the worker or the therapy; worker self-awareness and professional discipline are required here, because sometimes it can be very uncomfortable to listen to unflattering remarks from clients. Yet, when resistance is not addressed, the result is often misunderstanding about objectives, client dropout, or ineffective drifting during sessions.

INTERMEDIATE OBJECTIVES

The intermediate objectives of treatment are way stations on the road to the ultimate aim, means by which it is hoped the final objectives will be achieved. For guidelines to these subgoals, the worker relies upon the insights gained in the diagnostic study. The strengths and weaknesses and the dynamics of the person-situation systems have now been at least partially clarified; there is some degree of understanding of the major intermeshing factors that contribute to the problem. Again the field is studied, this time to see where modification may be possible. What factors seem to be salient in bringing about the difficulty? Which are not likely to change or will change only with great difficulty? Where are the weaknesses or idiosyncrasies in the client's personality, relationship patterns, or the larger environment? Where are the strengths that can be brought to bear on the dilemma?

Illustrations of intermediate goals may be useful. We speak of hoping to encourage a mother to send her child to camp or a husband to share his thoughts and feelings more fully with his wife. Or we say that we will endeavor to reduce the severity of the superego or to strengthen the client's ability to assert needs or to modify a tendency to project. These are "shorthand" descriptions of what may be a lengthy process. The plan to encourage a mother to send her child to camp was a treat-

ment objective in the situation of a woman who had been widowed a year before and knew she was overly dependent on her fourteen-year-old son. As a result, the son was being deprived of normal developmental experiences. The mother wanted her son to mature but found many reasons for not sending him to camp when this was suggested by the worker. It took many weeks of work to enable this mother to recognize her fears; to discuss her husband's death, her grief and resentment; to see that her dependence on her son was denying him companionship with boys his own age and that this was not good for him; and that she was postponing getting on with her own life by keeping her son so closely tied to her.

Such intermediate objectives are sought only because they are seen as necessary for the achievement of an ultimate goal of improved personal-social functioning. They are closely related to the *procedures* of treatment, and are often articulated in combination with them. A worker may say that he "hopes to reduce anxiety by developing acceptance and reassurance and by persuading the sister-in-law who lives nearby to visit daily," or that she "will try to reduce hostility toward a child by ventilation of parents' anger," or "help mother to see that her failure to set limits on her young son is increasing his anxiety," or "use a corrective relationship to help Mrs. George reduce her tensions about sex," or "try to help Mr. Brown recognize that his anger at his son is related to underlying hostility toward his father," or "urge Mrs. Field to reflect on the consequences of her impulsiveness in an effort to help her to regulate it." *None of these objectives is an end in itself,* but a way station on the road to better personal-social functioning. *Each is a means to the client's overall objective.* The connection between these intermediate goals and the client's wishes is usually discussed in detail with the client. Such discussion has the double advantage of increasing motivation to participate in treatment steps toward the client's goal and of recognizing the value of similar ways of handling problems that will arise in the future.

The Presenting Problem and Intermediate Objectives

Kaplan and Mason,[10] in their analysis of the help needed by a mother facing the crisis of the premature birth of a child, pointed to four distinct psychological tasks confronting the mother. Beginning with her expression of "anticipatory grief" in preparation for the possible loss of the child, she must also face feelings about her inability to deliver a normal full-term baby. If the infant survives, he or she may be kept in the hospital for as long as eight to ten weeks. The mother is thus confronted by the task of establishing her relationship with the child long after this would have developed through natural maternal contact and the child's response to her care. Finally, she has the task of understanding how a premature baby differs from a normal baby in its special needs and growth patterns. The accomplishment of each of these psychological tasks constitutes an intermediate goal of casework treatment.

Similar analyses could be made of many other situations that confront clients. In the previous chapter (page 259), the problem of an unwanted pregnancy was used to illustrate the significance of the problem classification for treatment. The points listed in that case were intermediate goals. Similarly, in the situation of Mrs. Kord, a sixty-five-year-old woman whose husband's mental and physical deterioration after several strokes appeared to require permanent institutional care, a worker could delineate a number of such subgoals: (1) to learn through a medical appraisal whether she was right in believing that institutional care was the best plan, (2) to help Mrs. Kord realize the need for this step, (3) to prepare Mr. Kord for this change insofar as this was possible, (4) to help Mrs. Kord work through her feelings of guilt over no longer being able to care for her husband, (5) to help Mrs. Kord work out the actual plans for her husband, (6) to involve close relatives who were concerned about Mr. Kord and unrealistically brought pressure to bear on Mrs. Kord to continue to keep him at home when she was physically unable to do so, (7) to help Mrs. Kord work through her guilt over the placement and her grief over losing her husband, and (8) to help Mrs. Kord resume former interests and pleasures.

The nature of the presenting problem itself, then, is an important determinant of both long-range and intermediate goals. Needless to say, tasks and subgoals are decided on the basis of many other factors also, including the personalities, preferences, and capacities of the individuals involved and the availability of resources.

Intermediate Objectives and Systems Considerations

Obviously, intermediate goals are related to the worker's *dynamic understanding* of factors contributing to the difficulty: the many factors that, taken together and interacting within a common system or among related systems, constitute the problematic condition. It is not enough, however, simply to locate what appear to be the salient contributing factors. A second question arises: *Which of these numerous factors lend themselves to modification?*

Unmodifiable Contributing Factors   Not infrequently, as we have said, the most important factor in the dynamics of the problem is not the most likely to yield to treatment. The most directly disturbing element in a family may, for instance, be the presence of a severely retarded son whose condition is not expected to improve. It is the other family members, however, particularly the parents, who have to determine how best to plan for this boy. There may be disagreement: one parent may favor institutional placement and the other for various reasons prefer to keep the child at home. There may be no suitable place to send him that does not have a long waiting list. It may be possible to find day care facilities for the boy at least to remove him from the home a large part of the time so that his needs do not dominate the household and deprive the other children of attention and care. Problems arising with other children in the family or exhaustion of the parents may lead to intrapsychic shifts that ultimately result in reconsideration of the question of placement of the retarded child.

Poor housing is often a factor that cannot be improved. High rents, a family's low income, and crowded conditions in the city may make it impossible to move to a better location. Attention may have to be focused on the children's peer relationships and on opportunities to build these up in the local community center and on health care or income management. Sometimes a marital and parent-child problem arises because of the physical deterioration, such as multiple sclerosis, of one parent which is not yet so serious as to require hospitalization but does require substantial modification of family roles and relationships. Although the major cause of the problem cannot be remedied, the family develops new patterns to accommodate changing circumstances.

Sometimes the unmodifiable contributing factor lies within the personality of the client. An illustration of this occurred in the case of a very attractive young woman who was extremely dependent and wanted to be cared for in a childlike fashion; this attitude led her to involve herself in unwise relationships with men who gave the appearance of strength but always turned out to have severe personality flaws that eventually caused her unhappiness and suffering. It became clear that her dependence was so strong and deep-seated that it was impossible to reduce it very much. However, the caseworker was able to help her to recognize her pattern and the consequences of her haste in trying to satisfy her needs and endeavored to strengthen

her perception and judgment so that she would be better able to find a suitable person to lean on. As it turned out, she did meet a stable, kind older man with many caretaking and other complementary qualities whom she eventually married and with whom she was able to be relatively content. Similarly, a man with a severe obsessive-compulsive personality disorder may never be able to experience pleasure or spontaneity or to enjoy relationships fully, but it may be possible for him to reduce his tendency to procrastinate and become less painfully perfectionistic.

Indeed, there is one whole group of contributing factors that can never in themselves be changed: harmful developmental experiences. The individual's *reactions* to these experiences can be modified, but not the experiences themselves. Sometimes clients can reevaluate them in the light of more mature judgment or can see that they have distorted the early picture. This was true, for example, of the woman described in Chapter 7 who blamed her parents for not letting her go to college although, as she later came to see, she had never let them know that college interested her. At other times, however, even the reactions cannot be modified, but some control can be gained over them as the client becomes aware of them and of their effects on current life. Thus, modifiability is related to assessment of strengths and weaknesses in the client's situation, to relative strengths of the various ego capacities, and sometimes to willingness to engage in extended treatment.

The Point of Intervention and Tipping the Balance   Since, as we know, any change in any element in a system has an effect on every other element, it is not necessary to work directly with every aspect of a problem. We discussed earlier how improvement in one part of a system can either bring improvement in another or can affect another part adversely. For instance, in a situation in which the presenting problem is a teenage boy's hostility to his mother, if this is accompanied by rivalry between father and son, encouraging a better mother-son relationship may result in greater father-son tension and greater husband-wife tension also. In such a situation, other approaches—or intermediate objectives—may be both possible and preferable. A better husband-wife relationship may need to precede work on the son's problem. Or it may be best, depending on other factors, to work first with the father, helping him with fear of being displaced by his son. Or it may be better to work with the boy himself, helping him to build greater security outside the family. Under most circumstances, the most effective approach would be to treat the total family problem in family interviews or to combine these with individual interviews.

The question of the order in which different aspects of the problem can best be considered can also be of importance. A pertinent illustration of this is found in the Russo case, described in Chapter 16, in which the father-daughter conflict was made an initial focus of family treatment. This was so for two reasons: first, because it was one of the problems the family was most willing to discuss in the early sessions and, second, because on assessment of the family system, it was predicted that an improved relationship between Mr. Russo and his daughter would diminish the force of the mother-daughter collusion, or "gang-up," against the father. Also, as mother and daughter became less dependent on one another, the treatment focus could then shift to the marital relationship.

In choosing which aspect of a dilemma to deal with, workers often make use of another characteristic of systems, the fact that there is usually in each system what is called a *point of maximum reverberation.* As was noted earlier, this refers to a salient spot in a system at which change will bring about the greatest amount of modification in other elements. One member of a family may be a "key person." The case of Joan (see pages 54 and 55) well illustrates how

a single change in the stepfather triggered resounding changes in the balance of the family system and the personalities of all of the members. In an employment problem, the key person may be the union representative rather than the supervisor, or it may be the client's wife or husband. Even a small amount of relaxation of the superego can help to free many ego functions that have been inhibited by harsh self-criticism. In Chapter 17 we will describe how seemingly intrapsychic phobic symptoms in women may be remarkably relieved when their husbands join them in treatment and become more involved and self-revealing. In other words, by looking at the interrelationships within and among systems, the worker can judge where the point of greatest potential effectiveness lies and thereby establish treatment objectives that begin to modify the balance of forces.

Clinical Diagnosis

As indicated in the previous chapter, the clinical diagnosis is in one sense supplementary to dynamic understanding. When relevant, it helps to clarify dynamics and increases sensitivity to elements that are likely to exist, even if they are not yet apparent. In this sense, it affects intermediate treatment goals in the same way that dynamic understanding does, with the additional value that it suggests some goals and provides information about what may or may not be acceptable or helpful to an individual.

For instance, often a person suffering from a hysterical neurosis is ready much sooner to understand and accept goals directed toward the well-being of another than a person with a narcissistic personality disorder. A client with an obsessive-compulsive neurosis may accept such a goal readily enough, but if the goal is not immediately achieved, unless care is taken to ward it off, there is risk of greater guilt and reinforcement of the already too punishing superego. When a narcissistic personality disorder is involved, the very early narcissistic injury must be kept in mind and great care taken not to expect consideration of altruistic objectives until a relationship of trust and acceptance is well established.

Broadly speaking, with neuroses, treatment objectives often relate to softening rigid or harsh aspects of the person's psychological apparatus, especially the ego defenses and superego, and to bringing into awareness events, thoughts, feelings, needs, and so on, that have been buried or diverted. References to such notions as *reduction, relaxation,* and *uncovering* are often included in the treatment plan for clients diagnosed as having neurotic disorders: "to reduce guilt or self-criticism"; "to reduce anxiety by 'giving' Mrs. Green permission to explore her own needs and feelings"; "to help Mr. Ortiz relax his severely restrictive superego so that he is less driven by rigid 'shoulds' and 'oughts'"; "to help Ms. Smith to uncover and recall some childhood experiences and feelings that seem to relate to current fears and tensions in close relationships"; and so on.

In contrast, people with personality disorders frequently need help in *building* and *integrating* a psychological structure that has gaps and lacks organization. Some or many of the ego functions and defenses often require *strengthening* rather than relaxing. Cognitive capacities often must be encouraged and reinforced. Many clients with personality disorders need help distinguishing one feeling from another, or their thoughts from their feelings, or their thoughts and feelings from reality. In treatment, amorphous global feelings (such as rage and emptiness) sometimes can be matured into feelings that are more specific. The "split" between "good" and "bad" feelings about self and others may need to be bridged. When realistic, it is often necessary to support a sense of continuity, an "emotional memory," that allows the individual to be aware that he or she will be all right, or that others will remain constant, even in the face of a minor setback or disagreement.

Greater independent functioning—less reliance on others for direction or for filling basic emotional needs—may need to be fostered by the development of more competence and confidence. As is often true of people with neuroses, but often more harshly and globally, many clients with serious personality disorders are severely self-critical and unforgiving of themselves; they frequently need help appraising themselves more realistically; almost always they need to develop a greater capacity for "self-soothing." The superego-ego ideal may need to be better or more evenly developed in various ways.[11]

The following illustrate some treatment objectives that may be formulated for clients with personality disorders: "to help Mrs. Altman become aware of the relationship between her cutting criticisms of her husband and his withdrawal"; "to help Mr. James to make 'ego-alien' his urge to belittle his son"; "to encourage Mrs. Chase to distinguish between what she *perceives* her husband is doing and saying and what she *fears*"; "to help Mr. Barnes to recognize feelings of sadness and fear rather than only pervasive fury"; "to foster Ms. Harris's tolerance for her past behaviors and to help her develop greater compassion for herself"; "to heal the 'split' and encourage Mr. Allen to begin to recognize that 'good' and 'bad' feelings toward himself and others can coexist"; "to help Jane believe that even if she receives poor grades in college, her emotional well-being or her relationship with her father will not be permanently jeopardized"; "to help Mrs. Carter realize that she has many worthwhile opinions of her own and need not rely so consistently on those of others"; "to help John begin to learn the good feelings he can enjoy through helping others"; "to promote a 'corrective' therapeutic relationship in order to facilitate the maturation of ego functions"; and so on.

As we said in Chapter 12, neurotic and personality disorders often overlap and are often observed in the same person. Some blend of both kinds of objectives may therefore be necessary, always depending on and related to the client's reasons for seeking treatment, of course. Furthermore, these objectives may be relevant when no clinical diagnosis is indicated but when a client's difficulties seem to arise in part from personality traits or behaviors that interfere with functioning or with the achievement of ultimate goals.

With psychosis in general, treatment objectives are usually closely related to developing a stronger and more accurate sense of reality, to coping with concrete problems, and to developing social and coping skills. In schizophrenia, in particular, one important subgoal is to establish a steady, nonjudgmental, caring but not-too-close relationship. Although it is important to convey acceptance and understanding, it is often equally important to protect a client with schizophrenia from becoming frightened of engulfment in the treatment relationship; if the relationship is experienced as warm or close, as much as this may be desired by the client, great anxiety about it may be stirred up. As noted earlier, it is often an objective when psychosis is evident to help the client accept psychiatric evaluation and medication.

INTERVENING VARIABLES

Thus far we have been discussing treatment goals from a client-centered perspective. A number of other factors must of necessity enter into the emergence of both intermediate and long-range goals.

Needs of Other Family Members

It is the exception rather than the rule that the worker can be concerned with the welfare of the individual client alone. The total client-situation system usually includes other members of the client's family, or at least other individuals of significance to the client. The social worker always has an indirect responsibility to

these other people. This constitutes another factor intervening between motivation, etiology, and treatment. As we mention at various points in this book, the worker must take into consideration the effect on others in the family of changes sought by or for the individual who for the moment is the focus of attention. This does not mean that the worker sacrifices the interests of one individual to those of another, but it is the worker's responsibility to bring into treatment planning awareness of pertinent interrelationships between the client and other members of the family. Nor is this an intrusion into the integrity of the treatment process, for neither worker nor client can move wisely without giving full consideration to the interactions among family members.[12] Because of the complementarity that exists in family relationships, a change in one part of the equilibrium not only brings changes in other parts but also results in feedback counterreactions that in turn affect the person with whom the change originated. Earlier in this chapter we gave examples of positive and negative reactions by family members that followed changes made by an individual in treatment, which then have repercussions on the entire family system.

Along the same lines, sometimes when a client has little motivation for making personal changes, interest can be mustered to make changes that will benefit others. The following case illustrates the point. In her family and on her job, a woman habitually took on the role of "martyr" or "go-between," doing a lot for others, seldom asking for anything for herself, and yet resenting that others did not show her the consideration she showed them. Her awareness of this long-standing pattern did not result in her making significant changes. However, when she realized that by being the one to mediate between her teenage son and his father, from whom she was divorced, she was interfering with the father-son relationship and actually infantilizing and promoting fear in her son, then and only then did she make efforts to modify her habitual behavior.

Peripheral Factors

Before going on to an examination of the choice of treatment procedures in the next chapter, we must consider a few additional variables—somewhat peripheral but nevertheless important—that intervene between treatment and the ideal objective of modifying or removing some of the factors contributing to clients' difficulties.

An obvious variable is *time*. If experience indicates that a certain type of change is likely to require a number of months of work and that the client will be available for only a few interviews, it is usually contraindicated to embark upon a line of treatment that will have to be interrupted midway. A decision on this factor is sometimes influenced by the special function of the agency (as in certain crisis or hospital services where contact is limited to a short time span), in which case, referral to another agency may become a major treatment objective. Circumstances affecting the client may also affect the timing; the matter about which the client is coming for help may have to be settled within a few days or a few weeks. Even in long-term treatment, the time factor may unexpectedly become important. After a few months of treatment a client or family may have to move to another city. Themes may be emerging at this point about which treatment decisions must be made. If they cannot be developed profitably within the time available, they should be circumvented rather than opened up and dealt with inadequately. If clients feel that their short-term or long-term goals have not been achieved, again considering a referral is important.

Another variable affecting the nature of treatment may be the way in which the *agency function* is defined. The course of a case in which there are both parent-child and marital problems is likely to differ if the client applies to a child-oriented clinic rather than a family service

agency. A woman who is deciding whether to separate from her ill but very difficult husband may be offered very different treatment if she goes to the social service department of the hospital for the mentally ill where her husband is being treated rather than to a mental hygiene clinic in her own community. Treatment planning and formulation of objectives may be significantly influenced by the role definition of the agency and the worker.

An agency's view of *priorities* in its function will often translate itself into other variables affecting the treatment process: offices that do or do not provide privacy or protection from interruption during interviews, caseloads that permit forty-five- to sixty-minute interviews per week for each client who needs the time, or caseloads that are too large to permit interviews of this length or frequency, and so on. Casework that has as its objective a substantial change in individual functioning usually requires uninterrupted and regular interviewing time. Exceptions to this do occur. Crisis treatment, for instance, of necessity often occurs in the midst of interruptions and unplanned interviews: in hospitals, schools, or storefront facilities, or at the scene of disaster. Here the intensity of emotion aroused by the crisis may make concentration possible in spite of distractions, and the immediate availability of interviews may be more important than other considerations. Of course, the availability of medical, psychiatric, educational, or other kinds of *consultation*, depending on client need, may significantly influence treatment goals and procedures.

The caseworker's *skill* is another intervening factor of great importance.[13] Different themes, aims, and procedures call on different kinds of skill. Individual, couple, and family treatment require different abilities and talents. Work with children and adolescents has its special demands. Clients with catastrophic illnesses and families of such clients do best with workers who have particular personal and professional experience and skill. It is essential that the worker define treatment objectives that lie within his or her range of competence and, within these limits, treat with skill rather than venture into treatment in which the worker is unprepared and unsure. This requirement, however, must not be taken to mean that treatment skill is static and cannot be further developed in workers but that development is achieved by *gradual* reaching just beyond the border of one's present well-established ability, not by luring the client into deep and troubled waters to sink or swim along with the worker!

Ideally, of course, the client's need should be met by whatever form of treatment will bring the greatest relief from discomfort. This means either that the agency function should be sufficiently flexible to adapt to varying needs or that, when necessary, transfers should be made to other agencies that offer the required treatment. It also means that within agencies clients should be referred to workers whose skill is adequate to meet their particular needs.

The ultimate objectives of treatment, then, are determined jointly by client and worker. The client's motivation as it relates to goals is central to treatment. Intermediate goals are means to the client's ultimate objective, often formulated by the worker and discussed with the client and acceptable to him or her. Intermediate goals rest on the nature of the problems to be dealt with, on dynamic understanding, and on the clinical diagnosis. They are guided also by the assessment of modifiability, of strengths, of weaknesses, and of points in the client's personality, family, or social system at which interventions are likely to be most effective. Certain intervening variables are also important. The objectives of treatment must be thought of as fluid, modified as changes develop in the clients' understanding of their needs and in their motivation and as the worker's understanding of the client's requirements and capacities grows. The client's response to treatment and

ability to use it are of major importance in these reformulations. Goals not only enable worker and client to avoid drifting along in a friendly, noneffective way but also make it possible to avoid blind alleys. Conscious treatment planning serves the purpose of trial action. It compels the therapist to think through the possibilities and consequences of a line of treatment before undertaking it and involving the client in fruitless effort. Well-focused and consciously planned therapy is likely to be effective therapy.

NOTES

1. See Chapter 8, note 14.

2. See Virginia Satir, *Conjoint Family Therapy*, rev. ed. (Palo Alto, Calif.: Science and Behavior Books, 1967), especially chapter 5, "Marital Disappointment and Its Consequences for the Child." The chapters on family and marital therapy in this book discuss this important issue more fully.

3. The subject of motivation is often discussed under the name of its opposite, that is, resistance, by which we mean any attitude or behavior of the client (of which he or she may be unaware) that interferes with the work of treatment. For a useful discussion of motivation and related factors, see Helen Harris Perlman, chapter 12, "The Client's Workability and the Casework Goal," in *Social Casework: A Problem-Solving Process* (Chicago: University of Chicago Press, 1957), pp. 183–203.

4. The term "contract" is generally used to describe the explicit common understanding of conditions and goals of treatment arrived at by client and worker. In psychosocial casework it is usually seen as an informal, ongoing process, with new agreements made as additional goals emerge. For the general subject of client and worker goal setting, see Beulah Compton and Burt Galaway, chapter 10, "The Contract Phase: Joint Assessment, Goal Setting, and Planning," in *Social Work Processes*, 3d ed. (Chicago: Dorsey Press, 1984). See also Anthony N. Maluccio and Wilma D. Marlow, "The Case for the Contract," *Social Work*, 19 (January 1974), 28–36 (also reprinted in the Compton and Galaway chapter); Michael A.

Rothery, "Contracts and Contracting," *Clinical Social Work Journal*, 8 (Fall 1980), 179–185; and Sonya L. Rhodes, "Contract Negotiation in the Initial Stage of Casework Service," *Social Service Review*, 51 (March 1977), 125–140. See also Brett Seabury, "The Contract: Uses, Abuses and Limitations," *Social Work*, 21 (January 1976), 16–21, for a very good discussion of the value of the contract, but also of its shortcomings and possible dangers.

5. See Chapter 11, note 4, for references on involuntary clients.

The idea of "joining the resistance" is not a new one, but it has taken a somewhat different turn with the emergence of so-called paradoxical interventions. For the most part, we eschew paradoxical approaches. We do not like the seeming "trickiness" of most of them; many of the techniques do not strike us as being respectful to clients. For ethical reasons, then, we prefer more straightforward approaches that allow for mutuality between client and worker. We also believe that paradoxical interventions can be confusing and that clients generally do better when they understand how the changes they have made came about. Nevertheless, for those readers who are interested in paradoxical treatment, we refer them to two of the most responsible volumes on the subject: Peggy Papp, *The Process of Change* (New York: Guilford Press, 1983); and Gerald R. Weeks and Luciano L'Abate, *Paradoxical Psychotherapy: Theory and Practice with Individuals, Couples, and Families* (New York: Brunner/Mazel, 1982).

6. Lillian Ripple, Ernestina Alexander, and Bernice Polemis, *Motivation, Capacity and Opportunity* (Chicago: University of Chicago Press, 1964), deal extensively with the foregoing in their study of the "discomfort-hope" balance in the client's use of treatment. For their conclusions, see pp. 198–206. Jerome Frank also stresses the importance of hope in "The Role of Hope in Psychotherapy," *International Journal of Psychiatry*, 5 (May 1968), 383–395, as does Angelo Smaldino in "The Importance of Hope in the Casework Relationship," *Social Casework*, 56 (July 1975), 328–333.

7. See, for example, Karen W. Bartz and Elaine S. Levine, "Child Rearing by Black Parents: A Description and Comparison to Anglo and Chicano Parents," *Journal of Marriage and the Family*, 40 (November 1978),

709–719; Anita Delaney and Emelicia Mizio, eds., *Training for Service Delivery to Minority Clients* (New York: Family Service Association of America, 1981); Dorcas Davis Bowles, "The Impact of Ethnicity on African-American Mothering: A Report of a Study in Progress," in Louise S. Bandler, ed., *Education for Clinical Social Work Practice: Continuity and Change* (New York: Pergamon Press, 1983), 77–86; Wynne Hanson DuBray, "American Indian Values: Critical Factor in Casework," *Social Casework*, 66 (January 1985), 30–37; Melvin L. Kohn, *Class and Conformity: A Study in Values* (Chicago: University of Chicago Press, 1977); Mirra Komarowsky, *Blue Collar Marriage* (New York: Random House, 1964); Hylan Lewis, *Culture, Class and Poverty* (Washington, D.C.: Cross Tell, 1967); Teresa Donati Marciano, "Middle Class Incomes, Working-Class Hearts," in Arlene S. Skolnick and Jerome H. Skolnick, eds., *Family in Transition* (Boston: Little, Brown, 1977), 465–476; Charles H. Mindel and Robert W. Habenstein, *Ethnic Families in America* (New York: Elsevier, 1976); Hyman Rodman, "Lower-Class Family Behavior," in Skolnick and Skolnick, *Family in Transition*, 461–465; Angela Shen Ryan, "Cultural Factors in Casework with Chinese-Americans," *Social Casework*, 66 (June 1985), 333–340; and Shirley Thrasher and Gary Anderson, "The West Indian Family: Treatment Challenges," *Social Casework*, 69 (March 1988), 171–176. See also many relevant papers in Monica McGoldrick et al., eds., *Ethnicity and Family Therapy* (New York: Guilford Press, 1982). For further references, see Chapter 12, note 7.

8. A case example presented by John P. Spiegel, "Conflicting Formal and Informal Roles in Newly Acculturated Families," in Gertrude Einstein, ed., *Learning to Apply New Concepts to Casework Practice* (New York: Family Service Association of America, 1968), pp. 53–61, illustrates this point. On the other hand, in recent years pluralism and increasing acceptance of a wide variety of lifestyles and family relationship patterns have led sociologists and clinicians to be more cautious than they were about viewing alternative modes and value differences as "pathological"; see Rodman, "Lower-Class Family Behavior." Furthermore, understanding family life of various cultures is a complicated matter indeed. For example, in a persuasive paper, Robert Staples' examination of theory and research on the black family leads him to conclude that much of it has been biased and fraught with myths and stereotypes; see his "Towards a Sociology of the Black Family: A Theoretical and Methodological Assessment," *Journal of Marriage and the Family*, 33 (February 1971), 119–135, reprinted in Skolnick and Skolnick, *Family in Transition*, 477–505. See also William Ryan's polemic against *Blaming the Victim*, rev. ed. (New York: Random House, 1976). The interested reader may also want to refer to Ludwig L. Geismer, "Family Disorganization: A Sociological Perspective," *Social Casework*, 59 (November 1978), 545–550, which raises important questions about linking family disorganization with low socioeconomic status.

9. Judith C. Nelsen, "Dealing with Resistance in Social Work Practice," *Social Casework*, 56 (December 1975), 588. In addition to this excellent article, we also recommend Carol M. Anderson and Susan Stewart, *Mastering Resistance: A Practical Guide to Family Therapy* (New York: Guilford Press, 1983); Renate Frankenstein, "Agency and Client Resistance," *Social Casework*, 63 (January 1982), 24–28; Alex Gitterman, "Uses of Resistance: A Transactional View," *Social Work*, 28 (March–April 1983), 127–131; Howard Goldstein, "A Cognitive-Humanistic Approach to the Hard-to-Reach Client," *Social Casework*, 67 (January 1986), 27–36; and Carl Hartman and Diane Reynolds, "Resistant Clients: Confrontation, Interpretation, and Alliance," *Social Casework*, 68 (April 1987), 205–213.

10. David M. Kaplan and Edward A. Mason, "Maternal Reactions to Premature Birth Viewed as an Acute Emotional Disorder," *American Journal of Orthopsychiatry*, 30 (July 1960), 539–547.

11. See especially Mary E. Woods, "Personality Disorders," in Francis J. Turner, ed., *Adult Psychopathology: A Social Work Perspective* (New York: Free Press, 1984), for a fuller discussion of treatment goals for clients with these conditions.

12. In addition to the numerous references on family and marital interaction and treatment cited elsewhere, see Arthur Leader, "The Notion of Responsibility in Family Therapy," *Social Casework* (March 1979), 131–137, in which he discusses the importance of helping family members to take responsibility for the effects of their communications and behavior on one another.

13. Mullen's and Reid and Shyne's findings concerning worker differences amply demonstrate variations in worker approach: Edward J. Mullen, "Differences in Worker Style in Casework," *Social Casework*, 50 (June 1969), 347–353; and William Reid and Ann Shyne, *Brief and Extended Casework* (New York: Columbia University Press, 1969), pp. 76, 84. Ripple et al., in *Motivation, Capacity and Opportunity*, demonstrate the effect of differences in worker warmth and encouragement. Frank, "Role of Hope in Psychotherapy," sees this aspect as one of primary importance. Research on the role in treatment effectiveness of various therapist attributes is reviewed in Larry E. Beutler et al., "Therapist Variables in Psychotherapy Process and Outcome," in Sol L. Garfield and Allen E. Bergin, eds., *Handbook of Psychotherapy and Behavior Change*, 3d ed. (New York: John Wiley & Sons, 1986). See also notes to Chapter 10, especially notes 1, 2, 5, and 18.

CHAPTER 14

Diagnostic Understanding and Choice of Treatment Procedures

When we turn to the choice of treatment procedures (described in Chapters 5 through 8) by which we hope to move toward long-range and intermediate goals, we see that certain overall decisions about procedures are dictated by both objectives and diagnostic understanding. Obviously, if one objective is to bring about environmental improvement, either *environmental treatment* or *extrareflection* is certain to be prominent. If there are problems of personal dysfunctioning and both diagnostic thinking and the client's motivation make self-understanding a reasonable objective, *intrareflection,* including, perhaps, *dynamic* and *developmental reflection,* will play a major role. Where the objective is improvement in interpersonal relationships, all aspects of current *person-situation reflection* will of necessity be in the forefront.

Not only does the broad initial diagnostic thinking guide the details of treatment, but also indispensable to the *immediate* choice of procedures is continuous sensitive understanding. For instance, after an interview in which a client had ventilated much feeling about her husband's "TV addiction," as she called it, the worker anticipated that there would be an op-portunity to encourage her client's beginning awareness that her intense annoyance at her husband's preoccupation with sports on TV paralleled a childhood reaction to her father's regular Saturday trips to the "Game," which always came before any family activity. However, as soon as the client entered the room for her next session, the worker noted her harassed expression and the recurrence of an eye twitch. The anticipated plan for the interview had to be set aside, and instead the worker sought to learn the cause of her client's present distress. Both basic diagnostic thinking and immediate perception of the client's need and readiness for one of these alternatives enter such decisions, decisions that must be made in a flash.

Each interview, then, is a constantly moving encounter between a clinician and an individual, couple, or family—occasionally with a collateral person present when objectives require this—undertaking a common task. The worker's part in that task includes being continuously alert to clients' immediate feelings and attitudes, thinking, and reactions. In communication language, this is alertness to feedback, feedback that reveals how the interaction is proceeding and guides the worker's next procedures. Accurate reception of these communications requires not only close attention but, even more important, empathy with the clients, a capacity to *feel with* each individual involved, at the same time one is *thinking* about what response will be most helpful. Of course, when one is unsure of exactly how clients are reacting, it is essential to seek as much information as possible through nonthreatening questioning rather than operating on guesswork.

ENVIRONMENTAL CHANGE

Many aspects of the relationships between diagnostic understanding and the procedures of treatment have been discussed in the chapters describing these procedures and their uses. Clearly, the identification of factors contributing to a client's dilemma is the first indicator of whether environmental treatment is needed. Also, as we have pointed out many times, changes in the environment often have immediate effects on the inner life of an individual and on interpersonal relationships. A job that is a better "fit" for a man than the one he has may increase self-esteem, reduce anxiety, and contribute to a more satisfying marriage with little or no need for intrareflection. Locating a cheerful and competent homemaker may relieve a woman with young children enough to permit convalescence from major surgery without additional casework help. If a change in the external situation would seem to benefit a client, a second indicator is the assessment of whether or not it is likely that the change can be brought about. If it appears that this might be possible, the next decision to be made is that of *how* to effect the change, through direct intervention by the worker or through helping clients to act for themselves.[1] Of course, the *general* preference of the psychosocial worker is to enable clients to do things for themselves whenever possible. So we must turn again to assessment: Is the client able or likely to become able to do this? Is the environment likely to respond to

the effort? Will the worker's intervention be more effective than the client's? The dynamic diagnosis will be involved: How immediate is the need for the change? Is it urgent that change be made faster than the client is likely to be able to bring it about? One further diagnostic consideration: What is the state of the client's motivation and trust in the worker? Is it important for the worker to win the client's confidence by immediately doing something that will better his or her situation?

If direct environmental work is decided upon, the actual steps taken will again depend upon diagnostic thinking about collaterals as well as about the client. In work with people in the client's social environment, some impressions can be formed from what the client has said to the worker, but much of one's understanding is arrived at on the spot, as the person consulted responds to the worker's approaches. Since details of environmental work and of the issues involved were discussed in Chapter 8, we need not deal with them further here.

INTERPERSONAL RELATIONSHIPS, INTERNAL CHANGE, AND PERSON–SITUATION REFLECTION

When we turn to problems that primarily concern interpersonal relationships and internal change, we find that the nature of the problem and the opportunities for effective solution determine which procedures we select. As just mentioned, sometimes inner distress or dissatisfaction in relationships is efficiently addressed by modifying some aspect of the environment. Similarly, as the chapters on family and couple treatment will describe, there are times when apparently intrapsychic symptoms (e.g., depression or panic attacks) can best be relieved when changes are made in the family or marital balance.

In most cases, interpersonal and personal difficulties lead us to emphasize procedures designed to promote both outwardly directed and inwardly directed understanding. The Hollis study of marriage counseling cases, for instance, showed that from the second interview onward over 50 percent of the worker's communications were of a reflective type: predominantly *person-situation reflection*.[2] (See Chapter 6 for a discussion of these reflective procedures and their uses.) The client responds by a gradual increase in reflective comments. Occasionally, diagnostic observation shows that a person is so depressed or grief-stricken that treatment at first is very heavily weighted with *sustainment*, *ventilation*, and some *direct influence* (see Chapter 5). But, characteristically, there is soon some movement into thought about the details of everyday living and an effort to expand the client's awareness of his or her own feelings beyond depression and grief per se to other emotions.

In family, marital, or individual interviews, as the worker listens to clients' discussions of interpersonal problems, the question constantly arises: Which thread of the communications should be picked up? The worker tries to find a way to enable clients to gain the understanding needed to deal with the dilemma more competently as rapidly as possible but without running the risk of overloading them with more new ways of looking at things than they can comfortably assimilate or are ready to take on. To go too fast may be to lose clients.

The Anxiety Factor in Early Interviews

The Hollis study, which compared fifteen clients with marital problems who continued in treatment with fifteen who dropped out after the first or second interview, found that the workers had made a markedly greater number of lengthy interpretations and explanations in the initial interviews with those who dropped out than in those with clients who continued. Furthermore, it was found that these communications in many instances had a distinct potential for arousing anxiety. In contrast, in early interviews with clients who continued, anxiety-arousing comments had in large part been avoided. This is not to say that

reflective techniques, even intrareflection, can never be used in early interviews. Sometimes a worker can be straightforward, even incisive, yet nonthreatening. If care is taken to assess the anxiety factor, introduction of some person-situation reflection into early interviews induces feedback that is often of great value to diagnostic understanding and to mutual clarification of the early objectives of treatment. This also gives the client a sample of what the contact will be like, providing something to be taken away as an immediate treatment gain.

> Mrs. Ford, a young single mother, was referred by a school psychologist to a family service agency because her eight-year-old son was daydreaming and crying in class. Projective tests revealed that he was consumed with rage and with fears that his family would abandon him. In the first interview, the mother, who had had a very unstable childhood herself, wept and said that she saw history repeating itself. She had lived with a series of men, had moved frequently, and had been hospitalized for a "nervous stomach" three times over the past two years. She was sad, she said, that she had not given better care to her son than her alcoholic parents had given her. Expressing understanding for this woman's deep distress, the worker said that it sounded as if Mrs. Ford were, perhaps, asking for some help in stabilizing her own life as well as that of her son. Mrs. Ford, looking relieved, said, "That's exactly what I want. I've been unhappy with myself for a long time." At the end of the first interview, it was clear that this client wanted to think introspectively about her own life and about her part in her son's problems. Mrs. Ford's openness to reflective thinking was a positive diagnostic sign and an indicator of her motivation for change.

When the sequence in which matters are taken up rests on the worker's choice in following one lead or another, assessment of the anxiety-arousing potential of each choice is highly pertinent. We referred earlier to the fact that when the worker recognizes tension and anger in family relationships, it is usually very important to give the client adequate opportunity for the expression of hurt and resentment. Interpretations concerning how the other person feels or why the other person acts as he or she does are more likely to be accepted if they come later, unless diagnosis shows unusual openness to self-awareness. It is usually more effective to help people to express their own feelings and to speak about themselves before encouraging them to empathize with a spouse. In most cases, when there is a significant amount of animosity, there is little readiness for appreciation of the way in which a client is hurting another person or provoking negative reactions, such as through withdrawal or counter-hostility. Assessment often indicates that not only ventilation of feelings but also acceptance by the worker of the hurt and of the desire to retaliate may be needed to prepare the way for understanding of the other's needs or consideration of his or her contribution to the troubles.

Personality Factors

Factors within the personalities of clients will greatly influence readiness to try to understand themselves, their behavior, its effects on others, and the needs or feelings of people with whom they are involved. This point is well illustrated by two contrasting marital counseling cases carried by the same worker. In the first case, the worker was very active during early contacts in promoting the wife's reflection concerning her husband. In the second, emphasis was placed instead on the wife's awareness of her own feelings. The reasons for the difference in treatment lay not in the situations but in the worker's diagnostic understanding of the personalities of the two women. Both women were very afraid of not being loved, both were volatile women, both were of southern European background, both were belittling their husbands and initially putting all the blame for family unhappiness on them. Both were intelligent and motivated to seek help. The first client, however, had no doubt of her love for her husband and had matured emotionally to the point that she was well related to other people and cared for their welfare as well as for her own. Clinically, one could say that her personality was relatively healthy and well developed, with evidence of some hysterical features. This client immediately responded with understanding to the worker's carefully worded questions about how her husband might feel, why he might be acting as he was, and what effect some of her impulsive hostility might be having on him. So it was possible for client and worker to proceed rapidly. The second client, clinically classified as having a narcissistic personality disorder, was a more dependent and self-centered person, preoccupied with her own anxieties; she clung to her husband but was less giving of love herself. She had less spontaneous interest in her husband's feelings and reasons for them. She wanted and needed to talk about herself and how he had hurt her. Her understanding of the nature of her own feelings toward her husband had to be given precedence over attempts to develop her understanding of him.

The quality of a person's capacity to love others, the ego's capacity for object relationships, is of primary importance in influencing readiness for understanding others and the effects of his or her own actions upon others. An individual greatly retarded in this capacity may lack motivation to look inward for the cause of difficulties. Such a person is not sufficiently attuned to others to appreciate their feelings easily or to see the ways in which he or she provokes and hurts them. These clients are often unable to put to good use treatment that requires much self-examination. There may be introspection, but it is a narcissistic or self-pitying type of introspection. The person often can be reached only to the extent that he or she feels very strongly the worker's interest for his or her own sake. Sometimes an individual with this difficulty can be led to think of the effects of behavior on others in the context of his or her own self-interest.

It is important to add that the willingness to engage in reflection about self and others can be significantly influenced by factors other than personality. If there is a crisis or significant external pressure of any kind, self-understanding and understanding of others may be affected either positively or negatively. A person who is generally self-absorbed may be jolted into understanding the needs of another when a spouse threatens separation, for example, or when a child develops severe psychological symptoms. On the other hand, if an individual becomes seriously ill or suffers a significant loss, there may be an increase in self-preoccupation and—at least temporarily—less concern for others.

Thought Processes and Self-Understanding

The client's capacity for logical thinking (another ego quality), experience with this type of thinking, and the degree to which secondary rather than primary processes are dominant also strongly influence the extent to which reflective procedures in general can be used and the direction and pace at which the work can proceed. Can the client make only rather simple connections, or is there capacity for more sophisticated thinking? Can the person be led to reason things through independently, or must the worker explain concretely step by step? Some people know a good deal about psychological mechanisms long before they see a worker. Others are psychologically naive and must have matters explained in detail. As noted earlier, greater intellectual knowledge sometimes leads to a superficial acquiescence or to a facile denial of the importance of an interpretation, even though it may be an accurate one.

In our experience, although normal intelligence certainly facilitates reflection, superior intellectual ability does not necessarily lead to readiness to be introspective or to understand others; the talent for these reflective processes seems to be a separate capacity.

The need for a worker to distinguish between a client's sophistication about psychological theory and his or her capacity for reflection that leads to change is illustrated by the following contrasting examples:

One client, a brilliant chemist, often talked at length in treatment sessions about the "cause" of his anger with his wife, which he related to the influence of his "overprotective" and "seductive" mother. In his view, his early experiences resulted in his being wary of women, always fearful that they wanted to control him. Therefore, he would explain, when his wife made affectionate or sexual overtures, he would convert his fright into hostility. To be sure, his appraisal of his difficulties had merit, but he seemed far better motivated to perfect his elaborate analysis of himself and his reactions than he was to make changes.

In contrast, Dick Jones (Chapter 3), who was seen in marital therapy with his wife, had no advanced education and little knowledge of psychological matters. Nevertheless, his capacity for introspection led to productive work in treatment far surpassing that of the chemist. Dick Jones's quickness in understanding the nature of his passivity, its effect on his wife, and the dysfunctional pattern of interaction that had developed between them was important to the marked improvement in the marital relationship that was achieved in brief treatment.

Often, behavior similar to that the worker is trying to help the client to understand is commonplace in children and can first be understood in them. "Look, have you ever noticed how when Verne is mad at Phil (older brother) he starts jumping on Stella (little sister)?" If the client's response shows understanding—"What about that! He sure does; he just takes it out on her"—the client will probably be able to understand the same defense mechanism in her own displacement from husband to son.

For some people, however, this sort of reasoning and carryover from one situation to another are impossible, even when the interpersonal adjustment problem is acute. If the shortcoming in thought processes is not accompanied by general emotional immaturity or a severe thought disorder, progress can sometimes be made by suggestion and advice. But this is not likely to be effective unless a strong positive relationship has been established, so that the client has confidence in the worker's goodwill and good sense.

Situational and Ethnic Factors

When families are plagued with severe environmental problems, these sometimes dominate the whole gestalt so completely that reflection about relationship problems seems of little importance. Casework should then concentrate on these practical problems. Once these are alleviated, perhaps there will be motivation for tackling strain in other parts of the system such as internal family stress.[3] This was the case in the Stone family described in Chapter 3. Family members can sometimes make progress toward learning to be mutually supportive in times of stress rather than taking frustrations out on each other. Family sessions are often the best way to move toward such a goal.

Ethnic factors are extremely diverse in their significance to treatment. In some cultures there is strong aversion to discussing family troubles and complaints with outsiders. In some, men especially regard the need for such help as a disgrace and a sign of weakness. Certainly, language differences of any major proportion can be a deterrent to the kind of communication necessary for intrapsychic reflection, yet in the Garcia case (Chapter 18) such reflection was possible in spite of the worker's meager knowledge of Spanish and Mr. Garcia's limited facility with English. Differences between worker and client, as discussed in Chapter 11, can create obstacles to treatment of any type, and sometimes—although far from always—are particularly problematic when there is the need for self-understanding. The degree to which potential difficulties are prevented depends heavily on how the differences are handled by the worker. Many problems involving dissimilarities are surmountable.

Diagnostic Understanding

The specific content of any interpretation or reflective comment by the worker is directly dependent on diagnostic understanding. The worker who tries to help an individual see another person more clearly depends upon the diagnostic impression of the meaning of the other person's actions. This understanding can be expected to be more accurate than the client's only to the extent that the worker has taken more factors into consideration than has the client, has looked at the matter from the other person's point of view, is more objective and is thus not hampered by the distortion of perception that skews things for the client, and makes use of knowledge that the client does not have concerning the functioning of personalities and of interacting systems. Obviously, if the worker has met the other or others, especially in conjoint sessions in which interactional patterns become apparent, the worker's interpretations about the other people are necessarily more precise and also can be checked out with them. Often, for example, what appears to be hostility in another person is actually fear or hurt, and the recognition of this can make a difference in the client's attitude and reactions. In the Russo case, described in Chapter 16, and in other cases discussed in the family and couple chapters, family members were frequently helped in conjoint sessions to understand one another more clearly.

Specifics of what the worker seeks to help the client to become aware of and understand will depend directly upon the ongoing diagnostic assessment of what factors are contributing to the social dysfunctioning, modified constantly by what the client can assimilate and what the goals of treatment are. Only as the worker recognizes (and, preferably, witnesses in vivo) dysfunctional responses and sees the factors in personal interactions that touch off such responses can he or she enable the client also to recognize them.

The choice of procedures within the various types of person-situation reflection obviously hinges very strongly upon the kind of problem the client is trying to resolve and the worker's assessment of the factors contributing to the problem. In interpersonal problems, treatment themes usually include both outwardly and inwardly directed reflection concerning the current interactional gestalt.

It is important to realize that *clinical* diagnosis per se does not immediately point us to the selection of treatment procedures. As we have indicated in several previous chapters, in order to arrive at the point of being able to think about themselves and their situations, clients diagnosed with severe personality disorders and psychoses often require special gentleness and a large amount of support: acceptance, reassurance, encouragement, and active involvement from the worker. However, other clients—such as those with neurotic features who are very anxious or those who are in the throes of crisis—may need just as much sustainment. For very disturbed people, direct influence may be necessary to promote trust or to provide structure if they are too disorganized to provide it for themselves. For others who are equally upset, advice may arouse suspicion or hostility. Although many clients need very few directive comments from the worker, many with and without serious personality problems seek and make good use of various kinds of advice. Ventilation is necessary and helpful for almost all of our clients, but for people who are extremely disturbed lengthy and intense emotional release can result in decompensation. For others, even those with mild neurotic disorders, ventilation may result in the emotions' snowballing, frightening the clients rather than relieving them. The extent to which people usefully engage in person-situation reflection also depends on many factors other than the clinical diagnosis. As we shall illustrate in the upcoming section, pattern-dynamic and developmental reflection is useful to clients with a broad range of diagnoses.

PATTERN-DYNAMIC AND DEVELOPMENTAL REFLECTION

The decision as to whether or not to lead the client to pattern-dynamic or developmental reflection (see discussions of these procedures in Chapter 7) or to expand on clients' own spontaneous moves in this direction is again guided in psychosocial casework by the worker's diagnostic understanding. These types of reflection are encouraged when the difficulty is one for which this type of help is useful and when the client appears to be capable of participating in the process of self-understanding and is willing to do so. Developmental and dynamic understanding can help clients see how and why they are reacting in unrealistic or dysfunctional ways, strengthen their grasp of patterns and their origins, and contribute to the ability to change them. Here we are talking about repetitive intrapsychic *patterns*, not isolated instances of behavior or responses.

Motivation

Opportunities for developing more than isolated bits of understanding arise primarily when clients are motivated to develop considerable self-understanding. Such motivation often occurs when individuals are caught in a crisis or faced by developmental changes within themselves or within members of their families. Instances of the latter are the birth of a child, especially the first one, a wife's decision to work outside the home, a husband's decision to change to a radically different form of work, the departure of grown children from the home, and death in the family. These rather sudden changes may overtax the ego defense system or upset a longtime balance of intrapsychic or family forces. Dynamic or developmental reflection is not always needed, but in many instances it is exceedingly helpful in enabling the client to deal with the new situation.

These procedures can also be particularly useful and interesting to clients when they are dissatisfied with their ways of relating to others or with feelings about themselves or when they feel that they are not living up to their abilities in study or work. Clients' motivation for developing pattern-dynamic and developmental understanding sometimes develops only after they finally recognize that they *cannot change other people* but *can* change themselves. The procedures can be very helpful in many family or other relationship problems when current person-situation reflection is not sufficient to enable the person to change dysfunctional ways of interrelating with others.

Widespread Use

Some years ago, when we were first attempting to understand the significance of the clinical diagnosis for choice of treatment procedures, some of us thought that one could generalize to the point of saying that efforts to help clients understand the dynamics of their psychological functioning and its development should be limited to individuals who appeared to be only mildly neurotic. This turned out to be extremely simplistic and misleading. Actual examination of work that was being done by skillful practitioners showed that these techniques were being used more widely than had been anticipated and that broad diagnostic classification was only, at best, a rough indicator of when they could be helpful. Finer criteria that related to assessment of various aspects of ego and superego functioning, ability to deal with anxiety, motivation, interpersonal and other situational factors, and so on, began to be developed.

The cases discussed in detail in other chapters of this book demonstrate how clients with a wide range of problems and clinical diagnoses were able to participate in pattern-dynamic and developmental reflection. These reflective procedures, combined with person situation reflection and frequent use of sustainment, were, to varying degrees, components of the long-term treatment of Mrs. Zimmer (Chapter 3), diagnosed as having a borderline personality disorder. Dick and Susan Jones (Chapter 3), both basically sound psychologically, were able to be introspective about their personality patterns and their early life experiences as they worked to resolve their relationship difficulties. Mrs. Barry (Chapter 21), diagnosed as having paranoid schizophrenia, astonished the worker with her capacity for making connections between her present situation, her father's alcoholism, and her position as the overlooked "middle child." Mrs. Stasio (Chapter 21), faced with terminal cancer and an awareness of some of her neurotic patterns, used these types of intrareflection a number of times in her treatment experience. Although originally involuntary clients, both Mr. and Mrs. Carter (Chapter 21) were able to reflect on patterns of behavior that had interfered with their functioning and family life. Jed Cooper (Chapter 21), whose anxiety had many hysterical features, was able to make helpful connections between his current difficulties and his complicated ties to his parents. Mr. Russo (Chapter 16), although not characteristically given to introspection, was able to reflect movingly in family sessions on how the early death of his mother and frequent changes of foster homes when he was a boy had contributed to the depression he suffered at the time his older daughter moved away from home. Tom and Kathy Brent (Chapter 18) were both able to link up the significant deprivations of their childhood with the dysfunctional interactional patterns of their marriage.

ANXIETY AND GUILT

Assessment of the degree of anxiety and understanding of the client's way of handling it are very important considerations in the choice of treatment procedures, and especially so in intrareflection. Although we have commented a number of times on the significance of this factor, further points remain to be considered and reemphasized. Anxiety and guilt may logically be discussed together, for guilt is one form of anxiety—in Anna Freud's words,[4] the ego's fear of the superego—and what is said about anxiety in general applies with equal force to guilt. Anna Freud also called attention to anxiety caused by the ego's fear of the instincts or drives: that is, fear that thoughts, feelings, and actions not approved by ego or superego will break through despite efforts to control them. This form of fear is especially prevalent in psychosis and in severe personality disorders.

Sensitivity to the actual existence of anxiety and to the degree to which it is present in the client at any one moment is essential, as is awareness of the extent to which the client chronically carries anxiety around or is vulnerable to its arousal. What particular elements in the client's present or past provoke this anxiousness? How does this anxiety show itself, and how does the client handle it? Does anxiety impel the client to behavior that creates problems or that he or she later regrets? Does it result in increased psychological or somatic symptomatology? What defenses does the cli-

ent use against it? Is the person immobilized? Will he or she run away from treatment? In what ways does the client try to get relief, and do they work?

Observation of Anxiety

In order to be alert to the presence of anxiety in the client, one must be aware of the ways in which it expresses itself. Occasionally, clients spontaneously say that they feel anxious. Sometimes, anxiety is shown physically, by trembling of body or voice, body tenseness, sweating or pallor, nervous gestures or excitement, and so on.[5] Sometimes the client reveals it by posture, sitting on the edge of the chair or at a distance, wrapping a coat tightly or refusing to take it off. When a person has been seen at least a few times, the worker may be able to spot anxiety because the client's demeanor has changed in some way. Most often, anxiety shows itself in increased use of the client's characteristic defense mechanisms. The intellectual may go off into theoretical, often contentious discussions; defensive hostility erupts in the challenge that treatment is not helping, with the implication that the worker is incompetent; rationalization, reaction formation, denial—any of the mechanisms of defense—may be brought into play in their characteristic role of attempting to protect the individual from experiencing anxiety. Avoidance may finally result in the client's skipping interviews altogether. If these signs of anxiety are recognized early enough, they can alert the worker to the presence of anxiety and the need to discuss the problem with the client. *Resistance* is often a manifestation of anxiety; ways of handling it are discussed in the previous chapter. Sensitivity to the presence of anxiety needs to be accompanied by awareness of the conditions under which anxiety tends to be high, both for clients in general and for the particular individual(s) with whom one is working.

Anxiety and the Treatment Process

We have already commented in earlier chapters on the many ways in which anxiety can be aroused by the use of various treatment procedures. A brief review at this point will emphasize the importance of this factor in applying diagnostic understanding to the treatment process. Reflective consideration of intrapsychic content is by no means the only set of treatment procedures by which anxiety is aroused. Merely describing, as part of the application process, life events of which one is ashamed may be a very painful, anxiety-provoking experience. Ventilation that involves the expression of emotions or desires of which the client is afraid may bring fear that talking will be a forerunner of acting. Guilt may very easily be aroused in a sensitive person by discussions that produce awareness for the first time of the harmful effects of his actions on others or even of needs of his child or wife to which he has been blind. The individual with a very severe superego will feel guilt very keenly whenever matters in which he or she appears to be even slightly in the wrong are raised. Even when the worker merely listens, such an individual anticipates criticism, often projecting his or her own self-condemnation onto the worker; the person then may fear loss of love or the worker's indifference and may in self-defense blame the worker or resort to outright denial or defensive hostility or even withdraw from treatment.

Even the giving of suggestions and advice, under certain conditions, can arouse anxiety.

In one case a worker was greatly concerned about the severity with which an impulsive mother was in the habit of disciplining her seven-year-old son. Early in the contact, the worker advised her against this and was gratified at the change in her client's handling of the child and his immediate improvement. Unfortunately, however, she had not made a careful diagnostic study of the mother or thought ahead to the possible consequences of her advice. In the first place, the child had never been controlled in any other way. His initial reaction was to be very good, but, as might have been foreseen, he soon began to explore the limits of his new freedom and became increasingly defiant of his now disarmed mother.

In addition to being impulsive, the mother had a great deal of compulsiveness in her makeup. A more thorough assessment would have identified the clinical signs of this, which is usually accompanied by a severe conscience and a strong wish to please. Along with her impulsivity, then, this woman had a need, carried over from childhood, to win the approval of others, especially those in authority. She tried very hard to be a good mother along the lines the worker suggested. In fact, however, after the initial good news of improvement in the child, she found it very hard to let the worker know that things were not going so well. This also could have been foreseen. Eventually, one day "all hell let loose," and her anger against her son burst forth in a potentially dangerous way. Then, to justify herself, she had to condemn the child as uncontrollable by any other means and turned completely away from the worker and her advice.

Self-Understanding   On the whole, the development of understanding of oneself and one's own functioning, whether in discussion of the current person-situation interaction or of personality patterns, tends to arouse more anxiety than do other treatment processes. The reasons for this are several. These are types of self-examination. As the client becomes involved in such treatment, he or she may become more acutely aware than previously of his or her faulty functioning. This realization can cause discomfort and pain, particularly, again, if the client has a severe superego. These discomforts, in turn, frequently stir up anger at the worker, the bearer of ill tidings, who causes the client still more discomfort.

Uneasiness may also arise when clients, in individual or conjoint treatment, develop enough self-awareness to realize the degree to which they have been attributing their emotional responses and behavior to the actions of others: "When he criticized me the other morning, I was too devastated to go to work." Or, "I will never be happy again now that my daughter plans to marry outside our faith." Or, "I can't tell my wife that I would like to go out in the evening with my friends occasionally, because she would get too angry with me." As will be discussed more fully in the family and couple chapters, very often in families where interactions are chronically dysfunctional, family members are hesitant to change well-established patterns—as a result of fear of abandonment, of being overwhelmed, of being disloyal, etc.—and therefore become extremely anxious about the prospect of making changes even when it becomes evident that these could bring relief and satisfaction.

Preconscious Material Anxiety can be great, too, when treatment involves the client's bringing to consciousness memories and realizations that have been hidden, or at least that a person has not talked about with others. These matters would not be hidden away if they were not in some way painful. It may be the pain of sorrow or frustration. Or the superego may be affronted, for the client may be defying parental standards in producing particular memories or becoming aware of certain feelings and attitudes. Adults who were victims of incest or abuse as children sometimes have totally or partially blocked recollections of their painful experiences and the fears, guilt, and confusion attached to them; if memories begin to return, spontaneously or in the treatment process, a

great deal of anxiety often accompanies them.[6] Anxieties surrounding preconscious material are similar to those experienced by patients in psychoanalysis, who feel them even more strongly in relation to deeply unconscious, repressed material, material that is generally not accessible through procedures used in casework. In analysis, this is recognized as a principal source of resistance, and in casework a similar factor is involved. Painful early experiences have sometimes been of such traumatic proportions that extreme anxiety would be involved in reliving them. In such cases there is usually strong resistance to recalling them, and this should serve as a caution signal to the worker. This can be true even for adults who, for example, suffered the extremes of persecution during the Holocaust or for men and women who witnessed or endured the horrors and atrocities of war. Some of these painful experiences were so very difficult to assimilate that they could be surmounted only as they could be walled off by suppressions and repressions that, more often than not, it would be unwise to disturb.

On the whole, a past experience that arouses anxiety deriving from the pain of reliving the experience is more easily borne than one that also arouses guilt or humiliation. If, for instance, the memory involves actions or even feelings and wishes that the individual thinks are shameful or wrong, fear of the worker's disapproval may be very strong. Guilt is frequently associated with childhood hostilities toward parents and others in families in whom such high value was placed on surface amiability that all anger had to be hidden. It is also associated in many people in our culture with childhood sexuality, with masturbation, with homosexual thoughts or behavior, and with so-called sexual perversions of various sorts. Both individual and cultural values are strong determinants here. For one person, hostile feelings will be taboo and shameful; for another, lying; for still another, erotic responsiveness.

Other Sources Even positive feelings in treatment can cause anxiety in some people. Some individuals who have been badly hurt in close relationships fear further suffering if they allow themselves to come too close to others; uneasiness may develop as they begin to experience warm feelings toward their worker. Others fear entrapment or engulfment. It is important, then, that the worker try to assess consequences of one's own expressions of warmth or strongly supportive communications, avoiding them when they might be misinterpreted or frighten a client.

Fear of change itself may be present in any form of treatment having as its goal some degree of change in personality functioning or behavior. Even though present ways of functioning cause discomfort, they usually also have some secondary advantages. Anticipated changes may require greater self-control, less expression of hostility, less blame of others, more altruistic and less self-centered behavior. The client may desire change but may also feel uneasy about it and reluctant to give up old ways—because of fear, as we said earlier—or because in some respects these ways are comforting and self-gratifying.

This is not to say that intrareflection is universally anxiety-arousing. Certain themes, even when they are dynamically or developmentally explored, may be fairly low in their anxiety potential and therefore can safely be explored even in so-called fragile personalities.

A case in point is that of a woman diagnosed as having a schizophrenic disorder who was able to see that her suspicious expectation of hostile attack from a woman in her current life was a displacement from childhood experiences in which she had been very badly treated by a harsh grandmother. Discussion of the circumstances not only did not arouse anxiety but actually allayed it. Talking about her memories of her grandmother's cruel behavior was not frightening because the worker did not attempt to explore whether the client was partly at "fault" but accepted the situation as having been extremely painful and a regrettable hardship. Recognition of the possibility of displacement also involved no blame for the client; instead, it gave her a rational explanation for some of her fears, so that she was able to look more realistically at the lack of evidence in the current situation to justify them.

Anxiety Reduction

Clients sometimes find great relief in talking about painful experiences in the presence of a sympathetic worker who is not overwhelmed by their ventilation. This process may help the ego to assimilate the memories, to be less afraid of them, to be more able to bear the pain involved, and to express the natural emotions of grief and anger associated with the experiences. Such verbal activity is similar to the play activities of children, in which they repeat painful and frightening experiences in an effort to assimilate them. When the happenings that are being aired are also responsible for some current reaction that is causing clients trouble, they may in the very same interview also experience a sense of relief from talking about them. For instance, a person who as a child had very critical parents, and consequent feelings of distrust in his or her abilities, may obtain almost immediate relief from talking about their unjust criticisms. By sensing the worker's confirmation that they were indeed unjust, the client can experience some freeing from the earlier acceptance of the parents' views. Reflective procedures may also be used to help the client think about why the parents were harsh or punitive; realization that their behaviors were derived from pressures or unhappiness in their own lives, having little to do with the client as a young child, often produces not only relief but a reduction of internalized self-blame. Of course, if the parents are living and able to attend conjoint sessions, acknowledgment and explanations from them usually can be more forceful than reassurances from the worker or speculations by the client.

In any event, the main reason that clients pursue understanding in spite of anxiety is the satisfaction gained from new realizations about themselves, their fears, self-criticisms, and inhibitions. A load is often lifted, and sometimes genuine excitement is felt as insight exposes an encumbering defense. Understanding gained about childhood sources of unhappiness or about parents' actions in and of itself often results in significant relief.

There is much the worker can do in helping the client deal with anxiety. Of primary importance is the worker's continuous attitude of support and acceptance, which softens the impact of comments. When this is communicated to clients, they can find support in a basic security with the worker; whatever the exigencies of the moment, clients can then hold to a strong underlying conviction that the worker feels positive toward them, respects them, and is endeavoring to help them. This conviction is inevitably obscured, from time to time at difficult moments in treatment, by transference elements and by projection of clients' own attitudes. Such distortions can be corrected, however, only if the actual relationship is a positive one and is fundamentally perceived as such by the clients. To achieve this basic relationship and keep it alive, both direct and indirect sustainment are important.

Worker Style and Client Anxiety

What might be called the "form" or "style" of worker communications used in promoting reflective thinking also has direct bearing on clients' potential anxiety. Worker comments can vary, as we have seen, from direct interpretation or explanation to completely nonsuggestive questions or comments that merely draw the client's attention to something the worker would like the person to consider. An illustration of the latter is the repetition of the last phrase or so of something the client has said. In general, the more open-ended a worker comment is the less likely it is to arouse anxiety, since it can be ignored; if clients are not ready to follow the worker's lead, they can easily respond without any recognition of the matter to which the worker is trying to draw attention. More direct comments and questions push clients harder, and interpretations, of course, formulate an opinion with which the client must deal. To illustrate these points, a worker might make one of the following comments to a woman whose father apparently sexualized his relationship with her when she was young: "Were there any other things about your experiences with your father that made you uneasy?" Or, "Is it possible that your father turned to you for some kind of affection or comfort since his relationship with your mother was so contentious?" Or, "It seems that there was a great deal of sexual tension between you and your father when you were a child." Other factors being equal, the more direct the comment the greater the possibility of stirring up anxiety.

A worker always searches for ways to express ideas that support rather than hurt, even though questions and comments may also generate anxiety. Sometimes interpretations can be softened by humorous wording. When clients have gained some understanding, the worker—who, naturally, is pleased—may "reward" them. Sometimes this is put into words: "Even though it was hard, you've done a good job of thinking that through." Just as often, facial expression and tone of voice communicate the feeling that the client has taken a step forward.

Balancing Anxiety and Movement

When a basically secure relationship has been established, clients often make very good use of anxiety-provoking comments. It is sometimes necessary to refrain from reassuring and comforting remarks at specific points in order to keep the client at work pursuing understanding of difficulties.

To illustrate: A woman who tends to be extremely critical of her husband tells the caseworker about an incident in which this tendency was prominent and half apologizes for her disparaging words. The worker may either make a reassuring remark about the distress she must have felt that prompted her to castigate her husband or comment more directly, if the basic relationship is a good one: "You *do* have a sharp tongue!" Or, with a light touch, "How did those cutting remarks affect your husband?" The latter procedures will not be very reassuring. They will increase rather than decrease the client's anxiety and, if the worker has correctly gauged her ego and superego qualities, will serve to motivate her to reflect on her overreaction or her communication style. Great care must be exercised in finding the balance by which to give enough warmth and security to nourish progress and protect the client from excessive anxiety and at the same time to maintain a level of tension conducive to motivation toward self-understanding.

A worker sensitive to either the likelihood of anxiety or its actual presence can often help the client bring this into the open, thereby reducing it. "Perhaps it scares you a little to tell me about this." Or, "I guess that was a tough question." Or, during an anxiety-arousing interview, "Let me know if you think we're going too fast." Remarks such as these may not only provide relief but also promote feedback from the client as part of his or her responsibility for guiding the treatment. If it seems wise to go on, the worker can proceed in a number of ways. Sometimes it is possible to draw the client's attention to defensiveness. At other times, it may be necessary to work first on the personality characteristic that makes the individual respond so strongly: with compulsive clients, for instance, the overly severe superego and perfectionism.

At other times it is necessary to have a period of relaxation in treatment, in which the worker says directly or in effect, "Perhaps later you will feel more able to talk about this." And at still other times, when the worker has good reason to think that the client is close to talking about certain experiences but is afraid to do so, ways can be found for framing a question or comment that relieve guilt or anxiety before the frightening content is actually expressed.

It can happen that after a difficult episode of self-understanding, the client, in the next interview, stays on superficial or self-congratulatory material. This relaxation may be necessary. A balance needs to be found between relaxing and sustaining measures, on the one hand, and procedures pressing toward self-understanding and change on the other.

When anxiety or guilt or shame is either chronically very high or aroused by the experiences the client is having when he or she comes for treatment, a goodly measure of sustaining procedures, especially indirect sustainment, is of particular value. There are times, for instance, when it is well to draw the client out about experiences in which he or she has played an especially helpful role. Or one may refer to good motivation even while pointing out mistakes a person has made. In individual or conjoint sessions, the situation can be reframed: "You obviously meant to be helpful to Johnnie even though you frightened him by treating him the same way your father treated you." Or, "You came across as angry at your wife even though you were trying to tell her how very hurt you were feeling." It is important, of course, that such supportive interpretations be realistic.

If the client is unable or unwilling to deal with anxiety, one can refrain from pursuing anxiety-arousing content. It may be possible later, when the client has gained strength or is more trusting of the worker, to reintroduce it; or, on the other hand, worker and client may agree that this particular content may have to remain untouched. Timing and sequence are always important. The worker's continuous diagnostic assessment of the client and sensitivity to current moods and reactions can enable him or her to avoid observations and insights for which the client is not yet—or, for that matter, may never be—ready.

If treatment is kept close to the realities of life, if person-situation reflection is the central focus, the client who develops more understanding usually experiences improvement in interpersonal relationships. Clients receive new responses from others in reaction to changes in their ways of handling matters. Indeed, in situations in which this is lacking, it is very difficult for clients not to become too discouraged to continue. This is one of the reasons—when at all possible—for seeing all individuals involved in problems of interpersonal adjustment.

If the worker is sensitively attuned to the client by means of accurate diagnostic assessment of both underlying personality patterns and nuances of feelings and reactions while interviews are in process, casework is not basically a painful process. There are, of course, ups and downs from interview to interview. But if efforts to develop understanding of self and others are well paced, clients can experience satisfaction and even excitement in their greater grasp of their dilemmas and increased ability to cope with them. They can also experience a strengthening of self-esteem, for the relationship in many ways is a nourishing one.

We have been endeavoring, in this chapter, to delineate ways in which the casework treatment procedures used to help a client rest upon the worker's differential understanding of a wide range of characteristics of the client and the personal-social situation. Treatment is always an individualized blend of the objectives mutually arrived at by client and worker, the themes or subgoals in the service of these objectives, and the procedures which develop these themes. The nature of the blend is not a matter of individual artistry or intuition, important though these may be. On the contrary, choice and emphasis follow definite principles and rest upon a most careful evaluation of the nature of clients' problems, external and internal etiological factors and their modifiability, and clients' objectives, motivation, and pertinent personality factors. In addition, there must be comprehension of the nature, effects, and demands of the different types of casework procedures and of the criteria by which the worker can match clients' needs and capacities with the particular combination of procedures most likely to be of value in enabling clients to overcome, or at least to lessen, their difficulties. As much as possible, treatment is a shared process in which client feedback is encouraged and often modifies the course the therapy takes. It should by now be clear that the process of diagnostic assessment is an ongoing one, with the emphasis in treatment varying in harmony with the changing needs, capacities, and wishes of the clients.[7]

We mention here a point that will be elaborated upon in the chapters on family and couple treatment. Obviously, conjoint interviews are more complex than individual treatment sessions. Nevertheless, *all of Hollis's six major categories of treatment procedures can be used in family and couple interviews as well as in one-to-one meetings.* Of course, the meaning of a particular worker communication may be different for every person who hears it, and therefore the worker must assess possible consequences of a particular intervention on *all* who are present.

NOTES

1. See good examples of this in Bernard Neugebore, "Opportunity Centered Social Services," *Social Work,* 15 (April 1970), 47–52. Many of the references in Chapter 8, note 9, also address this issue.

2. Florence Hollis, "Continuance and Discontinuance in Marital Counseling and Some Observation on Joint Interviews," *Social Casework*, 49 (March 1968), 167 174.

3. Good discussions of related points can be found in Geoffrey B. Barnes et al., "Team Treatment for Abusive Families," *Social Casework*, 55 (December 1974), 600–611; Thomas P. Brennan et al., "Forensic Social Work: Practice and Vision," *Social Casework*, 67 (June 1986), 340–350; Henry Freeman et al., "Can a Family Agency Be Relevant to the Inner Urban Scene?" *Social Casework*, 51 (January 1970), 12–21; Esther Krystal et al., "Serving the Unemployed," *Social Casework*, 64 (February 1983), 67–76; Norman Ostbloom and Sedahlia Jasper Crase, "A Model for Conceptualizing Child Abuse Causation and Intervention," *Social Casework*, 61 (March 1980), 164–172; Eleanor Pavenstedt, ed., *The Drifters: Children of Disorganized Lower-Class Families* (Boston: Little, Brown, 1967); and Arthur Pierson, "Social Work Techniques with the Poor," *Social Casework*, 51 (October 1970), 481–485.

4. Anna Freud, *The Ego and the Mechanisms of Defense* (New York: International Universities Press, 1946), pp. 58–60.

5. Lotte Marcus, "The Effect of Extralinguistic Phenomena on the Judgment of Anxiety" (doctoral dissertation, Columbia University School of Social Work, New York, 1969).

6. See Jill Blake-White and Christine Madeline Kline, "Treating the Dissociative Process in Adult Victims of Childhood Incest," *Social Casework*, 66 (September 1985), 394–402.

7. As supplements to references already cited in this chapter and previous chapters on casework diagnosis and treatment, the following are relevant. In addition to useful theoretical discussions of diagnosis and treatment, many of the readings also provide clinical case illustrations: Lucille Austin, "Dynamics and Treatment of the Client with Anxiety Hysteria," in Howard J. Parad, ed., *Ego Psychology and Dynamic Casework* (New York: Family Service Association of America, 1958). Bernice Ballen, "The Growth of Psychoanalytic Developmental Psychology and the Application of Technique," *Clinical Social Work Journal*, 8 (Spring 1980), 28–37. Bernard Bandler, "The Concept of Ego Supportive Psychotherapy," in Howard J. Parad and Roger R. Miller, eds., *Ego-Oriented Casework: Problems and Perspectives* (New York: Family Service Association of America, 1963). Catherine Bittermann, "Marital Adjustment Patterns of Clients with Compulsive Character Disorders: Implications for Treatment," *Social Casework*, 47 (November 1966), 575–582. Margaret C. Bonnefil, "Therapist, Save My Child: A Family Crisis Case," *Clinical Social Work Journal*, 7 (Spring 1979), 6–14. Margaret C. Bonnefil, "The Relationship of Interpersonal Acting-Out to the Process of Decompensation," *Clinical Social Work Journal*, 1 (Spring 1973), 13–21. Linde A. Chernos, "Clinical Issues in Alcoholism Treatment," *Social Casework*, 66 (February 1985), 67–75. Tamar Cohen, "The Incestuous Family Revisited," *Social Casework*, 64 (March 1983), 154–161. Joyce Edward, "The Use of the Dream in the Promotion of Ego Development," *Clinical Social Work Journal*, 6 (Winter 1978), 262–273. Miriam Elson, *Self Psychology in Clinical Social Work* (New York: W. W. Norton, 1986). Anne O. Freed, "Social Casework: More Than a Modality," *Social Casework*, 58 (April 1977), 204–213. Jennie S. Fuller, "Duo Therapy Case Studies: Process and Techniques," *Social Casework*, 58 (February 1977), 84–91. Howard Goldstein, "Toward the Integration of Theory and Practice: A Humanistic Approach," *Social Work*, 31 (September–October 1986), 352–357. Judith A. B. Lee and Susan J. Rosenthal, "Working with Victims of Violent Assault," *Social Casework*, 64 (December 1983), 593–601. Lois Lester, "The Special Needs of the Female Alcoholic," *Social Casework*, 63 (October 1982), 451–456. Celia Leikin, "Identifying and Treating the Alcoholic Client," *Social Casework*, 67 (February 1986), 67–73. Hilliard Levinson, "Communication with an Adolescent in Psychotherapy," *Social Casework*, 54 (October 1973), 480 488. Lorraine Pokart Levy, "Services to Parents of Children in a Psychiatric Hospital," *Social Casework*, 58 (April 1977), 204–213. Florence Lieberman, ed., *Clinical Social Workers as Psychotherapists* (New York: Gardner Press, 1982). Sophie Loewenstein, "An Overview of the Concept of Narcissism," *Social Casework*, 58 (March 1977), 136–142. Herta Mayer and Gerald Schamess, "Long Term Treatment for the Disadvantaged," *Social Casework*, 50 (March 1969), 138–145. Roger S. Miller, "Disappointment in Therapy," *Clinical Social Work Journal*, 5 (Spring 1977), 17–28. Judith Marks Mishne, *Clinical Work with Adolescents* (New York: Free Press, 1986). Ben A. Orcutt, "Family Treatment of Poverty Level Families," *Social Casework*, 58 (February

1976), 92–100. Joseph Palumbo, "Perceptual Deficits and Self-Esteem in Adolescence," *Clinical Social Work Journal*, 7 (Spring 1979), 34–61. Renee Pellman et al., "The Van: A Mobile Approach to Services for Adolescents," *Social Casework*, 58 (May 1977), 268–273. Wendy Ranan and Andrea Blodgett, "Using Telephone Therapy for 'Unreachable' Clients," *Social Casework*, 64 (January 1983), 39–44. Pauline I. Scanlon, "Social Work with the Mentally Retarded Client," *Social Casework*, 59 (March 1978), 161–166. Bertha G. Simos, "Grief Therapy to Facilitate Healthy Restitution," *Social Casework*, 58 (June 1977), 337–342. Max Siporin, "The Therapeutic Process in Clinical Social Work," *Social Work*, 28 (May–June 1983), 193–198. Harry Specht and Riva Specht, "Social Work Assessment: Route to Clienthood," Part I, *Social Casework*, 67 (November 1986), 525–532; Part II, *Social Casework*, 67 (December 1986), 587–593. Ronald L. Taylor, "Marital Therapy in the Treatment of Incest," *Social Casework*, 65 (April 1984), 195–202. Francis J. Turner, ed., *Adult Psychopathology: A Social Work Perspective* (New York: Free Press, 1984). Francis J. Turner, ed., *Differential Diagnosis and Treatment in Social Work*, 3d ed. (New York: Free Press, 1983). This is an excellent source for articles pertinent to the relationship between diagnostic factors and treatment. His prefaces to the three editions are included and recommended. M. Ellen Walsh, "Rural Social Work Practice: Clinical Quality," *Social Casework*, 62 (October 1981), 458–464. Pauline Young-Eisendrath, "Ego Development: Inferring the Client's Frame of Reference," *Social Casework*, 63 (June 1982), 323–332.

CHAPTER 15

Family Therapy and Psychosocial Casework: A Theoretical Synthesis

One of the most distressing paradoxes of recent decades is that at the same time that the support of the family structure is needed the most, the turbulence of the larger social system has endangered it. Federal and state governments have cut back on aid and services to families and children, with the result that large numbers of people are left wanting for the most basic necessities. As American society has become more impersonal and bureaucratized, it has rendered people in ever greater need of the shelter and solace of family life. Concurrently, rapid social changes and widespread shifts in traditional values have had a disturbing effect on the quality of family relationships, often depriving the individual members of essential built-in supports.

Indeed, the family is being challenged from within as well as from without. Families have given up some of their former functions: socialization of the very young and nursing care of the old and ailing, for example, are shared with the broader community. Although still discriminated against in the workplace, women are nevertheless more independent economically than ever before. It is estimated that, by 1990,

85 percent of married couples will have two employed spouses; the vast majority of women work at paying jobs and do most of the housework as well. Traditional sex-role relationships have been challenged and, to varying degrees, have undergone significant changes. Many customary family patterns have died out and unfamiliar lifestyles have sprung up. Often families splinter and disperse. The divorce rate is more than double what it was in 1967. Many children are now living in single-parent homes. Homeless families try to survive in cities and towns where housing is unavailable and temporary shelters are inadequate at best and life-threatening at worst. When the family has been weakened or fractured, it may be unable to fulfill its ideal—if never fully realized—function as a haven of love and acceptance. Spouse and child abuse, homicide, teenage suicide, and substance abuse are tragic indicators of how quality family life can buckle under the strain of internal and external assaults. With greater frequency than ever, we hear people denying any commitment to their families. Marriages are being delayed and large numbers of young people are choosing to remain unattached.[1] There

are even some who question whether the American family as an institution will survive the forces that threaten to undermine it.

In our view, however, it is inevitable that some form of family life will endure. No adequate substitute has been found for the nurturance and socialization of the young. The family has been central to molding personalities, to defining values and worldviews; the child's innermost emotional development is derived in large measure from experiences in the home. Family relationships cannot be compared to any other social connections in the depth and intensity of their effect upon individual members. And, indeed, "the family is the cell to which people revert in times of social disorganization."[2] In spite of the many changes it has undergone, and the diversity of lifestyles it now encompasses, the modern family is still seen by many of its members of all ages as the primary place for comfort and refuge from the larger, unpredictable world. We agree with Zimmerman that "most families, despite or because of changing structures and a frequently unfriendly environment, are performing their functions and meeting the needs of their members and society apparently better than society is meeting the needs of families."[3]

The failure of social institutions to provide adequate services to families, along with changing family structures and values, have required social workers to examine and expand their approaches to practice.[4] The burgeoning and ongoing expansion of the family therapy movement, now over thirty years old, has been, in part, a response to the need to counteract the disruption of the traditional family network in times of unsettling change.[5] It is beyond the limits of these chapters to present an overview of the literature or to review in detail the often disparate points of view that have flooded the family therapy field.[6] Nevertheless, our intent is to provide a synthesis of some of the basic concepts and to demonstrate that these relatively recent developments in family treatment have broadened casework theory and provide us with additional procedures for assessment and intervention. The psychosocial approach, with its commitment to understanding families and interpersonal relationships, is uniquely equipped not only to assimilate the principles but to contribute to their synthesis.

FAMILY GROUP TREATMENT AND THE SOCIAL CASEWORK TRADITION

The family outlook is woven into the fabric of the social work tradition. From the earliest days of the profession, social workers have recognized the importance of family life to the healthy development and functioning of its individual members. The report of the first White House Conference on Child Welfare in 1909 defined home life as "the highest and finest product of civilization" and urged that homes not be broken up for reasons of poverty alone.[7]

In her groundbreaking work of 1917, *Social Diagnosis,* Mary Richmond was remarkably cognizant of the need to study the individual in interaction with the environment. Recognizing what we, today, may take for granted, the pioneering Miss Richmond pointed out that the individual must also be regarded in the context of the family group:

> Family caseworkers welcome the opportunity to see at the very beginning of intercourse several of the members of the family assembled in their own home environment, acting and reacting upon one another, each taking a share in the development of the client's story, each revealing in ways other than words social facts of real significance.[8]

In less quaint language, perhaps, current family therapists, including those interested in home visits and nonverbal communication, share her approach to understanding the family.

Over sixty years later, Miss Richmond's advice can serve to remind us that "the man should be seen," and that other relatives (now referred to as the "extended family") must not be overlooked. How modern her ideas seem to us as we read "The need of keeping the family in mind extends beyond the period of diagnosis, of course." Without a family view, "we would find that the good results of individual treatment crumble away." Miss Richmond had a prophetic grasp of the "drift of family life," as she called it, that heralded casework's understanding of the complexities of family interrelationships.[9]

Social casework continued to emphasize the interdependence of people and their environments. Nevertheless, after World War I, the field began to take a serious interest in psychology, which strongly influenced the profession in the 1920s. In spite of keen concern with the problems of the "real world" during the depression years of the 1930s, Freudian ideas were also taking hold and by 1940 social work was inundated by psychoanalytic thinking. During these periods, social workers temporarily abandoned some of their interest in the broader social issues. Never, however, did these shifts to more intense fascination with the inner emotional life of the individual client totally obscure the significance of family history and interaction. Caseworkers, vital contributors to the mental hygiene and child guidance movements of the 1920s and 1930s, realized that the behavioral and emotional problems of children as well as the mental disorders of adults were profoundly influenced by family relationships. However reasonable—or even agreeably received—the worker's advice to a client's relatives was not enough. Family members needed treatment, too, if the problems of the individual (or, nowadays, the "index client" or "identified patient") were to be resolved.

By the late 1930s, caseworkers in family welfare (now family service) agencies were also working "above the poverty line," ministering to the emotional and interpersonal disturbances of family life as well as to the financial and environmental aspects. Although frequently the individual was of major interest, family case-

work objectives of almost a half century ago were broadened to include "remedial and preventive treatment of social and emotional difficulties that produce maladjustment in the family," "intrafamily harmony," and development of "the capacities of all family members to the fullest."[10] In short, neither environmental assistance to the family, on the one hand, nor treatment of the individual out of his milieu, on the other, were deemed sufficiently helpful. Many caseworkers recognized that the family as a whole required attention.

Gordon Hamilton, in her classic introductory text on psychosocial casework, built on the earlier casework approach to the family as the "unit of work." Today's family therapists would have little quarrel with her view:

> Using "group process" in family life does several things: it locates and clarifies the problem through discussion; it permits expression of opinions; it dissipates anxiety for each child, because the situation is shared with the other, as well as with the worker; and this participation releases ability to move toward action. Work with families inevitably includes children, adults, adolescents, young married couples, and the aged; none of these can be treated as isolated problems, because of the nature of social relationships themselves.

She added, "there are considerations of family balance and behavior as a group as well as from the point of view of each individual member." In the ordinary course of the child's development, she said, "first through identification and then through increasing the psychological 'distance' between the self and the persons around him...[he] moves healthily out of the 'undifferentiated unity'...of the parent-child relationship."[11]

Hamilton's concepts preceded the family therapy movement, yet they had much in common with ideas that followed. Jackson's work on "family homeostasis," Bowen's notion of the "undifferentiated family ego mass," and the concept of "individuation," are elaborations and refinements of these rudimentary formulations of Hamilton. Mudd, Josselyn, and Hollis, too, were among those who took early steps to develop a family-centered approach to family and marital problems.[12]

Modern-day family treatment, like casework, rests on a blend of knowledge, theory, and "practice wisdom" from various disciplines and sciences, with input from psychoanalytic, communication and systems theories, ego psychology, and several of the social sciences. Diverse schools of thought abound, however, with much controversy stirring within family therapy circles. The student (and, indeed, the practitioner, supervisor, or teacher) is faced with a staggering array of material about family dynamics and treatment procedures, as would be expected in a new field. One bibliography listed some two thousand articles and books published on family therapy between 1950 and 1970;[13] that number has probably tripled by now. The deluge confounds us less, however, as soon as we recognize that many of the new concepts and techniques can be embraced comfortably by the psychosocial framework. If, in the past, casework's family orientation was in some ways underdeveloped, the seeds were there. The ever growing family therapy movement adds impetus to the creative integration of the wealth of theory, specialized techniques, and research that flow from practice.

Social work professionals, although not always sufficiently credited with their contributions to the movement, can be proud of their place in the rapid growth of family treatment. They have not simply received and assimilated theory and procedures; they have been in the forefront of their development. In fact, Siporin reminds us, until recently, social workers were viewed as *the* experts in family practice; in mental health or child guidance clinics and hospitals, for example, the individual whom we now refer to as the "identified patient" was often seen by a psychiatrist or psychologist, but parents, spouses, and family groups were routinely assigned to social workers.[14] A most renowned trailblazer, Nathan Ackerman, credited much of his early work in family treatment to his association with a social work family agency Jewish Family Service.[15] Virginia Satir, Frances Scherz, Arthur Leader, Sanford Sherman, and Harry Aponte are among many others with social work backgrounds who have made substantial contributions to family treatment.[16] Many graduate schools of social work have developed curricula and research in family studies and treatment practices.[17] Some social workers view casework and family therapy as separate practices. We, on the other hand, see no need to choose between them. Later in this chapter we will discuss more fully how, in our view, the psychosocial framework can theoretically accommodate the principles of family treatment.

CHANGE, STRESS, AND FAMILY ADAPTATION

Without exception, families are repeatedly required to adapt to stress and change. Over time, roles must be modified, positions shifted, and patterns of behavior adjusted. As the familiar means of meeting needs become outmoded, new ways must be discovered. There are no "problem-free" families. Pressures may result from:

1. *A new development phase of an individual member of the nuclear or extended family*. When a child reaches adolescence, or a young adult leaves the family home for good, or a daughter challenges her parents' mores and chooses not to marry, or an elderly grandparent can no longer function independently, the family is required to adapt to new roles and rules and new patterns of interaction. Having a baby, however joyful, can create a crisis for a marriage. Each such change is often accompanied by a sense of loss, and a period of mourning and temporary regression on the part of at least one family member.

2. *Illness, injury, or impairment of a family member*. When one person gets sick, becomes emotionally distressed, or has an accident, or when a mentally or physically defective child is born to a family, the special needs of the situation call for reassignment of family roles and functions. Whether the outcome is recovery, institutionalization, or death, adaptations and readaptions will be required.

3. *External stress on an individual member.* A crisis on the father's job, a change in a child's school, the death of a close friend of the mother's, or an act of discrimination encountered by any member, all reverberate upon the family system.

4. *External stress on the entire family.* When the family home burns down, when urban renewal forces relocation, when the breadwinner loses his or her job, or when the economic situation compels a family to apply for public assistance, when a family suddenly becomes homeless and cannot locate another place to live, the whole family is directly affected, and mechanisms for coping must be activated. The addition to the household of a foster child, a new stepparent, or an elderly relative requires adjustments in the system to enlarge the family boundaries.[18]

Families facing transitions and stresses such as these are almost inevitably faced with conflict and pain. They fear change, yet they need to change. Feelings of bereavement can be profound when familiar relationships and patterns have to be modified. A period of disorganization and confusion may follow. For some families, the outcome is resolution and growth. Others, however, become chronically regressed, chaotic, or symptomatic. When, as caseworkers, we meet with a family, we require a framework for analyzing and assessing the relationships, interactions, and patterns that operate within its structure. Specifically, we must be able to evaluate whether the overall family style is essentially *functional* or *dysfunctional*. Usually, when a family comes for treatment, one or more of its members feels the pressure of a problem. We must be able to determine whether

the difficulty relates to a transient phase of stress, a transition to which the family must painfully accommodate, or whether the family process in and of itself is too dysfunctional or resourceless to regain its balance.

Some key concepts from family theory can assist us in our efforts to explore the family's structure and functioning. Combined with our knowledge of the individual personality, and of the interaction of the individual with the larger social environment, these concepts, which describe the internal workings of families, provide us with a clearer picture of the degree of health or disability in a particular family situation. From this understanding, we can proceed to fashion techniques of intervention.

Before presenting these concepts, let us be reminded of the diverse family roles and relationship patterns that exist in our society. In family therapy, as in all other methods of casework, we must be keenly sensitive to variations in style that are either culturally determined or idiosyncratic to a particular family group. However atypical, these modes of family relations may be functional and adaptive. For example, the extended "urban matriarchal" family, which can include grandmother, mother, and children, may operate well and even creatively if roles are well defined. The sharing and cooperation that can occur in poor families with this structure, or in communal living arrangements that have sprung up in recent years, sometimes allow for a good balance of mutuality and independence. Single parents, mothers or fathers, can successfully provide a home for children. (See Chapter 16 for a discussion of single-parent families.) Male-female roles based on individual preference rather than on traditional expectations can be adaptive. Homosexual couples, who must develop special role definitions, sometimes do raise children and need not be diagnosed as dysfunctional on the grounds of lifestyle alone. The quality of interactions and the nature of the family relationships are far more significant as indicators of family functioning than are the facts of the family's composition or role designations as such. How, more specifically, do we determine where a family falls on the functional-dysfunctional continuum? The following summary of some central concepts of family therapy provide us with useful criteria.

BASIC CONCEPTS OF FAMILY THERAPY

The early family research of the 1950s, which led to some of the central principles guiding the development of the family therapy movement, focused primarily on the study of schizophrenia.[19] Often stymied by the resistance of the schizophrenic process to therapeutic intervention, researchers and practitioners of various disciplines were spurred on to study the schizophrenic within the family environment. As the family therapy movement took hold, it became clear that many of the original concepts could be applied more broadly to families with various symptomatic members, or even to "normal" families. A review of casework and other journals reveals that increasingly clinicians have used the family approach with alcoholics, delinquents, the psychosomatically or terminally ill, and the aged, and with a broad range of marital and parent-child conflicts.

The purpose of this chapter and the one that follows is twofold. First, we will introduce and organize some of the central concepts that have emerged from the family therapy field. We hope the reader's appetite will be whetted sufficiently to study the literature further. Second, we intend to demonstrate the relevance of family therapy to the psychosocial orientation. In some social work and family therapy circles, there is resistance to relating concepts derived from the psychoanalytic study of the individual with those that describe the properties of the family as a unit. In our view, however, a theoretical synthesis of the two can be attained. We shall return to a fuller discussion of this later; it is enough, for the moment, to note that these chapters aim to bridge transactional and systems concepts with intrapsychic theory.

The concepts we have chosen to include here are those that we in practice have found useful in our work. In some instances, the language of family theory is so abstruse that it can seem hard to apply to the real people who visit our offices. In our presentation, however, we have attempted to connect the concepts as closely as possible to the human beings they attempt to describe. Needless to say, family theory has wide gaps, and the principles vary in their levels of abstraction and inclusiveness. Refinements and corrections will derive from ongoing research and clinical experience. Theories about intrapsychic phenomena and even small-group concepts have had a longer history of validation.

It is essential to note that concepts from various "schools" of family therapy often overlap and can be interrelated; frequently a similar idea is expressed by different terms. Indeed, the student of family therapy is barraged by an overabundance of names and labels. The constructs that follow represent our effort to extract and integrate key concepts from some of the seminal family theories and to provide a basic framework and language with which to describe and understand family life and functioning.

Differentiation and Boundaries

Central to family theory are two assumptions around which many of its principles can be organized.[20] First, it is believed that each human being strives for a sense of relatedness and closeness in associations with others. Needless to say, relationships may come and go over a lifetime, but the individual's need for sharing with others is ongoing. Second, and equally important, it is postulated that every person seeks a sense of personal identity, a self-definition, that has consistency and cohesion over time, in spite of emotional ups and downs or external pressures. Each new developmental phase, of course, will alter some aspects of an individual's self-definition. On the basis of these assumptions, we can see that difficulties arise when the pursuit of interpersonal relationships drives a person to negate a sense of self or, conversely, when an individual is so determined to maintain a sense of identity that the need to share his or her life intimately with others is forfeited.

The student of family literature will repeatedly come across a group of more or less analogous terms such as "differentiation," "individuation," and "autonomy." Equally prevalent are an assortment of words that express the opposite idea, including "enmeshment," "fusion," "undifferentiation," and "symbiosis." Generally speaking, these terms (many of which can be found as well in the writings of psychoanalysts and ego psychologists) refer to the degree to which individuals and subsystems within the family accept, or do not accept, themselves and each other as distinct, self-defined, and self-directing. According to our assumptions, growth occurs when individuals accept themselves, their thoughts, feelings, and qualities as uniquely theirs and separate or differentiated from those of others; at the same time, they recognize the need for close relationships. The functional family, then, provides its members and subgroupings (such as the marital pair or the sibling subsystem) with definite yet flexible boundaries and functions. In other words, one person or subsystem can operate independently and yet share intimately with other members.

The dysfunctional family, by contrast, whose members define themselves in relation to others, is often threatened by divergent or independent points of view or expectations. Often in families we see clinically, differences are resisted or denied. Making "I" statements ("I think," "I plan," "I stand for," "I want," "I feel") can seem risky to members of highly undifferentiated or enmeshed families because independent positions are believed to threaten the continuity of relationships. Put another way, when family members are constantly agreeing with or trying to please others at the sacrifice of achieving their own satisfactions or goals, these behaviors are often guided by the notion that they will thereby make their relationships safe; thus, fears of disapproval or abandonment can preclude autonomous functioning. A father who has made his living in a craft that has been handed down for several generations may see his son's interest in becoming a musician as disloyal or as a challenge to his way of life and to his value as a father; he may, therefore, react with angry or rejecting behaviors. In many troubled families, separation threats are used as a means of control; such threats often effectively keep family members fearful of abandonment and therefore anxiously attached and dependent.[21] By the same token, change and spontaneity are often resisted for fear that these will result in the deterioration of the family relationships without which the members fear they cannot survive.

Sometimes family members explain their own feelings, actions, or sense of personal worth on the basis of the behavior of others. "If it weren't for you, I'd be happy" is a sentiment frequently expressed in family meetings. A husband may remark about his wife, "If she feels good, then I feel good." In some families it can be hard to discern whose feelings are whose; a mother may say in all seriousness, "We are not feeling well" when, it turns out, her son is upset about a girlfriend's rejection of *him*. Parents often believe that their children's successes are more important than their own, and therefore their happiness can depend on their youngsters' choices of career, lifestyle, or mate. A wife may measure her self-esteem by the degree or type of affection she receives from her husband rather than relying on her *own* evaluation of herself. Carried to its extreme, in enmeshed families, each member operates on the myth or delusion that he or she cannot live without the other(s) and, therefore, has no independent existence.

Bowen suggests a basis on which to assess the level of an individual's self-differentiation. It is his theory that people can be placed on a "differentiation of self" scale, according to their *ability to distinguish their subjective feeling processes from their objective thinking processes*. The higher on the scale (i.e., the higher the level of differentiation) the more the individual, even under stress, can distinguish between emotions and intellect, between feelings and facts.

Well-defined individuals can make rational decisions or plan actions in their own best interests *even if emotional reactions strongly urge them in another direction*. For example, even in the face of severe fear, a person can decide to make a speech to a large group, disagree appropriately with a formidable authority figure or parent, go on a difficult job interview, and so on. Although deeply angry, one can speak in a civil manner to one's boss when any other action could threaten a pay raise or promotion—or the job itself. In spite of sadness and pain, one can still decide to visit a dying friend, go to a funeral, or explore difficult material in therapy. When temporarily separated from a loved one, a person can derive comfort from knowing that there will be a reunion. Furthermore, the well-differentiated person can be intimate with others without fear of fusion and loss of a sense of self. Close relationships are formed on the basis of choice rather than compulsion and fear. The person's definition of "self" is not severely shaken by the disapproval of others, nor must there be constant approval to feel adequate; people's reactions may be considered but are screened by one's own attitudes and judgments. It stands to reason that people who are on the high end of Bowen's scale are more flexible and better able to handle stress than those on the lower end. Of course, complete differentiation or emotional maturity, in Bowen's terms, describes a degree of functioning that none of us actually achieves.[22]

Poorly differentiated individuals, on the other hand, especially when stressed or anxious, often cannot distinguish feeling from fact. The intellect is so *flooded by emotion* that decisions are based on what will temporarily reduce anxiety rather than on rational assessments or beliefs. Emotions and thoughts are so commingled that their lives are ruled by immediate, unreasoned reactions. In psychoanalytic terms, ego functioning (especially judgment and impulse control) is impaired or overridden in the face of powerful instinctual drives. These individuals depend on the feelings and opinions of others to define them, and, as described previously, often cannot distinguish their own emotions from those of the people close to them, particularly those on whom they heavily rely. Relationships are often marked by extreme dependency. When things go wrong, it is common for people who are not well differentiated to see their difficulties as rooted in the behaviors or "faults" of others. It may not be their intention to place "blame," as such; rather they imbue others with far more power than they themselves have and therefore try to induce *the others* to make changes; they often have little sense that modifications that *they* make will have effect on their relationships. When physically healthy, intelligent adults unrealistically see others rather than themselves as essential to their well-being (or survival), they often place more burdens on relationships than are tolerable. Sometimes they are described as having a "bottomless pit" or never getting enough from the people around them; the truth is that those who are so poorly self-defined do not know that they have themselves to rely on. Obviously, we are not referring here to individuals who are realistically victimized by others or by noxious social conditions and powerless to take actions to free themselves.

In Bowen's view, and also in that of many other family and individual therapists from various schools of thought,[23] *helping people to become aware of the difference between their intellectual processes and their emotional processes* can be critical to helping them become better able to solve problems and improve overall functioning. People can learn to monitor their own emotional reactivity and thereby use their mental faculties to make thoughtful choices. They need not (and should not) deny their feelings, but they also need not be ruled by emotion. Once feelings do not automatically dominate actions, people are then freed to use judgment and discrimination in relationships with others and in life decisions.

Notions about differentiation are sometimes misunderstood. When we speak of independent, self-defined individuals, we do not imply that they operate exclusively in their own orbits or that they are necessarily self-absorbed, self-centered, or "selfish" in their relationships. To the contrary, as people learn to tolerate true intimacy (in contrast to enmeshment or "stuck-togetherness"), they can also be very responsive to the feelings and attitudes of others. Without sacrificing one's personal identity—one's values, one's goals, one's emotional life—one can also be altruistic. In fact, in our experience, those who can maintain a sense of themselves as uniquely special, separate, and self-directing people are better able to be thoughtful to others and giving and loving to those close to them than individuals who cannot function autonomously. The person who relies on others for self-definition, who operates out of fear and extreme dependency—whose *fundamental sense of self* "was acquired at the behest of the relationship system and . . . is negotiable in the relationship system"[24]—eventually harbors resentment toward those on whom he or she so thoroughly relies.

Returning now to Bowen, marriages, he believes, usually occur between two people of similar levels of self-differentiation. The lower the level of differentiation of family members, the greater the fusion or blending (or symbiotic dependency) with one another. For example, one spouse may appear to function more independently than the other. Close examination, however, reveals that the "strength" of one partner may be contingent on the "weakness" of the other. In clinical practice, we frequently observe the rapid decline of the "strong" family member when the "fragile" or "sick" one (e.g., spouse or adult child) separates or dies. The incompetence of one is required for the stability of the other. Bowen's concept of the "undifferentiated family ego mass"* describes the quality of fusion or "emotional oneness" that these kinds of family relationships evidence. Members of an undifferentiated family ego mass, particularly when under pressure, can become deeply involved in the feelings, thoughts, and fantasies of one another. Often the phase of extreme "we-ness," which can be overwhelmingly intense, is followed by a period of distance and even hostile rejection. We frequently see in practice marital pairs, or families with adolescents, going through such cycles of profound dependence and angry repulsion.

For many years, social workers have been aware of the phenomenon of positive and negative "complementarity" in marriages and in the interactional behavioral patterns of entire families. This concept, along with the concepts of dependence and symbiosis, long familiar to psychosocial workers, is closely related to some aspects of Bowen's theory.[25]

Boundaries are the means by which individuals, subsystems, and generations protect their differentiation and maintain a sense of identity. As Minuchin conceives them, boundaries at one pole are very rigid and the individuals and subgroups within the family are quite uninvolved with and disengaged from the others. At the other pole are those families with diffuse or loose inner boundaries; the family members and subsystems are enmeshed or fused with one another. Most families fall within a wide range between these extremes and have clear yet pen-

---

* Although Bowen discontinued using this phrase to describe a family's emotional fusion, it appears so frequently in family literature that we have chosen to include it.

etrable boundaries that permit close relationships among their members.

"The family system," writes Minuchin, "differentiates and carries out its functions through subsystems. Individuals are subsystems within a family. Dyads such as husband-wife or mother-child can be subsystems." Furthermore, "subsystems can be formed by generation, by sex, by interest, or by function."[26] Of course, in-laws also constitute subsystems and, along with other members of an extended family, often participate to some degree in the life of a nuclear family.

Experience has taught us that families usually operate optimally when the *spouse subsystem* has a boundary that can protect it from constant intrusion by other subsystems, particularly when children are small or aging parents have significantly prominent needs; the spouses need a refuge and stimulation, time together for mutual support, and opportunity to engage in adult interests. As Minuchin points out, the *parental subsystem,* comprising the same people as the spouse subsystem, is responsible for socialization of the children; the boundary should be permeable enough to provide children with access to *both* parents, while preventing them from assuming spouse functions.

The *sibling subsystem* "is the first social laboratory in which children can experiment with peer relationships." They "support, isolate, scapegoat, and learn from each other...how to negotiate, cooperate, and compete...how to make friends and allies, how to save face while submitting, and how to achieve recognition of their skills."[27] When it works well, training acquired from sibling interactions prepare children in important social skills, an opportunity not available to only children. But when there is too much parental intrusion or when the sibling activities and relationships are diverted in any way by personal or marital problems of the adults, the children's social development may be retarded.

Most family therapists believe that healthy family functioning requires individuals and

other subsystems to have clear boundaries. Within limits, the exact nature of the authority and responsibilities assigned to subsystems is not usually as important as the clarity with which these are defined. For example, a sixteen-year-old daughter may take considerable responsibility for younger children while parents work, but the limits and prerogatives of her power must be quite precisely delineated; furthermore, they should be agreed upon by mother and father to prevent dysfunctional alliances and blurring of parental boundaries. A grandmother may successfully carry out various functions for a family as long as these are primarily delegated by the parents and are distinctly understood by all involved. Cultural and idiosyncratic family variations in family structure should not be deemed dysfunctional, as long as the rules about who participates, and how, are generally unambiguous.

At various stages of a family's development, disengagement and enmeshment can coexist. For example, it is common to find a tendency toward enmeshment and diffusion of boundaries between a mother and her small children, while the father is more disengaged. A father and son, or mother and daughter, may become very close, enjoying an almost exclusive relationship when they avidly share a mutual interest, in sports, the arts, intellectual matters, and so on. Greater disengagement may occur, and boundaries may become firmer and less permeable, as adolescents and their families prepare for the natural separation associated with this life phase. In relation to developmental issues, Minuchin's concepts of disengagement (rigid boundaries) and enmeshment (diffuse boundaries) do not in themselves represent functional or dysfunctional family styles.

Families that consistently operate at one pole or the other, however, can be dysfunctional. Thus, a family system with rigid inner personal or subsystem boundaries can accept a wide range of individual differences, but the disengagement can be so marked that support from the family group is called forth only when the system is severely stressed. Otherwise, family members operate independently, with minimum help from the others and little sense of belonging.

> The professional parents of an eleven-year-old boy, both deeply immersed in their respective careers, were unaware that their youngster was being bullied and forced to hand over his carfare to older boys each day, until a sensitive janitor alerted the school social worker. The boy, trained to be self-reliant, had been walking home from school and suffering the humiliation of his plight without feeling free to seek his parents' guidance and comfort.

Discussing a similar family process, in different terms, Pittman writes:

> Family tension is hard to describe, but it is palpable. It may be seen as a measure of the members' experience of one another. Tension can be so low that no one feels involved in anyone else's life. Adolescents can develop severe drug habits, young adults can have affairs, and older ones can deteriorate with Alzheimer's, before anyone is aware of anything unusual.[28]

In the extremely enmeshed, fused, or overly dependent family, on the other hand, the most minor event occurring to one member immediately creates a stir of activity among others. Boundaries are so diffuse that privacy is minimal and the feelings of one person seem indistinguishable from those of another. In Pittman's words, "the emotional tension is so intense that one person's emotions are felt instantly by other family members and seem owned by the reactor rather than the originator."[29] The tasks of one member may be absorbed by others, often arresting the development of the individual's sense of competence and autonomy.

> A seventeen-year-old girl with recurrent headaches, for which no physical basis could be detected, was referred for treatment by her physician. In family sessions it was revealed that her mother, who had always thought of her daughter as "delicate," did a major portion of the girl's homework, recommended which friends she should or should not choose, and bought much of her clothing without consulting her about her preferences. The mother told the worker, "I know Alice's feelings better than Alice does." The father complained that his wife always put Alice's needs above his.

Caseworkers frequently meet families, such as this one, in which one parent is in an "undifferentiated alliance," or a symbiotically dependent relationship, with one or more children. In these situations the marital relationship is often distant or hostile, and the child frequently becomes symptomatic. Similarly, when a parent has remained fused or excessively involved with his or her parents, the marital boundaries are sacrificed to hostile-dependent relationships with families of origin. Reverberations upon the entire system are inevitable.

> A couple and their sixteen-year-old son (the youngest of four children and the only one living at home) were in family treatment because the boy, although extremely bright, was failing in school and was isolated from his peers. The mother's mother lived in an "in-law" apartment in the family home. Shortly before the boy's symptoms were exacerbated, his usually sullen and remote father, in a rage, pushed the grandmother against a wall, bruising her. Although the mother and grandmother argued frequently, it was clear that the mother kept trying to win her mother's rarely expressed approval. They spent many hours together during the day. Even after the father came home, the mother visited the grandmother for part of every evening. The boy "could do no wrong"

in his grandmother's eyes, and she often allowed him privileges denied by one or both parents.

In this situation, the individual, marital, and generational boundaries were repeatedly violated. The grandmother, who had little other life of her own, was excessively involved with her daughter and her daughter's marriage; she also intruded on the parenting of the boy. Rather than confronting his wife directly for being more closely connected to her mother than to him, the father attacked the mother-in-law. At other times, he displaced his rage and became critical of his son. The wife was more deeply invested in her relationship with her mother than that with her husband, or, for that matter, her son. The goals of family treatment were to help the marital pair to achieve a warmer, less hostile relationship; to assist the grandmother in developing some social group contacts that would bring her satisfaction and reduce her need to intrude on the life (or boundaries) of her daughter's family; and to support the boy in developing peer friendships as well as closer relationships with his older siblings, who could guide him in his efforts to differentiate from this complexly enmeshed family system. Family therapy progressed accordingly, and the boy became less burdened by the family pathology. Eventually, he was able to establish more comfortable relationships with every member of his family. His schoolwork improved and his friendships increased. When treatment terminated, every family member felt benefited by it.

In Chapters 17 and 18 cases which exemplify how members of undifferentiated families—in these illustrations, spouses—often carry psychic functions for and act out the expectations of others are discussed. When self-esteem is low, and individual boundaries are diffuse, introjected expectations may then be projected onto and assumed by others. For example, the father who believes that he is not worthy enough to pro-

duce a successful son may project this notion onto the boy with the result that the boy fails in the very areas his father anticipates he will. A mother, who was raised by a critical mother, may induce her daughter to find fault with or demean her in the ways her mother did. In both situations, the children are unconsciously accommodating the inner psychic functions of their parents.

The Family as a System

Family members can be viewed as interacting, interdependent parts of an organic whole. Some concepts from systems theory have been described elsewhere in this book (see especially Chapter 2). The family unit, like an intricately coordinated clock, is greater than the sum of its parts, because of the interactions and interrelationships within it. Without the interdependence, there is no family system, simply a cluster of individuals. Intrapsychic events alone cannot account for the movement and flow of the family system that develops its own patterns of behavior and affective expression, its unique rules and role expectations.

It follows that family dysfunction is not simply the sum total of the disturbances of individual members but the product of the family as an entity. The "identified patient" or "index client" (i.e., the individual who seeks treatment or is "chosen" by the family as the troubled member) often represents a family symptom through whom the family expresses its difficulties as a system. As Framo says, "although all symptoms are not interpersonally determined, they always have interpersonal relationship consequences which will determine their nature, course, preservation, or removal."[30] When a family comes for treatment, then, the therapist's focus may not be on individual pathologies as such (even though these may be included in the overall assessment) but on the family system or interactions that produce or sustain troublesome symptoms. Experience has taught us that family members frequently become symptomatic in shifts, with individuals taking turns. Often we find that when a problem child improves, a sibling then develops difficulties, or else marital strains of the parents are exposed.

Systems theories are repeatedly demonstrated in practice: When one person makes significant changes, all those in close emotional connection with him or her are required to make compensatory changes. In families burdened by dysfunctional processes, if one member is hurting, it can usually be assumed that the others are also in pain. Family processes are regulated and reinforced by corrective "feedback mechanisms" that work within the family's internal structure to maintain its stability.

In one family treatment case, the presence of an adult son in the home was the key to maintaining the balance of his parents' marriage; both parents were closer to him than they were to each other. Marital dissatisfactions remained hidden since the parents were united by their overinvolvement in their son's life. Moves the young man made toward independence were met with his parents' efforts to discourage him (feedback mechanisms) in order to maintain the status quo (or equilibrium) of the marital relationship.

Family Homeostasis The familiar term "family homeostasis" refers to the capacity of the family's internal environment to maintain a constancy or equilibrium, healthy or dysfunctional, by a continuous interplay of dynamic forces that restores it to its familiar state after disturbances in its balance. Such family equilibrium does not imply a static condition but a balance of its dynamic components comparable to the interacting factors that keep a bicycle balanced while in motion. The source of disturbance can be internal or external. In the preceding case, the son's attempt to separate from his family represented an internal disturbance that was followed by his parents' attempts to return the family system to its former steady state. Frequently, a change in the system is most possible when the homeostatic balance is upset. The notion that a family in crisis can be most accessible to growth-producing change derives from this principle. The entry of the family therapist on the scene can disturb the balance, and many family therapists recommend deliberately inducing an upset to make way for a new and healthier homeostasis. Developed by Bateson, Jackson, and others as a family concept, the idea was elaborated on by Ackerman, who described the homeostasis of the personality, of the family, and of the larger environment and the interdependence of the three.[31]

Hartman and Laird, citing Speer and others, correctly point out that the notion of family homeostasis can mistakenly be used to characterize family processes as static and unchanging.[32] When literally applied from other sciences to family processes, this concept may limit our expectations and our appreciation of the capacities families have for adaptation, change, and choice. Human beings have faculties for making *deliberate* and *immediate* modifications; no other organisms or systems have these abilities. Humans have the capacity to think of creative ways of solving problems and to institute life-enhancing innovations.

When we refer to the principle of "homeostasis," we intend it as Ackerman used it: to signify what he termed "controlled 'instability.'" Without "instability," he wrote, "there can be no growth, no adaptation, no learning, no creativity. But this is controlled 'instability,' controlled so as to offset a too rapid and destructive change. [W]e envisage the homeostatic principle as a kind of shock barrier, both for body and mind, which enables *expansion of the organism while protecting its integrity.*" (emphasis ours)[33] Although all families need to maintain stable properties—shared values, rules, a sense of continuity and coherence—it stands to reason that for functional and flexible families, adaptation and innovation come more easily than for rigid families systems in which any change is experienced as a threat. In some cases, a major gain in treatment is the family's recognition that change *is* possible and need not be feared.

Hartman and Laird describe three of the ways in which change in families may be initiated:

> First, change can occur as a result of new input or information from the world outside the family; second, change may emerge from the exchange of information among components within the system; and third, an autonomous or differentiated position taken by one member of the family system may become the spur to change. Clearly if change occurs in any one of these ways, it is likely to effect transformations in the others.[34]

Family Roles

A concept important to family theory, as Spiegel defines it, a role is "a goal directed pattern or sequence of acts tailored by the cultural process for the transactions a person may carry out in a social group or situation." Furthermore, "no role exists in isolation but is always patterned to gear in with the complementary or reciprocal role of a role partner."[35] Particular roles are defined in part by the cultural or subcultural values held by a family; thus, the larger society defines certain aspects of the husband-wife role or the mother-child role. Within the family, however, roles are additionally designated according to the family's particular needs or values. Sometimes an individual's role lasts the lifetime of the family: "the brain," "the black sheep," "the baby," and "the clown" are among many we see again and again. Over time, roles can be interchanged. Although all families designate roles, some are assigned to cloak a dysfunctional family balance.

A husband and wife came to treatment for severe marital problems. The husband was a heavy drinker at whom the wife self-righteously raged. After a brief period of treatment, the husband stopped drinking altogether, and the wife, to her own amazement, became depressed. Her low self-esteem and her deep-seated expectations of disappointment were masked by her husband's willingness to accept the "alcoholic" role. As long as she could rant about his behavior, she could maintain the illusion of superiority that protected her from facing her feelings of worthlessness and despair.

This case illustrates the reciprocal nature of roles. In no way do we mean to imply that the husband's drinking problem was "caused" by his wife's behavior. In fact, in a somewhat similar situation, over the course of treatment a wife stopped nagging her husband about his drinking; shortly afterward, the husband was fired from his job for stealing equipment. In treatment he began to recognize his stake in finding another way to provoke his wife to "scold" him; it was his effort to preserve their accustomed roles and the status quo. The point is that just as a change in one part of the system requires a shift in the other, so if one person modifies or drops a role, the role partner, too, will be compelled to make compensatory changes.

Roles are, functionally or dysfunctionally, assigned in families in order to accommodate real or assumed needs; they are patterns of behavior designed to fulfill family functions. There are families in which roles are haphazardly allocated; when there is too much "under-organization," essential functions may not be carried out at all. In these cases, families may deteriorate unnoticed, or they may be referred to some kind of social service, where, it is hoped, they can get help establishing role expectations.[36]

In families with dysfunctional role reciprocity, some member(s) may be labeled "dependent" or "helpless," with the apparent result that a "martyr," "hero," or "rescuer" is required to get things done; in fact, in some families, the underachievers become essential to the (albeit fragile) sense of well-being of the over-doers. In this connection, it is sometimes a child who is called upon to "rescue" parents who seem unable to fulfill parental roles; we often refer to such a child as "parentified." As Boszormenyi-Nagy and Ulrich write about *parentification*:

> In a healthy family, to the extent a child supplements the parents' resources, this can be an avenue of growth and enrichment, e.g., the child who comforts mother when mother has suffered a loss. Yet, when parents are set to draw heavily on a child, its whole life can get sucked into the captive devotion to becoming a parental figure.... The parentified child may be the "good sibling" who sacrifices all self-strivings so as to preserve the family balance.[37]

Similarly, those children who take on important family responsibilities may become more capable and less self-centered as adults than those who have been catered to, but when children are called upon to *take over for* rather than to *assist* their parent(s), important childhood needs may thereby be sacrificed.

Dysfunctional role reciprocity can also be referred to as *irrational role assignment*. Often symptoms develop in reaction to the roles: A parentified child may become depressed in order to escape from burdens that are stifling or are beyond him or her. When rewards for being the "martyr" severely diminish, yet the person is too frightened to refuse the role allocated by the dysfunctional family system, he or she may develop psychosomatic symptoms. In Chapters 17 and 18, on couple treatment, we will discuss this process in further detail.

An evaluation of the level of *cooperation* or *contention* among family members when carrying out role functions may provide vital information about family functioning and unexpressed feelings and attitudes; for example, complaints about assigned duties may reflect relationship dissatisfactions. When meeting with families, it is also useful to assess *role flexibility*. As important as it is to have roles (and boundaries) fairly clearly defined, it is equally important that

definitions be revised to meet new conditions. How does the role structure adapt under the stress of vicissitudes families inevitably face? Can roles be exchanged when necessary? Will a father take on responsibilities usually carried by his wife when she is indisposed? Or vice versa? Can the adolescent take care of the younger children if the mother has to go to work or care for an elderly relative? When there seems to be role rigidity, it can be predicted that the family will have less capacity for coping with crisis than the family with role flexibility.

Scapegoating In family therapy, the term "scapegoat" is frequently used to describe the individual—often the "identified patient"—who reflects the family pathology by becoming symptomatic. Hostility or unresolved disappointments between parents, for example, can be displaced onto a child who then "acts out." Frequently, clinicians view the "identified patient" as the scapegoated "victim" because his or her problems mask the problems among other family members. In reality, however, there is no single victim. Thus, the incorrigible child whose role is to obscure the marital tensions in the family may be "victimized" by carrying the burden of the parents' problems, but the rest of the family ultimately become the victim of the child's behavior. In this sense, *every* member is scapegoated by the hidden, often unconscious, issues that plague the family as a whole.

Although never fully accepting the view that the family is a system, Ackerman commented on the clinical situation in which one part of a family seems to "draw the breath of life at the expense of the other." Disturbed families, he hypothesized, threatened by differences among their members, create alliances that battle for dominance. A member or faction attacks, and the victim (scapegoat) finds family allies with whom to counterattack. Another member or faction, at times even the scapegoat, takes on the role of "healer." Thus the roles are fulfilled by particular members and, with the passage of time, by other members. Each is selected for the respective role by unconscious emotional processes within the family.[38]

Similarly, in families in which there is alcoholism, Wegscheider reports that in addition to the "alcoholic" (or "dependent") role, five other roles—"enabler," "hero," "scapegoat," "lost child," and "mascot"—are repeatedly, sometimes interchangeably, played out as an unhealthy way of "preserving the family system at whatever cost" (see the case of Jed Cooper in Chapter 21). Too frightened to confront their many practical and emotional problems, family members unconsciously adopt these roles, hiding their real feelings "behind an artificial behavior pattern." She sees each family member as carrying "a supporting role in the alcoholic drama, which seems to promise some kind of reward in a system that offers few.... Each role grows out of its own kind of pain, has its own symptoms, offers its own payoffs for both the individual and the family, and ultimately exacts its own price."[39]

Triangles   As we mentioned earlier, an idea emphasized by many family therapists is that the human being simultaneously strives for close relationships and for a sense of personal identity. The balance between the two, of course, can be difficult to maintain. When, as we have already illustrated, a close relationship between two people becomes tense (out of a fear of intimacy, through overdependency, or as a result of any unresolved conflicts), the pair may involve a third person on whom the anxieties are displaced. A mother, for example, disappointed by her emotionally distant husband, may try to fill her unmet needs in her relationship with her young son. The father, equally dissatisfied, may vent his feelings by criticizing the boy. By "triangulating" or pulling in the child in this way, the tension between the parents is displaced and reduced, the balance of the relationship is resumed, and the issues be-

tween them remain obscured. Triangulation can also describe the process when two people pull in a family pet, the television set, alcohol, or an external event to evade problems between them and to stabilize the relationship. Numerous triangles exist simultaneously in a family, but, over time, the emotional forces within it can reside mostly in one triangle. When this happens, the triangulated or "triadic" one, such as the boy in the example, takes on a role not unlike that of the scapegoat. Needless to say, the more undifferentiated the individuals, the more often triangulation will occur.

Minuchin has identified three sets of conditions that produce dysfunctional triadic structures: (1) When each parent demands that the child side with him or her against the other parent. (2) When marital stresses are expressed through the child and the illusion of parental harmony is thereby maintained; unconsciously, the parents may reinforce any deviant or "sick" behavior of the child and then unite to protect the youngster. (3) When one parent establishes a coalition with a child against the other parent.[40]

A nine-year-old boy was in treatment for encopresis (soiling), which was interfering with peer relationships and creating general embarrassment for him. Meetings with the family, including a fifteen-year-old daughter, mother, and father, further revealed that the girl was a severe nailbiter and underachieved in school. Seating positions of the first sessions were the same. The boy sat close to and interacted mostly with his mother; the girl assumed a similar position vis-à-vis her father. The parents, although polite to one another, sat as far apart as the office chairs allowed. When they spoke together they talked almost exclusively about their concern for the children. After four meetings, the worker was convinced that there were some charged issues between the parents and arranged a session without the children. With considerable difficulty—and much support from the worker—they disclosed that the father, a diabetic, and the mother, a rather timid woman, had not had sexual relations for three years. They had never shared with each other their feelings about this, nor had they made any attempts to adapt their sexual practices to accommodate the father's potency problem (a common symptom of diabetes). As their relationship became more distant, each turned to a child for emotional support to bolster waning self-esteem. The children, unable to bear the strain of demands they could not meet, became symptomatic.

In this family, both children were "triangulated" (or, one might say, scapegoated) by the marital pair. And, as we frequently find, the children became the "passport" for the parents' marital treatment. The symptoms of both children subsided after more than a year of marital treatment. The daughter's symptoms cleared up more quickly than the son's, perhaps because the father had many outside interests that he had pursued more avidly after the deterioration of his marital relationship; he was not totally dependent on his daughter to fulfill his emotional needs. The mother-son dyad, on the other hand, was the most intense connection in the mother's life, and achieving greater differentiation required more time for her and her son.

It is probably clear to the reader that various writers on family therapy may approach the same or similar points of view but often by using different language. For example, triangulation is one form of scapegoating in which a third person is blamed, alienated, or "chosen" to be symptomatic in order to obfuscate the conflict or stress between two people. In psychological terms, both of these concepts involve the ego defense of displacement and sometimes of denial: that is, the strain between family members is denied and then displaced onto another.

Pseudomutuality   All family relationships and roles are by nature, in some form, complemen-tary; compromises are required to achieve compatibility and smooth functioning. When there is *genuine* mutuality in a family, divergent interests, opinions, and feelings are tolerated; flexible role behavior can add stimulation and vitality to family life. Pseudomutuality, on the other hand, refers to the family's compulsive absorption with "fitting together" that, as Wynne describes it, creates "the illusion of a well integrated state even when that state is not supported by the emotional structures of the members."[41] Threatened by differences among its members, the family promotes the myth of harmony. To maintain it, the individual members must lock themselves into rigid roles and relinquish their personal identities. They must suppress or deny differences that they fear may destroy the family relationship. If sufficiently persistent, the resulting inhibition of self-expression can create severe personality disturbances in family members.

Neighbors complained to the police about an eighteen-year-old young man's exposing himself in the courtyard of the housing project where he lived with his parents and three younger siblings. Placed on probation, he was referred to a mental health clinic for treatment. He related superficially to his young male worker but contended that he had no problems. Referred for family therapy, the parents insisted they had a "perfect family" and that the boy was framed by jealous neighbors whose testimony had convicted him. Both parents were cordial and, on the surface, cooperative. It was not until some relatives of the mother came from the West Indies to live in the household that the family became intolerably stressed. At this point, family tensions surfaced and hidden grievances between the parents were uncovered. Work with the family could then begin.

In this situation, the parents had been unwilling to recognize the serious implications of their son's behavior. They feared that giving up the illusion that all was well with him—or, for that matter, with the marriage—would threaten the family structure. After the family was engaged in treatment, it became evident that the denial of all differences and problems among the members had placed such a strain on the young man's internal psychological system that he became symptomatic. The younger children, too, were manifesting stressed reactions to the family mandate to conform: to think, feel, and behave in a prescribed manner. Wynne sees no real victims in pseudomutuality since all members of the family participate. In this case, the young man, as well as his parents, maintained that family life was ideal, despite the high prices he paid as an individual; he, too, promoted the myth of harmony. Had external forces not stressed the family beyond endurance, family meetings, a contingency of the young man's probation, might have gone on as meaningless exercises. In all likelihood, without therapy, even more disturbing personality problems would have developed in this family.

Family Myths and Secrets   Myths serve the function for families that defenses serve for individuals.[42] To protect itself against conflict or ambivalent feelings and to maintain its balance, the family—or individuals within it—paint a picture of a situation or of relationships that, when explored, prove to be distorted or untrue. The myth may be shared by the family as a whole, or it may be promoted by one or more of its members. Role designations that misrepresent particular family members as "weak" or "bad" are myths. Myths may be perpetuated to avoid or to deny painful feelings of self-blame, as they often are in families that exclusively attribute their miseries or misfortunes to one family member. For example, the alcoholic in a family may be assigned the role of "culprit" to exonerate others of responsibility for family problems. Families may protect themselves against intrusions or judgment of the outside

world with myths, as with the myth of pseudomutuality described. Incest and extramarital affairs are often well-kept secrets. In families in which there is incest, usually it is children who are misused and sacrificed—often sworn to silence—to protect adults from resolving their own personal or relational issues. In cases of infidelity, too, the secret almost always is an indirect means for handling unresolved individual and/or relational issues (see Chapter 17). Myths and secrets may also go hand in hand to cloak "unspeakable" events of the past, or a family tragedy.

A nine-year-old girl with an incessant and obsessive fear of snakes was referred for family therapy after a period of unsuccessful individual treatment. The parents appeared to enjoy a loving relationship with each other and with their only child, Deborah. Yet the family climate seemed unexplainably strained. Only after several sessions, in response to a random question, did the worker learn that the mother suffered from a heart condition, a fact the parents had not shared with Deborah. The worker sensed that the mother's illness was more serious than the parents were acknowledging and hypothesized that the child had picked up the tension about it, as the worker had. Not understanding its meaning, Deborah, the worker suspected, had displaced her feelings of dread onto snakes. After some careful and sensitive work in family therapy, the child (and the worker) learned that both parents feared the mother's illness could prove fatal. With the support of the worker, the relationships among the three became more open and intimate. As the underground anxieties surfaced, the family members could share their feelings of heartbreak and affection. Deborah's fear of snakes all but disappeared. It was fortunate for the child that her symptoms were alarming enough to prompt her parents to seek outside help, because the mother died less than a year after treatment terminated. Had the family denial persisted, Deborah would have been left with guilt, lack of resolution about the loss of her mother, and—if she learned the truth—bitterness toward her parents for having promoted the myth that all was well in a household in which her mother was dying.[43]

In this family, the parents consciously kept the secret and perpetuated the "all-is-well" myth to "protect" Deborah. (The notion that children cannot tolerate tragedy is in large measure itself a myth.) The parents had been less aware of their *own* need to maintain the myth in order to obscure from themselves their feelings of terror and sadness.

Communication Concepts

Jackson, Haley, and Satir, among others, turned to communication theory to conceptualize the workings of the family system. Summarizing her view, Satir wrote:

A person who communicates in a functional way can:

a. Firmly state his case
b. yet at the same time clarify and qualify what he says,
c. as well as ask for feedback
d. and be receptive to feedback when he gets it.[44]

Work with family groups necessarily involved interventions by the therapist to focus and clarify the messages exchanged among members. Beyond this, the distortions and unexplored assumptions that generally pervade the communication process of disturbed families become the grist for treatment. The myths and misapprehensions on which the family operates must be exposed and dispelled. In family therapy, members can learn to inquire about the thoughts and feelings of others, and to share their own. Any tendency of family members to act on untested suppositions often can be re-

vealed more quickly in family therapy than in individual treatment. The child who believes his behavior caused his parents' divorce and the woman who erroneously assumes her daughter-in-law hates her have opportunities to correct their distortions in family group meetings.

Principles of communication set forth by Jackson and his colleagues have become important in family assessment and treatment.

Relationships and interactions depend not only on *what* is communicated, but on *how* the message is sent. Thus, the *quality* of the communication can reveal more about the relationship than the *content*. For example, the manner in which we ask someone to pass the salt (i.e., our tone of voice, inflection, physical gestures, and so on) can define a peer or a superior inferior kind of relationship. The content is similar, but the message about the relationship can be very different. A metacommunication (defined as a communication about a communication) serves to qualify the literal content of a message by means of a second verbal or nonverbal statement.

In a family session a usually passive and agreeable husband turned to his wife and said with feeling, "You make me angry." Immediately after this statement he smiled, adding, "I was only kidding." His second message, the metacommunication—it was later revealed—masked his fear of his wife's retaliatory anger.

In Jackson's view, verbal communications reveal less about relationships than nonverbal messages. The latter, however, can be more ambiguous: tears, smiles, and frowns have many meanings. Furthermore, he points out, it is impossible *not* to communicate. Silence and withdrawal are strong messages. If a family comes for treatment and the teenage son sits silently, or the daughter sits outside the family circle, these are nonetheless communications for the therapist to decipher.

Often, then, in trying to appraise the relationships of the family system, the therapist can learn more from the feeling tone and body language that accompany the intercommunications than from the message content itself. No message is simple. The family therapist looks for an accompanying, often abstract, message that confirms or denies the first.[45]

There are some families in which faulty communication patterns derive primarily from lack of knowledge; in these cases, misunderstandings and difficulties may be cleared up fairly quickly. The caseworker may act as "coach" to family members who simply never learned to make "I" statements or to speak directly to one another rather than *through* or *about* a third person. Needless to say, "go-betweens" and triangulation interfere with functional communication. Some families can be taught the value of allowing disagreement, even about "taboo" subjects. By the same token, the worker may help family members to listen rather than to interrupt, distort, or reinterpret what others are saying. Sometimes, out of habit, there are subjects which families have not talked about but which can be elicited with just a little support and encouragement. However, in other families, poor communication may reflect lack of differentiation, problems around boundaries and roles, and so on. Under these circumstances, more extensive treatment may be required to help family members become less fearful, more autonomous and self-defined, as well as more communicative.

The Double Bind   "Toward a Theory of Schizophrenia," a classic article written by Bateson, Jackson, and colleagues, describes the *double bind* as "a situation in which no matter what a person does, he cannot win."[46] The essential ingredients of this particular kind of communication situation are:

1. Two or more persons, one designated as "victim"

2. Repeated experience or a continuing condition

3. A primary negative injunction such as "Do this or I will punish you"

4. A secondary injunction conflicting with the first at a more abstract level, enforced by punishments, threats to survival, or promise of a reward

5. A situation in which the victim can neither leave the field nor comment on the discrepant messages

The child whose mother accuses him of not loving her enough is in a "no-win" situation when he tries to kiss her and she anxiously recoils, as though to say "go away." If this condition is repeated, it is double binding. The boy needs his mother, so he cannot leave. If he comments on the contradiction, he will be scolded. Obedience to one message results in disobedience to the other.

The double bind can be perpetrated by one or more individuals:

A father constantly complained that he wanted his twenty-one-year-old, unemployed son to get a job and "become a man." In words, the mother agreed, but whenever the young man found work, she told him it was either dangerous or "beneath" him. In a family session he told his mother he thought she was babying him. Both parents then called him "stupid."

In this case, if the son remained idle, his father belittled him. If he found a job, his mother disapproved. If he complained about the bind, his parents joined together to insult him. Unfortunately, this young man participated in the double-binding situation by defining himself as too weak to make a move without his parents' approval.

In a follow-up article, written in 1962, the same writers modified one aspect of this important theoretical contribution: "The most useful way to phrase double bind description is not in terms of a binder and a victim but in terms of people caught up in an ongoing system which produces conflicting definitions of the relationship and consequent subjective distress."[47] As illustrated in the above example, the participation of the "victim" is as essential to the perpetuation of the bind as are the parts played by the "binders." This modification is an important one for family therapists to remember when they find themselves feeling partisan to the "underdog" who, unless he or she is a very small child, has taken on the role and may (to the therapist's surprise) fight to protect it.

Mystification R. D. Laing coined the term "mystification" to describe an indirect means of handling differences or conflict. When A's perceptions contradict B's, for example, A may insist to B: "It's just your imagination" or "You must have dreamt it." Or, another example of mystification given by Laing: A child is playing noisily in the evening and his mother is tired. She could make a direct statement, such as "I am tired and I want you to go to bed." Or, a mystifying statement would be: "You are tired and should go to bed." Mystification becomes a serious matter when:

> ...one person appears to have the *right* to determine the experience of another, or complementarily, when one person is under an *obligation* to the other(s) to experience, or not to experience, himself, them, his world or any aspect of it, in a particular way.[48]

Thus, the not necessarily tired boy in the above example may or may not be confused about his own feeling state, but he may feel obliged at some level to disclaim his subjective experience. In mystification, Laing says, some kind of conflict is present, but evaded. (Perhaps in the above example, the mother was in conflict about wanting to be a "good mother," yet feeling too tired to tolerate her son's din. In order not to face her inner conflict, she projected her tired feelings onto the boy. In this way, she

could send him to bed yet avoid doubts about her "good mothering.") The double bind is necessarily mystifying, but mystification need not be truly double binding, if the one being mystified does not disclaim his or her own experience. Although the victim of the double bind cannot leave or comment on the bind, the person being mystified may protest or be aware that mystification need not affect one's inner experience. Laing's concept can be useful to clinicians when identifying family process.

A seven-year-old, very bright boy was behaving disruptively in school, and the teacher referred the mother to a family agency to arrange individual treatment for the child. In the first interview with mother and son, the worker noted that when the boy complained that his teacher never punished an equally mischievous student, the mother dismissed him with "the teacher wouldn't play favorites." At another point, the boy told his mother *with a smile* that he was frightened when she yelled at him, to which the mother responded, "You couldn't be or you would behave." The worker pointed out to the mother that she was denying the boy's experience, to which only he could attest. In this case (unlike many others), the mother, a hard-working and caring single parent, got the point immediately. She was able to acknowledge that the boy's school problem had been "one more pressure," and that she was probably trying to ignore it by insisting to her son that he saw and felt things differently than he did.

After a total of four joint sessions, the school reported significant improvement in this boy's behavior, and the mother commented that it was easier to listen to her son than to struggle with him. When the mystification was eliminated, the boy's symptoms did not return. Incidentally, it can be assumed that the boy protected himself by smiling; in the event that his mother had persisted in her "right" to define his experience, he was prepared to oblige by disavowing what he felt with a smile. We might add that the mother continued for some brief individual treatment, consisting mainly of emotional and environmental support. The worker offered encouragement and resource suggestions to help her broaden her social life. As she became more personally fulfilled, she was better able truly to "hear" her son. Had the worker decided on play therapy for the boy, the mystification might never have been revealed. By the same token, had the school symptoms been less vexing, this mother might have unwittingly participated in the creation of a deeper personality disturbance in her son.

THE PSYCHOSOCIAL FRAMEWORK AND FAMILY THERAPY

Is family therapy casework? Can the psychosocial framework comfortably accommodate principles and methods from the family therapy field? There are some who would insist that one must take sides and declare oneself as either a caseworker or as a family therapist. Among casework advocates of the either/or position are those who contend that family problems are fundamentally the function of the psychosocial difficulties of each individual member. From this point of view, improved family functioning depends on the resolution of individual problems.

On the other hand, there are some family therapists who claim that assessment or diagnosis of the individual family members is irrelevant for therapy purposes. From this standpoint, change for the family and the individuals in it requires therapeutic approaches aimed at the family structure: the transactions, behavior, and communication patterns of the dysfunctional family system. The individual's inner life, personality structure and dynamics, and even past history are downplayed or disregarded.[49]

In our view, the dichotomy is unfortunate. Certainly, a particular caseworker may feel better equipped by training or temperament—or may simply prefer—to concentrate on one treatment method rather than another. As individual practitioners we may be partial to particular kinds of clients, problems, or settings, and our propensities may lead us to choose among modalities as well. To confine ourselves theoretically to one point of view to the exclusion of another, however, is quite a different matter. We need not close out new information and approaches that can expand our knowledge base and enhance our effectiveness as caseworkers. Conversely, as we welcome new ideas, let us not assume that we must scrap traditional knowledge and methods of proven value.

The rationale for the incorporation of family therapy concepts by casework or clinical social work requires a review of some of the central features of our psychosocial framework.

The Person-in-Situation Social work treatment, by tradition and by definition, has never exclusively addressed either the inner life of the individual, on the one hand, or the social-environmental situation, on the other. In fact, despite variations in emphasis during different historical stages or in particular settings, social work thinking has always stressed person-situation interaction and the interdependence of the person and the context. The "person-in-situation" concept, as we pointed out in Chapter 2, has three components: (1) the person, including personality system, emotional life, and biological characteristics; (2) the situation or environment, including other people; and (3) the nature of the interactions between the two. Whatever the particular theoretical orientation, consistent attention to all three components has distinguished social work from the other helping professions.[50]

Of particular importance to casework's integration of family therapy principles is the interactional component. Human beings are influenced by their environments and, in turn, affect the people and circumstances around them. Often, the most salient feature of a person's environment is the family. The transactions and the quality of the interdependence between the individual and the family are of prime importance to casework diagnosis and treatment. Systems theory reminds us that "encounter between an organism and the environment *leave both changed*;[51] in fact, our clinical practice has always been based on this awareness. Although we can think of the person, the situation, and the interaction between them as discrete matters, casework recognized how each affects the others. As the concepts described in this chapter illustrate, internal and external phenomena are intertwined. When changes occur in a family system, the behavior and inner lives of individual members shift. Conversely, individual changes reverberate upon the family as a whole. The actions of one individual are both cause and effect of the actions of others. In contrast to the single-cause, linear approach to understanding human behavior, the psychosocial orientation is one that assesses the multidimensional, reciprocal influences of the personality, the family, and the larger social system, as each acts on and reacts to the others.

Psychiatry and Freudian theory have deepened our view of individual dynamics. The social sciences have advanced our understanding of the human environment. More recently, the ideas that have emerged from the family therapy movement equip us with means for studying the transactions of individuals in the family environment; new information about the properties of the family as a system has become available. Family concepts fill some real gaps in casework theory; the place for including them is provided by the psychosocial framework.

The Personality System Freud, whose ideas have been basic to the psychosocial approach, broke new ground with his proposition that personality is shaped by social as well as biological

forces. Neurosis, he asserted, is an outgrowth of the individual's family experience and inborn drives. The intrapsychic oedipal conflict, for example, is grounded in early parental relationships. In his well-known case of "Little Hans," Freud worked with the father, not with the boy himself. The successful treatment of the boy's horse phobia was achieved through interventions in the family system. Unfortunately, as psychoanalytic theory was passed down, some followers not only failed to expand on the interactional aspects of personality but narrowed the theory to minimize the social side of Freud's thinking, which, although not fully developed, was there all along.[52]

Concepts derived from the study of personality—*internalization* and *introjection*—point us to some of the significant theoretical links between intrapsychic and family systems phenomena. As we know, the child's superego internalizes or introjects the commands, prohibitions, and ideals of the parents or other authority figures, with the result that the youngster learns to conform to their demands and values even in their absence. Yet our understanding of a particular client requires an additional, interactional perspective. Take, for example, a man who feels hostile toward his mother, oppressed by demands he believes she makes on him. Often we discover that he is reacting to his early mother introject, which bears little resemblance to his mother of today; the demands—if she ever made them—are no longer hers but his own. Yet his negative attitude toward her may provoke angry or defensive responses from her that, in turn, tend to reinforce his internalized representation of her. To see the total picture, then, we must understand the client's inner life, the interdependence of the past and the present, and the circular nature of the mother-son interactions. Joint or family sessions may be the most efficient approach with which to expose and correct internalized distortions as they are played out in interpersonal relationships.

In this case, it is also probable that this man's introjected expectations, derived from his past (possibly *always* distorted) image of his mother, are also evident in other interactions; he may, for example, view his wife as "controlling," even when objective evidence does not support his perception. As many family therapists have emphasized, individuals emerge from their families of origin more or less "programmed" to reenact introjected roles and qualities that derive from family members, relationships, and experiences as they assimilated them in childhood. This process, often referred to as the *intergenerational transmission process* or *family projection process* becomes additionally complicated when *each* spouse brings his or her own internalizations to the marital relationship. Marital and family-of-origin sessions may most efficiently expose and correct internalized distortions as these are played and replayed in present interpersonal relationships. Chapters 17 and 18 discuss these issues as they are revealed in marital therapy.

Similarly, our understanding of the notion of externalization (sometimes referred to as projection) helps to bridge theories of individual dynamics and family relationships. *Externalization* refers to the act of attributing inner, subjective phenomena, including wishes, fears, conflicts, and thoughts, to the external world. We can see how such internal matters or aspects of one's self, once externalized, become part of an interactional process, particularly when they involve other people. For example, a client may tell us he is unhappily married but that he will not leave his wife for fear she will break down emotionally, although, in fact, he is externalizing his hidden concern about his own stability. Or a wife who says she wants to plan a vacation because her husband needs it may have difficulty giving *herself* permission for a holiday; furthermore, the husband may be in the habit of counting on his wife to accommodate *his* difficulty planning pleasures on his own behalf. Unacceptable dissociated inner experiences, in these examples, fears and wishes, once externalized are no longer discrete internal

events. They affect and are affected by the interpersonal arena; interactional forces take on a life of their own above and beyond the individuals involved.

Taking this process one step further, Wynne describes the *trading of dissociations*. This concept refers to the complementary and interlocking externalizations of intrapsychic dissociations. In other words, a man, unaware of a particular quality in himself, may see it located in the personality of his wife and believe his problem can only be relieved by changes in her. Similarly, the wife locates her own unacceptable qualities or ideas in her husband and sees her difficulties as a function of his personality. For example, a man may (accurately) view his wife as angry and bitter when, indeed, he has suppressed his own violent feelings; the wife, on the other hand, may see her husband's dependence on her while disclaiming hers on him. The fixed view that the man has of his wife is unconsciously exchanged for the fixed view she holds of him. The purpose of the reciprocal and shared trading of dissociations is twofold: first, both individuals protect themselves from experiencing their dreaded feelings; yet, second, each is able to "retain these qualities within his purview, at a fixed distance from his ego."

A teenage daughter may perceive her mother's punitively moralistic qualities, while dissociating those same features in her own personality; the mother, unaware of dreaded ("bad") sexual impulses within herself, become keenly attuned to those of her daughter. Each sees the need for change in the other, since each perceives aspects of the other that are outside that person's awareness. By externalizing inner, unacceptable parts of themselves, they may each persecute the other for these qualities rather than enduring what would otherwise be very painful self-castigation. It is easy to see how complicated and futile the relationship between this mother and daughter could become. As Wynne explains: "The trading of dissociations means that each person deals most focally with that in the other which the other cannot acknowledge. Thus, there can be no 'meeting,' no confirmation, no mutuality, no shared validation of feelings or experience."[53] This process can be extended to involve every family member in a network of traded perceptions. The individuals involved, as Wynne points out, might be diagnosed as ego-syntonic character disorders who may not be motivated for individual treatment. Often, these same people become engaged in family therapy because they recognize the need for other family members to get help. In family sessions, intrapsychic, dissociated aspects of individuals that they have located in the personalities of others can be identified.

Individual and family thinking merge again when we examine the writings and research findings of Bowlby, Spitz, Mahler, and others from the psychoanalytic tradition on *separation* and *individuation*.[54] Family theorists too, as discussed earlier in this chapter, have been keenly interested in these matters. There is general agreement that the development of a relatively autonomous, self-reliant personality depends heavily on two conditions of the individual's childhood: (1) consistent parental availability, responsiveness, and support; and (2) parental encouragement of the child's independence and self-direction appropriately timed to the child's age. Absence of either of these conditions can contribute to lasting separation anxieties in the youngster. A mother (and/or a father, grandmother, or other key person to whom the child is attached), sensing her child's emerging independence, may be threatened by separation feelings and withdraw more completely and abruptly than the child, who still requires steady reassurance and support, can bear. Or, on the other hand, the mother's anxiety may lead her to cling to the child; she may do this by overprotecting or "parentifying" the child (i.e., treating him or her as a parental substitute). In any case, the mother's separation and abandonment fears are transmitted to the child. Unwittingly,

parents may pass on to their children the unfulfilled longings, or wishes to retaliate, that grow out of their own childhood experiences.

Thus, the adult who in early life was abandoned, literally or emotionally, may cling to a person or even a memory out of fear of feeling alone again. Or the individual may set up interpersonal situations in which the experience of abandonment is painfully repeated over and over again. Similarly, the adult who was steadily discouraged from functioning independently may hold on desperately to others to maintain a sense of belonging. In family treatment, we frequently see families in which the members, sometimes alternately, cling to or abandon their parents, their spouses, or their children. Such overdependency and estrangement among family members can often be traced to earlier separation-individuation disturbances. The longings, fears, and anger derived from old parent-child experiences are transferred to current family relationships. It is Leader's hunch that "in the majority of families seeking help, the intergenerational theme of abandonment flows deep like an underground stream."[55] Family myths, roles, and interactions are patterned to guard against conscious and unconscious separation fears. As we have already illustrated, often family members deny inevitable differences of opinions, thoughts, or feelings among them, for fear that these will lead to separation or estrangement. In these situations, each individual is deeply enmeshed in the larger family process. Symptoms and troubled feelings, although in part a function of the dynamics of the personality, cannot be appraised fully in isolation from this outer reality.

In summary, the selected illustrations included in this section support our view that the psychosocial framework can accommodate family concepts. Caseworkers can improve their treatment skills when they are equipped with specific information about the nature of the complex interplay of forces that prevail in a family system. "How," asked Ackerman shortly before his death, "can we choose between the family and the person? The person is a subsystem within the family, just as the family is a subsystem within the community and culture."[56] We agree with Minuchin: "changes in a family structure contribute to changes in the behavior and the inner psychic process of the members of that system."[57] Repeatedly, in our clinical practice, we see how the moods and behavior of individuals change as their families change. However, with Ackerman, we would caution against a mechanistic approach to systems that tends to deny the force and integrity of the individual personality. Each family member has a private inner world, unique natural endowments, character structure, and personal identity that endure over time. The special qualities of the individual reverberate upon the family system as well. The greatest possible sophistication about the dynamics of the personality system and the family system, and the nature of the reciprocal influences between them is required to understand the problems individuals and families bring to treatment. As Moultrup says: "A family therapist who ignores the individual will enjoy the same success or lack of success as an individual therapist who ignores the family."[58]

In the chapter that follows we will demonstrate how, as we broaden our knowledge base, we increase our choices of treatment methods, strategies, and goals.

NOTES

1. For useful information on changing family situations, see Family Service America, *The State of Families 1* (Milwaukee, Wisc.: Family Service America, 1984); and *The State of Families II: Work and Family* (Milwaukee, Wisc.: Family Service America, 1987).

2. Kingsley Davis, "The Changing Family in Industrial Society," in Robert C. Jackson and Jean Morton, eds., *Family Health Care: Health Promotion and Illness Care* (Berkeley: University of California Press, 1976), pp. 1–16. See also George Peter Murdock, "The Universality of the Nuclear Family," and Talcott Parsons, "The Stability of the American Family System," in Norman W. Bell and Ezra F. Vogel, eds., *A Modern Introduction to the Family*, rev. ed. (New York: Free Press, 1968), pp. 37–47, 97–101. A discussion of the vital functions that families perform can also be found in Shirley L. Zimmerman, "Reassessing the Effect of Public Policy on Family Functioning," *Social Casework*, 59 (October 1978), 451–457. An excellent compilation of articles that examine recent shifts in family patterns and relationships can be located in Arlene S. Skolnick and Jerome H. Skolnick, eds., *Family in Transition*, 2d ed. (Boston: Little, Brown, 1977).

See also Charles Frankel's useful paper, "The Impact of Changing Values on the Family," *Social Casework*, 57 (June 1976), 355–365, in which he expresses concern about the decline in respect for the institution of the family.

3. Shirley L. Zimmerman, "The Family: Building Block or Anachronism," *Social Casework*, 61 (April 1980), p. 204.

4. See Anne O. Freed, "Building Theory for Family Practice," *Social Casework*, 63 (October 1982), 472–481; and Morton R. Startz and Helen F. Cohen, "The Impact of Social Change on the Practitioner," *Social Casework*, 61 (September 1980), 400–406.

5. See, for example, Sanford N. Sherman, "Intergenerational Discontinuity and Therapy of the Family," *Social Casework*, 48 (April 1967), 216–221; Nathan Ackerman, "Family Healing in a Troubled World," *Social Casework*, 52 (April 1971), 200–205; and Nathan W. Ackerman, *Treating the Troubled Family* (New York: Basic Books, 1966).

6. See especially, Irene Goldenberg and Herbert Goldenberg, *Family Therapy: An Overview*, 2d. ed. (Monterey, Calif.: Brooks/Cole, 1985), a very readable text that examines major theories and approaches to family treatment.

See also Carlfred B. Broderick and Sandra S. Schrader, "The History of Professional Marriage and Family Therapy," in Alan S. Gurman and David P. Kniskern, eds., *Handbook of Family Therapy* (New York: Brunner/Mazel, 1981); Vincent D. Foley, *An Introduction to Family Therapy* (New York: Grune and Stratton, 1974); Philip J. Guerin, Jr., ed., *Family Therapy* (New York: Gardner Press, 1976), Chapter 1; Lynn Hoffman, *Foundations of Family Therapy* (New York: Basic

Books, 1981); Marshall Jung, "Directions for Building Family Development Theory," *Social Casework,* 64 (June 1983), 363–370; and David Moultrup, "Towards an Integrated Model of Family Therapy," *Clinical Social Work Journal,* 9 (Summer 1981), 111–125.

7. Quoted in Frank J. Bruno, *Trends in Social Work: 1874–1956* (New York: Columbia University Press, 1957), p. 177.

8. Mary E. Richmond, *Social Diagnosis* (New York: Russell Sage Foundation, 1917), p. 137. For more on the roots of family treatment in social work history, see Frank Montalvo, "The Third Dimension in Social Casework: Mary E. Richmond's Contribution to Family Treatment," *Clinical Social Work Journal,* 10 (Summer 1982), 103–112; and Max Siporin, "Marriage and Family Therapy in Social Work," *Social Casework,* 61 (January 1980), 11–21. See also Lois Bravermann, "Social Casework and Strategic Therapy," *Social Casework,* 67 (April 1986), 234–239, for a discussion of social work's tendency to disregard early casework contributions to family therapy; the author offers possible explanations for this phenomenon.

9. Richmond, *Social Diagnosis,* pp. 134–159.

10. Greater detail on the history of the shifts in social work emphases can be found in Helen Leland Witmer, *Social Work* (New York: Rinehart, 1942), especially Chapters 8 and 17; Arthur E. Fink, *The Field of Social Work* (New York: Holt, 1942), especially chapter 4; and Kathleen Woodroofe, *From Charity to Social Work in England and in the United States* (Toronto: University of Toronto Press, 1962), especially Chapter 6.

11. Gordon Hamilton, *Theory and Practice of Social Case Work,* 2d ed. (New York: Columbia University Press, 1951), pp.95–97.

12. Emily Mudd, *The Practice of Marriage Counselling* (New York: Association Press, 1951); Irene Josselyn, "The Family as a Psychological Unit," *Social Casework,* 34 (October 1953), 336–343; and Florence Hollis, *Women in Marital Conflict* (New York: Family Service Association of America, 1949).

13. Ira D. Glick and Jay Haley, *Family Therapy and Research: An Annotated Bibliography* (New York: Grune & Stratton, 1971).

14. Siporin, "Marriage and Family Therapy in Social Work," p. 14.

15. Nathan W. Ackerman, *The Psychodynamics of Family Life* (New York: Basic Books, 1958), p. xi. This volume is one of the family therapy classics.

16. Among the many books and articles on family treatment written by these social workers are Virginia Satir, *Conjoint Family Therapy,* rev. ed. (Palo Alto, Calif.: Science and Behavior Books, 1967); Frances Scherz, "Theory and Practice in Family Therapy," in Robert W. Roberts and Robert H. Nee, eds., *Theories of Social Casework* (Chicago: University of Chicago Press, 1970), 219–264; Arthur L. Leader, "Current and Future Issues in Family Therapy," *Social Service Review,* 43 (January 1969), 1–11; Sherman, "Intergenerational Discontinuity and Therapy of the Family"; and Harry J. Aponte, "Underorganization in the Poor Family," in Guerin, *Family Therapy,* pp. 432–448.

17. See Siporin, "Marriage and Family Therapy in Social Work."

18. See especially the excellent compilation of pertinent articles in *The Family Life Cycle,* Elizabeth A. Carter and Monica McGoldrick, eds. (New York: Gardner Press, 1980). See also the still useful volume, Howard J. Parad, ed., *Crisis Intervention* (New York: Family Service Association of America, 1965), which contains some very good articles that describe the impact of various crises and stressful events on family life; of particular relevance to this section are those articles in Part 2, "Common Maturational and Situational Crises," pp. 73–190.

The ways in which family and individual developmental tasks necessarily run parallel is discussed more fully in Scherz, "Theory and Practice in Family Therapy," pp. 229–231. See also Trevor R. Hadley et al., "The Relationship Between Family Developmental Crisis and the Appearance of Symptoms in a Family Member," *Family Process,* 13 (June 1974), 207–214; in a study reported on in this article, a positive and significant relationship was found between the onset of symptoms in family members and two types of family crisis: the addition of a family member and the loss of a family member.

19. There were exceptions: Ackerman, *Psychodynamics of Family Life,* and John E. Bell, *Family Group Therapy,* Public Monograph No. 64 (Washington, D. C., U.S. Government Printing Office, 1961). Ackerman and Bell were among some of the early pioneers

in the study of the family environments of non-psychotic clients.

For an orientation to the rationale and historical development of the family therapy movement see the following: Gerald H. Zuk and David Rubinstein, "A Review of Concepts in the Study and Treatment of Families of Schizophrenics," in Ivan Boszormenyi-Nagy and James L. Framo, eds., *Intensive Family Therapy* (New York: Harper & Row, 1965), pp. 1–25. See also some of the references in note 6.

A number of studies about pathological family interaction in families with a schizophrenic member appeared in the 1940s and the 1950s. In these studies, emphasis was on dynamic relationships. Unsuccessful efforts were made to relate specific abnormal traits in parents to their children's abnormal traits or specific type of family to type of symptoms. Finally, the central object of attention became the pathological family system. See Don D. Jackson and Virginia Satir, "A Review of Psychiatric Developments in Family Diagnosis and Therapy," in Nathan W. Ackerman, Frances L. Beatman, and Sanford N. Sherman, eds., *Exploring the Base for Family Therapy* (New York: Family Service Association of America, 1961), pp. 29–49; Elizabeth H. Couch, *Joint and Family Interviews in the Treatment of Marital Problems* (New York: Family Service Association of America, 1969); Christian C. Beels and A. S. Ferber, "Family Therapy: A View," *Family Process*, 8 (1969), 280–318; Nathan W. Ackerman, "Family Psychotherapy Today," *Family Process*, 9 (1970), 123–126; and David Olson, "Marital and Family Therapy: Integrative Review and Critique," *Journal of Marriage and the Family*, 32 (1970), 501–538.

20. See Lyman C. Wynne et al., "Pseudomutuality in the Family Relations of Schizophrenics," in Bell and Vogel, *A Modern Introduction to the Family*; pp. 628–649; and Thomas Fogarty, "Marital Crisis," in Guerin, *Family Therapy*, pp. 42–90.

21. See Paul Argles, "The Threat of Separation in Family Conflict," *Social Casework*, 65 (December 1984), 610–614.

22. Murray Bowen, *Family Therapy in Clinical Practice* (New York: Aronson, 1978).

23. See, as examples, James L. Framo, *Explorations in Marital and Family Therapy* (New York: Springer, 1982); Frank S. Pittman, III, *Turning Points: Treating*

Families in Transition and Crisis (New York: W. W. Norton, 1987); and Carl R. Rogers, *On Becoming a Person: A Therapist's View of Psychotherapy* (Boston: Houghton Mifflin, 1961). See also Philip Rich, "Differentiation of Self in Therapist's Family of Origin," *Social Casework*, 61 (September 1980), 394–399, for useful discussions of differentiation issues.

24. Bowen, *Family Therapy in Clinical Practice*, p. 366.

25. See Chapter 12, note 11.

See also two excellent articles on intergenerational dependency and separation anxiety: Gerda L. Shulman, "Treatment of Intergenerational Pathology," *Social Casework*, 54 (October 1973), 462–472; and Arthur L. Leader, "Intergenerational Separation Anxiety in Family Therapy," *Social Casework*, 59 (March 1978), 138–144.

Sometimes an unequal yet complementary relationship is so necessary to the functioning of the individuals involved that it can be dangerous to disturb the balance even though it clearly involves a pathological adaptation; see Chapter 12, note 12, for references illustrating this point.

26. Salvador Minuchin, *Families and Family Therapy* (Cambridge, Mass.: Harvard University Press, 1974), p. 52. See Chapter 3, especially pp. 51–60, for further elaboration on Minuchin's ideas on family structure and boundaries.

27. Ibid., p. 59.

28. Pittman, *Turning Points*, p. 21.

29. Ibid., p. 22.

30. James L. Framo, "Symptoms from a Family Transactional Viewpoint," in Framo, *Explorations in Marital and Family Therapy*, p. 53. See also his thorough and readable chapter on many of the theoretical and technical aspects of family treatment, "Rationale and Techniques of Family Therapy," pp. 61–119. This chapter also appears in Boszormenyi-Nagy and Framo, eds., *Intensive Family Therapy*, along with many other articles we recommend to the student of family therapy.

31. Don D. Jackson, "The Question of Family Homeostasis," in Don D. Jackson, ed., *Communication, Family and Marriage: Human Communication*, vol. 1 (Palo Alto, Calif.: Science and Behavior Books,

1968), pp. 1–11; Don D. Jackson, "Family Interaction, Family Homeostasis and Some Implications for Conjoint Family Psychotherapy," in Don D. Jackson, ed., *Therapy, Communication, and Change: Human Communication,* vol. 2., pp. 185–203; and Ackerman, *Psychodynamics of Family Life,* pp. 68–79.

32. See a very highly recommended text: Ann Hartman and Joan Laird, *Family-Centered Social Work Practice* (New York: Free Press, 1983), pp. 93–96. See also David C. Speer, "Family Systems: Morphostasis and Morphogenesis, or 'Is Homeostasis Enough?'" *Family Process,* 9 (September 1970), 259–278.

33. Ackerman, *Psychodynamics of Family Life,* p. 71.

34. Hartman and Laird, *Family-Centered Social Work Practice,* p. 95.

35. John P. Spiegel, "The Resolution of Role Conflict Within the Family," in Bell and Vogel, *Modern Introduction to the Family,* p. 393.

36. Aponte, "Underorganization in the Poor Family"; and Salvador Minuchin, et al., *Families of the Slums* (New York: Basic Books, 1967).

37. Ivan Boszormenyi-Nagy and David N. Ulrich, "Contextual Family Therapy," in Gurman and Kniskern, eds., *Handbook of Family Therapy,* p. 169.

38. Nathan W. Ackerman, "Prejudice and Scapegoating in the Family," in Gerald H. Zuk and Ivan Boszormenyi-Nagy, eds., *Family Therapy and Disturbed Families,* pp. 48–57. See also the excellent paper by Ezra F. Vogel and Norman W. Bell, "The Emotionally Disturbed Child as the Family Scapegoat," in Bell and Vogel, *Modern Introduction to the Family,* pp. 412–427.

39. Sharon Wegscheider, *Another Chance: Hope and Health for the Alcoholic Family* (Palo Alto, Calif.: Science and Behavior Books, 1981), pp. 84–86.

40. Minuchin, *Families and Family Therapy,* p. 102. See also Murray Bowen's discussion of triangles in Guerin, *Family Therapy,* pp. 75–78; and Thomas Fogarty, "Systems Concepts and the Dimensions of Self," in Guerin, *Family Therapy,* pp. 147–148.

41. Lyman C. Wynne et al., "Pseudomutuality in the Family Relations of Schizophrenics," in Bell and Vogel, *Modern Introduction to the Family,* p. 628.

42. Antonio J. Ferreira, "Family Myth and Homeostasis," *Archives of General Psychiatry,* 9 (July–December 1963), 457–463. See also Helm Stierlin, "Group Fantasies and Family Myths," *Family Process,* 12 (June 1973), 111–125.

43. This case is described more thoroughly in Mary E. Woods, "Childhood Phobia and Family Therapy: A Case Illustration," in Florence Lieberman, ed., *Clinical Social Workers as Psychotherapists* (New York: Gardner, 1982), 165–178.

44. Satir, *Conjoint Family Therapy,* p. 70.

45. See the very important volume on communication by Paul Watzlawick, Janet Beaven, and Don Jackson, *Pragmatics of Human Communication* (New York: W. W. Norton, 1967). The reader who wishes to study body movement and communication will be interested in a collection of essays by Ray L. Birdwhistell, *Kinesics and Context* (Philadelphia: University of Pennsylvania Press, 1970). See also two articles by Albert E. Scheflen: "The Significance of Posture in Communications," *Psychiatry,* 27 (1964), 316–331; and Human Communication: Behavioral Programs and Their Integration in Interaction," *Behavioral Science,* 13 (1968), 44–55.

46. Gregory Bateson, Don D. Jackson, Jay Haley, and John H. Weakland, "Toward a Theory of Schizophrenia," *Behavioral Science,* 1 (October 1956), 251–264, reprinted in Jackson, *Communication, Family, and Marriage,* pp. 31–53.

47. Gregory Bateson et al., "A Note on the Double Bind—1962," *Family Process,* 2 (March 1963), 154–161, reprinted in Jackson, *Communication, Family, and Marriage,* p. 58.

48. Ronald D. Laing, "Mystification, Confusion, and Conflict," in Boszormenyi-Nagy and Framo, *Intensive Family Therapy,* p. 346. See also R. D. Laing and A. Esterson, *Sanity, Madness and the Family,* 2d ed. (New York: Basic Books, 1971); this book includes clinical studies of the families of schizophrenic patients and identifies mystification as an important aspect of the families' communication styles.

49. See, in particular, Jay Haley, *Problem Solving Therapy,* 2d ed. (San Francisco: Jossey-Bass, 1986). Salvador Minuchin, although to a lesser extent, also minimizes the importance of diagnosis of the individual.

50. In addition to other references on the history and practice of social work already cited in this book, see Bernice K. Simon, "Social Casework Theory: An Overview," in Roberts and Nee, *Theories of Social Casework*, especially p. 375; in spite of many variations in orientation among casework theoreticians, the person-in-situation concept is widely recognized by most points of view.

51. Gordon Hearn, in Francis J. Turner, ed., *Social Work Treatment: Interlocking Theoretical Approaches*, 2d ed. (New York: Free Press, 1979), p, 364.

52. Sigmund Freud, "Analysis of Phobia in a Five-year-old Boy," in James Strachey, ed., *The Complete Works of Sigmund Freud*, vol. 10 (London: Hogarth, 1964), pp. 5–148. See also Ackerman, *Psychodynamics of Family Life*, pp. 26–51, for an interesting approach to the integration of psychoanalytic concepts and the influences of the family environment.

53. Lyman C. Wynne, "Some Indications and Contraindications for Exploratory Family Therapy," in Boszormenyi-Nagy and Framo, *Intensive Family Therapy*, pp. 297–300.

54. See John Bowlby, "Grief and Mourning in Infancy and Early Childhood," in Ruth S. Eissler et al., eds., *The Psychoanalytic Study of the Child*, vol. 15 (New York: International Universities Press, 1965); Margaret S. Mahler, Fred Pine, and Anni Bergman, *The Psychological Birth of the Human Infant* (New York: Basic Books, 1975); Gertrude and Rubin Blanck, *Ego Psychology: Theory and Practice* (New York: Columbia University Press, 1974), pp. 40–60; and Shirley S. Taylor and Norma Siegel, "Treating the Separation-Individuation Conflict," *Social Casework*, 59 (June 1978), 337–344.

55. Leader, "Intergenerational Separation Anxiety," p. 141.

56. Nathan W. Ackerman, "The Growing Edge of Family Therapy," in Clifford J. Sagar and Helen Singer Kaplan, eds., *Progress in Group and Family Therapy* (New York: Brunner/Mazel, 1972), p. 451.

57. Minuchin, *Families and Family Therapy*, p. 9.

58. Moultrup, "Towards an Integrated Model of Family Therapy," p. 113. See also David E. Scharff and Jill Savege Scharff, *Object Relations Family Therapy* (Northvale, N.J.: Aronson, 1987), p. 13, for a similar statement.

CHAPTER 16

The Clinical Practice of Family Therapy

From the point of view expressed in the preceding chapter, it follows that we cannot fully understand individuals without knowledge of the families to which they belong. Conversely, as we build a conceptual system with which to evaluate a family's dynamics, the total picture requires a grasp of the characteristics of the individual members. In some case situations, the understanding of the biological and psychological qualities of the individual(s) is the most important guide to treatment; in others, the properties and transactions of the family system are of greatest consequence. In still other cases, of course, we must be particularly attuned to how individuals and families are influenced by and interact with the larger community and social system. We need not choose among these levels of conceptualization. Rather, as we collect the mass of information that clients bring, we must try to organize the germane data from as many perspectives as possible. After weighing the influence of diverse levels on each other and on the problem at hand, we are then in a position to select treatment methods and procedures.

To demonstrate the thinking that goes into arranging data and deciding whether or not to engage the whole family in treatment, we introduce the Russo case. This family will serve to illustrate how the theoretical framework presented in these two family chapters can be applied in practice.

AN INTAKE REQUEST: THE RUSSO FAMILY

Mrs. Russo telephoned the mental health clinic in her area, seeking an appointment for her husband, whom she described as depressed and withdrawn. He had not asked her to call and, in fact, she had not told him she was doing so. She believed she could persuade him to keep the appointment, however. Since Mrs. Russo was making the application, the worker recommended that she come in with her husband. From the telephone conversation the worker learned that this couple, in their late forties, had two daughters: Linda, age twenty-two (who moved with her husband from her parents' apartment building to Canada three months before Mrs. Russo's call to the clinic), and Angela, age seventeen (a senior in high school). At the time of intake, Angela was vacationing with her maternal grandmother, a widow for twenty years, who lived next door and to whom Angela had always been close.

During an extended interview with Mr. and Mrs. Russo, the worker found Mr. Russo to be quite severely depressed, self-blaming, and indecisive, yet still able to function on his job. Mrs. Russo came across as a very managerial and perfectionistic woman. She talked at length, often on her husband's behalf. On the basis of this first contact, the worker ordered and weighed the information she had gathered from four interpenetrating vantage points:

1. About his *biochemical* situation, she learned that during a previous depression Mr. Russo had responded favorably to mood-elevating drugs. To help relieve his symptoms, one treatment option would be to refer him to a psychiatrist who could evaluate him for medication.

2. On the *intrapsychic* level, the worker hypothesized that Mr. Russo's depression was rooted in early deprivation. His mother had died when he was three, after which he spent several years in a series of foster homes and institutions. His current depression developed shortly after his daughter Linda, with whom he had always had a warm relationship, moved to Canada. He regressed into a partial withdrawal and experienced a pervasive sense of emptiness and hopelessness. His negative feelings about himself tormented him, overwhelming his inner life. The worker surmised that the feelings of loss experienced in his young years had been reactivated. On the basis of her knowledge about early deprivation and depression, she tentatively concluded that Mr. Russo's tendency toward self-depreciation and low self-esteem were exacerbated when Linda left. Without Linda's kindness and interest in him, he felt abandoned and alone once again. Yet, unable to accept his anger at her, he turned it against himself.[1] The worker considered the option of individual treatment in which sustainment, some direct advice, and reflection could

take place in the context of a "corrective relationship."

3. Various aspects of Mr. Russo's *family relational* situation were revealed. Although Mrs. Russo was genuinely concerned about her husband, her tolerance for his morose dependency was strained and her anger poorly masked. The younger daughter, Angela, who was close to her mother, often ridiculed and demeaned her father. Fairly openly, the mother defended Angela's contempt for Mr. Russo, blaming it on his apathetic and self-pitying manner. The worker guessed that Angela was voicing feelings her mother could not express directly. From her knowledge of family systems, the worker hypothesized that the mother-daughter collusion provided the mother with external support and gratification (and probably gave the daughter some of the same), and the father had become the outsider, particularly now that the older daughter had moved away. Mr. Russo participated in the collusion and promoted his "odd man out" status by being so self-depreciating. Paradoxically, his pathetic demeanor also brought out the motherly side of Mrs. Russo, who was taking more and more responsibility for many areas of her husband's life. Thus, although the price both paid was high, she protected him from feeling totally alone. Family sessions, the worker considered, might foster a more mutually rewarding relationship between Mr. and Mrs. Russo, thus reducing Mr. Russo's depression and providing greater gratification for Mrs. Russo. In turn, this might assuage her anger and reduce her need to ally herself with Angela. Involving Angela in treatment, the worker suspected, could be preventive by helping her to separate from her mother enough to begin to establish her own life and plan for her college years. Without Angela's participation, furthermore, she might work against any progress made by her parents if her role in the family process continued.

4. The larger *socioeconomic* system had also influenced Mr. Russo's situation. In fact, Mr.

Russo blamed his depression mostly on a recent shift in his job. As a receiving clerk, Mr. Russo had been in charge of two other men and had successfully organized his small department. His boss had often commended him for his reliability, his willingness to work overtime, and his pleasing manner. Two months before the intake meeting, the company for which he worked was taken over by a large concern. Although given a promotion in terms of job title and salary, he no longer supervised other men and he had little contact with his old boss. Because of automation, his job no longer challenged his organizational talents and his work was duller and more routine. The impersonal climate of the new company provided little positive support for Mr. Russo. The worker speculated that referral to an employment service for vocational testing and placement in a smaller, more intimate establishment might better utilize his capabilities and fulfill his strong need for praise from others.

On the basis of the above facts about the past and the present reported by Mr. and Mrs. Russo, and her observation of the couple's behavior and interactions, the worker evaluated the Russo case on these four interdependent conceptual levels. No single hypothesis or conclusion reached at any one level could be considered more intrinsically "true" or "right" than any other. In fact, as the worker studied the Russo case from each perspective, the overall assessment became richer and more complete. The question of choice came up only as she considered which treatment approach could most effectively relieve Mr. Russo's depression. It was clear that she could address more than one level at the same time. For example, she could arrange an evaluation for medication and then set up individual or family sessions. Or, in addition to other treatment approaches, she could refer him to an employment service. Of particular interest to us in this chapter are the criteria that helped the worker determine whether she

should see Mr. Russo in individual treatment (with, perhaps, occasional family or couple meetings), or whether she should arrange to see the family as a unit.

INDICATIONS FOR CONSIDERING FAMILY TREATMENT

Although we will resume our account of the Russo family later on in this chapter, we pause now to consider the conditions under which a worker might decide on family therapy as the treatment of choice. There are differences among practitioners and writers on the question of indications (and contraindications) for family therapy. Yet, we often must ask ourselves: under what circumstances should we try to see the family as a group and when should we choose to work with individual members? In recent years, there has been a surge of research on the outcomes of marital and family therapy, some of which contrast these with the effectiveness of individual treatment. There are indications, for example, that family therapy is often more effective than individual treatment, *even for difficulties that are not presented as interpersonal*, but rather seen by clients as individual or intrapsychic in nature. There is also evidence that including the father in family meetings "clearly improves the odds of good outcomes in many situations."[2] But there is not yet a solid body of research that specifically identifies the treatment of choice for many categories of presenting problems, family situations, or relationship styles. Of course, whether we see one person, a subgroup, or an entire family in treatment, we use family and systems perspectives as well as psychodynamic concepts to assess our clients' psychosocial situations.

A typology of criteria for selecting the family therapy approach must rest, therefore, on empirical evidence and clinical experience. The list that follows represents a blend of selected recommendations made by several authors in the field,[3] combined with our own views, on the conditions under which family therapy might be considered the treatment of choice:

1. When the family as a group, whether in crisis or handicapped by long-standing problems, *requests* family treatment and defines its difficulties as involving all family members. As family therapy has become better known, more such requests are initiated by families.

2. When the presenting problem immediately suggests a family relationship difficulty, or, of course, more than one. Examples would include marital or parent-child conflicts, problems with extended family members, and strife among siblings.

3. When one or more of the family members want to make an appointment for another or want to bring another in for help.

4. When a child's disturbances or symptomatology is the impetus for seeking treatment. Exploration usually reveals that the child's symptoms are, at least in part, an expression of other difficulties in the family system. Also,as Sherman says: "The child's boundaries are so fluid and interlaced with the little world outside himself—primarily his family—that, in important respects, we cannot be sure what is inside him and what is outside him."[4]

5. When adolescents or poorly differentiated adults, particularly but not exclusively those living in their parents' home, either cling to or defensively disown their families. In these situations, boundaries are either diffuse or rigid and impenetrable. In either case, such individuals have been unable to separate effectively. Whether a person is submissively tied or rebelliously acting out, usually similar problems can be found in other family members. Individuation of the identified patient or index client may be discouraged by the family situation. Furthermore, we agree with Mitchell: "The clinical evidence is overwhelming that the human being does not separate from what he needs but has never had, until he finds it or its equivalent."[5] As we pointed out earlier, individuation is most successfully achieved when the family group supports the young person's (or immature adult's) growth and autonomy. Contrary to the view of some emerging adults (and, on occasion, their caseworkers), geographical distance from their family of origin does not in and of itself foster differentiation. A change in the pattern of relationships, which allows closeness and independence alike, often does.

6. When family communication appears impaired. When it is extremely distant, restrained, vague, or bizarre, or when messages are contradictory, double-binding, or mystifying. When family members seem to be acting on faulty assumptions about one another. Such communication patterns may be addressed most incisively in the context of the family group. Also, bewildering symptoms can sometimes be understood when viewed as a reaction to the family communication style.

7. When the index client believes that his or her distress or behavior is the function of the personality or personalities of *other* family members. When irrational role assignments seem to be interfering with healthy family functioning. Consistent externalization or "trading of dissociations" (see pages 328 and 329) can respond to intervention aimed at the interpersonal aspects of these processes. Since individuals who project in these ways are often not very amenable to intrareflection, family treatment may be preferred.

8. Similarly, when family members can express their feelings of distress but see them entirely as reactions to the symptoms or behavior of the index client. In these situations, the burden for the well-being of the entire family is unrealistically placed on the shoulders of the scapegoated one. Interventions that promote the sharing of responsibility for the difficulties call for the participation of the entire family in treatment.

9. When there is evidence of consistent violation of generational boundaries. For example, when parents "parentify" children, they

deprive them of needed nurturing and delegate authority to them that they cannot manage. When dysfunctional intergenerational coalitions become a way of life for the family, as when two family members team up against a third (mother and son against father, grandmother and grandchild against mother, and so on).

10. When it appears that one or some family members' perceptions of other members, or of family values and ideals, are seriously distorted. Or when myths and secrets appear to be the family style. These can be exposed and corrected in the family context.

11. When intrafamily relationships are affectively impoverished, chaotic, or hostile. The participation of all family members in the here-and-now may be the most effective way to help them to learn alternative styles.

12. When an individual is receiving inadequate physical or emotional support from the family and is therefore poorly cared for or lonely. This condition applies to many elderly or ill clients who are estranged from or neglected by family members, as well as to some psychiatrically ill or retarded individuals living at home, in halfway houses, or institutions. In some instances, it may not be possible or advisable, because of his or her condition, for the index client to be present at family sessions. Other members, however, often have conflicts and unresolved feelings about the client or among themselves that can be clarified in family group meetings and that may result in more support for the neglected member. Sometimes the family as a unit becomes the client and engages in treatment. In any event, the potential for improving the presenting situation can be explored by calling together the relatives.

13. When the index client is either unmotivated for or has been unsuccessful in utilizing individual treatment.

14. Similarly, when individual treatment for any family member is recommended but the member is resistant. He or she may need—at least temporarily—the support of being seen with the family. Although less true than in the past, in our experience there have been significant numbers of men, for example, who are more amenable to family or couple treatment than to individual therapy.

15. When the worker has not been able to decide on a treatment approach. To begin with family meetings reduces the probability that an individual will be reluctant to share the worker with other family members if family therapy becomes the treatment of choice. By the same token, the family may be less likely to believe in the worker's neutrality if the worker has had a longer relationship with one member than with the others. Arranging family sessions at the outset also diminishes the possibility that the worker will become strongly identified with the index client and thus unable to maintain "involved impartiality" so important to family (or any other) therapy. Individual meetings can always be arranged later. This is not to say that individual treatment cannot comfortably evolve into family therapy as well as vice versa. (In some situations, a phase of individual therapy, or concurrent individual treatment, may be necessary for one member. A severely scapegoated one, for example, may need extra support to relinquish this role.)

Even when one or more of the above conditions point to the selection of family therapy, there may be other factors that interfere. First, the worker may not feel comfortable or competent enough to treat the family as a group. In this instance, if family treatment is indicated, the worker would be best advised to refer the family to another therapist or to invite a more experienced colleague to act as cotherapist.

Second, a small percentage of families cannot be persuaded to enter treatment as a group. Or, some family members may adamantly refuse to be involved, with the result that family meetings are incomplete. In these cases, the worker will have to work either with the index client alone or with part of the family. The worker need not, however, abandon the family orientation or efforts to understand the family system. The worker should be alert to changes in the index client that may have repercussions on the family. (Sometimes, as we shall discuss later in this chapter, changes made by the motivated member can result in positive changes in others in the family.) Third, in some cases there are geographical obstacles. Often young adult clients, for example, live many miles away from their parents; even when family treatment would be helpful, it may be impossible to arrange. Also prisons, residential treatment centers, training schools, psychiatric hospitals and institutions for the retarded are often located at considerable distance from the family homes. Family treatment may be limited thereby, although not necessarily ruled out. In recent years, increased efforts have been made to involve families even when they do not live near the institution.[6]

Sometimes, after a series of family meetings, the worker may decide to move into individual treatment with one or more of the family members. This may occur when there seems to be motivation to explore personal issues. However, in making the shift, it is important for the worker to utilize all of the available knowledge about the workings of the particular family system. The worker must consider whether the family's dysfunctional equilibrium will be reactivated thereby and militate against changes the individual is working toward.

A worker did not object when a resistant family discontinued weekly sessions in order to give support to a twenty-three-old daughter, who wanted to work on her relationships with men. But, the young woman's problems were so intertwined with those of her parents that, as soon as she made moves to individuate and live an adult life, her mother and father began to interfere by infantilizing her, as had been their lifelong pattern, thus drawing her back into a dependent role. The daughter allowed and unconsciously encouraged this out of years of familiarity with the pattern. Progress achieved earlier was reversed until the worker resumed family meetings.

In families such as this, one member's effort to grow up can seem like an abandonment threat to the others, and tendencies toward enmeshment are intensified. In this case, the worker had been "inducted" into the family system (i.e., drawn in on the side of the family's defensive resistance to change) in the hope that the young woman's efforts to individuate might be better served. It became clear, however, that the homeostatic family process was so powerful that the daughter was unable to make changes from within herself when she was so pressured by the family from without. After a year of family work, including some marital treatment of the parents, the daughter was then able to make progress in individual treatment.

CONTRAINDICATIONS FOR FAMILY THERAPY

Under what conditions would we recommend against family group meetings? With Sherman, we agree that family therapy may "take" even under circumstances that seem to contraindicate it.[7] Nevertheless, we present a list of those situations that call for the exercise of particular caution as a worker considers the family therapy approach:

1. When a family member is in the throes of a psychotic break. Usually, it is best to wait until there is some stabilization of the most acute symptoms.

2. When a family member or family members are grossly deceitful, psychopathic, or paranoiac, and family work is thereby rendered virtually impossible.

3. When the family process or some of the members are so destructive that the intensely negative interactions have a snowball effect.

4. When a family member has a severe psychosomatic illness. There have been some reports from clinicians that in these cases family therapy occasionally sets off dangerous somatic reactions. In such situations, before embarking on family (or individual) treatment, medical or psychiatric consultation is advisable.

5. When a relationship (e.g., marital or parent and adult child) appears to be "pathological" yet stable and efforts aimed at change are likely to result in the emotional deterioration of one or more family members. Consultation or psychiatric advice may be required to identify such situations and to determine, on the basis of diagnostic appraisal, whether there are family members who are psychologically so delicately balanced that they cannot tolerate family meetings or who might decompensate over a course of intensive family therapy.

6. When an individual's defensiveness or anxiety would be so intensified by family group meetings that he or she would be too uncomfortable to benefit from them. Of course, to a degree, many clients will become apprehensive when family therapy is suggested. But, just as a worker treating an individual must be careful not to press hard for material that will stimulate immobilizing discomfort, so the family therapist must be able to assess differentially a particular client's level of anxiety about family group meetings before strongly encouraging them. The work with Jed Cooper, to be presented in Chapter 21, illustrates this type of situation, in which family therapy was contraindicated despite the fact that this client's difficulties were intimately intertwined with his relationships with his parents.

7. When family relationships are "dead" and family members cannot mobilize the energy to work on them. However, even divorcing or divorced couples sometimes work together effectively to separate, to sort out for each spouse the issues that led to the breakdown of the marriage, or to work out problems relating to the children.

8. When a client is strongly motivated for and prefers individual therapy, and is able to make progress in treatment without suffering setbacks caused by counterpressures from the family. Individuals who have established living arrangements and lives separate from their families, including many single young adults, often fall into this category. Frequently, one member of a family may have personal issues or particular problems to resolve that do not require the ongoing participation of the others. The large bulk of some clinical caseloads is comprised of such individuals. Nevertheless, occasional or intermittent joint and family meetings may be arranged to facilitate a particular piece of work with an individual client. Sometimes, as we have mentioned, family sessions may lead to a course of individual treatment for one or more members who are motivated to continue. When the entire family is in treatment, each individual is an equal participant in the therapy. When an individual is in treatment, and the family is invited for sessions, the worker still observes the family system, but the family members are viewed as part of the individual's environment; they are related to as collaterals—unless, of course, they are engaged subsequently in ongoing family treatment. (See Chapter 8 for a discussion of the use of family sessions in the service of individual treatment.)

In our experience, the feasibility of family therapy is often best tested during exploratory sessions. Sometimes the most unwieldy, disorganized, or uncommunicative families respond surprisingly well. In very difficult situations it may be wise to involve a cotherapist. Not only can two heads be better than one, but the dangers of being hopelessly "inducted" by the family pathology may be averted. The "blind spot" of one therapist may turn out to be readily discerned by the other. If they work well together, cotherapists can supplement each other as they address the multifarious and perplexing issues that can spring up in family meetings.

Finally, we share Wynne's view that it is easy to exaggerate the possible dangers of embarking on a program of family treatment: "The likelihood of bringing about drastic or precipitous changes unintentionally is extremely low." As in individual treatment, worrisome symptoms that reflect long-standing dysfunctions may emerge in the course of family therapy. In these instances, it is usually best not to terminate family sessions abruptly. Rather, the worker may have to work harder to devise a treatment strategy that will confront the dysfunctional system. As Wynne goes on to say, helping families to make real and enduring changes is a formidable task. We are less likely to contribute to unwanted change than we are to discover that the family system is so intransigent that it is difficult to foster any change at all![8]

ADVANTAGES OF FAMILY THERAPY

In cases where conditions favor treating the family as a unit, we have found this approach to have distinct advantages over individual treatment:

1. Observing the family as a group affords the worker a deeper and more complete understanding of the complex situations of the individual members. Direct observation is worth a thousand descriptive words. Reports from a client, however conscientiously rendered, are necessarily limited to material that is conscious. Much of the behavior and interpersonal transactions, verbal and nonverbal, that penetrate a dysfunctional system may be distorted by or be beyond the awareness of the family members. Of course, experience and diagnostic skills help the worker to make intelligent inferences about a family situation, even when only one family member is seen. But by sitting with the family as a whole, the worker can learn firsthand about the interlocking "fits," the quality of individual and subsystem boundaries, alliances, and the repetitive patterns that perpetuate the difficul-

ties. Data obtained in individual therapy rely heavily on conjectures; in family sessions, many more facts can be witnessed in the here-and-now.

2. Distortions, projections, myths, and family secrets that are burdening individual members can be exposed and challenged. When timed appropriately, the worker can raise questions sensitively, such as: "Have you any idea what makes your son think you prefer his sister?" "Do you always act as though your feelings don't matter?" "When you tell Johnnie that you are going to call the policeman to take him away do you really mean you would want him to go away for good? Johnnie seems to think you do." "Were you angry when you said that—as your husband assumes—or is that the way you act when you are frightened?" "Were you trying to protect your daughter by not telling her how sick your husband really is?" When people learn to speak for themselves, the process of individuation is enhanced.

3. On the same order, once identified, dysfunctional sequences can be addressed or interrupted *when they occur*. Bringing attention to them *in vivo* may have far more impact than talking about them in individual sessions where they can become intellectualized rather than experienced on the spot. For example, in a family meeting, a worker might inquire of a passive father, "Have you noticed that you often let others in the family answer questions for you?" Or, with a light touch, the family therapist might ask an angry adolescent girl, "What do you think would happen if you told your mother again how you feel about your early curfew, but this time without insulting her?"

4. Family sessions can provide the opportunity to shift the focus to the marital relationship when the problems of the children or adolescents appear to be a reflection of problems between the parents. Similarly, since parent-child relationships can be heavily influenced by relational patterns that were established between the parents and *their* parents, family sessions

provide an arena for exploring how introjects and intergenerational issues manifest themselves in the present family system. For example, the worker might ask a mother, "Do you notice that the things you hated most in your relationship with your mother are occurring here between you and Susan?"

5. In family meetings, family members can make new and real connections with each other and thereby gain the freedom to separate effectively. As discussed earlier, threats and fears of abandonment can stand in the way of family members accepting differences among them, or of allowing each other autonomy. In enmeshed families, since the issues of one member are so complexly intertwined with those of the others, it is often difficult to sort out the problems in individual treatment.

6. Family sessions provide the climate, with the support of the worker, for family members to learn about and empathize with one another as each shares experiences, feelings, and past history. So often in family therapy we hear "I never knew you felt that way." Or, "Gee, Dad, you never told me you played minor league baseball." Or, "Now that you have told me about your life as a child, I understand your stubbornness (or temper or reserve). Before this, I always took it personally." The fears about sharing vulnerable feelings or the belief that no one really cares can be dissolved as families learn to talk together.

7. Family meetings can circumvent the problems that arise when family members are suspicious or frightened about what the index client is doing or talking about in one-to-one therapy. Often unconsciously, those who are not in treatment may worry about changes in the family balance, and therefore interfere with or sabotage the efforts of those who are.

8. Whenever possible, it is far more effective to work with the "transferences" or projections *among family members* than with those between an individual client and a worker. Relationships within the family are intrinsically far more important than the treatment relationship. Moreover, transference to a therapist is not usually as intense, stable, or fully developed as it is with members of one's family, and hence it can be less accessible to intervention. This point, as it relates to couple treatment, will be discussed in greater detail in Chapter 18.

9. The way in which therapists use their personalities is important in every kind of treatment, but there is an added dimension to the impact they can have in family therapy. Workers not only encourage family exchanges by generating a climate of acceptance and trust, but their tenderness, ability to laugh at themselves and willingness to take chances in relationships with the family provide a model that can lead the members to risk new ways of relating to each other. In many families that we see clinically, despair and low self-esteem run rampant; this special kind of "corrective" experience provided by the worker can promote greater intimacy and a sense of belonging among family members, as well as an opportunity for the healing of old wounds.

THE INITIAL INTERVIEW: THE RUSSO FAMILY

Returning now to the Russo family, once the worker had organized the data from her first interview with Mr. and Mrs. Russo, as outlined earlier, she considered treatment approaches. She referred Mr. Russo to the clinic's consulting psychiatrist who prescribed a mild dosage of a mood elevating drug.[9] She decided it would be premature to refer him to an employment service until she had more information about his overall job situation, his interest in making the change, and the opportunities that might be available to him.

The important choice the worker had to make was whether to treat the entire Russo family. As she reviewed the conditions for considering family treatment, the following indications (see pages 337 to 340) seemed relevant:

Although the family was not requesting treatment for the entire group, Mrs. Russo had made the application and willingly participated in the interview with her husband. (Indications 1 and 3.)

Marital difficulties were not the impetus for treatment, but the strains between the couple were immediately apparent. Mrs. Russo's anger and Mr. Russo's depression seemed partially linked with the marital interaction. The parents did not complain specifically about Angela, but difficulties in her relationship with her father were reported. (Indication 2.)

The worker suspected that the mother and daughter were clinging to one another, to the detriment of the marriage. It also seemed possible that Angela would have difficulty separating. (Indication 4.)

Communication patterns were not yet fully understood by the worker, but she did note considerable restraint and indirectness. Mr. Russo did not reveal his feelings about his marriage or about Angela's attitudes toward him; instead, he retreated into silence or self-blame. Mrs. Russo spoke on behalf of her husband and daughter but expressed little about her own feelings. (Indication 5.)

Mrs. Russo believed her husband's behavior and depression were the only family problems to which she and Angela were reacting. Relief of his symptoms, she assumed, would resolve any discomfort the others were experiencing. (Indication 7.)

The worker sensed that Mrs. Russo and Angela frequently teamed up against Mr. Russo. She further speculated that Mrs. Russo's mother might be part of the coalition that cast Mr. Russo into the role of outsider. (Indication 8.)

Mr. Russo's motivation for individual treatment seemed minimal. Not given to introspection or reflection about his situation or dynamics, it seemed probable that he would be more amenable to group meetings. Should he (or any other family member) seek individual treatment in the future, there would be greater clarity about the family situation and all of the family members would have experienced the treatment situation. (Indications 12, 13, and 14.)

There were, then, several conditions that led the worker to favor the family therapy approach. She could think of no contraindications, but any which might exist would be revealed in exploratory family sessions. A week after the intake interview, Angela had returned from her trip and accompanied her parents to the initial family meeting. An abbreviated excerpted summary of the first session (in sufficient detail for the reader to see the complex process) follows.

After the worker and Angela were introduced, there were friendly exchanges between the worker and each family member individually. The worker then briefly brought Angela up to date on the previous meeting with Mr. and Mrs. Russo. Angela said she saw no reason for her being present since the problem was her father's "bad mood." The worker said that in her experience, when one person in the family is unhappy, the entire household is often affected. Mrs. Russo agreed: "We all seem to be getting on each other's nerves lately." She added that she was particularly concerned about how her husband's depression was causing Angela to be "cranky." "Sometimes," she commented, "Angela stays with her grandmother to get away." The worker asked Mrs. Russo whether she was finding the going rough herself, to which she replied, "Not really." She said she would feel better when her husband and Angela got along better. The worker said she thought one purpose of family meetings would be to help everyone in the family to understand one another better, adding that perhaps ways of improving relationships among all of them could be found to make the family a happier place. Angela said she thought her father was acting like a baby and just feeling sorry for himself.

Up to this point, Mr. Russo said almost nothing. Turning to him, the worker said she wanted everyone's opinion about the problem. He answered that he thought the medication was helping him a little and he hoped soon he would be "out of the dumps." He complained about his job change. Angela snapped at her father, saying, "You're stupid." She said the house was like a morgue lately, especially since her sister Linda, who used to visit frequently, had moved to Canada. She added that her father thought Linda was an "angel" and he was happy when *she* was there. Mrs. Russo smiled, apparently in appreciation of Angela's angry remarks. The worker asked the father how he accounted for Angela's sarcasm about him. Before he could answer, Angela blurted out, "You don't have to live with him!" Mrs. Russo began to make a comment supporting Angela. The worker interrupted by indicating that she wanted to hear from Mr. Russo, whose eyes had become watery. Angela sneered. The worker said to Mr. Russo that it looked like he was hurt by Angela's remarks. "I suppose I'm not much of a father to her," he replied. "That makes you sad, I imagine," the worker said. "Of course it does," murmured Mr. Russo. "She's my baby girl," he added almost inaudibly.

Then the worker addressed Angela: "Did you know it mattered to your father how you and he get on?" A little subdued, Angela replied, "He doesn't care." The worker asked Mr. Russo whether he ever let Angela know how disappointed he was about the way they get along. He said he supposed he hadn't but volunteered nothing further. Mrs. Russo began to explain Angela, saying that when Angela was young she "adored" her father, and she only turned on him this way when he started acting like a "zombie." Gently, the worker interrupted what she sensed would be a long defense of Angela, adding that she thought it would help more if each person spoke for himself or herself. The worker asked Angela what she thought. Angela said her mother was right. "Your mother understands you pretty well?" the worker offered. "She's the only one who does," Angela said, noting that she and her sister never got along because Linda was her father's "pet." "That must be hard to take," the worker said. Angela shrugged.

The worker then said to Mr. Russo that she gathered he had never gotten around to telling Angela how much she meant to him, and that perhaps it would be helpful if he did something about that. Mrs. Russo started to interject something when the worker said she thought that Dad and Angela had some things to straighten out with each other, reminding Mrs. Russo that she herself had said that their poor relationship bothered her. The worker added that there was no way she, Mrs. Russo, could do their work for them. Mrs. Russo, a little uncomfortably silent now, glared at Mr. Russo. Angela laughed nervously. The worker turned to Mr. Russo, who said, tearfully, "I love both my daughters. One is miles away and the other one hates me." Angela said nothing but did not seem to be sneering; for just a moment, she looked more softly at her father. Mrs. Russo started to say, "Angela doesn't hate him but...." "Good-humoredly, the worker cut in and reminded Mrs. Russo that it would be good if Angela spoke for herself. There followed some tentative but friendlier exchanges between Angela and her father. Shortly thereafter, characteristically, Mr. Russo withdrew in silence and Angela scoffed. Observing this interaction, the worker commented that she had some ideas about what often might happen between them: On the one hand, she pointed out, Mr. Russo seemed shy about telling Angela how much he cared about her, without putting himself down. On the other hand, Angela made it harder to find out her father's true feelings for her by sniping at him so regularly. Both mildly acknowledged the worker's remarks but said no more. The worker said she thought they could both learn to make their relationship a better one, but that it might take a little practice and willingness of both to stick their necks out.

Deciding to reinvolve Mrs. Russo in the interaction, on her own behalf rather than as a commentator, the worker told her she got the impression that she felt burdened sometimes by having to fix up the relationship between her husband and daughter, and by looking after Mr. Russo when he was depressed. "What," the worker asked, "do you want for yourself from the family?" Mrs. Russo replied that her children had been her life, real joys to her. She said she was glad that Linda was happily married, but she missed her and wished she hadn't gone so far away. The worker commented that Angela was growing up too, and recalled that college plans were in the offing. With feeling, Mrs. Russo said she hoped Angela would find a school nearby so she could live at home. "What would it be like if Angela moved away too?" the worker asked. Mrs. Russo became thoughtful and quiet, finally saying that she did not know what she would do. "Life would seem empty," she said. The worker spoke briefly about how difficult it is to make changes when one has been so devoted to one's children. Mrs. Russo cried. Now including Mr. Russo, the worker said to them both that when children grow up and go away, the parents often have to find each other again and this can be quite a challenge. In a positive but not imposing or directive way, the worker asked whether they thought they would like to work on that. It seemed, she continued, that some of the pleasures of family life had gotten lost in the shuffle with all of the recent problems they had been facing. Mr. Russo nodded. Mrs. Russo said she thought everything would feel a lot better if Mr. Russo got over his blues. Maybe, the worker said in a low-key tone, we can find some connection between the other family issues and Mr. Russo's unhappiness. Mrs. Russo indicated she understood and did not argue.

The worker suggested that the family meet together for six sessions (even though she suspected their work together might take longer) and then reevaluate the situation. Mrs. Russo asked whether she could call if Mr. Russo seemed very depressed. The worker told her that she certainly wanted to be available to them between sessions if absolutely necessary, but it would be preferable if they could bring the issues that concerned them into the family meetings. She further suggested that if Mr. Russo was depressed, he should be the one to call. In a matter-of-fact way, she added that she thought it would work best if any contacts made between sessions were shared at the next meeting so everyone could keep informed. Angela said she didn't want to come to every meeting because she had "better things to do." After giving Angela an opportunity to express her uneasiness about family sessions, the worker said she thought everyone's help would be needed, at least for the first six meetings. She added that she was impressed with the willingness and interest all of them had shown in talking about the family situation. It was a good sign, she told them. She thought they were the kind of people who would be able to work out some of their problems with each other. "He'll never change," Angela quipped, pointing to her father. "Don't be rude," the mother admonished. Mr. Russo seemed to brighten at this apparent show of support from his wife.

To the group, the worker said that she was pleased that the family had asked questions about the meetings and that she wanted them to share their feelings about the therapy as it went along. Sometimes, the worker said, she might make a comment that they would find irritating. When this happened, she would like them to tell her about it. After arranging their meeting schedule, the worker added in passing that at some point they might want to invite Mrs. Russo's mother to join them since she was so close to the family. The worker shook hands with all three as they left.

THE INITIAL INTERVIEW: GUIDELINES AND "GROUND RULES"

It is crucial for the family therapist to establish a tone and point of view that will help to engage the family in treatment. It is part of the "practice wisdom" of family work that the therapist as a matter of course moves back and forth between accommodating to the family style and taking positive leadership. As in any treatment situation, the worker must try not to "crash" family defenses by pressing for understanding or changes for which the family is not yet ready. Timing is of the utmost importance. In family therapy particularly, so much material is witnessed by the worker in such rapid-fire fashion that sometimes the temptation to interpret or intervene precipitously is difficult to resist. The discipline of the worker is thereby strenuously tested as the family drama unfolds and reveals itself by way of the many-leveled verbal and nonverbal interactions that occur in the treatment session. The worker refrains from over-zealous interventions, yet at the same time sets the stage for the therapy by defining its focus and by conveying leadership and expertise early in the relationship with the family. Escalation of negative interactions among family members is often prevented thereby.

In the initial Russo family interview described above, the worker carefully followed the cues of mood and the messages of the moment. She respected "where they were." For example, by accepting rather than interpreting Mr. Russo's statement that he had not been "much of a father" to Angela, she recognized his sadness and gave him room to express it. Had the worker made a comment such as "Your wife and daughter seem to gang up on you often," or if she asked him why he thought he hadn't been a better father, the emotion of the event—which led to a fleeting but touching moment between Mr. Russo and Angela—might have been lost. Similarly, only gently, toward the end of the hour, did the worker touch on the marital problem that was so glaringly evident all along. The point we make is that the art and empathy necessary to family treatment have much in common with those needed for individual therapy, but the family process by its very nature calls for special care. If the worker prematurely or heavy-handedly reacts to the profound emotional charge and the large amount of dynamic material revealed by the family interactions, especially during the early stages of therapy, the family may defensively try to regain its equilibrium by closing ranks and even bolting from treatment.

On the other hand, the worker for the Russo family did not succumb to the pitfalls of the opposite extreme and allow the family to control the therapy. In the course of the hour, she was able to weave into the process—usually explicitly, sometimes implicitly—a number of "ground rules." She thereby methodically paved the way for a working alliance with the family. Family therapy that lacks direction, focus, or structure can, at best, flounder and become chaotic. At worst, it can be so disenchanting to the family members that they terminate treatment.

In their chapter on family therapy outcome research, Gurman and Kniskern write:

> There exists an accumulating empirical literature supporting the relationship between treatment outcome and a therapist's relationship skills. This literature suggests that it is generally important for the marital-family therapist to be active and to provide some structure to early interviews, but not to confront tenuous family defenses very early in treatment. Excesses in this direction are among the main contributors to premature termination and to negative outcomes.[10]

As we suggest the ground rules itemized below, we cannot caution the beginning family therapist enough about the importance of offering them to a family, as the worker for the Russos did, in a matter-of-fact yet easygoing and caring way that is in harmony with the process of the meeting. These can be effectively introduced *only* when they are relevant to the evolving interactions. At no time should they be delivered as a series of pronouncements. As the reader studies the following ground rules, it may be clarifying to refer to the Russo interview and to be cognizant of when and under what circumstances the worker used them to guide the treatment.

1. Telephone or interview contacts with one or more family members and the worker prior to the beginning of family therapy should be mentioned at least briefly to the entire group.*

2. The notion that unhappiness or pain in one family member usually involves everyone close to this member should be made explicit.

3. The purposes of family meetings should be defined as: (a) an effort to help everyone in the family to understand one another better; and (b) an attempt to search for ways to improve family relationships so that family life can be more satisfying for all. Even when the initial problem appears to be the symptom of one member, how this affects and is affected by other relationships should be explored with the family.

4. It should be made clear that if contacts between the worker and individual family members occur outside the regular meeting sessions, these should be shared or at least referred to at the next meeting.*

5. In words and actions, the worker must demonstrate an "involved impartiality." It should be made clear that the worker takes no one's side and is equally interested in each member. Family therapists must show that they are not concerned with "blame" or "fault," but with working together toward resolution of the difficulties. By giving support to each family member, and by directing reflective or interpretive remarks to all members on a more or less equal basis, or to the family as a whole, a worker may quell concerns about partiality or about who will be "blamed."

6. If not volunteered, at some point during the initial interview each family member's point of view usually should be elicited with questions such as: "What do you think is wrong?" "What changes in the family would you like to see?" Or, "How are you hoping these family meetings will help?"[11]

7. Directly or indirectly, family members must be encouraged to speak for themselves rather than for others. "Mind reading" should be discouraged. Family members should be asked to put their assumptions in the form of questions to each other.

8. After a period when family members tend to talk directly to the worker, it is often best to encourage them to talk to one another. This shift must be carefully timed. Sometimes, the members are too uncomfortable to do this in initial interviews. Occasionally, they talk or fight tenaciously with one another. In these cases, the worker may reverse the general rule and continue to engage each member in interaction.

9. When realistic, the family's willingness to work on problems should be supported and optimism about possible improvement should be conveyed.

10. When a relative (or housekeeper, close family friend, etc.) appears to be important to the family situation, the worker should prepare the family for possibly including that person at future meetings on an as-needed basis.

11. Feedback from the family about the therapy and about the worker should be encouraged. This keeps the worker informed, demonstrates to the family ways of relating openly, and encourages the family to take a share of the responsibility for how the treatment progresses.

12. To reduce resistance to family meetings, it is often important to establish a limited time structure that is definite, yet flexible enough to change later if necessary. A plan for evaluation, after a period of family therapy, in which the family and the worker share reactions, should be announced at the onset of treatment.

FAMILY CONCEPTS AND THE RUSSO FAMILY

Many of the family concepts described in Chapter 15 are illustrated by the Russo family and

* See discussion of privacy and confidentiality, pages 353 and 354.

were identified by the worker after the two interviews (one marital, one family) described earlier. For example, *lack of differentiation* among family members (or *enmeshed* family relationships) was apparent. Mrs. Russo tended to speak for her husband and for Angela and not for herself. Angela, the worker surmised, voiced contemptuous feelings about Mr. Russo in part because Mrs. Russo was unwilling to express these directly. Mr. Russo allowed others to speak for and define him without correcting or commenting on what they said. *Individual boundaries*, then, tended to be unclear and diffuse.

Generational boundaries and *marital boundaries* were frequently violated. Mr. and Mrs. Russo did not look to each other for refuge and primary support. Mr. Russo had gotten most of his comfort in the family from his daughter, Linda, until she married and moved away. Mrs. Russo apparently looked to Angela to act out her own feelings. The relationship between Angela and her mother was closer and more mutually supportive than that between Mr. and Mrs. Russo. The worker suspected that the grandmother joined Mrs. Russo and Angela in criticism of Mr. Russo, thus intruding on marital and generational boundaries; this hunch was later substantiated.

Systems concepts are illustrated by the changes that occurred in the entire family when Linda left home, when Mr. Russo's job situation changed, and when the possibility that Angela might go away to college was considered. Every family member was affected. The process of *family homeostasis* is evident in the family's reluctance to change, even though the present balance was clearly dysfunctional in several of its aspects. In fact, the worker included Angela in the treatment thinking that without her participation she might unconsciously impede positive changes made by her parents. Or else, her sense of responsibility for maintaining the family equilibrium might prevent her from individuating and going away to college.

There are many examples of *family roles* in the Russo case, some of which were perfectly functional. These include work and school roles, for example. However, dysfunctional roles were also apparent. Obviously, Mr. Russo took on the *scapegoat* role. He became the symptomatic one, taking the blame and being blamed for the family's troubles. *Irrational role assignments* were made; dysfunctional role reciprocity was present. Mr. Russo behaved in some respects like the "helpless" one, requiring and supporting Mrs. Russo's tendency to be "overresponsible." Linda was the "angel" who could soothe Mr. Russo's sadness. Angela "acted out" her mother's unexpressed negative feelings. Some of the *triangles* in the Russo family functioned to dilute and externalize tension and lack of resolution in the marital relationship. Dysfunctional *triangulation* was most evident in the fact that each parent was more allied with one of the children than with each other.

Family *communication processes* in the Russo family were not as dysfunctional as sometimes observed in families. Yet unhealthy patterns were very apparent. A few comments in the sessions could be thought of as indirect, *mystifying messages*. Mrs. Russo and Angela each had the habit of defining Mr. Russo's feelings, thoughts, and motives rather than talking about what they themselves really meant. Furthermore, Mr. Russo did not protest the remarks his wife and daughter made about his inner experience. By far, the most flagrant communication abuses were seen when family members frequently failed to make "I" statements about thoughts or feelings; they were much more likely to speak for one another than for themselves.

Even though several family concepts describing family dysfunction are illustrated in the process of the Russo sessions, there are others—such as the *double bind, pseudomutuality, myths, and secrets*—that were *not* part of this family's style. Furthermore, the family had solid strengths. Openness and flexibility were revealed early on. Many families who come for treatment are far more rigid and defensive than the Russos. For example, Mr. Russo was able to move away from his role as "scapegoat" and speak a little for himself in the first family session. Mrs. Russo responded more kindly to him after this change. Briefly, Angela seemed to soften toward her father. Toward the end of the family session, the unhealthy alliance between Mrs. Russo and Angela was weakened when the mother supported her husband and rebuked her daughter for being "rude" to him. Because dysfunctional patterns were not too entrenched and recalcitrant, they were accessible to the worker's interventions. It is essential to remember that when using family concepts to assess family functioning, the *severity* as well as the *presence* of dysfunctional processes must be evaluated.

More examples of family concepts are illustrated by the Russo family. The reader may wish to become more familiar with ideas basic to family thinking by reviewing the case material presented earlier in the chapter and identifying additional examples.

TREATMENT PROCEDURES AND TECHNIQUES IN FAMILY THERAPY

The Hollis typology of treatment procedures (see Chapters 5 through 9 in this book) can be adapted to study worker and client communications in joint and family treatment.[12] Certainly, multiperson interviews are far more complex and the classification system requires additional dimensions with which to analyze the interactional process. It is our hope, nevertheless, that the dynamics of marital and family interviews will become an important subject for researchers. Among the many issues that could be studied are: Which treatment procedures and combinations of procedures prove most effective in family (or marital) therapy? How does family therapy compare with individual treatment as a means of resolving the problems people bring to treatment? Under what conditions and for what types of problems is one modality more effective than the other? Do family therapists use the procedures they say they do? The more answers we have to these

and other questions, the more effective our practice can become and the better able we will be to teach others how we work.

By reviewing the earlier chapters, the reader will see that all of Hollis's six major categories of worker and client communications can be applied to the analysis of a family session. For example, the first four casework procedures can be located in the initial interview with the Russo family. The worker employed *sustainment* procedures throughout the course of the meeting. She used this procedure when she said to Angela, "That must be hard to take." When she praised the family as a whole for its interest and willingness to talk about the family situation, she used sustaining techniques. In addition to the numerous verbal samples of sustainment there were, of course, the many unrecorded nods, smiles, and gestures that conveyed her interest, her wish to help, and her understanding. Procedures of *direct influence* were important to this first meeting as the worker conveyed the "ground rules" about the treatment process. When she suggested that Mrs. Russo step back so that Mr. Russo and Angela could work on their own relationship, the worker was giving direction to all three family members. These procedures are perhaps more commonly employed in family sessions than in individual sessions, as Ehrenkranz discovered in her sample of joint marital interviews.[13]

Exploration, description, and *ventilation* are evident in many worker and family communications in the Russo session. As Angela described the change in her father since Linda moved away, she also ventilated some bitterness about her sister's being an "angel" in her father's eyes. When the worker explored Mr. Russo's relationship with Angela, she opened the door for him to ventilate some of his sadness about it. The worker also paved the way for ventilation about the treatment process. *Person-situation reflection* was encouraged by the worker at several points and occasionally was volunteered by family members. Examples of this category include Mr. Russo's saying about Angela, "I suppose I'm not much of a father to her"; the worker's asking Mr. Russo how he accounted for Angela's sarcasm about him; and Mrs. Russo's reflecting, in response to the worker's question, about how empty life would seem after both daughters left home.

In the initial meeting, neither *pattern-dynamic* or *developmental reflections* were encouraged by the worker, nor were they volunteered by the Russo family members. These procedures were sparingly employed by the worker in subsequent sessions in much the same way they would have been in individual interviews. The difference is that the other family members were privy to the process. For instance, with the worker's help, in one very moving interview, Mr. Russo was able to reflect on how the early death of his mother and frequent changes of foster homes as a boy contributed to the sadness he felt when his daughter Linda moved. His recognition of this was touching to the rest of the family (including his mother-in-law, who was present). This was one of the events of the therapy that helped to reduce the hostility of the others toward him and that brought the Russo family closer together. The fact that these procedures can be used in family treatment may be encouraging to those who are concerned that family therapy is not as "deep" as one-to-one treatment. Finally, *environmental* work was considered by the worker in connection with Mr. Russo's job situation; in some family therapy cases it can be as important an intervention as it is in any casework treatment.

Particularly exciting, although technically complicated for researchers, is the potential for classifying the diverse meanings of the same communications to each family member. For example, as the worker explored Mr. Russo's positive feelings toward Angela in the initial interview, *his ventilation of sadness* about their relationship appeared to be *sustaining for Angela*. Similarly, when the worker spoke to Mrs. Russo *in a sustaining way* about the burden she carried by having to "fix up" the relationship between Mr. Russo and Angela and by looking after Mr. Russo when he

was depressed, this very same communication suggested a *directive* (which the worker had already given more explicitly) to Mr. Russo and Angela: that they would have to take more responsibility for their own relationship and problems. These examples only begin to touch on the many ways the Hollis classification could be employed to examine the multilevel dynamic events that occur in family therapy.

In this connection, it is interesting to note that when Ehrenkranz studied joint marital interviews in 1967, she discovered that in her particular sample, most of which came from one agency, the workers rather consistently failed to use procedures that in the literature were considered important to joint interviewing. Specifically, they employed few techniques that would lead to on-the-spot clarification of the marital interactions; definition of the treatment focus; or reflective consideration of either the treatment process or the relationship with the worker. She also concluded that workers were tempted to make interpretations to the marital pair too quickly, and that the clients were either unable to respond, or reacted with hostility. We can speculate that the findings of a more broadly based and up-to-date study might be different. At the time of the Ehrenkranz research, caseworkers (and others in the helping professions) were, as a group, less advanced than they are now in conjoint interviewing procedures. Perhaps because of their lack of experience, they were overwhelmed by the intensity and complexity of the marital interactions. Only further research, however, will reveal just what we do in marital and family treatment, and whether we actually do what we say we do.

SPECIAL EMPHASES IN PSYCHOSOCIAL FAMILY THERAPY

It is important to mention at this point that there are some family therapists who declare that they discourage procedures that would lead to the following: the expression (ventilation) of emotion; the development of self-awareness or the understanding of inner dynamics (reflection), which they believe is unlikely to foster change and therefore is irrelevant to treatment; and the exploration of past history, since they believe that the past is manifested in the present family relationships.[14] It is our hunch that if the family interviews of these writer-practitioners were scrutinized in a research study, we would find that they address these issues much more frequently than they advocate doing. When we see them in action, in live interviews or on videotapes, we sense that the psychoanalytic influence or training that is part of the backgrounds of many of the leading family therapists has become second nature to their treatment repertoire, in spite of the protestations of some. How interesting it would be to apply the Hollis typology to the work of those who claim their successes depend exclusively on interventions that address the structure, communication patterns, and behavior sequences of the family.

Along similar lines, some of these same family therapists consider it unnecessary—or even detrimental to treatment—to make interpretations or to share with the families what they think about what they see. Certainly, as we demonstrated in our discussion of the Russo family interview, interpretations, observations, and interventions of all kinds should be measured and carefully timed. The therapist selects first for intervention those aspects of the family interaction that seem most accessible. As we pointed out earlier, in the first session with the Russos the worker chose to work very little with the marital relationship since the energy in the family could be directed most comfortably to the conflict between father and daughter and the mother's go-between role in it. Defenses against other explorations were respected for the time being. However, for both ethical *and* practical reasons, we strongly disagree with the point of view that admonishes against even well timed interpretations and the sharing of observation and opinions by the therapist.

Our reason for taking this position is threefold: *First,* we believe that client family members have the right to know what the worker thinks and, on principle, should be privy to as much information as they can understand or tolerate.

Second, we believe that when the therapist consistently withholds impressions, the treatment relationship degenerates into an "expert-idiot" format in which the family is at the mercy of manipulations by the worker—which the worker never explains. Interpretations or opinions openly shared, on the other hand, give the family the opportunity to accept, reject, or modify them. Indeed, sometimes the therapist can be operating under a misapprehension that the family can correct. We advocate a treatment environment with as much equality as possible, in the sense that worker and family members, all fallible people, are sitting together, sharing thoughts and feelings and searching for solutions to the dilemmas and aches in the family's life. Family therapists are, of course, experts, trained to understand family processes; they have developed methods and techniques, based on theory and experience, about how people change. Family members, however, are equally important experts on their own experience, on what their hopes and goals are, on what choices and changes they want to make, and on how they feel their therapy is progressing. A climate that promotes such mutual sharing between worker and family is one that encourages the family members to take responsibility for their lives and for their work in therapy. If they are kept in the dark about the worker's maneuvers, their passivity and dependence is encouraged and their initiative is discouraged. Many clients we see in family and individual treatment who have problems involving differentiation have little confidence in their own abilities to make choices and changes. They have habitually given more value to the opinions of others than to their own. If the worker implies that he or she is in *total* charge of the therapeutic process, the tendency of some clients to give too much power away to others will be reinforced.

Third, in our view and experience, when people can understand and give meaning to their feelings and behavior they are in a far better position to use their intelligence to find their own solutions and to work toward change than when they submissively follow the leadership of the family therapist.

In response to some critics of family treatment, we want to emphasize that, as far as we know, there are few family therapists who believe that *excessive* ventilation of negative or destructive feelings and so-called total frankness support the purposes of family meetings. There is legitimate concern about the dangers of "free-for-all" communications and "brutal honesty" that some fear are encouraged in family therapy.[15]

Caution is certainly essential. As indicated earlier, if negative interactions are too intense or destructive, and family members seem unwilling or unable to work together in a more positive fashion, it may be best to arrange individual interviews, at least temporarily, until a less vituperative climate can be promoted. In some families, however, the worker need not be too thin-skinned about insults and anger flying about in family meetings and can understand that in many instances these abuses are everyday occurrences. (In such families, the members are often more frightened by their own and each other's tender feelings than they are by the violence of affect to which they are so tragically accustomed.) If we keep in mind that beneath the bitter attacks and expressions of hostility there is often pain, disappointment, and sadness, the worker can encourage the expression of *these feelings*, which are frequently more "honest" than the anger that masks them.

Furthermore, the family therapist must develop a style with which to respond to ongoing abusiveness among family members. In the Russo family, for example, in essence the worker relabeled Angela's anger at her father

as disappointment. Pittman, when confronted with a family of blaming attackers, remarked paradoxically in his low-key manner: "It seems kind of unpleasant to me, but I wouldn't want to change something y'all enjoy so much."[16] Any intervention or technique, consonant with worker style, that fosters reflection about the behavior that reinforces the problems the family wants to resolve can help us to avoid the trap some warn against.

"Brutal honesty" of other kinds—as in the case of the husband who enthusiastically describes his secretary's bust measurements to his jealous wife—must be explored to determine the underlying meaning of the communication. More specifically, in this situation the worker would try to find out why the man wants to hurt his wife in this manner. Some critics are concerned about negative effects of the exposure of differences among family members in conjoint sessions, fearing that conflict will be exacerbated rather than reduced. It is our opinion that the revealing of previously undisclosed disparate thoughts and feelings among family members can be helpful and, when handled skillfully by the family therapist, can actually reduce hostility. The purpose of family therapy is not to discourage differences, but to help family members to recognize that these need not be feared, and that relationships need not be lost because of them. In fact, when such fears are quelled, family members often find that diverse feelings, interests, and points of view are stimulating and enrich their relationships.

"Honest communication" also does not imply that the privacy of family members should be violated. Certainly, married couples share intimacies that need not be the property of their children or their parents. Adolescents, as they grow toward independence, are well known for their wish to conceal certain facets of their lives. In this connection, we refer the reader to the ground rules for family therapy suggested earlier in this chapter. We made the point that contacts between family members and the worker between family sessions should be shared with the entire group. This does not mean every aspect of the content need be revealed. For example, during one phase of treatment, Mr. and Mrs. Russo were seen in joint sessions, without Angela and the grandmother, to explore their marriage and sexual relationship. The *fact* that they met was revealed, but the couple and the worker indicated to the others that they were working on issues that were private to the marital relationship. Confidentiality was respected and marital boundaries were supported. On the other hand, when Mrs. Russo telephoned to report on her husband's depression, this information was part of the work of the whole family, and particularly of Mr. Russo. If the worker had concealed it, inadvertently she would have been inducted into a collusion with Mrs. Russo, thus reinforcing the latter's managerial tendencies and Mr. Russo's passivity. In short, outside sessions, communication from a family member to the worker about *other* family members are discouraged and usually revealed. Under most circumstances, information that is personal to a family member or members is treated confidentially. Only under special conditions, such as the pregnancy of a twelve-year-old daughter or a danger that a family member will attempt suicide, is confidentiality breached. In *every* instance, however, before revealing personal information, the worker should seek the consent of the individual and explain why it must be disclosed.

ON DIAGNOSIS, GOALS, AND THE HEALTHY FAMILY

Over the years, attempts have been made to conceptualize family diagnosis by developing classifications of family types or typologies of family dysfunction.[17] These attempts were divergent in orientation. Some were grounded in the diagnostic assessments of the intrapsychic or social functioning of individuals; others described medical or socioeconomic conditions of families. Such designations as "the schizophrenic family," "the phobic family," "the alcoholic family," "the lesbian family," "the unemployed family," the "anorectic family," "the family in poverty," and so on, failed to describe overall family functioning. Other attempts at classification were so general or so limited (e.g., "the enmeshed family") that they did not grasp the complexity of the family dynamics. Under some circumstances such categories invite stereotyping. Certainly, the achievement of a classification of dysfunctional families would enhance the theory on which family practice is based. Unfortunately, in spite of brave efforts to build a scheme of family diagnosis, no single, satisfactory system has emerged.

As in other modalities, the purpose of diagnosis is to guide treatment. There are some family therapists who claim that diagnosis is irrelevant to family work. Satir is quoted as saying that categorizing families does not help in therapy, adding, "Family diagnosis does not have the practical value of physical, medical diagnosis where specific diagnosis requires a specific treatment."[18] Indeed, a comprehensive diagnostic scheme has thus far eluded us, but *if* the complexities and multiple dimensions of family process could be classified by designating clusters of factors often found together, it would aid us in our selection of treatment procedures. Research would be required to determine which procedures would be most effective in the treatment of particular types of family dysfunction. In spite of widespread concern about diagnosing or labeling, as caseworkers we are always making generalizations, based on the facts before us, in order to determine the nature of clients' problems and strengths. It is true that no two families are precisely alike, but the more grounds we have on which to organize and classify data, without stereotyping or in any way denying the uniqueness of each family situation, the more effective our treatment will become.

Ackerman and others have urged the development of a model or set of normative standards that would capture the characteristics of the healthy family.[19] More recently, Framo has suggested some principles that can be used to describe the well-functioning family. He makes the essential point, "nearly every person, family, and marriage, over the course of their lives, goes through periods of turmoil and disorganization that at the time appear pathological."[20] Nevertheless, one can view his ideas as providing a framework against which the current functioning of a family can be measured. They can also be used to consider ideal goals toward which a family might move.

An abbreviated summary of principles of "normal" family functioning described by Framo is as follows: (1) well-differentiated parents with a "sense of self" developed before they separated from families of origin; (2) clear generational boundaries, with children not expected to "save" parents or the marriage; (3) realistic perceptions and expectations by parents of each other and the children; (4) loyalty to family of procreation greater than to family of origin; (5) spouses' putting themselves and each other before others, including children, but without excluding children; (6) children not encouraged to feel that loyalty to one parent means disloyalty to the other; (7) identity development and autonomy encouraged for all family members; (8) nonpossessive warmth and affection expressed among all family members; (9) open, honest, and clear communication and ability to deal with issues directly; (10) realistic, adult-to-adult relationship of parents with members of families of origin; (11) involvement with others outside the family.[21]

Even without a satisfactory scheme for family diagnosis as such, our own theoretical framework can guide us. As outlined in Chapter 12, the psychosocial approach to diagnosis is one that scans the whole field and builds up a body of facts and assumptions about the multiple aspects of the person-situation gestalt, including the transactional aspects. Choices about therapeutic interventions derive from the worker's assessment of those features of the situation that must be modified to relieve the problem at hand and those aspects that can be strengthened to improve family functioning. In the Russo family, for example, we saw that the worker decided to treat the family as a group rather than Mr. Russo individually, on the basis of her observations of the characteristics of the individuals and of the family's interactions. She chose to intervene in those areas she assumed would be most modifiable.

The family therapy concepts included in the previous chapter may contribute to a systematic typology of family types or family dysfunction. These concepts contain many of the components necessary for the development of a diagnostic system. At this point, they provide us with tools, in addition to those we use to assess personality dynamics, with which to describe and evaluate interpersonal patterns and family relationships. Although unordered in terms of their levels of importance or degree of abstraction, they provide a basis for assessing the strengths and troubled areas of a family's functioning.

Some sample questions, among many derived from family concepts, that a worker might consider when assessing a family are: Is the index client's symptom a reflection of difficulties in either the larger family or the marital relationship? How well differentiated are family members? Are individual and subsystem boundaries distinct, on the one hand, yet permeable, on the other? Are boundaries either overly rigid or dysfunctionally diffuse in various parts of the family system? What are the roles and role relationships? Are they appropriate to ages and generations? Is a child being "parentified"? Is the mother being infantilized as she clings to a managerial grandmother? Who is scapegoated? Are family members taking turns as the symptomatic or scapegoated one? Who is triangulated, and how? Is communication clear, or is it confused, amorphous, mystifying, or double-binding? What nonverbal communications can be deciphered? What metacommunications qualify the verbal statements?

Further areas the worker may explore concern the significance of introjects and projections of family members as they are played out in the interpersonal arena of the family. Can "trading of dissociations" be identified? Are the family supports consistent enough to promote growth in individual members? Do family members cling to each other? Are they estranged? How strong are resistances to change? What kinds of defenses does the family use to maintain a dysfunctional balance? Are there myths and secrets? How are family rules enforced? What is the emotional climate of the family? Are expressions of anger taboo? Are feelings of tenderness, sadness, and disappointment discouraged? Does the family tolerate differences of ideas and feelings among family members?

These and other diagnostic questions start to flow as the worker sits with a family in therapy. Understanding of individual dynamics and the workings of the larger social system is supplemented if the worker is grounded in family theory. Diagnosis and treatment go hand in hand. The more the worker knows about a family, the clearer it will be which problems must be addressed. When attempting to effect changes in the family system, the worker will learn more about the areas of accessibility and vulnerability, which, in turn, will influence further treatment strategies and techniques.

POSTSCRIPT: THE RUSSO FAMILY

Family therapy for the Russos lasted ten months. In six of the thirty-six sessions, Mr. and Mrs. Russo met together, without any other family members, to work on their marital and sexual relationship. Of the remaining thirty sessions, Angela attended all except the last two, which were scheduled after she left for college, several hundred miles away. Linda, on a trip home, came to one session, eager to settle some misunderstandings that had developed between her and her mother.

The maternal grandmother attended three sessions. A deeply religious woman of middle-class, northern Italian background, Mrs. Russo's mother had been critical of Mr. Russo's occupational status and lack of interest in the church since the day she met him. Class and educational differences between Mr. and Mrs. Russo, influenced by Mrs. Russo's mother's attitude about these, played a role in the family conflicts. Mrs. Russo had attended college briefly, and Linda and Angela both aspired to professional careers that placed Mr. Russo, a high school dropout, in an inferior position in his eyes and the eyes of his family.

On the other hand, the worker's knowledge of cultural factors played only a small part in her work with this family. Both Mr. and Mrs. Russo were third-generation Italian Catholics and yet, even with the differences in their class backgrounds, as a family they were part of an upwardly mobile, lower-middle-class, heterogeneous community. In a minor way, the family members, particularly Mrs. Russo's mother, had a traditional reluctance about bringing their "dirty linen" to a stranger; she believed that if help was needed, the family should speak with a priest. Yet, as frequently occurs with Italian families, every member of the Russo family was able to be quite expressive emotionally in therapy sessions. Mr. Russo was able to cry and to speak of tender and sentimental feelings; at the same time he berated himself for being less than a "man" as he compared himself unfavorably to his father, a domineering, occasionally violent person. The girls both attended parochial grammar schools, but went on to public high schools, which they preferred; only the grandmother had been disappointed by their choice. Although both parents were reluctant to see their daughters leave home, they did not—as some Italian parents do—resist these moves on the basis of concern about sexual behavior or vulnerability away from the family.

On balance, Angela probably benefited most from family treatment. Without guilt or fear, she was able to follow through on her wish to leave the household and prepare for her own life and career. Mrs. Russo became less intrusive in the relationship between Angela and Mr. Russo and, over the months of treatment, father and daughter enjoyed a warmer relationship than they had for years. During several sessions in the middle phase of therapy, Angela fought hard with her mother, as adolescents often do (but as Angela previously had not done), for the "right" to make her own decisions, large and small. Although reluctantly, Mrs. Russo was able to give her daughter some credit for being almost adult. In the last session before she left for college, Angela gave genuine thanks to her parents for their support and shared loving feelings with them both. Family therapy was clearly preventive for Angela, who, without it, might have given in to her mother's dependence on her and remained at home. Or she might have left defiantly for college, burdened with many unresolved feelings about her decision.

At the end of treatment, Mr. Russo was less depressed and was no longer taking medication. Periodically, he slipped back into "the dumps," but these episodes were less intense and of shorter duration than they had been. Without self-blame, he was able to announce to his family, including his mother-in-law, that he felt neither capable nor secure enough to face the "jungle" of the job market and seek employment with more prestige or personal reward. He had made peace, he said, with his current employment situation. The confidence with which he made this choice enhanced his self-respect and, in turn, resulted in far less criticism from his wife, his daughter, and even his mother-in-law. Involving Mrs. Russo's mother in the therapy exposed and diminished her contribution to the family alignment against Mr. Russo. A few weeks before termination, his mother-in-law broke her leg and Mr. Russo willingly gave her practical help he had never offered before.

Mrs. Russo, whose motivation was essential to the therapy, made more gains than she expected, since she had assumed that her husband would have to make all of the changes. Of course, she did benefit from his progress and the greater family harmony achieved through treatment. But by being less intrusive and managerial—not easy for her—she also won appreciation from both her daughters and a new kind of closeness with them that was no longer primarily based on mutual dependency. Furthermore, it turned out, Mrs. Russo had many cultural and intellectual interests that her husband did not share. As she became less critical in general, she was able to stop complaining to Mr. Russo about his "narrow mind." Instead, she found friends to join her in activities she could enjoy apart from her husband.

The couple's sexual relationship, which had never been satisfactory, improved only slightly, if at all. However, the resentment they both felt about it was reduced, and neither was motivated to explore the matter further at the time of termination. On the whole, Mr. and Mrs. Russo were able to listen to each other better and to accept their differences more comfortably. Each made personal choices without resorting to self-blame or recriminations. They no longer clung to their daughters' love out of despair over their marriage. All family members expressed positive feelings about the treatment experience and wanted to make sure they could return should the need arise.

Would individual therapy for Mr. Russo have worked well? Medication and supportive casework might have relieved his depression. His improved self-esteem might have resulted in positive repercussions throughout the family. From the point of view of the worker, however, Mr. Russo could not have bucked the collusion of the other family members. Without the participation of them all, the worker believes, he would have retreated again into depression and self-blame. It also seems probable that Angela would not have made the gains she did without the support of family sessions.

Some families continue to grow and change after treatment ends. Others return during crises or setbacks or resume treatment to achieve further goals. In some cases, individual members continue in treatment after family meetings are terminated. Many families change more remarkably than the Russo family did. Others make far fewer gains. In families with limited intellectual and emotional resources, or with patterns of long-standing dependency and poor differentiation, change may be minimal. It is the task of the family therapist to travel with the family toward mutually agreed upon goals, and to identify the point at which progress ceases. As in any casework treatment, in the final analysis, the worker cannot expect more change for clients than they wish for themselves.

We move on from the Russo family now and turn to other subjects of importance to the clinical practice of social work. The remaining sections of this chapter will discuss transference and countertransference, resistance, single-parent families, and stepfamilies.

TRANSFERENCE AND COUNTERTRANSFERENCE IN FAMILY THERAPY

Much of the discussion in Chapter 10 about unrealistic reactions of the individual client and the worker toward one another applies to family work as well. But there are some real differences. In some instances, transference and countertransference reactions may be more diluted in family therapy than in individual treatment, where the emotional forces are totally concentrated on the one-to-one relationship. More often, however, the complexity of the family process intensifies, for both worker and family, the tendency to subjectify reactions. Patterns and defenses within any family group have been functioning for a long time, and the family has an established set of (often unrealistic) attitudes and responses with which to face any threat, including the intrusion of a family therapist!

These reactions from the family can keenly affect the worker's perspective.

In any therapy situation, the person who applies for help to some degree feels vulnerable. Old childhood feelings, derived from relationships with parents, authority figures, and siblings, or feelings associated with later relationships can be reactivated as clients acknowledge to a professional that they cannot solve their problems by themselves. Fear of blame and disapproval, as well as hopes, warm feelings, awe, and longings for approval, are among the many "portable" reactions that people bring into treatment from other parts of their lives. In family group therapy, such transferences can become contagious and travel from one family member to another. Or they can be a function of the system as a whole, as may happen when, in a defensive effort to protect the homeostatic balance, family members band together to block the worker by assigning him or her a distorted negative role.

In a family of rigid, critical parents (who both had disapproving parents themselves) and two adolescent sons, the family treated the worker with suspicion. As a group, family members falsely accused him of making judgmental statements about them all to the high school guidance counselor who had referred them for treatment. They joined together and displaced their negative experiences with their respective parents onto the worker. Only after many weeks, as greater trust was established, was the family able to risk exposure to the worker without the fear of his disapproval.

In other cases, deprived or dependent families may attribute to the worker the role of family "savior," a role impossible for anyone to fill.

To further complicate the picture, a family's unrealistic attitudes and responses may be divisive in the therapy situation. For example, the father who experienced himself as the "black sheep" of his original family may assume that his wife will get better attention than he will from the therapist (as perhaps his sister did from his mother). If the wife in this situation brings from *her* past a seductive or manipulative manner with which to curry favor from parental or authority figures, the husband's fears may be reinforced. On the basis of experiences in their family, children and adolescents, too, may bring various transference responses to the therapy, such as expectations of being favored, blamed, or required by the worker to try to rescue other family members. When family members have divergent responses to the therapist, angry or rivalrous feelings can be aroused within the family group. Of course, if there are cotherapists, the family may assign one the role of "good parent" and the other that of "bad" one. As unsettling as some family reactions may be, the worker who encourages open discussion and begins to challenge or interpret some of the distortions, can use them to help family members learn more about themselves, each other, and the repetitive patterns that hamper the growth of the entire family. The focus of family treatment, as we have said, should be shifted as soon as possible to the complexities of "transferences" and projections *among* family members. Unrealistic responses to the therapist must be addressed, of course, but not induced. Ideally, the worker takes on the role of neutral "coach" or "facilitator," helping family members to recognize unrealistic attitudes that pervade and taint the family process itself. This issue will be discussed further in Chapters 17 and 18 on couple treatment.

The family caseworker, too, may displace early or unrealistic feelings or attitudes onto the family being treated. In fact, as important as it is for a worker interested in family work to master the theory and techniques of family therapy, it is equally essential that one be constantly alert to countertransference and countertherapeutic reactions. In individual treatment, when listening to descriptions of the family situation, the therapist can more often maintain an objectivity that may be elusive in the face of powerful family forces operating in vivo.

As we indicated earlier, when we speak of "induction" in family therapy, we usually mean that the worker is inadvertently pulled into the family system, on the side of its defenses and resistance.

A mother who was diabetic, arthritic, and had suffered a "nervous breakdown" many years earlier, was seen by the father and by the children as fragile. The mother's demeanor invited this view. In frequent telephone conversations with the worker, the father expressed concern that family therapy would be detrimental to his wife's health. The worker allowed his own clinical judgment about the mother's very evident strengths to be discounted and was persuaded to treat her with "kid gloves" as the family did. Only after it was clear that therapy was at a standstill did the worker begin to challenge the family myth about the mother that, it turned out, was promoted by the father to shield himself from facing worries about his own emotional well-being. Had the worker allowed his induction to continue, the family resistance would have won out and treatment would have failed.

Such family forces at work can place extraordinary stresses on the most mature worker and thereby sap his or her effectiveness. It takes a secure therapist indeed to feel comfortable in a family that pressures him as this one did. It is even harder, perhaps, to maintain one's perspective when faced with a family that closes ranks and isolates the worker as the worker begins to touch on patterns and interlocking defenses that have taken years to develop. Similarly, it can be difficult for the therapist to hold on to hope when meeting with a family immobilized by apathy or rigidity, or a family in which there has been violence, incest, or other kinds of abuse. In some instances, the therapist may be prompted to work too hard, too fast, or to attack the family.

There are other pitfalls to be avoided. The worker may overidentify with a family member or subgroup or fail to empathize with others. The problem is compounded in a family that attempts to involve the worker in collusions or alignments with one member or subgroup against others within the family. Angry, competitive, or protective feelings may be stirred in the worker. For example, a particular worker may feel hostile toward the parents of an abused or scapegoated child and may want to prove she is a better "mother." Or another worker may be tempted to take the part of a "henpecked" husband against a controlling wife, if he loses sight of the hand-in-glove aspects of their relationship, which can be equally painful to both partners. Young workers may find it easy to identify with rebellious adolescents. Older workers, facing the trials of raising their own teenage children, may tend to feel partial to the beleaguered parents. A worker who has (or had) either an angry or overly dependent relationship with either of his or her parents (or with a sibling, grandparent, etc.), may transfer feelings about that person to the relationship with the corresponding member of the client family. Finally, more often than we would wish, family therapists are tempted to repair the marriages of clients in ways that they have never been able to influence their own parent's relationships— or, for that matter, their own marriages. Countertransference problems, then, can be provoked by patterns of family interaction as well as by the characteristics of an individual family member.

The goal for workers who choose to treat families is to maintain "involved impartiality." Without involvement, there can be no working relationship. Without impartiality, the worker will be hopelessly inducted into the family system. If the worker consistently takes sides, sooner or later some or all of the family members are likely to refuse to continue in therapy. To be free to work for the benefit of the family, one must be as secure as possible about oneself and one's competence, and must be ever alert to one's "Achilles heel" or unresolved feelings about one's own family relationships. If the worker suspects that countertransference attitudes or responses are impeding progress with a family, supervision or consultation can be effective ways of regaining lost perspective. In many agencies, family therapists have made good use of one-way mirrors, videotape, "live supervision," and cotherapists as aids against slipping into unrealistic, countertherapeutic reactions. In attempting to help troubled families change, the worker is well advised to heed Whitaker's counsel that the therapist "must be available to each person of the family, yet belong to none; he must belong to himself."[22]

RESISTANCE AND FAMILY THERAPY

Much of what we said about resistance in Chapter 13 applies equally to family treatment. Above all, when we speak of resistance we must ask, resistance to what? Sometimes families resist ideas or suggestions of the worker because the worker has not explained them adequately. Perhaps the worker has explicit or implicit goals for the family that the family does not share. The worker with "hidden agendas" obstructs the work and also may stimulate hostility or premature terminations. So-called resistance is sometimes described pejoratively by workers: "She is resistant to separating from her alcoholic husband." Or, "The parents are resistant to sending their son to camp." Obviously in these cases, if these goals are the therapist's only, insufficient attention is being given to "where the client is."

Even though well-meaning, workers sometimes are dogmatic or rigid and try to persuade clients of particular points of view. When families oppose such suggestions, the worker may respond with countertherapeutic reactions of anger or pessimism. These responses, in turn, often engender further reluctance in the family to engage in the difficult work of family treatment. The importance of mutuality has been mentioned several times in this book. When the therapist shares observations and opinions and attends closely to the family's priorities, clients are then in the best position to make informed decisions. Resistance is inevitable, but therapists can intensify or diminish it on the basis of their respect for and their flexible responses to families and their situations. It is the worker's responsibility to explain the link between the family difficulties and the therapeutic suggestions and interventions. It is also the worker's responsibility to find out what family members think will help.

Family resistance often occurs immediately. During the intake telephone call, clients may oppose the idea of meeting conjointly. Sometimes such reactions have a cultural component. Clients may have concerns about privacy or about sharing of intimate family matters with outsiders. Some are concerned about secrets being uncovered in family meetings. Often family members fear they will be blamed for the problems by other family members or by the therapist. Initial reluctance may be dealt with in various ways. When speaking with a mother of a symptomatic child, for example, a worker might say, "If Peter is going to get the best help I can offer, it will be important for me to get to know the world he lives in, the people who matter the most to him." Or, "Although families can't be blamed for a problem like Peter's, they can usually be helpful in the solution." Or, "The work often goes faster when all who are involved put their heads to it." When resistance persists, the worker might suggest, "Why don't we get the whole family together for the first meeting and then decide on the best way to proceed after that?"

Some families want to exclude one or more family members from sessions. A mother may say the father is too busy or too critical of the child to be a helpful participant. Parents sometimes want to leave out the "well" siblings or other family members for fear of upsetting them. There are a few family therapists who will not see families unless every member comes.[23] In our opinion, this rigid stance can result in some families' never getting much-needed treatment. When our best efforts to persuade the caller to bring the entire family to the first meeting fail, we may "join the resistance" and see whoever is willing or available. Occasionally, there may be good reasons, which the family understands better than the worker, for not meeting with the entire group. In any event, one can always try to expand the membership later, after family members have been given fuller explanations of the rationale for including the entire family and the worker has a better understanding of the reluctance to do so.

Forms resistance takes at any point during family treatment are too many to mention. Among common forms of resistance are lateness or missed sessions, missing members, complaints about lack of progress, hopelessness (i.e., denial of family strengths), refusal to discuss relevant issues, disruptive behavior by children or by fighting adults, persistent focus on one member (present or absent), constant blaming, unwillingness to talk, sessions monopolized by one member, intellectualization, and pseudomutuality (i.e., denial that there are problems). In every case, it is important to find ways to discuss evidence of possible resistance with family members without conveying the idea that they have been "caught" in something. Sometimes behaviors that seem resistant to the therapist have entirely different meanings to family members; they must be given the opportunity to explain *their* interpretations.

Resistance frequently derives from fear of change, of the family as a whole or of individuals within it. Homeostasis operates to counteract change. Moreover, family members who willingly come for family sessions, such as Mrs. Russo, often come with the idea of trying to change *other* family members, thus resisting the prospect of making changes themselves. Old patterns are hard to break. People often feel most comfortable carrying out familiar family roles and behaviors, even when these no longer work well for them. As Anderson and Stewart write in their useful book on resistance in family therapy:

> It is easy to understand why people resist changing their habits of relating, as the saying goes, "better a known devil than an unknown saint." The prospect of change in intimate personal relationships is more threatening to an individual's sense of emotional security than most other changes. It is not surprising that most people respond with fear and resistance. Change is frightening and could result in a situation that is worse than the current one. *Loss of one sort or another always accompanies change.* In order to change, individuals must give up something valued or thought to be essential, often giving up reality as they see it [emphasis ours].[24]

When the worker understands the discomfort—at times the terror—induced in some clients by the prospect of change, it is easier to be empathic. Furthermore, the reality of some risks feared by clients must be acknowledged. If the family meets as a group, the members indeed *may* face criticism. Dissatisfactions probably *will* be expressed. Unsettling secrets *may* be revealed. Feelings of uneasiness about these possibilities should be normalized. In a comfortable therapeutic climate the fear of change may be dissipated to some degree. Motivation—the wish for relief from pain, worry, and stress—counteracts some resistance. In every case, it is the worker's task to find the delicate balance between accommodating defensive resistance and providing leadership toward change.

SINGLE-PARENT FAMILIES

Early family research and theory usually described the intact family of procreation. The marital relationship, as we have said, was found to

be an important key to modifying conditions for the entire family. In recent years, because of the dramatic increase in single-parent families in all walks of life, family theorists and therapists have turned their attention as well to special issues facing this group. In contrast to earlier views about the consequences of "broken families," clinicians have come to recognize that these nontraditional families are not necessarily more problem-prone than any other families.[25] Although there may be some differences in the ways single parents adapt to their circumstances, depending in part on class or ethnic factors, many of the issues they have to deal with and the difficulties they encounter apply across the board.

Some of the principles pertaining to intact families also apply to one-parent families. When any child becomes symptomatic, he or she is often sending out an "SOS" that the family is in trouble. A child's development may be distorted in an effort to diminish or absorb a parent's pain.[26] Children can be infantilized, parentified, presented as a parent's "best foot forward," neglected, or unduly criticized by a single parent as well as by parents living together. There *are* differences, however. For example, issues in the single-parent family can depend in part on how the parent became single. Some such parents were never married. Others were separated, divorced, or abandoned. Some have spouses who have been incarcerated for many years. Still others lost spouses through death. Attitudes may vary according to whether the one-parent family resulted from choice, rejection, a sudden loss, and so on.

Other special issues are considered in the assessment of single-parent families coming for help. Some of the common ones follow. Generally they can apply to female or male parents.

1. When children are overly relied upon by a single parent, they may become symptomatic. Unfulfilled needs can lead a parent to seek major companionship from children or see them

as the "reason for living." A parent who has been rejected, even the noncustodial parent, may try to bolster self-esteem by proving adequacy as a parent at the child's expense or at the expense of the child's relationship with the other parent. Under these circumstances, a child may feel overly responsible for the parent's feelings or well-being. Some children do not develop age-appropriate peer relationships because of the intensity of the bond with a lonely parent. As a consequence of the extreme importance bestowed upon a child, problems around hierarchy and consistency may develop in single-parent homes. For example, one minute a child may be an intimate confidante to an unhappy parent, yet only a moment later be disciplined like a child. Adolescents acting out sexually or with drugs are sometimes protesting a parent's neediness. One-parent, one-child families can be particularly vulnerable to difficulties as they try to fill all of each other's relational needs.

2. Single parents can be enormously burdened. Most single parents work. Many do not have enough money and get little or no financial support or help with the children. Bitterness about responsibilities, about their lives and losses, can induce feelings of resentment about children's needs. The result may be neglect or apparent indifference. Negative feelings parents have about themselves—for example, when they feel they have failed at marriage or have been rejected—can be projected onto children. When the noncustodial or absent parent is idealized by a child to compensate for disappointment in the overwhelmed or angry parent, bitterness may develop. Children of angry or distracted single parents may seek security (healthy or destructive) elsewhere in order to feel less criticized or ignored. When they find teachers, families of friends, or others who show a genuine interest in them, some children are saved from serious damage.

3. When one parent has disappeared or is dead, the custodial parent and child often have fantasies about the absent one. A parent, for example, may see the child as a "double" for the parent who is gone. In some such cases, when the marital relationship was positive, the child can "do no wrong"; when it was negative, the youngster may be unable to "do right." Both types of projections are unrealistic and destructive. Children in such situations may have secret longings for the absent parent, idealizing him or her to such an extent that the "in-house" parent can never match the fantasized image of the other one. Problems inevitably follow.

4. Some single parents, whether custodial or noncustodial, are steeped in guilt because the child has been deprived of a two-parent home. There may be less money than there was, the child may be alone a lot, the parent may have less time or patience than previously. The initiator of a marital breakup often feels guilt most acutely. Good judgment about what is best for children may be impaired by a parent's wish to reduce the guilt or to "make up" to the child for what was sacrificed by the breakup of the marriage.

5. There is a large group of single-parent families burdened by the effects of various kinds of unfinished business. Examples include (a) children who feel guilty, overly responsible, or heartbroken about the dissolved relationship; (b) as in intact homes, children of separated parents who become symptomatic, bringing the focus on themselves, hoping to unite their mother and father (especially when the breakup is in some manner incomplete, children may be preoccupied with hopes of reconciliation); (c) parents whose feelings about the separation are unresolved often compete for the child's loyalty. A child may be coaxed to side with the parent who seems "pathetic" or "misused." Loyalty to one parent may be seen as disloyalty to the other. Many triangles and conflicts may emerge. A parent may say: "I'll send you to your father/mother if you don't behave." Or, "Why don't you go live with your father if you think he is

so great?" Unhealthy polarizations and alliances often develop, with children caught in the middle.

6. Relationships with families of origin are often supportive to single-parent families but they may also complicate matters. Some parents of the single parent may take a "you made your bed, now you must sleep in it" or "I told you so" approach. Others, going through changes in their own lives (e.g., widowhood, loneliness of the "empty nest"), may overtly or covertly welcome being needed by the grieving or overburdened single parent and the children. Sometimes hierarchical problems develop; grandparents may infantilize or demean the single parent and act to preempt major parental responsibilities.

Single-parent households among blacks have increased at an even more rapid rate than among other groups in the population. In some black families, as well as in some families from other groups, the mothers had babies when they were very young and the three generations live together, often in female-headed households. In addition to economic problems many such families face (in too many cases they live in poverty and must also contend with a capricious welfare system), the grandmothers bear enormous burdens; sometimes they are involved in raising their own children as well as those of their daughters (or sons). In these families, as we shall mention again shortly, it is often particularly important to help the young person (usually the mother) to assume her responsibility as parent without rejecting the needed help of the grandmother.

Treatment Considerations

Special systems issues can arise when treating single-parent families. Some single parents, for example, are eager to share parenting responsibilities with the worker. Especially those with meager support networks may look to the worker on an ongoing basis to share concerns about children, to help in disciplining them, or to provide adult companionship. One single parent said to her family therapist, "You are the first adult I have talked with since I saw you last week!" Although the worker wants to be available to such a parent, it is equally important for the worker to help her to reflect on ways to expand her support systems. If the worker continues to be a parent's *major* comfort, the parent in turn may unconsciously encourage children's symptoms. Otherwise, there might be no need to keep coming to see the worker!

Conversely, some single parents feel rivalrous toward the family caseworker. In such cases, children may not relinquish symptoms, for example, and thereby save the mother or father from humiliation—humiliation that the worker "succeeded" in helping after the parent had failed. It is with constant amazement that we witness the many and creative ways that children "tune in" to their parents' feelings and try to take care of them.

Worker overresponsibility can be a major pitfall when treating troubled single parents and their children. Sympathy and concern for these clients who are so often lonely or overwhelmed can induce workers to try to do more than they realistically can do. One can develop an "urge to rescue" when burdened parents feel helpless, when "latch-key" children seem to get little guidance or tender parenting, or when children are so involved in trying to take care of their parent(s) that they are not getting their own developmental needs met. As in all other kinds of casework, it is important for us to be realistic about what we can and cannot do. Otherwise we may seem to make promises we cannot possibly keep.

Treatment Emphases

In our experience, working with troubled single-parent families often requires attention to the following areas:

1. *Generational boundaries, privacy, and de-triangulation.* When a parent and child are enmeshed and overly reliant on one another, when there is either infantilization or parent-ification of a child, firmer generational boundaries may be required. Children may have to be helped to understand that they cannot be privy to some strictly adult concerns. Although children in some single-parent families may carry significant responsibilities for providing practical and emotional assistance to parents, generational distinctions are nevertheless essential. Adolescents who have been close to their single parents may need special support when explaining that certain aspects of their lives are now "off limits." It is quite common for children to be triangulated in various ways by separated parents; frequently these children are burdened by being in this position and need help to get out of the middle. It can be extremely important for some single parents to differentiate their children's feelings toward absent spouses from their own attitudes; children's experiences with their parents are necessarily different from those between unhappy spouses. In the three-generational family with a single parent, especially a young one, the family therapist may help a grandparent move into the position of *consultant* to the parent; this can discourage a wholesale appropriation of the parental role. In some cases, triangulation of the children by the grandparent can be prevented by clarification of role definitions. Under the best circumstances, inexperienced single parents can receive important guidance from their older family members without being stripped of their own status as parent.

2. *Grief over losses, completion of unfinished business.* Commonly, as we have said, single parents and their children coming for help have not completed their mourning or resolved problems in relationships. Understandably, there is often resistance to discussing past painful experiences, even though the lack of resolution of these may be contributing to the difficulties that brought them to treatment. Parents may believe they are protecting their children, or vice versa, by never discussing sad experiences. In some families, deaths, divorces, desertions, institutionalizations literally have never been mentioned, yet the effects of these continue to fester in some form or another.

3. *Reflection on realistic hardships and inequities borne by the single parent.* In the next chapter we will discuss in greater detail how, as a group, separated and divorced women are far worse off financially than their estranged husbands. In at least nine out of ten cases, women are the custodial parents, and child support payments from fathers are often meager or nonexistent. Working full time and keeping a home for youngsters, without practical or moral support, can be extremely grueling. Single parents often blame themselves for feeling burdened or for being less than perfect, and recognition of the realities can be supportive. By the same token, children who blame their parents for their deprivations can be helped to see their situations in perspective; parent-child relationships can be enhanced when children realize that the reason they are doing without many benefits is not that their mothers are withholding from or punishing them.

4. *Supportive networks and resources.* Because of the countless needs and strains experienced by many single-parent families, the caseworker often can be instrumental in providing opportunities to the adults and children. Legal assistance may be needed. Self-help support groups can be located in many communities or can be sponsored by agencies serving single-parent families; a sense of community can be very comforting to isolated and beleaguered parents. Women's centers that have sprung up over recent years often provide a multitude of services of interest to single mothers. Day care centers, camps, after-school activities may make significant differences in the children's lives and bring needed relief to parents. Economic hardships experienced by many single parents may ultimately be relieved by referring them to job training programs or other educational opportunities. Self-esteem, too, may be bolstered when single parents who have no marketable skills are enabled to become independent and respected members of the work force.

Expansion of networks for children and for single parents often leads to a healthy differentiation of needs and activities that are appropriate to their various ages; in a natural way generational boundaries are strengthened. Because of their heavy responsibilities or a tendency to be inordinately child-focused for practical and/or emotional reasons, some single parents need "permission" to seek adult companions, friends or lovers, who are special to them. Children who feel responsible for their parents' happiness may need encouragement to seek peer relationships. Treatment of single-parent families, especially those that tend to be insular, is often heavily focused on exploring new opportunities for every member.

STEPFAMILIES

The constraints of space make it impossible to discuss in depth an often extremely complex lifestyle that is on the increase: the step, "blended," or "reconstituted" family. It is estimated that one out of four children born in the 1980s will live in a stepfamily by the time they are eighteen. For additional information on this diverse group and on treatment considerations, the reader is urged to turn to references supplied in the notes.[27] Here we will touch only on a few of the central issues confronted by these families and by the clinicians who are attempting to help them.

In this discussion, the terms "spouse" and "marriage" can often be applied to many partners and relationships that are committed on an ongoing basis, even if no legal bonds exist. Gay and lesbian couples, too, raise children; many of our comments here can also apply to these families.

Whether one person without children is married to (or living on a consistent basis with) a person with a child or children, or whether both mates bring children to the relationship, under the best of circumstances significant adjustments are required by everyone involved. Additional complications can arise, of course, when the couple subsequently has a child together. In a large number of cases, the children have permanently lost a parent, through death or desertion. It is not uncommon for children never to have met their real parent. Sometimes babies were conceived when the mother was very young and the relationship with the father was a brief one; casual sexual encounters are responsible for some births. In some stepfamilies, the children's real parents are both very much a part of the children's lives. In others, the nonresident parent—usually, but not always, the father—is only peripherally involved, if at all.

Some of what we have said about single-parent families applies to step or combined families. In most cases, these families are born of loss and disappointment—if not conflict or rejection—of some sort. The loss of a "perfect" first marriage or family, the loss of a dream, is often deeply felt. Problems can arise because families are trying to adjust to the addition of a new member or new members. Often, family members have to deal with moving to new homes or changing schools, friends, and jobs. The normal stresses associated with the creation of a step or blended family can be compounded by a number of factors:

1. If there is extreme sadness or bitterness about the first marriage in either of the original partners and these feelings prevent the bonding of the new relationship

2. If the children profoundly long for or idealize their real father or mother, who is dead, absent, or neglectful, and have not resolved their feelings about the situation

3. If the children have not accepted the breakup of their parents

4. If there is competition between stepchildren and stepparents for the affections of a parent/spouse

5. If the children are placed in the middle of a hostile relationship between their parents and are conflicted about their loyalties or feel guilty for having a loving relationship with a stepparent

6. If a parent and the children have had such close relationships prior to the addition of the stepparent that the latter is hopelessly "shut out"

7. If resentment about financial or visitation arrangements is felt by any of the adults involved

The stepparent is often faced with enormous pressures. In an effort to be immediately successful, they sometimes set themselves up for difficulties, if not failure. Stepmothers, for example (perhaps especially those who never had children of their own), may bring excessive enthusiasm for mothering: to finally have a chance to be a parent, to replace the mother who died, to be a better mother than the real mother (whom the father may criticize), to win her new husband's approval, and so on. When there is an expectation, by the stepmother or stepfather, that the child will feel "instant devotion" to the new family member and this does not occur, disappointment, anger, and self criticism can sweep over the entire family.

In other cases, stepmothers may feel conflicted about taking on the responsibilities of children. They may want to please the new husband yet feel cheated of time for the marital relationship. This can be particularly problematic when the children were not originally part of the "package" but subsequently came to live with father and his wife. Of course, when the stepmother brings children of her own to the marriage, competition among the children can create tensions which, if either fostered or not handled competently and cooperatively by the adults, can create tremendous family tension.

Stepmothers who do not live with their husbands' children also face some of the same demands as those who do, even if not on an everyday basis.

Stepfathers, too, have their special pressures. They also can have unrealistic expectations. They may have the urge to rescue a family that has been bereft. They may feel they have to be the "strong" one or the "disciplinarian" in the family, often making it harder for the children to accept the "intruder," especially if the mother is torn between the wishes of her new husband and the complaints of the youngsters. Stepfathers who have children who are not living with them can feel resentful and/or guilty that they are spending so much time and energy on their wife's children. Often the mother and children have developed patterns of doing things in the home, and they resent any interference with their established routines. Marital conflicts may result. When the children treat the stepfather as an interloper, he may become harsh toward the youngsters or withdraw from them, in turn, adding to tensions between the couple. Often financial problems develop. If a stepfather has children of his own, his wife may begrudge the money he has to give to the other family. A man who has never been married before may resent sharing his paycheck with a spouse, to say nothing of children.

Grandparents often have complicated roles when a stepfamily is formed. In some cases, grandparents were heavily relied upon for babysitting or financial help when the family was a single-parent unit. Certainly some grandparents are glad to be relieved of these responsibilities when their daughter or son remarries, but others can feel displaced and deserted. It can happen that grandparents, like some stepchildren, resent or feel threatened by the new family member and actively denigrate him or her. The parent may be torn between his or her parents and the new spouse; children may be forced into complicated loyalty conflicts that involve three generations. Remarriages of both parents can result in the children's having eight sets of grandparents, requiring adjustments by all involved to the suddenly expanded network.

Combining unrelated children can be very difficult in some families. Territorial problems often develop if there is a new need to share living and sleeping space. Rivalry between stepsiblings can develop out of fear of losing a sense of ''specialness'' in relationship to one's own parent. Different backgrounds, styles, interests, rules, and ways of doing things make it hard for some families to feel comfortable when trying to blend together. Because of this or because of unresolved feelings about the loss of the original parent or family, children often overtly or covertly do what they can to break up the new family, sometimes in hopes of getting the old one back.

We have mentioned many difficulties that can arise when step- or blended families are formed. We want to emphasize that large numbers of such families find creative and loving ways to overcome and adapt to the problems of adjustment. In some cases, families feel an immediate benefit from adding a new member or members and adapt fairly readily. And, even when there are relationship problems that require professional help, it is important to remember that at the bottom of a great deal of the trouble are sadness, hidden grief, and fear. More often than not, antagonisms and rivalries are not primarily related to the actual characteristics of the former spouse or stepparent but rather to the unresolved feelings of all involved. There may be fears of loss of position or role (favorite grandparent, oldest or smartest child, for example), or of self esteem. There may be worry about losing relationships: children may fear their father will withdraw because the stepfather is in the picture; grandparents may feel discarded. Some parents who left a spouse to enter into a new relationship and marriage may feel particularly vulnerable and behave in dysfunctional ways in order to justify themselves. Others are still reeling under feelings of rejection by the former spouse, with children caught in the middle; divided loyalties, pressures to join alliances, or fears of losing allies are often at the root of the trouble. The possibilities, of course, are endless. When step- and blended families seek our help, we must try to determine what particular issues are creating pain.

Treatment Considerations

Because of the variety of problems that can be uncovered when stepfamilies find themselves in trouble, it is impossible to be very specific here about treatment goals. However, we offer the following general treatment suggestions:

1. As in many other family situations, with an eye to timing, it is usually important to try to *transcend the content and capture the spirit* of many specific complaints. Children, for example, may grasp at concrete matters (such as ''I hate the way my stepfather chews gum'' or ''My stepmother doesn't cook good meals'') to explain their distress when, in fact, they are struggling with grief, rejection, or fear. In family meetings, these feelings can often be tapped when the children feel comfortable and self-aware enough to express themselves. Adults, too, may blame children's behavior or minor idiosyncrasies of others for their unhappiness. They may try to feel better by vociferously castigating former spouses. It is the therapist's job to seek to understand the more basic issues, including the hidden feelings that foster violations of generational boundaries and scapegoating.

2. It is often very important to help family members feel *less threatened about differences* of feelings among them. Many variations are inevitable when new relationships form. For example, children often need permission to express sadness over losing their own mother, particularly when the stepmother is being very kind and unrealistically hopes to ''make up'' to the children for their loss and help them to forget it. In some cases, former spouses are very

angry at one another and pressure the children to feel as they do. In family meetings adults can be helped to realize that the children's relationships to their parents are not at all the same as those of the disillusioned former mates; the children's adjustments will be far more comfortable if their feelings and experiences are respected rather than opposed.

In order to reduce conflict and rivalry, and to bring a warmer climate to the complicated relationships, grandparents can be part of the treatment. When their importance is acknowledged and their feelings of loss understood, bitter feelings about being displaced can be eased; in turn, the grandparents will then be less likely to try to enter into dysfunctional alliances with their children or grandchildren. Stepparents, too, sometimes need special understanding; for example, many need to know that it is natural to have feelings for their own children that they do not have (and may never have) for their stepchildren.

Although careful assessment is necessary, there are some situations when it is extremely helpful to bring the former spouses, at times with their new spouses, together to facilitate the resolution of "unfinished business" and to work out differences about handling of the children. There is plenty of evidence that tells us that children are more likely to thrive when the adults in their lives work out problems between them, including separation problems. Not only the children are helped in this process; the new spouses often feel less threatened when their mates are not so intensely preoccupied, negatively or positively, with their old relationships. Sometimes family meetings with former spouses can include children who are caught in the middle or who need some relief from the trauma of the breakup. In these cases, of course, it is important to make it crystal clear to the children that the parents are not seeking reconciliation, as the youngsters often unrealistically hope, but rather are interested in working together to make life better for them.

3. Often it is essential to *expose and dispel myths*.[28] Although most families operate on some myths that are idiosyncratic to them, many stepfamilies are burdened with specific and recurring demands. Perhaps the major one is the expectation that there will be "instant love" among all members of a newly constituted family. As unrealistic as it usually is, stepchildren and stepparents often feel compelled to try to feel close to each from the start. Stepsiblings are admonished to get along with one another, often without recognition of the need for time to make adjustments to the changes that have been thrust upon them. It can be comforting for newly constituted families to know that it frequently takes as long as two years for the members to feel settled down and emotionally connected—and that blended family life simply cannot be perfect from the outset.

In some families, the myth of the "wicked stepmother" still prevails, although it is our impression that with the increasing numbers of blended families, this notion is losing ground. However, just as children are often scapegoated for the problems that arise, so are stepparents of either gender. Family meetings can provide an opportunity to support the spousal relationships and diffuse the tendency to blame the "intruder" for the problems of adjustment.

Related Issues

In therapy with stepfamilies, it is not uncommon to meet with subgroups in addition to or instead of the family as a whole. The new couple may need sessions to cement the relationship and make decisions about how to handle situations involving the children. A displaced grandparent may meet with his or her son and daughter to mend the hurt feelings stemming from the change in the family structure. Stepsiblings may have sessions without the adults. And, as we said, former spouses may need to resolve old or ongoing conflicts.

This section would not be complete without mention of some of the problems around sexuality that are particular to stepfamilies. The air is often sexually charged because the new couple is in the throes of a "honeymoon phase"; sometimes they can be careless about ensuring privacy for themselves and protecting the children from overstimulation. When stepsiblings, especially but not exclusively adolescents, are thrown together, sexual excitement often follows, even though it may not be acted upon. Stepfathers and stepdaughters, stepmothers and stepsons can feel sexual attractions toward one another. Many clinicians observe that when there has been no bonding between adult and child when the latter is very young, sexual feelings are less likely to be repressed. Under serious circumstances, this reality can lead to sexual abuse of children in stepfamilies. More frequently, jealousies between spouses evolve, or adults become overly strict with the children in an effort to contain the feelings and counteract their impulses.

We conclude by emphasizing that in stepfamilies, as in most families, it is the adults who must take the leadership and bear the burden for making many of the changes, even though as often as not it is the children's symptoms that bring the families into treatment. When the adults resolve their own conflicts and handle their own relationships, old and new, they not only provide a happier climate for the children but are better able to help their youngsters go through the pains and adjustments that accompany the breakup of one family and the formation of another. And, when stepparents, who are taking on the responsibility of raising children who are not their own, do not have the support and nurturance of their spouses, the entire family is bound to suffer. Much of the family work, therefore, must be directed toward the relationship issues among the adults.

It has taken two long chapters to present some of the basic theoretical and practical concepts required for engaging, assessing, and treating families. Although we, the authors, favor family group treatment when it is indicated and feasible, we also emphasize the importance of family and systems perspectives in our work with individuals. Individual and family dynamics interplay. As we have said very often throughout this text, whatever affects one part of a system necessarily affects the other parts to some degree. Positive shifts in a family's structure or climate can result in profound personality modifications of individual members. Changes in an entire family can occur after one member has been in treatment and makes changes. Because of this, we need not despair if we cannot gather the entire family together. When possible—whether we are seeing one family member, a subgroup, or an entire family—we search for the most accessible aspect of the system, the part that will be most responsive to intervention.[29]

In the two chapters that follow, some of the principles already discussed will be expanded upon as we direct our attention to the assessment and treatment of couples who turn to us for help with their relationships.

NOTES

1. See Janice Wood Wetzel, *Clinical Handbook of Depression* (New York: Gardner Press, 1984), especially Chapter 2.

2. Alan S. Gurman and David P. Kniskern, "Family Therapy Outcome Research: Knowns and Unknowns," in Gurman and Kniskern, eds., *Handbook of Family Therapy* (New York: Brunner/Mazel, 1981), p. 750. See especially pp. 748–761 for a generally encouraging review of research, still in its infancy, on the outcome of family therapies. See also Jack Santa-Barbara et al., "The McMaster Family Therapy Outcome Study: An Overview of Methods and Results," *International Journal of Family Therapy*, 1 (Winter 1979), 304–323, for a report of one exploratory study of brief family therapy with a large sample size that showed positive outcome results for over three-fourths of the families treated. Richard

A. Wells and Alan E. Dezen, in "The Results of Family Therapy Revisited: The Nonbehavioral Methods," *Family Process*, 17 (September 1978), 251–274, discuss some of the problems to researchers, one of the important ones deriving from the diversity of treatment methods and approaches in family work.

3. See Lyman C. Wynne, "Some Indications and Contraindications for Exploratory Family Therapy," in Ivan Boszormenyi-Nagy and James L. Framo, eds., *Intensive Family Therapy* (New York: Basic Books, 1965); Nathan Ackerman, *Treating the Troubled Family* (New York: Basic Books, 1966), pp. 111–112; Daniel Offer and Evert VanderStoep, "Indications and Contraindications for Family Therapy," in Max Sugar, ed., *The Adolescent in Group and Family Therapy* (New York: Brunner/Mazel, 1975), pp. 145–160; and Frances H. Scherz, "Family Treatment Concepts," *Social Casework*, 47 (April 1966), 234–240.

See also Arthur Leader's excellent article, "The Relationship of Presenting Problems to Family Conflicts," *Social Casework*, 62 (October 1981), 451–457, for a discussion of the importance of establishing connections between presenting problems and family conflicts and of determining how these connections guide the therapy.

4. Sanford N. Sherman, "Family Treatment: An Approach to Children's Problems," *Social Casework*, 47 (June 1966), p. 369. See also Adena R. Frager, "A Family Systems Perspective on Acting-Out," *Social Casework*, 66 (March 1985), 167–176, for a discussion of acting-out as a response to, and an attempt to repair, systemic dysfunction. The reader may also be interested in an early article by Nathan W. Ackerman, "Psychiatric Disorders in Children—Diagnosis and Etiology in Our Time," in Paul H. Hoch and Joseph Zubin, eds., *The Diagnostic Process in Child Psychiatry* (New York: Grune & Stratton, 1953), 205–230, in which he discusses the importance of viewing children's difficulties in the context of family and social experiences.

5. Celia Mitchell, "The Therapeutic Field in the Treatment of Families in Conflict: Recurrent Themes in Literature and Clinical Practice," in Bernard Reiss, ed., *New Directions in Mental Health* (New York: Grune & Stratton, 1968), p. 75. See also a pertinent article by Sharon L. Wechter, "Separation Difficulties Between Parents and Young Adults," *Social Casework*, 64 (February 1983), 97–104.

6. See Salvador Minuchin et al., *Families of the Slums* (New York: Basic Books, 1967), which describes treatment of families of boys referred to a private residential treatment center (Wiltwyck School for Boys), most of whom lived a considerable distance from the institution. See also William R. McFarlane, ed., *Family Therapy in Schizophrenia* (New York: Guilford Press, 1983), for several very good articles on the involvement of families in the care and rehabilitation of mentally ill family members. Of interest, too, is Eda Goldstein's report of a study of young adult inpatients, which strongly suggests the importance of parental involvement in the treatment process, in "The Influence of Parental Attitudes on Psychiatric Treatment Outcome," *Social Casework*, 60 (June 1979), 350–359.

7. Sanford N. Sherman, "Family Therapy," in Francis J. Turner, ed., *Social Work Treatment*, 2d ed. (New York: Free Press, 1979), pp. 471–472.

8. Wynne, "Some Indications and Contraindications," pp. 321–322.

9. See the study by Myrna M. Weissman and Eugene S. Paykel, *The Depressed Woman* (Chicago: University of Chicago Press, 1974), in which all of the 150 moderately depressed women studied responded favorably (i.e., experienced some reduction of symptoms) to a period of four to six weeks of drug therapy; social adjustment (not affected by medication) was enhanced by those who received weekly psychotherapy in addition to drugs.

10. Gurman and Kniskern, *Family Therapy Outcome Research*, p. 751.

11. Many beginning family therapists have found that very useful guidelines are provided by Jay Haley in Chapter 1, "Conducting the First Interview," in *Problem-Solving Therapy* (San Francisco: Jossey-Bass, 1987). See also, Helm Stierlin et al., *The First Interview with the Family* (New York: Brunner/Mazel, 1980).

12. An exploratory study of joint marital treatment in which the Hollis typology was used is reported by Shirley M. Ehrenkranz in her doctoral dissertation, "A Study of the Techniques and Procedures Used in Joint Interviewing in the Treatment of Marital Problems" (Columbia University School of Social Work, New York, 1967). Two articles summarizing this ex-

cellent beginning effort to use the Hollis classification to examine conjoint treatment were published: "A Study of Joint Interviewing in the Treatment of Marital Problems," *Social Casework*, 48 (October–November 1967), pp. 498–503, 570–574. See also Florence Hollis, "Continuance and Discontinuance in Marital Counseling and Some Observations on Joint Interviews," *Social Casework*, 49 (March 1968), 167–174. The findings reported by Ehrenkranz and Hollis, however, were based on small samples and, as they indicated, further refinements of the typology would be required to study the many dimensions and complex interactions found in multiperson interviews.

13. Ehrenkranz, "A Study of Joint Interviewing," pp. 499–500.

14. See, for example, Jay Haley, *Problem-Solving Therapy*, pp. 125, 176, 198–199, and 228; and Salvadore Minuchin, *Families and Family Therapy* (Cambridge, Mass.: Harvard University Press, 1974), p. 14.

15. See, for example, Scott Briar and Henry Miller, *Problems and Issues in Social Casework* (New York: Columbia University Press, 1971), pp. 191–192.

16. Frank S. Pittman, III, "The Family That Hides Together," in Peggy Papp, ed., *Family Therapy: Full Length Case Studies* (New York: Gardner Press, 1977), p. 2.

17. For discussions of some of the attempts to develop classifications or nosologies of family disorders, see Frances H. Scherz, "Family Treatment Concepts," *Social Casework*, 47 (April 1966), pp. 234–240; Nathan W. Ackerman, Frances L. Beatman, and Sanford N. Sherman, *Expanding Theory and Practice in Family Therapy* (New York: Family Service Association of America, 1967); Nathan W. Ackerman, *The Psychodynamics of Family Life* (New York: Basic Books, 1958), pp. 329–330; Group for the Advancement of Psychiatry, "The Field of Family Therapy," 78 (New York: Group for the Advancement of Psychiatry, March 1970); Eleanor S. Wertheim, "Family Unit Therapy and the Science and Typology of Family Systems II," *Family Process*, 14 (September 1975), 285–309; and George S. Greenberg, "The Family Interactional Perspective: A Study and Examination of the Work of Don D. Jackson," *Family Process*, 16 (December 1977), 385–412. See also James Framo's

informal scheme for classifying marriages in "Marital Therapy and Family of Origin," in Framo, *Explorations in Marital and Family Therapy* (New York: Springer, 1982), pp. 202–203.

18. Quoted in Vincent D. Foley, *An Introduction to Family Therapy* (New York: Grune & Stratton, 1974), p. 145.

19. Nathan W. Ackerman. "The Growing Edge of Family Therapy," in Clifford J. Sagar and Helen Singer Kaplan, eds., *Progress in Group and Family Therapy* (New York: Brunner/Mazel, 1972), p. 454. See also Thomas F. Fogarty, "Systems Concepts and the Dimensions of Self," in Phillip J. Guerin, ed., *Family Therapy* (New York: Gardner Press, 1976), pp. 149–150; and James L. Framo, "Marital Therapy and Family of Origin," pp. 199–201, for informal attempts to classify well-functioning families and marriages.

20. Framo, "Marital Therapy and Family of Origin," p. 199.

21. Ibid., pp. 199–200.

22. Carl A. Whitaker et al., "Countertransference in the Family Treatment of Schizophrenia," in Boszormenyi-Nagy and Framo, *Intensive Family Therapy*, p. 335. See also James L. Framo, "Rationale and Techniques of Intensive Family Therapy," in the same volume, pp. 194–198; and Helm Stierlin, "Countertransference in Family Therapy with Adolescents," in Sugar, *The Adolescent in Group and Family Therapy*, pp. 161–177.

By becoming more differentiated in their relations with their own families of origin, family therapists can learn to develop greater objectivity and less reactivity toward their clients. For readings on this, we recommend: Elizabeth A. Carter and Monica McGoldrick Orfanidis, "Family Therapy with One Person and the Family Therapist's Own Family," in Guerin, *Family Therapy*, 193–219; Philip Rich, "Differentiation of Self in the Therapist's Family of Origin," *Social Casework*, 61 (September 1980), 394–399; and Peter Titelman, ed., *The Therapist's Own Family: Toward the Differentiation of Self* (Northvale, N.J.: Aronson, 1987).

23. Augustus Y. Napier and Carl A. Whitaker, *The Family Crucible* (New York: Harper & Row, 1978).

24. Carol M. Anderson and Susan Stewart, *Mastering Resistance* (New York: Guilford Press, 1983), pp. 25–26.

25. For readings on single-parent families, see especially, Anita Morawetz and Gillian Walker, *Brief Therapy with Single-Parent Families* (New York: Brunner/Mazel, 1984). See also Geoffrey L. Greif, "Single Fathers and Noncustodial Mothers: The Social Worker's Helping Role," *Journal of Independent Social Work*, 1 (Spring 1987), 59–69; Tina U. Howard and Frank C. Johnson, "An Ecological Approach to Practice with Single Families," *Social Casework*, 66 (October 1985), 482–489; and Daniel S. Nieto, "Aiding the Single Father," *Social Work*, 27 (November 1982), 473–478.

26. Virginia Satir, *Conjoint Family Therapy*, rev. ed. (Palo Alto, Calif.: Science and Behavior Books, 1967), especially Part I.

27. See especially, Emily B. Visher and John S. Visher, *Stepfamilies: A Guide to Working with Stepparents and Stepchildren* (New York: Brunner/Mazel, 1979); and Esther Wald, *The Remarried Family: Challenge and Promise* (New York: Family Service Association of America, 1981). See also, Harriette C. Johnson, "Working with Stepfamilies: Principles of Practice," *Social Work*, 25 (July 1980), 304–308; Marilyn O. Kent, "Remarriage: A Family Systems Perspective," *Social Casework*, 61 (March 1980), 146–153; Elinor B. Rosenberg and Fady Hajal, "Stepsibling Relationships in Remarried Families," *Social Casework*, 66 (May 1985), 287–292; and Greta W. Stanton, "Preventive Intervention with Stepfamilies," *Social Work*, 31 (May–June 1986), 201–206.

According to an article in *Psychology Today*, "Stepdaughter Wars," by Joshua Fischman (November 1988), one child in ten now lives with a stepparent; this makes the expected increase reported by Fischman—that is, that one out of four children born in the 1980s will live in a stepfamily by age eighteen—particularly striking.

28. See Gerda Schulman, "Myths That Intrude on the Adaptation of the Stepfamily," *Social Casework*, 53 (March 1972), 132–139.

29. In addition to references cited in this chapter and in Chapter 15, readers may find the following readings relevant to the further study of the practice of family therapy: Harry J. Aponte, "Diagnosis in Family Therapy," in Carel B. Germain, ed., *Social Work Practice: People and Environments* (New York: Columbia University Press, 1979). Harry J. Aponte, "If I Don't Get Simple, I Cry," *Family Process*, 25 (December 1986), 531–548. Ivan Boszormenyi-Nagy and Geraldine M. Spark, *Invisible Loyalties* (New York: Harper & Row, 1973). Anna M. Chase et al., "Treating the Throwaway Child: A Model for Adolescent Service," *Social Casework*, 60 (November 1979), 538–546. Christine A. Dietz and John L. Craft, "Family Dynamics of Incest: A New Perspective," *Social Casework*, 61 (December 1980), 602–609. Virginia Goldner, "Feminism and Family Therapy," *Family Process*, 24 (March 1985), 31–47. Felisha S. Gwyn and Allie C. Kilpatrick, "Family Therapy with Low-Income Blacks: A Tool or Turn-Off?" *Social Casework*, 62 (May 1981), 259–266. Carol Hardy-Fanta and Elizabeth MacMahon-Herrera, "Adapting Family Therapy to the Hispanic Family," *Social Casework*, 62 (March 1981), 138–148. Ann Hartman, "The Extended Family as a Resource for Change: An Ecological Approach to Family Centered Practice," in Germain, *Social Work Practice*, pp. 239–266. Harriette C. Johnson, "Emerging Concerns in Family Therapy," *Social Work*, 31 (July–August 1986), 299–306. Arthur L. Leader, "Family Therapy for Divorced Fathers and Others out of the Home," *Social Casework*, 54 (January 1973), 13–19. Arthur L. Leader, "Therapeutic Control in Family Therapy," *Clinical Social Work Journal*, 11 (Winter 1983), 351–361. Monica McGoldrick and Randy Gerson, *Genograms in Family Assessment* (New York: W. W. Norton, 1985). Salvador Minuchin et al., *Psychosomatic Families: Anorexia Nervosa in Context* (Cambridge, Mass.: Harvard University Press, 1978). Gerda L. Schulman and Elsa Leichter, "The Prevention of Family Breakup," *Social Casework*, 49 (March 1968). Michael J. Shernoff, "Family Therapy for Lesbian and Gay Clients," *Social Work*, 29 (July–August 1984), 393–396. Donna R. Weaver, "Empowering Treatment Skills for Helping Black Families," *Social Casework*, 63 (February 1982), 100–105. Arthur Weidman, "Therapy with Violent Couples," *Social Casework*, 67 (April 1986), 211–218. Jack Weitzman, "Engaging the Severely Dysfunctional Family in Treatment: Basic Considerations," *Family Process*, 24 (December 1985), 473–485.

CHAPTER 17

Couple Treatment: Problems in Relationships

Joint interviewing of couples is an aspect of just about every caseworker's function. This chapter will discuss the psychosocial casework approach to marital relationships. It includes a brief historical perspective, some assessment and general treatment considerations, a typology of couple relationships and problems, and discussions of unique concerns of "nontraditional" couples, of women, and of marriages in which there have been extramarital affairs. Using case illustrations, Chapter 18 will focus on specific treatment issues and approaches.

It should not surprise us that at the very time the institution of marriage is believed to be in serious jeopardy, when approximately one-half of first marriages and over 40 percent of second marriages end in divorce,[1] that more and more people are seeking professional help to understand and mend their marital relationships. Even though presenting complaints brought to family agencies, mental health clinics, protective and other services have always included marital unhappiness, treatment of marital problems often evolved only *after* children's symptoms were explored. In recent years, however, parents seem to be more aware of the effects

their marriage has on the emotional well-being of their children; as a result, children may not be required so often (as unconsciously they sometimes are) to be "passports" for troubled parents getting help.

Indeed, couples with or without children, separated and divorced couples concerned about the ongoing destructive effects of their conflictual relationships on their children, unmarried people of all ages who are living together, gay pairs, couples interested in premarital counseling, others looking for "enrichment" and solutions to "midlife crises" or "empty-nest syndromes"—*all* are frequently seen by social workers in various kinds of agencies and clinics and in private practice. In these two chapters on couple treatment, even when we specifically use terms such as "marriage," "marital relationship," and "spouse," our discussions usually can apply to nontraditional as well as traditional couples.

A BRIEF HISTORICAL PERSPECTIVE

Like family therapy, couple therapy has roots in the casework tradition.[2] However, the emphasis on psychological matters in the 1920s, followed by the ever-increasing influence of psychoanalytic ideas in the 1930s, tended to lead casework thinkers and practitioners to work primarily with individuals and favor seeing marital partners separately, even when marital difficulties were a major treatment focus.[3] In her book published in 1949, *Women in Marital Conflict*, Hollis wrote:

> If treatment is to go beyond environmental support and clarification, if it involves extensive use of psychological supportive processes, and particularly if insight development is contemplated, it is more economical and effective in the end *for each person to have his own worker* [emphasis ours!]. Otherwise much time and effort will be dissipated in dealing with rivalry and misunderstanding created by attitudes toward the common worker, tremendous care will have to be taken to avoid and straighten out misquotations, and the worker will face a difficult task in establishing himself as both sympathetic and impartial in the minds of both clients.[4]

There are many professionals, including some social workers, who still hold these notions today, often for the same or similar reasons. However, we, the authors of this text, now believe that for many, if not most, marital or couple difficulties, joint interviewing proves to be most effective. We agree with Framo that the likelihood of divorce is greater if partners go to two therapists separately. He writes, "In treating a couple one must consider that there are three patients: the husband, the wife, and the relationship." Marriage therapy, he goes on, "not only deals with the intrapsychic dynamics of each spouse but also examines *the interlocking nature of the marital bond*." [emphasis ours].[5] Obviously, when spouses are seen separately, the complexities of the bond between them cannot be as effectively addressed as when they are observed in vivo by couple and worker together. We will say more about this later, especially in Chapter 18. As we shall also discuss there, joint interviewing requires the worker's

"involved impartiality" (discussed in Chapter 16); we now believe this is not only possible but essential.

Contraindications to conjoint couple therapy do exist, however, and are similar to those that apply to family sessions (see pages 340 and 341). There are situations in which treatment involving separate interviews or, more occasionally, even different workers may seem to be the wisest approach to a particular couple. Also, as discussed in Chapter 16, when a member of a family or couple is unavailable or unwilling to participate in treatment, shifts in the family or marital system can be fostered by changes and efforts made by one member in individual treatment.[6] In this connection, it is interesting to note that Hollis made this point in her 1949 study on marital conflict, over a decade before systems concepts as such were introduced into casework or mental health thinking:

> The writer...would definitely not agree with those who take the position that it is impossible to help in marriage conflict unless both partners are willing to participate in treatment. Many cases in this study demonstrate the opposite—that a change in one partner may in itself decrease the total conflict or even go further and *bring about a responding change in the other person involved*. [emphasis ours].[7]

Over the years, our clinical experiences have substantiated one of the basic premises of current family therapy practice: If one person changes, all others in emotional relationships with him or her are likely to make compensatory changes.

ASSESSMENT AND GENERAL TREATMENT CONSIDERATIONS

In Chapter 15, we discussed our rationale for integrating systems and psychodynamic approaches in casework with families. Marital and some other types of couple work represent a subtype of family therapy; as such, from the psychosocial point of view, the same reasoning applies.[8]

Joan and Bill were referred by Family Court for psychiatric evaluations and social work treatment after charges and countercharges of physical and verbal abuse. Both had endured extraordinarily deprived childhoods. In addition to Alcohol Abuse, Bill was given a DSM-III diagnosis of Antisocial Personality Disorder. Joan was believed to meet the criteria for a diagnosis of Histrionic Personality Disorder with paranoid features. When they were seen first in individual and then in couple treatment by a social worker in a spouse abuse service, the interlocking nature of the marital transactions became apparent. Briefly stated, when Joan thought (often accurately) that Bill was lying to her or seeing other women, she wrote letters to various members of his family accusing him of wanting to poison her. Particularly after bouts of excessive drinking, Bill responded by assaulting her and they engaged in treacherous physical battles. As it turned out, the destructive pattern between them was so entrenched that they did not respond to casework efforts and the marital balance or homeostasis was maintained; for their protection the couple's children, who were constantly triangulated in the cross fire, were placed in foster care. Only after Bill was killed in an automobile accident a year later was Joan (who voluntarily returned to casework treatment) able to disentangle herself sufficiently from her enmeshment with Bill (as well as from members of her family of origin) to begin to embark on the work of self-differentiation. Even though the couple's motivation or capacity for change had not been sufficient prior to Bill's death and the power of the marital bond had seemingly prevented movement by either partner, subsequently Joan successfully built on the work that she had only just begun while Bill was alive.[9]

In this case, the caseworker assessed individual behavior and marital processes which were complexly intertwined. By the time Joan and Bill were married, each had already internalized many self-defeating behavioral and emotional patterns and poor self-esteem. Subsequently, the marriage itself, with its own destructive patterns, blocked efforts either to improve or to terminate their relationship.

When Joan's suspiciousness and Bill's defensive aggressiveness became part of the marriage, these along with other individual qualities interacted to form new and repetitive *marital* dynamics. *Interactional processes always go beyond the inner lives and behaviors of the individuals.*

In spite of the forcefulness of the marital interaction, we want to emphasize that there are many enduring, "portable" personality qualities in people that are expressed under most circumstances. In fact, as discussed more fully in Chapter 2, important influences on personality occur at very young ages. The nurturance of the relatively autonomous, self-reliant personality requires two basic conditions of "good enough parenting": (1) consistent parental availability, responsiveness, and support; and (2) parental encouragement of the child's independence and self-direction, appropriately timed to the child's age. Absence of either of these can result in the child's not internalizing an independent, stable concept of self; this in turn can impair the capacity for relating to others. Many of the clients we see with personality disorders, including Joan and Bill, have come out of backgrounds of inconsistency, neglect, or overprotection. Mate selection is often made on the basis of a need to "complete" oneself and to bolster self-esteem.[10] Unfortunately, as often as not in these cases, destructive marital patterns emerge and serve to incapacitate further rather than to strengthen the individual personalities. When spouses look to one another to feel "whole," they usually place more of a burden on the relationship than it can handle. On the other hand, marital dysfunction can be seen as a desperate attempt by both partners to *solve* psychological conflicts; the couple's troubles can be viewed as a drive for health, a constructive perspective which diminishes blame and offers hope.[11] As we shall see, at its best, the marital relationship can also become a force that heals, a nurturing environment in which spouses can provide one another with "corrective" experiences.

Assessment of marital relationships calls on concepts illuminating personality development, ego functions, psychopathology, communication and feedback processes, homeostasis, triangulation, and enmeshment—among others. We emphasize the need for multilevel assessment and intervention because the power of the interactional phenomena is frequently overlooked, especially by practitioners and theoreticians primarily rooted in personality and intrapsychic theory. For example, to our amazement, Christopher Dare's search of the papers published in the three most influential and prestigious psychoanalytic journals found them "noticeably lacking in even passing references to marriage as an important feature of people's psychological life." Over a recent ten-year period, Dare reports, there are "no articles on marriage, although there are copious references to other family dyads; no extensive accounts of psychological features or causations of marital relations; and only passing references to the fact that many of the people represented in case histories, so extensively reported, are married."[12] How troubled marriages are derived from and yet also transcend the personalities of the individual partners is a major emphasis of these chapters on couple treatment.

SPECIAL ASSESSMENT CONCERNS

In couple treatment, understanding and intervening require attention to the following interpenetrating points:

1. When changes occur in the marital system, the behavior and inner lives of individuals also change. For example, when a man makes positive changes requested by his wife—such as spending more time at home, participating more with the children, becoming more interested in sexual relations—the wife actually may become indifferent, feel uncomfortable, or articulate a new complaint (sometimes to the surprise of the inexperienced worker). Between spouses there is often an "agreement" about the degree of distance or intimacy to be maintained; thus, when one person makes a move, the other adjusts to maintain the accustomed balance. Along similar lines, when a partner who has had the role of "pursuer" withdraws, often the "distancer" begins to approach the former pursuer. When an alcoholic spouse stops drinking, it is not uncommon for the other one to become depressed. When the "weak" partner dies, we often find that the "strong" one breaks down. In a sense, the couple may become "one self," with each partner (whether apparently so or not) dependent on the other to feel "whole."

To illustrate further: a spouse who takes on the role of "rescuer" usually requires a "helpless" mate to fend off fears of unworthiness, disapproval, or abandonment; the mate who "agrees" to be rescued out of fear may disown his or her own strengths in order to assure the spouse's attachment and concern. In this case, if the "rescuer" begins to resent and resist the burden of taking care of his or her spouse or the "rescuee" makes moves toward independence, it can be expected that there will be a reaction by the other to restore the status quo. The actions of one spouse are both cause and effect of the behaviors and feelings of the other. Like chicken and egg, cause and effect are inseparable.

2. In spite of pressures to pinpoint clinical diagnoses, we must give full recognition to the influence of the immediate social context as well as to abiding personality features. Feelings, attitudes, and actions of each spouse and the quality of the marital dynamics itself can be viewed as accommodations to the conditions under which they exist, within and outside the marriage. For example, in the case of Bill and Joan described above, Joan was unable to make moves toward self-improvement during her marriage; the marital interactions were greater than the personalities of both. Yet after Bill died she could develop new, more satisfying ways of leading her life by addressing long-standing personality issues of her own. A man may be labeled "impulse-ridden" or "aggressive" because of the manner in which he torments his wife but be described as "mild-mannered, well-disciplined, and hardworking" on his job. The wife in this marital situation may suffer from "depression," and it is only after she is working at a job in which she feels competent and valued that feelings of cheerfulness make her realize that her "depression" is situation-bound.[13] When the context changes, symptoms or certain so-called character traits may also change.[14]

3. It is clear that when one spouse is in therapy, without the participation of the other, the situation can produce a powerful intrusion on the marital system. When a relationship is faltering or even when there are no immediate complaints about the marriage, individual treatment may be an important contributing factor to its dissolution. The woman mentioned above learned that when at work and away from her husband, she did not feel depressed; without marital sessions she might have left her husband, never exploring the possibilities for change in their unhappy relationship. In another case, a woman who sought treatment for discontent with many aspects of her life developed a strong, positive transference to her male therapist, idealizing him to such an extent that in her eyes her husband compared very unfavorably. She ended her marriage. Had there been joint sessions, the transference to the therapist might not have emerged so powerfully and the issues *between the spouses* might have been addressed instead. In the next chapter we will discuss the issue of transference in couple therapy.

(The writers usually urge involvement of both spouses at the beginning of treatment, even in cases in which the presenting complaint of an individual appears unrelated to the marriage. Alerting the couple that sometimes there are important repercussions on the relationship when only one partner makes changes may encourage both spouses to engage in the therapy. At least, they are then in a better position to make informed choices.)

4. Taking the above points a step further, if an individual's symptoms are assessed as arising totally from intrapsychic issues, important opportunities for helping may be overlooked. Neurotic conflicts or developmental deficits may not altogether explain a person's behavior, attitudes, or feelings that on first glance seem very personal. In fact, in the experience of the writers, there are few complaints presented by married clients that are not powerfully influenced by the marital relationship; the difficulties of one spouse, to one degree or another, are lived and acted out in combination with the other. It follows, then, that symptoms are often most effectively addressed in the context of the marriage.

In this connection, Woods has studied, case by case from her own clinical practice, more than a dozen married women suffering from phobias and anxiety attacks. In each situation the husband was asked to participate (sometimes puzzling or even annoying the wife, who was usually sure that her marriage had no bearing on the problem). As it turned out, when the husband joined the treatment, in each case symptom relief for the wife and improved marital functioning resulted. Prior to the husband's participation (or in the rare instances when husband, wife, or both refused to be seen jointly), much less progress occurred.

By far, the majority of these were marriages in which there was no threat of divorce and there were mutual caring and general concern for one another. However, almost without exception, a common pattern was revealed: The husbands, although extremely concerned about their wife's welfare (in some instances to the point of taking on the role of "rescuer"), tended to display little emotion and talked very little about themselves. The wives, particularly after becoming symptomatic, were often quite emotive: tearful, "hysterical," or angry. Yet, like their husbands, they seldom addressed their hopes or disappointments about their lives and marriages. Neither the husbands nor the wives seemed able to speak or make requests directly to their partners. In terms of intimacy, all led lonely lives. It can be speculated that the women's symptoms were, in part, communications, unconscious attempts to draw their husbands closer.

There were some dramatic moments when the men began to express themselves and take "I" positions in sessions; almost without exception the women showed signs of relaxation, some almost immediately, others eventually. Even when the men were expressing complaints or concerns about the relationship that they assumed their spouses would not want to hear, the wives soon were more gratified than threatened because they felt closer and less alone. In nearly all of these situations, the women indicated that they realized they had felt lonely (and sometimes "crazy" for being unhappy when they had such good mates). It was important to them to know what their husbands thought and felt. The men, most of whom had been trained in one way or another to discount their inner lives, were amazed at how much more they began to enjoy themselves and their marriages once they had the experience of having their secret or disowned "real" selves revealed and understood by their wives. As Loewenstein said, "The need to be understood can be as urgent as the need for self-understanding."[15]

After an unsuccessful course of behavioral therapy, Barbara, age thirty-three, came for treatment of anxiety and phobic symptoms that were seriously curtailing her activities.

She was constantly terrified that she would have an anxiety attack; when one occurred, she had acute fears of death. For over a year she had been unable to drive a car or leave her house unless her husband, Al, was with her. She was so preoccupied that she could not give first-rate attention to her two young children. As is often true of people with these symptoms, Barbara had not successfully separated from her family of origin. She came from an enmeshed family in which family members did not deal directly with one another and yet all were intricately intertwined. Barbara and her mother spoke on the phone several times a day about how to help the father and younger sister with their problems. Barbara was the "good" girl, in contrast to her sister, who was "bad," "difficult," and "selfish." She was very much involved in trying to mediate her parents' marital problems. It was also expected that she should take inordinate responsibility for caring for grandparents and for rescuing her sister from one predicament after another. Barbara did not protest her family's expectations and vehemently disagreed with the worker's suggestion that her symptoms might be a reaction to the responsibilities she carried. It was almost impossible for her to claim, at least directly, any needs or wants of her own. She had a martyred demeanor, often self-righteously complaining that it is the "good" ones—of whom she saw herself as one—who suffer. Her sister, she grumbled, had no disabling symptoms in spite of her self-absorption. Barbara was extraordinarily sensitive to criticism, especially if she thought it challenged her selflessness. She saw herself and Al as among the very few who care about others.

Only after several individual sessions was Barbara even willing to consider having Al join the treatment with her. She "owned" her own symptoms and resisted the notion that her husband had any part in them. She seemed to fear that she might "rock the boat" of her marriage, which she convincingly described as loyal and committed. Gently but repeatedly the worker suggested that solid relationships such as hers and Al's can have powerful healing powers; rather than emphasizing problems, the worker framed her recommendation in terms of the strengths of the marriage. Because of the acuteness of her symptoms, Barbara finally agreed to bring Al to sessions.

In his family of origin, as the oldest child, Al had the role of being the "strong, silent" one. Apparently he had gotten the message from his parents that he would be most admired and loved if he was self-reliant and helpful to others. Rarely was he aware of his own wishes or feelings. Al's demeanor was matter-of-fact, not overtly warm, yet he was extremely helpful to Barbara and showed genuine concern for her which, on the surface, she seemed to take for granted.

The therapeutic work was slow. Individual and interactional styles were firmly set. Barbara and Al were not open to the suggestion that—other than Barbara's symptoms—there were any individual, marital, or family-of-origin concerns which they needed to address. Meanwhile, Barbara's phobias were becoming more pervasive and paralyzing, finally becoming serious enough to upset the delicate, yet heretofore stable, balance of the marriage.

Al played an important role in the breakthrough that occurred. After many months, rather than just presenting himself as a helper to Barbara, he cautiously began to express some of his own feelings. At first he spoke of his resentment about the negative effect on their children for the entire focus of the family to be on Barbara's problems. Barbara, always verbose, began talking more and more rapidly, seemingly trying to drown out Al's remarks. For a brief period, Al retreated from speaking for himself. However, during one session Barbara, who habitually spoke

for Al, mentioned that he did not mind how often she and her mother spoke on the telephone. Flushed and furious, Al uncharacteristically exclaimed, "I've had enough!" and stormed out of the office. The following week he dropped Barbara off but did not come in. He returned for the next appointment and was able to tell her how neglected he felt by all the attention and caretaking she required. Furthermore, he told her that he thought he ranked fourth with her: after her family, the children, and her "damn fears." At first Barbara attacked Al and tried to discredit his complaints, but he doggedly persisted. He announced that he was "on a roll" and this time could not be stopped.

It took only a few weeks for Barbara to accept what Al was saying. She went on to admit for the first time that she had always feared that she was not "good enough" in his eyes, just as she never felt "good enough" to her family, in which so much attention went to her sister.

At last the work could begin. Both Barbara and Al realized that they had not paid much attention to their own feelings and needs. She was oppressed by the unending demands of her family and her inability to be of any lasting help to them. He was constantly trying to come to her aid, and though he kept doing more and more for her, her symptoms grew worse. Barbara began to be less self-righteous, talking about herself instead of others and what they needed or "should" do.

As treatment continued, both Barbara and Al benefited tremendously from learning how to speak for themselves. They discovered that they would not be unloved or abandoned even if they spoke from the depth of their own (negative or positive) feelings. They recognized how, when both "sold their souls," they continually reinforced their loneliness and underrated the potentials in their relationship. They declared that they would not allow themselves to be "swallowed up" by external demands ever again and agreed that their marriage would become a primary priority. By the time treatment terminated, two years after it began, Barbara's symptoms (which may have had some physiological as well as psychosocial basis[16]) had greatly diminished and both were pleased with their enriched, more openly tender relationship in which there was genuine give-and-take between them for the first time.[17]

It cannot be overemphasized that in *all* marriages, intense, interlocking dynamics transcend the inner lives of the individuals. It is not uncommon for two (or more) people in close relationships to make unconscious, unspoken "bargains" whereby they collusively carry out psychic functions for one another. By disowning his own needs, Al provided Barbara with attention she could never get from her family of origin. By becoming phobic, Barbara gave Al the opportunity to repeat the role he played with his parents, as the helpful, self-reliant one who made no demands on others. The whole *is* greater than the sum of its parts!

Furthermore, as illustrated in the case of Al and Barbara, trouble often develops when people believe, consciously or unconsciously, that they have to bury or disown important aspects of themselves: feelings, thoughts, values or purposes. They can become symptomatic or unhappy: angry, confused, hopeless. Their marriages, at best, leave each wanting in some way. When we speak of facilitating autonomy or differentiation, we are talking about helping people to claim themselves and develop those hidden or unevolved parts that were compromised out of fear of losing love or of being overwhelmed. In couple therapy, therefore, not only is the opportunity for self-understanding offered but *being deeply understood by the people who count the most* (and this should not mean therapists!) can be one of the most meaningful outcomes. This potential is not intrinsic to individual treatment.

A TYPOLOGY OF COUPLE RELATIONSHIPS AND PROBLEMS

Classifications of marital problems have been attempted by some writers and practitioners, although emphases among them differ and agreement on a single typology has not been achieved.[18] There are, however, some very distinct types of marital conditions that may significantly affect treatment goals and strategies. Some of these are revealed at the outset; others emerge as treatment evolves. Furthermore, the factors that influence the course a marriage takes are complex and not always altogether clear, to the couple or to the worker. In this section we will be presenting an informal breakdown (or rough classification) of some of the types of dilemmas that frequently emerge when clients come to couple therapy; it is based on our experience, and its purpose is to provide possible guidelines for assessment and treatment.

Several factors concerning the somewhat arbitrary divisions of our classification should be kept in mind:

1. They frequently overlap. That is, a couple's situation may straddle two or more categories.

2. They may describe marital situations in which there has been *chronic* distress or dissatisfaction. Or, conversely, the marriage may be, to some degree, in *crisis*, mild or acute.

3. They are applicable whether a couple has sought treatment voluntarily, is in joint therapy because of concern about a symptomatic child, or has been mandated by the court or protective services to get help.

4. Consideration must be given to strengths and healthy adaptive features of the relationship as well as to dysfunctional and "pathological" aspects (intelligence, talents, emotionality, honesty, ability to empathize, flexibility, lack of extreme defensiveness, etc.). Though not specifically mentioned here, such positive qualities significantly affect the course of treatment and must be assessed.[19]

5. In some instances a category may suggest the degree of severity of the problem but usually is *not* a reliable predictor of the difficulty of the treatment or of the outcome. Some troubles seem relatively minor and yet yield very little to therapeutic efforts; other serious relationship problems may be remarkably susceptible to changes.

6. Along similar lines, it is also true that some individuals who seem deeply disturbed nevertheless have successful marriages, and others whom we would not diagnose as having significant psychological problems are involved in painfully destructive relationships.[20] In these latter situations, interactional patterns usually become the major focus of attention.

Categories of Relationships

The categories of couples and their relationships seen in casework treatment include the following.

1. Essentially Solid, Committed Relationships with Minor Dysfunctions Whether newly formed or longstanding, these usually require relatively small shifts or adjustments to alleviate the difficulties. In some instances, an educational approach brings significant relief. This may involve assistance with communication skills, universalization (helping the couple to realize that many others experience the same or similar difficulties), provision of information about the dynamic aspects of the marriage or guidance around crises or "expectable" life cycle transitions, and examination of the stresses and tasks often associated with these. Many couples in this category are minimally defensive and are able to reflect on their situations and on their patterns of interaction, often making significant improvements quite quickly. When better understanding is achieved, empathy for one another may come naturally. It is not unusual for these couples, with the worker's help, to design "homework" derived from

new perspectives and "tools" gained in treatment. Gains made between sessions can be rewarding and can reassure the couple that it is not the worker who is ultimately responsible for the improvement they are enjoying. Dick and Susan Jones's relationship, described in Chapter 3, belongs in this group.

There are couples in this category with rigid personality traits and/or interactional patterns, who make changes surprisingly slowly in spite of a high level of emotional differentiation and capacity for caring and understanding. The changes they *do* make usually "stick," but there may be many sessions in which nothing seems to happen. There are other couples for whom enrichment of the marriage is a primary goal. In our experience it is futile and antitherapeutic to insist on brief treatment or a fixed number of sessions just because the couple is essentially healthy and stable; if there is dissatisfaction with the status quo and motivation for change and growth, couples should not be penalized by impatient workers or unbending agency requirements because treatment is taking longer than someone thinks it should.

2. Couples Stressed by Life Cycle Transitions Difficulties may be associated with:

• The adjustment to a newly committed relationship

• The shifts—in the couple relationship and in job, financial, and other lifestyle arrangements—mandated by parenthood

• The changes that are required, often by the mother, when the last child is ready to go to school

• The tribulations induced by children's moving into adolescence

• The strains placed on the couple by the deterioration and death of aging parents

• The change to being alone for the first time in many years after the "children" become young adults and leave home

• The planning for retirement

• The adjustments required by stresses imposed by the later years, including physical deterioration and concerns about illness and death

All of these natural events in the couple's life require accommodations.[21]

Some of the major factors that influence the successful (or unsuccessful) adaptation of the couple to new life phases and circumstances are:

• The nature of social system supports, such as socioeconomic status, employment and housing conditions, effects of social attitudes about sex roles, parenting, etc.
• Extended family relationships: the extent to which members of the couple are differentiated from, or severely enmeshed with, their families of origin. Are in-law relationships strained? (See category 7 for further discussion of extended family issues). Along similar lines, are there culturally supported family attitudes that facilitate, retard, or distort life cycle transitions?
• Overall level of marital or couple functioning, such as stability of the relationship; competence at communication, negotiation, resolution of conflict; flexibility; level of differentiation; capacity for caring and empathy; degree of trust and intimacy.
• Personality qualities, such as stability and maturity, autonomy, and capacities for initiative, compromise, and optimism.

3. Couples in Which There Is One Symptomatic Partner

When the symptom is of the "acting-in" variety (energy is turned against the self), such as in depression, extreme "nervousness" or anxiety attacks, phobias, compulsivity, and even sometimes addictions, it is often the symptomatic partner who seeks individual help. In these cases, the client's partner may willingly become involved. Some others do not want or see the need to participate in treatment; still others volunteer as collaterals and try to help the spouse or the therapist.

When the symptom is one of "acting out," or is in some way more conspicuously interactional in nature and consequence (sexual or physical abuse, violent rages), it is often, but not always, the asymptomatic spouse or some outside agency worker who arranges for help.

When one spouse has symptoms, as we have said, it is usually most effective to have both partners join the treatment, at least in the beginning. Individual sessions can always be planned at a later point. In the case of Al and Barbara, it became clear that Barbara's seemingly individual symptoms were significantly influenced by personality features of both partners and unrevealed strains in the relationship. Without a doubt, joint meetings became the most efficient treatment modality.

In some situations, when spouses of individuals with acting-out symptoms apply for help, it may be difficult, although often not impossible, to encourage couple sessions. Understandably the symptomatic partners may feel defensive or assume they will be blamed by the worker as well as by their mate. Although every effort should be made to include both partners, in severe situations of spouse abuse or other antisocial behaviors, the spouse who has been abused may be too frightened to meet in joint sessions. Also, the asymptomatic spouse may want help to become more self-directed and less reactive. Practical as well as psychological aid may be required for the spouse to get out of the "victim" position, with or without the relationship.

Couples with specific, sometimes severe, types of sexual dysfunction (e.g., premature ejaculation, inability to ejaculate, or so-called frigidity) belong to this group. Frequently the partner having the difficulty comes for help. Occasionally there are medical factors involved or truly functional disorders; of course, these should always be explored. Like phobias, symptoms often reflect overt or covert relationship issues and are diminished when the problems are exposed and addressed.

4. Chronically Conflictual Relationships In these there is usually more bickering and disagreement than fulfillment. Quarrels are not necessarily limited to one issue. More often than not, they involve a wide range of topics, such as money, sex, child rearing, sharing of responsibilities, and ways to deal with jobs, in-laws, and so on. Clinicians have come to realize that frequently the resolution of a presenting issue does not settle the marital distress (and, when it does, the relationship probably belongs to category 1). More often than we would wish, settling one matter uncovers another. In couple treatment, it becomes apparent that the dysfunctional interactional *process* is entrenched, and the function of particular, often interchangeable, *content* complaints is to maintain the status quo. Successful treatment requires attention to issues that are often concealed and reach beyond specific areas of discontent. Therefore, these often joyless—even if committed—relationships may be better understood and treated when viewed in the light of the categories that follow.

5. Relationships in Which Avoidance Is a Way of Life When a spouse is "work-addicted," is a substance abuser, has an affair, or is deeply absorbed in the children, friends, family-of-origin, or outside activities, often there is little opportunity to nurture the relationship or to deal with dissatisfactions. As with conflictual relationships just discussed, unless simply bringing the problems out in the open induces positive changes and reverses the pattern of avoidance, the underlying problematic issues may be illuminated by referring to categories that follow. (Of course some couples *do* live comfortably when each spouse is deeply involved in individual activity and time together is limited. As we said in Chapter 15, families can fall within a wide range between the extremes of disengagement and enmeshment without feeling distressed or being viewed as dysfunctional.)

6. Couples Strained by One or More Extraordinary External Pressures War, unemployment, natural disasters, insufficient money, discrimination, unavailability of decent housing or safe living conditions, necessity of living with in-laws, chronic illness of one partner or other close family member, premature deaths: these are only a few of the many possible outside impingements that can seriously affect the quality of a love relationship.

Along somewhat different lines, social and/or extended family negative attitudes about intergroup marriage or homosexuality may also seriously strain a couple's relationship. (When such negative reactions reflect family emotional processes instead of value differences, then category 7 may be more relevant. We shall also discuss these problems in more detail in a later section of this chapter: "'Nontraditional' Couple Situations.")

Sometimes practical assistance and concrete services can alleviate difficulties flowing from external pressures; help with mourning may be required; or intergenerational sessions can address some of the issues involving the extended family. In some situations, the caseworker may take on the role of advocate in some of the various ways described in Chapter 8. In all cases, the chances for relief are best when spouses react to external pressures by working with rather than against one another.

7. Couples in Which There Are Dysfunctionally Enmeshed or Otherwise Disturbed Family-of-Origin Relationships Many family therapists agree that when spouses have not successfully separated from their original families, they are usually not well differentiated in their nuclear families.[22] In these cases, loyalties,[23] or attachments for whatever reasons, to extended family members may be more powerful and compelling than bonds between the spouses. We often find that generational boundaries are blurred. As Framo comments, these spouses have "never really left home."[24] Complaints and jealousies about in-laws are common in these relationships.

Lack of differentiation from families of origin is a frequent treatment issue: sometimes the ties binding the generations are complex, but sometimes they are rather easily resolved when the couple relationship is strengthened. In the Russo family (see Chapter 16), Mrs. Russo's relationship with her mother was one of the factors retarding the marital relationship; by the same token, Mr. Russo's sadness about his early family life diverted his energy from feelings toward his wife. When the couple worked on some of the difficulties between them, intergenerational difficulties diminished. Understandably, Mrs. Russo's mother's relationships with all members of the family subsequently improved. When Al and Barbara, described earlier in this chapter, made improvements in their marriage, Barbara defined her relationships with members of her family of origin much more clearly. As discussed in the family therapy chapters, enmeshment is often accompanied by a high level of anxiety; when family members are poorly differentiated, they may have fears of engulfment or of abandonment. Under these circumstances, "triangulation" is common; it will be remembered that in the Russo family, there were several examples of dyads that involved a third person in order to reduce stress and maintain the balance of the relationship.

Of course, "emotional cutoffs" (i.e., refusal to associate with some member or members of the families of origin) are as symptomatic of lack of differentiation as are overinvolvements; indeed, they are opposite sides of the same coin because they both arise from emotional intensity (rather than indifference) toward extended family members. Again, fears of rejection or fusion usually prompt the individual's efforts to avoid the interactions at all cost. Extreme reactivity reveals lack of individuation. In one case, a woman in her sixties had not spoken with her only sister, with whom she had been extremely close in childhood, for forty years, purportedly

because of a relatively minor misunderstanding at her own wedding. When she reflected on this in therapy, she began to realize that it had been "easier" for her to make a sharp break in anger than to bear the inevitable separation brought about by her marriage. Ironically, some of the marital problems she had had over the years arose in large part from unresolved feelings about her sister.

Unfinished business with families of origin can seriously impact a marital relationship in many ways. For example, a husband who, for whatever reasons, has not separated comfortably may stop off at his mother's house for dinner before coming home to his increasingly angry wife. If a wife teams up with her mother (perhaps out of a need to please or appease her) to denigrate her husband, he will undoubtedly feel like an outsider and become more and more hurt, angry, or depressed. This was the situation in the Russo family. When husbands or wives have cut off or have been cut off by their parents, the unresolved grief, anger, and longing can overload the marital relationship. Often one spouse makes unrealistic demands on the other in hopes of compensating for "lost" parents. The quality of the marital relationship of a spouse's parents—even if it is negative—can powerfully influence expectations of marriage and ways of interacting, especially if there has not been much differentiation from the parents.[25]

It is necessary to add, as indicated in category 2 above, that important events in the lives of extended family members inevitably and naturally affect the marital relationship to an often considerable degree. A father's death, a mother's illness, a sister's divorce, a brother's alcoholism: all can negatively burden the marital system. On the other hand, it is well known that couples sometimes are able to grow closer, on their own or in treatment, in the face of distress in extended families.

When there are identifiable complications arising from relationships with families of origin, we may recommend family-of-origin meetings.[26] And, as we shall soon see, sometimes these are suggested even when the intergenerational influences are not so immediately apparent. These sessions may be held with an individual and his or her original family, without the spouse. The presence of the "outsider" (the spouse) may constrain or distract the work, providing an opportunity to resist differentiation of relationships between the generations, a difficult enough task without the addition of inhibiting forces.

8. Couples in Which Projections and Irrational Role Assignments Are Negatively Affecting the Relationship Dysfunctional roles, attitudes, emotional styles, and behaviors are expected and imposed on one another. (At this point the reader may want to review pages 327 to 329, where family projection processes are discussed.) In an almost uncanny way, each spouse induces in the other behaviors and attitudes that correspond to introjects from the past, usually derived from perceptions of parent figures, but sometimes of siblings or others. Repressed object relationships are recreated in the relationship with the marital partner. Experiences of roles, rules, and "programming" from the family of origin may be introduced into the marriage.[27] Clinical experience supports the conclusion that when individuals are insufficiently differentiated, they often want to avoid aloneness at all cost; they will, therefore, reproduce these emotionally familiar, sometimes hurtful, situations that connected them to their original families. For example, a woman who as a child felt criticized and undervalued by members of her original family may subtly invite negative judgments, contempt, or condescension from her husband. The man who felt overly depended on or suffocated by his overprotective mother may encourage his wife to pursue him, as his mother did, but if she does so, he may push her away.

People often marry products of their fantasies, with little regard for the spouse's actual ability to meet demands made on him or her to fulfill an idealized image. In such instances, disillusionment is bound to result. People can marry their worst—rather than their ideal—fantasy or induce behaviors that guarantee that their negative expectations will become self-fulfilling. In clinical practice and in life we have all encountered individuals who feel deprived or offended by circumstances others would consider trivial. In treatment it may be revealed that these people never had experience at defining what they want or negotiating for it, and thus they feel disappointed. Often these individuals seem almost driven to project their own negative expectations onto their marital relationship.

In some cases, mates are chosen who have qualities that are positive and nurturing. Under the best of circumstances marriages can provide each partner with a "corrective" experience, in various ways "making up" for and adding to original parenting experiences, even in cases in which the individuals have been emotionally deprived or abused. In fact, as many marital and family therapists know, good marriages sometimes provide the basis for the best therapeutic experiences. However, when the mates are unconsciously locked into a rigid, closed system—and the couple colludes to repeat the negative introjects or unrealistic expectations—problems in the relationship are part of an *intergenerational transmission process* and are perpetuated by the projection of the internalized past onto the present.[28]

In clinical practice we frequently see how spouses assume for themselves and imbue their mates with many kinds of roles in order to feel safe. For example, in order to carry on the role of "caretaker" or "hero," the spouse must try (often unconsciously) to induce dependency or neediness in the other and view him or her as "weak." If a woman learned to gain her parents' attention by acting "confused" or "hysterical" (albeit the attention was ridiculing and controlling), in her marriage she may repeat the same behavior and elicit the same results. For every "martyr" in a marriage there must be a partner who is seen as abusive, irresponsible, uncooperative, or distant.

Similarly, it is not uncommon for couples to promote connections that are held together by the familiar "glue" derived from family-of-origin experience. Some families—and subsequently couples—maintain a sense of connection through worry (e.g., telephoning each other very frequently to make sure "everything is all right"). Insults and teasing are often used by family members to touch base with one another, and these behaviors may then be brought into marriages. Depression or pessimism sometimes becomes the predominant feature of a family's climate and, when transported to the couple's life, results in endless complaining, sullenness, perennial "victimization," or some other demoralizing behavior. Certainly angry interactions and even abuse, as painful as these are for the members, can become the "adhesive" for families and couples. These methods for maintaining relatedness are often passed down over many generations.

When losses in the original family have not been mourned and resolved,[29] not only is it difficult to bring full commitment and emotional energy to current relationships but introjects, either idealized or loathed, may be brought into the marriage. A woman whose father deserted or died when she was young may find ways in her marriage to reexperience the familiar feelings of longing so familiar to her as a child; she may either encourage her husband to be distant or be so immersed in the old feelings that she cannot absorb his affections. The man whose mother cast him in the role of "stand-in" for his father (living and unavailable or dead) may be particularly anxious about marital intimacy for fear of being smothered or overly relied upon once again.

It is fortunate when adult children have the opportunity to deal with introjects from the past by addressing their relationships with their parents in the present. Frequently, as we said, marital partners come to recognize that, in fact, the difficulties between them are not as powerful as family-of-origin issues, however buried these latter may be. Often with the explanation and encouragement coming at first from the couple's therapist, enmeshment, emotional cutoffs, unresolved losses, guilt, and excessive sense of responsibility can be most effectively addressed directly with parents. When it is possible to have sessions with extended family members, the problems and the projections that have been transferred to the marriage can be dealt with in the relationships where they originated. In our experience this can bring immediate benefit to the marriage.[30] When such intergenerational work is not possible, couple treatment can still provide opportunities to understand families of origin in new ways, as will be demonstrated in the case of Tom and Kathy Brent discussed in Chapter 18.

9. Second Marriages Which Introduce Special Difficulties for One or Both Partners If a previous spouse has died, there may be unresolved mourning, preventing a full commitment to the present relationship. Jealousies can be felt when the first relationship is unfinished for whatever reason; as mentioned in the family chapters, obviously this problem is further complicated when children of previous alliances necessitate continued involvement (personal and/or financial) with the former partner. Situations involving stepchildren can place strains on new relationships. Second marriages, by definition, follow failed or lost relationships; they can, therefore, be constant reminders of the precariousness of the marital union. In troubled second marriages, whatever the other problems, help is often needed to separate from the past, strengthen trust between partners, and solidify the new family relationships.[31]

10. A Variety of Couples Who Share What Some Clinicians Refer to as "Calcified" Marital Styles Generally, these do not bode well for successful marital treatment. In some instances, separation or divorce therapy may evolve as the agreed-upon goal. In other cases, perhaps in the majority, even though deep unhappiness is felt by both partners and solutions seem to be out of reach there is inability, reluctance, or refusal to consider separation. Often couples in this mixed group have attempted various kinds of treatment, all seemingly to no avail. Some have been referred as involuntary clients because of the repercussions their disastrous interactions have on other family members, particularly children. Relationships in this category may be distant and more or less "dead" on the one hand, or chronically vituperative and vicious on the other, with the couple caught in repetitive, deeply destructive interactional cycles. Others can be loveless or "brother-sister" arrangements which disappoint one or both of the spouses. Although some of these marriages are long-standing, others may be relatively new but equally unmovable. When improvement seems impossible and separation is not seen as an option, sometimes the individuals can be helped to find satisfactions in other aspects of their lives—in their jobs, activities, friendships, etc.—with the added result that the disagreeable aspects of the marital relationship may be somewhat diminished.

11. Couples in Which One Spouse Wants to Leave the Relationship and the Other Wants to Save It Marital therapy is the effort of last resort. Sometimes joint meetings last a very short time, just long enough for the one who wants separation to get courage, "permission," or justification to go ahead with it. "Often," as Framo says, "the partner who is finished with the marriage would like to exit from the therapy and leave the partner with the therapist."[32] When one spouse has firmly closed the door on the marriage, frequently his or her affections have shifted to a new lover. Divorce therapy may follow the initial phase of treatment. Fairly often the rejected spouse continues in individual treatment to deal with the repercussions. Occasionally, the marriage gets a second wind and the relationship can be modified and enhanced.

Special caution may be required of the worker in treating couples in this category. When pained by the disappointment of the spurned spouse or concerned about effects of a breakup on children, the worker may try too hard to help resurrect a marriage even when the spouse who wants to terminate it continues to show no motivation for working on it.

12. Marriages That Have Come to an End by Mutual Agreement If they seek casework help, it is usually for the purpose of addressing the problems involved in separating. Divorce therapy or mediation has gained prominence in recent years;[33] in some therapeutic circles it is viewed as a specialty requiring additional training and, perhaps, some sort of certification. Issues such as money, property, custody, and arrangements for the children are part and parcel of divorce. Some couples, concerned about escalating battles when lawyers become involved, prefer to try to negotiate these matters in a therapist's office. Needless to say, such negotiations can be difficult since the very problems of communication, negative and entrenched behaviors, projections, and individual personality problems that defeated the marriage in the first place may equally thwart the best-intentioned efforts to end it without rancor.

When it comes to difficulties in intimate relationships, too often history repeats itself for individuals who blame the marriage or the other spouse for their unhappiness, and the same distortions, projection processes, and negative behaviors recur in new contexts. Therefore, in the writers' experience, the most hopeful outcome for these couples occurs when both spouses are willing to examine the problems that destroyed the relationship; they are then better able to mourn their losses, let go of each other and of the dreams that brought them together, and go on to the next phase of their lives. If each partner is able to identify his or her particular contributions to the problems, future relationships and choices of mates may result in happier experiences.

"Nontraditional" Couples

Committed love relationships, regardless of specific lifestyle, have more similarities than differences. Yet some do have special characteristics. The ones we shall mention here are premarital couples, unmarried pairs living together, cross-cultural relationships, and gay couples. Obviously these categories may overlap: one may have as clients two lesbian lovers, from divergent cultural backgrounds, in the process of determining whether or not they want to live together.

Premarital Relationships Customarily, two people planning to marry—equally committed to one another and experiencing no major difficulties in functioning or in the relationship—have sought "premarital counseling" (if they sought it at all) from pastoral advisers, family doctors, self-help groups, and the like. For the most part, they have not consulted marital therapists.[34] In the throes of anticipating marriage—with passion and optimism at a peak, when no distress or symptoms are apparent—preventive measures are not usually a high priority. Couples who do go to therapists for premarital counseling are often in their thirties, with one or both members having been married before.[35] With some notable exceptions, caseworkers and others who do couple work have not developed interventive approaches to relationships *before* trouble comes. Certainly this is an area of prevention that requires more at-

tention than it receives from clinical social workers.[36]

Premarital treatment usually covers particular areas. Of course, as is true of married couples, each pair is unique; each has special concerns and priorities. It is also true that repetitive patterns are less entrenched than they are with couples who have been together a long time. Yet, whatever the presenting issues are, person-situation, pattern-dynamic, and even developmental reflection is often required; in premarital treatment, as well as marital therapy, enhancing awareness of self and other may be a major goal of the work.

Several overlapping areas commonly emphasized in premarital therapy include:

1. *Communication and interactional styles and skill.* Learning early on to make self-defined, clear "I" statements instead of "you" or "we" statements, especially during important discussions about the relationship or in efforts to resolve conflicts, may prevent many later misunderstandings and disappointments. More open emotional expressiveness may be required to facilitate some significant communications. When each partner learns how his or her verbal or nonverbal behavior impacts the relationship positively or negatively compatible styles of interacting can be established early, before dysfunctional patterns emerge.

2. *Respect for differences.* Too often couples, especially those coming from enmeshed families or those who subscribe to the romantic notion that "togetherness" means that thoughts, opinions, and feelings are identical, are afraid to admit and accept dissimilarities.

3. *Mutual disclosure and discussions regarding values, attitudes, and basic emotional requirements, including needs for distance and closeness, dependence and independence.* Frankly shared statements from each can educate and prepare the other about important expectations. Becoming aware of and realistic about one's exaggerated visions of the role the other will play (e.g., "He

will be able to save me from myself'' or ''She will be able to take care of me'') is often an important focus of premarital treatment.

Encouragement from the couple's therapist may be essential here. Many idealistic—often but not always young—people preparing for marriage underestimate the importance of their own individual views and, in their excitement, are all too willing to put them aside. Or else they are reluctant to be straightforward about some facets of themselves for fear that the future spouse will disapprove. Those with low self-esteem may be especially afraid that if they reveal too much about themselves they will no longer be loved. Couples will find that they must learn to compromise on various issues, but negotiations cannot occur until they begin to speak honestly.

4. *The need to develop methods for confronting inevitable changes, crises, or conflicts.* There are no marriages without outside pressure and inner strife; quite naturally, when these occur, loving feelings can be overshadowed by anxiety or frustration. Evolving flexible means for coping with life's transitions and ordeals can help couples approach these events with more confidence and less fear.

5. *Open discussions about sexuality in general and expectations of their own sexual relationship in particular.* Obviously the direction this work takes will depend in part on whether or not the couple has been sexually active. How comfortable or sophisticated they are about sexual matters will also influence the premarital work. There are some couples, even those married for many years, who have never had *any* open talks together about sexual likes and dislikes, worries, difficulties, etc. The knowledge that such sharing is *normal* and *essential* can be preventive.

6. *The transition from family of origin to the nuclear family.* Premarital treatment provides an opportunity to begin to cement the bond of the upcoming marriage while constructively separating from parents. At best, these shifts are

lovingly achieved. When couples, for whatever reasons, do not establish boundaries differentiating them from their extended families and defining what their relationships with the original families will be, marriage may be plagued with conflict and stress. Needless to say, couples from different backgrounds or with particular personal preferences will draw the limits differently; the critical point is that the boundaries should be unambiguously established.

Many of the areas described above require intense attention from troubled couples who come later on in the marriage for treatment. Optimally, many unhappy situations can be prevented through premarital exploration.

Unmarried Couples Living Together This is a broad and varied group. In terms of age it includes young premarital couples at one extreme and, on the other, elderly companions who have reasons for not marrying, e.g., protection of social security or other benefits or fear of disapproving relatives (some adult children find it hard to believe that older people still desire sexual and romantic relationships!) Between 1970 and 1980 the number of unmarried couples living together tripled and it is estimated that this number will continue to increase.[37]

Many dilemmas this divergent group brings to therapy are also presented by married couples. Yet, there are some differences. Examples of unmarried couples seen by caseworkers include, among others:

1. *Live-in relationships that are truly transitory.* These would include college students or people temporarily assigned to work in geographical areas away from home. In spite of the absence of commitment, emotional involvements may lead to problems concerning unplanned pregnancy, dependency, or separation. Concern about AIDS has stimulated considerable caution about casual sexual liaisons.

2. *"Trial marriages" to determine whether the relationship will survive under one roof.* According to some experts, there is no firm evidence that living together before marriage decreases the risk of divorce.[38] Nevertheless, often in these situations when discussions about marriage have reached some sort of stalemate, for one or both partners, or when problems similar to those found in married relationships arise, professional help is sought.

3. *Couples unable to marry because one or both of the members are already legally married.* Divorce may be difficult or impossible because of financial considerations, disappearance of a spouse, or a spouse's confinement in prison or a mental institution. Differential assessment is required in working with these couples. In some cases, the unmarried status is not a problem to either member; unrelated issues prompt them to seek treatment. In other instances, when legitimizing the relationship is a concern, the worker may help the couple to obtain legal help to learn about their rights and options. When it is compatible with the goals of the couple, the caseworker can assist in various ways in the resolution of practical and emotional issues needed to dissolve previous unions.

4. *Couples to whom commitment seems risky.* Again, if neither member is uncomfortable about the legally uncommitted arrangement, this situation will not be the presenting problem. But sometimes couples come for help to overcome fears about marriage. Quite commonly a pair living together will seek therapy specifically because one member is beginning to press for marriage and the other is resisting marriage. If this is the true problem, brief treatment may resolve the matter. The reluctant partner may be helped to overcome apprehensions. It can also happen that the person seeking permanency comes to realize that he or she will have to look for it elsewhere.

In some cases, there is an unexpressed (and usually unconscious) pact: one "agrees" to express the ambivalence and the other claims to

be ready to plunge into marriage. Yet, as it develops, when one changes his or her position, the other will then take the opposite side. In large part, the work in therapy is to help each partner "own" his or her particular ambivalence, to resolve it, and then to be in a position to decide for or against commitment. The importance of working through indecision is underscored by the repeated complaints of many married couples coming for help who feel that their relationships were far more satisfactory when they were living together than after they married. When fears of intimacy (of engulfment, entrapment, rejection, or abandonment) underlie ambivalence, defensiveness may significantly increase almost immediately after the wedding.

5. *Couples comfortable with their status but pressured by parents or others to marry.* Some parents are ashamed or morally offended; others are eager for grandchildren. Some may express simple disapproval; others use punitive financial or emotional strategies to try to force marriage. Obviously, resolution requires differentiation from families of origin and redefinition of the couple's relationships as adults to their parents. The couple may need help making independent decisions in spite of parental objections. The choice not to marry may be more related to leftover rebelliousness or reaction to parental control than to philosophical or emotional attitudes against getting married.

6. *Couples in which there have been previous marriages, particularly those with children.* All too often, either because of the bitterness of the former spouse or attitudes of the children (possessiveness, loyalty to the other parent, or some combination of these) the new live-in partner is scapegoated by the former family. Family meetings with the parent and children may provide an opportunity to resolve the difficulties so that the new love relationship is not destructively triangulated. Some of the difficulties encountered by stepfamilies (see Chapter 16) may apply here. Issues from previous marriages, intertwined with early family influences, can combine to influence current relationship troubles.

7. *Gay couples.* In the eyes of the law, gay couples are unmarried, and they are subject to particular pressures and conditions. They will be discussed later in this section.

Cross-Cultural Relationships   In the literature of social work, sociology, and related fields, much has been written about the stresses experienced by couples whose members have different ethnic, religious, or racial backgrounds. Failure to understand one another or to appreciate each other's values and lifestyle, disapproval of family and friends, and outright social discrimination are among difficulties encountered by some cross-cultural couples.[39] "Generally," writes Monica McGoldrick, "the greater the difference between spouses in cultural background, the more difficulty they will have in adjusting to marriage."[40] There is research to suggest that ethnically mixed couples are more likely than others to get divorced, have personal problems, and experience difficulties with extended families and children.[41]

In clinical practice we are less likely to see those intermarriages that *are* working successfully. In the case of Dick and Susan Jones (Chapter 3), racial differences played an insignificant part in their relatively minor difficulties; in-laws on both sides did not have intense negative reactions to the marriage, and the couple's two children appeared to be unusually well adjusted. In our view there is a tendency to underemphasize the potential for stimulation and new experiences and the opportunities for special kinds of complementarity that derive from differences.[42] Margaret Mead spoke to both sides of the issue: "If you are not going to marry the boy next door—and if you do you may die of boredom—then you are going to have to work much harder."[43]

In an article we highly recommend, McGoldrick and Preto[44] present several factors they believe influence the degree of adjustment required by cross-cultural marriages. They conclude that the more similar the values (e.g., between Puerto Rican and Italian mates in contrast to Irish and Italian) probably the less difficult the adjustment will be. Great differences between spouses in acculturation (such as between fourth- and first-generation immigrants) can lead to misunderstandings. Religious differences in addition to cultural ones may increase the possibilities for disharmony. In therapy, intermarried couples can be helped to become aware of differences deriving from their cultural backgrounds. "Just as understanding family patterns, the role of sibling position, and life cycle stages is important for couples, so is understanding the impact of ethnic differences."[45] We agree with McGoldrick that couples may have a "sudden and remarkable shift in response when they come to see the spouse's behavior fitting into a larger ethnic context rather than as a personal attack."[46]

Difficulties experienced by cross-cultural couples are frequently believed to be strongly influenced by the negative reactions of families of origin, especially parents of the spouses.[47] Disapproval, refusal to "permit" the marriage or to attend the wedding, and emotional cutoffs (some of which last for years) are all reactions that can strain the relationship. Of course, family systems involve *all* family members and a son or daughter in an enmeshed or autocratic family may marry outside his or her culture in order to try to gain emotional distance or independence. The choice of spouse may serve as an expression of anger and defiance. The young person who has been "chosen" by the parents to be triangulated (or dysfunctionally overinvested in by one or both) in order to defuse stressful marital intensity and evade difficulties may be the very one who intermarries as the route for confrontation or escape.

In an important—perhaps to some, controversial—article, Friedman, who has had extensive experience with intermarried couples, persuasively argues that cultural differences are often used as "cultural camouflage."[48] In other words, parents will often claim their objection to a mixed marriage is based on practical, philosophical, or religious concerns, when in actuality the disapproval represents an effort to avoid emotional processes in the family. At times of stress, differences—cultural or other kinds—can become the focal point and hide the true concerns in the family. For example, the young adult who has been important in maintaining the marital balance of his or her parents (usually, according to Friedman, the oldest or only child) is the one from whom the parents find it hardest to separate. Obviously, the greater the difficulties the parents have in letting go of the triangulated child, the more intense the pressure on him or her, and the harder it is for that child to leave home. Often, the more intensely entangled, the "further out" the young person will marry (e.g., interracially as well as interreligiously). As Friedman says: "More powerful circuits need more powerful circuit breakers."[49]

Certainly, the broader social context, in addition to the extended family context, in which the intermarried couple functions can tip the balance of the relationship. The interplay between the marital system and other systems can support or be devastatingly destructive to the fabric of the marriage. Ethnocentrism, racism, and other forms of bigotry in the community, in schools the children attend, or in the workplace can place heavy demands on the couple's emotional resources. When intolerance isolates the couple, realistic distrust of others can result and, too often, the spouses can begin to blame themselves or each other for their unhappiness. Self-esteem can be severely battered. In addition to helping such couples recognize what has happened and validating their sense that *indeed they have been victimized*, caseworkers often can provide encouragement and information about self-help groups and organizations in which mutual support and opportunities for socialization with others facing similar difficulties can be found.

As for every couple coming to the attention of the caseworker, appropriate intervention requires careful assessment. To summarize, in cross-cultural unions, it is important to determine whether differences are contributing to distress or whether their function is to divert attention from other issues. When the couple is troubled, the difficulties may be strongly, mildly, or minimally influenced by the varied backgrounds or by family and social reactions to the marriage. When differences are a problem *within* the relationship, we can often help couples understand and even value these instead of taking them personally. Finally, as caseworkers, sometimes we can encourage couples to take one further step. As McGoldrick and Preto write:

> Under the best of circumstances, the challenge of differences in a relationship may open the possibility for productive personal changes. For instance, a WASP female who has difficulty expressing anger for fear of losing control and who becomes instead depressed or symptomatic may learn to be more direct and comfortable with her anger by marrying an Italian male who tends to be confrontive and spontaneous with his feelings. Or a Jewish husband may teach his WASP wife a new repertoire of emotional expression, freeing her to experience her feelings more fully, while she may teach him that there is a time to stop analyzing feelings and to just get on with things.[50]

Gay and Lesbian Couples   Gays—singly or in pairs, men or women—have been consistently stigmatized in the United States.[51] Even in this era of heightened sexual enlightenment, gays are frequently viewed as morally or psychologically deviant. Gay males, perhaps always the target of special ridicule and ostracism, now must endure the increasingly violent reaction to their sexuality triggered by the advent of AIDS. Recent polls reveal significant numbers of radically hostile responses; some believe that AIDS is a just punishment for sinful behavior; others call for segregating homosexuals, an idea that actually preceded the AIDS panic.[52] Furthermore, gay males and females have been the subject of discrimination and disapproval—subtle and overt—by family, friends, coworkers, and employers as well as by the larger social systems.

Lesbians and gay men have responded to destructive attitudes in various ways. In order to minimize the effects of social disapproval and hatred, many have denied their sexual preferences (to others and/or to themselves), hidden and lied, developed "secret worlds," and had "counterfeit relations" with associates, friends, and family.[53] As is true of any stigmatized group, gay men and women are vulnerable to low self-esteem and self-hate. Prejudice and overt discrimination can take a toll on the hardiest personalities. Those who have stayed "in the closet" often have borne the burden of deep feelings of shame about their differences. There is evidence that *when* "coming out" is motivated by a growing sense of self-acceptance, this act, in turn, can foster pride and an enhanced sense of belonging. Gay support and action groups have provided a sense of community that was far less available even twenty years ago. In spite of recent efforts to scapegoat the AIDS victims, political pressure from the gay community and its allies has contributed to increased enlightenment among heterosexuals. According to Loewenstein: "Longtime lesbian women who had to live in hiding for years seem to harbor more self-hatred than lesbians of the newer generation who have reaped the benefits of new and enlightened sexual attitudes."[54]

Let us add a note of caution here. Sometimes as a result of pressure from peers who have "come out" and sometimes as a way of expressing pent-up rage about social and/or family biases against same-sex love relationships, gay clients feel compelled to enter into ill-considered confrontations—at work, with parents, or with friends—in a manner that will ensure hostile if not rejecting reactions. The approach taken may thus hamper resolution and actually contribute to further pain and isolation. Although revealing one's sexual orientation may yield personal and political rewards in the long run,[55] the questions of how, when, and where (and, of course, whether) may take time and careful reflection.

For years, the mental health community labeled homosexuality as "abnormal" and "pathological"; only relatively recently has this view been somewhat modified, although social workers and others are hardly unanimous in their views on the matter.[56] Saghir and Robins described research in which a battery of psychological tests was administered to lesbian and nonlesbian women to determine differences between them. The only significant negative distinction found was a higher incidence of alcoholism in the lesbian group.[57]

As is true of people from other oppressed groups, resilience and the human capacity for adaptation have saved many from severe psychological damage and despair. Recognition of gay clients' strengths in the face of alienation and abuse can be an important therapeutic function. Validation of the reality of the injustice perpetrated by society's attitudes can have meaning to those gay clients who have been blaming themselves all too long for the prejudices they have experienced. Some clients, affected by prevailing negative opinions, need affirmation that homosexual relationships are a viable lifestyle and can be as fulfilling and productive as "straight" ones; they can benefit from a treatment relationship in which they are not viewed as "sick," "bad," or even in a "second best" kind of arrangement.

There are times, however, when clients and their caseworkers alike are inclined to dwell almost exclusively on the brutality of the "system," thereby neglecting the work that *can* be accomplished. As is true in all therapy, it does not promote progress to ventilate endlessly about issues outside of one's control, but it is also true that when those who are motivated (in this instance, the gay couples) make changes, corresponding changes in other parts of the larger system may occur, especially in relationships with family, friends, and coworkers.

Problems encountered by gay pairs, in spite of society's reluctance to accord them first-class status, are remarkably similar to those for which other couples seek help: difficulties dealing with various life transitions; symptomatic members who are depressed, anxious, sexually dysfunctional, etc.; conflictual or disengaged relationships; troubled family-of-origin relationships; projections and irrational role assignments; unresolved former relationships, including problems involving children from former marriages; and so on. The typology of relationship problems discussed earlier in this chapter can apply to same-sex as well as to heterosexual relationships. There can be confusion about role expectations in heterosexual relationships and these issues can cause difficulty for gay couples also.

Some of the comments we made about the "camouflage" or "red herring" function of transcultural marriages vis-à-vis families of origin can apply as well to gay couples and their families. Emotional problems can be masked by a fixed focus on the subject of sexual orientation just as negative reactions to intermarriage can cloak family difficulties. There are also other issues that pertain specifically to gay couples and their families. For example, parents can deny, sometimes even when they are clearly told, that their "child" is in gay relationship; this is not as likely when the relationship is a cross-cultural one.[58] Also, while parents of children who choose to intermarry may assume some guilt, parents of gay offspring seem to harass themselves more cruelly with self-blame (e.g.: "Where did we go wrong?"), inappropriately taking responsibility for their children's behavior and measuring their own competency as parents or as people in relation to it. No wonder some parents, consciously or unconsciously, are inclined to refuse to believe even obvious facts about their child's sexual orientation.

In enmeshed family systems, denial of gay relationships also can function to obstruct separation. Fears of differentiation can postpone—sometimes indefinitely—the establishment of a distinct and committed gay couple relationship. If the original family sees their child's same-sex partner as only a "friend" or "roommate," and the couple does not draw clear boundaries around their relationship, both generations can perpetuate the notion that the younger person never really left home after all. In that sense, a gay "child" can protect the balance of such families in ways that the heterosexual cannot.

In any event, even when there are only minimal negative or avoidance reactions, the gay relationship is rarely viewed by families as having the same importance as the heterosexual marriage. Denial and avoidance are not the only reasons. The fact is that gay relationships, even those that are stable, monogamous, and enduring, when contrasted with "straight" relationships, do not have socially established role definitions, traditions, and powers to guide and protect them. As Loewenstein writes in her article about lesbian women:

> Our society gives no kinship recognition to homosexual bonds. As a result, there are additional stresses during times of sickness and hospitalization or death of one partner, with no legal rights regarding inheritance or child guardianship. One wonders how many heterosexual unions would survive without the benefit of social sanctions and financial or parenthood considerations. Women are faced with the difficult task of building new relationships that are not necessarily bound by available traditional heterosexual models.[59]

Indeed, gay couples have to work harder than others to delimit the rules, roles, boundaries, and loyalties which give meaning and substance to their union; this is particularly true of defining how it will function in the context of family and larger social systems. Ambiguity can result when outside expectations run counter to the spirit of their relationship: pressure to take a "date" of the opposite sex to a function, for example, or invitations to go "home" as a single person for holidays, which could preclude the couple from spending special times together.

When working with gay couples it is essential to know that, contrary to the notions some people have, most partners in gay relationships do not take on roles that simulate stereotypical "male" and "female" roles. A number of studies reveal that there are widely diverse behavioral and role patterns among both gay men and lesbians. Saghir and Robins report that their findings support other studies: "Role behavior among homosexual women appears to be most often related to group and individual preference rather than to any basic psychologic imperatives of masculinity or femininity."[60] Furthermore, even though there are fewer established guidelines for defining roles within the gay relationship, many couples can grow to view the opportunity for flexibility and choice about distribution of functions positively.

Women in Couples

Although times are changing, traditionally women have been expected to be selfless, nurturing, and focused on the needs of others rather than on their own. Even unmarried women of all classes have been guided by social role definitions into occupations of "service," as teachers, nurses, nurses' aides, domestic and child care workers, secretaries, and the like. Only recently have substantial numbers of women, especially from the middle class, chosen "masculine" careers in which money, status, and power constitute primary rewards. Others have sought fulfillment by putting creative or artistic careers ahead of traditional "women's work." Many have done so despite discouraging opposition, discrimination, and even ridicule. By describing "instrumental" (rational and task-oriented) roles of men in the work world and "expressive" (emotional and

nurturant) roles of women in the family, in 1955 Parsons and Bales in effect endorsed these as "normal" and necessary to carrying out economic functions and family relationships.[61] Surprisingly, these fixed role definitions are still believed by large numbers of people to be fundamental to the well-being of all, even if the woman also has to supplement family income by going to work. Although there have always been role variations in some marriages, these have tended to be, and sometimes still are, viewed as deviant.[62]

Married women's denial of self, then, has been strongly reinforced by the larger social system: self-esteem and competence were to be achieved in the home, as comforter of hardworking husband, nurturer of children, mediator, and manager of household operations. Autonomous strivings that did not give top priority to caretaking functions were strongly discouraged. Although women are often the "hub" of the family, in charge of many of the interactions there (and, as we frequently see in clinical practice, sometimes possessively so), as often as not this is a thankless job. Family problems seem to be more consistently blamed (sometimes even by family therapists) on "overcontrolling" or "intrusive" wives and mothers than on "distant" or "ineffectual" husbands and fathers. Men, too, have been expected to deny personal ambitions and fulfillments when these diverge from the norm; in particular, those who do not vigorously and successfully carry out the breadwinner role generally are not accorded full status as "men." It is important for the caseworker to recognize that men's as well as women's positions have been powerfully influenced by social values and expectations and to identify the ways in which this is so.

In couple treatment, then, although we may focus primarily on the processes *within* the confines of the marital system, the dynamics and influences of greater systems—even if these are not immediately open to change—must be acknowledged. As Goldner points out in her excellent article: "Erecting a conceptual boundary around the family was clearly essential for the development of family systems theory, but it also deflected theoretical attention away from an encounter with the ways in which participation in family life is not merely an idiosyncratic accommodation to the 'needs of the family system' but is regulated by social forces operating above and beyond the family's affective field."[63] Systems far more powerful than the family impact the patterns, including the gender patterns, of couple processes.

It is true that gender roles are now less rigidly defined than they were (this varies in different cultural and economic groups and geographical areas). The trend toward egalitarian marriages that began in the middle classes is also spreading to the working class.[64] Nevertheless, the inequities continue. Women's average earnings are less than two-thirds those of men, and, in spite of equal opportunity laws, women are still paid less than men for doing the same work.[65] Only about one in four women work full time in the home, yet one study found that women who have jobs do more than five times as much housework as their husbands.[66] Although the number of working wives and mothers continues to increase, day care provisions are less available than they were a few years ago. Society's message is that even though women's earnings are often required to maintain a minimal standard of living for the family, it is still the woman's job to see to it that the children receive adequate supervision as well as other basic requirements.

It is important to note here that substantial research suggests that for various reasons there is often reluctance (sometimes unexpressed) among wives as well as husbands to relinquish traditional roles. This is true even among those who subscribe to the idea of reciprocal sharing and support in job and family responsibilities.[67] Although less often than in previous years, in part because of the differential in earning power, women are still expected (and expect) to give up their jobs and activities and uproot themselves to adjust to their husband's educational or occupational moves from one place to another. The reverse can occur but less commonly.

Some of the most serious inequities become apparent when there is a question of separation and divorce. Men are less stigmatized socially for leaving their spouses and children behind. Women, expected to "keep the home fires burning," are often subtly or not so subtly blamed for marital breakup, especially when it is their decision to end the marriage. And, without a doubt, women who leave their children in the care of their husbands or others are viewed by most as having failed in meeting their responsibilities. (After divorce, only about one woman in ten does not have full custody of the children.) Clinicians, hardly immune from traditional judgments, must be alert to the possibility of countertherapeutic reactions to such women.

Without a doubt, the aftermath of divorce affects men and women very differently. Goldner reports on the findings of one study: one year after divorce, "women's 'economic well-being' (income minus expenses) dropped 73 per cent, whereas their ex-husbands' showed a 42 per cent improvement." Furthermore, child support payments "are received by only 34 per cent of female-headed families, and only 68 per cent of those receive the full amounts intended, which are modest in any case."[68] And, as Pittman points out:

> Gender relationships cannot be truly equal so long as the economy makes divorce more disadvantageous economically for women than for men, and fashion determines that middle-aged men are considered more desirable marriage partners than middle-aged women. Women may not be able to achieve equality within marriage, but they are even less able to do so outside marriage. Our cur-

rent gender arrangements mean that women must value their marriages more than men do—an inherent inequality.[69]

The important point to be made here is that when we are treating couples, differentials in the power of men and women, as these have been influenced by superordinate social forces, must be recognized by the worker and openly discussed with the couple. One cannot assume, for example, that important decisions—whether the woman with children will take a job, whether the family will relocate to accommodate the husband's career, or whether the couple will separate—have equal implications for each spouse. Even though the couple has little control over society's expectations and norms, frank discussions about gender disparities permit more informed reflections and choices by both partners.

EXTRAMARITAL RELATIONSHIPS

Chapters on marital treatment would not be complete without some mention of the common yet culturally frowned upon, usually complicated, often heartbreaking subject of the extramarital relationship. Although statistics on the frequency of sexual unfaithfulness in marriage differ, it seems safe to say that infidelity of some kind occurs in more than 50 percent (some say 70 percent) of marriages, with 30 to 60 percent of men and 25 to 40 percent of women unfaithful at some point during their married life. Traditionally men have been the "philanderers," but in recent years apparently more and more women are becoming involved in outside liaisons.[70]

Affairs can take various forms, including the single or occasional occurrence, recurrent extramarital activity, relationships in which the attraction is primarily or entirely sexual, deep friendships of long standing, and those in which there is a great deal of ongoing passion, often including strong feelings of being "in love." Some extramarital relationships are abruptly "confessed" to or discovered by the other

spouse; others are, on some level or another, known by the spouse but never discussed. Sometimes spouses ignore obvious "telltale" evidence of their mates' affairs, consciously or unconsciously not wanting to know. And then there are situations in which the secret is very well kept and therefore never even suspected.

Exposure of an affair may bring a couple to treatment. In some cases, spouses may use couple sessions to admit unfaithfulness: sometimes to rid themselves of guilt, sometimes to rid themselves of the marriage. Extramarital relationships are frequently disclosed in individual therapy or in couple treatment in which individual sessions with the worker have been arranged or sought.

There is no single explanation for sexual unfaithfulness. Usually it is helpful to view it as a *symptom*, an indirect expression, of some intrapsychic or interactional process. In our view, it would be a mistake to assume that the affair arises solely from individual conflicts on the one hand or from failure of the marriage (or spouse) on the other. In interviewing a couple or an individual, disclosure of the past or current affair(s) requires careful assessment. In some situations, extramarital relations may, at least in part, express early developmental deficits and distortions or oedipal or other unresolved issues. Some people have extramarital relationships to boost self-esteem by seeking constant reassurance of their sexual attractiveness. Affairs can arise in response to life cycle transitions, such as those popularly referred to as "midlife crises." There are also people who always want to feel the way they did when they were first married; usually the "high" of those days is not sustained in marriage and thus affairs can be the way to maintain the illusion of being perpetually "in love."

The marital relationship itself may be an important factor in the affair:

1. In some cases, the couple's need for distance—for protection against feeling engulfed

or overly dependent—may be accommodated by one or both spouses having an affair.

2. Infidelity can be a means for ventilating anger, disappointment, or despair about one's marriage.

3. The extramarital relationship may be a solution to serious deficits in the marriage or make an intolerable situation—a marriage that is dead, distant, or deeply irritating—tolerable. In clinical practice it is not uncommon to hear (sometimes as rationalization and sometimes not) that the affair allows spouses to be more considerate, patient, and interested in their mates and families when they enjoy outside sexual and emotional replenishments not available within the marriage.

4. Sometimes when a spouse cannot find the courage to terminate his or her marriage forthrightly, the discovery of infidelity may become the precipitant to its dissolution.

5. In some instances, the affair and its revelation can have a constructive function by provoking a marital crisis which ultimately may facilitate communication and resolution of longstanding marital conflicts.

The treatment approach to a couple for whom extramarital relations have played a part will depend on the assessment of the many factors mentioned above. It will be necessary to try to understand the individual and marital dynamics that influenced the situation. Some clinicians insist that there cannot be couple treatment if either spouse is actively involved in an outside relationship. In many cases, however, the couple may be coming to determine whether or not the marriage is viable. Certainly, in most situations, whether the marriage continues or not, the one whose spouse has been extramaritally involved must deal with a broad range of feelings: anger, hurt, betrayal, rejection, fear of loss, and so on. The one who has had the affair may be ridden with guilt, self-doubt, or other feelings. Sometimes both spouses use treatment to mourn the end of an unhappy marriage. In most cases, even if the person involved in the affair is having individual treatment, it is the authors' preference to encourage that person to bring in his or her spouse to confront the marital issues; often the impasse in the marriage (and in the treatment of the individual) can thereby be resolved one way or the other. By the same token, when the one whose mate has been having an affair comes for help, participation of both spouses can be the most effective approach either to building a better relationship or to coming to decisions about the marriage that are as comfortable as possible for all concerned. Above all, of course, it is important to determine what both spouses want to do about their relationship, why they are coming for treatment, and whether what they are hoping for is realistic in terms of the state of the marriage and the attitudes of their mates.[71]

In Chapter 18 we will discuss specific treatment issues and techniques in couple work.

NOTES

1. Family Service America, *The State of Families I* (Milwaukee, Wisc.: Family Service America, 1984), p. 8.

2. In addition to references cited elsewhere, especially in Chapters 15 and 16, see Max Siporin, "Marriage and Family Therapy in Social Work," *Social Casework*, 61 (January 1980), 11–21.

3. See, for example, Gordon Hamilton, *Theory and Practice of Social Casework* (New York: Columbia University Press, 1951), where no specific discussion of joint interviews can be found except in connection with home visits. See also Helen Leland Witmer, *Social Work* (New York: Rinehart, 1942), who wrote (p. 94): "with respect to the institution of the family the function of social work is to facilitate the family's normal activities through counseling with individuals about the difficulties they encounter in family life."

4. Florence Hollis, *Women in Marital Conflict* (New York: Family Service Association of America, 1949), p. 183.

The reader may be interested in an article by Charles W. Hefner and James O. Prochaska, "Concurrent vs. Conjoint Marital Therapy," *Social Work,* 29 (May–June 1984), 287–291, who report results of a small study in which there were no significant differences in outcome between concurrent and conjoint treatments, although improvement occurred in both groups. See also Richard A. Wells and Vincent J. Giannetti, "Individual Marital Therapy: A Critical Reappraisal," and Alan S. Gurman and David P. Kniskern, "Commentary," *Family Process,* 25 (March 1986), 42–65.

5. James L. Framo, "Marriage and Marital Therapy: Issues and Initial Interview Techniques," in *Explorations in Marital and Family Therapy* (New York: Springer, 1982), pp. 123–140.

6. See Elizabeth Carter and Monica McGoldrick Orfanidis, "Family Therapy with One Person and the Family Therapist's Own Family," in Philip J. Guerin, *Family Therapy* (New York: Gardner Press, 1976), 193–219; and Murray Bowen, *Family Therapy in Clinical Practice* (New York: Aronson, 1978).

7. Florence Hollis, *Women in Marital Conflict,* p. 182.

8. For discussion of various, often overlapping, models of marital therapy, see Neil S. Jacobson and Alan S. Gurman, eds., *Clinical Handbook of Marital Therapy* (New York: Guilford Press, 1986).

9. For readings on spouse abuse see Jerry Finn, "The Stresses and Coping Behavior of Battered Women," *Social Casework,* 66 (June 1985), 341–349; Marybeth Hendricks-Matthews, "The Battered Woman: Is She Ready for Help?" *Social Casework,* 63 (March 1982), 131–137, in which the concept of "learned helplessness" is discussed; Peter H. Neidig et al., "Domestic Conflict Containment: A Spouse Abuse Treatment Program," *Social Casework,* 66 (April 1985), 195–204; John W. Taylor, "Structured Conjoint Therapy for Spouse Abuse Cases," *Social Casework,* 65 (January 1984), 11–18; and Jack Weitzman and Karen Dreen, "Wife Beating: A View of the Marital Dyad," *Social Casework,* 63 (May 1982), 259–265.

10. See, especially, Virginia Satir, *Conjoint Family Therapy,* rev. ed. (Palo Alto, Calif.: Science and Behavior Books, 1967), pp. 8–10; and, for case illustrations, Celia F. Rice, "Marital Treatment with Narcissistic Character Disorders," in Judith Mishne, ed.,

Psychotherapy and Training in Clinical Social Work (New York: Gardner Press, 1980), 261–273.

11. See a useful article by Marquis Earl Wallace, "A Focal Conflict Model of Marital Disorders," *Social Casework,* 60 (July 1979), 423–429, in which the author proposes an approach to the synthesis of psychoanalytic and family systems concepts.

12. Christopher Dare, "Psychoanalytic Marital Therapy," in Jacobson and Gurman, eds., *Handbook of Marital Therapy,* p. 15.

13. Florence Wexler Vigilante, "Use of Work in the Assessment and Intervention Process," *Social Casework,* 63 (May 1982), 296–300.

14. Sophie Freud Loewenstein, "Inner and Outer Space in Social Casework," *Social Casework,* 60 (January 1979), 19–29.

15. Ibid., p. 28.

16. American Psychiatric Association, *Diagnostic and Statistical Manual of Mental Disorders,* 3d ed., rev. (Washington, D.C.: American Psychiatric Association, 1987), p. 113.

17. See a book we recommend: Frank S. Pittman, III, *Turning Points: Treating Families in Transition and Crisis* (New York: W. W. Norton, 1987), especially p. 242. It is interesting that Pittman, in his work with families, also found a relationship between phobic symptoms and the "need for connectedness." See also R. Julian Hafner, "Marital Therapy for Agoraphobia," in Jacobson and Gurman, eds., *Clinical Handbook of Marital Therapy,* 471–493, who also recommends marital interviews for women who present as agoraphobic.

18. See, for example, Framo, "Marriage and Marital Therapy," pp. 126–130; and Pittman, *Turning Points,* Chapter 1.

19. James L. Framo, "Symptoms from a Family Transactional Viewpoint," in Framo, *Explorations in Marital and Family Therapy,* p. 15.

20. Marion F. Solomon, "Treatment of Narcissistic and Borderline Disorders in Marital Therapy: Suggestions toward an Enhanced Therapeutic Approach," *Clinical Social Work Journal,* 13 (Summer 1985), 141–156. See also Wallace, "A Focal Conflict Model of Marital Disorders."

21. See Elizabeth A. Carter and Monica McGoldrick, *The Changing Family Life Cycle: The Framework for Family Therapy* 2d ed. (New York: Gardner Press, 1988); Pittman, *Turning Points,* Chapter 4; and Morton R. Startz and Claire W. Evans, "Developmental Phases of Marriage and Marital Therapy," *Social Casework,* 62 (June 1981), 343–351.

22. See, for example, Bowen, *Family Therapy in Clinical Practice;* James L. Framo, "Family of Origin as a Therapeutic Resource for Adults in Marital and Family Therapy: You Can and Should Go Home Again," in Framo, *Explorations in Marital and Family Therapy,* 171–190; Michael E. Kerr, "Obstacles to Differentiation of Self," in Alan S. Gurman, ed., *Casebook of Marital Therapy* (New York: Guilford Press, 1985), pp. 111–153; and Ann Hartman and Joan Laird, *Family-Centered Social Work Practice* (New York: Free Press, 1983), p. 85.

23. Ivan Boszormenyi-Nagy and Geraldine Spark, *Invisible Loyalties: Reciprocity in Intergenerational Family Therapy* (New York: Harper & Row, 1973).

24. Framo, "Marriage and Marital Therapy," p. 128.

25. See Arlene S. Fontane, "Using Family of Origin Material in Short-Term Marriage Counseling," *Social Casework,* 60 (November 1979), 529–537, for a good discussion of this point.

26. See James L. Framo, "The Integration of Marital Therapy with Sessions with Family of Origin," in Framo, *Explorations in Marital and Family Therapy,* 191–224.

27. See David E. Scharff and Jill Savege Scharff, *Object Relations Family Therapy* (Northvale, N.J.: Aronson, 1987), pp. 18–19. See also Henry V. Dicks, *Marital Tensions* (New York: Basic Books, 1967); Dicks was one of the early integrators of psychodynamic and relational concepts.

28. See Bowen, *Family Therapy in Clinical Practice;* and Framo, "Symptoms from a Family Transactional Viewpoint," pp. 11–57.

29. Norman L. Paul, "The Role of Mourning and Empathy in Conjoint Marital Therapy," in Gerald H. Zuk and Ivan Boszormenyi-Nagy, eds., *Family Therapy and Disturbed Families* (Palo Alto, Calif.: Science and Behavior Books, 1967), 186–205.

30. See Robert L. Beck, "Beyond the Transference: Interviews with Adults and Their Parents in Psychotherapy," *Clinical Social Work Journal,* 12 (Spring 1984), 57–68; and Framo, "Family of Origin as a Therapeutic Resource for Adults in Marital and Family Therapy."

31. See John Goldmeier, "Intervention in the Continuum from Divorce to Family Reconstitution," *Social Casework,* 61 (January 1980), 39–47, for a useful discussion with case illustrations.

32. Framo, "Marriage and Marital Therapy," p. 129.

33. See Morna Barsky, "Strategies and Techniques of Divorce Mediation," *Social Casework,* 65 (February 1984), 102–108; Ann L. Milne, "Divorce Mediation: A Process of Self-Definition and Self-Determination," in Jacobson and Gurman, *Clinical Handbook of Marital Therapy,* 197–216; and Helen R. Weingarten, "Strategic Planning for Divorce Mediation," *Social Work,* 31 (May–June 1986), 194–200. See also Mary M. Senger-Dickinson and Cyrus S. Stewart, "Caseworker Recognition of Marital Separation," *Social Casework,* 68 (September 1987), 394–399, for a useful discussion of the importance of clinical intervention during the separation phase of the divorce process.

34. Ellen M. Berman and Martin Goldberg, "Therapy with Unmarried Couples," and Howard J. Markman et al.,"Prevention," which both appear in Jacobson and Gurman, eds., *Clinical Handbook of Marital Therapy,* pp. 301–319; 173–195.

35. Berman and Goldberg, "Therapy with Unmarried Couples," p. 302.

36. See Markman et al. (p. 173), who cite references that indicate that "among marriages that do not end in divorce, 50% are not happy marriages and only 10% of all marriages reach their full potential."

37. Berman and Goldberg, "Therapy with Unmarried Couples," p. 301.

38. Ibid., pp. 305–306.

39. See John A. Brown, "Casework Contacts with Black-White Couples," *Social Casework,* 68 (January 1987), 24–29.

40. Monica McGoldrick, "Ethnicity and Family Therapy: An Overview," in Monica McGoldrick et al., *Ethnicity and Family Therapy,* p. 20.

41. Monica McGoldrick and Nydia Garcia Preto, "Ethnic Intermarriage: Implications for Therapy," *Family Process,* 23 (September 1984), 347–364.

42. Ibid., p. 349.

43. Quoted by Celia Jaes Falicov, "Cross-Cultural Marriages," in Jacobson and Gurman, *Clinical Handbook of Marital Therapy,* p. 429.

44. McGoldrick and Preto, "Ethnic Intermarriage," pp. 349–350.

45. Ibid., p. 362.

46. McGoldrick, "Ethnicity and Family Therapy," p. 21.

47. Falicov, "Cross-Cultural Marriages," pp. 429–450; and McGoldrick and Preto, "Ethnic Intermarriage," pp. 347–364.

48. Edwin H. Friedman, "The Myth of the Shiksa," in McGoldrick et al., *Ethnicity and Family Therapy,* 499–526.

49. Ibid., p. 506.

50. McGoldrick and Preto, "Ethnic Intermarriage," p. 349.

51. Laura S. Brown and Don Zimmer, "An Introduction to Therapy Issues of Lesbian and Gay Male Couples," in Jacobson and Gurman, *Clinical Handbook of Marital Therapy,* 451–468; Erving Goffman, *Stigma* (Englewood Cliffs, N.J.: Prentice Hall, 1963); and Carol Warren, "Homosexuality and Stigma," in Judd Marmor, ed., *Homosexual Behavior* (New York: Basic Books, 1980), 123–141.

52. See, for example, *New York Times,* August 30, 1987, p. 20, reporting a Gallup Poll of 1,607 adults interviewed around the United States in which 42 percent agreed with the statement "I sometimes think that AIDS is a punishment for the decline in moral standards." Fortunately, 43 percent disagreed.

Carol Warren in "Homosexuality and Stigma" reports (p. 125) on a 1977 California poll in which 5 percent of the respondents "said that homosexuals should be punished and kept away from 'normal' people," and 43 percent "said that homosexuals should be tolerated, but only if they do not publicly show their way of life."

53. Carol Warren, "Homosexuality and Stigma"; and Barbara Ponse, "Lesbians and Their Worlds," in Marmor, *Homosexual Behavior,* pp. 157–175.

54. Sophie Freud Loewenstein, "Understanding Lesbian Women," *Social Casework,* 61 (January 1980), p. 32.

55. Sallyann Roth and Bianca Cody Murphy, "Therapeutic Work with Lesbian Clients: A Systemic Therapy View," in Marianne Ault-Riche, ed., *Women and Family Therapy* (Rockville, Md.: Aspen, 1986), 78–89.

56. In a study of seventy-eight social work graduate students' attitudes toward homosexuality, 84 percent were seen as nonhomophobic and 16 percent scored in the homophobic range. Although these are fairly positive findings, to us they are not good enough. See Laura Friedman, "Attitudes of Mental Health Professionals toward Homosexuality: A Study of Graduate School Students" (unpublished Professional Seminar paper, Hunter College School of Social Work, May 1987). Among other things, Friedman recommends that social work students learn more about lesbians and gay men before working with them, that there be increased opportunities in graduate school for interactions between heterosexuals and homosexuals, and that issues related to homosexuality become an integral part of curriculum in course work and at field placements.

57. See Loewenstein, "Understanding Lesbian Women," p. 31.

58. See Roth and Murphy, "Therapeutic Work with Lesbian Clients"; and Jo-Ann Krestan and Claudia S. Bepko, "The Problem of Fusion in the Lesbian Relationship," *Family Process,* 19 (September 1980), 277–289.

59. Loewenstein, "Understanding Lesbian Women," p. 34.

60. Marcel T. Saghir and Eli Robins, "Clinical Aspects of Female Homosexuality," in Marmor, *Homosexual Behavior,* p. 285.

61. T. Parsons and R. F. Bales, *Family, Socialization, and the Interaction Process* (New York: Free Press, 1955).

62. For very useful and thought-provoking articles about the general lack of recognition given to feminist ideology in family theory and practice, see

Virginia Goldner, "Feminism and Family Therapy," *Family Process*, 24 (March 1985), 31–47; and Rachel T. Hare-Mustin, "A Feminist Approach to Family Therapy," *Family Process*, 17 (June 1978), 181–194.

63. Goldner, "Feminism and Family Therapy," p. 33.

64. See Audrey D. Smith, "Egalitarian Marriage: Implications for Practice and Policy," *Social Casework*, 61 (May 1980), 288–295.

65. *New York Times*, October 3, 1983, p. B 15; see also Family Service America, *The State of Families, II: Work and Family* (Milwaukee, Wisc.: Family Service America, 1987), pp. 18–27.

66. Goldner, "Feminism and Family Therapy," p. 37.

67. See the interesting study and discussion by Audrey D. Smith and William J. Reid, "Role Expectations and Attitudes in Dual-Earner Families," *Social Casework*, 67 (September 1986), 394–402. There are indications that both husbands and wives may be ambivalent about equal sharing of household and child care functions; the authors recommend helping couples clarify "covert contracts" that tend to be influenced by traditional roles.

68. Goldner, "Feminism and Family Therapy," p. 42.

69. Pittman, *Turning Points*, p. 52.

70. See Larry L. Constantine, "Jealousy and Extramarital Relations," in Jacobson and Gurman, *Clinical Handbook of Marital Therapy*, p. 412.

71. For readings on extramarital affairs, see Pittman's "Infidelity" chapter in *Turning Points*, pp. 97–128; Sonya Rhodes, "Extramarital Affairs: Clinical Issues in Therapy," *Social Casework*, 65 (November 1984), 541–546; Herbert Strean, "The Extramarital Affair: A Psychoanalytic View," *Psychoanalytic Review*, 63 (Spring 1976), 101–113; and Robert Taibbi, "Handling Extramarital Affairs In Clinical Treatment," *Social Casework*, 64 (April 1983), 200–204.

CHAPTER 18

Couple Treatment: Clinical Issues and Techniques

In the previous three chapters, our discussions of family and marital treatment have been grounded in concepts that integrate intrapsychic and systems thinking. We use these same concepts when working with individual clients, but in family and marital therapy we work with the relationship system in vivo. From the psychosocial point of view, behavior, emotions, and symptoms cannot be appraised apart from the systems in which they exist; often the marital relationship is the most salient and most accessible impinging system of all.

Even when severely stressed by negative socioeconomic conditions, an individual or couple has to make decisions about how to circumvent or transcend them or how to try to join others to temper the noxious influences. Obviously when spouses are able to work *with* rather than *against* each other, when they are able to be gratified rather than deprived by their marriage, they have a far better chance at negotiating the other systems in their lives. Sometimes, a small tip in the balance of personality or marital systems or of living conditions can result in remarkable differences in couple functioning. In other cases, the work can be very slow or little progress seems possible, at least

with the helping methods developed so far. Probably most cases, like the case of the Brent couple that follows, fall between these extremes.

TOM AND KATHY BRENT

Some couples with difficulties, unable or unwilling to confront their own unhappiness, tenaciously cling to the notion that it is their child and the child only who needs therapy. Other parents present a child's problem, but very quickly the symptom diminishes or seems less important. In these situations, as in the Brent case, the child truly seems to function as a "passport" for marital treatment.

Tom and Kathy Brent (see genogram[1]) requested help from a family agency for their daughter, Melissa, age thirteen, who was underachieving in school. Three family meetings were held with the parents, Melissa, and her brothers, Tommy, age fourteen, and Randy, age twelve. It soon became apparent to the worker and to the parents that the core difficulties resided in the parental relationship; the children's issues were not critical and responded quickly to the brief family therapy. Tom and Kathy

THE BRENT FAMILY
GENOGRAM

KATHY'S MATERNAL GRANDPARENTS
Born and died in Ireland

"Strict" and "cold"

KATHY'S AUNT

Kathy lived with aunt in U.S.A. from age 8

KATHY'S MOTHER

Living in Ireland; Kathy visited her only once in 27 years

KATHY'S FATHER

Died in accident when Kathy was 5

KATHY
35
Born in Ireland

RN: visiting nurse; "perfectionistic," conscientious

Married 16 years

RANDY
12

MELISSA
13

Identified client; underachiever in school

TOMMY
14

TOM'S MATERNAL GRANDPARENTS
Lived with Tom's family until Tom was 12

Born in U.S.A.

English–Irish

TOM'S FATHER
Canadian

Deserted family when Tom was 10 months; died of alcoholism when Tom was 2

As a boy, felt like an "outsider," betrayed by mother, a "loner"

TOM
38

Meter reader; hard worker; reserved

TOM'S MOTHER

Married 35 years

JIM COOK

Tom's stepfather; "belittled" Tom

TOM'S BROTHER
30

TOM'S BROTHER
21
Student

TOM'S SISTER
26

TOM'S BROTHER-IN-LAW

□ Male
○ Female
✕ Deceased
■ and ● Members of nuclear family
□ and ○ Members of extended family

actually seemed relieved to have the opportunity to focus on their marital difficulties; with no apparent resistance, therefore, couple sessions were arranged. On the basis of information gathered from the Brents and from her own observations of family and marital interactions, the worker summarized Tom and Kathy's histories and their current relationship:

Tom, age thirty-eight, a meter reader for a utility company, was the oldest of four children, the only child of his mother's first marriage. His own father, who was Canadian-born, deserted the family when Tom was ten months old and died of alcohol-related diseases when Tom was two. His mother, of English-Irish heritage, remarried when he was three and she and her second husband, Jim Cook, had three children, ages thirty, twenty-six, and twenty-one at the time of intake. From Tom's perspective, his stepfather had rejected and competed with him. When he paid him attention at all, it was critical or ridiculing. Jim seemed partial and more loving to his own children; they, Tom's half-siblings, in turn admired their father and got along well with him. Tom said that his mother, probably to "keep the peace" with her husband, did not defend or protect him from his stepfather's treatment.

Tom's maternal grandparents, who lived with the family until Tom was twelve, had strongly disapproved of his mother's first marriage. Apparently for this reason they never seemed fully able to accept Tom either. The effect of all of this, Tom reported, was that he felt like an outsider in his own family. Furthermore, he described his mother, stepfather, and grandparents as frequently "deceitful." When Tom's siblings graduated from elementary school, for example, monies were deposited in a bank for their future use, but, when Tom inquired about this (no money had been given to him) he was told it was not true. Only later did one of his sisters confirm his suspicions. In one of the first sessions, Tom readily admitted to having a quick temper, which he attributed to the anger

he had felt toward his family all of his life. At the time he came into couple treatment, Tom's mother, stepfather, and siblings were alive and resided within one hundred miles of the Brent home.

Tom, a very serious man with a strong sense of responsibility, functioned well at work. In addition to his regular job, he sometimes worked at a gasoline station to make ends meet. The Brents had managed to save enough to buy a modest house in the small city in which they lived. Tom took pride in work he did around his home and garden. Although his relationships with his children were in some ways distant, he was deeply concerned about their well-being; he was also determined not to show any of the favoritism he himself had experienced. Under most circumstances, Tom was reserved and did not initiate conversation. At times his manner seemed sullen to the point that his children often viewed him as unapproachable and were especially fearful that his inner anger would erupt, as it occasionally and unpredictably did. In contrast to his usual quiet demeanor with others, with Kathy he was often verbally cruel and attacking. In many respects, Tom emerged from his childhood feeling lonely, like an "outsider," angry, betrayed by his mother, suspicious, and wary of trusting anyone.

Kathy, age thirty-five, a registered nurse, was born in Ireland. She was an only child whose father died in an accident when she was five. At age eight, her mother sent her to live in the United States with her maternal aunt, whom Kathy described as a strict, cold, matter-of-fact woman; as Kathy remembers it, her aunt "always had 20/20 vision when it came to flaws but was visually impaired when it came to positive achievements!" Not surprisingly, Kathy worked hard to please and, indeed, became a perfectionist. From the time she was sent away from home she felt rejected by her mother and grew to resent her; throughout her childhood, she longed for and idealized her father. For reasons different from Tom's, Kathy also thought of herself as an "outsider." She was "different" from other children in the northeastern city in which she lived: her strict aunt made her wear clothes that other children laughed at and prohibited her from many activities enjoyed by her peers. At the time of intake, Kathy's mother still lived in Ireland; Kathy had visited her only once in twenty-seven years, just before her marriage to Tom sixteen years previously. The aunt who raised her lived near the Brents and was Kathy's only close relative.

Kathy's quick, curious mind and wry, sometimes caustic humor were part of her basic style. Generally she was outgoing and conveyed confidence; with Tom, however, she could be withdrawn and elusive. A practical, conscientious, and very hardworking woman, she had an excellent reputation at the visiting nurses agency where she began to work when all of the children grew to school age. Kathy ran her home with a firm hand, conveying expectations of her children that they complained were often impossible to achieve. She recognized that sometimes her treatment of her children was similar, although considerably less severe than, that she had received from her aunt. Childhood experiences influenced her to have feelings of isolation and sadness; she felt rejected and criticized by others and was often consumed by self-criticism and shame. Although she thought of herself as never able to please others, she never stopped trying to be "perfect."

Interactional Patterns

Interactional patterns of the Brent couple were established quite early in their marriage and became increasingly entrenched over the years. As is true of many couples, when they got married, Tom and Kathy both longed for someone to love them, to take care of them emotionally, to help them feel "whole," and to provide the self-esteem that each lacked. They started out trying to do everything they could to please each other. They each denied (often to themselves and usually to each other) their own thoughts,

feelings, or attitudes in the belief that these might jeopardize caring from the other. Out of fear they were not openly expressing their wishes or concerns. As might be expected, after the sexual and romantic ecstasy subsided, feelings of resentment began to accumulate. They then seemed less perfect to one another; disappointment and distrust set in. The dream that brought them together began to fade: they had looked to each other for surcease from childhood pain, for the comfort and safety of togetherness. Instead their idols had fallen, and illusions of "happiness everafter" were shattered.[2]

As disenchantment became more pervasive, the patterns that ultimately led them into treatment began. When Kathy felt alone and misunderstood, she clammed up and sometimes hid information from Tom that she thought would make him angry and critical. For Tom, Kathy's withdrawal and evasion triggered his early experiences of being ignored; he became suspicious, made unwarranted assumptions about what she was thinking or doing, and followed these with verbal violence. He heaped upon his wife the outrage that he could not express in his youth. In turn, Kathy felt still more hurt and unappreciated. Tom's anger left her feeling like the small child her aunt had criticized. She became more distant and reluctant to share even the most trivial matters with Tom. Certainly the disclosure of intimacies, which had seemed safe in the glow of their early marriage, now felt very dangerous. The negative, vicious cycle that we described in theory in Chapter 17 was played out between the Brents as it is, with variations, between many spouses: couples so often begin with high hopes for everlasting joy, then believe they have to disown aspects of themselves in order to protect it, and then recreate situations from their childhood which they both expect and dread.

Behaviorally, by expressing inner representations of themselves (introjects), as unworthy, "bad," and "imperfect," Tom and Kathy were externalizing expectations onto the other that they would be unloved and let down. Specifically, Tom projected his sense of being ignored and betrayed as though it were Kathy's deliberate intention to mistreat him. Kathy projected her feelings of being misunderstood, disapproved of, and rejected, as if Tom's essential purpose were to criticize and scorn her. Each, immersed in unhappiness, was thus unable to realize that in large part the other was motivated by fear, by need for self-protection, and by the magnetism of familiar conditions. Neither had the confidence to believe that a positive change could be made *unless the other changed*. Of course, the more the negative interactions continued, the more convinced each became: secretly of his or her own unworthiness and ineffectiveness, explicitly of the other as rejecting and untrustworthy.

Reluctance to Change

Unknowingly, Tom and Kathy each had participated in inducing in the other the very behavior and attitudes that had brought them such sorrow as children. Indeed, their worst dreams had come true. Yet, as painful as the situation was, as much as they yearned for a return to the early days of their marriage, and as motivated as each was to come for marital therapy, both were also clearly afraid of change.

Why, we often wonder as we sit with couples earnestly seeking relief, do they often cling so hard to collusively hurtful patterns? Each pair, of course, has its own "reasons" for being reluctant to open up and to explore possibilities for repair and growth. Tom and Kathy were chosen for discussion here because, in some respects, they represent many "stuck" couples seen in clinical practice. They illustrate common issues facing marital pairs who are stymied by more or less unconscious reluctance to modify their situations.

In the case of Tom and Kathy, from the worker's point of view, the obstacles to change included:

1. *The natural tendency for any system, including a marital system, to maintain a dynamic but steady balance (homeostasis), as discussed in Chapter 15.* Negative interactional patterns became entrenched and predictable. Irrational role assignments (the reciprocal projections of introjects) were firmly set. Demoralizing communication patterns were stabilized. Efforts to make changes that would extend beyond the range of their set patterns were met by counterforces that resisted those efforts, thereby maintaining the equilibrium of the marital system.

However, when the demand for change, whether from external events or inner motivation based on the intolerability of the present circumstances, upsets the balance sufficiently to *require* new adaptations, treatment usually progresses—sometimes rapidly. When couples seek help because inner and/or outer forces are demanding change, the resultant anxiety and need to find new ways of living facilitate the work of treatment. But, like Tom and Kathy Brent, many couples are *not* totally desperate and therefore they resist disturbing the status quo. In the Brent case, had any of the children been severely symptomatic, the family might have been thrown into crisis, thus necessitating immediate and drastic changes.

2. *The attraction of the familiar.* In their marriage, Kathy and Tom actually re-created the circumstances and emotional climate that they experienced as children. As we have said, sometimes people tend to induce others to fulfill their negative expectations, not only to accommodate inner self-hate or self-doubt but also to shape relationships similar to those to which they are accustomed. In short, some kind of connection with others is better than none at all and, unless one has experienced a more gratifying kind, the tendency is to fall back on what is *known*, especially in the face of disappointments that *always* occur in intimate relationships.

3. *Fear of the pain of losing hope and love again.* Tom and Kathy, and many other couples, are wary of bringing tender feelings back into their

relationship. Often this is expressed explicitly. With sadness and resolution, one woman told her marital worker over and over, "My heart is closed." She was terrified to risk disappointment again after discovering that her husband had had an affair. When they married, Tom and Kathy believed that they had found in each other the answer to their deepest inner yearnings. But once disenchanted, neither felt strong enough to try again until their daughter led them to treatment.

HOW DO WE INTERVENE?

There are, as we have said, a significant number of couples in distress who can be helped with a little environmental relief (employment for one of the spouses, support groups, resources for the children or elderly relatives, etc.). In some cases, a comfortable state can be attained with a small tip in the balance of forces. A significant number of couples seen by caseworkers are naive about communication skills and interactional styles and require only brief supportive and educational treatment. Of course, goals must be mutually established with each couple. Making a couple aware of interactional behavior and providing information about *how* to approach one another to achieve goals are frequently the caseworker's functions. Dick and Susan Jones (Chapter 3) provide an illustration of this kind of short-term marital treatment. There are brief examples of others later in this chapter.

But when problems are more deeply entrenched, as they were with Tom and Kathy, how do we interrupt destructive interactional cycles? Before outlining steps that often lead to success, we insert some caveats:

Five Cautions

At the *beginning of treatment*, when dysfunctional cycles resist the couple's or the worker's efforts to change:

1. We do *not* encourage ongoing, freely exchanged ventilation of current negative emotion, such as angry blaming, hostility, and bitterness toward one another. Of course it is important that the feelings be stated and understood. However, in our view, repetitive venting is usually futile at best and dangerous to the relationship at worst. If it does not release inner pressure or help in mutual understanding very quickly, the likelihood is that this kind of exchange will become an acrimonious "free-for-all," escalating as it feeds on itself, thus alienating the spouses even more. Unbending expectations each partner has about how he or she will be treated in the marriage are further validated as distortions and dysfunctional patterns are reinforced. Moreover, in the minds of the spouses, the harrowing experience of reciprocal ventilation can become associated with therapy, discouraging them from continuing to come for help. Equally important is the fact that most often negative emotion is a "cover" for softer feelings such as disappointment, hurt, sadness, loneliness, fear, inadequacy, and helplessness. Generally, then, it is more productive to create a climate in the sessions that will elicit *these* feelings than to facilitate the escalation of defensive attacks that make such sharing riskier.

2. We do *not* promote hand holding, hugs, or other kinds of physical closeness. Some therapists try, and probably occasionally succeed, to break through negativity by urging exercises that include some sort of touching. From our point of view, such interventions should be very carefully considered because they may not be sensitive to "where the clients are": clients can feel misunderstood and, perhaps, frightened if the worker pushes them into behaviors that feel unsafe. If the climate between the spouses warms up, there may be times when a worker gently suggests that they sit near one another or reach out in some way, but, as often as not, we think it best to follow the couple's lead in this area. When they feel closer, they are likely to make affectionate moves *that suit them*; such voluntary moves are far better than those prompted by the worker.

3. We do *not* suggest that each spouse ask the other for what he or she wants or claims to need from the other. Again, exercises of this kind can be helpful when problems are not serious, or in the context of "marriage enrichment" workshops and the like, or later on in treatment when the climate of the marriage has improved. However, when difficulties are as entrenched as they were in Tom and Kathy's case, the spouses are usually not yet ready to listen and do not feel like giving much to the other. When requests partners make of each other are rejected, by words or actions, the upshot can be more confirmation of the unlovability of self and/or of the intractability of the other.

4. We do *not* urge spouses to listen responsively and creatively to one another, to try to put themselves in the other's shoes, and to empathize with their spouse's feelings. Again, when they first seek help, often couples are too angry to do this; or, even if the spouses are not inclined to be vicious or blaming, usually they are too stuck, self-absorbed, or frightened to be able to react constructively to one another. As for the preceding caveat, efforts to encourage such sensitivity are likely to lead to disappointment and reinforce the often considerable disillusionment in the marriage.

5. We do *not* encourage warming up a fight or disagreement that occurred some days ago. Couples usually want to go over such material—sometimes needing the opportunity to ventilate—and hence this kind of reporting will not be altogether prevented. But it is usually the worker's job to foster "here-and-now" communications during the session and respond most intensely to those. In this way, the quality of the couple relationship and reciprocal interactions can be addressed directly *as they are going on*. "Talking about" marital dynamics can lead to intellectual insight; we often see couples, including those who have been in therapy be-

fore, who are able to explain themselves and their relationships in very enlightened terms but have failed to put their excellent understanding to use. When deeper (more emotionally resounding) insight is achieved *within* the session, in the interactive experience, it has a better chance of fostering awareness which, in turn, can lead to changes in feelings and behavior. Occasionally, when couples battle viciously, it *can* be useful to help them examine what happened from a distance, at a time when they are less flooded by emotion and therefore can be more objective.

To reiterate: Some of the approaches described in these above "cautions" may be used to advantage as treatment progresses, when clients are less frightened and defensive and have more understanding of themselves, their spouses, and their relationships.

Treatment Steps

How, then, do we proceed? The following measures taken by the caseworker in couple sessions are recommended in cases, like the Brents', in which there is serious marital distress:

1. Convey through action and words the worker's warm interest, sensitivity, trustworthiness, and "involved impartiality" (to be discussed in greater detail later in this chapter). Above all, for the work to be successful, the spouses must feel that they are in a safe place and that the worker is fair and nonblaming. There is a continuous balance to be maintained between intense concern and detachment from judgment. *Therapeutic listening requires respect for and understanding of the couple's reality rather than imposition of the caseworker's point of view.* On a regular basis, feedback about the couple's experience of the sessions and of the worker's approach should be solicited; the commitment to mutuality is respectful to the clients and helpful to the worker and also may provide the

spouses with an experience in teamwork, a model for their own conduct within the marital relationship. In fact, the Brents expressed their appreciation for the worker's ability to listen, understand, and avoid taking sides. They felt their own objectivity was enhanced by her example. Many couples may feel the benefit of this attitude and yet not put it into words.

2. Seek enough history to help the worker and ultimately the spouses to identify and reflect upon the underlying bases for the repetitive projection of old introjects onto the current marital relationship. As was true in the case of Tom and Kathy, early family background information can help to decipher the basis for expectations and reactivity between the spouses.

3. Help the couple to become conscious of their individual and joint dysfunctional behaviors and cycles. It is the caseworker's responsibility to assist each spouse in revealing and pinpointing vulnerable areas that contribute to the escalation of negative, disappointing reactions. Early in treatment, for example, Tom and Kathy were able to see how, when Kathy was afraid she would be criticized, she became evasive. And they learned how, in turn, when Tom's anger and suspiciousness were triggered, Kathy withdrew even further. It is equally important, of course, to support and facilitate the couple's *positive* patterns. Both Tom and Kathy were very principled people with a well-developed social conscience; each had a solid sense of fairness. Hence, as treatment progressed, it became possible for the worker to bring attention to these qualities, as they were often revealed in relation to their children and other people in their lives, and help them use these same qualities to bring more balanced, less blaming attitudes to marital interactions.

4. Carefully try to determine the original basis for their attraction to one another and the strengths they see in one another and in the marriage. If there are positive memories or attitudes to be uncovered, these may help the couple to sustain some optimism about the rela-

tionship in spite of painful issues that brought them to treatment. However, it is not uncommon for those who feel deeply angry or misunderstood to be unable to perceive or admit that there are redeeming features in the other or in the marriage. Almost always when this is so, it is best not to press for unavailable feelings since doing so may make it seem that the worker is not listening or is not comprehending how grave the problem really is. In the early phases of treatment, Tom and Kathy were unable to remember with intensity the depth of their early feelings for one another; they knew they had been "in love" and had had high hopes for the marriage, but keen feelings of disappointment overshadowed positive memories. Each was aware of admirable qualities, such as conscientiousness and concern for the children, in the other, but neither saw these as relevant to their current marital situation.

5. On the basis of the worker's hypotheses about underlying, disowned aspects of each spouse, begin to reframe (i.e., define in different ways) current attitudes, feelings, behavior, and communications. *This process of uncovering suppressed or consciously hidden material is often at the heart of marital (and also individual) therapy.* Openly expressed emotions or attitudes, as such, are not the fundamental problem in many unhappy marital relationships, but often they function to cover up others that are unexpressed. When this is so, it is the worker's task to coax the obscured feelings into awareness. Manifest, defensive feelings can be understood by each individual, and eventually by each spouse, as a way of hiding vulnerabilities and not necessarily as a wish of punishing or abandoning the other. Such reframing requires empathy, if not intuition. It also requires gentle and careful work.

For example, one might say softly to Kathy, "Do you think it is easier for you to evade and withdraw and say you don't care rather than to let yourself, or Tom, know how long you have yearned to have affection and approval or how very scared you are of trusting these when you do get them?'' Or, to Tom, with kindness, ''Is it safer for you to try to 'mind read' Kathy, badger or blame her than to tell her of the depth of your disappointment and sadness?'' Or, to either, ''Do you think you were afraid that when the other really got to know you, he/she wouldn't love you and that you expressed that fear through anger?'' Or, ''When you get scared of being left, rejected, disapproved of, and the like, do you feel like striking out (Tom) or crawling into a shell (Kathy)?''

These reframed statements or interpretations are hunches, however well thought out, and as such are always open to correction by clients. The worker may be wrong; even if the assessments are accurate, the clients may be too afraid to acknowledge them. When there is disagreement, then the worker and the spouses must continue to seek clearer understanding of the meanings behind feelings and behaviors.

There are many other examples of reframing: of a wife with small children, a worker might ask: ''Do you think you turned away from your husband and toward your sons for affection because you felt you were less likely to be rejected?'' Or, to a ''no-nonsense,'' very logical husband who lost his mother when he was a small boy: ''Is it possible that when your mother died you had to put your love and sadness away, 'deciding' that the best way to survive was to take very practical approaches to life?'' And, later: ''Because of the ways you handled soft emotions in childhood, does it make you uneasy now when your wife clamors for more tenderness?''

In many cases it is helpful for clients to understand how children often creatively protect themselves by disowning vulnerabilities and how they may continue to do so as adults even when this interferes with their lives and relationships. For example, it could be helpful to the ''no-nonsense'' man just mentioned to know that ''putting feelings away,'' when he was young and dependent and had no one to listen to his sad side, was probably the most adaptive

thing he could have done at the time. However, this man might also come to realize that in his current adult life covering up emotions no longer works well for him or for his marriage.

6. Help each spouse to listen to contradictions between the other's typical (usually negative) attitudes and the more genuine feelings that come to the surface when reframed. Ultimately, new understandings and responses may emerge. In the Brent case, Kathy began to realize that Tom's angry behavior covered disappointment and fear derived from his childhood. Tom learned that it was not Kathy's intent to ignore him; instead, her evasive behavior had been developed as protection against hurt during her early years. As we shall discuss soon in greater detail, it is our view that one of the major benefits of joint sessions is that it provides the opportunity for spouses to understand one another during the treatment; when genuine feelings are mutually revealed and understood, defensiveness decreases and intimacy is enhanced.

Timing of interventions is crucial, of course, because if one spouse is encouraged to open up before the other is ready to be truly attentive, defensiveness may reemerge. Needless to say, the work will be slowed down. When one spouse is very angry and therefore cannot listen, he or she may laugh at or attack or try to negate the authenticity of the other's expressions. Suppose a worker did suggest to the ''no-nonsense'' man that he must have put loving feelings away at a young age, when his mother died. If the wife was filled with rage, she might make a reply such as, ''That's ridiculous! He never had loving feelings for anybody!'' For this man, who would probably feel extremely vulnerable revealing emotions that had been hidden so long, there could be a lot of pain and a serious setback in the work as a result of the worker's premature efforts to expose his tender side to his still bitter wife.

7. Educate and reinforce. When progress is made it is important for the worker to predict

the probability of recurrence of old defensive interactions. Particularly under stress, there may be a tendency in both spouses to disown some facets of themselves again and to lose sight of their newly found understandings of themselves and of each other. The urge to blame is sometimes revived, and, if it is, the worker may have to remind both spouses of the progress that followed increased awareness of individual issues that contributed to marital distress. There is usually a need to review regularly the changes each has made and the way change in one necessitates change in the other.

Over and over again, intrapsychic experience is related to interactions and vice versa. For example, the worker might say to Tom: "Under stress, when you again have fears of being betrayed or of being an outsider, your impulse to attack and badger seems to crop up again. You can understand, though, that it is at those points that Kathy clams up." Or, to Kathy: "When you fear disapproval and rejection, you crawl right back inside yourself again, don't you? Can you see, though, how this triggers Tom's feelings of being left out?"

As this phase of therapy progresses, both spouses can become clearer and clearer that they need not live reactively by giving up power to one another. In other words, they need not assume that their behavior or feelings are "caused" by the other but rather that they can take charge of their own conduct and communications, and even bring positive initiative to the climate of the relationship. As Pittman describes, often both husband and wife "see the marriage as belonging to their spouse, who uses it as a form of tyranny over them, as if they are being held captive. They take little responsibility for making the marriage work...."[3] When they are no longer so deeply entrenched in feeling like victims of one another, ideally each will learn to recognize and interrupt the negative cycles, rather than waiting for a change of behavior from the spouse. Kathy learned not to withdraw automatically when she feared criticism. Tom almost completely ceased his verbally abusive behavior; instead he made a point of telling Kathy directly what was on his mind, including how frightened he became when he thought he might lose her.

During this final step, it is often necessary for the worker to continue to teach communication skills, helping the spouses to make "I" statements and to talk with one another in autonomous, emotionally meaningful terms. By now, if the treatment has been successful, both are in a much better position to hear and respond accurately. As greater satisfactions arise, they give up negative, destructive, and lonely patterns. Ideally, they become better at delicately balancing intimacy and independence.[4]

RAPID ASSESSMENT, BRIEF TREATMENT, AND REFERRAL

In many agencies, both brief and extended marital treatment are provided by social workers according to the mutually agreed upon need. However, in a broad range of settings—including substance abuse programs, inpatient and outpatient hospital social services, hospices, prisons, employment assistance programs, agencies specializing in spouse abuse, and services to AIDS victims—casework is limited by the agency's functions and the clients' reasons for being involved in treatment. Those facilities unable to provide ongoing help to couples often have experienced workers who make rapid assessments and provide time-limited treatment and, when needed, referrals. Three brief case illustrations follow:

Rita, a seventeen-year-old woman, was hospitalized for bulimia at a twenty-one-day experimental inpatient hospital service devoted to the evaluation and referral of adolescents with eating disorders. Two meetings with Rita's parents quickly revealed that, although rarely openly conflictual, both were depressed and unable to approach each other about the emptiness of their marriage. The father had two almost full-time jobs and when he was at home, he was usually sleeping. The mother devoted most of the hours during the day (she worked as a waitress in the evenings) to visiting her recently widowed mother. Neither spouse knew how to bring closeness back to their drifting relationship. The skillful worker was able to arouse their interest in a referral to a family agency for couple therapy; she also arranged for Rita to join a group for teenagers with eating disorders. A follow-up call several weeks later revealed that Rita was doing well and that her parents had begun to communicate their disappointments and to clarify their misunderstandings; after only a few marital sessions, trust between them was beginning to be renewed.

In this case, the worker had to engage the couple's confidence quickly since she had only three weeks to prepare for a transfer to another service.

In a hospital counseling service for AIDS patients, John and his lover, Arthur, with whom he had lived for seven years, were seen together for several months before John died. The social worker helped them both with their terrors about the illness; the men shared their outrage and sadness. From the worker's point of view, without her encouragement, John and Arthur would have been too frightened to mourn together; instead, they would have related superficially in the precious time they had left. In the process of saying good-bye, and as John grew weaker and weaker, he found some peace and developed some acceptance of his tragedy. Arthur's positive experience with the hospital social worker stimulated him to seek a referral for his own ongoing treatment. By being helped to grieve, he was released to begin to redefine his life and, ultimately, to seek new relationships.

Because of the constraints of hospital policy, the worker could not continue with Arthur after John died; however, her strong relationship with him and her commitment to his welfare as well as to John's were central to the successful referral.

In preparation for his parole, Jim, a thirty-year-old prisoner, was seen by a social worker. Jim was becoming increasingly anxious; he worried especially about his jealous feelings toward his wife, Charlene. He had been arrested after severely assaulting a man he had believed was interested in her. Even though Charlene had visited him fairly regularly during his two-year incarceration, he was consumed by the fear that she would reject him now. Six weekly marital sessions held with the prison worker while Jim was still in jail brought some of Jim's worries out in the open; Charlene also had serious unexpressed concerns about the marriage. In the brief period of treatment it was established that the relationship was very important to them both and they wanted to protect and build on it. The couple were referred to a community mental health clinic to continue the work after Jim returned home.

By being responsive to Jim's apprehensions, the worker provided a service that was sufficiently helpful to both Jim and Charlene that they were willing to continue their couple treatment after Jim was released. Without the brief treatment, often not available to prisoners, it is probable that the marriage would have deteriorated and it is equally probable that Jim's jealous rage would have led to another arrest.

In each of the three cases just described, it was important that social workers were on the scene and saw beyond the immediate or practical concerns of their primary clients. It seems safe to say that without the encouragement of the workers, not one of those who accepted referrals would have sought help independently;

yet, in all three situations, the referrals were successful and the clients were gratified by the opportunity to continue the work they began in the short-term services.

Tipping the Balance: Brief Treatment of Multiple Problems in a Marriage

Helen and Jake Garcia and their four children living at home, who ranged in age from nineteen to five, were referred by Child Protective Services to a clinical social worker in private practice. The family had originally come to the attention of the protective agency because of allegations made by the thirteen-year-old daughter, Maria (the only girl), that her father had fondled her genitals on two occasions when he was intoxicated. A summary of the full investigation by the protective workers and the probation officer of family court where the case had been heard concluded that Jake was very remorseful about his behavior (he did not remember it but he did not deny it) and had successfully abstained from alcohol for a two-month period. He was attending Alcoholics Anonymous meetings and planned to continue. The family was being referred to the private practitioner, who worked closely with the protective services and the court, because of multiple problems. The child protective workers believed that if the problems were not alleviated, alcoholic behavior and sexual abuse could recur. Serious difficulties included the following: Jake, who had few work skills and spoke little English, through no fault of his own had recently lost his job as a chauffeur; the learning-disabled eleven-year-old son was truant from school; the nineteen-year-old son was not taking initiative to find work; Helen had never been employed outside the home and for many reasons was reluctant to look for a job in spite of the current financial crisis.

After two meetings with the entire family, it became apparent that the most critical unresolved issues were within the parental relationship. Except for Maria, who had been "parentified" and was habitually protective of her mother, the children did not want to attend meetings. The worker offered resources for vocational counseling to the oldest son; she also contacted the teacher of the eleven-year-old in hopes of getting him special remedial and supportive attention at school.

Some separate meetings were also held with just the parents and Maria concerning the specific experiences she had with her father and her feelings of betrayal because she had not been protected by her mother (who at first did not believe the child's statements about the sexual abuse). Maria was also bitter because she felt that she had taken better care of her mother over the years than her mother had of her. In these meetings, Jake told Maria of his regret and shame. Although Helen was defensive at first, the worker was able to help her to *really* listen and respond to Maria's outlook on their relationship and the roles they had fallen into with each other.

Over a four-month period, the worker held twelve marital sessions with Jake and Helen. In addition to the serious practical problems, it was soon revealed that unspoken resentments between them were quite close to the surface, even though each had a polite, almost deferential demeanor vis-à-vis the other as well as toward the outside world. As it turned out, Helen was harboring twenty-year-old anger pertaining to their courtship; in particular, she felt that their first sexual experience had been forced upon her. Because of cultural and family beliefs, she had thought she had no choice but to marry Jake even though she did not respect him. Helen also blamed Jake for various actions which she felt had alienated her from her extended family.

Over the years, Jake had reacted to Helen's nonverbal sullen and critical attitudes toward him by becoming increasingly distant, morose, and alcoholic. Neither had directly discussed the unhappiness between them; therefore, neither understood the other and each experienced the other's behavior as attacking and rejecting. In couple therapy, the mutual disclosure of feelings and assumptions was intense and extremely difficult for both Jake and Helen at first, but after only a few sessions each reported enormous relief, greater trust, and more closeness. They reviewed scores of events in their lives that had led to pain and misunderstanding.

By the time the short-term treatment ended, the positive potential in the relationship had been uncovered. Once the grudges dissipated and there was greater fulfillment in the relationship, Jake and Helen were able to work together on other serious problems facing their family. Jake continued to go to AA, was not drinking at all, and was offered a secure job by a distant, well-to-do relative of Helen's from whom the Garcias had been estranged until Helen initiated a reconciliation during the treatment.

Certainly all of the problems in this case were not settled, and they may never be. Longstanding personality problems were only briefly addressed. However, the balance of the marital system shifted, allowing the strengths of the partners and the relationship to emerge. Helen and Jake were thereby freed to build on rather than to continue to obscure their capacities for affection and problem solving.

At a follow-up family meeting six months after termination, it was apparent that the Garcia couple and the family continued to make progress. Communication among them all was vastly improved; the older son was working and the younger was getting better grades and enjoying school more. Maria seemed more relaxed and less involved in her parents' issues. Jake and Helen worked together with less rancor and more mutual respect. Experience has taught us that if the couple relationship works well, parenting issues are usually vastly simplified. Even extremely destructive behaviors, such as incest and alcoholism, can be prevented or corrected when the marital relationship changes. In this case, as in many other intact families who

come for family therapy, very soon after the initial explorations the mutual decision is made to work mainly with the parents. And in some situations significant alleviation of long-standing dysfunction can occur in a short period of time.

COUPLE VERSUS CONCURRENT INDIVIDUAL SESSIONS

Many of the indications, contraindications, and advantages that pertain to family therapy, as discussed in Chapter 16, pertain as well to conjoint couple treatment and, therefore, need not be repeated here. However, when marital matters are involved, there are some specific issues relating to conjoint and concurrent individual sessions that we want to emphasize.

It is not uncommon for workers, even those who prefer conjoint to individual concurrent therapy for spouses with marital difficulties, to arrange a meeting or two with each spouse separately. Many therapists believe that rapport with each person is established more quickly by using this approach. It gives some spouses freedom to talk more easily about difficult material, including "secrets," such as extramarital affairs,[5] and collusions of various sorts with other family members (often parents or children). There is disagreement among clinicians about how such "classified" information should be handled. Some workers promise confidentiality, at times strongly encouraging that the information be revealed to the nonattending spouse, at other times dealing with the pros and cons of keeping the material hidden. Many clinicians declare at the outset that they will not keep secrets. This approach has the advantage of protecting the therapist from collusion; it can also protect either spouse from feeling betrayed by the therapist who participated in withholding important information. Pittman describes his point of view: "I have found it helpful to offer one separate individual session for each marital partner. Most jump at this opportunity to charm me and tell me their secrets, even though I make clear I won't agree to keep the secrets. People just need to check out the safety of revealing things in their fragile marriage."[6]

As stated in the discussion of extramarital relationships in Chapter 17, it is our view that each situation has to be assessed individually. Understanding the function that the secret information plays in the relationship may be more important than sharing the details with the spouse. In any event, it is of utmost importance that the worker make his or her position about secrets and confidentiality exquisitely clear *from the outset* in order to prevent later misunderstandings.

Whether or not there are occasional separate sessions with individual spouses, it is our general view that unless there are contraindications (such as those listed on pages 340 and 341), conjoint meetings are an easier, more direct and efficient approach to alleviating marital distress than concurrent individual sessions. Although we mentioned some of our reasons for this point of view earlier, we summarize here those we consider most important:

1. The complexity of the marital bond cannot be as thoroughly understood or addressed when it is not observed in action. The energies involved in the interactional patterns—the emotional intensity of the interlocking process—transcend the dynamics of each individual and take on a life of their own. Emotions, especially those connected to the marriage, will be talked about but rarely experienced as keenly in individual sessions. By the same token, people are not usually aware of the intricacy of their marital patterns and therefore cannot fully describe them.

2. Experience has taught us that internalized objects (introjects) indeed can change in the presence of the original object. (Early inner images of one's parents and corresponding self-images can often be corrected in the context of current, realistic relationships and meaningful communications with them.) Similarly, when a spouse has projected, for example, an inner representation of a critical father onto his or her mate, it is still possible to amend it "secondhand"; in other words, a positive marital relationship can provide a "corrective experience" and be instrumental in rectifying the old introjects, thereby freeing people to experience their mates and themselves as they actually are. Family-of-origin meetings with each spouse can be very valuable in remedying and/or updating internalized images of parents, but often this is not possible because the parents are not available or because the clients refuse to involve them.

3. In casework as well as in most therapies, the transference to the therapist is not usually as intense or as stable or as fully developed as it is with a spouse, and hence not as accessible to reflection and insight. We will be saying more about transference in the context of marital therapy in the next section.

4. The interchangeability and instability of individual symptomatology become much more apparent to the worker and to the couple in marital sessions. When one person's symptom diminishes, often that person's spouse may manifest some sort of new problem. Along the same lines, the meanings of the symptoms, such as the phobias described in the case of Barbara and Al (see Chapter 17), are frequently uncovered when the marital relationship is explored.

5. When both spouses are present, each becomes better able to understand the basis of the feelings and behavior of the other, which too often are taken personally as rejections or attacks. It often becomes apparent that negative emotions expressed by a spouse are "covers" for other, usually softer, feelings. It can be extraordinarily relieving to learn that some unpleasant attitudes of one's partner are derived from early childhood experiences and not primarily from the marriage. Obviously, when spouses are not defensive, they are much more likely to be able to hear and empathize with one another.

THE COUPLE–WORKER RELATIONSHIP

Much of what we said in Chapters 10 and 16 about realistic and unrealistic responses, transference, and countertransference applies to couple treatment as well as to individual and family therapy. However, there are some special issues, particularly in connection with transference and countertransference, that relate specifically to marital treatment and require mention here.

Transference

As described in previous chapters, in individual therapy the therapeutic relationship can be used as a "laboratory" for client self-understanding. In particular, client transference reactions (in contrast to realistic responses) to the worker can be examined in order to reveal parental introjects, inner images of self, manifestations of lack of differentiation (including tendencies to become enmeshed), assignment of unrealistic powers to others, etc. The relationship with the worker can help clients gain awareness of their characteristic ways of relating to others (positively and negatively). A worker may provide well-timed feedback when appropriate to the purposes of the treatment. Strictly speaking, transference refers to the transfer of the client's past feelings, attitudes, and behaviors—often from childhood—*to the therapist*. In couple (and family) therapy this definition is usefully expanded.

Whenever possible, in marital treatment, a major focus should be on the complexities of the "transferences" *between the spouses*, not toward the worker. Often, but certainly not always, unrealistic reactions to the therapist are of minimal importance, as in the case of Dick and Susan Jones (see Chapter 3). When these do occur, usually they should be addressed in order to keep communication open between client and worker and to sustain feelings of trust. As we shall see, discussion about unrealistic attitudes toward the worker can provide important opportunities for self-understanding. But, in contrast to some instances in individual treatment, in our view, it is usually best not to divert the marital work by deliberately inducing or searching out transference reactions to the worker.

As we saw in the case of Tom and Kathy Brent, introjects rooted in childhood experiences are revealed through projections, patterned defenses, and emotional attitudes as these are transferred back and forth in vivo between the spouses. Optimally, if it can be saved, the marriage itself ultimately becomes a "corrective" experience. It makes far more sense for spouses to learn in therapy how to be nourished in a reparative marital relationship, where the emotional intensity and investment actually reside, than to try to make up for what is lacking through a strong connection to the worker. Even when couple treatment results in separation, analysis of the processes that have gone on between them in a "real-life" relationship can usually throw a broader light on individual and interactional dynamics than examination of the more circumscribed relationship with the worker.

Put another way, our clients are not always wrong when they "resist" or "deny" powerful transference connections to the worker. Protests from clients about their relationships to their therapists are frequently heard: "But this is not a 'real' relationship!" "I don't really know you at all and you know 'everything' about me!" "It's so one-sided!" These complaints may be a defense against therapeutic work, but they also contain profound truths: What really matters (or, realistically, should matter) to our clients are the people with whom they have shared or are sharing their lives, for whom they feel deep loving feelings or from whom they have sought kindness, acceptance, affection, and companionship. Hence, conjoint interviews often have a better chance of uncovering transference distortions and childhood origins of marital dysfunction than efforts to locate these in the reactions of a spouse or couple to the worker.

The worker's approach to the couple treatment is critical to maintaining the focus on transferences between spouses. Frequently, intense transference to the worker can be prevented simply by not encouraging it. In our experience, this is best achieved when workers remain outside the marital system and present themselves as neutral but concerned facilitators or "coaches,"[7] whose purpose is to help spouses learn about their relationships; to get to know themselves and each other in new ways; to be understood, especially by each other; and to communicate genuinely and meaningfully in their marriage. Ideally, if there is transference to the worker, it is to a kind aunt or uncle, a benign grandparent, a special teacher, or the like. For the most part, such transferences need not be probed or emphasized. Needless to say, this approach requires that the worker maintain, to the best of his or her ability, "involved impartiality," which we will discuss in the next section, on countertransference.

In spite of the best efforts by the worker, however, there are points in many marital cases when transference reactions to the worker do require recognition and exploration. Sometimes, especially early in the treatment, one or both members of a couple indicate directly or indirectly that they expect the worker to show partiality. In fact, as in all therapy, later misunderstandings can be prevented if the worker makes routine inquiries about a couple's reaction to his or her approach, including whether they sense partiality. (One might simply say to both spouses, "If at any point you feel disturbed by something I say, or feel that there is bias, or that I am not understanding your point of view, it is extremely important that you let me know.") When the expectation that the worker will take sides is a distortion, rather than a reaction to countertherapeutic behavior by the

worker, it can become "grist for the mill" of the therapy, an opportunity for spouses to explore current attitudes and their sources.

During the initial phase of marital therapy with his wife, Laura, Bob was able to say that he feared the worker would judge him to be the one who was "wrong." It became apparent that this expectation arose from his original family, in which—or so it seemed to him—his parents always thought his younger sister was "right," and Bob never received positive recognition. Upon hearing Bob's concern, Laura admitted that she was afraid the worker was not taking her seriously. Since the worker knew this was far from true, he helped Laura reflect on her childhood experience in her family. As the youngest of several children, she had the role of "baby," the "cute one" who made other people laugh but whose intelligence and common sense were never acknowledged. From time to time Bob actually seemed to try to induce the worker to blame him; similarly, Laura occasionally related to the worker in childish ways, in accordance with the the role assigned to her by her family of origin.

Tom and Kathy Brent also brought their characteristic expectations of others to the therapist: Tom assumed that he would be the "outsider" in relation to Kathy and the worker; Kathy imagined that however hard she worked in treatment, she would never gain the worker's approval. In each of the marital cases, distortions were discussed openly and their sources explored. Also, because the workers in both cases consistently demonstrated warmth and fairness to these couples, after the first few weeks of therapy worries about partiality faded, replaced by concerns about themselves and the dynamics of their marital relationships.

The reader will recall Barbara, who had phobic symptoms (see pages 379 to 381), and her husband, Al. From the beginning, it was clear that Al thought the worker would not be interested in *his* feelings but only in how he could be helpful to Barbara. Barbara seemed to expect that no one, including the worker, could really care about her, so she put her energies into making lengthy, self-righteous statements about how "good" people suffer the most and get the least recognition. In the initial months of treatment, these transference reactions could not be explored because neither was able to be introspective. Rather, the worker waited patiently for opportunities to help them gradually to become less defensive and more reflective about themselves and their life together.

Sometimes in couple treatment it is revealed that, as a child, one of the spouses has had a "special" relationship with one parent, often the parent of the opposite sex, with the other parent being left as "odd person out" in the triangle. In couple therapy this spouse may try to charm or induce the worker's favoritism, thus re-creating the situation with his or her parents. Although people with this background often have had anxiety about "winning" against the other parent, they may be equally frightened of being "excluded." This kind of transference to the three-person treatment format may or may not be influenced by the sex of the therapist.

If couples are fearful of change or if the worker pushes them too hard, the two spouses may gang up against the worker, preventing him or her from working effectively. In these cases, there is a kind of "united transference" by the couple that exceeds the responses of each individual. Workers try hard not to get into this position because sometimes the attitudes harden and the couple ends treatment abruptly and prematurely, without an opportunity for closure. However, if such a situation develops, it is important for the worker to do everything possible to interpret the situation and, when appropriate, to take responsibility for his or her part in the difficulty.

Countertransference

In its narrowest sense, *countertransference* refers to workers' reactions to their clients—fantasies, feelings, attitudes, behavior—which reflect distortions and displacements stemming from their own childhood experiences. In this book we use the term more broadly to include not only unrealistic responses but also those that may be realistic but are countertherapeutic. Some of the frequent countertherapeutic snares that pertain specifically, although not exclusively, to couple work follow:

1. One of the common pitfalls one can fall into is to experience—and, more importantly, act upon—*feelings of partiality.* (Since this chapter is about couple treatment, we are referring to countertherapeutic responses in joint sessions; however, it is important to keep in mind that even if one never sees a client's spouse, involved impartiality is equally essential.) If, for example, the worker shows partiality to a wife she may resent it and indignantly defend the husband she had just been criticizing. Or else, by taking sides, one may be inadvertently colluding with projections, leaving distortions spouses have about each other unchallenged. Clients' feelings of helplessness and victimization may thereby be reinforced.

The worker can and should be able to empathize with a client about experiences that *feel* negative, whether or not they would seem upsetting to most people. Furthermore, when the behavior of one spouse *is* offensive or abusive, this certainly should be acknowledged. In conjoint treatment, both spouses may need feedback from the worker when actions of one are hurtful, destructive, or dangerous to the other. In the case of Tom and Kathy, the worker made it clear to Tom that it should not surprise him that Kathy felt hurt and criticized by his verbal attacks. Since he had been an "outsider" in his family, it had hardly occurred to him that his behavior, positive or negative, could impact anyone. If destructive behavior continues, it is not helpful for the worker to join with "victims" to assail the integrity or motivations of abusers; it is far more productive to help clients who are being maltreated to reflect on what they want to do to change their circumstances (rather than futilely trying to change their spouses) and to consider how this might be done. When legal assistance, temporary shelters, or other resources are required, the worker may be instrumental in locating these.

It can be particularly difficult to maintain a nonjudgmental stance when addictions, compulsive gambling, battering, incest, or other extremely destructive behaviors have been involved; however, experience has taught us that focusing all of the concern on the victims, often the wives, without involving the abusers whenever possible, frequently results in resumption of the same marital patterns and behaviors by both spouses. In every marriage, including abusive ones, it is important to try to enlist the help of husband and wife (and, in family matters, other family members) to explore what has happened that allowed the unhappy or destructive interactions to develop and how these can be changed. When we permit feelings of partiality to interfere with this stance, we may dissuade people from taking responsibility for making changes and thereby contribute to their staying stuck in roles of victim and victimizer.

Reasons for having the impulse to take sides are many and sometimes idiosyncratic to the worker. For some, there may be competitive feelings toward a spouse of the same sex. More often than we would wish, workers develop a strong attraction to the spouse of the opposite sex. Others may be so sensitive to the second-class status that women traditionally have endured that they feel like blaming the husband. If inequalities do exist, it is far more appropriate to point these out and help the couple determine how *they* want to deal with them. A worker who feels partiality to one of his or her parents and blames the other may replicate these attitudes in marital work. When our responses to a couple are similar to our attitudes toward our own parents, we may find ourselves reacting to one spouse or both in ways we did as children, by trying to please, by being charmed, by being intimidated, by being persuaded by one that the fault lies totally with the other, by feeling pity or revulsion—all of which can contribute to attitudes of partiality.

2. When marital systems are dysfunctional but stable, the interactional and defensive patterns entrenched, and problems "calcified," it is common for workers to have two divergent countertherapeutic reactions: One is to *work too hard* instead of enlisting the efforts of the spouses to determine what changes each wants to make. People in chronically unhappy marriages often feel helpless, believing that the other spouse controls them and the marriage; these feelings of powerlessness can induce overdetermined efforts by the conscientious worker, who eventually learns that he or she has no real control over the relationship but can only try to help the spouses take charge of themselves. The second reaction is to *throw up one's hands.* Out of feelings of helplessness, a worker may attack such couples, sometimes to the extent that they leave treatment. Or the worker may become passive and sit back and let couples run the sessions, getting little or no help from the inactive worker. These reactions result in the continuation of the same dysfunctional patterns that caused the couple to seek help.

3. *The worker's childhood position or role in his or her family of origin* may be countertherapeutically replicated in the relationship with a couple. Workers who had the role of "mediator" or "rescuer" with their parents may feel overly responsible for the fate of their clients' marriages. These workers sometimes have too few expectations of the couples and underestimate their part in solving the problems. As we have said, people, including workers, tend to carry original family roles with them into adulthood and, if self-esteem is derived in part from efforts to save their parents' relationship, they may be reluctant to let go of that role. The *reductio ad absurdum* of this situation would be the subtle, unconscious sabotaging of any progress made by a couple since improvement would eliminate the worker's function!

If it was the worker's role in his or her family to become symptomatic when the parents were having difficulties, countertransference reactions could lead that worker to become physically ill, tired, or depressed or to act out. Sometimes when couples are battling, feeling helpless, or acting in other ways that are reminiscent of parental behaviors, old feelings are reactivated and a worker can feel enormously angry or sad.

4. Most people are emotionally affected by loss, even when they are only witnesses to the process. Those who provide marital therapy inevitably share in experiences of *separation* and *family breakup* with some couples. Of course, reactions to these are unique to each worker. Some will deny that the marriage is over and keep trying to resurrect it. Others, as a result of anxiety about separation, may become angry or have the impulse to attack one or both of the spouses. Still others handle their feelings by detaching, perhaps in order to prevent the pain associated with loss or breakup. In these situations the workers may then be, to one degree or another, unavailable to couples during separation or to those spouses who want help afterward.

5. When couples in treatment are of a *different socioeconomic class, racial or ethnic background, or sexual orientation* than the worker, countertransference reactions can arise. For some, cross-cultural relationships stir up negative feelings. The worker's prejudice against particular groups or blatant stereotyping obviously creates serious countertherapeutic problems; such feelings must be immediately recognized and handled if the therapy is to be effective, rather than destructive. More often, in subtle ways, workers can have difficulty being empathic with some couples because their experiences or their ways of interacting with one another (more apparent when two people are seen together) are so divergent from those of the workers.

As we have said many times over the course of this book, it is imperative that we be familiar with some of the wealth of written material relevant to the people with whom we work. Many of our clients have been severely stigmatized and oppressed as a result of their social status, background, or lifestyle. But we need more than facts about the indignities endured by a particular group; to the best of our abilities, we need to *feel with* as well as intellectually understand relevant life experiences. Above all, we need to learn that differences in ways of being— patterns of thinking, feeling, acting—are not necessarily better or worse than the worker's ways; they are just different! (Of course, sometimes people who are not at peace with their own identities, racial/ethnic backgrounds, or lifestyles can react negatively to couples *simply because they belong to the same group;* this problem, too, requires keen self-awareness and efforts toward resolution by the worker.)

And, in order to understand our clients as well as possible, and not impose our own biases, we need to be willing to *learn from them.* It is they who can best help us to see their situations and their relationships *as they see them.* It is their lead we must follow if we are to engage them and stay in touch with their needs and aspirations. It is also our job to be attuned to suspicious or defensive attitudes among clients who expect, on the basis of painful life experience, to be misunderstood, patronized, or demeaned because of background or sexual preference. We must work toward relaxation and openness, toward frank discussions of differences when necessary, taking every precaution possible to avoid responding anxiously or angrily to couples who are reluctant to trust us.

Countertransference reactions are, as we discussed in Chapter 10, unavoidable occurrences in the life of the caseworker. Marital therapy, like family therapy, brings its own hazards that derive from the force of interactional events. There are no simple safeguards. But a number of preventive measures, measures that should continue for as long as one continues in the work, can cut down on the quantity and intensity of countertherapeutic responses to couples. Certainly personal therapy can be very valuable in reducing the influence of conflicts and negative reactions stemming from childhood or current stresses and in developing self-awareness, including familiarity with one's "Achilles' heels." Participation in one's own couple and/or family treatment can sharpen sensitivity to countertherapeutic reactions. Ongoing discussions with colleagues about dynamics, treatment procedures, transference and countertransference phenomena are absolutely necessary. Supervision and/or peer consultation with trusted professionals—sometimes using one-way mirrors and audio- or videotapes—are invaluable aids to sorting out the objective from the subjective, the realistic from the unrealistic. Cotherapists sometimes help to protect each other from pitfalls in the treatment, although economic considerations usually preclude ongoing cotherapy in couple work. Marital treatment can be intellectually and emotionally demanding, and we need to find opportunities to keep learning from one another, to share our worries and mistakes, and to let off steam when necessary. Destructive effects of countertransference reactions are greatly reduced thereby, much to the benefit of troubled couples who seek our professional help.

POSTSCRIPT: KATHY AND TOM BRENT

Tom and Kathy were in marital treatment on a more or less weekly basis for just over two years. Toward the latter part of treatment, the three children attended four sessions with their parents. No other family members were invited to attend. Both Tom and Kathy were adamantly opposed to including any of them even though occasionally the worker suggested it, operating on the notion that many of their earlier unhappy experiences could be more deeply understood by them and—perhaps—in some ways modified in the present relationships.

During the first year the worker was extremely active and followed treatment steps described earlier in the chapter. Over and over again, with acceptance and warmth, she helped both Tom and Kathy to understand themselves, in the past and present, so that they could begin to speak frankly about their own thoughts and feelings. Although the development of self-awareness and trust came slowly, after the first year with only occasional setbacks under stress—they were able to talk to each other freely about heretofore hidden matters, with the result that each had increased appreciation of the other and listened more often without becoming defensive. Once self-awareness and communication were enhanced, focus on the problematic, dysfunctional aspects of their lives greatly diminished. By the end of the first year of therapy, the marital relationship was no longer the demoralizing, painful experience it had been when they first sought help.

The second year of therapy, therefore, could be devoted to building on strengths and expanding potentials of the individuals and of the relationship. Tom and Kathy used their sessions to channel energies previously depleted by fear and self-doubt. They discussed vocational and educational plans: Tom decided to enroll in a technical school and prepare for a career as an electronics technician; Kathy contemplated an advanced degree in nursing, hoping eventually to become supervisor of her office at the visiting nurse association. Each felt supported by the other in these explorations and decisions. Because their families, both of which were experienced by them as emotionally barren, had provided them with few examples of creative and loving relationships, they literally had to learn how to bring tenderness and positive direction to their marriage. The worker's kind, honest, self-confident, but nonauthoritarian style offered a model that undoubtedly influenced the course of this phase of treatment. Tom and Kathy were able to learn by example that their own energies and initiatives could enhance every aspect of their lives. Thus both the marriage and the "good aunt" transference to the worker provided a rich, reparative experience.

After years of silent dissatisfaction with their sexual life, Tom, with considerable difficulty but without blame, raised the subject in a session. The result was that they openly discussed how they felt about it and what they wanted. As often happens, outside the sessions, rather than in the worker's presence, they began talking about some of the most intimate details. In a very short time they delightedly reported renewed pleasure in their love life. For most of their lives they had been guided by what they thought were the expectations or attitudes of others or "rules" they had been raised by, with little sense that they could shape their own experiences in the ways *they* wanted. Whether in relation to sex or to a host of other matters, initially each had implicitly assumed that the fate of their marriage was determined by the other. Neither had confidence that his or her actions could influence the outcome of the relationship. During the second year of marital therapy, however, there were times of shared exhilaration as they enjoyed the rewards of the hard work both had put into the treatment.

Issues involving the children were discussed comfortably rather than defensively by them. The children were involved in the four family sessions at the suggestion of Tom, not because there were any apparent difficulties but rather so that they could participate with their parents in some of the changes that had been made. To the worker, they all seemed more relaxed and outgoing than they had when treatment began. In spite of easier communication with each other and with the worker, Tom and Kathy's char-

acteristic reserve at times still inhibited them from being as open with their children as they wanted to be. However, in the brief family therapy, they were able to be more forthcoming than they had been, with the result that there were several very touching moments in which all five members were able to share some feelings—primarily positive, often poignant—that had been "under cover" until then. Melissa, now almost sixteen, who the reader will remember was the "identified client" when the Brents first came for treatment, summed up the current family situation in the final family meeting: "We used to be more like an army troop than like a family. We all did everything we were supposed to do, on schedule, but it never seemed to matter how we felt about it. No one hardly ever laughed or cried except at the movies. But since Mom and Dad came for help, they both seem happier and have more patience about what concerns us. Dad's temper used to be very scary to me and he seemed so unapproachable; Mom was like a 'top sergeant,' keeping us in line. The difference is, now we can talk to them and they listen and really care about our feelings. Now, too, we can have fun as a family." Clearly, the improvement of the marital relationship yielded innumerable benefits for the children even though they were only peripherally involved in the actual therapeutic process. Successful marital treatment often has significant preventive ramifications; dysfunctional family patterns handed down from generation to generation can be diminished, if not altogether arrested, when parents interrupt the process by becoming self-defined and constructively taking charge of themselves and their relationships.

To summarize: Couples of all ages,[8] walks of life, and lifestyles are seen by social workers in a broad range of contexts in brief and extended treatment. As discussed in Chapter 16, the Hollis typology of treatment procedures and worker-client communications can be adapted for conducting and studying interviews with more than one person. Obviously, marital sessions provide the worker with opportunities for intervention not available in individual therapy. The intensity of marital interactions can make joint interviewing difficult and confusing and adopting an attitude of neutrality takes practice, particularly with couples who activate subjective responses. But the worker who strives for self-awareness and has seen couple after couple can become comfortable and skillful working with troubled marriages. Often one has the privilege of participating in a positive growth process that ultimately reaches many more people than the two who actually came for help.

NOTES

1. The genogram, which organizes useful information and provides a quick picture of a family tree and relationship patterns over generations, is valued by many individual, marital, and family therapists. For an excellent reference on how to construct and "read" genograms, see Monica McGoldrick and Randy Gerson, *Genograms in Family Assessment* (New York: W. W. Norton, 1985). See also Philip J. Guerin and Eileen G. Pendagast, "Evaluation of Family System and Genogram," in Philip J. Guerin, *Family Therapy* (New York: Gardner Press, 1976), Chapter 26; and Ann Hartman and Joan Laird, *Family-Centered Social Work Practice* (New York: Free Press, 1983), Chapter 10.

2. For two books that discuss illusions, myths, and disillusionments in intimate relationships, see William J. Lederer and Don D. Jackson, *The Mirages of Marriage* (New York: W. W. Norton, 1968); and

Joel Shor and Jean Sanville, *Illusion in Loving: Balancing Intimacy and Independence* (New York: Penguin Books, 1979).

3. Frank S. Pittman III, *Turning Points: Treating Families in Transition and Crisis* (New York: W. W. Norton, 1987), p. 14.

4. For readings on couple treatment not cited in this chapter or in Chapter 17, we recommend Robert L. Beck, "Redirecting Blame in Marital Psychotherapy," *Clinical Social Work Journal*, 15 (Summer 1987), 148–158, which includes a case example; Sylvia Jo Ann Larsen, "Remedying Dysfunctional Marital Communication," *Social Casework*, 63 (January 1982), 15–23; and Robert L. Pugh, "Encouraging Interactional Processes With Couples in Therapy," *Clinical Social Work Journal*, 14 (Winter 1986), 321–334. We also recommend Philip J. Guerin, Jr. et al., *The Evaluation and Treatment of Marital Conflict: A Four-Stage Approach* (New York: Basic Books, 1987); and Richard B. Stuart, *Helping Couples Change* (New York: Guilford Press, 1980).

5. For references on extramarital affairs, see Chapter 17, note 71.

6. Pittman, *Turning Points*, p. 85.

7. Murray Bowen, *Family Therapy in Clinical Practice* (New York: Aronson, 1978); Elizabeth A. Carter and Monica McGoldrick Orfanidis, "Family Therapy with One Person and the Family Therapist's Own Family," in Philip J. Guerin, *Family Therapy*, 193–219.

8. See references in Chapter 17. See also George S. Getzel, "Helping Elderly Couples in Crisis," *Social Casework*, 63 (November 1982), 515–521; and Mary Ann Wolinsky, "Marital Therapy with Older Couples," *Social Casework*, (October 1986), 475–483.

Crisis Intervention and Brief Treatment

Throughout this book there are discussions and case illustrations of brief treatment of individuals, couples, and families. Chapter 19 summarizes some basic principles and approaches to crisis intervention and other brief therapies.

For years it was assumed by most caseworkers that a contact should be continued until the needed help was given, or the client withdrew, or the worker decided there was nothing more to be done. But many clients withdrew after only a few interviews. Others continued for many months, sometimes for several years. The "functional" school of social work, strongly influenced by Otto Rank's thinking, as early as the 1930s began advocating the setting of time limits for the length of contact at the outset.[1] Proponents of this approach believed that the client worked best against such limits, that the will was mobilized and growth and individuation were fostered by the establishment of planned endings. Subsequently, for many reasons related to expediency and to clinical judgment, some of which we shall touch upon in this chapter, caseworkers from all schools of thought began to assess differentially when

short-term treatment might be *as* effective as or even *more* effective than unlimited therapy. Various devices were tried to bring help more quickly, among them briefer services with more limited and specific goals.

CRISIS INTERVENTION

A major form of brief service is crisis treatment.[2] Originally seen only as an emergency measure, a holding operation until longer-term treatment could be arranged, crisis treatment in which *help was offered immediately* and at the scene of the crisis when necessary, often proved effective in preventing long-range or devastating effects of traumatic events. A pioneer in crisis intervention, Erich Lindemann, worked with the families of victims of the 1943 Boston Coconut Grove nightclub fire.[3] Finding remarkable uniformity in the "normal" grief reactions of the survivors, he described the "acute grief syndrome" and delineated phases of "grief work" through which the bereavors had to proceed in order to begin to free themselves from binding ties to the deceased, to readjust to life without that person, and to form new relationships. Lindemann's work led the way for others to outline predictable *phases* and *tasks*, typologies designed to guide interventions, associated with a broad range of hazardous events or developmental and transitional crises. We will say more about the benefits and limitations of such typologies shortly.

Categories of Crises

A crisis may be defined *as any major event or change that requires individuals or families to restructure their ways of viewing themselves, their world, and their plans for living in it.*[4] It may be precipitated by a specific trauma or series of traumas or a circumstance (or set of circumstances) that has been building up over time. One may think of crises as *anticipated* or expectable or as *unanticipated*. Anticipated crises include *developmental* or *maturational* events, such as adolescence, midlife, and old age. Anticipated crises also embrace *transitional* points in the life of an individual or family such as starting a new job or school, moving to a new geographic area, living in the "empty nest," or retiring. Unanticipated crisis events include various kinds of *losses*: death of a family member, desertion or divorce, a disabling accident, mental or physical illness of an individual or family member, loss of a job, a miscarriage, and so on. Many changes can be experienced as *loss,* such as the behavior problem of a previously "model" child, the affair of a spouse, the alcoholism of a family member, or alienation among family members. *Additions,* too, may precipitate an unanticipated crisis: the birth of a new sibling, introduction of a foster child or elderly relative into the home, merger of households required by shortage of housing, illness or death of a parent. And, of course, *external blows* and conditions create unanticipated crises: floods, earthquakes, fires, economic depression, war, assault, and rape are a few of many such hazardous events.

The Crisis State

Whatever the precipitant, crisis induces an upset in the equilibrium (the homeostatic balance) of the individual personality or family system. Although the actual duration of the *acutely* disturbed state varies widely, it is by nature time-limited. The tension and anxiety induced by the crisis mount until some sort of resolution occurs (often during a period of up to six weeks) with or without professional help. As described by Rapoport and by Galon,[5] the individual or family may perceive the crisis and the subsequent circumstances as a *threat* to the sense of well-being (reacting with anxiety), as a *loss* (reacting with depression and grief), or as a *challenge* (experiencing mobilization of positive energy and motivation for growth). Depending on a number of factors we shall discuss shortly, including what kinds of coping mechanisms are activated, the resolution can result in a condition that is better than it was prior to the crisis, return to the previous state, or deterioration and adoption of dysfunctional patterns of living. In any case, *once the crisis state subsides and some resolution occurs, individuals and families are far less likely to be accessible to outside intervention* than when they are feeling vulnerable, unsettled, or disorganized *immediately* after the crisis, when rapid change is possible within a short time.

Outcomes of Crisis

Tension induced by crisis calls for relief. When individuals and families are in an unsteady state, egos are fluid, defenses are shaken, emotions are at a peak; there are often a great deal of floundering and a search for comfort and answers. Thus some sort of action is taken, and it, in turn, produces an outcome. Overlapping *positive* outcomes include (1) resolution, (2) redefinition of the problem or expectations, and (3) relinquishment of goals.

Resolution can be as specific as the location of a homemaker or the activation of a support network that comforts during a catastrophic or transitional time. A child may be encouraged to take a favorite doll to kindergarten until adjustment to school is achieved. A man who has lost his job may be retrained for another. On the other hand, resolution and return to equilibrium may require that people go through a process, a series of stages, as they do in grief reactions.

Redefinition is often necessary to resolve the situation that brought on the crisis. For example, among other things, psychoeducation provides families of severely disturbed individuals with a realistic understanding of mental illness and attempts to diminish feelings of blame or failure.[6] Often when working with families with adolescents, an effort is made to help both the parents and the teenagers realize that the anger or behavior exhibited by either "side" is not intended to hurt but rather arises from fear, frustration, self-doubt, or other negative emotions. Mr. Russo (see Chapter 16) was able to reframe his employment situation; this capacity led to his decision to continue on in his familiar job rather than to seek work with more prestige.

Relinquishment of unavailable objectives and dreams often occurs through a process of mourning and, ultimately, redirection of energies. Over and over again, people must restructure their ways of looking at the world and their relation to it. Rejection from medical schools may lead a person to give up a lifelong career ambition and consider another profession for which he or she is better qualified. A father may have to let go of hope that his son will join him in the family business. Parents who have fixed notions about how they want their children to lead their lives as adults find they must relinquish these when they realize that their son or daughter intends to remain single, is gay, or plans to intermarry.

When positive solutions do *not* occur, however, greater—sometimes seemingly irreversible—disorganization may follow. When coping mechanisms habitually employed by individuals or families do not successfully resolve the current situation, maladaptive patterns often develop. *Chronic* grief and depression may set in after a loss. In order to handle painful events, people sometimes withdraw or refuse to associate with family members whom they blame for their troubles, thus intensifying feelings of anger or hurt. Others blame themselves so harshly for what has happened to them that problem-solving mechanisms are paralyzed.

Preventive Intervention

Of course, everyone does not need or want professional help in order to go through a crisis and restore or improve previous emotional balance. However, over the course of recent decades, social workers and other clinicians have been increasingly innovative in their approaches to victims of crisis and disaster and to populations "at risk." Mobile crisis units, telephone "hot lines" directing people to help they need, special services providing assistance to victims of crime, mental health teams offering *immediate* attention to those who need it, and so on, have emerged in an effort to respond to people when they are most amenable to help and can best use it. These opportunities are designed to *prevent* disabling aftereffects. Brief help during this period, when people need to ventilate and are more open to reflection and advice, is usually far more effective than long-term treatment after the crisis is over. In fact, clients already in ongoing therapy often make the most rapid gains when a crisis arises.

In recent years, concerns about *prevention* have also been behind the development of other programs. These programs offer services *before* a crisis occurs. "Rap groups" in schools and community centers offer support and direction to adolescents during an often tumultuous developmental phase. Relatives of cancer victims are sometimes seen in groups during the admission process at hospitals; not only are support and information supplied but social workers *screen* for individuals who need and want more extensive services. Under the best circumstances, family members are routinely seen by social workers in hospital emergency rooms, psychiatric facilities, nursing homes, and so on, not just to enlist help for the patients but also to determine who else may need assistance of some sort to prevent or minimize the effects of the patients' situations.[7]

(Unfortunately, as we said in Chapter 8, support for these preventive services is often dependent on the priorities of current political administrations. When funding is inadequate, sporadic, or suddenly cut back, the effect is frequent interruptions of help. Some potential clients never receive assistance. The effects of innovations in practice cannot always be properly evaluated because, as a result of the interruptions, they are too short-lived or fragmented.)

Generic Stages: Do They Occur in Reaction to Crisis? What About Time-Limited Tasks and Interventions?

Originally, crisis intervention was seen as primarily relevant to intact, well-functioning individuals who faced hazardous events or developmental transitions. Notions were then developed about predictable   so-called normative—reactions to a broad range of such situations. Kubler-Ross's typology of reactions to the diagnosis of terminal illness is well known: (1) denial and isolation, (2) anger, (3) bargaining, (4) depression, and (5) acceptance. It seems that there is hardly any maturational crisis, profound life change, or hazardous event that has not been studied and about which time-limited stages of reaction and tasks required for resolution have not been proposed.[8] These, in turn, have led clinicians to design interventive strategies. However, as Lukton points out in her important article, "generally, proof is lacking that the coping tasks must be performed in a preordained sequence, or that being able to conceptualize the stages helps to perform the

tasks." Generic interventive principles can be useful when flexibly applied, but they do not help workers differentiate one client from another. Lukton writes, "When we fail to explore the unique experience of the crisis for each client, we may force the data into our own preconceived categories and may miss discovering the meaning of the event for the individual." She adds, "we have been remarkably untroubled by the lack of agreement among the experts as to the nature of the normative tasks for various age groups." Some clinical writers view disengagement as one of the normative tasks of aging. Others take the opposite view, that active interaction with the environment is normative. Lukton reminds us that we must think of older people and *all* people as diverse, with widely divergent, sometimes unique needs that actually may conflict with rigid typologies of normative tasks and time frames.[9]

Taking Lukton's points a little further, on several grounds we believe it is misleading to design generic approaches to catastrophes or life stages for *intact and well-functioning people* on the assumption that they *react similarly to particular situations within a specific time frame.* First of all, people who are not so "intact" often creatively resolve crises and grow from the experience. Second, the generic approach tends to discount life experiences of clients in crisis that might influence the course reactions and resolutions take. For example, some people who faced similar circumstances in the past may cope more easily as a result. On the other hand, previous, possibly unresolved, experiences can exaggerate current reactions, necessitating attention to both past and present difficulties. Third, the environmental context in which the events are occurring can be of utmost importance to the outcome of the crisis. Available opportunities as well as quality of support systems and living conditions may dramatically affect resolution. Fourth, the personalities of the people undergoing the crisis—their strengths and capacities, defense systems, characteristic methods for handling problems and stress—are all very pertinent to crisis reactions and resolutions. Depending on a number of factors, then, crises that appear to be the same can have very different meanings and run very different courses. In crisis treatment, as in all other forms of psychosocial therapy, we need to think in systems terms rather than in linear terms.

We see it as unfortunate, then, that there has been a tendency to develop rigid typologies of interventive strategies designed for specific crises. It is equally unfortunate that crisis intervention is too often delegated to paraprofessionals or others with minimal training.

A woman who had recently been the victim of a vicious attempted rape was referred to a clinical social worker. She had first been seen individually and in a group by an earnest and caring woman police officer who headed a police department's Victims Assistance Service. Briefly trained in crisis techniques and operating on the notion that it was essential for this client to express her anger within a four- to six-week period after the assault, the officer kindly but persistently prodded the woman to "get in touch" with her rage. As it turned out, the woman characteristically had an extraordinarily peaceful, soft personality. She was numb and shocked, she was frightened by what had happened, she was having flashbacks of the terrible experience, but she had *no* awareness of anger. In her first visit with the social worker she asked, "Is there something wrong with me because I am not angry?" As it turned out, this woman's anger did not emerge at all until almost nine months after the incident, and the course of her reaction to the crisis took well over a year to subside, in part because of the nature of her personality and in part because her assailant was out on bail as the trial dragged on for eleven months. As a result of her limited training, the police officer was not equipped to assess the fact that for

these reasons this victim's fear transcended and blocked out her outrage for a far longer period of time than the generic approach suggested.

This case calls our attention to an important treatment consideration. If we always assume that crisis resolution must occur within a short time period, we may find ourselves pushing clients too fast and too hard. In the case of Mr. Kennedy (see Chapter 3), his daughter had moved away six months prior to intake; however, it was not until he had tried to work things out "his way" that he was willing to seek help. In other words, *ideally* interventions are made as soon as possible after the precipitating event. However, they may have to wait until the *cumulative* effects of the situation are so disturbing, and efforts at problem solving so unproductive, that the search for new solutions becomes essential. One researcher on trauma suggests, "The common belief that people recover after a few weeks from disaster is based on mistaking denial for recovery."[10] It sometimes takes months or even years for a person to assimilate fully the emotional impact of a catastrophic event. *Each situation has to be individually assessed.*

Crisis and the Assessment Process

It is essential, then, to evaluate the *severity* of the crisis, the individuals going through it, the interplay with the environment, and the supports available. Fortunately, rapid diagnosis is often possible because the homeostatic balance has been upset. Among the interpenetrating areas to be assessed are the following.

The Meaning of the Crisis to the Individuals and Their Families   In every situation, it is essential to evaluate the implications of the crisis to the people going through it. Although rape necessarily has a negative impact, the reaction of a person who has never had sexual intercourse is different from that of one who does not have the added concern of loss of virginity. When a worker expressed sympathy to a woman with several children whose husband had recently been killed in an industrial accident, the woman replied, "Yes, it was terrible, but imagine how much worse it would have been if I had loved him!" Unemployment for an actor or actress may be less unexpected and less traumatic than for an assembly line worker thrown out of work when the factory permanently closes. Some losses seem to be more symbolic than "real" yet are profoundly felt; for example, parents may need to be helped to take seriously their teenage son's reactions to a fender dent on the automobile he had saved for and pampered.

Current Adaptive Capacity Are the clients able to implement new methods of coping required by the present circumstances? How creative and flexible are they? Are functioning and problem-solving abilities impaired? In the case of Mr. Kennedy, for example, when he was first seen by the worker it was clear that there had been a significant loss of adaptive skills because he was so angry, depressed, and disorganized. In contrast, both Dick and Susan Jones (also Chapter 3) functioned almost as well as ever in spite of their acute distress.

Preexisting Personality Patterns and Structure
As already suggested, an individual's or family's characteristic strengths, outlook, adaptational patterns, and defenses are often rapidly revealed when in crisis. In the Kennedy case, the worker quickly ascertained that Mr. Kennedy had been an active man with many interests who had relied heavily on his daughter for support; he had tried to adjust to his losses himself but simply could not achieve a comfortable balance in his life without help. When making an assessment, one may gain some clues to personality functioning by comparing the particular reaction to a crisis to what might be an "ex-

pectable" reaction. One person may seem more thrown by a transient disappointment than another who has been given a diagnosis of cancer. It has been suggested that the more invulnerable one feels prior to a severe crisis, and the more one views the world as benign, the more devastating the catastrophe will be.[11]

Relevant Prior Life Experiences Generally, in crisis treatment, we focus on present circumstances, coping mechanisms, and supports required for mastering the situation. Nevertheless, clients often spontaneously link previous events, feelings, or difficulties to the current disturbance. One woman who had been raised in a large and very poor family agonized when her apartment was burglarized: "I never, ever before had anything of my own." Poorly resolved old conflicts or losses may be revealed and reexamined in the course of working on the crisis at hand. The woman described earlier who had endured an attempted rape was able to work on her difficult marital relationship while she was in treatment because her husband was more available to her than he had been in the past; the crisis had shifted the balance of the marital system. Adaptive capacities strengthened through resolution of a crisis frequently carry into the future, when new situations arise. Even though Mr. Kennedy spoke little about past history, his characteristic ways of handling loss and dependency were quickly revealed and modified. In the face of their current crisis, the Jones couple came to understand antecedents to maladaptive patterns and made changes that promised to be lasting.

Family Circumstances and Attitudes When an individual is in a crisis, the approach taken by family members can make a big difference. Obviously, unintrusive but positive support provides the individual with the optimal context in which to endure and come to grips with the ordeal. Equally obviously, when family members blame the victim, become dictatorial, or overprotect him or her, the course of resolution may be diverted or distorted. Sometimes dysfunctional family patterns are intertwined in the crisis situation, as when, for example, a woman who has been extremely dependent on her grown children loses her husband and pressures at least one of them to return "home." When families as a whole are facing a crisis, it is important to assess the potential for mutual aid and support. In many crises family meetings or conjoint meetings with relatives are helpful in arriving at accurate assessments and often can be crucial to a healthy outcome.

Support Systems: Needed Resources and Opportunities   Each crisis event has its own requirements of the environment; these depend in part on the assessment of all of the factors discussed. For Mr. Kennedy, the acquisition of a part-time job with a rent-free apartment was fortunate on both financial and emotional grounds. First-rate medical evaluation for a baby with an organic brain defect, adequate educational facilities for extraordinary children of all kinds, housekeeping help for an accident victim living alone can all provide an enormous amount of reassurance and practical assistance. Therapeutic and self-help groups sometimes are more effective than individual treatment in assisting people who have been victimized by catastrophic events.

Individualized Crisis Treatment

On the basis of the evaluation, crisis treatment usually includes the following.

Active, Decisive Intervention   During and after the rapid assessment, the worker is usually more direct than in long-term treatment, less often waiting for the client's spontaneous insights. To an overwhelmed woman with small children who has just learned that her husband has an inoperable brain tumor, the hospital social worker may say, "It's going to be essential that we make plans now for the care of the children when they arrive home from school." Or, after listening carefully to a distraught woman who is immobilized by news that her mother, from whom she has been estranged for many years, is critically ill, "It sounds as if you won't forgive yourself if you don't make the trip to see her." Frequently, we may state emphatically that to come to grips with the situation quickly, it will be important for family members to join in the treatment process. In short, people who are "swept away" by the immediate impact of a crisis often require a worker who presents as a confident, competent authority.

Clear Explanations Offered by the Worker   On the basis of information gleaned from clients, including experiences with and observations of them, the worker often offers interpretations about reactions to the crisis. These must suit the individual and not simply follow an outline of "normative" stages of reaction. To the woman who had been the victim of the attempted rape, the worker said, "It's perfectly normal to feel numb after such a shocking experience." To another woman who had had a very similar experience but had a different personality, "Of course you are angry." To a man who had experienced many losses but had trouble expressing the depth of his feelings about them, "One more deadly illness in the family is more than anyone would find bearable."

Encouragement of Cognitive Reflection and Prevention of Disabling Regression   To the extent possible, the worker attempts to enlist the client's thinking processes in order to understand the situation more clearly and to prevent emotional flooding. Although the ventilation of clients' feelings provoked by the crisis is *critically* important to healthy resolution, it is equally important that a balance between emotions and understanding be maintained. Clients can be helped to realize personal meanings of traumatic experiences and to identify maladaptive coping skills interfering with recovery. A worker asked a man who had lost his mother when he was young and who had withdrawn from his wife after his teenage son's suicide, "Is it usual for you to isolate yourself when unspeakable tragedy strikes?" Another worker observed to a woman railing at family members after a crisis, "It seems that when you feel frightened (sad, disappointed) you express it as anger." Over and over again, when diagnostically indicated, we say to clients in the throes of crisis, "Even though you feel as though you can't bring yourself to take the actions you have to take and make the decisions you have to make, I'm certain you will find that you can. Would it help to begin by taking this (specific) step?" Throughout treatment, the worker endeavors to promote and restore hope, mastery, competence, and autonomy as quickly as possible. Often, after an initial interview, the client gains relief from the ventilation of feeling and from being understood. Security can be derived from setting realistic tasks. In the Stone case (Chapter 3) Mrs. Stone was helped to regain an active role in taking charge of her family and her situation, thereby preventing a decline into hopelessness.

Involvement of Needed Supports and Resources   On an individualized basis, as suggested above, the worker either actively searches for or assists the client in locating networks, assistance, or opportunities that will be the right "fit" for that person. Again, accurate assessment makes the difference. There is no point in referring people to places they will not go or in offering opportunities they will not accept.

Goals   Lydia Rapoport, in her now classic article on crisis intervention, aptly summarizes objectives:

> The goals of crisis-oriented brief treatment can be...specified as follows: (1) relief of symptoms; (2) restoration to the optimal level of functioning that existed before the present crisis; (3) understanding of the relevant precipitating events that

contributed to the state of disequilibrium; (4) identification of remediable measures that can be taken by the client or family or that are available through community resources.

These are the minimum goals that should be achieved as part of crisis resolution. In addition, where the personality and social situation are favorable, and the opportunity presents itself or can be created, work can be done to: (1) recognize the current stresses and their origins in past life experiences and conflicts; (2) initiate new modes of perceiving, thinking, and feeling and develop new adaptive and coping responses that will be useful beyond the immediate crisis resolution.[12]

Even after an initial interview, relief sometimes is promoted by setting specific goals and defining tasks required to achieve them.

"Crisis-Prone" Clients

An initial assessment of individuals or families may quickly reveal that the clients being seen characteristically experience small changes or simple problems as emergencies. Whether the recent precipitating event is serious or not, it sometimes becomes apparent that there has been a chronic pattern of self-defeating behaviors and attitudes that promote extreme anxiety, disorganization, failure, and inability to cope with life's minor vicissitudes, to say nothing of major disasters. In these cases, it is not very useful to think in terms of "restoration to a preexisting optimal level of functioning." One hopes to help clients *strengthen* capacities for coping.

When the precipitating event is truly minor, and there is evidence that panic and confusion have been a way of life, clients are often reassured when the situation is put into perspective. Although we must be careful to acknowledge their feelings, clients may gain relief when they see that the current situation is not an emergency at all but simply one that they can learn to handle differently. As with all crisis victims, we attempt to bolster cognitive functions and allay regressive tendencies, to do all we can to support self-esteem, mastery, and autonomy; but in contrast to most crisis situations, in these cases we usually do not encourage repetitive ventilation. Clients with such difficulties often need longer treatment than crisis intervention ordinarily requires; brief treatment may be a "band-aid," but it is almost inevitable that a new small occurrence will bring on another overwhelming response and, perhaps, another cry for professional help. In our experience, a significant number of crisis-prone clients are helped to recognize that ongoing treatment, in which they learn to build on their strengths, can help them to avoid recurrent and agonizing ups and downs. Principles that apply to the treatment of personality disorders are usually relevant; when there are no extenuating external circumstances to account for extreme reactions, clients with this chronic problem frequently have serious ego deficits.

OTHER BRIEF TREATMENTS

It is beyond the scope of this book to discuss the many variations of the brief treatment model that have come into being over the past forty-five years.[13] Suffice it to say that from World War II on, caseworkers became increasingly concerned about long agency waiting lists, more and more applicants seeking help, budget cuts, demands for accountability, questions raised regarding casework effectiveness, etc. Furthermore, many clients for whom long-term treatment was being planned chose not to continue after a few sessions. Close scrutiny of casework and other kinds of treatment revealed that much, if not most, therapy was in fact brief. Clients were feeling helped more quickly than their caseworkers had believed possible. These realities led practitioners from the mental health professions to develop treatment strategies for short-term services. Once viewed as superficial and expedient, brief services now are often *preferred* by clients and clinicians alike. Over the years, research has assured us that *for a wide range of problems and clients*, effective, and sometimes lasting, results can be achieved through a short period of treatment. Even people with severe and chronic problems can be helped by brief treatment methods if reasonable goals are set.[14] In general, then, caseworkers no longer simplistically assume that more treatment is better treatment.

Crisis intervention, by definition, tends to be self-limiting. In *planned time-limited treatment*, a specific or approximate time for ending is usually set up at the beginning of the treatment relationship; in most brief treatment models, the time contract is open to renegotiation if resolution of the problem at hand takes more time than was estimated or if helping with additional problems is requested. The length of contact in short-term treatment may vary from as few as two or three interviews to a period of three to six months. The literature on brief therapy generally considers twenty-five sessions the upper limit of brief treatment.[15] Obviously, there is a large overlap between short-term and crisis treatments, but many clients in brief treatment deal with difficulties or dilemmas that are *not* urgent or catastrophic. However, both planned time-limited and crisis therapies usually require that the worker make rapid assessments, intervene actively, make pertinent interpretations quickly, and give direct advice when appropriate. Often a number of interviews are held within a short time span. When it fits the treatment plan, clients and workers together plan tasks and "homework" assignments.

In a few approaches to short-term therapy, the contract made about time arrangements is *non-negotiable*. In our experience—and in that of others, including many proponents of brief treatment—the decision about the actual number of months or sessions the work will require often cannot be definitely determined immediately, even when it is agreed that the treatment will probably be of short duration. In the psychosocial approach, a time frame is frequently suggested by the worker *with the un-*

derstanding that there will be a reevaluation at points along the way and when the period is up. The Jones couple in Chapter 3 "contracted" for ten sessions but were clear that the therapy could be extended after an evaluation at that time; they chose to have a final, eleventh meeting in which they summarized and reinforced the work they had done. In the Russo case (Chapter 16) the worker suggested that the family meet together for six sessions and then evaluate the situation, even though she suspected the work would take longer. As it turned out, the family attended thirty-six sessions over a period of ten months. When client motivation and need are present, extending a contract for brief treatment can lead to productive and more intricate work than short-term therapy allows, as it did for the Russos. Various ways in which time can be set were discussed under "Deciding on Length of Treatment" in Chapter 11.

Selection of Clients

Which clients are best suited to short-term work? There are some clinicians who recommend a course of brief therapy for all clients or patients seeking help. If no improvement occurs, then a course of long-term treatment can be suggested. In our view, we do not yet have adequate or firm knowledge of diagnostic indicators that determine for whom brief services are definitely indicated. Some who seem to have complex problems are able to make large gains with which they are satisfied very quickly. Sometimes, for example, brief help with communication skills can vastly improve the quality of family relationships. Or, as was true in the Garcia brief treatment case (pages 415 and 416), a relatively small change in one part of a family with multiple problems can have significant effects on every family member, including those who do not participate in the treatment. On the other hand, there are clients whose requirements for help initially appear to be quite circumscribed, yet change comes slowly

or else they subsequently decide to explore additional issues.

Nevertheless, a broad range of criteria for selection of those believed to be best suited for brief therapy have been suggested by clinicians and researchers:[16] (1) those whose difficulties began recently and whose concerns relate primarily to current matters; (2) those who view or can be helped to view their problems as specific and concrete rather than diffuse and abstract; (3) those whose previous level of functioning has been satisfactory; (4) those who have a rapid ability to relate realistically, flexibly, and honestly to the therapist; (5) those whose relationships, past or present, demonstrate a capacity for depth and reciprocity; (6) those who are able to experience and express feelings fairly easily and freely; (7) those who have high initial motivation for change and will make the necessary sacrifices to achieve it; (8) those willing and able to participate *actively* in working on problems and tasks; (9) those who are "psychologically minded," who have the capacity for introspection and for emotional as well as intellectual insight; (10) those who are initially reluctant to accept any help at all but are reassured by the suggestion of time limits.

Those generally considered *unsuited* for brief therapy include people who have serious personality disorders or deficits and who both need and want extensive personality change or reconstruction in order to live more satisfying lives. Severe dependency, anxiety, antisocial or "acting out" behaviors usually cannot be reversed in a short time. Clients with deep-seated narcissistic, borderline, passive-dependent, masochistic, or self-destructive traits do not make basic changes quickly. Extreme rigidity and negativism do not easily yield to even the most skillful therapeutic intervention; change usually requires extended treatment. In short, individuals and families who seek help for problems deriving from *chronic, recalcitrant* personal and relationship problems often are not appreciably helped over the course of brief treatment.

William J. Reid, who has been studying and developing a special form of short-term treatment since the 1960s, has identified types of clients for whom his brief *task-centered* approach is usually *not* indicated: (1) those not interested in taking action to solve specific problems but who want an understanding person with whom to explore "existential" issues, such as concerns about life goals, identity, stresses and losses; (2) those who for various reasons are unwilling or unable to isolate precise problems and carry out the relevant tasks; (3) those involuntary clients mandated by others to seek treatment who wish no help and cannot or will not arrive at a problem definition.[17]

Characteristics and Benefits of Brief Therapies

Under what circumstances would we consider time-limited service the treatment of choice? What are some of its common characteristics? How does it compare with extended therapies? What special advantages may it have? Although there are no definitive answers, we offer comments here that relate to these often-posed questions:

1. When the client and worker define a problem or problems that are precise, that have specific solutions, time limits are often appropriate. In *task-centered* and many other types of brief treatment, client and worker together identify specific difficulties, goals and tasks and decide upon the duration of the treatment. The agreement they reach constitutes the contract for treatment. In general, the issues addressed and the tasks agreed upon are quite precise and concerned with the "here-and-now." Although there may be some some discussion of early history, dreams, transference, and so on, *extensive* exploration of these matters is less common than in some forms of long-term therapy. In order to maintain the limited foci, some practitioners conducting brief psychotherapy simply will not respond to material raised by the client that is not related to the agreed-upon problems and tasks. When successful, this exercise not only achieves the immediate goal but enhances confidence and competence. The expectation is that because the client's problem-solving capacities and autonomous functioning are strengthened through the treatment process, ability to handle difficulties that arise in the future will be maximized.

In this connection, it is important to add that therapy *of any length* is not a "cure" or an end-all. Rather, it provides a foundation for self-awareness and continued growth. Clients may become aware of self-defeating patterns and devise ways to avoid them. Ideally, during treatment clients adopt "tools" for coping and problem solving which they continue to use and build upon as new situations arise. Individuals, couples, and families are encouraged to continue to work independently even after treatment ends. Thus, particularly in brief treatment, immediate accomplishments may be modest, but over time, as Wolberg reports, continued application of methods learned during treatment will help bring about ongoing changes.[18]

We want to emphasize here that much of brief treatment involves pattern-dynamic and developmental reflection, as well as person-situation reflection and the other treatment procedures described in this text; the entire Hollis typology of techniques is applicable to treatments of all lengths. Short-term treatment definitely does not address only concrete matters, as many illustrations throughout this book demonstrate. In still another example, a woman concerned about her relationship with her seven-year-old daughter realized very quickly that she had transferred old anger at her now-deceased mother onto her child. On the basis of this developmental understanding, she reflected on possibilities for modifying her behavior; she set tasks for herself, implementing them between sessions, to deal differently with her daughter. In a few weeks the relationship between mother and daughter improved remarkably.

Most of us with clinical practice in family therapy have seen dramatic and rapid changes occur when one member of the family makes changes in attitude or behavior. For instance, one seemingly small initiative taken by a heretofore "distant" father sometimes has immediate and lasting repercussions on the relationships and inner lives of all family members. (See an example of this on pages 54 and 55.) When a mother gives up the "go-between" role, other changes in the family system often follow quickly, as in the Russo case (Chapter 16), even though treatment of this family was extended to deal with additional issues.

Much of brief treatment, then, requires careful and rapid assessment of psychodynamic, interpersonal, and systems issues. A positive therapeutic relationship is important to treatments of every length, even those that require only a few sessions. It should be apparent to the reader that the processes and goals of most brief therapy methods are totally compatible with the psychosocial approach presented in this text.

2. Sometimes clients are urged to remain in treatment even though they express satisfaction with their accomplishments. By recognizing the value of short-term contacts, caseworkers can avoid the implication that people choosing to terminate "prematurely" are leaving in an "impaired" or unfinished condition. Even a subtle message of this sort can be demoralizing to clients; it tends to dampen confidence in the progress achieved and may foster dependency. Mutuality is certainly better served when we support clients in what they have done rather than judge them for what they choose not to do.

3. When time limits are established—and workers and clients are focused on achievements, tasks, and goals—usually less drifting and less aimless exploration occur. Many clinicians believe that "regressive," open-ended treatment can be a disservice to clients who, prior to the development of the problem that

led them to seek help, were satisfied with their lives and functioning.

4. In long-term, unfocused treatment, clients may cease growing or may even regress, as they increasingly rest on a comfortable, dependent treatment relationship rather than seek meaningful companionship in their "real" lives. In James Mann's view,[19] open-ended therapy stimulates the unconscious longing for fusion, while time-limited treatment provides an opportunity for a maturational event, a leap toward autonomy, an opportunity to resolve difficulties surrounding separation and individuation.

5. As the "functionalists" asserted over a half century ago, time limits and the dynamic use of time as a variable in treatment indeed can help to mobilize clients' strengths and foster motivation; there can be greater incentive to work more quickly and productively than when the contact is totally open-ended. Workers, too, may concentrate their efforts more consistently when they know that time is not unlimited.

6. We mentioned earlier that when the problem at hand appears to be one that can be resolved quickly, clients who might otherwise resist treatment may agree to brief treatment. Concern about being trapped in an endless process may be allayed when a time frame for the contact is suggested.

7. The function of the agency or service and other factors beyond the control of workers and clients are highly relevant to the duration of treatment. Social workers attached to inpatient services in hospitals, crisis teams, residential treatment centers, prisons, or day care centers, for example, remain active with individuals and families only as long as these clients are directly involved with the service or facility. (Examples of short-term work with couples in settings in which contact is limited by agency function can be found on pages 413 to 415.) Similarly, when social work interns or staff members will soon be leaving their agencies or clients plan to move to another locale, the therapy is necessarily time-limited. If the contact has been a positive ex-

perience for clients and further treatment is wanted and needed, abbreviated treatment can be a springboard for future service elsewhere. When contacts are ended by circumstances rather than by clients' choices or requirements, it is important that social workers utilize special skills necessary for effecting successful referrals. Needless to say, it is essential to identify *appropriate resources* that are a good "fit" for the particular people involved. It is equally important that workers share with clients all the information they have about the resource. Clients' feelings and attitudes about the transfer must be discussed with sensitivity and in detail. Chapter 20 addresses termination issues.

8. We note an important additional benefit: because of its structure and often clearer focus, the planned brief treatment is especially suited to research, providing excellent opportunities for measuring treatment effectiveness and for studying and improving our methods of helping clients in need.

Further Comments on Brief and Extended Treatment

What are the limitations of brief treatment? We have outlined some client characteristics and problems that are usually not amenable to abbreviated therapies. To add to that, we believe that we do not yet have reliable guidelines to inform us exactly when time-limited treatment is preferable and when longer help is needed. Even though there is considerable evidence that short-term approaches can be extremely effective and well received by clients and in many cases result in greater gains for clients than open-ended therapies, research findings are nevertheless contradictory and inconclusive when it comes to comparing long-term and brief treatments.[20] In our experience, furthermore, benefits often accrue in unlimited treatment that are not measured by research methods, particularly those that do not solicit the reactions of clients themselves.

It is, as we have said, usually not possible to predict at the beginning of treatment exactly how many sessions, weeks, months, or even years will be necessary to achieve particular clients' goals. In view of this it seems reasonable, when a limit is set, to keep the option open for reconsideration in case, as the work proceeds, further treatment seems desirable. Some studies have demonstrated that as many as *60 percent of brief-treatment patients return for additional therapy.*[21] When clients aspire to extensive understanding of self and of relationships in order to bring about changes in feelings, attitudes, and ways of living, therapy often takes a long time or requires a series of contacts.

Although there may be some demonstrable advantages to non-negotiable time contracts, as Mann and a few others claim, we believe that the benefits rarely justify the practice. Currently, most proponents of time-limited therapies assert that contracts should be open to renegotiation when the client and the worker agree on further work to be done.

Without a doubt, brief treatment approaches have alerted us to the need to maintain focus, to avoid drifting, and to guard against regressive client dependency. We have also become acutely aware that when time limits are too flexible, reactions that naturally accompany termination may be evaded. However, workers aware of these hazards can pay attention to conducting well-focused sessions; they can indicate to clients their reluctance to continue along the same path if, over a significant period of time, no movement is occurring. By the same token, the consolidation of gains made, the expression of joys, sorrows, and disappointments that are part of many terminations need not be lost if, when treatment goals have been reached, there is a planned process for evaluation and ending.

When psychosocial casework is extended, it involves either contact over a lengthy period or intermittent contact of varying duration and intensity, sometimes over years. The latter requires *continuity* of understanding and of the treatment process, even though there may be long or short intervals in which contact is not needed. It is often well to prepare the client for the possibility of return and, when feasible, for the client to be seen each time by the same worker. Work with children, the elderly, the handicapped, deinstitutionalized mental patients, adolescent mothers, and many others often benefit from the "open door" approach. When people's circumstances or aspirations change, or old dysfunctional coping patterns revive under stress, or unanticipated catastrophic events occur, it is humane and gratifying to be available to help returning clients regain equilibrium or advance to new levels of functioning.

As important as brief treatment methods and research have been to the advancement of casework practice, we do not want to overestimate the usefulness of the short-term approach, as administrators are sometimes tempted to do, as a way of solving fiscal or other problems. There is no way to measure the value of personal development in quantitative terms. One can waste as much money, time, and human potential by giving too little service as by encouraging inappropriate long-term treatment. Mrs. Zimmer (Chapter 3) provides a case in point: we are convinced that little or nothing would have been accomplished by her within a three- or six-month time limit. Although cost to the agency is a valid consideration, it should not be an overriding one. Furthermore, if this client had been forced to terminate, she might have mustered the motivation to start all over again elsewhere, but we believe the first period of treatment probably would have been a virtual waste; she simply would not have been able to sustain the benefits of the rudimentary gains achieved in a few months.

Along similar lines, we fervently caution against stereotyping "lower-class" clients who are presumed to prefer and benefit more from time-limited therapies than from open-ended treatment.[22] Even if this is *statistically* accurate,

if we act arbitrarily and make policy decisions on the basis of this information, services will be withheld from those who do not fit the generalization. Our many years of practice and those of our colleagues convince us that *many* lower-socioeconomic-class clients make *excellent* use of long-term treatment. We urge that they not be denied such opportunities for reasons of cost or because of biases promoted by statistics!

We conclude this chapter on crisis and other brief treatments with a few additional remarks. The use of brief treatment is expanding; it is employed in more and more settings with an increasing number of clients and presenting problems. It is our opinion that some special training is required for the successful practice of time-limited therapy. Like conjoint treatment, brief therapy rests comfortably on the psychosocial theoretical base, but additional knowledge and skill are required to develop expertise in this demanding and complex modality. Active engagement and a direct approach, rapid assessment and intervention, task assignment and implementation all require a pace, focus, and knowledge that are not always seen as essential to open-ended treatment. Yet we firmly believe these special skills are useful to *all* clinicians, first, because, as we have said, until treatment is in progress, we usually cannot be sure how long it will take, and, second, because most treatments can benefit from these methods at various junctures: long-term clients may face catastrophic events; task-centered activities can help *any* client translate understanding into action. We therefore strongly recommend that as a matter of course clinical social workers read about various brief treatments and attend courses, workshops, or seminars on time-limited approaches and techniques. Third, in the opinion of many researchers and clinicians, brief treatment is the preferred modality in many, if not most, cases and situations.

Of his carefully researched time-limited, task-centered social work model, Reid writes: "Although there are limits on its range of application, it is offered as a basic service for the majority of clients dealt with by clinical social workers. The core methods of the approach, notably activities designed to help clients plan and implement problem solving tasks, can be used within most practice frameworks."[23] Although we believe that there are many situations in which brief methods are not sufficient, we thoroughly endorse the notion that all clinicians should be solidly grounded in the concepts and practices that have emerged from over forty years of studying short-term approaches.

NOTES

1. See Elizabeth C. Lemon, "Planned Brief Treatment," in Aaron Rosenblatt et al., eds., *Clinical Social Work* (San Francisco: Jossey-Bass, 1983), pp. 401–419; and Ruth E. Smalley, "The Functional Approach to Casework Process," in Robert E. Roberts and Robert E. Nee, eds., *Theories of Social Casework* (Chicago: University of Chicago, 1970), pp. 79–128, for discussions of the functional approach to time limits and time phases.

Readers are also referred to John H. Presley, "The Clinical Dropout: A View from the Client's Perspective," *Social Casework*, 68 (December 1987), 603–608; and Ronald W. Toseland, "Treatment Discontinuance," *Social Casework*, 68 (April 1987), 195–204. Both articles report on studies that find that many discontinuing clients, even those who drop out after one session, report benefit from the treatment.

2. A great deal has been written on crisis theory and practice by and for social workers. Special mention is made of the early compilation that still is in wide use and provides very valuable reading: Howard J. Parad, ed., *Crisis Intervention: Selected Readings* (New York: Family Service Association of America, 1965). See also Gerald Caplan, *Principles of Preventive Psychiatry* (New York: Basic Books, 1964); Caplan was also among the major developers of crisis theory, which was based, in part, on his studies at the Family Guidance Center, Harvard School of Public Health, in 1954.

For other readings, see also Margaret Ball, "Issues of Violence in Family Casework," *Social Casework*, 58 (January 1977), 3–12; Samuel L. Dixon and Roberta

G. Sands, "Identity and the Experience of Crisis," *Social Casework*, 64 (April 1983), 223–230; Paul and Lois Glasser, eds., *Families in Crisis* (New York: Harper & Row, 1970); Naomi Golan, "Crisis Theory," in Francis J. Turner, ed., *Social Work Treatment*, 3d ed. (New York: Free Press, 1986), pp. 296–340; Naomi Golan, *Treatment in Crisis Situations* (New York: Free Press, 1978); Judith H. Goldring, *Quick Response Therapy: A Time-Limited Treatment Approach* (New York: Human Services Press, 1980); David L. Hoffman and Mary L. Remmel, "Uncovering the Precipitant in Crisis Intervention," *Social Casework*, 56 (May 1975), 259–269; Charlotte Kirschner, "The Aging Family in Crisis: A Problem in Living," *Social Casework*, 60 (April 1979), 209–216; Diego J. Lopez and George S. Getzel, "Helping Gay AIDS Patients," *Social Casework*, 65 (September 1984), 387–394; Danuta Mostwin, "Social Work Interventions with Families in Crisis of Change," *Social Thought*, 2 (Winter 1976); Jeanette Oppenheimer, "Use of Crisis Intervention in Case Work with the Cancer Patient and His Family," *Social Work*, 12 (April 1967), 44–52; Lydia Rapoport, "Crisis Intervention as a Mode of Brief Treatment," in Roberts and Nee, *Theories of Social Casework*, 265–311; Gwen Schwartz-Borden, "Grief Work: Prevention and Intervention," *Social Casework*, 67 (October 1986), 499–505; Larry L. Smith, "A Review of Crisis Intervention Theory," *Social Casework*, 59 (July 1978), 396–405; Larry Smith, "Crisis Intervention in Practice," *Social Casework*, 60 (February 1979), 81–89; and Reva S. Wiseman, "Crisis Theory and the Process of Divorce," *Social Casework*, 56 (April 1975), 205–212.

3. Erich Lindemann, "Symptomatology and Management of Acute Grief," in Parad, *Crisis Intervention*, 7–21.

4. See Lemon, "Planned Brief Treatment," pp. 404–406, for discussions about definitions of crisis; we have adopted the definition offered by C. Murray Parkes, quoted by Lemon.

5. Rapoport, "Crisis Intervention as a Mode of Brief Treatment," and Golan, "Crisis Theory."

6. Kayla F. Bernhein and Anthony F. Lehman, *Working with Families of the Mentally Ill* (New York: W. W. Norton, 1985).

7. See, for example: Anne Bergman, "Emergency Room: A Role for Social Workers," *Health and Social*

Work, 1 (February 1976), 32–44; and Gerald W. Grumet and David L. Tractman, "Psychiatric Social Workers in the Emergency Department," *Health and Social Work*, 1 (August 1976), 114–131. See also relevant articles in Gerald F. Jacobson, ed., *Crisis Intervention in the 1980s* (San Francisco: Jossey-Bass, 1980). Refer also to Chapter 8, note 2.

8. Elizabeth Kubler-Ross, *On Death and Dying* (New York: Macmillan, 1969).

See Golan, "Crisis Theory," for a discussion of the broad range of events and a rich bibliography on transitional events and processes that are now included under the rubric of "crisis." See also, Naomi Golan, "Intervention at Times of Transition: Sources and Forms of Help," *Social Casework*, 61 (May 1980), 259–266, for a very useful discussion of treatment of "normal people with normal troubles."

9. See Rosemary Creed Lukton's excellent and highly recommended article, "Myths and Realities of Crisis Intervention," *Social Casework*, 63 (May 1982), 276–285.

10. *New York Times*, November 26, 1985, p. C 1. See also *New York Times*, August 8, 1989, p. C1: "Research suggests normal range of reactions to grave loss is far wider than thought."

11. Ibid., pp. C 1 and C 9.

12. Rapoport, "Crisis Intervention as a Mode of Brief Treatment," pp. 297–298.

13. There is a wealth of literature on brief and time-limited treatments. See, for example, Simon H. Budman and Alan S. Gurman, *Theory and Practice of Brief Therapy* (New York: Guilford, 1988); Norman Epstein, "Techniques of Brief Therapy with Children and Parents," *Social Casework*, 57 (May 1976), 317–324; Arlene S. Fontane, "Using Family of Origin Material in Short-Term Marriage Counseling," *Social Casework*, 60 (November 1979), 529–537; Raymond Fox, "Short-Term, Goal-Oriented Family Therapy," *Social Casework*, 68 (October 1987), 494–499; James Mann, *Time-Limited Psychotherapy* (Cambridge, Mass.: Harvard University Press, 1973); Jennie Sage Norman, "Short-Term Treatment with the Adolescent Client," *Social Casework*, 61 (February 1980), 74–82; Genevieve B. Oxley, "Short-Term Therapy with Student Couples," *Social Casework*, 54 (April 1973), 216–223; William J. Reid and Ann W. Shyne, *Brief*

and Extended Casework (New York: Columbia University Press, 1969); Peter E. Sifneos, *Short-Term Dynamic Psychotherapy: Evaluation and Technique*, 2d ed. (New York: Plenum, 1987); Ram Naresh Singh, "Brief Interviews: Approaches, Techniques, and Effectiveness," *Social Casework*, 63 (December 1982), 599–606; Leonard Small, *The Briefer Psychotherapies* (New York: Brunner/Mazel, 1971); Lewis Wolberg, *Handbook of Short-Term Psychotherapy* (New York: Thieme-Stratton, 1980).

In the 1960s William J. Reid and Laura Epstein combined the brief treatment approach with techniques of task planning and implementation. See their books: *Task-Centered Casework* (New York: Columbia University Press, 1972), and *Task-Centered Practice* (New York: Columbia University Press, 1977). See also William J. Reid, *The Task-Centered System* (New York: Columbia University Press, 1978). For a useful summary of the task-centered approach, see William J. Reid, "Task-Centered Social Work," in Turner, *Social Work Treatment*, pp. 267–295.

See also Martin J. Blizinsky and William J. Reid, "Problem Focus and Change in a Brief Treatment Model," *Social Work*, 25 (March 1980), 89–93; Elin Cormican, "Task-Centered Model for Work with the Aged," *Social Casework*, 58 (October 1977), 490–494; Anne E. Fortune, "Communication in Task-Centered Treatment," *Social Work*, 24 (September 1979), 317–323; Dean H. Hepworth, "Early Removal of Resistance in Task-Centered Casework," *Social Work*, 24 (July 1979), 317–323; Jo Ann Larsen and Craig T. Mitchell, "Task-Centered, Strength-Oriented Group Work with Delinquents," *Social Casework*, 61 (March 1980), 154–163; and William J. Reid, "A Test of a Task-Centered Approach," *Social Work*, 20 (January 1975), 3–9.

14. See Mary P. Koss and James N. Butcher, "Research on Brief Psychotherapy," in Sol L. Garfield and Allen E. Bergin, eds., *Handbook of Psychotherapy and Behavior Change* (New York: John Wiley, 1986), 627–670; David Malan, *The Frontier of Brief Psychotherapy* (New York: Plenum, 1976); and Reid and Shyne, *Brief and Extended Casework*.

15. Koss and Butcher, "Research on Brief Psychotherapy," p. 629.

16. See Koss and Butcher, "Research on Brief Psychotherapy"; Lemon, "Planned Brief Treatment";

Reid, "Task-Centered Social Work," in Francis J. Turner, *Social Work Treatment: Interlocking Theoretical Approaches* (New York: The Free Press, 1986), pp. 267–295; Wolberg, *Handbook of Short-term Psychotherapy*.

17. Reid, "Task-Centered Social Work," p. 289.

18. Wolberg, *Handbook of Short-Term Psychotherapy*, pp. 47, 243–244.

19. James Mann, *Time-Limited Psychotherapy*.

20. Koss and Butcher, "Research on Brief Psychotherapy," especially pp. 656–663; the authors make the following important point (p. 657): "Studies that employ rating scales that purport to reflect dynamic change such as personality reorganization or structural changes as opposed to overt behavioral change are more likely to favor long-term psychotherapy than studies where outcome measures focus on concrete behavior change."

Yet Libbie G. Parad, in her excellent and highly recommended paper "Short-Term Treatment: An Overview of Historical Trends, Issues and Potentials," *Smith College Studies in Social Work,* 41 (February 1971), 119–146, discussed (p. 144) effectiveness studies and concluded almost two decades ago: "In those studies which have compared the outcome of *planned* short-term treatment with open-ended treatment, the short-term cases have shown a significantly greater rate of improvement. This holds true even in those studies in which the therapists involved did not have a special commitment to short-term treatment." Libby Parad is also convincing when she writes (p. 120): "The evidence would seem to indicate that in reality the bulk of casework practice has always been short-term."

For an opinion about indications and contraindications for task-centered treatment, see Joel S. Kantor, "Reevaluation of Task-Centered Social Work Practice," *Clinical Social Work Journal,* 11 (Fall 1983), 228–244. See also Richard O'Connor and William J. Reid, "Dissatisfaction with Brief Treatment," *Social Service Review,* 60 (December 1986), 526–537, for a discussion of research indicating that in spite of generally optimistic reports on brief treatment outcomes, there are substantial numbers of clients in many studies of the subject who express some form of dissatisfaction with time-limited treatment.

21. Koss and Butcher, "Research on Brief Psychotherapy," p. 657.

22. Ibid., p. 645.

23. Reid, "Task-Centered Social Work," p. 290.

CHAPTER 20

Termination

It may seem paradoxical that successful treatment leads to separation from the very relationship that nurtured the progress. Yet, as we well know, when children and adolescents move from one developmental phase to another, they must forego certain aspects of dependency to achieve greater growth and autonomy. In therapy, too, where a feeling of childlike dependency, among many other feelings, is often present, the attainment of mutually agreed upon goals is often, sometimes painfully, "rewarded" by loss. For many clients, the loss is profound because treatment has provided an extraordinary opportunity to be accepted, listened to, and encouraged to grow. Grief and mourning, expressed in stages that include denial, anger, sadness, and acceptance, can be at the core of the termination process for some (but certainly not all) clients. There can be additional responses, such as anxiety stemming from a conflict between dependence and independence, excitement about accomplishments and goals that have been achieved, optimism about the future, and, sometimes, disappointment that for one reason or another expectations of treatment could not be realized. Termination is a time to consider the gains that have been made and ways these can be consolidated and built upon after treatment is over. An examination of the therapeutic alliance can lead clients to reflect on ways they handle other important relationships. When relevant, transfer to another worker or agency may be part and parcel of the ending phase. For the benefit of workers and agencies, as well as for clients, feedback about the treatment experience is essential.

In both brief and long-term contacts, the way the termination process is managed can have significant implications for clients, sometimes long after treatment ends. The worker's role can be critical. This chapter will discuss some basic principles, gleaned from practical experience and the literature, involved in an *individualized* approach to termination.

SPECIAL FEATURES OF TERMINATION

Although careful handling of the *beginning* phase of treatment can be extremely important, the process of *ending* a therapeutic relationship often requires even greater skill, sensitivity, and self-awareness.[1] This is true for many reasons. *First,* when clients initially come to see a worker, they are usually feeling pressured by the difficulties that led them to seek help, and, often with very little encouragement, they become involved in the treatment process if they feel the worker is interested and accepting. During termination, however, even when complex issues are involved, there may be more reluctance to address them because they can be difficult, sometimes painful, and more easily denied or shelved than those that surround presenting problems. Thus, the worker may need far more persistence to promote a therapeutic climate that fosters openness and honesty between client and worker.

Second, especially when treatment is going well, there may be a minimum of discussion about the feelings *between* clients and worker. In many cases of individual and conjoint therapy, much more emphasis is placed on internal concerns or family relationships or on matters outside the interviewing room. Termination, on the other hand, generally requires some acknowledgment by clients of the meaning of the therapy and of their feelings toward the worker.

Third, many practitioners agree that when termination is incorrectly or carelessly handled, gains made in treatment may be interfered with or even totally reversed. Growth that is expected to continue after treatment is over may be stunted. If the ending is experienced negatively by clients, even if earlier phases seemed productive, there may be reluctance to become involved with social or therapeutic services again should the need arise. Because time is short, mistakes made by the worker at the conclusion of the contact are less likely to be corrected than at any other point. *Fourth*, as we shall discuss further, termination is complicated by special factors, including whether the termination is planned or unplanned, who initiates the idea to end, and whether it is mutually accepted.

Finally, an issue we shall also expand upon is that terminations can often be very difficult for the worker. Ambivalence is more likely to be present around endings than beginnings. The worker's feelings toward the client and the treatment experience, the worker's general way of handling separations, the worker's current emotional and relational situation can all profoundly influence the course termination takes. Obviously, for workers as well as clients, experiences with previous losses may critically affect how separation is handled. Difficulties involving intimacy also may inhibit the worker's awareness of feelings aroused during the final phase of treatment.

ASSESSMENT OF CLIENT REACTIONS TO TERMINATION

Ideally, in every case, there will be time to address relevant issues around the ending of treatment, time to say a good-bye that is appropriate to the client's feelings about the experience and the relationship with the worker. In order to do so, one has to assess, with the client's active help, the factors that will influence the course the termination will take.

Intensity of the Relationship

The intensity of the treatment relationship, or the emotional investment clients have in their workers, is a critical factor. When there is strong involvement, there is often, but not always, an abundance of positive feelings. Ambivalent relationships can also stimulate powerful emotions. Generally speaking, the more intense the involvement of clients with their workers, the more acute the response to ending will be.* In

---

* Strong reactions can also occur when clients are offhandedly dismissed because they have come to the wrong agency. This is because often clients have had to muster considerable courage to ask for help and can be humiliated or defeated by uncaring responses of receptionists or workers. Elsewhere we have dealt with the importance of skill in making referrals.

any event, clients have very diverse reactions to the treatment relationship, ranging from profound attachment to little awareness of feelings toward the worker, with many falling somewhere between the extremes. These reactions to the worker significantly affect termination experiences.

The differences in the worker-client relationships are based on several factors, including the unique aspects of a therapeutic contact, cultural and personality factors, transference reactions, and the meaning the treatment has had for the clients.

For some clients, the relationship with the worker is the first one ever experienced in which full attention is paid, unconditional acceptance is given, and little is asked in return. It is easy to understand, then, how deeply tied to their workers they sometimes feel and how reluctant they can be to give them up. On the other hand, there are clients who have or have had close, nurturing relationships and therefore are not so profoundly touched by or dependent upon the worker-client connection. On the basis of personal style or cultural tradition, some clients are effusive and others maintain a formal reserve from beginning to end, even in long-term treatment; many, of course, fall in a middle range between the two. Clients who function relatively autonomously often do not feel shaken by termination. Dick and Susan Jones (Chapter 3), for example, clearly respected and appreciated the worker and her help, but they had turned to her primarily as an expert in marital relationships and expected little nurturance beyond that; in their case, therefore, separation was not laced with complex reactions. In contrast, for Mrs. Zimmer (also Chapter 3), whose capacity for autonomous functioning and for object relations was unevenly developed, treatment and—to some degree—termination were tempestuous, fraught with separation-individuation conflicts; alternately she clung to and angrily lashed out at the worker, blaming her for her distress. Clients with prominent

schizoid features, who generally prefer to be "loners" and seem to be indifferent to personal relationships, if they do have contact with caseworkers, are not likely to have significant emotional reactions during treatment or at termination. The degree to which clients have mastered separation-individuation crises and the manner in which they have characteristically coped with conflicts about dependence and independence can influence responses to termination for better or worse.

The nature and depth of transference involvement during the treatment process can significantly influence the separation process. Dependent therapeutic attachments often resemble early relationships, or longed-for relationships, with parents; thus, the positive and negative aspects of these attachments can arouse sadness and anxiety when it is time to leave the relationship that fostered growth during the treatment. *Equally important*, of course, are the exhilaration and pride that usually accompany the realization that one has achieved one's goals, has become independent, and can now carry on without the worker's help. It is Palumbo's view that when treatment has been successful for clients with personality disorders, grief and mourning need not be present during the termination phase because the client has internalized the functions of the therapist and therefore no longer requires the fused relationship that was present during earlier phases.[2] It is our experience, too, that by the time such treatments end, the extreme intensity of the attachment has often diminished considerably. However, we also agree with Webb, who writes: "The fact that one is happy and exhilarated about the prospect of being on one's own does not negate the possibility of some anxiety about the prospect, nor the feeling of some loss connected to missing the person who helped make the independence possible."[3]

Other kinds of transference responses to the worker may also shift during the final phase. For example, those clients who incorrectly tend to feel that people either want to cling to or get rid of them may use termination with the worker as an opportunity to correct these distorted expectations. Clients who have customarily related to others either deferentially or arrogantly may become able to say good-bye to the worker as one equal to another. People who sought help during treatment to reduce self-centeredness may take the opportunity of termination to focus on reciprocity in the therapeutic relationship.

Individuals and families who have shared catastrophic or other extraordinary emotional experiences with their workers are far more likely to be invested in the treatment relationship than others whose lives were less turbulent during therapy. Just as people may feel more grateful to surgeons who have saved their lives than to allergists who give weekly shots, so even brief casework treatment during an acute crisis may lead to stronger client-worker attachment than some less eventful long-term treatments.

In our experience and that of others,[4] therapeutic relationships are often more profound in intensive individual therapy than in equally intensive conjoint treatment. Complex dependency and transference relationships are more likely to occur in the exclusivity of one-to-one treatment. As we have pointed out in the chapters on family and couple treatments, the focus of these therapies is usually less on the worker-client interaction and more on the relationships among family members. It stands to reason, then, that often there will be less mourning by couples and families when they terminate than when individuals leave treatment. Of course, each member will have his or her particular responses to ending therapy. Nevertheless, when couples and families do experience a deep sense of loss, this can be shared among themselves; clients in individual therapy may find it harder to find others who can understand what the meaning of the client-worker relationship has been.

Client Satisfaction

The degree of *satisfaction* or *dissatisfaction* with the worker and with the treatment can significantly influence termination. Obviously, if clients feel the worker was either incompetent or unable to offer the right kind of help, leaving that worker will usually be accompanied by few positive feelings. More likely, there will be anger or indifference; some clients may get some relief by taking the initiative to terminate and seek help elsewhere.

It is not uncommon for people to have exaggerated expectations of what the treatment or the worker can provide; if during the period of treatment there has been no resolution of these unrealistic hopes, disappointment is bound to emerge at termination time. Similarly, there are clients who desperately want to change but because of lack of capacity or opportunity simply cannot; in these cases, too, there are bound to be regrets.

Experiences with Loss

Previous experiences with loss and characteristic ways of handling it can have enormous influence on client responses to termination. Some people confront loss of an important relationship by distancing from it, by maintaining a "stiff upper lip," or by hastily expressing farewells. Others become overwhelmed by sorrow or fear and want to prolong the contact. Many of our clients have been traumatized by early separations or emotional abandonment, and reactions to termination often mirror responses to previous losses.

Sanville writes:

Most of our patients would probably subscribe to the old French proverb, "to part is to die a little," for they often experience separation or impending aloneness as threatening psychic extinction, if not as stirring up actual suicidal impulses. These are frequently persons who have had too early and too often to face the trauma both of miserable relationships and of unchosen breakings up. Most tend to react by a desperate search for new ties, and their very urgency makes for a tendency to repeat past patterns. Others resolve, "Never again" and rigidly avoid commitments. Neither is left with a sense of free choice.[5]

These reactions can emerge at the end of treatment and, when dealt with at the time, can provide important opportunities for growth.

Current Life Circumstances

Current issues in clients' lives and situations can shape emotional reactions to termination. If there are no extraordinary external pressures and clients feel competent and confident about handling themselves and their circumstances, termination may feel less problematic than when they are in a state of distress. But when clients are in the midst of change or turmoil or problems have not been comfortably resolved, extremely painful feelings may emerge when the conclusion of treatment draws near.

Social Supports

The state of clients' *social network* is often very relevant to how termination is experienced. Because of personality idiosyncrasies, illness, advanced age, or various situational factors, some people have meager social connections. When relationships are impoverished and supports are sparse, the ending process with the worker may be keenly felt.

Conditions of Endings

Client reactions can be affected by whether termination is *planned* or *unplanned*, by *who* terminates, and by whether termination is *permanent* or an *"open-door"* arrangement is possible. It can happen that contacts are precipitously interrupted because clients withdraw and refuse to return. Extraordinary circumstances related to worker or client occasionally force an abrupt ending to a treatment relationship. In these cases of unplanned discontinuance, there is no opportunity to review the treatment process or to resolve feelings—such as anger, abandonment, or sorrow—that are stirred by termination.

When clients decide, for whatever reason, that they want to leave treatment, they can at least feel the satisfaction that accompanies the making of a choice. Even if the decision to leave is based on dissatisfaction with the treatment, or from the worker's viewpoint is for the "wrong reasons," it is nevertheless a self-directed step; although possibly reactive, on some level it is positive. On the other hand, when the worker is leaving the service or declares that there is no purpose in continuing or agency policy requires that treatment be discontinued, such endings will have very different meanings to clients. There may be feelings of rejection and unworthiness; old losses may be reawakened. When the decision to discontinue is mutually accepted, it is much more likely to be an organic choice, and feelings around termination—whatever they are—have a better chance of resolution. In every case, effort should be made to take whatever time is required to discuss the treatment experience and the meanings of ending it.

Many clinicians, including the authors, endorse an "open-door" policy, which allows clients to return to see their worker on an "as-needed" basis, when possible. Some clients do their best work in spurts. Under these conditions, of course, termination experiences are tempered by the realization that "good-bye" can actually mean "until we meet again." But, when students or other workers leave the agency, or the clients are no longer eligible for the service where the worker is employed, feelings around the loss of the relationship cannot be cushioned by thoughts of future meetings.

Of course, *how the worker handles the termination* strongly influences clients' experiences of the separation. We will soon be discussing the social worker's role and tasks.

TERMINATION AND THE TREATMENT PROCESS

The manner in which worker and client join together to conclude treatment frequently determines the degree to which progress sustains and continues. In fact, *termination itself—which sometimes can be compared to a crisis—is often a period of rapid growth.* An extra leap toward self-reliance may occur when the process of ending is set in motion. Important features of successful termination include the following.

Anticipatory Preparation by the Worker

Whether treatment is time-limited by contract or not, the worker is often able to think ahead to the final phase of treatment. With far greater accuracy than when preparing for the initial interview, client needs and reactions to termination can be anticipated. With the benefit of first-hand experience with clients, the worker can bring knowledge, sensitivity, and tentative planning to the work that will be required to make the ending as meaningful as possible.

Eliciting and Dealing with Clients' Feelings

Just as there are no definite "normative" emotional responses or ordered tasks associated with particular crises, so each individual and family has its own unique way of handling reactions to termination. As indicated above, the range of responses is very broad indeed. The subphases of the final lap of treatment can vary greatly in emphasis. Shock, denial, anger, sadness, fear of aloneness, feelings of betrayal, euphoria, disappointment, relief that a painful or inconvenient process is over, loving and/or hateful feelings toward the therapist, and gratitude for help given can all be included in the mix, in every possible sequence. Sometimes, even when treatment has been extremely successful, there will be moments of regression and discouragement, doubts that progress really occurred. Because of fear, perfectionism, or desire to forestall the ending of a meaningful relationship, clients may introduce new issues on which they want to work.[6] It is the worker's role to be available to and accepting of whatever combination of feelings the client expresses, at the same time maintaining a realistic view of clients' accomplishments and capacity for self-direction and ongoing growth.

It is necessary to be aware of two opposite risks when helping a client handle feelings about termination. The first is the risk of exaggerating or *overestimating* the importance the treatment or the relationship has had for the client. When a worker presses for positive feelings that are not there or are not expressed in the way the worker wants to hear them, clients may think the worker is self-involved or wants attention or praise; they may conclude that the worker does not want them to leave and thus they may feel guilty for doing so. Some people, as we have said, for various reasons do not become very attached to their workers even when they are very pleased with the outcome of treatment. Although there are clients who are effusive in their gratitude and shower the worker with affection or even with farewell gifts, others express equal appreciation by shaking hands and saying, "Thank you for your help." We want to be careful not to induce feelings of guilt or inadequacy by attempting to elicit nonexistent or inaccessible reactions. It follows that for some clients, termination can be a fairly brief, matter-of-fact process; for others it requires many sessions to resolve deep, complex, or ambivalent feelings.

On the other side of the coin, it is equally important not to *underestimate* the significance of the therapeutic experience to clients. Because of modesty, embarrassment, boredom, or unrealistic hopes for client change, workers may diminish client expressions of satisfaction, gratitude, warmth, and so on. Under these circumstances, clients may leave feeling misunderstood or disappointed in the worker's unwillingness to join in the sharing of good feelings. It may seem to clients that the worker thinks not enough was accomplished, that they will not make it on their own, or that their positive feelings are somehow unacceptable.

Evaluation of Progress

In order to consolidate the gains made by clients and to prepare for ongoing growth, it is important that during the final phase clients and worker review changes and achievements together. Very often "tools" that have been acquired have proved helpful to clients in managing themselves, their relationships, and other aspects of the world around them. By going over what they have learned, they are likely to gain confidence that they can confront problems that will inevitably arise when treatment is over and the worker is no longer there as "coach" or "cheerleader." They may be helped to locate others, such as family members and friends, with whom they can talk things over in the future. In conjoint therapy, clients are often enabled to turn to family members for support and advice. "The goal of treatment," wrote the wise Gordon Hamilton forty years ago, "is always to help the person return as soon as possible to natural channels of activity with strengthened relationships."[7] Communication skills, methods for handling and expressing emotion, constructive approaches to self assertion, ability to negotiate social service systems and advocate for oneself, plans for future tasks: all are among many concrete matters that people often take away from treatment. The more explicitly they are recapitulated, the more likely they will hold up over time. Very often the process of evaluation arouses sadness about giving up old ways of thinking, feeling, and being and regrets about precious time lost in the past, as well as pride in progress made.

Opportunities for Growth

We have already indicated that for some clients, particularly those with various kinds of developmental deficits, termination can provide the context for a maturational event. In spite of sadness about separation or fear of independence, often accompanied by feelings of abandonment or inadequacy, a positive parting from the worker can support strengths and autonomy. The worker's confidence and encouragement, with "no strings attached," can provide a corrective experience that helps to liberate clients who have felt that family "strings" tied them down.

During termination, clients who have difficulty handling contradictory emotions, such as some of those who have personality disorders, can sometimes achieve better integration of positive and negative feelings. Growth occurs when there is a deep recognition that extreme variations in feelings can coexist. Similarly, the "emotional memory," the awareness that one will be all right even when a caring person is not right there, is reinforced. Clients can be helped to recognize that the progress and the functions of the worker that were "borrowed"—including self-esteem and self-direction—are now internalized and can be taken with them when they go.

Very often when people have had painful or unfinished losses, the shared process of termination between client and worker can become an extraordinary opportunity for resolution and release. When clients are mourning the end of treatment and the loss of the relationship with the worker, termination sometimes stimulates a crisislike state. Emotions from past losses often spontaneously rise to the surface and are linked to the current situation. When enough time is allowed to handle reactions to termination, the momentum of emotion may even reach old injuries that were never before explored.

When Indicated, Referral or Transfer

Generally, discussions during the final phase include consideration of future help, should it be needed. Even when there are no specific plans for transfer or referral, a worker often asks clients, "Do you think you would seek help again if the need arises?" If the worker is in a special setting, such as a crisis or hospital in-patient service, it is important that clients know what resources are available to them should they wish to seek additional treatment. When clients request an immediate referral it is important, as we have said in other chapters, that the worker be sure that the clients will be accepted. More often than not, it is best for the worker to contact the other agency and prepare the way for an easy reception.

When a worker is leaving a service and clients want to continue treatment with someone else at the agency, it is the worker's responsibility to make the transfer as smooth as possible. Ideally, toward the end of therapy with the original worker, the new therapist can be introduced and join one session or part of a session (not the last one, of course, which should be reserved for worker and clients to say their final good-byes). Sometimes, because of the pressure of time or the worker's own ambivalence about leaving, transfers are too quickly or casually managed. Some resigning workers "close down" emotionally because their eyes have already turned to new beginnings. The experience of ending may feel like rejection to clients. Particularly when it is the worker's recommendation that clients continue with someone else, they often need time to consider the transfer; feelings about being shuttled off can be especially painful for those who have had multiple separations.[8]

The departing worker's possessive feelings about clients may also interfere with a successful transfer. Inadvertently, a worker may sabotage the shift to a new therapist or another agency by sending a covert message such as

"No one will be as caring (skillful, helpful) as I." Needless to say, if clients feel either rejected or only conditionally released from the treatment relationship, they are likely to feel betrayed, misunderstood, unfinished, or confused. They may discredit the worker or doubt the merit of the work that was done; gains may be diminished or reversed.

Feedback from Clients

Information obtained from clients' assessments of their experiences in treatment can be invaluable to the worker's ever-accumulating body of knowledge of treatment techniques and approaches. Clients help us to understand how these vary according to modality, client situations and needs, family and socioeconomic backgrounds, and so on. Even though every individual and family is different, common principles do emerge. We can learn from clients what was helpful and what was not, and under what circumstances. Because clients have been in a uniquely intimate relationship with their workers, they sometimes offer insights about treatment approaches or personal styles that supervisors do not see. If, for example, one hears from several clients that they frequently felt criticized or that the worker seemed uninterested, it is incumbent on the worker to consider this information carefully, rather than defensively attributing it only to client transference or personality problems.

Often clients say most, either positively or negatively, about their treatment experience during the termination phase. It is a rare worker who, over years of experience, is not occasionally taken by surprise when a seemingly formal, reserved, or self-absorbed client at the end says something like "Your kindness and confidence in me are what saw me through this year." By the same token, negative comments or complaints that were withheld for various reasons during treatment may be brought to the surface during the feedback process: "It always annoyed me that you answered the telephone during our sessions." Or, "There were times when you really hurt my feelings, like when you said...." What we learn from one set of clients will aid us in being even more helpful to the next.

Although it is obviously best for clients to be forthcoming and direct about their positive and negative experiences, it is equally essential to the worker and to the agency that communications from clients be elicited and taken seriously. We agree with Germain and Gitterman: "Creating the climate that will permit the client to be candid in his assessment of the service is a measure of worker skill."[9]

The Final Ending: The Worker Speaks

While clients are going through evolving feelings about ending treatment, obviously the worker stays closely attuned to their requirements for response. One cannot be stony silent and expect that clients will take all of the risks of revealing emotions associated with the therapeutic relationship without any reciprocity from the worker. Yet a delicate balance must be maintained. Workers must carefully time and monitor the expression of their own feelings about the meaning of the treatment experience, the relationship, and the upcoming separation. Positive feelings expressed prematurely, for example, may tend to inhibit clients' negative reactions. In some cases, for reasons that relate to the worker's personality and past or present circumstances, the ending may be more emotionally moving to the worker than to the client. In these cases, if the worker shares the strong feelings, clients may feel a demand is being made on them that they cannot satisfy; termination may leave them feeling guilty or deficient. Thus, even the expression of warm feelings must be guided by what is in the best interests of the client, *not* by what feels good to the worker. Assessment skills and disciplined use of self are crucial to the very end.

A FEW MORE WORDS ON WORKER SELF-AWARENESS

In concluding this chapter on endings, the importance of workers' being alert to their own feelings about termination cannot be overstated. The success of this phase depends heavily on the worker's attitudes toward the individual or family involved, toward separation, and toward his or her current professional and personal situation.

It can be tempting, especially when we have very positive feelings toward clients, to wish more for them than they wish for or are able to achieve for themselves. For example, had the worker who treated the Russo family (Chapter 16) urged Mr. and Mrs. Russo to continue in treatment to work on their sexual relationship, about which they had little motivation, the overall progress that had benefited every family member might have been negatively affected, if not overturned.

Levinson writes in his now classic article on termination:

> If the therapist sees separation and termination not as a matter of growth but as a traumatic event for the patient, then he will find himself acting in a variety of ways to postpone the eventual day of termination. Subsequently, this delay will retard the patient's progress toward finding new solutions to old problems. It will also block constructive growth processes...depriving him of the encouragement or expectation of a self-directed attitude. Simply put, the patient cannot take steps away from a therapist who holds him back from moving on.[10]

Our impulse to cling to certain clients, to evade the pain of separating from them, to want to make up to them for their childhood deprivations or injuries certainly humbles us and helps us to empathize with many parents we see in practice who hold on to their adult children. Our reasons for prolonging treatment may not differ much from those of the parents: before letting go, we may want to keep trying for a "perfect" result; characteristically, we may associate endings with fears of aloneness; we may be getting satisfactions from mutual attachments with clients that make up for deficits in our own intimate lives.

It is also possible subtly to encourage clients to terminate. If we are bored, frustrated, or inconvenienced, we may find reasons to justify discontinuance without giving ample consideration to clients' needs or to the meaning of the therapy to *them*. Also, as we said, once the decision to terminate has been made, we may be tempted to detach. Those of us with problems with intimacy may want to maintain distance from clients' feelings about us and ours about them. When we feel rejected by clients, because they did not progress in ways we had hoped, because they were dissatisfied, or because they decided to terminate, we may be inclined to end the treatment in a brusque, countertherapeutic fashion.

Until recently, relatively little had been written by social workers about termination. Yet, the act of saying a planned good-bye to individuals, couples, and families requires that every component of our competence—our ethics, our knowledge, our skills, and our self-awareness—be brought to bear creatively, with extraordinary discipline and finesse.

NOTES

1. For recommended readings on termination, see: Beulah Compton and Burt Galaway, *Social Work Processes*, 3d ed. (Chicago: Dorsey Press, 1984), Chapter 14; Evelyn Fox, Marion Nelson, and William Bolman, "The Termination Process," *Social Work*, 14 (October 1969), 53–63; Carel B. Germain and Alex Gitterman, *The Life Model of Social Work Practice* (New York: Columbia University Press, 1980), Chapter 6; Terry A. Kupers, *Ending Therapy: The Meaning of Termination* (New York: New York University Press, 1988);

Hilliard Levinson, "Termination of Psychotherapy: Some Salient Issues," *Social Casework*, 58 (October 1977), 480–488; and Helen Northen, *Clinical Social Work* (New York: Columbia University Press, 1982), Chapter 9.

2. Joseph Palumbo, "The Psychology of Self and the Termination of Treatment," *Clinical Social Work Journal*, 10 (Spring 1982), 15–27.

3. Nancy Boyd Webb, "A Crisis Intervention Perspective on the Termination Process," *Clinical Social Work Journal*, 13 (Winter 1985), p. 334.

See also, Anne E. Fortune, "Grief Only? Client and Social Worker Reactions to Termination," *Clinical Social Work Journal*, 15 (Summer 1987), 159–171, for a report on a study suggesting that terminations more often include positive affect and evaluation of treatment goals than negative affect; these findings correspond with results of other studies mentioned by her.

4. Compton and Galaway, *Social Work Processes*, pp. 562–563.

5. Jean Sanville, "Partings and Impartings: Toward a Nonmedical Approach to Interruptions and Terminations," *Clinical Social Work Journal*, 10 (Summer 1982), p. 123.

6. See Levinson, "Termination of Psychotherapy," pp. 485–486.

7. Gordon Hamilton, *Theory and Practice of Social Casework*, 2d ed. (New York: Columbia University Press, 1951), p. 236.

8. See Stacia I. Super, "Successful Transition: Therapeutic Interventions with the Transferred Client," *Clinical Social Work Journal*, 10 (Summer 1982), 113–122, for a very useful discussion, with case examples, of suggestions for how the new worker to whom the client has been transferred can best handle the transition.

9. Germain and Gitterman, *The Life Model of Social Work Practice*, p. 279.

10. Levinson, "Termination of Psychotherapy," p. 484.

CHAPTER 21

The Psychosocial Approach: Clinical Case Examples

To complete our discussion of casework methods of psychosocial study, diagnosis, and treatment, we have selected four cases in which the relationship between diagnostic thinking and treatment methods and objectives can be demonstrated. These particular cases have been chosen because they illustrate very different treatment problems. The presenting difficulties, the dynamics of the personalities and situations, and the clinical diagnoses called for considerable variation in emphasis. Nevertheless, almost all of the major types of procedures discussed in earlier chapters were used, at one point or another, in each of the cases.

Although abbreviated, the material is presented in ample detail. The purpose is to provide the reader with as precise an understanding as possible of the actual practice of psychosocial therapy. Specifically, attention will be given to demonstrating (1) how the clinical social workers arrived at diagnostic assessments, (2) how they worked with the clients to define and move toward mutually agreed upon goals as these evolved over the course of treatment, and (3) how treatment procedures were selected and how, as the needs and capacities

of the clients changed, the worker adjusted the blend of these procedures. In each case, it will be seen, differential understanding of the clients and their situations led to individualized clinical judgments. As the fund of knowledge grew and as client trust developed, the worker accordingly made shifts in treatment methods. The importance of worker self-awareness is also addressed.

PSYCHOSIS: SHORT-TERM INPATIENT TREATMENT

Louise Barry, a thirty-four-year-old black woman, was involuntarily committed to the inpatient facility of a county psychiatric hospital with the diagnosis of paranoid schizophrenia.[1] It was her fourth such hospitalization in four years. On the day she was admitted she had gone to a medical clinic for treatment of a stomach virus. When the doctor attempted to give her an injection of an antibiotic, she began to scream wildly and accuse the doctor of trying to kill her. Since it was feared she might physically attack some member of the clinical staff, she was forcibly restrained and taken to the psychiatric hospital. Once admitted, she began to scream, "All men are trying to kill women" and "People are trying to kill me." Shortly thereafter, she began to sob uncontrollably and repeat over and over, "It's no use. I just want to die."

The caseworker, later assigned to Mrs. Barry, was first brought into the case to speak with Mr. Barry, who had been notified at work of his wife's hospitalization. He arrived within minutes, clearly shaken by the recurrence of her illness. He spoke openly and impressed the worker as being extremely devoted to his wife of eighteen years, genuinely concerned for her welfare.

Mr. Barry said that his wife's present breakdown followed the pattern of the others. Prior to hospitalization, she would suddenly decide to stop taking medication on which she had been maintained since her first breakdown. The past week, without medication, she had been unable to sleep; she sat at the foot of their bed until late at night, wrapped in blankets, muttering to herself, and asking Mr. Barry questions that he interpreted as intended to "trap" him. She would say, for example, "How would you like to go out Friday night with Alice and Joe?" When Mr. Barry agreed "too quickly," she would then accuse him of being sexually interested in Alice. He emphatically denied involvement with Alice or with any other women. Aside from her "mental troubles," and the fact that she was deeply disappointed that they seemed unable to have children, he felt their marriage had been harmonious and satisfying, at least to him. He could not suggest any reasons or precipitating events, other than her refusal to take medication, that would account for her becoming disturbed at this particular time.

Mr. Barry and his wife grew up in a small town in the south but rarely went back to visit. Shortly after they were married (she was sixteen and he was nineteen), they came north to settle in the city in which they now lived. The major reason they moved was that Mr. Barry

had wanted to pursue a career as a musician, but his efforts failed. Instead, he found employment as a repairman with the telephone company, the job he still held.

He spoke about his wife with pride, describing her as a very bright woman. She had not finished high school but now was studying for an equivalency examination. She had also begun taking courses in electronics and television repair. Mr. Barry not only accepted his wife's interests but actively encouraged them. Recalling that Mrs. Barry had repeatedly screamed, "All men are trying to kill women," the worker wondered to herself whether Mr. Barry's enthusiasm for her studies had been perceived by his wife as pressure. Apparently, Mr. Barry had also encouraged her to supplement their income by working part time as a waitress.

It was obviously painful to him that his wife became suspicious when she had these breakdowns. She also had blamed him for "locking her up" in the past and for the fact that she had never become pregnant. Actually, neither he nor his wife had consulted any doctors about the latter problem in recent years. Since it was a sensitive subject for Mr. Barry, the worker did not press the matter or ask how he felt about having no children. She did inquire, however, whether he had ever been involved in outpatient therapy with his wife and learned that though it had been suggested, he had been reluctant. At this point, he said, he would be willing to "do anything" if it would help.

Later the same day the caseworker introduced herself to Mrs. Barry, suggesting that they might speak together. Mrs. Barry responded angrily: "You don't want to talk to me. *I* don't know. My husband knows." Softly, the worker replied that she was sure that Mrs. Barry knew a lot, especially about how unhappy she was feeling. She said she hoped they would be able to talk about it while she was in the hospital. Mrs. Barry complained that everyone talked with her husband behind her back to get her locked up. Challengingly, she added that people should talk to them together "to find out how things really are." The worker told her that she had seen Mr. Barry, even though she would have preferred to meet with her first, explaining that he had come to the hospital worried and wanting to talk with someone. The worker added that in the future she would let Mrs. Barry know beforehand if she planned to be in touch with him; she, too, hoped the three of them could arrange to talk together. Mrs. Barry said no one in the hospital had offered this before. She was suspicious of her husband's willingness to join in sessions with her. Nevertheless, she listened carefully to the worker's account of the meeting with him.

From her knowledge of schizophrenic episodes, the worker recognized that her first encounter with Mrs. Barry had to be one in which she conveyed clearly and quickly her caring and sincerity. As important as these therapist qualities are for any client, they are crucial for the acutely disorganized, decompensating, frightened person with paranoid ideation. A break in reality such as Mrs. Barry was experiencing is usually accompanied by diffuse suspiciousness. On the other hand, the worker was aware, as she reached out to Mrs. Barry to gain her trust, that she should not press for greater closeness than Mrs. Barry could tolerate.

It is well known among clinicians who work with such patients that they cannot only fear encroachment, but often are keenly sensitive to a therapist's mood, indifference, or lack of genuineness. In this case, the worker's attentiveness and words of understanding were also accompanied by facial expressions and gestures to convey to Mrs. Barry that she felt "with" and "for" her in her unhappiness.

On this first day of hospitalization, Mrs. Barry was alternately lucid and incoherent. When the worker gently asked how she had come to the hospital, she muttered that men are trying to kill her and that someone had "wired my head so I can't think right." The worker commented on how frightening it must be to feel that way, saying she imagined it was exhausting always to have to be on guard against getting hurt.

Without suggesting that she believed the delusional statements to be true, the worker related to the emotional affects. Furthermore, knowing that schizophrenic patients, particularly those who are delusional, are likely to respond poorly to probing questions, the worker refrained from making inquiries that could be construed as intrusive and that could exacerbate Mrs. Barry's hostility or withdrawal from reality. Even an effort to seek background information might well have resulted in undoing the worker's efforts to establish a trusting relationship.

Mrs. Barry was unwilling to sign voluntary commitment papers as she had in the past. Without pressure, the worker suggested that she consider this because it worried her and others that Mrs. Barry was saying she wanted to die. But Mrs. Barry insisted that she did not need help. She knew, however, that the doctors might recommend commitment and the worker agreed that this was so because they were concerned for her safety and well-being. Mrs. Barry's desire to talk was a good prognostic sign in the worker's view. Although even the sickest person usually wants human contact, some schizophrenics are so frightened and withdrawn that they cannot or will not communicate. Mrs. Barry, however, was actively attempting to reach out in spite of her suspiciousness. Moreover, the worker felt hopeful because of Mrs. Barry's evident strengths: she had functioned well in various areas of her life over the years, she had mastered new skills, she was able to hold a job.

As it turned out, Mrs. Barry was committed to the hospital for twenty days. The hope was that she would respond well in this period of time as she had to similar hospitalizations in the past. However, the worker and the psychiatrist assigned to Mrs. Barry were in disagreement about some aspects of the treatment. The psychiatrist believed that since this patient was denying the need for help, her prognosis was probably poor. Since she was so "uncooperative," he said, he would not try to work with her until the medication began to take effect; even then he doubted she would respond to psychotherapy.

The worker knew she faced a delicate situation. First, she and the doctor had significant ideological differences. For example, he saw treatment as a process in which the patient is passive. He was primarily interested in medication and tended to see this as the major, if not the only, treatment procedure of value to schizophrenic patients. Second, of European, aristocratic origin, he seemed unable to understand or relate well to people with divergent cultural or economic backgrounds. He appeared to give up on such patients, especially those who were poor and black. Third, his position at the hospital was in jeopardy; he had recently been demoted, and he handled his insecurity about this by being authoritative with the worker.

Although the worker found the doctor exasperating, she knew it was important not to antagonize him. If she challenged his views, it might limit her helpfulness to Mrs. Barry, since he was in charge of the case. Furthermore, she was truly sympathetic about his tenuous position at the hospital and realized he was reacting defensively. Consequently, the worker stressed their areas of agreement; she told him that she, too, believed medication was of primary importance to Mrs. Barry's treatment. She then added that she wanted to meet with Mrs. Barry and to keep in touch with her husband since she felt they both would benefit from a show of personal interest. She offered to share any information that would be helpful. He said the worker would be wasting her time, but agreed to her plan, adding, with a paternal smile, that he saw it as the worker's need rather than the patient's.

As discussed in the chapter on environmental work, a worker's understanding of the power structure and hierarchy of an agency, and of the particular professionals who staff it, is essential to good service. With this doctor (as with collaterals in general), tact and understanding were of prime importance to the treatment.

During the first week of Mrs. Barry's hospitalization, the caseworker saw her three more times and subsequently at least three times weekly. At first her visits were brief, since Mrs. Barry was often acutely confused. She had many delusions, to which the worker listened carefully, in order to determine what they might be expressing about how Mrs. Barry perceived herself in relationship to other people and to the world around her. This client had several repetitive complaints: she believed her husband was persecuting her because he wanted her to work in the restaurant where all the other waitresses hated her; she thought her money was being stolen at the hospital; she believed people were tampering with her brain; and she thought the nurses were deliberately passing her over by giving medication first to other patients, even when she was at the head of the line. The worker did not employ reflective procedures designed to help Mrs. Barry understand what these recurring themes meant; at this point, any such attempts might have been construed as invasions or demands.

Recognizing that Mrs. Barry truly believed she was singled out for bad treatment at the hands of others, the worker made special efforts to be considerate of her. For example, she tried to see Mrs. Barry afternoons, when she had more uninterrupted time; she also made a point of telling her early in the day the exact time of their meeting; she looked for ways in which she could give her genuine compliments, and greeted her in passing as she made her rounds through the hospital. She also investigated what might be causing misunderstandings, such as Mrs. Barry's feelings of being passed over in the medication line, and learned that the nurses, to whom Mrs. Barry frequently complained, viewed her as a "demanding" patient. On the other hand, the nurses reported that Mrs. Barry would say she wanted to be "invisible" and then seem to hope she would be noticed spontaneously.

The caseworker observed that when she came to the floor, Mrs. Barry would respond cheerfully when waved to, but if the worker was briefly intercepted by another person, Mrs. Barry's smile would fade and she would become absorbed elsewhere and not acknowledge the greeting they just exchanged. In one interview, when Mrs. Barry seemed particularly well related and relaxed, the worker tentatively asked whether at medication time she did something similar by trying to "fade into the woodwork" when another patient broke into line in front of her. Mrs. Barry then revealed, with self-awareness that astonished the worker, that she felt she had never really been noticed, much less preferred, by her parents when she was growing up. Her older brother was her mother's favorite; her very "pretty" and "clever" younger sister, whom Mrs. Barry referred to as "spoiled," was her father's "pet." She, on the other hand, was the "plain" one who had gotten little encouragement or recognition. With feeling, she told the worker that she had developed a habit of pretending not to care whether she was noticed and to hide her feelings of resentment and sadness. With words and by her attitude, the worker gave recognition to Mrs. Barry for being able to understand herself so well.

The worker sensed that Mrs. Barry had truly begun to trust her. With her client's consent, she shared some of this information with the nurses to help them understand their patient better and feel less antagonistic. She also gave them suggestions about ways Mrs. Barry might be drawn out in patient therapy groups, since she tended to be reticent there and try to make herself "invisible."

The first task of treatment, then, was to attempt to establish a solid relationship. Only when this was achieved, and after Mrs. Barry had become somewhat better organized with the help of medication, was the worker able to help her reflect on some of the issues and feelings she had never before shared in detail with anyone. Feelings of alienation, so pervasive in disturbed clients, can often be alleviated when a warm and personal interest is taken in their private feelings and thoughts. The worker's next treatment objective was to help Mrs. Barry understand the importance of medication, without which it seemed probable that this client would periodically decompensate. In this setting, where patients were hospitalized for a maximum of sixty days, it was important to help her with this quickly.

While eliciting Mrs. Barry's attitudes about medication, the worker looked for comments that might throw light on her refusal to take it prior to admission. Was there a connection between the medication and Mrs. Barry's notion that people were tampering with her brain or "wiring" her head wrong? Similarly, did Mrs. Barry's interest in electronics represent her way of attempting to gain control over her "brain"?

In one meeting, Mrs. Barry protested, "Why do *I* have to take medication and everybody else in the world doesn't?" When asked how she felt about that, she simply answered, "Crazy." The worker said that many other people *did* in fact take medication, for example, many diabetics use insulin, because body chemistry is different in everyone and does not always provide what is needed to stay well and feel good. The worker added that she herself also had to take medication regularly. Her approach was designed to help Mrs. Barry consider the reality of the situation; at this point, she did not pursue intrapsychic issues.

As they talked, however, Mrs. Barry admitted that, to her, being on medication meant she was not only "different" and "crazy" but "weak" as well. It made her feel she could not make it on her own, that she needed a "crutch"; and that this was why she had wanted to test herself by trying to get along without it from time to time. She said she had always been "disgusted" by her alcoholic father, whom her mother had belittled for needing drink to "lean on." The worker helped her to examine ways in which she might view her situation differently: In contrast to her father, who was incapacitated when he drank, she, Mrs. Barry, functioned well and felt better when she took medication. The need to make up for a biochemical deficit was quite different from the excessive use of alcohol.

During subsequent meetings, Mrs. Barry indicated she had given thought to these talks about medication. Until now, she had not looked at it in these ways. Probably never before had she linked her perception of herself to her father's "weakness." Since the issue of control is important to most paranoid patients, and was clearly so to Mrs. Barry, the worker pointed out that when she was on medication she was able to control herself so that other people did not think she was sick and put her in the hospital against her will.

As Mrs. Barry became increasingly less confused, it seemed likely that some of her money *had* been stolen at the hospital, as she had suspected. Mr. Barry confirmed his wife's assertion that she always carried a ten-dollar bill pinned on her person. Although the money was not listed among her belongings in the property office, Mrs. Barry was convinced that it was being kept from her there. The worker took Mrs. Barry to the safe—other staff members had refused to do so on the grounds that she was delusional—and they looked for it together. It was not there, but the worker said that it was indeed very possible that her ten dollars could have disappeared in the struggle on the day she was admitted. Together, they "mourned" the loss of the money. The worker said she knew how helpless and out of control one feels when carefully kept possessions disappear. Mrs. Barry spoke about an occasion when she found a wallet belonging to a coworker and how "of course" she returned it, adding that she never did expect people would treat her as well as she treated them. To this, the worker responded that when these things happen, it certainly makes it harder to trust others.

In the session following her trip with the worker to check the safe, there was a marked change in Mrs. Barry. She greeted the worker with the statement that she felt she was "too suspicious"; she could not understand why she did not trust people and had to "see everything with my own eyes" before she could believe it. She had not believed the worker when she said the money was not there. The worker repeated that when people have been hurt or disappointed, it can be difficult to trust. At this, Mrs. Barry began talking about her husband and his early promises that he would give her everything when he became a successful musician. Now, not only were her husband's wages low but he was a reckless spender. Moreover, in recent years he went out by himself much more often than he had in the early years. She felt lonely and often thought he must be seeing another woman. She believed her husband was sterile. He knew how much she wanted to have children, and she felt that if he truly cared he would have himself checked.

For the most part, the caseworker listened to Mrs. Barry and expressed her understanding of how disappointed she felt. She said she hoped they could arrange a session with her husband so they could talk over some of these matters. On speaking to the psychiatrist in charge of Mrs. Barry's case, however, the worker learned that the doctor disapproved of the idea of conjoint sessions; it was his belief that Mrs. Barry was trying to "control" the treatment and "manipulate" the worker. Tactfully, but with conviction, the worker shared her view that in spite of Mrs. Barry's illness and paranoia, there seemed to be some important reality aspects to the marital relationship that required Mr. Barry's participation. Reluctantly, the psychiatrist agreed to "go along" with the worker, who then scheduled a joint session.

During the third week of hospitalization, in spite of her improvement, Mrs. Barry was still periodically confused. But self-awareness was keener than it had been, and she often commented on how frustrated she became when she had difficulty expressing herself. The worker reassured her that she was sounding clearer than she had and encouraged her to take the time she needed to pull her thoughts together. When less pressured by others, she was often able to be more coherent and relaxed. Mrs. Barry acknowledged this and said she wished her husband would pressure her less about her high school equivalency test.

On the day before Mrs. Barry's twenty-day commitment was to expire, and a few hours before the joint session with her husband was scheduled, the worker found her to be depressed, withdrawn, and uncommunicative. She was unresponsive to the worker's overtures. Returning an hour later, the worker asked Mrs. Barry whether she were apprehensive about going home or about the meeting planned with her husband. Mrs. Barry said she wanted to stay in the hospital to make sure she would feel well when she left. Moreover, she wanted to have more than one meeting with her husband; she did not want to go home until certain matters that she was afraid to bring up alone were discussed. She signed voluntary papers to remain another week, adding that this time she would be in the hospital "for myself, not for the court."

During this last week in the hospital, the three individual sessions turned out to be the most productive of all. It was Mrs. Barry who had chosen to extend her hospitalization, and she seemed determined to benefit from it. She was able to reflect further on her decision to stop medication that had resulted in her "going crazy." Aside from viewing medication as a hated "crutch," she had also been extremely fearful that she would not be "smart enough" to pass the high school equivalency examination. Fearing that she would fail and prove to

others, particularly her husband, who had such high expectations of her, that she was worthless and had "mixed-up brains," she supposed that she had played it "safe" by getting sick; she knew that if she discontinued medication she would be rehospitalized. Again, she related her fear of failure to having felt like the "plain" and "stupid" middle child. Once she was able to share her understanding and feelings with the worker, she also brought them up in the group therapy sessions where she got further support.

There were two conjoint meetings with Mr. and Mrs. Barry. Mrs. Barry was able to tell her husband that his encouragement about the test felt like pressure to her, and that his enthusiasm about her courses in electronics made her feel that she would disappoint him if she did not do well. She told him it angered her that he wanted her to work at the restaurant she despised. Mr. Barry had a tendency to evade, but he did listen to her complaints and try to understand them. He realized there might be some misunderstandings between them and made efforts to change. Even though he had little insight into his wife's problems or his contribution to them, he agreed to marital therapy, reassuring her that he loved her and did not want her to get sick again.

The worker had the impression that Mr. and Mrs. Barry were in competition with one another, that Mrs. Barry was trying to measure up to her husband, who was skilled in telephone repair, and that there were hidden mixed feelings below his overly determined interest in his wife's achievements. In these joint meetings, however, the focus was limited almost entirely to the problem of pressure. The worker chose not to open up other issues of the marriage, even though many of these seemed problematical, for fear of further upsetting the marital relationship. They had little time to work. Instead, prior to Mrs. Barry's discharge, a referral for marital therapy was arranged that the worker was not too optimistic about. First, Mr.

Barry was resistant to it and, second, the choice of resources was limited. In the clinic near the Barrys' home, there was only one therapist, a pastoral counselor, who provided marital therapy, and it was the worker's hunch that he might not do well with this particular couple. Fortunately, Mrs. Barry was also interested in joining an outpatient group, in which the worker expected she would do well.

From time to time after she left the hospital, Mrs. Barry telephoned the worker. She said that they had gone only once for marital treatment and then discontinued, feeling they did not need it. She attended group therapy sessions regularly for four months until the group disbanded after a cut in funding to the clinic. A year and a half after Mrs. Barry's discharge, the worker made a follow-up telephone call to her. She learned that Mrs. Barry felt she was doing well. She had continued to take medication despite the fact that she was suffering side effects (constipation, blurred vision, dryness of the mouth, and so on). She kept her appointments at the medication clinic regularly. She also told the worker that when she left the hospital she had decided not to take the equivalency test. The following year, however—on her own and not because her husband expected it—she went back to study for it, took it, and failed by only a few points. She did not seem discouraged and said she would try again soon. Mrs. Barry also told the worker that if she felt further treatment was necessary she would definitely go for it. She wanted to stay as well as she was.

This case illustrates how diagnosis and treatment go hand in hand, and how even short-term treatment can be effective in laying the ground for more extended therapy when needed. It demonstrates how the often discouraging clinical diagnosis of "paranoid schizophrenia" need not, in and of itself, lead to despair about a client's ability to grow and change to make more satisfactory adjustments to life. In this case, the worker's primary objective was to help Mrs. Barry recompensate with the help of

medication, and resume her previous adjustment. However, within a short time, further goals of awareness of self-defeating behavior and of improvement of the marital relationship seemed possible.

The worker's assessment evolved and changed as she learned more about her client. Similarly, her treatment approach shifted as Mrs. Barry began to be better related, to trust the worker, and to be ready for self-understanding. In the context of a great deal of support, Mrs. Barry was able to pour out many pent-up feelings and emotionally charged memories. Careful timing made it possible to help her gain understanding about her decision to stop taking medication, without which she might have discontinued it again after her discharge. Contrary to the view of those who believe that the mentally ill cannot benefit from procedures other than those that are supportive or directive, the work with Mrs. Barry demonstrates that she was able to think reflectively on several levels: about herself, her situation, and her patterns of thinking and behaving, and on influential aspects of her childhood experiences.

Effort was also made to improve the quality of service for Mrs. Barry by working closely with the nurses to help them treat their patient with greater understanding. Attuned to the client-situation interplay, the worker identified how certain features of the hospital milieu, such as the staff's refusal to allow Mrs. Barry to examine the safe, tended to exacerbate her delusions. In spite of the pessimistic approach of the psychiatrist in charge, the worker was able to find a way of working with him without alienating him; she was able to persuade him to accept her plan for conjoint meetings, a plan that the worker believed was not only diagnostically sound but imperative to the success of Mrs. Barry's treatment. As a result, Mr. Barry was no longer viewed simply as a consultant about his wife's illness but also as an important participant in her environment.

This case also shows how important it is for clients, even those as disturbed as Mrs. Barry was, to take an active part in their own treatment. At several points, the work was guided by directions Mrs. Barry chose: the worker supported Mrs. Barry's wish to include her husband in treatment and helped to arrange it; she accepted Mrs. Barry's request to see for herself if the money was in the hospital safe. And, of utmost importance, Mrs. Barry worked most productively when *she* made the decision to remain in the hospital. In each instance, her autonomy and self-esteem were reinforced.

It is important to note that the handling of this case differed significantly from what it would have been three or four decades ago. Prior to the development of antipsychotic drugs, Mrs. Barry's future surely would have been less hopeful; it is possible that she would have become a chronic schizophrenic, hospitalized for years or for the rest of her life. Furthermore, deinstitutionalization has resulted in shorter periods of inpatient treatment and greater emphasis on outpatient services (which, as this case confirms, are still far from adequately financed or staffed in many areas). Happily, Mrs. Barry's chances for a relatively adequate adjustment, particularly if she returns for treatment when necessary, are far greater than they would have been just a generation ago.

TERMINAL ILLNESS[2]

Anna Stasio, age forty-four, telephoned a mental health clinic asking for an appointment with a woman therapist as soon as possible, to discuss "serious personal problems." As it happened, the worker assigned to intake on the day she called was a man. He asked her if there were any particular reason why she thought he could not help her. She replied abruptly, "I haven't got time for that." She asserted that under no circumstances would she agree to see a man, adding that she needed someone mature and

experienced. In response to her request, an experienced woman worker was assigned.

At the beginning of the first interview, with startling directness, Mrs. Stasio stated that a malignant tumor had been discovered on one of her lymph nodes several months previously. More recently, it was determined that the cancer had spread throughout her system. She was receiving chemotherapy. Although the doctors believed she was now in remission, she was, as she put it, "sitting with a time bomb." She had no idea how long she would live, having been given estimates ranging from six months to two years, but she knew her days were numbered and she wanted to have someone who was "dispassionate" to talk with on a regular basis. Her father was old, her mother had a serious heart condition, and she described her husband as "weak" and "neurotic." None of them were comforting to her, she said, because she felt *she* had to soothe *them* when she talked about her illness. She had insisted on a mature woman because she felt women were "stronger" than men. Furthermore, she did not want to see a social worker who was "wet behind the ears" or unduly frightened by a dying woman. The worker, a senior on staff with many years of experience, was genuinely moved by this woman's courage and determination to get what she needed for whatever time she had left to live. By gesture, tone of voice, and mood, she conveyed this. She agreed it was important for Mrs. Stasio to feel satisfied with the person she was seeing, urging her to tell her if she felt uncomfortable. Operating on Mrs. Stasio's clue that she was a person who tended to feel protective of the feelings of others, even at her own expense, the worker assured her that though she would be pleased to work with her, she would not feel hurt if Mrs. Stasio decided she was not the right therapist. At this, Mrs. Stasio visibly softened; her eyes filled and she said gently, "I liked you from the moment we met."

In taking this straightforward approach, the worker conveyed that she, too, was a strong person who could, in the interest of her client, tolerate a rejection. This was undoubtedly supportive to Mrs. Stasio, who seemed to need someone whom she felt was as fearless as she saw herself to be. As she sat with this remarkable woman, the worker considered how her own emotional resources were being put to the test. Paradoxically, Mrs. Stasio came across as attractive, vital, and colorful, yet she was dying. As the client talked about herself, she did so with a wide range of feeling: at times she was angry and impatient; at times she spoke with tenderness and sadness; in spite of everything, she had a sense of humor. In every instance, her emotions were expressed vividly. The worker realized she would have to prepare herself now to be intimately associated with the many physical and emotional processes associated with terminal illness.

In early interviews with Mrs. Stasio, the worker learned that she came from a middle-class, intellectual family; her mother had been a professional ballet dancer and her father a college professor of literature. Her father was English born, her mother of Italian origin. Both parents were of Protestant background but neither was religious; Mrs. Stasio described herself as an atheist. She was an only child and had always been thought of as "headstrong." In college, she majored in fine arts; at that time she married her first husband, an actor with whom she lived for five years. They had an exciting but stormy marriage that ended because they were both too "stubborn" and aggressive. Each fought to overpower the other. When she married again, she chose a man of the opposite extreme; she portrayed Mr. Stasio, an engineer who had worked at the same government job for twenty years, as insecure, passive, and dull, but very kind. He was not well paid but had not had the courage to get his master's degree or to seek more challenging work. They had two children, Roger, age fifteen, and Elizabeth, age thirteen. The marriage had never been a truly happy one for her, but she had resigned herself

to it, knowing that her domineering qualities had led her to choose him. For the past few years, she and a woman friend (with whom she had had a brief sexual affair) had operated a small picture-framing business that had been fairly successful and important to the family income. Mrs. Stasio had had two years of intensive psychotherapy when her children were small; it had helped her to understand herself better, and to feel less angry and disappointed about her husband.

In her characteristically definite way, Mrs. Stasio declared she did not want family therapy or joint meetings with her husband. The worker had not yet suggested these, but, once again, this client was taking charge of getting the kind of treatment she wanted. She would find her own way of saying good-bye to her family; she did not need help with this. What she did want, she said, was someone whom she could use as a sounding board, to help her think over how to plan the rest of her life. There were also certain aspects of her behavior she wanted to change, particularly toward her husband and her daughter. She did not want to continue to feel guilty, as she did, about the way she took out her anger over her illness on Mr. Stasio. She was falling into the pattern she had been in when she went into therapy the first time; she belittled her husband and raged at him over minor matters. After all, it was not his fault that she had "settled" for a marriage that bored her. When she learned that she would soon die, she realized she would never experience a better relationship, a fantasy that had kept her anger "in check" in recent years. She worried about the effect of her hostility on the children, who would have only their father when she died; she did not want to contaminate their future relationship by her actions toward her husband now.

She felt concern for both children. But Roger, she thought, would handle himself; she described him as an "all-American boy": a fine student, an athlete, with many friends.

Elizabeth, however, who had been born with a cleft palate and had had many operations since infancy, was a withdrawn, immature girl who did not do well in school and had very few friends. Mrs. Stasio said that she tended to overprotect her daughter and did not want to do this now that Elizabeth would have to learn to be self-reliant. The worker pointed out that, if it seemed indicated, the children—or at least Elizabeth—might benefit from individual sessions. Mrs. Stasio opposed this idea as strongly as she resisted family treatment; emphatically, she said that changes in her own behavior would be the most helpful thing for Elizabeth. Mrs. Stasio's characteristic need to control, undoubtedly reinforced by her illness, necessarily limited treatment options.

Very early in therapy, Mrs. Stasio said that she would like to meet twice weekly, if possible. She had a lot to talk about and very little time. Although it was a general rule at the clinic to make appointments with clients on a once-a-week basis, for two reasons the worker arranged to make an exception. First, she wanted to be responsive to this client's wishes, and, second, Mrs. Stasio did indeed have many issues to talk over. From the worker's knowledge of this kind of cancer (which she later verified with a medical consultant), it very often resulted in rapid decline and early death. For the next five months, except when Mrs. Stasio had to go into the hospital for treatment, they met twice weekly.

After the first month of therapy, Mrs. Stasio came in saying that her husband also wanted to see the worker, that he was "falling apart." She still did not want to have meetings with him, but said she had no objection to his seeing her worker on his own. In fact, she was urging him to come.

Indeed, Mr. Stasio, although hardly "falling apart," did want someone to talk to, with whom he could share his very mixed emotions. He was frightened and grief-stricken; he both resented and admired his wife. He also wanted suggestions about ways the children should be handled during this time. An intelligent man, Mr. Stasio was not usually introspective, but he needed a great deal of support and an opportunity to ventilate and to discuss the practical problems he was facing. Occasionally, the worker offered direct advice about the children, but primarily she encouraged him to make his own decisions, helping him to evaluate various options. During the course of their work together, as his wife became weaker, Mr. Stasio took on more and more responsibility for the household and child care. He was concerned about money now that Mrs. Stasio was no longer working and was having difficulty with Elizabeth, who was clinging to her mother and seemed irritable and sarcastic with him. Since he did not want to upset his wife, he preferred to share these worries with the worker. He, too, opposed family meetings, wanting to establish close relationships with his children on his own. In his view, to have a "mediator" would detract from his efforts to strengthen family bonds. For too long he had been in his wife's "shadow," and now he did not want to "hide behind" the worker.

Some clinicians might take the view that the worker should have pressed harder for family meetings (or for individual treatment for the children), particularly since Elizabeth appeared to be having difficulties. The worker believed that some avoidance was operating for both parents, but decided not to urge them to involve the children. She thought she could persuade Mr. Stasio to change his mind but was quite sure that any attempt to convince his wife could be deeply damaging to the therapeutic relationship. Furthermore, she believed it was important to respect Mrs. Stasio's method of handling her illness and her wish to do as much as she could herself. For Mr. Stasio, the decision not to urge family meetings may well have been one of the factors that encouraged him to function more independently with his children. It was he who would have to learn to take charge of the family and, if the worker conveyed the opinion that he could not do this without her direct help, she might have fostered his dependency. Under different circumstances, the worker might have been more forceful in recommending family meetings. As it was, both Mr. and Mrs. Stasio discussed in detail their relationships with the children, reflecting on how they could be most helpful to them.

From meeting to meeting, Mr. Stasio would report on his increasingly effective efforts to get closer to the children. He was able to talk with them about the sadness they shared; he found he could enlist their help around the house in ways he never had before. They were showing him more respect than previously and this gratified him, but he regretted that he had waited until his wife was dying to change his "image." Mrs. Stasio was no longer berating him frequently and he attributed this, in part, to the changes he had made. The worker was supportive of his new role but disagreed with him when he gave her more credit than he gave himself for the changes. She pointed out that he had worked hard and wondered why now he would want to downplay the importance of his own efforts and only recognize hers.

After three months, it became apparent to the worker that Mrs. Stasio's condition was rapidly deteriorating. Chemotherapy was no longer effective in forestalling the advance of the malignancy. Nevertheless, she remained mentally clear and actively engaged in all aspects of her life. She was grateful to her husband for taking more initiative at home; she spoke with appreciation of his good qualities and now found it comforting to view him as a "friend." She had neither the energy nor the inclination to belittle him now, and she was glad to achieve one of her major objectives: to behave differently toward him. By expressing her anger in the sessions, rather than directly at him, she had relieved the tension between them. She was also proud of the fact that she had been able to have loving talks about her condition with both children and had been able to listen to their concerns and questions. In a moving discussion with Elizabeth, which she had "rehearsed" with the worker beforehand, she told her daughter that she had probably "babied" her too much and that she regretted that, particularly now that Elizabeth would have to become increasingly independent. Mrs. Stasio spoke with compassion of her parents, now sick and old, who would have to face the loss of their only child; she gave a good deal of thought to how she could make it easier for them, fully aware that even now she was relating to them in a caretaking way, as had been her lifelong pattern.

Particularly after Mrs. Stasio had achieved the relationships she wanted with her family— or, perhaps, because she knew she was close to death—she began to use her sessions to reflect spontaneously, sometimes in minute detail, on various periods of her life. She talked with regret about never having had a fulfilling marital relationship. Her most satisfying sexual experiences, she confided, had been with women; she was glad now that she had allowed these, although she had felt very guilty about them at the time. Sharing these confidences, she said, had a "cleansing" effect. She joked that even though she was not religious, she seemed to have the need to "confess." Her relationship with her parents, both of whom tended to be passive, indecisive people, interested her. In her view, she had become a "powerhouse" because they were so unassertive and needed her leadership, even when she was very young. If this situation had been a liability for Mrs. Stasio, she saw it now as an asset. From her standpoint, her aggressiveness had served her well. She had been part of life, and had not simply watched from the sidelines as she felt her parents had.

As she spoke of her marriage, she said that her angry domination of her husband had, in some way, represented her effort to "make him over" into the strong man her father never was. As she saw it, she had taken on the role of the "man" in her parents' home, and again in her current family. Her disappointment in her father had led her to choose her first husband, who she viewed as his opposite. Unable to tolerate the power struggles that ensued, she made sure her next husband would be easier to manage! Her occasional homosexual affairs, she assumed, were a response to frustrations with the men in her life.

It had always been Mrs. Stasio's inclination to be introspective; moreover, her two years of psychotherapy several years earlier had contributed to her sophisticated self-understanding. In contrast to many treatment situations in which change in emotional or behavioral patterns is a primary objective, for Mrs. Stasio this phase of treatment (which involved dynamic and developmental reflection) was important to her attempts to come to peace with or "make sense" out of her life. There was no attempt on her part or the worker's to help resolve long-standing conflicts or neurotic issues; reflections on these matters were important only to the degree that Mrs. Stasio was interested in them.

Since Mrs. Stasio could not control her disease, she was determined to manage its effects. She would take charge of her own dying. Unlike many terminally ill patients, at no point did she use the defense of denial against the *fact* of her impending premature death. If she exhibited any denial, as the worker believed she did, it was denial or repression of anxieties and helplessness naturally associated with terminal illness. She handled these through "counterphobic" behavior. In the face of death, she continued to orchestrate: how her therapy would be handled, how her husband would get treatment, and how she would say good-bye to her children. To one session she brought three long typewritten letters, one to her husband and one to each child, to be read after she died. In these she gave instructions about her funeral and made suggestions about the management of finances, detailing ideas for them all to follow in the future. Gently, the worker asked Mrs. Stasio

if she thought the letters conveyed her doubts about whether the family would be able to manage without her. After thinking it over between sessions, Mrs. Stasio returned with a new set of letters, having discarded the first; in them she told each how much she cared, expressing confidence in them all. The only instructions included were those related to her funeral arrangements.

Diagnostically, Mrs. Stasio was seen as a woman who approached life intensely, even in the face of her debilitated physical condition. She had many well developed ego functions that helped her master difficult situations in health and in illness. She had a clear sense of values and a capacity for self-criticism and change, even in the last months of her life. Her chief defenses, repression and some denial of her fear of imminent death, allowed her to function effectively, not only for her own benefit, but for that of her family. She helped them prepare for the inevitable, and offered them an opportunity to grieve with her while she still lived. Her characteristic mode of handling anxiety, as she often said, had been to "grab life by the tail," and this style served her through these days of illness. As already noted, there were character problems and neurotic patterns that Mrs. Stasio had never resolved, although she was aware of some of them. Her inordinate need to control undoubtedly masked a long-standing fear of dependency; she allowed herself to rely on the worker only after she was absolutely sure that the worker could "take it." Her ambivalence toward men and uncertain sexual identification were evident. The worker's diagnostic understanding was of utmost importance to the treatment. It was essential, for example, for the worker to respect Mrs. Stasio's need for control and to recognize which defenses were necessary to protect her from overwhelming anxiety or despair. By getting to know her client as well as she did, the worker was also able to stay empathically attuned to the great vicissitudes of feeling Mrs. Stasio experienced during this final phase of her life.

Throughout the therapy, sustaining procedures were highly important. The worker used
several forms of support. Mrs. Stasio needed
the worker's strength, consistent interest, and
encouragement. She enjoyed the worker's
praise about the changes that led to warmer family relationships. A woman keenly connected
to her emotions and experiences, Mrs. Stasio
required an intense therapeutic relationship.
She originally requested a worker who could
be "dispassionate," but evidently she meant
someone who did not need to be taken care of;
she did not mean (and would not have tolerated!) a therapist who was emotionally unavailable. Following Mrs. Stasio's lead, the worker
shared how genuinely privileged she felt to have
gotten to know her; they spoke of their time
together as a special kind of "journey." Empathically, the worker shared Mrs. Stasio's anger at the arbitrary way illness chooses its victims. She truly understood her client's tears of
frustration and sadness: Mrs. Stasio had always
wanted to live a long life; now she would never
see her children become adults; now she would
miss out on her grandchildren; now she would
have no "third chance" at a better marriage. The
worker refrained from offering false reassurances; Mrs. Stasio counted on her to share in
the agony of accepting the inevitability of her
early death.

With Mr. Stasio, the worker was also supportive. She reinforced his capacity for independent functioning, and helped him to be aware
of his strengths, which he generally underestimated. With the worker's encouragement, he
was able to take more initiative with his children, particularly when not faced with his wife's
extraordinary aggressiveness. As Mrs. Stasio related more softly with him, he, in turn, could
be more confident and assertive. It proved important for Mr. Stasio to have someone to whom
he could vent his long-standing resentments.
He was then free to feel less conflicted in his
loving feelings for his wife. He began truly to
grieve for her and to face his fears about life

without her. Like his wife, he never denied
the reality of her condition, and this enabled
them to share their pain. From his point of
view, and Mrs. Stasio's as well, their times together became more tender and meaningful
than ever.

In addition to sustaining procedures and
those that fostered ventilation, the worker
helped Mr. Stasio reflect on the many day-to-
day difficulties and decisions that faced him.
He became more aware of his pattern of either
withdrawing or deferring to others, particularly
his wife but at times the worker too. Occasionally, he mentioned his relationship with his
domineering mother, to whom he was still
close, and recognized some of the roots of his
current behavior. But, in general, there was little emphasis on developmental reflection; he
had no interest in concentrating on his early life.
The most productive work seemed to come from
the use of procedures that addressed his present
feelings and behavior.

In what turned out to be her last office session, Mrs. Stasio looked very ill; she was failing
quickly but, though subdued, remained mentally alert. She said she had talked over all the
important matters that concerned her when she
first came. She wanted the worker to know how
much their meetings had meant. The following
day she entered the hospital.

By telephone, a few days later, Mrs. Stasio
asked the worker to visit. When she got there,
she saw that Mrs. Stasio had many bruises, the
result of falls when she tried to get out of bed.
She said she did not want to the worker to visit
her again. She did not want anyone to see her
in this weakened condition or to be remembered
as a hospital patient. She knew she would die
soon. She had said good-bye to her children,
her parents, and a few close friends. She allowed only her husband to see her now; he was
there many hours each day. She took the worker's hand, held it tightly for a minute, and then
turned away. The worker touched Mrs. Stasio's
shoulder, said good-bye, and left sadly, real-

izing that her client's battle for life was ending. She had turned over the controls: to her illness, to the doctors, to death itself.

Two weeks later, Mr. Stasio called to say that his wife had died. At the funeral, for the first time, the worker briefly met the children, who stayed close to their father throughout.

Mr. Stasio returned to therapy for a period of seven months. He expressed his grief and anger; he and the worker shared memories of Mrs. Stasio. The fact that the worker was unashamed of her own sadness helped Mr. Stasio to express his feelings of loss. He said it comforted him to speak with someone who had known his wife so well and who could understand the range of emotions he was experiencing. He was both consoled and frustrated as he reviewed the final weeks of his wife's life when they had become closer than ever before. He used his sessions to discuss issues related to the children who, on the whole, were relating well with each other. And they truly respected him now, too. He talked over practical plans and decided to move to another town, at some distance from the clinic, which would be closer to his mother, who could help with care of the children. Having a woman to lean on was still important to him, he said. Roger was doing well, but Elizabeth seemed unhappy and Mr. Stasio sought information, which the worker gave, about a mental health service in the area where they would be living. He was a lonely man now, but strikingly more confident about his ability to take charge of his family.

The process of dying is as individualized as the process of living. Similarly, the style of one's grief is idiosyncratic. Every adaptation, every expression of outrage and despair about death takes its own form, depending on the personalities of the dying patient and of those who are left behind. In contrast to the Stasios, the gravity of terminal illness is minimized by some patients and their families, who cling to hope for recovery long after the doctors have given up. Sometimes relatives feel they must "protect" patients by giving false reassurance, in order to make their last days as untroubled as possible. In other situations, such avoidance is maintained to shield the family members themselves from anxiety and depression. Some doctors do not believe terminal patients should be given the whole truth about their condition, although this is less frequently so than it was only a few years ago. In every instance, the social worker has to take the lead from the client and family. One cannot recklessly intrude on defenses against death any more than one should push hard against any defense that has been erected to protect an individual from overwhelming emotion; otherwise, the psychological balance of some clients might be serious endangered. On the other hand, there is increasing evidence that, when possible and diagnostically indicated, the opportunity for dying patients to share grief with those who will survive protects them from feelings of alienation and the sense that they are being dealt with dishonestly. Furthermore, often openness can provide a family with the opportunity to begin to face grief, to reduce potential guilt, and to prepare for adapting to life after the patient has died.

Almost two years after Mr. Stasio terminated treatment, he telephoned the worker asking for a joint session with a divorcee whom he planned to marry. For the most part, he and his family had done well since he last saw the worker. But he wanted help with problems related to tensions occurring between his and his fiancée's adolescent children. The worker met with the couple twice. However, Mr. Stasio's future wife, who appeared to have strong managerial tendencies and definite opinions, took a dark view of psychological help; she had always worked out difficult problems herself, she said. Efforts to explore this woman's adamance were met with unyielding resistance. Reluctantly, with only a token protest, Mr. Stasio acceded to her wishes not to meet again. The worker thought the children might be responding to unspoken struggles between the adults. But, under the circumstances, exploration was not possible. It seemed that once again Mr. Stasio was planning his life with a woman who, in a somewhat different manner from Anna Stasio, was, nevertheless, determined to take charge of situations her way.

In every treatment situation, the clinical social worker has to accept limitations imposed by the client. One can suggest other options, as the worker in this instance did, but the work can go on only to the extent that the client is willing to participate. Although she had been tremendously helpful to Mr. and Mrs. Stasio during the months before the latter died, and to Mr. Stasio for a period thereafter, she saw no way to help forestall problems that might well ensue in this new family unless they were willing to examine the issues. Only time would tell whether the couple, whom the worker was careful not to alienate, would return if, in fact, difficulties did arise.

A FAMILY'S CRISIS: INVOLUNTARY CLIENTS ACCEPT HELP

It was almost three o'clock on a hot summer Friday afternoon when a case supervisor from Child Protective Services telephoned a very experienced senior worker at the Crisis Unit of the Family Guidance Center, whom she knew well. They had worked together on several cases. The supervisor briefly summarized her reason for calling: In her office at that moment were Lloyd and Sara Carter, a black couple, ages forty-seven and thirty-four, respectively. Their two children, Robert, eleven, and Denise, eight, had been placed in a foster home on an emergency basis on Monday. After an anonymous call, alleging child abuse and neglect, a child protective worker had gone to the home. The family lived in a large, well-kept apartment in a run-down building in "Southside" (the area where most blacks in the small city lived). When the protective worker arrived there in the af-

ternoon, she found the children frightened by her visit and unwilling to answer her questions. At home with them was an elderly aunt of Mrs. Carter's, Mrs. Williams, who lived with the family; she said very little also but did admit that Robert had had several marks across his back and buttocks as the result of a beating his father had given him because the boy had taken money out of his sister's drawer. Robert nodded when the worker asked him whether all of this were true.

The protective worker contacted Mr. Carter at a local factory where he was employed loading tractor-trailers; Mrs. Carter, who worked nights for an office-cleaning service, could not be located. Reading from the worker's report, the supervisor said that when Mr. Carter arrived home he was outraged at the worker's intrusion and launched into an intense argument with her, waving his arms and calling her names; he said that he had "whipped" Robert with a belt, that it was his right as a father to do so, that the boy deserved it and was not hurt, and that it was nobody's business but his and his wife's. He was not, he repeatedly insisted, a "child-beater." "Does this look like a house that doesn't take care of children?" he shouted, pointing to the neat, well-furnished apartment and the children's large rooms. Over and over he demanded, "Do these children look neglected?" directing the worker's attention to the children's healthy appearance. "I work two jobs and my wife works also to send these children to private [parochial] school." He either could not or would not say where Mrs. Carter was. "There's an adult here," he said, referring to Mrs. Williams. "That's all that should matter to you."

The worker, who reacted strongly to Mr. Carter's fury, was concerned that the children were not safe. She took steps the same day to have them declared "at risk" on an emergency basis; they were removed from the home that afternoon. Today, the supervisor said, the Family Court judge told Mr. and Mrs. Carter, who want the children returned to them, that they would have to accept a referral for counseling before he would release them. The supervisor said that they had spoken with the school principal, even though classes had ended; from their investigation, it appeared that there had *not* been a history of abuse. However, the principal thought that there might be marital difficulties. Something may be wrong, the supervisor said. Mrs. Carter seems uncommunicative; perhaps she has emotional problems, she speculated. The principal thought that Mrs. Carter was "strange" sometimes. Reluctantly, the parents accepted a referral to the Guidance Center, realizing that the children would remain in placement until they agreed to get help. Mr. Carter especially, the supervisor warned, was very, very angry: "a difficult man to deal with," she said. The supervisor concluded by saying that she had been out of town when the children were placed. Without exactly saying so, she left the impression that she thought the protective worker and substitute supervisor had acted too hastily.

The Guidance Center worker had to handle some misgivings about becoming involved immediately. She weighed in her own mind whether she should make the appointment for early next week or whether she should agree to see them right away, as the supervisor urged. She realized that if she had the meeting, she would have to put aside her own end-of-the-week fatigue; she would have to call home, as she had to fairly often, to say she would be late and then deal once again with her family's disappointment. Without doubt, the meeting would be a long and difficult one; she wondered to herself whether she had the energy for it. On the other hand, she had enough information to be able to empathize with the anger and desperation these parents must feel about the precipitous removal of their children. She thought she might be able to engage them most quickly if she could be available to them now, when they were so distraught. They were

probably not feeling very trusting of "helping people," given the events of the week. Thinking through her own issues and negative feelings and taking a few moments for anticipatory preparation,[3] helped to diminish her reluctance. She asked the supervisor to put one of the Carters on the telephone; in a controlled voice, Mr. Carter spoke with her and they arranged for an immediate appointment.

This initial appointment lasted almost two hours. The first hour was taken up with Mr. Carter's furious complaints about the way the protective services handled their investigation. The worker listened, expressing understanding and caring about how the couple must have experienced the entire episode, without presuming to judge the merits of every detail that Mr. Carter presented. The worker thought to herself that Mr. Carter seemed to be a very proud and private man who undoubtedly felt deeply humiliated by what had happened. When asked how it had been for her, Mrs. Carter said she felt that their case had been handled badly and that the worker had taken action without knowing the facts. "This would not have happened like this to a white family," she added. The protective services worker had a "mean way about her"; the supervisor they saw today was much more understanding. Mr. Carter agreed. Viewing it as a strength, the worker noted to herself that they were able to differentiate the personalities in spite of their distress; they were not indiscriminately blaming everybody equally. In a flat, phlegmatic tone Mrs. Carter added that neither her husband nor she physically abused the children; this was the worst physical punishment either Robert or Denise had ever received, and it had occurred after several warnings to Robert about taking money in the house. The worker believed her. If there were marital problems, they were not letting their conflicts interfere with their primary objectives: to have the children returned as soon as possible and to restore their reputation as conscientious, nonabusing parents. This, the worker thought, was another strength: when threatened, they stood together.

Both parents, but particularly Mrs. Carter, responded to questions about the children. Robert was sometimes difficult to manage; he got into minor difficulties in school fairly often. He did not get very good grades. But, the mother said, "He has a very sweet nature." Denise is "like a little old lady"; she gossips with adults and tries to boss other children, including her brother. She loves school and does well there. Sometimes, when Mrs. Carter has to go to work early, Denise cooks supper for her father and brother. The worker had the impression that Denise was special to Mr. Carter and that Robert was closer to his mother than to his father. Mrs. Carter said that both children were very frightened by their sudden removal from the home and hate being away, even though the foster family is nice to them. Together and separately, the parents had visited the children several times since they were placed on Monday. Another strength, the worker noted.

Deliberately, the worker did not explore the marital relationship except to ask at one point, in a low-key way, whether they fought physically; they denied that they did. Her immediate goals were to encourage the couple to express their feelings about their situation and to enlist their trust. She wanted them to know that she would do whatever she could to help them, without reassuring them that she would use her influence to get the children home immediately. Although Mr. Carter was very angry at having to take time off from work, he was much calmer now and agreed to return with his wife on Monday so that they could "get all this over with."

As the worker drove home, she thought about the Carters. She had no difficulty understanding how desperate and misused they felt. She suspected that the child protective worker had been frightened by Mr. Carter's rage and, perhaps, this had provoked her to arrange for the emergency placement. Physical abuse, she

thought to herself, is not the problem; she felt quite sure of this, and her impressions were supported by the protective services investigation. But *something* was wrong. Certainly, Mr. Carter had quite a temper, yet apparently he usually controlled it. But was there anything beyond the immediate situation that accounted for Mr. Carter's anger? It was impossible to assess the quality of the couple's relationship; during the entire meeting there had been very little interaction between them. Except for Mr. Carter's anger, little emotion was expressed. Something about Mrs. Carter's listless manner and general demeanor was puzzling. Was there a drug or alcohol problem? Perhaps she could find a way to explore this, she thought, but first she needed to make sure she had their trust. And whatever the problem was, she believed it would be revealed only after the present crisis was resolved. She knew that the Carters would come to the Guidance Center for a few months at least, as long as the Family Court probation department remained active; they would do nothing to jeopardize their children. As she parked and prepared to make the most of the remainder of the evening with her family, the worker felt glad that she had decided to see this couple right away. Although she could not be sure, she thought that they had begun to have confidence in her.

The second meeting confirmed the worker's earlier impressions; she felt certain that the children were not at risk for physical abuse. The couple agreed to continue counseling, understanding that return of the children would be contingent upon this. The worker asked whether the Carters felt comfortable with her; counseling is a very personal experience, she said, and it was important that they see someone who feels right to them. She wondered whether they found it difficult to speak with a white worker. They could see another worker if they preferred. In a matter-of-fact way, both Carters said they wanted to stay with her. The protective services supervisor joined the Guidance Center worker in recommending to Family Court that the children be released. On Wednesday, they went home.

At the worker's request, Mr. and Mrs. Carter brought the children to the next meeting. They were pleasant but seemingly guarded; definitely on their best behavior, the worker thought. They did say that they had not been happy in the foster home. There was very little spontaneity during the entire session, except for Mr. Carter's continuing expressions of anger at the actions that had been taken against their family. Although indirectly he indicated that he appreciated the worker's help in getting the children returned, he made it very clear that he did not like to be forced to come for counseling. Mrs. Carter was quieter than ever. Although she had nothing concrete to base it on, intuitively, from some subtle cues in the woman's demeanor, the worker suspected an alcohol problem. She knew, however, that if she were going to be helpful to this family, she would still have to wait for the opportunity to raise the question when she had the best chance of getting a nondefensive answer. The time was not now, she realized. This meeting was one in which everyone, including the worker, seemed to be treading water.

Less than an hour after the session ended, the worker received an agitated, almost unintelligible, call from Mr. Carter. "I need help," he said over and over again. Finally, the worker was able to make sense of what he was saying: When the family left the session, they had gone to a nearby shopping mall; Mrs. Carter went to the restroom, and when she returned Mr. Carter could tell ("I can always tell," he said) that she had been drinking. "She promised she wouldn't do this again," he said. "Can you help?" Mr. Carter was calling from a phone booth. The worker made an appointment for Mr. Carter to return to the office with his wife the following day.

When the couple came in, both looked exhausted. They had been arguing bitterly since yesterday. Mr. Carter, close to tears now, kept asking his wife how she could have done this to him and to the children. Once he was a little calmer, the worker turned her attention to Mrs. Carter. The history of her alcoholism unfolded: She had had several bouts of heavy drinking over the years. Three years ago she attended AA meetings for a while but stopped going when her drinking seemed to be under control. Mr. Carter sometimes drank at home or with friends, occasionally to excess, but Mrs. Carter never openly drank. "You've tried to keep it a secret," the worker suggested. Mrs. Carter nodded. On a hunch, the worker gently inquired whether she also used pills. Mrs. Carter looked down and, after several moments, nodded. "Is it time to get help?" the worker asked. Mrs. Carter nodded again.

Actually, the worker did not get the details of when Mrs. Carter had begun drinking again or of what drugs she had been taking. Rather, she focused on her medical needs. She guessed that Mrs. Carter's drinking had not been immediately exposed, even to Mr. Carter in spite of his claims, because she was also taking pills; tremors and other telltale signs of alcohol abuse sometimes can be masked by drug use. When Mr. Carter raised the question of AA, the worker said that she thought Mrs. Carter needed attention from a doctor and suggested hospitalization at the detoxification unit of the local hospital. At first, Mr. Carter protested; he thought his wife could stay at home and get help. The worker looked at Mrs. Carter. "I'll go," she said. Arrangements were facilitated by the worker's call to social service at the hospital. Mr. Carter called later to say that his wife had been admitted.

Twice during her twenty-one-day inpatient treatment Mrs. Carter telephoned the worker. The second time, when she was about to be released, the worker noted how vital her voice sounded, in contrast to her former flat way of speaking. Enthusiastically, she told the worker that the children had visited her several times and that she was looking forward to going home. She had attended AA meetings in the hospital and would continue in AA; the twelve-step program made a lot of sense to her, she said.

Couple sessions began after Mrs. Carter returned home. Over an eight-month period, including three months after Family Court closed its case, there were twenty-seven meetings; two of these were attended by the children. In a general sense, the worker was not surprised to learn that Mr. Carter had been the oldest of four children; his father deserted the family when he was ten, leaving him to be his mother's "right arm." She counted on him to help care for his siblings while she worked. By the time he was a young teenager, he had a full-time job; he left school after the eighth grade. His super-responsible role in his current family, his pride, his anger, his difficulty in asking for help, the worker thought, all were understandable in view of childhood circumstances that forced him to put his own needs aside and grow up quickly.

Mrs. Carter's early years were filled with deprivation and fear. Her mother, now dead for five years, had Mrs. Carter, her only child, when she was sixteen. She lived with several men during Mrs. Carter's childhood. Some of them were alcoholic; one of them sexually abused her when she was twelve. She never thought her mother liked or wanted her; she tried desperately to please her but never thought she succeeded. Her brightest childhood memories were about summers spent with her maternal grandmother, who lived in the south. "I always knew she loved me, and that helped see me through the winter times," she told the worker.

Mr. and Mrs. Carter met when she was a teenager in the town where her grandmother lived and Mr. Carter was raised. At that time, Mr. Carter was married to someone else, with whom he had three children, who were now adults. It was not until after they met again at the grandmother's funeral, when Mrs. Carter was twenty-two and Mr. Carter was separated, that they became interested in one other. After a brief courtship, they decided to move north, where they lived together until Mr. Carter's divorce came through. Robert was born before their wedding.

Now that Mrs. Carter was not drinking and was regularly attending AA meetings, the couple and the worker discussed treatment goals. Although no longer resentful about the sessions, Mr. Carter did not see the need for them. He was coming because of the court requirement and, as it turned out, because Mrs. Carter found treatment helpful. She reviewed unhappy and terrifying childhood experiences; she was able to express anger and sadness when talking about her mother. As time went on, Mr. Carter said that he would do anything he could to help his wife stay sober; he participated in the treatment less reluctantly, as long as the focus remained on Mrs. Carter.

However, with the worker's well-timed encouragement, the marital relationship was explored. Predictably, Mr. Carter said that there were no problems as long as the drinking did not resume. Tentatively, Mrs. Carter began to talk about dissatisfactions. Her major complaint was that her husband always wanted to take charge: "His way is *the* way," she told the worker. When she was younger, she said, she needed a strong man—someone on whom she could depend, someone who would tell her and show her what to do—she had been very insecure as a result of the erratic circumstances of her childhood and her mother's rejection of her. But now she felt belittled and frustrated by his takeover style. Since she quit drinking, she had gotten very positive support from AA members; her sponsor, an older and kindly woman, "is like the mother I never had," Mrs. Carter said. Because she felt more confident, the very traits that attracted her to her husband now filled her with resentment.

For several sessions, Mr. Carter minimized his wife's complaints. When she persisted, he became belligerent, telling her she was just making excuses for her own shortcomings. As she grew stronger and more outspoken, his anger accelerated. The worker's countertransference reactions to his behavior were neutralized by her recognition of how threatened he was at having his authority challenged. In a sense, for many years, his "strength" was sustained by his wife's "weakness." If he no longer feels needed, the worker hypothesized to herself, he is afraid he will lose his wife. From his perspective, she surmised, his close relationship to his mother was based on the fact that he had taken care of her. Furthermore, his behavior was supported by traditional male-female relationships that had been highly valued in his family of origin. When irritated by Mr. Carter's bullying manner, the worker reminded herself of how frightening it is to shed familiar roles when there is no certainty that relationships will survive without them.

Mrs. Carter would not be intimidated. She had felt the relief and exhilaration of her newly found independence; she would not, could not, turn back. Tension mounted in the marital relationship. Concerned that Mr. Carter's anger might be displaced onto the children, the worker asked the parents to bring them to a few sessions. Issues involving Mrs. Carter's alcohol problem, of which the children were aware, were discussed. The worker articulated what the children also knew: that their parents were coming for sessions to work out some problems between them. The worker observed to herself, as she had previously, that Mr. Carter seemed to turn to Denise for comfort and that he and Robert were rather distant. Although the children were a little more relaxed than when she first met them, they were not very forthcoming in the two sessions they attended and had little interest in being there. The worker was reassured that they were not direct targets of Mr. Carter's perturbed state. She also believed that the children would become more expressive and more appropriately related to their parents only

when the marital relationship was better resolved. After the next family session, she decided, she would recommend that they return to couple meetings.

As it turned out, Mr. and Mrs. Carter appeared alone for the next appointment. Mr. Carter looked shaken and disheveled. He told the worker that after an argument with his wife last night, he went out drinking, something he had not done since Mrs. Carter was hospitalized. When he got home, he accused his wife of having affairs. He told her that he had never believed that Robert was his son. Instead of his usual angry diatribes, however, he became what Mrs. Carter described as "hysterical." He "cried and cried," she said, until he finally fell asleep. Uncharacteristically (he rarely missed a day of work), he asked her to call his employer and say he was sick. "That's what I was and that's what I am," Mr. Carter groaned. "I need help," he added. When he said it this time, however, he knew it was for *him*. The worker did not have to reply. Mrs. Carter turned to her husband and said, "I'll help you."

This was the turning point. Very quickly, Mr. Carter realized how frightened he had been for his entire married life. He had never dared to lean on his wife. Most of the time he did not even know that he wanted or needed to. Mrs. Carter reassured him that Robert was his son and that she had never been unfaithful to him; she had no desire to leave him, unless he reverted to his domineering, stubborn ways. She told him that she felt much closer to him when he acted like a "normal" person, instead of a superman. She, too, liked to feel needed. She liked it when he talked with rather than at her; she had been very lonely before.

During the next to the last session, the couple and the worker all became tearful as Mr. Carter told a story of how frightened he had been at age eleven when he was sexually assaulted by a male friend of the family; he did not dare tell his mother, not because she would blame him but because she would feel sorry for him, a response that he would have found intolerable. He was only now allowing his wife's tenderness to touch him; in his mind it had always been mixed up with pity, he said.

The decision to terminate felt right to Mr. and Mrs. Carter and to the worker. "There will always be problems," Mrs. Carter said, "but we've got a hold on them now." Together they reviewed the many phases of their relatively short treatment. Mr. and Mrs. Carter each realized how when one made changes, the other grew too. The worker gave them a lot of credit for the courageous way they had tackled difficult issues. She also asked whether there were anything they wished she had done differently. Mr. Carter wondered whether the children should have been involved; he would have preferred to leave them out of it. His wife disagreed, saying that she thought it had helped them to know they were trying to make things better for the family. Mrs. Carter, who had been so listless when they first met, expressed her gratitude to the worker in almost flowery terms. She appreciated the worker's confidence in her and in their marriage; she said she never felt judged. "I'll never forget you," she added. Mr. Carter was less effusive than his wife, but when he left, he shook her hand, looked her in the eye, and said, "I thank you." As she watched them walk away from her, the worker thought: Now it is going to be *his* turn to learn from *her*.

A few months after they ended their sessions and again four years later, Mrs. Carter called to refer AA friends for therapy. She was proud of her sobriety; she continued to attend AA meetings regularly and still had the same caring sponsor. The children were doing well, although Robert was going through his "teenage ups and downs." As for the marriage, they had some "bumpy" times, she said, but nothing that compared to the way things used to be.[4]

The success of this treatment relied heavily on strengths the couple brought with them and the worker's recognition of them. Throughout this text we have stressed the importance of focus on health as well as "pathology," of realistic optimism, of empathy, of warmth and genuineness. We have urged flexibility and have emphasized the importance of tailoring each piece of work to the needs and personalities of the particular clients being seen. Had the worker believed that involuntary clients are intractably "resistant" or that she had to confront Mrs. Carter's alcoholism before the timing was right, she would not have gained this couple's confidence. If she was convinced that lower-socioeconomic-class, relatively poorly educated black clients were unable to use casework assistance, her negative attitude probably would have stifled her best efforts. Fortunately, this worker preferred to make individualized assessments rather than to base her thinking on stereotypes that, as often as not, do not hold up in reality.

ANXIETY ATTACKS: THE ADULT CHILD OF AN ALCOHOLIC FATHER

At the suggestion of his sister, who worked in the mental health field, Jed Cooper, twenty-two, made an appointment with a clinical social worker in private practice. In his first interview, he said he felt tongue-tied. He blushed frequently and shifted uneasily in his chair. When he tried to explain why he had come, he became flustered and inarticulate. In this session, therefore, the worker took a very active, supportive role; she told Jed that it was hard for most people to talk to a strange person about personal matters. She added that she thought it would become easier for him as they went along, saying too, that it can become more difficult if one tries too hard, before one feels more relaxed. Mostly, the worker asked factual questions, to which Jed responded fairly comfortably, postponing, for the time being, those related to his reasons for wanting help.

She learned that Jed was the youngest of four children; his three sisters were married and now only he lived at home with his parents. His father, a retired policeman, was working as a security guard. Recently, his mother had begun working part time as a saleswoman in a department store. His mother was born in Ireland and his father was second-generation Irish; both were Catholic. At his mother's insistence, Jed had attended parochial schools. After graduating from high school, he had held various jobs and, for the past year, was learning carpentry by working as an assistant to a cabinetmaker. He seemed most at ease talking about his work and smiled for the first time when he answered questions about his job; he said he wanted to become an "A-1" craftsman. Speaking more spontaneously now, Jed said that his employer was "like a father" to him. Rather than inquiring immediately about this, the worker waited a moment, at which point Jed volunteered that he hated his father, who was an alcoholic and had been for as long as he could remember. Once this was said, Jed's tension obviously mounted again and the worker, while demonstrating that she understood his strong feelings, did not explore the matter further. She simply agreed that it must feel good to have a boss he could really enjoy.

When the session ended, it was still unclear just what had precipitated Jed's request for help. Only in the last few minutes was he able to say that he tended to get "nervous" and his sister thought he should have "someone to talk to." At this point, the worker did not have enough information to assess the nature of Jed's difficulties. She *was* aware that his anxiety was high and that supportive measures designed to reduce it took precedence over getting more information. She considered cultural factors that might have contributed to his uneasiness. Clients with a strong Catholic background are sometimes loath to share personal material with outsiders, particularly those not connected with

the church. As yet, she had no way of knowing whether some particular event had catalyzed Jed's acute state of anxiety and embarrassment. Some early childhood fears may have been activated. The possibility that Jed was severely disturbed could not be ruled out. But, seemingly well oriented, he functioned constructively on his job, and there was no apparent thought disorder. His affect was restricted, but when relaxed, he seemed emotionally responsive. In order to convey her caring and yet elicit Jed's motivation for and participation in treatment, the worker asked whether he wanted to meet again. When he nodded, she offered him three alternative dates for the next session, ranging from three to ten days away from the first interview. Jed chose the nearest date and left, firmly shaking the worker's hand and thanking her.

The Course of Treatment

In the second meeting, again Jed was tense and constricted for the first few minutes but became calmer more quickly than in the initial session. Still blushing frequently, he was able to say fairly fluently that he had become worried when, two weeks before, he had been sitting in the living room with his father watching a ball game and suddenly became extremely "nervous" and dizzy. When he tried to get up, his knees buckled and he fell to the floor. The episode did not last long, but afterward he began to sob uncontrollably. He went to work the next day but could not concentrate. He was so frightened that he spoke with his oldest sister, who suggested that he see a doctor, who told him there seemed to be nothing physically wrong. Again, at the suggestion of his sister, he called the worker. He had come, he said, to find out what was wrong with him. When the worker said that the incident must have worried him, Jed asked, "Does it mean I'm crazy?" He did not seem "crazy" to her, she said, but it did sound as though something were frightening him a lot. Jed volunteered that he had a similar "spell" two years before, again when he was alone with his father. He asked the worker whether she had ever heard of anything like this before. He seemed to be asking to be reassured, either that the worker was competent to help him or that his situation was not unique or hopeless. She answered that indeed she had known of other people who had responded to intense feeling or fear in similar ways, but that it might take a little time to find out why this had happened to him. "Is there a cure?" Jed asked. The worker, knowing that Jed was functioning normally in his daily life, said that the worst of his "attack" seemed to be over, adding that she thought it was possible some of his nervousness may have come from fear that he was "crazy." Jed agreed but added that he tended to be a nervous person, especially when he was at home. The worker could not be totally reassuring, since she still did not understand all of the dimensions of his symptoms, but she did say very positively that usually when people learn about themselves and their feelings they get considerable relief. Jed seemed encouraged.

For many meetings to come, Jed would arrive and say he did not know what he "should" talk about. His thoughts would block until he could find a comfortable subject—often his job, his car, the weather—from which he could then ease into more difficult material. In one session, after about two months of treatment, Jed asked the worker to come out to his car to see a bureau he had built and brought to show her. She was genuinely impressed with his work and freely told him so. Jed evidently needed support and encouragement, not only to reduce his anxiety but to be reassured that the worker thought of him as a competent, worthwhile man.

Positive—as well as negative—countertransference is important for a worker to recognize. In this case, the worker was aware of very warm feelings for Jed; she saw him as an appealing, sensitive person who sparked in her a "motherly" response, a wish to look after him. She made a conscious effort to keep the expression of some of her strongest feelings in check and still provide the sustaining climate he required. Furthermore, since one's subjective reactions to a client can often be helpful in diagnosis, the worker was alerted to the possibility that Jed's manner might elicit overly protective responses from other people in his life, including, perhaps, his mother, about whom he had said very little.

Jed had particular difficulty talking about his feelings toward his parents. Although he discussed his woman friend Laura, of whom he was very fond, he also shied away from any discussion of their intimate relationship. When Jed became flustered, even by gently placed questions, the worker would make remarks such as "Perhaps you'll feel more like discussing that at another time," or, "Maybe you can let me know when you feel comfortable enough to tell me something about that." Of these troublesome subjects, Jed was least inhibited about his anger at his father, for being unavailable to and critical of him as a child, for being a "whiner," for his excessive drinking and for the fact that he had let Jed's mother "wear the pants." He felt that his father had never liked him. His resentment was conscious and strong. Nevertheless, once he could ventilate it, he said it felt really good; in his family, people rarely shared deep feelings about anything. He said he usually did not confide in anyone, even his woman friend. Only when he became very frightened by his "attack" had he told his sister about it.

Aided by the worker's consistently calm, accepting, supportive approach, Jed slowly but surely took more initiative in starting sessions and in getting into the issues he had been sidestepping. He still needed sustainment, but to a far lesser degree. Having ventilated his anger at his father, he seemed relieved enough to begin to talk about his mother, whom he described as domineering and a "nag," although he knew she loved him. She had always catered to him, more than she did to his sisters and father. As he revealed more, it turned out that even when he was a small child his mother complained to him about his father, and this always made him feel very uncomfortable; in fact, it still did. His mother often asked him personal questions, about what he was doing and where he was going. She seemed hurt when he went out in the evenings. In the last year, since he had been dating Laura, his mother plied him with inquiries about her, giving him the impression that she was eager to find something to criticize. Mostly, he evaded her questions, but they annoyed him and made him "nervous." His mother, he complained, went through his bureau drawers, ostensibly searching for laundry. He never said anything to her about it but made sure he didn't keep anything private there. Jed also said he felt sorry for her because she had had "such a hard life," especially with his father.

By the time Jed had revealed this much, after about three months of therapy, he reported that on the whole he was feeling more relaxed than he had "for years." He was no longer afraid of "going crazy." Periodically, however, he felt guilty or, as he put it, "disloyal." He felt justified complaining about his father; but talking about his mother, he said, made him very uncomfortable. He felt he was hurting her, even though he knew she could not know what he was saying. He had not even told her he was in therapy.

Although initially it was difficult to evaluate the seriousness of Jed's problems, by this point in treatment the worker had formulated a fairly well-rounded diagnostic assessment. She viewed him as a man with intelligence, competence, and talents who functioned well in many areas. He had the capacity for good interpersonal relationships. Although shy and not given to sharing intimacies with others, he had several friends of long standing with whom he hunted and camped. When he spoke of his friend Laura, he did so with tenderness and sensitivity. He related warmly and positively to the worker. He had a clear sense of his own values and ethical standards. On the whole, then, ego and superego functions were well developed.

Although in early meetings Jed appeared quite disturbed, in time it appeared that some of his conflicts were centered in the psychosexual area. The worker surmised that his perception of his mother's intrusiveness and, perhaps, actual seductiveness, influenced Jed to feel guilty and conflicted about his relationship with her. He loved her but feared her impingement on his life. Furthermore, his father's lack of assertiveness and degraded status in the family had deprived Jed of a strong male model to admire and emulate. From the psychoanalytic point of view, the worker speculated that Jed's unconscious "castration fears" (derived from repressed incestuous wishes and fears of his father's retaliation), as well as his conscious anger at his father, were expressed through anxiety attacks, both of which had occurred in his father's presence. The worker speculated that unresolved oedipal issues were defended against primarily through defenses of inhibition, suppression, and repression. The clinical diagnoses the worker considered was "anxiety hysteria."[5] Subtle doubts about his masculinity, evidenced by his strong need for confirmation as a "male" (e.g., the manner in which he sought praise from the worker and his employer for his carpentry skills), lent further support to this diagnosis. There also appeared to be some unfulfilled needs related to having been either ignored or criticized by his often moody father and "babied" by his unhappy, apparently controlling mother. The DSM-III-R diagnosis of "panic disorder" also seemed to describe Jed's presenting problem.

There was still another perspective from which the worker could have assessed Jed's situation, had the information been available at the time the treatment took place. He was one of many adult children of alcoholic parents, a group that was not studied intensively until the last decade. Jed and the Cooper family as a whole were obviously deeply affected by many of the problems that frequently develop around alcoholism. Jed's descriptions of his family suggested rigidity, a characteristic of many families with alcoholic members, rather than flexibility. Certainly Jed's inhibitions prevented much spontaneity. His difficulty talking about himself or his family was consistent with the spoken or unspoken rule in many families with alcoholics: "Don't talk; don't feel; don't trust."[6] Children are often taught to hide the truth about the family situation from others. Families with alcoholic members may isolate themselves; the family system is often "closed," resistant to the involvement of "outsiders." When children are taught not to need others, it is hard (often impossible) for them, when they are young and when they are older, to ask for help. It was apparent that Jed had to struggle to reveal himself to the worker. Only when he was terrified by his symptoms did he talk to his sister about his concerns and seek treatment.

Thus, children of alcoholics often grow up learning not to talk about issues that really matter; to deny powerful emotions of terror, rage, and grief; to pretend to themselves that problems in the family do not exist. Obviously, many of Jed's feelings were repressed and suppressed. The children may take on false roles ("hero," "scapegoat," "lost child," "mascot," "placater") which serve to disguise and distract attention from the alcoholism and the feelings that derive from the family situation. We see such roles, efforts to adapt to and survive in the dysfunctional alcoholic system, assumed by children at a very young age. Although Jed was not as "lost" or as much of a "loner" as many of those who fall into the "lost child" category, to some degree he did share qualities of that role, such as his low profile, his choice of rather isolated vocational and recreational activities,

his anxieties about intimacy, his tendency to seek or expect little help from others, and his subtle doubts about his sexual identity. On the other hand, Jed was not the "forgotten child" that some in this role are; his special relationship with his mother, for better and worse, probably prevented him from being as isolated as some "lost children" are. As inhibited and embarrassed by his feelings as he was, he was not as emotionally stunted as many "lost" people are. Jed was capable of warmth and sensitivity to others, including Laura. Just as all diagnostic categories must be used cautiously, without stereotyping and sacrificing the assessment of the individual, it is equally important to avoid pinning roles on adult children of alcoholics without very careful evaluation of the unique qualities of the person in question.

Confusion naturally derives from the unpredictability and inconsistency that are almost always part of the experience of growing up in a house in which there is alcoholism. Particularly at the beginning of treatment, Jed seemed to be unsure of what kind of reactions he could expect from the worker. Personal and generational boundaries are often violated in alcoholic families. Certainly, Jed felt his privacy was invaded by his mother; his father's criticisms were probably mostly projections rather than related to actual qualities of Jed's and, as such, were intrusions. Because authentic interest in and affirmation of children of alcoholics is often uneven at best, self-esteem can be seriously flawed. Jed's parents were too self-involved to praise and validate him in his own right consistently; confidence was therefore not as well developed as it should have been. Yet, as the worker was aware, Jed's strengths were many and, in spite of his handicaps, he seemed motivated to continue coming to treatment until he felt better.

In the early months of Jed's therapy, the worker concentrated on procedures that were sustaining or that led to description and ventilation. On the whole, reflective procedures were limited to those related to current, practical matters. (For example, at one point Jed wondered whether he should consider moving out of his parents' home since he was so uncomfortable there. He decided that he was financially unprepared to make the change since he wanted to save money for the time when he would marry. He concluded that instead he would spend as little time at home as possible, a decision which, incidentally, may have contributed to his greater relaxation at this juncture.)

The worker made few interpretations except those that were reassuring. The "corrective" relationship—one that was consistent, accepting, and neither seductive, intrusive, nor possessive—was in contrast to the one he perceived he had with his mother. Although individual situations differ, in this case it was probably helpful that the worker was a woman roughly in his mother's age group and yet treated him with understanding and as an adult. It was also fortunate that concurrent with therapy he was benefiting from what might be called a corrective relationship with his employer, who, apparently unlike Jed's father, truly liked Jed, treated him "like a man," and admired his talents.

Throughout this early period, the worker refrained from encouraging reflection about issues close to Jed's psychosexual conflict, even though she suspected many of these were conscious or preconscious. Her reason for this was that trial questions, about his woman friend or his parents, that could have tapped greater awareness in these areas were generally evaded by Jed. She knew it would not help to press him to the point that he would become blocked or immobilized by anxiety; nor, of course, did she want to risk the possibility that he would bolt from therapy.

Gradually, after Jed had been in treatment close to six months, he began talking more about the discomfort he felt when he was around his parents. He wanted to understand it, realizing that his anxiety attack was related in some way. He also discussed some of his concerns about his relationship with Laura (heretofore he had only spoken of his pleasant, tender feelings for her), now confiding that he thought he had a "sexual hangup." He blushed when he said this but did not block or evade. He explained further that he would often spend the day excitedly thinking about Laura but, when they got together for intercourse, as often as not he lost his erection. Laura was very understanding, and he knew she loved him anyway, but he felt deeply humiliated.

Once he felt safe enough to approach these subjects, the worker began to elicit more and more relevant material. He could reflect now on how his anxiety when he was with his father related to unexpressed anger, but Jed could see that this was only a small part of a larger picture. He had known he was angry, and talking about it had brought relief, but he searched for more. He became interested in early memories. He recalled a frequent scene at home when he was young: his father would come from work, still wearing his gun and holster and he, Jed, would run in terror to his bedroom. On his day off, Jed's father would sit in the living room, drinking continuously, and Jed would imagine that as his father became increasingly intoxicated, he might grab him and beat him. In reality, his father never assaulted him, but the fear remained. Jed recalled recurrent childhood nightmares related to his fear of his father. As he reviewed these early events, he realized that his mother had wanted him as an ally against his father, frequently complaining about what a "bum" the latter was and telling Jed that she hoped he would not grow up to be a "drunk." Evidently, she turned to him to try to make up for her disappointing marriage. The more he talked, the more resentful of her he became for berating his father, who "didn't have a chance" in the face of her attacks.

Spontaneously, Jed recognized that there was something "sexy" about his mother's intrusiveness and overprotection of him. He remembered being uncomfortable at age five or six when his mother seemed "too eager" to help him with his bath. He once asked whether his father could bathe him instead, a request that insulted his mother. Jed was torn between wanting to "wriggle out" from her grip and wanting to please her. From a very young age he guarded his private thoughts and fantasies, knowing that by being secretive he was disappointing her. On the other hand, he helped her with her chores and would run all the way home to show her his good report card. Some of his happiest moments were when she told him he was the "nicest boy in the world." Much of this material was conscious; in fact, Jed said that he sometimes felt his head "swimming" with thoughts about his early years. Some of the memories were preconscious (such as those about his baths) but came to the surface over the course of treatment. An important aspect of this phase of therapy was that Jed was able to see his anger at his parents in another perspective; he knew he resented his father, but he had never dared to feel more than mild annoyance toward his mother.

There were some connections Jed never actually made. For example, if his intense uneasiness in the presence of his father derived in part from "castration anxiety," this was an unconscious fear generally not tapped by casework treatment. Similarly, incestuous wishes were also repressed. He reflected at some length, however, on the connections between his mother's need to intrude and his anger at his father for not taking charge of the situation and protecting him from her. The more he thought about it, the surer he was that what he had always believed was not true: his father *did* like him. He now saw him as a "coward" in the face of a domineering wife. Jed even remembered occasions when his father had invited him for a day of hunting and his mother said it was too dangerous and did not allow it. Instead of confronting her, Jed's father dropped the matter.

One of the high points in treatment came when Jed realized with sadness that his father was not anyone to fear at all, but a pathetic man. Thus, although the actual oedipal issues were not uncovered, many of the residues and related matters were, with the result that Jed no longer irrationally feared his father as he had.

It is true that a client sophisticated about psychological matters might be able to express his difficulties by using such terms as "castration anxiety," "mutilation fears," "sexual identity" problems, "incestuous wishes," and so on, but this does not necessarily mean that unconscious material would be brought to consciousness any more than it was for Jed. In general, clinical social workers concentrate on the derivatives that, in Jed's case, greatly reduced not only his fear but also his anger and guilt. Toward the latter phase of therapy, his anger at his father had dissipated and he was left primarily with the sadness that the older man's drinking and passivity had deprived them both of years that could never be recaptured. After the surge of resentment he felt toward his mother and the sense of guilt that accompanied it for being "disloyal," Jed realized too that she was a lonely woman who probably tried to control others because she felt so helpless herself. By the time treatment terminated, Jed's greater comfort with himself also led him to feel genuine sympathy for his parents' unhappiness.

After Jed revealed his sexual problem with Laura, there was very little further discussion about this. Intuitively, Jed seemed to know that it was related to experiences with and feelings about his parents. Undoubtedly, having grown up in an alcoholic family system affected Jed's capacity for intimacy and his self-esteem and interfered with confidence in his masculinity, as discussed earlier. One can only speculate about other connections. For example, were his fears about sexual intercourse related to his fear of his father's anger? to anxiety about incest stimulated by his mother's seductiveness? to guilt about betraying his mother? to fear of losing his sense of privacy? to the fact that a parental model for adult love and intimacy was lacking? Most likely, some combination of all of these was involved. In any event, as he was freed to express and work through some of his feelings about his childhood and the ways these related to his present situation, his sexual relationship with Laura markedly improved. He rarely had difficulty now maintaining an erection, and he felt more deeply satisfied than ever with their sexual life. By the time the treatment (which lasted a little over a year) ended, Jed was planning to share an apartment with Laura, whom, he assumed, he would eventually marry. After the final session, Jed asked the worker to come outside to meet Laura, who was waiting for him. As the worker recorded it, "It was hard to tell whether Jed was more proud of himself or of Laura."

To summarize, the complexity of diagnosis, the importance of the treatment relationship, and the selective, carefully timed use of treatment procedures are all well illustrated by this case. As is often true of clients with acute anxiety and strong inhibitions, at first Jed appeared to be more disturbed than he was. As his many strengths, including his capacity to engage in a warm relationship with the worker, became apparent, so did the assessment and treatment plan. Even though Jed was basically sound psychologically, the worker recognized he sorely needed a relationship he could trust without fear of being criticized or overwhelmed by the needs of another. He needed a caring, reliable, and "tuned in" person who could help him to uncover the way he felt and to express his feelings without fear or guilt. The worker affirmed his achievements, his many fine personal qualities, and—of utmost importance—his right to feel "like a man."

The mutual long-range goals, more or less explicitly shared by Jed and the worker, were to enable him to feel less anxious about himself and about "going crazy." As therapy progressed, he also wanted to improve his sexual

functioning. Intermediate goals, primarily determined by the worker, were to provide a climate that would foster positive transference, necessary for providing the "corrective" experience and for helping him feel safe enough to be reflective. His anxiety and timidity, combined with his Catholic school and family training (where emotional expression was strongly discouraged), required an extended period of sustainment. When the diagnostic picture becomes clear, it is sometimes difficult to resist premature interpretations. However, it was fortunate that this worker was sufficiently empathic with the intensity of Jed's anxiety to wait. Once ready, he made good use of reflective procedures and was in large measure freed of burdensome inner pressures and confusions. It is important to note again that the successful treatment was undoubtedly expedited by the reassuring, "man-to-man" relationship he had with his employer, a relationship he could never have with his father.

Readers may wonder why family therapy or family group meetings were not considered in this case, since Jed's difficulties were so intertwined with his relationships, past and present, with his parents. The worker was experienced in family therapy but did not view it as the treatment of choice. As discussed in Chapter 16, family treatment is contraindicated when a client's defenses or anxiety would be so intensified by group meetings that he could not benefit from them. Jed's inhibitions and anxiety were so marked, even when he was not in the presence of his parents, that the worker felt certain his blocking and discomfort would have presented insurmountable problems in family sessions. Only close to the end of therapy, when Jed had resolved the major issues that handicapped him, would he have been able to relax enough to express himself meaningfully to his parents. Furthermore, Jed was able to make progress in individual treatment. Only if counterpressures from his family had prevented him from moving forward or had resulted in setbacks, would family therapy have been indicated. In addition, the fact that Jed was in treatment on his own and taking charge of resolving his difficulties supported his wish to feel adult and self-reliant. And, as a result of the work he did on himself, his relationships with his parents felt much less threatening, more relaxed, although never truly close or comforting.

Recent and increasing attention that the helping professions are giving to the damaging consequences of growing up in an alcoholic family system has been enormously helpful to psychosocial assessment and treatment. In fact, according to the worker who treated Jed, this knowledge would have been extremely valuable had it been available at the time he was originally seen, even though both Jed and the worker felt the therapy had been very successful. Among many other benefits, it would have been reassuring to Jed to realize that his problems were common to many other adult children of alcoholics and that he was not a "freak" or "crazy." Nevertheless, the framework used by the worker was adequate to free Jed from most of his crippling inhibitions and to help him to lead a life free of many of the unresolved issues that had been signaled by the eruption of his anxiety attacks.

Postscript on Jed Cooper

Eight years after termination, Jed contacted the same worker and was seen for five sessions. He had been experiencing some anxiety—"not attacks like I had before"—and felt uncomfortable and worried that he might have similar episodes again. Jed had married Laura; their relationship had worked out very well, he reported. They had a five-year-old daughter, with whom he was obviously delighted. He had taken over his employer's small business after the latter retired and moved away; he still enjoyed his work but missed his friend and mentor. Six months before Jed called the worker, his father died; he had been severely disabled

by emphysema and other complications for over two years but only stopped drinking and smoking a few months before his death. Jed said he "felt nothing" at the funeral and burial and still was mostly detached, although sad that his father had been "such a waste." For the first time in his life, after his father's death, Jed began drinking frequently—to excess, he feared. Realizing that he might be vulnerable to the addiction that destroyed his father, he gave up all alcohol "cold turkey." He did not and would not go to AA. It is hard enough to talk to one person, he said. Emphatically, he told the worker that "group conversations" held no interest for him whatsoever. Characteristically, he had taken care of it himself and was proud that he had. Knowing Jed as she did, the worker did not suggest that he join a group for adult children of alcoholics. Again, individualized assessment is essential; although such groups are helpful to very many, others simply will not or cannot benefit from them. Nevertheless, Jed was very interested and reassured when the worker shared some of the insights that have come to light about common experiences of those who have grown up in an alcoholic family system.

Jed said that his mother seemed depressed and "lost" since his father's death. Although they had gotten along quite well, even if superficially, over the recent years, now he began to feel pressured by her again in a way he hadn't since terminating treatment the first time. Jed spent most of his therapy this time expressing feelings about both of his parents; he told the worker he remembered how helpful this had been before. After the second session, he was greatly relieved. He was able to be more compassionate toward his mother without feeling he should take care of her. He stayed for the three additional sessions for "insurance." At the suggestion of the worker, Laura attended the final session. This turned out to be particularly helpful because she felt that Jed had withdrawn from her in recent months. In the session, he shared with her the material and feelings about his parents he had discussed in treatment. With the worker's help, Jed could recognize that his anxieties, in part precipitated by the recent changes in his family of origin, were exacerbated because he had simultaneously retreated from his wife, from whom he could have received understanding and comfort (in which case he might never have had to return to see the worker!) Just as when he was a child, under stress, he "got lost." Once aware of how his old habits had reemerged, Jed vowed he would try not to let this happen again. The point was not lost on Laura either; by nature, she was a person who liked to reach out, especially when reassured that she was wanted, and Jed was able to respond. Both realized that they had to make a point of spending more "private time" together.

Interestingly, Jed's sister June, the sister who was seven years older than Jed and had originally urged him to seek help, came to see the worker shortly after Jed terminated for the second time. She had learned from her brother how helpful therapy had been for him. In contrast to Jed, she is overweight ("Food is my addiction," she announced), gregarious, and laughs and cries easily. When she came for treatment, she had just separated, painfully, from her alcoholic and verbally abusive husband. A social worker, working with disturbed children, June had many of the qualities of the "placater." She was the mediator and caretaker in her family; she recalled trying to break up fights between her parents when her father was drunk. She had tried to comfort her mother and felt responsible for her younger brother and sister. She had repeatedly pleaded with her father to stop drinking. In large part, she had put aside her own needs, focusing mostly on trying to "fix" the problems and feelings of others. As treatment progressed, she began to realize how her marital relationship replicated many of her childhood experiences. At the time of this writing, June, an outgoing and friendly woman, is

a member of an Adult Children of Alcoholics group and finds it extremely helpful. She is also in treatment working hard at trying to understand her own family experiences and to determine what she needs, wants, feels rather than being so totally preoccupied with rescuing and placating others. The rules, roles, and behaviors of the alcoholic family tend to be transmitted down through the generations, but at least two of the Cooper children, Jed and June, have interrupted the process. Without doubt, they and their children will live far healthier, more autonomous and fulfilled lives as a result of their having done so.

Successful treatment, of course, requires a worker with the personality, intuition, talent, and concern to do the work; it calls for enough personal security and flexibility to accept the pains and defeats as well as the pleasures and achievements of the clients we see. But as important as these worker characteristics are, they are not enough. A broad body of knowledge of people, their situations, and how these interact is required to individualize the particular client who asks for help. Responsible treatment rests on a theoretical framework, tested through practice, combined with a knowledge of the nature and effects of clinical methods and procedures. The cases presented in this chapter are certainly not offered as "proof" either of theories or results but as demonstrations of the relationships among psychosocial study, diagnostic understanding, and treatment presented in previous chapters. They are among the cases on which the theories developed in this book are based.

NOTES

1. For an excellent and comprehensive work on schizophrenia, see Silvano Arieti, *Interpretation of Schizophrenia,* 2d ed. (New York: Basic Books, 1974); the reader may be particularly interested in the discussion of psychotherapy, pp. 525–664, as companion reading to this presentation. See also Robert

Cancro et al., *Strategic Intervention in Schizophrenia* (New York: Behavioral Publications, 1974), for several good papers on treatment; and Judith Nelsen's two excellent articles: "Treatment-Planning for Schizophrenia," *Social Casework,* 56 (February 1975), 67–73; and "Treatment Issues in Schizophrenia," *Social Casework,* 56 (March 1975),145–151.

2. See Elisabeth Kubler-Ross, *On Death and Dying* (New York: Macmillan, 1969); Elizabeth R. Prichard et al., eds., *Social Work with the Dying Patient and the Family* (New York: Columbia University Press, 1977); Gwen Schwartz-Borden, "Grief Work: Prevention and Intervention," *Social Casework,* 67 (October 1986), 499–505; and Avery D. Weisman, *On Dying and Denying: A Psychiatric Study of Terminality* (New York: Behavioral Publications, 1972).

3. For discussions of anticipatory preparation, see Carel B. Germain and Alex Gitterman, *The Life Model of Social Work Practice* (New York: Columbia University Press, 1980), Chapter 2; and Alfred Kadushin, *The Social Work Interview,* 2d ed. (New York: Columbia University Press, 1983), Chapter 6. See also the discussion of this issue in Chapter 11.

4. See Chapter 11, note 4, for references on involuntary and hard-to-reach clients.

For readings on alcoholism, see Linde A. Chernus, "Clinical Issues in Alcoholism Treatment," *Social Casework,* 66 (February 1985), 67–75; Lois Lester, "The Special Needs of the Female Alcoholic," *Social Casework,* 63 (October 1982), 451–456; Jerome D. Levin, *Treatment of Alcoholism and Other Addictions: A Self-Psychology Approach* (Northvale, N.J.: Aronson, 1987);

and Sheldon Zimberg et al., eds., *Practical Approaches to Alcoholism Psychotherapy* (New York: Plenum, 1978).

5. See Lucille N. Austin, "Dynamics and Treatment of the Client with Anxiety Hysteria," in Howard J. Parad, ed., *Ego Psychology and Dynamic Casework* (New York: Family Service Association of America, 1968), pp. 137–158. See also Hilde Bruch's paper, which offers helpful information about treatment of anxiety, "The Sullivanian Concept of Anxiety," in William E. Fann, ed., *Phenomenology and Treatment of Anxiety* (New York: Spectrum, 1979), pp. 261–270. In the same volume, see Robert M. Gilliand's "Anxiety: A Psychoanalytic View," pp. 251–260, for a theoretical discussion of anxiety from the psychoanalytic point of view.

6. Claudia Black, *It Will Never Happen to Me!* (Denver, Colo.: MAC Publications, 1982). There is rich material available on Adult Children of Alcoholics, including: Robert J. Ackerman, *Children of Alcoholics: A Guidebook for Educators, Therapists and Parents* (Holmes Beach, Fla.: Learning Publications, 1983); Wayne Kritsberg, *The Adult Children of Alcoholics Syndrome: From Discovery to Recovery* (Pompano Beach, Fla.: Health Communications, 1985); and Phyllis Tainey, *Adult Children of Alcoholics: Workshop Models for Family Life Education* (Milwaukee, Wisc.: Family Service America, 1988).

See also Bryan E. Robinson, *Working with Children of Alcoholics: The Practitioner's Handbook* (Lexington, Mass.: D. C. Heath, 1989); and Sharon Wegscheider, *Another Chance: Hope and Health for the Alcoholic Family* (Palo Alto, Calif.: Science and Behavior Books, 1981).

In Conclusion

As we wrote at the outset, it has been the purpose of this book to describe and analyze the psychosocial approach to casework. It has not been our aim to *prove* that it is the best approach for helping troubled people or people seeking to make improvements in themselves and their situations. However, we have observed its effectiveness in our own practice and in that of many students and colleagues. Its empirical base is well documented in a great many reports of single cases and small groups of cases as well as in larger studies. There is no need to repeat here the discussion of research issues and methodology in Chapter 1, except to reiterate our conviction that further study by practitioners of psychosocial casework methods and their effects continues to be greatly needed. Better techniques are now more available than formerly for small case studies analyzing in detail the effects of various procedures, as well as providing an overall estimation of the extent to which clients with various problems do or do not improve in their functioning and sense of well-being. As Frank Turner points out in his Foreword to this book, we need to be humble in our expectations of research and recognize that knowledge comes slowly. Also, in our eagerness to demonstrate the effectiveness of our work, we must be ever careful to evaluate whether the tools we are using to do this are capable of measuring the full range and complexity of the changes that our clients are seeking and making.

DIVERSE APPROACHES

We do not intend to summarize here the psychosocial framework. It has taken this entire text to try to do that! We also cannot offer a comparative discussion of diverse points of view and approaches in social work.[1] A rich array of theories or "models" of social work treatment have emerged over the past quarter century; these attest to the fact that clinical social workers are in touch with other therapeutic fields and with new developments in the social sciences and are actively engaged in formulating their own ideas. Many practitioners do not routinely follow accepted methodology without knowledge of new findings and theories. Indeed, each new theory throws additional light on some aspect of the helping process.

There are overlaps in practice between workers who follow different approaches, with each group's often borrowing ideas and techniques from the others. This may account in part for the observation that differences in practice among workers are often not as great as differences in the theories they supposedly follow. However, there are also distinct differences between some theories that make them truly incompatible. In order to make informed choices about the use of diverse approaches, one needs to be clear about these incompatibilities. Theories vary in many ways. They differ greatly, for instance, in the emphasis they put upon the client-worker relationship: its nature and its importance in treatment. Some theories refer often to such concepts as acceptance, caring, sympathy, empathy, respect. Others, even when not necessarily opposing such ideas, seem to give them very low priority in treatment. The concept of self-determination is also widely accepted, but there are great variations in the degree to which this quality is emphasized or adhered to in practice. The notion of mutuality is interpreted differently, depending on the point of view. In the chapters on family treatment we pointed out that among family therapists there are variations of opinion concerning the expression of emotion, the use of past history, the development of self-awareness, the sharing of impressions and interpretations by the therapist, the need for assessing individual personality dynamics, and so on. As we indicated, some of the points of view involving these issues are not compatible with the psychosocial point of view for ethical as well as practical reasons.

Obviously, too, current approaches are based on differing perspectives on personality development and dynamics. Some personality theories have many common elements; others are far apart on such matters as the influence of past experiences on present behavior and the question of the unconscious. Ego psychology, its knowledge of ego functions and defenses, is not included in some theories. There are also great variations in concepts about the ways in which people can best be helped. As has been clear from reading this book, psychosocial caseworkers do not restrict themselves to cognitive measures or to educational and behavioral techniques, for example, as some others tend to do, although the psychosocial approach has incorporated some of these ideas and methods into its broader framework.

Theories differ also in their definitions of the "problem to be worked on." This aspect of practice ranges from those who would deal only with the presenting problems and symptoms to those who feel that in many cases there should be some exploration at the outset for the possible existence of other related problems with which casework could be helpful. Some would limit work to the "interface" of interacting systems; others would limit their concerns to intrapsychic phenomena; still others would see a much more inclusive gestalt of dynamic, interlocking factors.

When reading about various points of view, it is important to note that some writers have insufficient or inaccurate knowledge of the viewpoints of others. There are authors, for instance, who write as if psychosocial casework were tied to a narrow linear type of causation that relies largely, or even primarily, on past events. Some seem not be be aware of the relationships between psychosocial concepts of causation and systems theory. We hope that in this edition we have made the connections between these clearer than ever. Some people still believe that psychosocial casework is merely a watered-down version of psychoanalytic theory and practice. This text should dispel such misconceptions. When mentioning other points of view in this book, we have made every effort to represent them accurately; we welcome corrections from the proponents of any theory who feel we have misunderstood their ideas.

WHOM DO WE SERVE?

To what extent is psychosocial casework class-bound? In the 1930s we set out to demonstrate that interpersonal and social problems were not a monopoly of the poor or near poor but were experienced by people of all degrees of income and education and that all these groups could and would use casework help. By the 1960s this had been so well established that concern shifted to the notion that casework was a middle-class therapy that was not effective with low-income families. Some urged that it readapt itself to work with the poor. Others thought it could have nothing to offer the poor. In actuality, casework as a field has never stopped serving the poor even though it has served those from all other income groups as well. In medical and psychiatric clinics, in child placement agencies, in preventive and protective services, in agencies serving youth, among many others, caseworkers see many low-income clients. In child guidance clinics and family service agencies, many clients have always been—and still are—from low-income families.[2] As we mentioned in Chapter 1, of all mental health practitioners, clinical social workers provide most psychotherapeutic services; they outnumber psychiatrists who offer psychotherapy almost two to one. Social workers help people with a great variety of problems, in all walks of life.

It is certainly harder to help people who are beset with a host of problems that accompany lack of income; whether in the inner city or in rural areas, poverty and despair go hand in hand. Homelessness, poor housing, inferior schooling, crime-infested neighborhoods, unemployment, poor medical facilities, inadequate and often undignified public assistance, public indifference, prejudice, and contempt all mitigate against even a minimal quality of life for many people. AIDS, once overwhelmingly identified with gay men, now ravages the lives and families of the poor and the minorities. At the time of this writing, drug addicts, their sexual partners, and babies are increasingly being afflicted by the devastating disease. The widespread use of illegal drugs has resulted in the increase in addicts of all ages. In the most vulnerable communities, greedy drug dealers are promoting drug dependency in grade school children. These are tragedies that are far beyond the influence of casework alone. Progress sometimes can be made client by client, family by family, case by case, but these are total community—often nationwide—problems that must be tackled by community and government action. It is the obligation of social workers to come forth with information, leadership, and energetic advocacy for the changes that are essential to healthy living; we who see the devastating effects of the social conditions under which millions of Americans live must bring our expertise and our collective influence to bear.

At the same time, we must not assume casework cannot be effective with disadvantaged individuals and families. In examples in this book, help was offered and used by clients to find new solutions in spite of many handicapping circumstances. Sometimes, with encouragement and optimism provided by the caseworker, the right resources, the opportunity to reflect on their situations, clients can arrive at creative solutions to extremely difficult problems. Certainly when family members are working together rather than at odds with one another, they have a better chance of battling oppressive forces; often social workers can facilitate this kind of cooperative approach.

The poor have family relationships that go awry; they are also affected by illness, tragedies, loss through death. Poor people—even some of those who seem to have been toppled by oppressive conditions, by hopelessness and addictions—still have aspirations for themselves and for their children. Caseworkers have fought—and may have to continue to fight—to make financial help free of interference in personal matters. We must also keep on putting equal effort into seeing that first-rate service is *easily* available to those who lack money but want help. Structures must be developed and publicly supported to make this possible.

PRIVATE PRACTICE

For many years there was resistance to the private practice of clinical social work on the grounds that we should primarily serve people who cannot afford private fees and we should not take strength away from agencies set up for that purpose. We, the authors, differ from this point of view and believe that the increasing recognition and professional sanction of private practice in the main constitutes a positive step. In our opinion, the ideal of private practice should be to divide one's time between agency practice and independent work, thus ensuring that all experienced practitioners will devote part of their time to consultation, training, field instruction, or direct service with nonpaying or low-fee-paying clients. We hope that most private practitioners will continue to divide their time this way. We also hope that those who decide to engage in private practice will offer sliding fee scales to accommodate lower-income clients. In spite of those who complain that private practice excludes the poor, we are personally familiar with a number of private practitioners whose clientele ranges from the well-to-do to the economically disadvantaged. Those independent workers who have the will to do so can be available to referrals from many sources, including those agencies—children's and geriatric services, the courts, the schools, and many more—that are seeking high-quality clinical services for clients who cannot pay much, if anything. It is consonant with our professional values to devote a percentage of our private practice hours to such individuals and families. Ironically, independent clinicians, who often have lower overhead expenses than agencies, can sometimes absorb nonpaying clients more comfortably than those organizations that strug-

gle with inadequate budgets and therefore have to charge fees that are as high as or higher than those set by private practitioners. In our experience, agencies seeking referral sources are grateful to have collaborative relationships with experienced and skilled independent workers.

A further advantage of the spread of private practice for social work itself is the fact that, as we become better known as independent clinicians, our profession will be more widely recognized as the challenging and personally rewarding work that it really is. This, in turn, will attract a greater number of well-qualified candidates to professional study. It will also mean that as social work becomes more and more valued as a profession by society at large, when it speaks out for human rights and against social injustice it will have a better and better chance of being heard. Members of other professions and their societies, such as those of the medical and legal professions, have brought pressure to bear (certainly not always in ways that we wish they would!) because of the status and respect they enjoy. If social work is going to influence broad social policies, it must become better known as a strong profession based on strength and high principles.

A justified concern about private practice has been that independent practitioners may have fewer supports than those employed in agencies of high standards, where various types of in-service training and consultation can be readily available and where the agency vouches for the competence of its workers. People served by private practitioners deserve the equivalent of this protection. Through licensing and other standard-setting measures, including competency exams, reexaminations, and peer review, taken by government bodies and professional societies, it can be expected and required that caseworkers qualifying for independent practice have advanced training and experience in clinical social work, are continuing their education, and are making use of peer consultation.[3]

EDUCATIONAL ISSUES

In Chapter 1 we briefly discussed education for the specialization of clinical social work. There, we also referred the reader to references that elaborate on the authors' points of view on this subject.[4] Our major concern is that there is a need for intensive concentration in the study of *casework,* in the training of social work clinicians.

We have referred many times to the great expansion over the years of the body of knowledge now needed for the practice of clinical social work. To review this for emphasis: Skill is needed in family treatment and in work with formed groups as well as in work with individuals. Knowledge of crisis and brief treatments, including task-centered treatment, as well as open-ended and long-term treatment, required by some clients who seek extensive personality changes, is important. Content of theories of personality, systems and ecological relations, communications, and adaptive and maladaptive social functioning is constantly increasing. Every decade new information about our clients' situations emerge; since the last revision of this book, knowledge of geriatric services, stepfamilies, and alcoholic family systems—among many, many other subjects—has advanced considerably. Insights relating to cultural and socioeconomic factors as they affect our clients and the casework relationship are becoming more refined. Knowledge of the social environment has expanded greatly; all workers are now expected to understand how agencies, institutions, and social factors interrelate in the delivery of casework services. As we have said, caseworkers must be firmly grounded in social work's unique knowledge base, its traditions and ethics. Some knowledge of various theoretical approaches is also necessary. Increasingly, competent practitioners are also expected to be informed about, and often to participate in, research with its modern complexities.

A *beginning* understanding of some parts of these requirements can be secured in undergraduate BSW work and also in the generalist form of study in master's degree work. But to prepare for even beginning practice as a clinical social worker, making use of the full range of psychosocial treatment, in the opinion of the writers, requires a two-year concentration in casework at the master's degree level.

Individuals are so unique that in social work, despite well-developed practice knowledge and skill, we are constantly confronted by difficult choices. Again and again, decisions about treatment have to be made without knowing for sure what is best. Probably this is better than that, so we do this. Therefore, the worker must have sufficient personal and professional security to act on his or her own best judgment, without undue anxiety. The worker must also be flexible, alert to indications that some other course might be better, ready to modify an approach in the light of new understanding.

No blueprint of treatment can ever be given, any more than a skier can know each twist and turn he or she will have to take on a steep, unknown course. Like the skier, the worker knows the general direction, but the worker, too, may be able to see only a little way ahead and have to adapt the technique to the terrain quickly. To do this, it is necessary to be a skilled—well-educated, up-to-date—practitioner, who knows what to do to accomplish what and when a given procedure is necessary. A great contribution can be made to the quality of social work practice by the clinical doctorate as such programs become more widely available. We hope and expect that increasing numbers of clinical social workers will undertake this advanced study. It is not beyond our imagination, given the extent of the theoretical knowledge and practical experience that must be assimilated, that sooner or later the clinical doctorate will be the degree required as preparation for the practice of clinical social work.

LOOKING FORWARD

It is impossible to forecast the many areas in which casework and clinical services will advance in the next decade. We can only be sure that changes will come, that approaches to practice that seem modern today will be revamped as additional understandings emerge. On the basis of new information and experiences, reformulations and refinements go on all the time. It is incumbent upon us all, therefore, to keep up with the literature in social work and related professions; to share new ideas with colleagues, informally and professionally; to take courses, seminars, and workshops that keep us current as casework attempts to meet the challenges of changing times.

We anticipate that case management, an approach still in its infancy at the time of this writing, will be of increasing importance in the future. Currently a subject of confusion and differences of emphasis among social workers, it is nevertheless an approach deriving from the critical need to link clients to complex service delivery systems successfully. Use of case managers and incorporation of case management principles by all caseworkers should help to coordinate and facilitate the provision of various services at the time they are most needed. Ideally, clients will not "fall through the cracks" so easily as they often have in the past because they got lost in the complexity of modern-day bureaucracies and service delivery systems. Whether case management will become a specialization in and of itself within casework or whether the clinical social worker generally will take on the tasks of case management in addition to therapeutic functions is yet to be seen. Perhaps social work will take both directions, depending on the particular setting and the needs of the clients being served there.[5]

We welcome and urge all students and practitioners to read Dorothy Fahs Beck's study, *Counselor Characteristics: How They Affect Out-*comes, which was based on a large body of data from seventeen family service agencies.[6] It has many implications for education and for future research. For example, counselors *without* significant graduate-level education were found to be more effective in helping people with such matters as concrete services, information and referral help, and home visits, than those *with* professional education. Only when it came to the treatment of complicated family relationship problems did it seem that graduate workers may have had an edge, in terms of outcome and fewer dropouts, over those who had not been professionally trained. These findings certainly suggest that we may not be providing essential knowledge and experience to graduate students or that these functions are not sufficiently valued by schools of social work, students, and/or practicing clinicians.

Perhaps even more surprising are Beck's findings that matching clients and counselors on the basis of age, sex, race, marital status, parenthood, and socioeconomic status did not significantly affect outcomes. In fact, in some cases, differences between clients and counselors seemed to be advantageous. Obviously, these findings may not apply to other than family service settings, and further research is required in any event. However, Beck's study, which contains a great deal of information important to us all, certainly prompts us to take a second look at many of our assumptions and preconceptions about casework effectiveness and case assignments.

TOWARD WHAT ENDS?

Psychosocial casework seeks to strengthen individuals through helping them deal with current dilemmas, find answers to these dilemmas insofar as possible, and emerge from periods of stress with greater competence, more self-confidence, increased self-respect, and enhanced ability to respond positively to life. In working toward these ends, the clinical social worker seeks first to establish a positive and caring human relationship so that honest communication can take place and trust can develop. A *common ground* for work together must be found, with clarity about the client's goals and wishes to proceed along lines that the person or the worker may propose. The individual client-in-situation must be understood if the worker is to provide help geared to the motivation, needs, and capacities of the individual and to the opportunities and the modifiability of the environment.

Casework is not an agent of social control. Our effort is distinctly *not* to bend the client to the social system but rather to increase his or her ability to deal with the complexities of modern organizations, enhancing rather than diminishing his or her autonomy. It is often the worker's responsibility to attempt to modify rather than to reinforce social institutions, either in the short run for a particular client or in the long run for the good of us all.

Now more than ever, with the centralization of power in the modern state and in modern industry, and with the mechanization of so much of our lives, society needs a profession that is not aligned with these impersonal or oppressive forces but rather with the well-being of persons, of people: for individualization, and against depersonalization in all of its forms.

The essence of psychosocial casework is concern for individual human beings, for their relationships with others, their well-being in a grossly imperfect society, their achievement of an enhanced sense of their own value and increased competence in dealing with the vicissitudes of living. In a world where distrust is rampant, alliances and loyalties constantly shifting, values in flux, and bureaucracies ever more powerful and remote, individuals must develop strength and skill to meet their needs to effect changes in the external world without surrendering autonomy. They must learn to assess their situations realistically and to stand up for themselves. They must use their capacity for love to build islands of refuge and strength in families, with friends, and with neighbors, so that they and their children may be nourished to come to value, respect, and trust themselves and one another. This is what social work is all about.

NOTES

1. For an excellent introduction to many of these approaches, see Francis J. Turner, ed., *Social Work Treatment: Interlocking Theoretical Approaches*, 3d ed. (New York: Free Press, 1986).

2. For a picture of family service agency clients, see Dorothy Fahs Beck and Mary Ann Jones, *Progress on Family Problems: A Nationwide Study and Clients' and Counselors' Views on Family Agency Services* (New York: Family Service Association of America, 1973).

3. See Robert L. Barker's very useful volume, *Social Work in Private Practice: Principles, Issues, and Dilemmas* (Silver Spring, Md.: National Association of Social Workers, 1984). The reader may also be interested in the quarterly *Journal of Independent Social Work* (Binghamton, N.Y.: Haworth Press), which began publication in fall 1986; Barker is editor-in-chief of this journal, that has articles covering a variety of issues related to the independent practice of social work.

4. See Chapter 1, note 27.

5. See Chapter 8, note 18.

6. Dorothy Fahs Beck, *Counselor Characteristics: How They Affect Outcomes* (Milwaukee, Wisc.: Family Service America, 1988). See also Chapter 8, note 5.

A Note on the Reliability of the Classification*

Before using a research tool in formal study it is, of course, most important to know the degree of its reliability. Preliminary figures on the reliability of the classification when two judges are coding the same data are encouraging. Several reliability tests were run during the course of developing and experimenting with the typology. In the early stages a running record of agreement percentages was kept. There were times when we were greatly encouraged to find agreement rates in many of the categories that stayed above 80 percent and sometimes reached 90 percent or more for a series of three or four interviews. Then suddenly the agreement rate for an interview would drop to 70 percent, or even lower, either because the dictation was obscure or because it was particularly hard to decide whether the client was really reflecting. Such sudden drops revealed several pitfalls in reliability testing into which it is easy to slip. If reliability had simply been checked until a desirable level was reached, as is sometimes done, a high agreement rate could have been reported fairly early. But this would really have meant that we had stopped playing when we were winning.

A high rate could also have been established, as is sometimes done, by setting up an experiment in which examples of the different types of material are typed on cards that are then coded. This is a useful device to show at least that the system is conceptually clear, but it tells nothing about the borderline instances that are the real cause of disagreement between coders. To avoid these pitfalls, in the two reliability tests 19 and 20 interviews were used, respectively, and coded over an arbitrarily selected time span.

The principal measure of reliability used in the tests was the Spearman Rank Order Correlation Coefficient.[1] John Dollard and Frank Auld have pointed out the error introduced by relying, as is sometimes done, on a simple percentage agreement, the significance of which is so strongly influenced by the number of alternative choices available.[2] When only two choices are possible in a dimension, chance alone would yield 50 percent agreement even if the coding were completely unreliable. With each addition to the choices, however, the probability of chance agreement lessens. It is reduced to 33 percent when there are three possible choices, and to only 20 percent when there are five choices (assuming equal distribution over all alternatives). In other words, an agreement rate of 60 percent in the first instance would represent only 20 percent better than chance; in the second it would be almost twice as good as chance; and in the third three times as good.

* Taken by permission of *Social Casework* from "The Coding and Application of a Typology of Casework Treatment," *Social Casework*, 48 (October, 1967).

With this in mind it was decided not to use percentage agreement but, instead, to use rank order correlations over a sample comparable in number of cases to the size of sample for which the classification was likely to be used. In this kind of test the number of alternatives available in a given dimension does not have a bearing on the significance of the score. If one assumes that errors are randomized, this test gives a guide to the extent to which, in an actual study of the same number of cases, errors of judges in a given category may obscure differences or similarities that can be located with a more exact research tool.

Reliability scores can be reported on the major means categories and on subject matter categories 1, 2, and 3 used in the exploratory-descriptive-ventilative material and on the change context categories.[3] For the most part, as the accompanying tables show, the Spearman test was used. Three of the major categories were used so rarely that they could not be tested by the Spearman formula. For these Fisher's Exact Probability Test was used, basing the test on the simple presence or absence of the given procedure in the respective interviews.[4]

The figures in Table I represent the average of the two reliability tests administered in the next to the last and the last year of the study. The figures in Table II were obtained in the later test. In some categories there was substantial progress in reliability be-

TABLE II

Agreement Between Judges as Measured by Fisher Exact Probability Test

Category	Agree		Disagree	Sig. Level
	Present	Absent		
Client E	1	18	1	.10
Client F	5	13	2	.005
Worker B	4	11	5	.05
Worker E	0	18	2	N.S.
Worker F	2	16	2	.05

tween the first and second tests. For example, the analyses on the average score of .69 given for client C3 represent a rise from .60 to .79 between tests, the score of .36 for worker C3 represents a rise from .03 to .70, the .56 for client d represents a rise from .46 to .67.

The chief categories remaining in difficulty at the time of the second test were client b and worker d. These tables give a minimum estimate of the present reliability of the typology, however, since work was done subsequently to define the weaker categories further.

Though it is hoped that, eventually, all items can be brought up to a reliability score of .80, a score of .70 represents a substantial improvement not only over chance but also over judgments arrived at in a global way. For greatest reliability, two judges should be used on all material, the average of the two sets of coding being used in the analysis. When this averaging method is used, an agreement level of .80 between coders gives a reliability level of .88; agreement of .70, a reliability of .82; agreement of .65 a reliability of .79. (Using the Spearman-Brown formula,[5] inter-rater r is multiplied by 2 and divided by $1 + $ inter-rater r.) If double coding is not possible because of financial limitations, as is often true of doctoral dissertations, the author may be consulted concerning measures that should be taken to safeguard reliability as much as is possible with a single coder.

TABLE I

Agreement Between Judges as Measured by Spearman r

Category	Client	Worker
A	—	.83*
C	.82*	.87*
D	.76*	.75*
C1	.89*	.86*
C2	.78*	.74*
C3	.69†	.36
a[6]	.70†	.70†
b	.45	.65†
c	.73*	.84*
d	.56	.30

*Significance level ≤.001
†Significance level ≤.005

NOTES

1. Hubert M. Blalock, Jr., *Social Statistics* (New York. McGraw-Hill, 1960), pp. 317–319.

2. John Dollard and Frank Auld, Jr., *Scoring Human Motives: A Manual* (New Haven, Conn.: Yale University Press, 1959), p. 306.

3. Subject matter categories have not been useful and have since been dropped.

4. Blalock, *Social Statistics*, pp. 221–225.

5. J. P. Guilford, *Fundamental Statistics in Psychology and Education*, 4th ed. (New York: McGraw-Hill, 1965), pp. 457–458.

6. Small letters correspond to arabic numerals, 1, 2, 3, and 4 in text.

Bibliography

ABRAMSON, MARCIA. "The Autonomy-Paternalism Dilemma in Social Work Practice." *Social Casework,* 66 (September 1985), 387–393.

ACKERMAN, NATHAN W. "The Diagnosis of Neurotic Marital Interaction." *Social Casework,* 35 (April 1954), 139–147.

———. "Family Healing in a Troubled World." *Social Casework,* 52 (April 1971), 200–205.

———. "Family Psychotherapy Today." *Family Process,* 9 (1970), 123–126.

———. "The Growing Edge of Family Therapy." In Clifford J. Sagar and Helen Singer Kaplan, eds., *Progress in Group and Family Therapy.* New York: Brunner/Mazel, 1972.

———. "Prejudice and Scapegoating in the Family." In Gerald H. Zuk and Ivan Boszormenyi-Nagy, eds., *Family Therapy and Disturbed Families.* Palo Alto, Calif.: Science and Behavior Books, 1969, pp. 48–57.

———. "Psychiatric Disorders in Children—Diagnosis and Etiology in Our Time." In Paul H. Hoch and Joseph Zubin, eds., *The Diagnostic Process in Child Psychiatry.* New York: Grune & Stratton, 1953, 205–230.

———. *The Psychodynamics of Family Life.* New York: Basic Books, 1958.

———. *Treating the Troubled Family.* New York: Basic Books, 1966.

———, FRANCES L. BEATMAN, and SANFORD N. SHERMAN. *Expanding Theory and Practice in Family Therapy.* New York: Family Service Association of America, 1967.

ACKERMAN, ROBERT J. *Children of Alcoholics: A Guidebook for Educators, Therapists and Parents.* Holmes Beach, Fla.: Learning Publications, 1983.

AINSWORTH, MARY D. "The Effects of Maternal Deprivation: A Review of Findings and Controversy in the Context of Research Strategy." In *Deprivation of Maternal Care: A Reassessment of Its Effects.* Geneva: World Health Organization, 1962.

ALEXANDER, JEANETTE. "Alternate Life Styles: Relationship Between New Realities and Practice." *Clinical Social Work Journal,* 4 (Winter 1976), 289–301.

ALLEN-MEARS, PAULA, and BRUCE A. LANE. "Grounding Social Work Practice in Theory: Ecosystems." *Social Casework,* 68 (November 1987), 515–521.

ALLPORT, GORDON. "The Open System in Personality Theory." *Journal of Abnormal and Social Psychology,* 61 (November 1960), 301–310.

AMBROSINO, SALVATORE. "Integrating Counseling, Family Life Education, and Family Advocacy." *Social Casework,* 60 (December 1979), 579–585.

AMERICAN PSYCHIATRIC ASSOCIATION. *Diagnostic and Statistical Manual of Mental Disorders,* 3d ed. rev. Washington, D.C.: APA, 1987.

ANDERSON, CAROL M. and SUSAN STEWART. *Mastering Resistance: A Practical Guide to Family Therapy.* New York: Guilford Press, 1983.

ANDERSON, GARY D. "Enhancing Listening Skills for Work with Abusing Parents." *Social Casework,* 60 (December 1979), 602–608.

ANDERSON, LINDA M., et al. "Training in Family Treatment: Needs and Objectives." *Social Casework,* 60 (June 1979), 323–329.

ANGELL, ROBERT C. *The Family Encounters the Depression.* New York: Scribner's, 1936.

APONTE, HARRY J. "Diagnosis in Family Therapy." In Carel B. Germain, ed., *Social Work Practice: People and Environments.* New York: Columbia University Press, 1979.

———. "If I Don't Get Simple, I Cry." *Family Process,* 25 (December 1986), 531–548.

———. "Underorganization in the Poor Family." In Philip J. Guerin, ed., *Family Therapy.* New York: Gardner Press, 1976, 432–448.

APPEL, GERALD. "Some Aspects of Transference and Counter-Transference in Marital Counseling." *Social Casework,* 47 (May 1966), 307–312.

APTEKAR, HERBERT H. *The Dynamics of Casework and Counseling.* Boston: Houghton Mifflin, 1955.

ARGLES, PAUL. "The Threat of Separation in Family Conflict." *Social Casework,* 65 (December 1984), 610–614.

ARIETI, SILVANO. *Interpretation of Schizophrenia,* 2d ed. New York: Basic Books, 1974.

ARONSON, H., and BETTY OVERALL. "Treatment Expectation of Patients in Two Social Classes." *Social Work,* 11 (January 1966), 35–41.

ATTNEAVE, CAROLYN L. "Social Networks as the Unit of Intervention." In Philip J. Guerin, Jr., ed., *Family Therapy.* New York: Gardner Press, 1976, 220–232.

ATWOOD, NANCY. "Professional Prejudice and the Psychotic Client." *Social Work,* 27 (March 1982), 172–177.

AUSLANDER, GAIL K., and HOWARD LITWIN. "Social Networks and the Poor: Toward Effective Policy and Practice." *Social Work,* 33, (May–June 1988), 234–238.

——— and ———. "The Parameters of Network Intervention: A Social Work Application." *Social Service Review,* 61 (June 1987), 305–318.

AUSTIN, LUCILLE. "Dynamics and Treatment of the Client with Anxiety Hysteria." In Howard J. Parad, ed., *Ego Psychology and Dynamic Casework.* New York: Family Service Association of America, 1958.

———. "Qualifications for Psychotherapists, Social Caseworkers." *American Journal of Orthopsychiatry,* 26 (1956), 47–57.

———. "Trends in Differential Treatment in Social Casework." *Journal of Social Casework,* 29 (June 1948), 203–211.

AYERS, ALICE Q. "Neighborhood Service: People Caring for People." *Social Casework,* 54 (April 1973), 192–215.

BAILEY, MARGARET. "Casework Treatment of the Alcoholic and His Family." In *Alcoholism and Family Casework.* New York: Community Council of Greater New York, 1968, 67–108.

BALDWIN, KATHERINE. "Crisis-Focused Casework in a Child Guidance Clinic." *Social Casework,* 49 (January 1968), 28–34.

BALL, MARGARET. "Issues of Violence in Family Casework." *Social Casework,* 58 (January 1977), 3–12.

BALLEN, BERNICE. "The Growth of Psychoanalytic Developmental Psychology and the Application of Technique." *Clinical Social Work Journal,* 8 (Spring 1980), 28–37.

BANDLER, BERNARD. "The Concept of Ego Supportive Psychotherapy." In Howard J. Parad and Roger R. Miller, eds., *Ego-Oriented Casework: Problems and Perspectives.* New York: Family Service Association of America, 1963, 27–44.

BANDLER, LOUISE. "Casework—a Process of Socialization: Gains, Limitations, Conclusions." In Eleanor Pavenstedt, ed., *The Drifters: Children of Disorganized Lower-Class Families.* Boston: Little, Brown, 1967, 255–296.

BANKS, GEORGE P. "The Effects of Race on One-to-One Helping Interviews." *Social Science Review,* 45 (June 1971), 137–146.

BARKER, ROBERT L. *Social Work in Private Practice: Principles, Issues, and Dilemmas.* Silver Spring, Md.: National Association of Social Workers, 1984.

BARNES, GEOFFREY B., et al. "Team Treatment for Abusive Families." *Social Casework,* 55 (December 1974), 600–611.

BARSKY, MORNA. "Strategies and Techniques of Divorce Mediation." *Social Casework,* 65 (February 1984), 102–108.

BARTLETT, HARRIET. *The Common Base of Social Work Practice.* New York: National Association of Social Workers, 1970.

BARTZ, KAREN W., and ELAINE S. LEVINE. "Child Rearing by Black Parents: A Description and Comparison to Anglo and Chicano Parents." *Journal of Marriage and the Family*, 40 (November 1978), 709–719.

BATESON, GREGORY, et al. "A Note on the Double Bind—1962." *Family Process*, 2 (March 1963), 154–161.

———, DON D. JACKSON, JAY HALEY, and JOHN WEAKLAND. "Toward a Theory of Schizophrenia." *Behavioral Science*, 1 (October 1956), 252–264.

BEATRICE, DORY KRONGELB. "Divorce: Problems, Goals, and Growth Facilitation." *Social Casework*, 60 (March 1979), 157–165.

BECK, DOROTHY FAHS. "Counselor Burnout in Family Service Agencies." *Social Casework*, 68 (January 1987), 3–15.

———. *Counselor Characteristics: How They Affect Outcomes.* Milwaukee, Wisc.: Family Service America, 1988.

——— and MARY ANN JONES. *Progress on Family Problems.* New York: Family Service Association of America, 1973.

BECK, ROBERT L. "Beyond the Transference: Interviews with Adults and Their Parents in Psychotherapy." *Clinical Social Work Journal*, 12 (Spring 1984), 57–68.

———. "Redirecting Blame in Marital Psychotherapy." *Clinical Social Work Journal*, 15 (Summer 1987), 148–158.

BECKETT, JOYCE O. "Plant Closings: How Older Workers Are Affected." *Social Work*, 33 (January–February 1988), 29–33.

BEELS, C. CHRISTIAN, and A. S. FERBER. "Family Therapy: A View." *Family Process*, 8 (1969), 280–318.

BEHRENS, MARJORIE, and NATHAN ACKERMAN. "The Home Visit as an Aid in Family Diagnosis and Therapy." *Social Casework*, 37 (January 1956), 11–19.

BELL, JOHN E. *Family Group Therapy*, Public Monograph No. 64. Washington, D.C., U.S. Government Printing Office, 1961.

BELLAK, LEOPOLD, et al. *Ego Function in Schizophrenics, Neurotics, and Normals.* New York: Wiley, 1973.

———. "Psychiatric Aspects of Tuberculosis." *Social Casework*, 31 (May 1950), 183–189.

BENDER, BARBARA. "Management of Acute Hospitalization Anxiety." *Social Casework*, 57 (January 1976), 19–26.

BENEDICT, RUTH. *Patterns of Culture.* New York: Houghton Mifflin, 1934.

BENNY, CELIA, et al. "Clinical Complexities in Work Adjustment of Deprived Youth." *Social Casework*, 50 (June 1969), 330–336.

BERGER, DAVID M. *Clinical Empathy.* Northvale, N.J.: Jason Aronson, 1987.

BERGER, RAYMOND M. "Social Work Practice Models: A Better Recipe." *Social Casework*, 67 (January 1986), 45–54.

BERGLER, EDMUND. *Unhappy Marriage and Divorce.* New York: International Universities Press, 1946.

BERGMAN, ANNE. "Emergency Room: A Role for Social Workers." *Health and Social Work*, 1 (February 1976), 32–44.

BERKOWITZ, SIDNEY. "Some Specific Techniques of Psychosocial Diagnosis and Treatment in Family Casework." *Social Casework*, 36 (November 1955), 399–406.

BERLATSKY, MARJORIE. "Some Aspects of the Marital Problems of the Elderly." *Social Casework*, 43 (May 1962), 233–237.

BERLIN, SHARON. "Single Case Evaluation: Another Version." *Social Work Research and Abstracts*, 19 (Spring 1983), 3–11.

BERMAN, ELLEN M., and MARTIN GOLDBERG. "Therapy with Unmarried Couples." In Neil S. Jacobson and Alan S. Gurman, eds., *Clinical Handbook of Marital Therapy.* New York: Guilford Press, 1986, 301–319.

BERNHEIM, KAYLA F., and ANTHONY F. LEHMAN. *Working with Families of the Mentally Ill.* New York: W. W. Norton, 1985.

BERTALANFFY, LUDWIG VON. *General Systems Theory: Foundations, Development, Application.* New York: Braziller, 1968.

BETZ, JACQUELINE, PHYLLIS HARTMANN, ARLENE JAROSLAW, SHEILA LEVINE, DENA SCHEIN, GORDON SMITH, and BARBARA ZEISS. "A Study of the Usefulness and Reliability of the Hollis Treatment Classification Scheme: A Continuation of Previous Research in This Area." Master's thesis, Columbia University School of Social Work, New York, 1961.

BEUTLER, LARRY E., et al. "Therapist Variables in Psychotherapy Process and Outcome." In Sol L. Garfield and Allen E. Bergin, eds., *Handbook of Psychotherapy and Behavior Change*, 3d ed. New York: John Wiley & Sons, 1986, 257–310.

BIBRING, GRETE L. "Psychiatry and Social Work." *Journal of Social Casework,* 28 (June 1947), 203–211.

BIDDLE, BRUCE J., and EDWIN THOMAS, eds. *Role Theory: Concepts and Research.* New York: Wiley, 1966.

BIESTEK, FELIX. *The Casework Relationship.* Chicago: Loyola University Press, 1957.

BILLINGSLEY, ANDREW. *Black Families in White America.* Englewood Cliffs, N.J.: Prentice-Hall, 1968.

BINTZLER, JANET. "Diagnosis and Treatment of Borderline Personality Organization." *Clinical Social Work Journal,* 6 (Summer 1978), 100–107.

BIRDWHISTELL, RAY L. *Kinesics and Context.* Philadelphia: University of Pennsylvania Press, 1970.

BISNO, HERBERT. *The Philosophy of Social Work.* Washington, D.C.: Public Affairs Press, 1952.

BITTERMAN, CATHERINE. "Marital Adjustment Patterns of Clients with Compulsive Character Disorders: Implications for Treatment." *Social Casework,* 47 (November 1966), 575–582.

BLACK, CLAUDIA. *It Will Never Happen to Me.* Denver: MAC Publications, 1982.

BLAKE-WHITE, JILL, and CHRISTINE MADELINE KLINE. "Treating the Dissociative Process in Adult Victims of Childhood Incest." *Social Casework,* 66 (September 1985), 394–402.

BLANCK, GERTRUDE, and RUBIN BLANCK. *Beyond Ego Psychology: Developmental Object Relations Theory.* New York: Columbia University Press, 1986.

———. *Ego Psychology: Theory and Practice.* New York: Columbia University Press, 1974.

———. *Ego Psychology II.* New York: Columbia University Press, 1979.

BLANCK, RUBIN. "The Case for Individual Treatment." *Social Casework,* 47 (February 1965), 70–74.

———. "Countertransference in Treatment of the Borderline Patient." *Clinical Social Work Journal,* 1 (Summer 1973), 110–117.

BLAZYK, STAN, and MARGARET M. CANAVAN. "Therapeutic Aspects of Discharge Planning." *Social Work,* 30 (November–December 1985), 489–496.

BLIZINSKY, MARTIN J., and WILLIAM J. REID. "Problem Focus and Change in a Brief Treatment Model." *Social Work,* 25 (March 1980), 89–93.

BLOCH, JULIA. "The White Worker and the Negro Client in Psychotherapy." *Social Work,* 13 (April 1968), 36–42.

BLOOM, MARTIN. "Social Prevention: An Ecological Approach." In Carel B. Germain, ed., *Social Work Practice.* New York: Columbia University Press, 1979, 326–345.

BLOOM, MARY LARKIN. "Usefulness of the Home Visit for Diagnosis and Treatment." *Social Casework,* 54 (February 1973), 67–73.

BOATMAN, LOUISE. "Caseworkers' Judgments of Clients' Hope: Some Correlates among Client-Situation Characteristics and among Workers' Communication Patterns." Doctoral dissertation, Columbia University School of Social Work, New York, 1974.

BOIE, MAURINE. "The Case Worker's Need for Orientation to the Culture of the Client." *Proceedings of the National Conference of Social Work.* Chicago: University of Chicago Press, 1937, 112–123.

BONNEFIL, MARGARET C. "The Relationship of Interpersonal Acting-out to the Process of Decompensation." *Clinical Social Work Journal,* 1 (Spring 1973), 13–21.

———. "Therapist, Save My Child: A Family Crisis Case." *Clinical Social Work Journal,* 7 (Spring 1979), 6–14.

BOOKIN, DEBORAH, and RUTH E. DUNKLE. "Elder Abuse: Issues for the Practitioner." *Social Casework,* 66 (January 1985), 3–12.

BOSZORMENYI-NAGY, IVAN, and JAMES L. FRAMO, eds. *Intensive Family Therapy.* New York: Harper & Row, 1965.

——— and GERALDINE SPARK. *Invisible Loyalties: Reciprocity in Intergenerational Family Therapy.* New York: Harper and Row, 1973.

——— and DAVID N. ULRICH. "Contextual Family Therapy." In Gurman and Kniskern, eds., *Handbook of Family Therapy.* New York: Brunner/Mazel, 1981, 159–186.

BOWEN, MURRAY. *Family Therapy in Clinical Practice.* New York: Aronson, 1978.

BOWLBY, JOHN. *Attachment and Loss,* vol. 3. New York: Basic Books, 1980.

———. "Grief and Mourning in Infancy and Early Childhood." In Ruth S. Eissler et al., eds. *The Psychoanalytic Study of the Child,* Vol. 15. New York: International Universities Press, 1965.

———. *Maternal Care and Mental Health,* 2d ed., Geneva: World Health Organization, 1952.

BOWLES, DORCAS DAVIS. "The Impact of Ethnicity on African-American Mothering: A Report of a Study in Progress." In Louise S. Bandler, ed., *Education for Clinical Social Work Practice: Continuity and Change.* New York: Pergamon Press, 1983, 77–91.

BRAGER, GEORGE A. "Advocacy and Political Behavior." *Social Work,* 13 (April 1968), 5–16.

—— and STEPHEN HOLLOWAY. *Changing Human Service Organizations.* New York: Free Press, 1978.

BRAVERMAN, LOIS. "Social Casework and Strategic Therapy." *Social Casework,* 67 (April 1986), 234–239.

BRENNAN, THOMAS P., et al. "Forensic Social Work: Practice and Vision." *Social Casework,* 67 (June 1986), 340–350.

BRENNAN, WILLIAM, and SHANTI KHINDUKA. "Role Discrepancies and Professional Socialization: The Case of the Juvenile Probation Officer." *Social Work,* 15 (April 1970), 87–94.

BRIAR, SCOTT M. "Use of Theory in Studying Effects of Client Social Class on Students' Judgments." *Social Work,* 6 (July 1961), 91–97.

—— and HENRY MILLER. *Problems and Issues in Social Casework.* New York: Columbia University Press, 1971.

BRIARD, FRED K. "Counseling Parents of Children with Learning Disabilities." *Social Casework,* 57 (November 1976), 581–585.

BRIGGS, DEAN. "The Trainee and the Borderline Client: Countertransference Pitfalls." *Clinical Social Work Journal,* 7 (Summer 1979), 133–145.

BRITTON, CLARE. "Casework Techniques in Child Care Services." *Social Casework,* 36 (January 1955), 3–13.

BRODERICK, CARLFRED B., and SANDRA S. SCHRADER. "The History of Professional Marriage and Family Therapy." In Alan S. Gurman and David P. Kniskern, eds., *Handbook of Family Therapy.* New York: Brunner/Mazel, 1981, 5–35.

BRONFENBRENNER, URIE. "Socialization and Social Class Through Time and Space." In Eleanor E. Maccoby, Theodore M. Newcomb, and Eugene L. Hartley, eds., *Readings in Social Psychology.* New York: Holt, Rinehart & Winston, 1958.

BROWN, CAREE ROZEN, and MARILYN LEVITT HELLINGER. "Therapists' Attitudes Toward Women," *Social Work,* 20 (July 1975), 266–270.

BROWN, JOHN A. "Casework Contacts with Black-White Couples." *Social Casework,* 68 (January 1987), 24–29.

——. "Clinical Social Work with Chicanos: Some Unwarranted Assumptions." *Clinical Social Work Journal,* 4 (Winter 1979), 256–265.

BROWN, LAURA S., and DON ZIMMER. "An Introduction to Therapy Issues of Lesbian and Gay Male Couples." In Neil S. Jacobson and Alan S. Gurman, eds., *Clinical Handbook of Marital Therapy.* New York: Guilford Press, 1986, 451–468.

BROXMEYER, NEAL. "Practitioner-Research in Treating a Borderline Child." *Social Work Research and Abstracts,* 14 (Winter 1978), 5–10.

BRUCH, HILDE. "The Sullivanian Concept of Anxiety." In William E. Fann, ed., *Phenomenology and Treatment of Anxiety.* New York: Spectrum, 1979, 261–270.

BRUNO, FRANK J. *Trends in Social Work: 1874–1956.* New York: Columbia University Press, 1957.

BUDMAN, SIMON H., and ALAN S. GURMAN. *Theory and Practice of Brief Therapy.* New York: Guilford, 1988.

BURGESS, EARNEST W., and LEONARD S. COTTRELL, JR. *Predicting Success or Failure in Marriage.* New York: Prentice-Hall, 1939.

BURNS, CRAWFORD E. "White Staff, Black Children: Is There a Problem?" *Child Welfare,* 50 (February 1971), 90–96.

CALIGOR, LEOPOLD, and MILTIADES ZAPHIROPOULOS. "Blue-collar Psychotherapy: Stereotype and Myth." In Earl G. Witenberg, ed., *Interpersonal Explorations in Psychoanalysis.* New York: Basic Books, 1973, 218–234.

CANCRO, ROBERT. "An Overview of the Schizophrenic Syndrome." In Cancro et al., eds., *Strategic Intervention in Schizophrenia.* New York: Behavioral, 1974.

CAPLAN, GERALD. *Principles of Preventive Psychiatry.* New York: Basic Books, 1964.

CARTER, ELIZABETH A., and MONICA McGOLDRICK, eds. *The Changing Life Cycle: A Framework for Family Therapy,* 2d ed. New York: Gardner Press, 1988.

CAPUTO, RICHARD K. "The Role of Research in the Family Service Agency." *Social Casework,* 66 (April 1985), 205–212.

CARTER, ELIZABETH A., and MONICA McGOLDRICK ORFANIDIS. "Family Therapy with One Person and the Family Therapist's Own Family." In Philip J. Guerin, ed., *Family Therapy.* New York: Gardner Press, 1976, 193–219.

CAVAN, RUTH SHONIE, and KATHERINE HOWLAND RANCK. *The Family and the Depression.* Chicago: University of Chicago Press, 1938.

CHAMBERLAIN, EDNA. "Testing with a Treatment Typology." *Australian Journal of Social Work,* 22 (December 1969), 3–8.

CHANDLER, SUSAN MEYERS. "Self-Perceived Competency in Cross-Cultural Counseling." *Social Casework,* 61 (June 1980), 347–353.

CHASE, ANNA M., et al. "Treating the Throwaway Child: A Model for Adolescent Service." *Social Casework*, 60 (November 1979), 538–546.

CHERNUS, LINDE A. "Clinical Issues in Alcoholism Treatment." *Social Casework*, 66 (February 1985), 67–75.

CHESCHEIR, MARTHA W. "Some Implications of Winnicott's Concepts for Clinical Practice." *Clinical Social Work Journal*, 13 (Fall 1985), 218–233.

CHIANCOLA, SAMUEL P. "The Process of Separation and Divorce: A New Approach." *Social Casework*, 59 (October 1978), 494–499.

CINGOLANI, JUDITH. "Social Conflict Perspective on Work with Involuntary Clients." *Social Work*, 29 (September–October 1984), 442–446.

CLOWARD, RICHARD A. "Illegitimate Means, Anomie and Deviant Behavior." *American Sociological Review*, 24 (April 1959), 164–176.

———— and FRANCES FOX PIVEN. "Notes Toward a Radical Social Work." In Roy Bailey and Mike Brake, eds., *Radical Social Work*. New York: Pantheon Books, 1975, vii–xiviii.

COHEN, NATHAN E., ed. *Social Work and Social Problems*. New York: National Association of Social Workers, 1964.

COHEN, PAULINE C., and MERTON S. KRAUSE. *Casework with Wives of Alcoholics*. New York: Family Service Association of America, 1969.

COHEN, TAMAR. "The Incestuous Family Revisited." *Social Casework*, 64 (March 1983), 154–161.

COLLINS, ALICE H., and JAMES R. MACKEY. "Delinquents Who Use the Primary Defense of Denial." In Francis J. Turner, ed., *Differential Diagnosis and Treatment in Social Work*, 2d ed. New York: Free Press, 1976, 64–75.

———— and DIANE L. PANCOAST. *Natural Helping Networks: A Strategy for Prevention*. Washington D.C.: National Association of Social Workers, 1976.

COLLIS, JOHN STEWART. *The Vision of Glory*. New York: Braziller, 1973.

COMBS, TERRI D. "A Cognitive Therapy for Depression: Theory, Techniques, and Issues." *Social Casework*, 61 (June 1980), 361–366.

COMPTON, BEULAH, and BURT GALAWAY. *Social Work Processes*, 3d ed. Chicago: Dorsey Press, 1984.

CONSTANTINE, LARRY L. "Jealousy and Extramarital Relations." In Neil S. Jacobson and Alan S. Gurman, eds., *Clinical Handbook of Marital Therapy*. New York: Guilford Press, 1986, 407–427.

COOK, ALICIA S. "A Model for Working with the Elderly in Institutions." *Social Casework*, 61 (April 1980), 234–239.

COOPER, SHIRLEY. "A Look at the Effect of Racism on Clinical Work." *Social Casework*, 54 (February 1973), 76–84.

————. "The Master's and Beyond." In Judith Mishne, ed., *Psychotherapy and Training in Clinical Social Work*. New York: Gardner Press, 1980, 19–35.

————. "Reflections on Clinical Social Work." *Clinical Social Work Journal*, 5 (Winter 1977), 303–315.

———— and LEON WANERMAN. *Children in Treatment*. New York: Brunner/Mazel, 1977.

CORCORAN, KEVIN, and JOEL FISCHER. *Measures for Clinical Practice: A Sourcebook*. New York: The Free Press, 1987.

CORMICAN, ELIN. "The Task-Centered Model for Work with the Aged." *Social Casework*, 58 (October 1977), 490–494.

CORMICAN, JOHN D. "Linguistic Issues in Interviewing." *Social Casework*, 59 (March 1978), 145–151.

CRANE, JOHN A. "The Power of Social Intervention Experiments to Discriminate Differences Between Experimental and Control Groups." *Social Service Review*, 50 (June 1976), 224–242.

DARE, CHRISTOPHER. "Psychoanalytic Marital Therapy." In Neil S. Jacobson and Alan S. Gurman, eds., *Handbook of Marital Therapy*. New York: Guilford Press, 1986, 13–28.

DAVIS, INGER P. "Advice-Giving in Parent Counselling." *Social Casework*, 56 (June 1975), 343–347.

————. "Use of Influence Techniques in Casework with Parents." Doctoral dissertation, University of Chicago, March 1969.

DAVIS, KINGSLEY. "The Changing Family in Industrial Society." In Robert C. Jackson and Jean Morton, eds., *Family Health Care: Health Promotion and Illness Care*. Berkeley: University of California Press, 1976, 1–16.

DAVIS, LIANE VIDA. "Role Theory." In Francis J. Turner, ed., *Social Work Treatment*, 3d ed. New York: Free Press, 1986, 541–563.

DECKER, NORMAN. "Anxiety in the General Hospital." In William E. Fann et al., eds., *Phenomenology and Treatment of Anxiety*. New York: Spectrum, 1979, 287–298.

DE LA FONTAINE, ELISE. "Cultural and Psychological Implications in Case Work Treatment with Irish

Clients." In *Cultural Problems in Social Case Work.* New York: Family Welfare Association of America, 1940, 21–37.

DELANEY, ANITA, ed. *Training for Service Delivery to Minority Clients.* New York: Family Service Association of America, 1981.

DELGADO, MELVIN. "Social Work in the Puerto Rican Community." *Social Casework,* 55 (February 1974), 117–123.

DEVORE, WYNETTA. "The Life Model and Work with Black Families." *Social Casework,* 64 (November 1983), 525–531.

DEYKEN, EVA Y., et al. "Treatment of Depressed Women." In Francis J. Turner, *Differential Diagnosis and Treatment in Social Work,* 3d ed. New York: Free Press, 1983, 168–183.

DICKS, HENRY V. *Marital Tensions.* New York: Basic Books, 1967.

DIETZ, CHRISTINE A., and JOHN L. CRAFT. "Family Dynamics of Incest: A New Perspective." *Social Casework,* 61 (December 1980), 602–609.

DIXON, SAMUEL L., and ROBERTA G. SANDS. "Identity and the Experience of Crisis," *Social Casework,* 64 (April 1983), 223–230.

DOLAN, MARY M., and BETSY S. VOURLEKIS. "A Field Project: Single-Subject Design in a Public Social Service Agency." *Journal of Social Service Research,* 6 (Spring–Summer 1983), 29–43.

DOLGOFF, RALPH L. "Clinicians as Policymakers." *Social Casework,* 62 (May 1981), 284–292.

DOMANSKI, TERESA P., MARION M. JOHNS, and MARGARET A. G. MANLY. "An Investigation of a Scheme for the Classification of Casework Treatment Activities." Master's thesis, Smith College School for Social Work, Northampton, Mass., 1960.

DOUGHERTY, NORA. "The Holding Environment: Breaking the Cycle of Abuse." *Social Casework,* 64 (May 1983), 283–290.

DUBRAY, WYNNE HANSON. "American Indian Values: Critical Factor in Casework." *Social Casework,* 66 (January 1985), 30–37.

DUEHN, WAYNE D., and NAZNEED MAYADAS. "Starting Where the Client Is: An Empirical Investigation." *Social Casework,* 60 (February 1979), 67–74.

DUNKEL, JOAN, and SHELLIE HATFIELD. "Countertransference Issues in Working with Persons with AIDS." *Social Work,* 31 (March–April 1986), 114–117.

ECKRICH, SHERRY. "Identification and Treatment of Borderline Personality Disorder." *Social Work,* 30 (March–April 1985), 166–171.

EDWARD, JOYCE. "The Use of the Dream in the Promotion of Ego Development." *Clinical Social Work Journal,* 6 (Winter 1978), 262–273.

EFFRON, ANNE KURTZMAN. "Children and Divorce: Help from an Elementary School." *Social Casework,* 61 (May 1980), 305–312.

EHLINE, DAVID, and PEGGY O'DEA TIGUE. "Alcoholism: Early Identification and Intervention in the Social Service Agency." *Child Welfare,* 56 (November 1977), 584–592.

EHRENKRANZ, SHIRLEY M. "A Study of Joint Interviewing in the Treatment of Marital Problems." *Social Casework,* 48 (October and November 1967), 498–502, 570–574.

———. "A Study of the Techniques and Procedures Used in Joint Interviewing in the Treatment of Marital Problems." Doctoral dissertation, Columbia University School of Social Work, New York, 1967.

ELLIOTT, MARTHA W. "Hospitality as a Professional Virtue." *Social Casework,* 65 (February 1984), 109–112.

ELSON, MIRIAM. *Self Psychology in Clinical Social Work.* New York: W. W. Norton, 1986.

EPSTEIN, IRWIN. "Pedagogy of the Perturbed: Teaching Research to the Reluctants." *Journal of Teaching in Social Work,* 1 (Spring/Summer 1987), 71–89.

EPSTEIN, NORMAN. "Techniques of Brief Therapy with Children and Parents." *Social Casework,* 57 (May 1976), 317–324.

——— and ANNE SHAINLINE. "Paraprofessional Parent-Aides and Disadvantaged Families." *Social Casework,* 55 (April 1974), 230–236.

ERIKSON, ERIK. *Childhood and Society.* New York. Norton, 1950.

———. *Identity and the Life Cycle.* New York: International Universities Press, 1959.

EWALT, PATRICIA L., ed. "Toward a Definition of Clinical Social Work." *The National Association of Social Work Conference Proceedings.* Washington, D.C.: National Association of Social Workers, 1980.

——— and JANICE KATZ. "An Examination of Advice Giving as a Therapeutic Intervention." *Smith College Studies in Social Work,* 47 (November 1976), 3–19.

FAIRBAIRN, W. R. D. *Object-Relations Theory of Personality*. New York: Basic Books, 1954.

FALICOV, CELIA JAES. "Cross-Cultural Marriages." In Neil S. Jacobson and Alan S. Gurman, *Clinical Handbook of Marital Therapy*. New York: Guilford Press, 1986, 429–450.

FAMILY SERVICE AMERICA. *The State of Families*. Milwaukee, Wisc.: Family Service America, 1984.

———. *The State of Families. II: Work and Family*. Milwaukee, Wisc.: Family Service America, 1987.

FANN, WILLIAM E., et al., eds. *Phenomenology and Treatment of Anxiety*. New York: Spectrum, 1979.

FANSCHEL, DAVID, and EUGENE B. SHINN. *Children in Foster Care: A Longitudinal Investigation*. New York: Columbia University Press, 1978.

FANTL, BERTA. "Preventive Intervention." *Social Work*, 7 (July 1962), 41–47.

FARBER, LAURA. "Casework Treatment of Ambulatory Schizophrenics." In Francis J. Turner, ed. *Differential Diagnosis and Treatment in Social Work*, 3rd ed. New York: Free Press, 1983, 325–336.

FEINSTEIN, SHERMAN C., and PETER L. GIOVACCHINI, eds. *Adolescent Psychiatry: Developmental and Clinical Studies*. Chicago: University of Chicago Press, 1978.

FERMAN, LOUIS A., ed. *Poverty in America*. Ann Arbor: University of Michigan Press, 1965.

FERREIRA, ANTONIO J. "Family Myths and Homeostasis." *Archives of General Psychiatry*, 9 (July–December 1963), 457–463.

FIBUSH, ESTHER, and BEALVA TURNQUEST. "A Black and White Approach to the Problem of Racism." *Social Casework*, 51 (October 1970), 459–466.

FIEDLER, FRED E. "The Concept of the Ideal Therapeutic Relationship." *Journal of Consulting Psychology*, 14 (August 1950), 239–245.

FINCH, WILBUR A., JR. "Social Workers Versus Bureaucracy." *Social Work*, 21 (September 1976), 370–374.

FINK, ARTHUR E. *The Field of Social Work*. New York: Holt, 1942.

FINN, JERRY. "The Stresses and Coping Behavior of Battered Women." *Social Casework*, 66 (June 1985), 341–349.

FISCHER, JOEL. "Is Casework Effective? A Review." *Social Casework*, 18 (January 1973), 5–20.

——— and HENRY MILLER. "The Effect of Client Race and Social Class on Clinical Judgments." *Clinical Social Work Journal*, 1 (Summer 1973), 100–109.

FLAVELL, JOHN. *The Developmental Psychology of Jean Piaget*. Princeton, N.J.: Van Nostrand, 1963.

FOGARTY, THOMAS. "Systems Concepts and the Dimensions of Self." In Philip J. Guerin, ed., *Family Therapy*. New York: Gardner Press, 1976, 144–153.

FOLEY, VINCENT D. *An Introduction to Family Therapy*. New York: Grune and Stratton, 1974.

FONTANE, ARLENE S. "Using Family of Origin Material in Short-Term Marriage Counseling." *Social Casework*, 60 (November 1979), 529–537.

FOREN, ROBERT, and BAILEY ROYSTON. *Authority in Social Casework*. New York: Pergamon Press, 1968.

FORTUNE, ANNE E. "Communication in Task-Centered Treatment." *Social Work*, 24 (September 1979), 317–323.

———. "Grief Only? Client and Social Worker Reactions to Termination." *Clinical Social Work Journal*, 15 (Summer 1987), 159–171.

FOX, EVELYN, MARION NELSON, and WILLIAM BOLMAN. "The Termination Process." *Social Work*, 14 (October 1969), 53–63.

FOX, RAYMOND. "Short-Term, Goal-Oriented Family Therapy." *Social Casework*, 68 (October 1987), 494–499.

FRAGER, ADENA R. "A Family Systems Perspective on Acting-Out." *Social Casework*, 66 (March 1985), 167–176.

FRAIBERG, SELMA. *Every Child's Birthright: In Defense of Mothering*. New York: Basic Books, 1977.

———. *The Magic Years*. New York: Scribner's, 1959.

FRAMO, JAMES L. *Explorations in Marital and Family Therapy*. New York: Springer, 1982.

———. "Rationale and Techniques of Intensive Family Therapy." In Ivan Boszormenyi-Nagy and James L. Framo, eds., *Intensive Family Therapy*. New York: Harper & Row, 1965, 143–212.

FRANK, JEROME D. "The Dynamics of the Psychotherapeutic Relationship." *Psychiatry*, 22 (February 1959), 17–39.

———. "The Role of Hope in Psychotherapy." *International Journal of Psychiatry*, 5 (May 1968), 383–395.

FRANK, MARGARET G. "Casework with Children: The Experience of Treatment." In Francis J. Turner, ed., *Differential Diagnosis and Treatment in Social Work*, 3d ed. New York: The Free Press, 1983, 5–14.

FRANKEL, CHARLES. "The Impact of Changing Values on the Family." *Social Casework*, 57 (June 1976), 355–365.

FRANKENSTEIN, RENATE. "Agency and Client Resistance." *Social Casework*, 63 (January 1982), 24–28.

FRANKLIN, DONNA L. "Does Client Social Class Affect Clinical Judgment?" *Social Casework*, 67 (September 1986), 424–432.

FREED, ANNE O. "The Borderline Personality." *Social Casework*, 61 (November 1980), 548–558.

———. "Building Theory for Family Practice." *Social Casework*, 63 (October 1982), 472–481.

———. "Differentiating Between Borderline and Narcissistic Personalities." *Social Casework*, 65 (September 1984), 395–404.

———. "The Family Agency and the Kinship System of the Elderly." *Social Casework*, 56 (December 1975), 579–586.

———. "Social Casework: More than a Modality." *Social Casework*, 58 (April 1977), 204–213.

FREEDBERG, SHARON. "Self-Determination: Historical Perspectives and Effects on Current Practice." *Social Work*, 34 (January 1989), 33–38.

FREEMAN, EDITH M. "Multiple Losses in the Elderly: An Ecological Approach." *Social Casework*, 65 (May 1984), 287–296.

———, et al. "Clinical Practice with Employed Women." *Social Casework*, 68 (September 1987), 413–420.

FREEMAN, HENRY, et al. "Can a Family Agency Be Relevant to the Inner Urban Scene?" *Social Casework*, 51 (January 1970), 12–21.

FREUD, ANNA. *The Ego and the Mechanisms of Defense.* New York: International Universities Press, 1946.

FREUD, SIGMUND. "Analysis of Phobia in a Five-year-old Boy." In James Strachey, ed., *The Complete Works of Sigmund Freud*, Vol. 10. London: Hogarth, 1964, 5–148.

FRIEDMAN, DONNA HAIG, and STEVEN FRIEDMAN. "Day Care as a Setting for Intervention in Family Systems." *Social Casework*, 63 (May 1982), 291–295.

FRIEDMAN, EDWIN H. "The Myth of the Shiksa." In Monica McGoldrick et al., eds., *Ethnicity and Family Therapy*. New York: Guilford Press, 1982, 499–526.

FRIEDMAN, LAURA. "Attitudes of Mental Health Professionals Toward Homosexuality: A Study of Graduate School Students." Unpublished Professional Seminar Paper, Hunter College School of Social Work, May 1987.

FULLER, JENNIE S. "Duo Therapy Case Studies: Process and Techniques." *Social Casework*, 58 (February 1977), 84–91.

GARCIA, ALEJANDRO. "The Chicano and Social Work." *Social Casework*, 52 (May 1971), 274–278.

GARFIELD, SOL L. "Research on Client Variables in Psychotherapy." In Sol Garfield and Allen E. Bergin, eds., *Handbook of Psychotherapy and Behavior Change*, 3d ed. New York: Wiley & Sons, 1986.

——— and ALLEN E. BERGIN, eds. *Handbook of Psychotherapy and Behavior Change*. New York: John Wiley & Sons, 1986.

GARRETT, ANNETTE. *Interviewing: Its Principles and Methods*. New York: Family Service Association of America, 1942.

———. "Modern Casework: The Contributions of Ego Psychology." In Howard J. Parad, ed., *Ego Psychology and Dynamic Casework*. New York: Family Service Association of America, 1958, 38–52.

———. "The Worker-Client Relationship." In Howard J. Parad, ed., *Ego Psychology and Dynamic Casework*. New York: Family Service Association of America, 1958, 53–82.

GEISMER, LUDWIG L. "Family Disorganization: A Sociological Perspective." *Social Casework*, 59 (November 1978), 545–550.

———. "Thirteen Evaluative Studies." In Edward J. Mullen, James R. Dumpson, et al., eds., *Evaluation of Social Intervention*. San Francisco: Jossey-Bass, 1972.

——— et al. *Early Supports for Family Life: A Social Work Experiment*. Metuchen, N.J.: Scarecrow Press, 1972.

——— and KATHERINE M. WOOD. "Evaluating Practice: Science as Faith." *Social Casework*, 63 (May 1982), 266–275.

GEIST, JOANNE, and NORMAN GERBER. "Joint Interviewing: A Treatment Technique with Marriage Partners." *Social Casework*, 41 (February 1960), 76–83.

GELMAN, SHELDON R. "Esoterica: A Zero Sum Game in the Helping Professions." *Social Casework*, 61 (January 1980), 48–53.

GERMAIN, CAREL B. "The Ecological Approach to People-Environmental Transactions." *Social Casework*, 62 (June 1981), 323–331.

———. "The Life Model Approach to Social Work Practice Revisited." In Francis J. Turner, ed., *Social Work Treatment*, 3d ed. New York: Free Press, 1986, 618–643.

———. "Social Context of Clinical Social Work." *Social Work*, 25 (November 1980), 483–488.

———, ed. *Social Work Practice: People and Environ-*

ments. New York: Columbia University Press, 1979.

——— and ALEX GITTERMAN. *The Life Model of Social Work Practice.* New York: Columbia University Press, 1980.

GETZEL, GEORGE S. "Helping Elderly Couples in Crisis." *Social Casework,* 63 (November 1982), 515–521.

GHALI, SONIA BADILLO. "Culture Sensitivity and the Puerto Rican Client." *Social Casework,* 58 (October 1977), 459–468.

GILBERT, NEIL, and HARRY SPECHT. "Advocacy and Professional Ethics." *Social Work,* 21 (July 1976), 288–293.

GINSBERG, LEON H. *The Practice of Social Work in Social Welfare.* New York: Free Press, 1983.

GIOVACCHINI, PETER L. *Developmental Disorders.* Northvale, N.J.: Jason Aronson, 1986.

GITTERMAN, ALEX. "Uses of Resistance: A Transactional View." *Social Work,* 28 (March–April 1983), 127–131.

——— and ALICE SCHAEFFER. "The White Professional and the Black Client." *Social Casework,* 53 (May 1972), 280–291.

GLASSER, PAUL, and LOIS GLASSER, eds., *Families in Crisis.* New York: Harper & Row, 1970.

GLICK, IRA D. and JAY HALEY. *Family Therapy and Research: An Annotated Bibliography.* New York: Grune & Stratton, 1971.

GOFFMAN, ERVING. *Stigma.* Englewood Cliffs, N.J.: Prentice Hall, 1963.

GOIN, MARCIA K. et al., "Therapy Congruent with Class-Linked Expectations." *Archives of General Psychiatry,* 13 (August 1965), 133–137.

GOLAN, NAOMI. "Crisis Theory." In Francis J. Turner, ed., *Social Work Treatment,* 3d ed. New York: Free Press, 1986, 296–340.

———. "Intervention at Times of Transition: Sources and Forms of Help." *Social Casework,* 61 (May 1980), 259–266.

———. *Treatment in Crisis Situations.* New York: Free Press, 1978.

GOLDBERG, GALE. "Breaking the Communication Barrier: The Initial Interview with an Abusing Parent." *Child Welfare,* 54 (April 1975), 274–282.

GOLDENBERG, IRENE, and HERBERT GOLDENBERG. *Family Therapy: An Overview,* 2d ed. Monterey, Calif.: Brooks/Cole, 1985.

GOLDMEIER, JOHN. "Helping the Elderly in Times of Stress." *Social Casework,* 66 (June 1985), 323–332.

———. "Intervention in the Continuum from Divorce to Family Reconstitution." *Social Casework,* 61 (January 1980), 39–47.

GOLDNER, VIRGINIA. "Feminism and Family Therapy." *Family Process,* 24 (March 1985), 31–47.

GOLDRING, JUDITH H. *Quick Response Therapy: A Time Limited Treatment Approach.* New York: Human Services Press, 1980.

GOLDSTEIN, EDA G. "Clinical and Ecological Approaches to the Borderline Client." *Social Casework,* 64 (June 1983), 353–362.

———. *Ego Psychology and Social Work Practice.* New York: The Free Press, 1984.

———. "The Influence of Parental Attitudes on Psychiatric Treatment Outcome." *Social Casework,* 60 (June 1979), 350–359.

GOLDSTEIN, HOWARD. "A Cognitive-Humanistic Approach to the Hard-to-Reach Client." *Social Casework,* 67 (January 1986), 27–36.

———. "The Neglected Moral Link in Social Work Practice." *Social Work,* 32 (May–June 1987), 181–186.

———. "Starting Where the Client Is." *Social Casework,* 64 (May 1983), 267–275.

———. "Toward the Integration of Theory and Practice: A Humanistic Approach." *Social Work,* 31 (September–October 1986), 352–357.

GORDON, WILLIAM. "Basic Constructs for an Integrative and Generative Conception of Social Work." In Gordon Hearn, ed., *The General Systems Approach: Contributions Toward A Holistic Conception of Social Work.* New York: Council on Social Work Education, 1969.

———. "Knowledge and Value: Their Distinction and Relationship in Clarifying Social Work Practice." *Social Work,* 10 (July 1965), 32–35.

GOTTESFELD, MARY L., and FLORENCE LIEBERMAN. "The Pathological Therapist." *Social Casework,* 60 (July 1979), 387–393.

GOTTLIEB, WERNER, and JOE H. STANLEY. "Mutual Goals and Goal-Setting in Casework." *Social Casework,* 48 (October 1967), 471–477.

GOULD, ROBERT. "Dr. Strangeclass: Or How I Stopped Worrying About Theory and Began Treating the Blue-Collar Worker." *American Journal of Orthopsychiatry,* 37 (January 1967), 78–86.

GOULDING, MARY MCCLURE, and ROBERT L. GOULDING. *Changing Lives Through Redecision Therapy.* New York: Brunner/Mazel, 1979.

GOURSE, JUDITH E., and MARTHA W. CHESCHEIR. "Authority Issues in Treating Resistant Families." *Social Casework*, 62 (February 1981), 67–73.

GRANITE, URSULA. "Foundations for Social Work on Open-Heart Surgery Service." *Social Casework*, 59 (February 1978), 101–105.

GRAY, WILLIAM, FREDERICK J. DUHL, and NICHOLAS D. RIZZO, eds. *General Systems Theory and Psychiatry*. Boston: Little Brown, 1969.

GRAYER, ELINOR DUNN, and PATRICIA R. SAX. "A Model for the Diagnostic and Therapeutic Use of Countertransference." *Clinical Social Work Journal*, 14 (Winter 1986), 295–307.

GRAZIANO, ROBERTA. "Making the Most of Your Time: Clinical Social Work with a Borderline Patient." *Clinical Social Work Journal*, 14 (Fall 1986), 262–275.

GREENACRE, PHYLLIS, ed. *Affective Disorders: A Psychoanalytic Contribution to Their Study*. New York: International Universities Press, 1953.

GREENBERG, GEORGE S. "The Family Interactional Perspective: A Study and Examination of the Work of Don D. Jackson." *Family Process*, 16 (December 1977), 385–412.

GREENBERG, LOIS I. "Therapeutic Grief Work with Children." *Social Casework*, 56 (July 1975), 396–403.

GREENBERG, SHIRLEY. "The Supportive Approach to Therapy." *Clinical Social Work Journal*, 14 (Spring 1986), 6–13.

GREENE, MARY JANE, and BETTY ORMAN. "Nurturing the Unnurtured." *Social Casework*, 62 (September 1981), 398–404.

GREIF, GEOFFREY L. "Single Fathers and Noncustodial Mothers: The Social Worker's Helping Role." *Journal of Independent Social Work*, 1 (Spring 1987), 59–69.

GRIMM, JAMES W., and JAMES D. ORTEN. "Student Attitudes toward the Poor." *Social Work*, 18 (January 1973), 94–100.

GRINNELL, RICHARD M., JR., and NANCY S. KYTE. "Environmental Modification: A Study." *Social Work*, 20 (July 1975), 313–318.

GROSSER, CHARLES. "Local Residents as Mediators Between Middle-Class Professional Workers and Lower-Class Clients." *Social Service Review*, 40 (March 1966), 56–63.

GROUP FOR THE ADVANCEMENT OF PSYCHIATRY. "The Field of Family Therapy." New York: Group for the Advancement of Psychiatry, 1970.

GRUMET, GERALD W., and DAVID L. TRACTMAN. "Psychiatric Social Workers in the Emergency Department." *Health and Social Work*, 1 (August 1976), 114–131.

Guerin, Philip J., ed., *Family Therapy*. New York: Gardner Press, 1976.

——— et al. *The Evaluation and Treatment of Marital Conflict: A Four-Stage Approach*. New York: Basic Books, 1987.

——— and EILEEN G. PENDAGAST. "Evaluation of Family System and Genogram." In Philip J. Guerin, ed., *Family Therapy*. New York: Gardner Press, 1976.

GUNTRIP, HARRY. *Personality Structure and Human Interaction*. London: Hogarth Press, 1961.

GURMAN, ALAN S., and DAVID P. KNISKERN. "Family Therapy Outcome Research: Knowns and Unknowns." In Gurman and Kniskern, eds., *Handbook of Family Therapy*. New York: Brunner/Mazel, 1981, 742–775.

GWYN, FELISHA S., and ALICE C. KILPATRICK. "Family Therapy with Low-Income Blacks: A Tool or Turn-Off?" *Social Casework*, 62 (May 1981), 259–266.

GYARFAS, MARY GORMAN. "A Systems Approach to Diagnosis." In Judith Mischne, ed., *Psychotherapy and Training in Clinical Social Work*. New York: Gardner Press, 1980, 49–63.

HAAS, WALTER. "Reaching Out—a Dynamic Concept in Casework." *Social Work*, 4 (July 1959), 41–45.

HADLEY, TREVOR R., et al. "The Relationship Between Family Developmental Crisis and the Appearance of Symptoms in a Family Member." *Family Process*, 13 (June 1974), 207–214.

HAFNER, JULIAN, R. "Marital Therapy for Agoraphobia." In Neil S. Jacobson and Alan S. Gurman, eds., *Clinical Handbook of Marital Therapy*. New York: Guilford Press, 1986, 471–493.

HAGEN, JAN L. "Income Maintenance Workers: Technicians or Service Providers?" *Social Service Review*, 61 (June 1987), 261–273.

HALEY, JAY. *Problem Solving Therapy*, 2d ed. San Francisco: Jossey-Bass, 1987.

HALLOWITZ, DAVID. "Counseling and Treatment of the Poor Black Family." *Social Casework*, 56 (October 1975), 451–459.

HALLUM, KENNETH C. "Social Class and Psychotherapy: A Sociolinguistic Approach." *Clinical Social Work Journal*, 6 (Fall 1978), 188–201.

HAMILTON, GORDON. "Basic Concepts in Social Casework." *The Family*, 18 (December 1937), 263–268.

———. "Basic Concepts upon Which Case Work Practice Is Formulated." *Proceedings of the National Conference of Social Work*. Chicago: University of Chicago Press, 1937.

———. *Psychotherapy in Child Guidance*. New York: Columbia University Press, 1947.

———. "The Role of Social Casework in Social Policy." *Social Casework*, 33 (October 1952), 315–324.

———. *Theory and Practice of Case Work*. New York: Columbia University Press, 1940.

———. *Theory and Practice of Social Case Work*, 2d ed. New York: Columbia University Press, 1951.

———. "A Theory of Personality: Freud's Contribution to Social Work." In Howard J. Parad, ed., *Ego Psychology and Dynamic Casework*, New York: Family Service Association of America, 1958, 11–37.

———. "The Underlying Philosophy of Social Case Work." *The Family*, 18 (July 1941), 139–148.

HAMMER, EMANUEL F. "Interpretive Technique: A Primer." In Hammer, ed., *Use of Interpretation in Treatment: Technique and Art*. New York: Grune and Stratton, 1968, 31–42.

HANKINS, FRANK. "Contributions of Sociology to Social Work." *Proceedings of the National Conference of Social Work*. Chicago: University of Chicago Press, 1930.

HARDCASTLE, DAVID A. "The Indigenous Nonprofessional in the Social Service Bureaucracy: A Critical Examination." *Social Work*, 16 (April 1971), 56–63.

HARDMAN, DALE. "The Matter of Trust." *Crime and Delinquency*. 15 (April 1969), 203–218.

HARDY-FANTA, CAROL, and ELIZABETH MACMAHON-HERRERA. "Adapting Family Therapy to the Hispanic Family." *Social Casework*, 62 (March 1981), 138–148.

HARE-MUSTIN, RACHEL T. "A Feminist Approach to Family Therapy." *Family Process*, 17 (June 1978), 181–194.

HARTMAN, ANN. "The Extended Family as a Resource for Change: An Ecological Approach to Family Centered Practice." In Carel B. Germain, ed., *Social Work Practice: People and Environments*. New York: Columbia University Press, 1979, 239–266.

——— and JOAN LAIRD. *Family-Centered Social Work Practice*. New York: Free Press, 1983.

HARTMAN, CARL, and DIANE REYNOLDS. "Resistant Clients: Confrontation, Interpretation, and Alliance." *Social Casework*, 68 (April 1987), 205–213.

HARTMANN, HEINZ. *Ego Psychology and the Problem of Adaptation*. New York: International Universities Press, 1958.

———, ERNST KRIS, and R. LOEWENSTEIN. "Comments on the Formation of Psychic Structure." In Ruth S. Eissler et al., eds., *The Psychoanalytic Study of the Child*. vol. 2. New York: International Universities Press, 1946, 11–38.

HASHIMI, JOAN KAY. "Environmental Modification: Teaching Social Coping Skills." *Social Work*, 26 (July 1981), 323–326.

HAVINGHURST, ROBERT J. "Social and Psychological Needs of the Aging." *The Annals*, 279 (January 1952), 11–17.

HEARN, GORDON. In Francis J. Turner, ed., *Social Work Treatment: Interlocking Theoretical Approaches*, 2d ed. New York: Free Press, 1979.

HEFNER, CHARLES W., and JAMES O. PROCHASKA. "Concurrent Versus Conjoint Marital Therapy." *Social Work*, 29 (May–June 1984), 287–291.

HEINEMAN-PEIPER, MARTHA. "The Future of Social Work Research." *Social Work Research and Abstracts*, 21 (Winter 1985), 3–11.

HELLENBRAND, SHIRLEY. "Client Value Orientations: Implications for Diagnosis and Treatment." *Social Casework*, 42 (April 1961), 163–169.

———. "Main Currrents in Social Casework, 1918–36." Doctoral dissertation, Columbia University School of Social Work, New York, 1965.

HENDRICKS-MATTHEWS, MARYBETH. "The Battered Woman: Is She Ready for Help?" *Social Casework*, 63 (March 1982), 131–137.

HENRY, JULES. *Pathways to Madness*. New York: Random House, 1971.

HEPWORTH, DEAN H. "Early Removal of Resistance in Task-Centered Casework." *Social Work*, 24 (July 1979), 317–323.

HEYMAN, MARGARET M. "Some Methods in Direct Casework Treatment of the Schizophrenic." *Journal of Psychiatric Social Work*, 19 (Summer 1949), 18–24.

HIRSOHN, SID. "Casework with the Compulsive Mother." *Social Casework*, 32 (June 1951), 254–261.

HO, MAN KEUGH. "Social Work with Asian Americans." *Social Casework*, 57 (March 1976), 195–201.

———— and EUNICE McDOWELL. "The Black Worker-White Client Relationship." *Clinical Social Work Journal,* 1 (Fall 1973), 161–167.

HOFFMAN, DAVID L., and MARY L. REMMEL. "Uncovering the Precipitant in Crisis Intervention." *Social Casework,* 56 (May 1975), 259–261.

HOFFMAN, LYNN. *Foundations of Family Therapy.* New York: Basic Books, 1981.

HOLLINGSHEAD, AUGUST B., and FREDERICK C. REDLICH. *Social Class and Mental Illness.* New York: Wiley, 1958.

HOLLIS, FLORENCE. "Analysis of Two Casework Treatment Approaches." Unpublished paper, read at Biennial Meeting of the Family Service Association of America, 1956.

————. "Casework and Social Class." *Social Casework,* 46 (October 1965), 463–471.

————. "Casework in Marital Disharmony." Doctoral dissertation, Bryn Mawr College, 1947. Micro filmed, Ann Arbor, Mich.: University Microfilms, 1951.

————. "Continuance and Discontinuance in Marital Counseling and Some Observation on Joint Interviews." *Social Casework,* 49 (March 1968), 167–174.

————. "Environmental (Indirect) Treatment as Determined by Client's Needs." In *Differential Approach in Casework Treatment.* New York: Family Welfare Association of America, 1936.

————. "Evaluation: Clinical Results and Research Methodology." *Clinical Social Work Journal,* 4 (Fall 1976), 204–222.

————. "How It Really Was." *Smith College School for Social Work Journal,* 10 (Fall 1983), 3–9.

————. "On Revisiting Social Work." *Social Casework,* 61 (January 1980), 3–10.

————. "Principles and Assumptions Underlying Casework Practice." *Social Work,* (London), 12 (1955), 41–55.

————. *Social Casework in Practice: Six Case Studies.* New York: Family Welfare Association of America, 1939, 295–298.

————. "A Study of Joint Interviewing in the Treatment of Marital Problems." *Social Casework,* 48 (October–November 1967), 498–503, 570–574.

————. "The Techniques of Casework." *Journal of Social Casework,* 30 (June 1949), 235–244.

————. *A Typology of Casework Treatment.* New York: Family Service Association of America, 1968.

————. "And What Shall We Teach? The Social Work Educator and Knowledge." *Social Service Review,* 42 (June 1968), 184–196.

————. *Women in Marital Conflict.* New York: Family Service Association of America, 1949.

HOLMES, SALLY ANN. "A Holistic Approach to the Treatment of Violent Families." *Social Casework,* 62 (December 1981), 594–600.

———— et al. "Working with the Parent in Child-Abuse Cases." *Social Casework,* 56 (January 1975), 3–12.

HOROWITZ, AARON NOAH. "Guidelines for Treating Father-Daughter Incest." *Social Casework,* 64 (November 1983), 515–524.

HOWARD, TINA U., and FRANK C. JOHNSON. "An Ecological Approach to Practice with Single Families." *Social Casework,* 66 (October 1985), 482–489.

HOWE, MICHAEL W. "Casework Self-Evaluation: A Single-Subject Approach." *Social Service Review,* 48 (March 1974), 1–23.

HUTCHISON, ELIZABETH D. "Use of Authority in Direct Social Work Practice with Mandated Clients." *Social Service Review,* 61 (December 1987), 581–589.

ICARD, LARRY, and DONALD M. TRAUNSTEIN. "Black, Gay, Alcoholic Men: Their Character and Treatment." *Social Casework,* 68 (May 1987), 267–272.

IVANOFF, ANDRE, BETTY J. BLYTHE, and SCOTT BRIAR. "The Empirical Practice Debate." *Social Casework,* 68 (May 1987), 290–298.

JACKSON, DON D. "Family Interaction, Family Homeostasis and Some Implications for Conjoint Family Psychotherapy." In Don D. Jackson, ed., *Therapy, Communication, and Change: Human Communication,* vol. 2. Palo Alto: Science and Behavior Books, 1968, pp. 185–203.

————. "The Question of Family Homeostasis." In Don D. Jackson, ed. *Communication, Family and Marriage: Human Communication,* vol. 1. Palo Alto, Calif.: Science and Behavior Books, 1968, pp. 1–11.

———— and VIRGINIA SATIR. "A Review of Psychiatric Developments in Family Diagnosis and Therapy." In Nathan W. Ackerman, Frances L. Beatman, and Sanford N. Sherman, eds., *Exploring the Base for Family Therapy.* New York: Family Service Association of America, 1961, 29–49.

JACOBSON, GERALD, F., ed. *Crisis Intervention in the 1980's.* San Francisco: Jossey-Bass, 1980.

JACOBSON, NEIL S., and ALAN S. GURMAN, eds. *Clinical Handbook of Marital Therapy*. New York: Guilford Press, 1986.

JANSSON, BRUCE S., and JUNE SIMMONS. "The Survival of Social Work Units in Host Organizations." *Social Work*, 31 (September–October 1984), 448–453.

JAYARATNE, SRINIKA, and WAYNE A. CHESS. "Job Satisfaction, Burnout, and Turnover: A National Study." *Social Work*, 29 (September–October 1984), 448–453.

JEFFERS, CAMILLE. *Living Poor*. Ann Arbor, Mich.: Ann Arbor Publishers, 1967.

JOHNSON, HARRIETTE C. "Emerging Concerns in Family Therapy." *Social Work*, 31 (July–August 1986), 229–306.

———. "Working with Stepfamilies: Principles of Practice." In Francis J. Turner, ed., *Differential Diagnosis and Treatment in Social Work*, 3d ed. New York: The Free Press, 1983, 829–839.

JOHNSON, PETER J., and ALLEN RUBIN. "Case Management in Mental Health: A Social Work Domain?" *Social Work*, 28 (January–February 1983), 49–55.

JOLESCH, MIRIAM. "Casework Treatment of Young Married Couples." *Social Casework*, 43 (May 1962), 245–251.

JONES, MARY ANN, RENEE NEUMAN, and ANN W. SHYNE. *A Second Chance for Families*. New York: Child Welfare League of America, 1976.

JONES, TERRY. "Institutional Racism in the United States." *Social Work*, 19 (March 1974), 218–225.

JOSSELYN, IRENE. "The Family as a Psychological Unit." *Social Casework*, 34 (October 1953), 336–343.

JUNG, MARSHALL. "Directions for Building Family Development Theory." *Social Casework*, 64 (June 1983), 363–370.

KADUSHIN, ALFRED. "The Racial Factor in the Interview." *Social Work*, 17 (May 1972), 88–89.

———. *The Social Work Interview*. 2d ed. New York: Columbia University Press, 1983.

KANTOR, DAVID, and WILLIAM LEHR. *Inside the Family*. San Francisco: Jossey-Bass, 1975.

KANTOR, JOEL S. "Reevaluation of Task-Centered Social Work Practice." *Clinical Social Work Journal*, 11 (Fall 1983), 228–244.

KAPLAN, DAVID M., and EDWARD A. MASON. "Maternal Reactions to Premature Birth Viewed as an Acute Emotional Disorder." *American Journal of Orthopsychiatry*, 30 (July 1960), 539–547.

KAPLAN, HAROLD I., and BENJAMIN J. SADOCK, eds. *Comprehensive Textbook of Psychiatry*, 4th ed. Baltimore, Md.: Williams and Wilkens, 1985.

KAPLAN, LILLIAN, and JEAN B. LIVERMORE. "Treatment of Two Patients with Punishing Super-Egos." *Journal of Social Casework*, 29 (October 1948), 310–316.

KARDINER, ABRAM. *The Individual and His Society*. New York: Columbia University Press, 1939.

KASE, HAROLD M. "Purposeful Use of Indigenous Paraprofessionals." *Social Work*, 17 (March 1972), 109–110.

KASSEL, SUZANNE D., and ROSALIE A. KANE. "Self-Determination Dissected." *Clinical Social Work Journal*, 8 (Fall 1980), 161–178.

KEEFE, THOMAS. "The Economic Context of Empathy." *Social Work*, 23 (November 1978), 460–465.

———. "Empathy Skill and Critical Consciousness." *Social Casework*, 61 (September 1980), 387–393.

———. "Empathy: The Critical Skill." *Social Work*, 21 (January 1976), 10–14.

KEITH-LUCAS, ALAN. *The Giving and Taking of Help*. Chapel Hill: University of North Carolina Press, 1971.

KELLER, GORDON N. "Bicultural Social Work and Anthropology." *Social Casework*, 53 (October 1972), 455–465.

KEMPE, HENRY C., and RAY E. HELFER, eds. *Helping the Battered Child and His Family*. Philadelphia: Lippincott, 1972.

KENDALL, KATHERINE A. "A Sixty-Year Perspective of Social Work." *Social Casework*, 63 (September 1982), 424–428.

———, ed. *Social Work Values in an Age of Discontent*. New York: Council on Social Work Education, 1970.

KENT, MARILYN O. "Remarriage: A Family Systems Perspective." *Social Casework*, 61 (March 1980), 146–153.

KERNBERG, OTTO. "Borderline Personality Organization." In Michael H. Stone, ed., *Essential Papers on Borderline Disorders*. New York: New York University Press, 1986.

———. *Borderline Conditions and Pathological Narcissism*. New York: Aronson, 1975.

———. *Severe Personality Disorders*. New York: Yale University Press, 1984.

KERR, MICHAEL E. "Obstacles to Differentiation of

Self." In Alan S. Gurman, ed., *Casebook of Marital Therapy*. New York: Guilford Press, 1985, 111–153.

KHINDUKA, S. K., and BERNARD J. COUGHLIN. "A Conceptualization of Action." *Social Service Review*, 49 (March 1975), 1–14.

KING, CHARLES. "Family Therapy with the Deprived Family." *Social Casework*, 48 (April 1967), 203–208.

KIRSCHNER, CHARLOTTE. "The Aging Family in Crisis: A Problem in Living." *Social Casework*, 60 (April 1979), 209–216.

KLEIN, EMANUEL. "The Reluctance to Go to School." In Ruth S. Eissler et al., eds. *The Psychoanalytic Study of the Child*, vol. 1. New York: International Universities Press, 1945, 263–279.

KNAPP, MARK. *Essentials of Nonverbal Communication*. New York: Holt, Rinehart and Winston, 1980.

KNOLL, FAUSTINA RAMIREZ. "Casework Services for Mexican Americans." *Social Casework*, 52 (May 1971), 279–284.

KOEHLER, RUTH T. "The Use of Advice in Casework." *Smith College Studies in Social Work*, 23 (February 1953), 151–165.

KOGAN, LEONARD S. "The Short-Term Case in a Family Agency." *Social Casework*, 38 (June 1957), 296–302.

KOHN, MELVIN L. *Class and Conformity: A Study in Values*. Chicago: University of Chicago Press, 1977.

KOHUT, HEINZ. *The Restoration of the Self*. New York: International Universities Press, 1977.

KOMAROWSKY, MIRRA. *Blue Collar Marriage*. New York: Random House, 1964.

———. *The Unemployed Man and His Family*. New York: Dryden Press, 1940.

KOSS, MARY P., and JAMES N. BUTCHER. "Research on Brief Psychotherapy." In Sol L. Garfield and Allen E. Bergin, eds., *Handbook of Psychotherapy and Behavior Change*. New York: John Wiley, 1986, 627–670.

KOUNIN, JACOB., et al. "Experimental Studies of Clients' Reaction to Initial Interviews." *Human Relations*, 9 (1956), 265–293.

KRAMER, PHILIP. "The Indigenous Worker: Hometowner, Striver, or Activist." *Social Work*, 17 (January 1972), 43–49.

KRESTAN, JO-ANN, and CLAUDIA S. BEPKO. "The Problem of Fusion in the Lesbian Relationship." *Family Process*, 19 (September 1980), 277–289.

KRIS, ERNST. "Notes on the Development and on Some Current Problems of Psychoanalytic Child Psychology." In Ruth S. Eissler et al., eds., *The Psychoanalytic Study of the Child*, vol. 5. New York: International Universities Press, 1950, 24–46.

KRITSBERG, WAYNE. *The Adult Children of Alcoholics Syndrome: From Discovery to Recovery*. Pompano Beach, Fla.: Health Communications, 1985.

KRUG, OTILDA. "The Dynamic Use of the Ego Functions in Casework Practice." *Social Casework*, 36 (December 1955), 443–450.

KRYSTAL, ESTHER, et al. "Serving the Unemployed." *Social Casework*, 64 (February 1983), 67–76.

KUBLER-ROSS, ELISABETH. *On Death and Dying*. New York: Macmillan, 1969.

KUPERS, TERRY A. *Ending Therapy: The Meaning of Termination*. New York: New York University Press, 1988.

KUTCHINS, HERB, and STUART A. KIRK. "DSM-III and Social Work Malpractice." *Social Work*, 32 (May-June 1987), 205–211.

LAING, L. P. "The Use of Reassurance in Psychotherapy." *Smith College Studies in Social Work*, 22 (February 1952), 75–90.

LAING, RONALD D. "Mystification, Confusion, and Conflict." In Ivan Boszormenyi-Nagy and James L. Framo, eds., *Intensive Family Therapy*. New York: Harper & Row, 1965, 343–363.

——— and A. ESTERSON. *Sanity, Madness and the Family*, 2d ed. New York: Basic Books, 1971.

LAIRD, JOAN. "An Ecological Approach to Child Welfare: Issues of Family Identity and Continuity." In Carel B. Germain, ed., *Social Work Practice: People and Environments*. New York: Columbia University Press, 1979, 174–209.

——— and ANN HARTMAN, eds. *A Handbook of Child Welfare: Context, Knowledge, and Practice*. New York: Free Press, 1985.

LAMMERT, MARILYN. "Experience as Knowing: Utilizing Therapist Self-Awareness." *Social Casework*, 67 (June 1986), 369–376.

LARSEN, JO ANN. "Remedying Dysfunctional Marital Communication." *Social Casework*, 63 (January 1982), 15–23.

——— and CRAIG T. MITCHELL. "Task-Centered, Strength-Oriented Group Work with Delinquents." *Social Casework*, 61 (March 1980), 154–163.

LASSERS, ELISABETH, et al. "Steps in the Return to School of Children with School Phobia." *American Journal of Psychiatry*, 130 (March 1973), 265–268.

LAUGHLIN, HENRY P. *The Ego and Its Defenses*, 2d ed. New York: James Aronson, 1979.

LAZLO, ERVIN, ed. *The Relevance of General Systems Theory*. New York: Braziller, 1972.

LEADER, ARTHUR L. "Current and Future Issues in Family Therapy." *Social Service Review*, 43 (January 1969), 1–11.

———. "Family Therapy for Divorced Fathers and Others Out of the Home." *Social Casework*, 54 (January 1973), 13–19.

———. "Intergenerational Separation Anxiety in Family Therapy." *Social Casework*, 59 (March 1978), 138–144.

———. "The Notion of Responsibility in Family Therapy." *Social Casework*, (March 1979), 131–137.

———. "The Relationship of Presenting Problems to Family Conflicts." *Social Casework*, 62 (October 1981), 451–457.

———. "Therapeutic Control in Family Therapy." *Clinical Social Work Journal*, 11 (Winter 1983), 351–361.

LEDERER, WILLIAM J., and DON D. JACKSON. *The Mirages of Marriage*. New York: W. W. Norton, 1968.

LEE, JUDITH A., and CAROL R. SWENSON. "Theory in Action: A Community Social Service Agency." *Social Casework*, 59 (June 1978), 359–370.

——— and SUSAN J. ROSENTHAL. "Working with Victims of Violent Assault." *Social Casework*, 64 (December 1983), 593–601.

LEE, LAURA J. "The Social Worker in the Political Environment of a School System." *Social Work*, 28 (July–August 1983), 302–306.

LEIKIN, CELIA. "Identifying and Treating the Alcoholic." *Social Casework*, 67 (February 1986), 67–73.

LEMON, ELIZABETH C. "Planned Brief Treatment." In Aaron Rosenblatt and Diana Waldfogel, eds., *Handbook of Clinical Social Work*. San Francisco: Jossey-Bass, 1983, 401–419.

LESHAN, EDA. "Learning to Say Good-bye." In Francis Turner, ed., *Differential Diagnosis and Treatment in Social Work*, 2d ed. New York: Free Press, 1976.

LESOFF, REEVA. "What to Say When. . . ." *Clinical Social Work Journal*, 5 (Spring 1977), 66–76.

LESTER, LOIS. "The Special Needs of the Female Alcoholic." *Social Casework*, 63 (October 1982), 451–456.

LEVIN, JEROME D. *Treatment of Alcoholism and Other Addictions: A Self-Psychology Approach*. Northvale, N.J.: Aronson, 1987.

LEVINE, RACHEL A. "Treatment in the Home." *Social Work*, 9 (January 1964), 19–28.

LEVINSON, HILLIARD. "Communication with an Adolescent in Psychotherapy." *Social Casework*, 54 (October 1973), 480–488.

———. "Termination of Psychotherapy: Some Salient Issues." *Social Casework*, 58 (October 1977), 480–488.

LEVY, CHARLES S. "Advocacy and the Injustice of Justice." *Social Service Review*, 48 (March 1974), 39–50.

———. "Labeling: The Social Worker's Responsibility." *Social Casework*, 62 (June 1981), 332–342.

———. *Social Work Ethics*. New York: Human Services Press, 1976.

LEVY, LORRAINE POKART. "Services to Parents of Children in a Psychiatric Hospital." *Social Casework*, 58 (April 1977), 204–213.

LEVY, RONA L. "Overview of Single-Case Experiments." In Aaron Rosenblatt and Diana Waldfogel, eds., *Handbook of Clinical Social Work*. San Francisco: Jossey-Bass, 1983, 583–602.

LEWIS, HAROLD. "Ethical Assessment." *Social Casework*, 65 (April 1984), 203–211.

———. *The Intellectual Base of Social Work Practice: Tools for Thought in a Helping Profession*. New York: The Haworth Press, 1982.

———. "Teaching Ethics Through Ethical Teaching," *Journal of Teaching in Social Work*, 1 (Spring/Summer 1987), 3–14.

LEWIS, HELEN BLOCK. *Shame and Guilt in Neurosis*. New York: International Universities Press, 1971.

LEWIS, HYLAN. *Culture Class and Poverty*. Washington, D.C.: Cross Tell, 1967.

LEWIS, MARIAN F. "Alcoholism and Family Casework." *The Family*, 18 (April 1937), 39–44.

LIBASSI, MARY FRANCES. "The Chronically Mentally Ill: A Practice Approach." *Social Casework*, 69 (February 1988), 88–96.

LIDE, PAULINE. "Dynamic Mental Representation: An Analysis of the Empathic Process." *Social Casework*, 47 (March 1966), 146–151.

———. "An Experimental Study of Empathic Functioning." *Social Service Review*, 41 (March 1967), 23–30.

LIDZ, THEODORE. *The Person: His Development Throughout the Life Cycle*. New York: Basic Books, 1968.

LIEBERMAN, FLORENCE, ed. *Clinical Social Workers as Psychotherapists*. New York: Gardner Press, 1982.

———. *Social Work with Children*. New York: Human Services Press, 1979.

——— and MARY L. GOTTESFELD. "The Repulsive Client." *Clinical Social Work Journal*, 1 (Spring 1973), 22–31.

LINDEMANN, ERICH. "Symptomatology and Management of Acute Grief." In Howard J. Parad, ed., *Crisis Intervention*. New York: Family Service Association of America, 1965, 7–12.

LINDSEY, ELIZABETH W., et al. "Evaluating Interpersonal Skills Training for Public Welfare Staff." *Social Service Review*, 61 (December 1987), 623–635.

LINZER, NORMAN. *The Jewish Family*. New York: Human Sciences Press, 1984.

LOEWENSTEIN, SOPHIE. "Inner and Outer Space in Social Casework." *Social Casework*, 60 (January 1979), 19–29.

———. "An Overview of the Concept of Narcissism." *Social Casework*, 58 (March 1977), 136–142.

———. "Understanding Lesbian Women." *Social Casework*, 61 (January 1980), 29–38.

LOGAN, SADYE L. "Race, Identity and Black Children: A Developmental Perspective." *Social Casework*, 62 (January 1981), 47–56.

LOPEZ, DIEGO J., and GEORGE S. GETZEL. "Helping Gay AIDS Patients." *Social Casework*, 65 (September 1984), 387–394.

LORION, RAYMOND P., and ROBERT D. FELNER. "Research on Mental Health Interventions with the Disadvantaged." In Sol L. Garfield and Allen E. Bergin, eds., *Handbook of Psychotherapy and Behavior Change*. New York: John Wiley & Sons, 1986, 739–775.

LOEWENSTEIN, RUDOLPH. "The Problem of Interpretation." *Psychoanalytic Quarterly*, 20 (January 1951), 1–14.

LUCENTE, RANDOLPH L. "N = 1: Intensive Case Study Methodology Reconsidered." *Journal of Teaching in Social Work*, 1 (Fall/Winter 1987), 49–64.

LUKTON, ROSEMARY CREED. "Myths and Realities of Crisis Intervention." *Social Casework*, 63 (May 1982), 276–285.

——— and RUTH EHRLICH BRO. "An Alternative Model for Curriculum Building in Clinical Social Work Education: The California Institute for Clinical Social Work." *Clinical Social Work Journal*, 16 (Spring 1988), 8–21.

LUM, DOMAN. "The Psychosocial Needs of the Chinese Elderly." *Social Casework*, 61 (February 1980), 100–106.

———. "Toward a Framework for Social Work Practice with Minorities." *Social Work*, 27 (May 1982), 244–249.

LUTZ, WERNER A. *Concepts and Principles Underlying Social Casework Practice*. Washington, D.C.: National Association of Social Workers, 1956.

MAAS, HENRY S. "Socio-cultural Factors in Psychiatric Clinic Services for Children." *Smith College Studies*, 25 (February 1955), 1–90.

MAGURA, STEPHEN. "Clients View of Outcomes of Child Protective Services." *Social Casework*, 63 (November 1982), 522–531.

MAHLER, MARGARET S., et al. *The Psychological Birth of the Human Infant: Symbiosis and Individuation*. New York: Basic Books, 1975.

MALICK, MILDRED D. "A Situational Perspective in Casework Theory." *Social Casework*, 58 (July 1977), 401–411.

MALAN, DAVID. *The Frontier of Brief Psychotherapy*. New York: Plenum, 1976.

MALTSBERGER, JOHN, and DAN BUIE. "Countertransference Hate in the Treatment of Suicidal Patients." *Archives of General Psychiatry*, 30 (May 1974), 625–633.

MALUCCIO, ANTHONY N. *Learning from Clients: Interpersonal Helping as Viewed by Clients and Social Workers*. New York: Free Press, 1979.

———. "Promoting Competence Through Life Experiences." In Carel B. Germain, ed., *Social Work Practice: People and Environments*. New York: Columbia University Press, 1979, 282–302.

——— et al. *Permanency Planning for Children: Concepts and Methods*. London: Tavistock, 1986.

——— and WILMA D. MARLOW. "The Case for the Contract." *Social Work*, 19 (January 1974), 28–36.

MANN, JAMES. *Time-Limited Psychotherapy*. Cambridge, Mass.: Harvard University Press, 1973.

MARCIANO, TERESA DONATI. "Middle Class Incomes, Working-Class Hearts." In Arlene S. Skolnick and Jerome H. Skolnick, eds., *Family in Transition*. Boston: Little, Brown, 1977, 465–476.

MARCUS, LOTTE. "The Effect of Extralinguistic Phenomena on the Judgment of Anxiety." Doctoral dissertation, Columbia University School of Social Work, New York, 1969.

MARINE, ESTHER. "School Refusal: Review of the Literature." *Social Service Review*, 42 (December 1968), 464–478.

MARSH, JEANNE C. "Research Innovation in Social

Work Practice: Avoiding the Headless Machine."
Social Service Review, 57 (December 1983), 582–598.

MARZIALI, ELSA. "The First Session: An Interpersonal Encounter." *Social Casework,* 69 (January 1988), 23–27.

MASSERMAN, JULES, ed. *Depressions: Theories and Therapies.* New York: Grune and Stratton, 1970.

MASTERSON, JAMES F. *Psychology of the Borderline Adult.* New York: Brunner/Mazel, 1976.

MAVOGENES, NANCY, et al. "But Can the Client Understand It?" *Social Work,* 22 (March 1977), 110–112.

MAYER, HERTA, and GERALD SCHAMESS. "Long Term Treatment for the Disadvantaged." *Social Casework,* 50 (March 1969), 138–145.

MAYER, JOHN E., and NOEL TIMMS. "Clash in Perspective Between Worker and Client." *Social Casework,* 50 (January 1969), 32–40.

——— and ———. *The Client Speaks: Working Class Impressions of Casework.* New York: Atherton, 1970.

McADOO, HARRIET PIPES. *Black Families,* 2d ed. Newbury Park, Calif.: Sage, 1988.

McCULLUM, AUDREY T. "Mothers' Preparation for Their Children's Hospitalization." *Social Casework,* 48 (July 1967), 407–415.

McDERMOTT, F. E., ed. *Self Determination in Social Work.* London: Routledge and Kegan Paul, 1975.

McFARLANE, WILLIAM R., ed. *Family Therapy in Schizophrenia.* New York: Guilford Press, 1983.

McGOLDRICK, MONICA. "Ethnicity and Family Therapy: An Overview." In Monica McGoldrick et al., *Ethnicity and Family Therapy.* New York: Guilford Press, 1982, 3–30.

——— and NYDIA GARCIA PRETO. "Ethnic Intermarriage: Implications for Therapy." *Family Process,* 23 (September 1984), 347–364.

——— and RANDY GERSON. *Genograms in Family Assessment.* New York: W. W. Norton, 1985.

McINTYRE, EILENE L. G. "Social Networks: Potential for Practice." *Social Work,* 31 (November–December 1986), 421–426.

MEAD, MARGARET. *Sex and Temperament in Three Primitive Societies.* New York: Morrow, 1935.

MEISSNER, WILLIAM W. "Theories of Personality and Psychopathology: Classical Psychoanalysis." In Harold I. Kaplan and Benjamin J. Sadock, eds., *Comprehensive Textbook of Psychiatry,* 4th ed. Baltimore, Md.: Williams and Wilkens, 1985, 337–418.

MENCHER, SAMUEL. "The Concept of Authority and Social Casework." *Casework Papers, 1960.* New York: Family Service Association of America, 1960, 126–138.

MENDES, HELEN A. "Countertransferences and Counter-Culture Clients." *Social Casework,* 58 (March 1977), 159–163.

MEYER, CAROL. "Complementarity and Marital Conflict: The Development of a Concept and Its Application to the Casework Method." Doctoral dissertation, Columbia University School of Social Work, New York, 1957.

———. "Editorial." *Social Work,* 29 (July–August 1984), 323.

———, ed. *Preventive Intervention.* Washington, D.C.: National Association of Social Workers, 1975.

MILLER, ROGER, R. "Disappointment in Therapy." *Clinical Social Work Journal,* 5 (Spring 1977), 17–28.

———. "Student Research Perspectives on Race in Casework Practice." *Smith College Studies in Social Work,* 41 (November 1970), 10–23.

MILLON, THEODORE. *Disorders of Personality.* New York: John Wiley & Sons, 1981.

MILLOY, MARGARET. "Casework with the Older Person in the Family." *Social Casework,* 45 (October 1964), 450–456.

MILNE, ANN L. "Divorce Mediation: A Process of Self-Definition and Self-Determination." In Neil S. Jacobson and Alan S. Gurman, eds., *Clinical Handbook of Marital Therapy.* New York: Guilford Press, 1986, 197–216.

MINAHAN, ANNE. "Editorial Page: 'Burn-out' and Organizational Change." *Social Work,* 25 (March 1980), 87.

MINDEL, CHARLES H., and ROBERT W. HABENSTEIN. *Ethnic Families in America.* New York: Elsevier, 1976.

MINUCHIN, SALVADORE. *Families and Family Therapy.* Cambridge, Mass.: Harvard University Press, 1974.

——— et al. *Families of the Slums.* New York: Basic Books, 1967.

——— et al. *Psychosomatic Families: Anorexia Nervosa in Context.* Cambridge, Mass.: Harvard University Press, 1978.

——— and BRAULIO MONTALVO. "Techniques for Working with the Disorganized Low Socio-Economic Families." *American Journal of Orthopsychiatry,* 37 (October 1967), 880–887.

MISHNE, JUDITH MARKS. *Clinical Work with Children.* New York: The Free Press, 1983.

———. *Clinical Work with Adolescents.* New York: Free Press, 1986.

MITCHELL, CELIA. "The Therapeutic Field in the Treatment of Families in Conflict: Recurrent Themes in Literature and Clinical Practice." In Bernard Reiss, ed., *New Directions in Mental Health.* New York: Grune & Stratton, 1968.

MITTLEMANN, BELA. "Analysis of Reciprocal Neurotic Patterns in Family Relationships." In Victor W. Eisenstein, ed., *Neurotic Interaction in Marriage.* New York: Basic Books, 1956, 81–100.

MIZIO, EMELICIA. "Commentary." *Social Casework,* 58 (October 1977), 469–474.

———. "White Worker-Minority Clients." *Social Work,* 17 (May 1972), 82–86.

MONTALVO, FRANK. "The Third Dimension in Social Casework: Mary E. Richmond's Contribution to Family Treatment." *Clinical Social Work Journal,* 10 (Summer 1982), 103–112.

MONTGOMERY, MITZIE I. R. "Feedback Systems, Interaction Analysis and Counseling Models in Professional Programs." Doctoral dissertation, University of Edinburgh, 1973.

MONTIEL, MIGUEL, and PAUL WONG. "A Theoretical Critique of the Minority Perspective." *Social Casework,* 64 (February 1983), 112–117.

MOORE-KIRKLAND, JANET. "Mobilizing Motivation: From Theory to Practice." In Anthony N. Maluccio, ed., *Promoting Competence in Clients: A New/Old Approach to Social Work Practice.* New York: Macmillan, 1981, 27–54.

MORAWETZ, ANITA, and GILLIAN WALKER. *Brief Therapy with Single-Parent Families.* New York: Brunner/Mazel, 1984.

MOSTWIN, DANUTA. "Social Work Interventions with Families in Crisis of Change." *Social Thought,* 2 (Winter 1976).

MOULTRUP, DAVID. "Towards an Integrated Model of Family Therapy." *Clinical Social Work Journal,* 9 (Summer 1981), 111–125.

MOYNIHAN, ROSEMARY, et al. "AIDS and Terminal Illness." *Social Casework,* 69 (June 1988), 380–387.

MOYNIHAN, SHARON K. "Home Visits for Family Treatment." *Social Casework,* 55 (December 1974), 612–617.

MUDD, EMILY. *The Practice of Marriage Counselling.* New York: Association Press, 1951.

MULLEN, EDWARD, J. "Casework Communication." *Social Casework,* 49 (November 1968), 546–551.

———. "Casework Treatment Procedures as a Function of Client Diagnostic Variables." Doctoral dissertation, Columbia University School of Social Work, New York, 1968.

———. "Difference in Worker Style in Casework." *Social Casework,* 50 (June 1969), 347–353.

———. "The Relation Between Diagnosis and Treatment in Casework." *Social Casework,* 50 (April 1969), 218–226.

MURDACH, ALLISON D. "Bargaining and Persuasion with Nonvoluntary Clients." *Social Work,* 25 (November 1980), 458–461.

MURDOCK, GEORGE PETER. "The Universality of the Nuclear Family." In Norman W. Bell and Ezra F. Vogel, eds., *A Modern Introduction to the Family.* Revised ed. New York: Free Press, 1968, 37–47.

MURPHY, ANN, et al., "Group Work with Parents of Children with Down's Syndrome." *Social Casework,* 53 (February 1972), 114–119.

MURRAY, HENRY A. *Explorations in Personality.* New York: Oxford University Press, 1938.

MULTSCHLER, ELIZABETH. "Evaluating Practice: A Study of Research Utilization by Practitioners." *Social Work,* 29 (July–August 1984), 332–337.

NADEL, ROBERT. "Interviewing Style and Foster Parents' Verbal Accessibility." *Child Welfare,* 46 (April 1967), 207–213.

NAPIER, AUGUSTUS Y., and CARL A. WHITAKER. *The Family Crucible.* New York: Harper & Row, 1978.

NATHANSON, DONALD L., ed. *The Many Faces of Shame.* New York: The Guilford Press, 1987.

NATIONAL ASSOCIATION OF SOCIAL WORKERS, AD HOC COMMITTEE ON ADVOCACY. "Champion of Social Victims." *Social Work,* 14 (April 1969), 16–22.

NEIDIG, PETER H., et al. "Domestic Conflict Containment: A Spouse Abuse Treatment Program." *Social Casework,* 66 (April 1985), 195–204.

NELSEN, JUDITH C. *Communication Theory and Social Work Practice.* Chicago: University of Chicago Press, 1980.

———. "Communication Theory and Social Work Treatment." In Francis J. Turner, *Social Work Treatment,* 3d ed., New York: Free Press, 1986, 219–244.

———. "Dealing with Resistance in Social Work Practice." *Social Casework,* 56 (December 1975), 587–592.

———. "Issues in Single Subject Research for Non-Behaviorists." *Social Work Research and Abstracts,* 17 (Summer 1981), 31–37.

———. "Treatment Issues in Schizophrenia." *Social Casework*, 56 (March 1975), 145–151.

———. "Treatment-Planning for Schizophrenia." *Social Casework*, 56 (February 1975), 67–73.

NEMIAH, JOHN C. "Psychoneurotic Disorders." In Armando M. Nicholi, Jr., ed., *The Harvard Guide to Modern Psychiatry*. Cambridge, Mass.: Harvard University Press, 1978, 173–197.

NEUGEBORE, BERNARD. "Opportunity Centered Social Services." *Social Work*, 15 (April 1970), 47–52.

NICHOLLS, GRACE K. "Treatment of a Disturbed Mother-Child Relationship: A Case Presentation." In Howard J. Parad, ed., *Ego Psychology and Dynamic Casework*. New York: Family Service Association of America, 1958, 117–125.

NIETO, DANIEL S. "Aiding the Single Father." *Social Work*, 27 (November 1982), 473–478.

NORMAN, JENNIE SAGE. "Short-Term Treatment with the Adolescent Client." *Social Casework*, 61 (February 1980), 74–82.

NORTHEN, HELEN. *Clinical Social Work*. New York: Columbia University Press, 1982.

———. "Psychosocial Practice in Small Groups." In Robert W. Roberts and Helen Northen, eds., *Theories of Social Work with Groups*. New York: Columbia University Press, 1976, 116–152.

———. *Social Work with Groups*. New York: Columbia University Press, 1969.

NUEHRING, ELANE M., and ANNE B. PASCONE. "Single-Subject Evaluation: A Tool for Quality Assurance." *Social Work*, 31 (September–October 1986), 359–365.

O'CONNOR, GERALD O. "Case Management: System and Practice." *Social Casework*, 69 (February 1988), 97–106.

O'CONNOR, RICHARD, and WILLIAM J. REID. "Dissatisfaction with Brief Treatment." *Social Service Review*, 60 (December 1986), 526–537.

OFFER, DANIEL, and EVERT VANDERSTOEP. "Indications and Contraindications for Family Therapy." In Max Sugar, ed., *The Adolescent in Group and Family Therapy*. New York: Brunner/Mazel, 1975, 145–160.

OLMSTEAD, KATHLEEN A. "The Influence of Minority Social Work Students on an Agency's Service Methods." *Social Work*, 28 (July–August 1983), 308–312.

OLSON, DAVID. "Marital and Family Therapy: Integrative Review and Critique." *Journal of Marriage and the Family*, 32 (1970), 501–538.

OPPENHEIMER, JEANETTE. "Use of Crisis Intervention in Casework with the Cancer Patient and His Family." *Social Work*, 12 (April 1967), 44–52.

ORADEI, DONNA M., and NANCY S. WAITE. "Admissions Conferences for Families of Stroke Patients." *Social Casework*, 56 (January 1975), 21–26.

ORCUTT, BEN A. "Casework Intervention and the Problems of the Poor." *Social Casework*, 54 (February 1973), 85–95.

———. "Family Treatment of Poverty Level Families." *Social Casework*, 58 (February 1976), 92–100.

ORMSBY, RALPH. "Interpretations in Casework Therapy." *Journal of Social Casework*, 29 (April 1948), 135–141.

ORNSTEIN, ANNA. "Supportive Psychotherapy: A Contemporary View." *Clinical Social Work Journal*, 14 (Spring 1986), 14–30.

OSTBLOOM, NORMAN, and SEDAHLIA JASPER CRASE. "A Model for Conceptualizing Child Abuse Causation and Intervention." *Social Casework*, 61 (March 1980), 164–172.

OVERTON, ALICE. "Establishing the Relationship." *Crime and Delinquency*, 11 (July 1965), 229–238.

———. "Serving Families Who Don't Want Help." *Social Casework*, 34 (July 1953), 304–309.

OXLEY, GENEVIEVE B. "Involuntary Clients' Responses to a Treatment Experience." *Social Casework*, 58 (December 1977), 607–614.

———. "Short-Term Therapy with Student Couples." *Social Casework*, 54 (April 1973), 216–223.

PALMORE, E., ed. *Normal Aging and Normal Aging II*. Durham N.C.: Duke University Press, 1970, 1974.

PALUMBO, JOSEPH. "Borderline Conditions: A Perspective from Self Psychology." *Clinical Social Work Journal*, 11 (Winter 1983), 323–338.

———. "Perceptual Deficits and Self-Esteem in Adolescence." *Clinical Social Work Journal*, 7 (Spring 1979), 34–61.

———. "The Psychology of Self and the Termination of Treatment." *Clinical Social Work Journal*, 10 (Spring 1982), 15–27.

———. "Spontaneous Self Disclosures in Psychotherapy." *Clinical Social Work Journal*, 15 (Summer 1987), 107–120.

———. "Theories of Narcissism and the Practice of Clinical Social Work." *Clinical Social Work Journal*, 4 (Fall 1976), 147–161.

PANTER, ETHEL. "Ego-Building Procedures That Foster Social Functioning." *Social Casework*, 48 (March 1967), 139–145.

PAPP, PEGGY. *The Process of Change*. New York: Guilford Press, 1983.

PARAD, HOWARD J., ed. *Crisis Intervention*. New York: Family Service Association of America, 1965.

———, ed. *Ego Psychology and Dynamic Casework*. New York: Family Service Association of America, 1958.

——— and ROGER R. MILLER, eds. *Ego-Oriented Casework: Problems and Perspectives*. New York: Family Service Association of America, 1963.

PARAD, LIBBIE G. "Short-Term Treatment: An Overview of Historical Trends, Issues and Potentials." *Smith College Studies in Social Work*, 41 (February 1971), 119–146.

PARSONS, TALCOTT. "The Stability of the American Family System." In Norman W. Bell and Ezra F. Vogel, eds., *A Modern Introduction to the Family*, rev. ed. New York: Free Press, 1968, 97–101.

——— and R. F. BALES. *Family, Socialization, and the Interaction Process*. New York: Free Press, 1955.

PATTI, RINO J. "Limitations and Prospects of Internal Advocacy." *Social Casework*, 55 (November 1974), 537–545.

PAUL, NORMAN L. "The Role of Mourning and Empathy in Conjoint Marital Therapy." In Gerald H. Zuk and Ivan Boszormenyi-Nagy, eds., *Family Therapy and Disturbed Families*. Palo Alto, Calif.: Science and Behavior Books, 1967, 186–205.

PAVENSTEDT, ELEANOR, ed. *The Drifters: Children of Disorganized Lower Class Families*. Boston: Little, Brown, 1967.

PEARLMAN, MARGARET H., and MILDRED G. EDWARDS. "Enabling in the Eighties: The Client Advocacy Group." *Social Casework*, 63 (November 1982), 532–539.

PELLMAN, RENEE, et al. "The Van: A Mobile Approach to Services for Adolescents," *Social Casework*, 58 (May 1977), 268–273.

PERLMAN, HELEN HARRIS. *Relationship: The Heart of Helping People*. Chicago: University of Chicago Press, 1979.

———. *Social Casework: A Problem-Solving Process*. University of Chicago Press, 1957.

PETRO, OLIVE, and BETTY FRENCH. "The Black Client's View of Himself." *Social Casework*, 53 (October 1972), 466–474.

——— and ———. "Social Work with the Wealthy," *Social Casework*, 57 (April 1976), 254–258.

PHARIS, DAVID B. and TONY TRIPODI. *Evaluative Research for Social Workers*. Englewood Cliffs, N.J.: Prentice Hall, 1983.

PIAGET, JEAN. *The Child's Conception of the World*. New York: Harcourt, Brace, 1937.

——— and SUSAN ISAACS. *Social Development in Young Children*. New York: Harcourt, Brace, 1937.

PIERSON, ARTHUR. "Social Work Techniques with the Poor." *Social Casework*, 51 (October 1970), 481–485.

PILSECKER, CARLETON. "Help for the Dying." In Francis J. Turner, ed., *Differential Diagnosis and Treatment in Social Work*, 3d ed. New York: Free Press, 1983, 145–154.

PINDERHUGHES, ELAINE B. "Teaching Empathy in Cross-Cultural Social Work." *Social Work*, 14 (July 1969), 312–316.

PITTMAN, FRANK S., III. "Children of the Rich." *Family Process*, 24 (December 1985), 461–472.

———. "The Family That Hides Together." In Peggy Papp, ed., *Family Therapy: Full Length Case Studies*. New York: Gardner Press, 1977.

———. *Turning Points: Treating Families in Transition and Crisis*. New York: W. W. Norton, 1987.

——— and KALMAN FLOMENHAFT. "Treating the Doll's House Marriage." *Family Process*, 9 (June 1970), 143–155.

POLANSKY, NORMAN A., and JACOB KOUNIN. "Clients' Reactions to Initial Interviews: A Field Study." *Human Relations*, 9 (1956), 237–264.

POLANSKY, NORMAN A., et al. "Loneliness and Isolation in Child Neglect." *Social Casework*, 66 (January 1985), 38–47.

POLLAK, OTTO. *Social Science and Psychotherapy for Children*. New York: Russell Sage Foundation, 1952.

———. "Systems Theory and the Functions of Marriage." In Gertrude Einstein, ed., *Learning to Apply New Concepts to Casework Practice*. New York: Family Service Association of America, 1968, 75–95.

PONSE, BARBARA. "Lesbians and Their Worlds." In Judd Marmor, ed., *Homosexual Behavior*. New York: Basic Books, 1980, 157–175.

POWELL, THOMAS J. "Negative Expectations of Treatment: Some Ideas About the Source and Management of Two Types." *Clinical Social Work Journal*, 1 (Fall 1973), 177–186.

PRAY, KENNETH. "A Restatement of the Generic Principles of Social Casework Practice." *Journal of Social Casework*, 28 (October 1947), 283–290.

PRESLEY, JOHN H. "The Clinical Dropout: A View from the Client's Perspective." *Social Casework*, 68 (December 1987), 603–608.

PRICHARD, ELIZABETH R., et al., eds. *Social Work with the Dying Patient and the Family*. New York: Columbia University Press, 1977.

PROCTOR, ENOLA. "Defining the Worker-Client Relationships." *Social Work*, 27 (September 1982), 430–435.

PRODIE, RICHARD D., BETTY L. SINGER, and MARIAN WINTERBOTTOM. "Integration of Research Findings and Casework Techniques," *Social Casework*, 48 (June 1967), 360–366.

PRUNTY, HOWARD E., et al. "Confronting Racism in Inner-City Schools." *Social Work*, 22 (May 1977), 190–194.

PUGH, ROBERT L. "Encouraging Interactional Processes with Couples in Therapy." *Clinical Social Work Journal*, 14 (Winter 1986), 321–334.

RANAN, WENDY, and ANDREA BLODGETT. "Using Telephone Therapy for 'Unreachable' Clients." *Social Casework*, 64 (January 1983), 39–44.

RAPAPORT, DAVID. *Organization and Pathology of Thought*. New York: Columbia University Press, 1951.

RAPOPORT, LYDIA. "The Concept of Prevention in Social Work," *Social Work*, 6 (January 1961), 19–28.

———. "Crisis Intervention as a Mode of Brief Treatment." In Robert W. Roberts and Robert H. Nee, *Theories of Social Casework*. Chicago: University of Chicago Press, 1970, 265–311.

RATLIFF, NANCY. "Stress and Burnout in the Helping Professions." *Social Casework*, 69 (March 1988), 147–154.

REAMER, FREDERIC B. *Ethical Dilemmas in Social Service*. New York: Columbia University Press, 1982.

REDLICH, FREDERICK C., AUGUST B. HOLLINGSHEAD, and ELIZABETH BELLIS. "Social Class Differences in Attitudes Toward Psychiatry." *American Journal of Orthopsychiatry*, 25 (January 1955), 60–70.

REID, KENNETH E. "Nonrational Dynamics of Client-Worker Interaction." *Social Casework*, 58 (December 1977), 600–606.

REID, WILLIAM J. "Task-Centered Social Work." In Francis J. Turner, ed., *Social Work Treatment*, 3d ed. New York: Free Press, 1986, 267–295.

———. *The Task-Centered System*. New York: Columbia University Press, 1978.

———. "A Test of a Task-Centered Approach." *Social Work*, 20 (January 1975), 3–9.

——— and LAURA EPSTEIN. *Task-Centered Casework*. New York: Columbia University Press, 1972.

——— and ———. *Task-Centered Practice*. New York: Columbia University Press, 1977.

——— and ANN W. SHYNE. *Brief and Extended Casework*. New York: Columbia University Press, 1969.

——— and BARBARA SHAPIRO. "Client Reaction to Advice." *Social Service Review*, 43 (June 1969), 165–173.

——— and PATRICIA HANRAHAN. "Recent Evaluations of Social Work: Grounds for Optimism." *Social Work*, 27 (July 1982), 328–340.

REINER, BEATRICE SIMCOX. "The Feelings of Irrelevance: The Effects of a Nonsupportive Society." *Social Casework*, 60 (January 1979), 3–10.

RESNICK, HERMAN. "Effecting Internal Change in Human Service Organizations." *Social Casework*, 58 (November 1977), 546–553.

REYNOLDS, BERTHA CAPEN. "A Study of Responsibility in Social Case Work." *Smith College Studies in Social Work*, 5 (September 1934).

REYNOLDS, ROSEMARY, and ELSIE SIEGLE. "A Study of Casework with Sado-Masochistic Marriage Partners." *Social Casework*, 40 (December 1959), 545–551.

RHODES, SONYA L. "Contract Negotiation in the Initial Stage of Casework Service." *Social Service Review*, 51 (March 1977), 125–140.

———. "Extramarital Affairs: Clinical Issues in Therapy." *Social Casework*, 65 (November 1984), 541–546.

———. "The Personality of the Worker: An Unexplored Dimension in Treatment." *Social Casework*, 60 (May 1979), 259–264.

RICE, CELIA F. "Marital Treatment with Narcissistic Character Disorders." In Judith Mishne, ed., *Psychotherapy and Training in Clinical Social Work*. New York: Gardner Press, 1980, 261–273.

RICH, PHILIP. "Differentiation of Self in the Therapist's Family of Origin." *Social Casework*, 61 (September 1980), 394–399.

RICHMOND, MARY E. *Friendly Visiting Among the Poor: A Handbook for Charity Workers*. New York: Macmillan, 1899.

————. *The Long View*. New York: Russell Sage Foundation, 1930.

————. *Social Diagnosis*. New York: Russell Sage Foundation, 1917.

————. *What Is Social Casework?* New York: Russell Sage Foundation, 1922.

RIGBY, B. D., ed. *Short-Term Training for Social Development: The Preparation of Front-Line Workers and Trainers*. New York: International Association of Schools of Social Work, 1978.

RIPPLE, LILLIAN, ERNESTINA ALEXANDER, and BERNICE POLEMIS. *Motivation, Capacity and Opportunity*. Chicago: University of Chicago Press, 1964.

ROBERT W. ROBERTS, and ROBERT H. NEE, eds. *Theories of Social Casework*. Chicago: University of Chicago Press, 1970.

ROBINSON, BRYAN E. *Working with Children of Alcoholics: The Practitioner's Handbook*. Lexington, Mass.: D. C. Heath, 1989.

ROBINSON, VIRGINIA. *A Changing Psychology in Social Case Work*. Chapel Hill: University of North Carolina Press, 1930.

RODMAN, HYMAN. "Lower Class Family Behavior." In Arlene S. Skolnick and Jerome H. Skolnick, eds., *Family in Transition*. 2d ed. Boston: Little, Brown, 1977, 461–465.

RODWAY, MARGARET T. "Systems Theory." In Francis J. Turner, ed., *Social Work Treatment*, 3d ed. New York: The Free Press, 1986, 514–539.

ROGERS, CARL R. "Client-Centered Therapy." In C. H. Patterson, ed., *Theories of Counseling and Psychotherapy*. New York: Harper and Row, 1966.

————. *On Becoming a Person: A Therapist's View of Psychotherapy*. Boston: Houghton Mifflin, 1961.

————. "The Therapeutic Relationship: Recent Theory and Research." In Floyd Matson and Ashley Montagu, eds., *The Human Dialogue*. New York: Free Press, 1967, 246–259.

ROONEY, RONALD H. "Socialization Strategies for Involuntary Clients." *Social Casework*, 69 (March 1988), 131–140.

ROSEN, AARON. "Barriers to Utilization of Research by Social Work Practitioners." *Journal of Social Service Research*, 6 (Spring–Summer 1983), 1–15.

ROSENBERG, BLANCA N. "Planned Short-Term Treatment in Developmental Crises." *Social Casework*, 56 (April 1975), 195–204.

ROSENBERG, ELINOR B., and FADY HAJAL. "Stepsibling Relationships in Remarried Families." *Social Casework*, 66 (May 1985), 287–292.

ROSENBLOOM, MARIA. "Implications of the Holocaust for Social Work." *Social Casework*, 64 (April 1983), 205–213.

ROTH, FREDERICK. "A Practice Regimen for Diagnosis and Treatment of Child Abuse." *Child Welfare*, 54 (April 1975), 268–273.

ROTH, SALLYANN, and BLANCA CODY MURPHY. "Therapeutic Work with Lesbian Clients: A Systemic Therapy View." In Marianne Ault-Riche, ed., *Women and Family Therapy*. Rockville, Md.: Aspen, 1986, 78–89.

ROTHERY, MICHAEL A. "Contracts and Contracting." *Clinical Social Work Journal*, 8 (Fall 1980), 179–185.

ROYCE, DAVID D., and GLADYS T. TURNER. "Strengths of Black Families: A Black Community's Perspective." *Social Work*, 25 (September 1980), 407–409.

RUBIN, ALLEN. "Practice Effectiveness: More Grounds for Optimism." *Social Work*, 30 (November–December 1985), 469–476.

RUBIN, JULIUS. "Drug Addiction." In George Wiedeman, ed., *Personality Development and Deviation*. New York: International Universities Press, 1975, 358–373.

RUCKDESCHEL, ROY A., and BUFORD E. FARRIS. "Assessing Practice: A Critical Look at the Single-Case Design." *Social Casework*, 62 (September 1981), 413–419.

RUE, ALICE W. "The Casework Approach to Protective Work." *The Family*, 18 (December 1937), 277–282.

RUEVENI, URI. *Networking Families in Crisis*. New York: Human Services Press, 1979.

RUMELHART, MARILYN AUSTIN. "When Understanding the Situation Is the Real Problem." *Social Casework*, 65 (January 1984), 27–33.

RYAN, ANGELA SHEN. "Cultural Factors in Casework with Chinese-Americans," *Social Casework*, 66 (June 1985), 333–340.

RYAN, WILLIAM. *Blaming the Victim*, rev. ed. New York: Random House, 1976.

SAGIR, MARCEL T., and ELI ROBINS. "Clinical Aspects of Female Homosexuality." In Judd Marmor, ed., *Homosexual Behavior*. New York: Basic Books, 1980, 280–295.

SALCIDO, RAMON M. "Problems of the Mexican-American Elderly in an Urban Setting." *Social Casework*, 60 (December 1979), 609–615.

SELEEBEY, DENNIS. "The Tension Between Research and Practice: Assumptions of the Experimental Paradigm." *Clinical Social Work Journal*, 7 (Winter 1979), 267–284.

SALOMON, ELIZABETH. "Humanistic Values and Social Casework." *Social Casework*, 48 (January 1967), 26–32.

SALZMAN, LEON. *The Obsessive Personality*. New York: Science House, 1968.

SANTA-BARBARA, JACK, et al. "The McMaster Family Therapy Outcome Study: An Overview of Methods and Results." *International Journal of Family Therapy*, 1 (Winter 1979), 304–323.

SANVILLE, JEAN. "Partings and Impartings: Toward a Nonmedical Approach to Interruptions and Terminations." *Clinical Social Work Journal*, 10 (Summer 1982), 123–131.

SATIR, VIRGINIA. *Conjoint Family Therapy*, rev. ed. Palo Alto, Calif.: Science and Behavior Books. 1967.

SCANLON, PAULINE L. "Social Work with the Mentally Retarded Client." *Social Casework*, 59 (March 1978), 161–166.

SCHAMESS, GERALD. "Boundary Issues in Countertransference: A Developmental Perspective." *Clinical Social Work Journal*, 9 (Winter 1981), 244–257.

SCHARFF, DAVID E., and JILL SAVEGE SCHARFF. *Object Relations Family Therapy*. Northvale, N.J.: Aronson, 1987.

SCHEFLEN, ALBERT E. "Human Communication: Behavioral Programs and Their Integration in Interaction." *Behavior Science*, 13 (1968), 44–55.

———. "The Significance of Posture in Communications." *Psychiatry*, 27 (1964), 316–331.

SCHERZ, FRANCES H. "Family Interaction: Some Problems and Implications for Casework." In Howard J. Parad and Roger R. Miller, eds., *Ego-Oriented Casework: Problems and Perspectives*. New York: Family Service Association of America, 1963, 129–144.

———. "Family Treatment Concepts." *Social Casework*, 47 (April 1966), 234–240.

———. "Theory and Practice in Family Therapy." In Robert W. Roberts and Robert H. Nee, eds., *Theories of Social Casework*. Chicago: University of Chicago Press, 1970, 219–264.

SCHEUNEMANN, YOLANDA R., and BETTY FRENCH. "Diagnosis as the Foundation of Professional Service." *Social Casework*, 55 (March 1974), 135–141.

SCHLOSBERG, SHIRLEY B., and RICHARD M. KAGAN. "Practice Strategies for Engaging Chronic Multiproblem Families." *Social Casework*, 69 (January 1988), 3–9.

SCHORR, ALVIN. "Editorial Page." *Social Work*, 11 (July 1966), 2.

SCHUERMAN, JOHN R. "Do Family Services Help?" *Social Service Review*, 49 (September 1975), 363–375.

SCHULMAN, GERDA L. "Myths that Intrude on the Adaptation of the Stepfamily." *Social Casework*, 53 (March 1972), 131–139.

———. "Treatment of Intergenerational Pathology." *Social Casework*, 54 (October 1973), 462–472.

——— and ELSA LEICHTER. "The Prevention of Family Breakup." *Social Casework*, 49 (March 1968), 143–150.

SCHWARTZ, MARY C. "Helping the Worker with Countertransference." *Social Work*, 23 (May 1978), 204–209.

SCHWARTZ-BORDEN, GWEN. "Grief Work: Prevention and Intervention." *Social Casework*, 67 (October 1986), 499–505.

SEABURY, BRETT. "Communication Problems in Social Work Practice." *Social Work*, 25 (January 1980), 40–44.

———. "The Contract: Uses, Abuses and Limitations." *Social Work*, 21 (January 1976), 16–21.

SENGER-DICKINSON, MARY M., and CYRUS S. STEWART. "Caseworker Recognition of Marital Separation." *Social Casework*, 68 (September 1987), 394–399.

SEWELL-COKER, BEVERLY, JOYCE HAMILTON-COLLINS, and EDITH FEIN. "Social Work Practice with West Indian Immigrants." *Social Casework*, 66 (November 1985), 563–568.

SHANNON, BARBARA. "Implications of White Racism for Social Work Practice." *Social Casework*, 51 (May 1970), 270–276.

SHAW, SHARON B. "Parental Aging: Clinical Issues in Adult Psychotherapy." *Social Casework*, 68 (September 1987), 406–412.

SHEA, MARGARET M. "Establishing the Initial Relationships with Schizophrenic Patients." *Social Casework*, 37 (January 1956) 25–29.

SHERMAN, SANFORD N. "Family Therapy." In Francis J. Turner, ed., *Social Work Treatment*, 2d ed., New York: Free Press, 1979.

———. "Family Treatment: An Approach to Children's Problems." *Social Casework*, 47 (June 1966), 368–372.

———. "Intergenerational Discontinuity and Therapy of the Family." *Social Casework*, 48 (April 1967), 216–221.

SHERNOFF, MICHAEL J. "Family Therapy for Lesbian and Gay Clients." *Social Casework*, 29 (July–August 1984), 393–396.

SHOR, JOEL, and JEAN SANVILLE. *Illusion in Loving: Balancing Intimacy and Independence*. New York: Penguin Books, 1979.

SHULMAN, LAWRENCE. *The Skills of Helping Individuals and Groups*. Itasca, Ill.: F. E. Peacock Publishers, 1984.

SIEGEL, DEBORAH J. "Defining Empirically Based Practice." *Social Work*, 29 (July–August 1984), 325–331.

SIFNEOS, PETER E. *Short-Term Dynamic Psychotherapy: Evaluation and Technique*, 2d ed. New York: Plenum, 1987.

SILVERMAN, PHYLLIS R. "A Reexamination of the Intake Procedure." *Social Casework*, 51 (December 1970), 625–634.

SIMON, BERNICE K. "Social Casework Theory: An Overview." In Robert W. Roberts and Robert H. Nee, eds., *Theories of Social Casework*. Chicago: University of Chicago, 1970, 353–394.

SIMOS, BERTHA G. "Grief Therapy to Facilitate Healthy Restitution." *Social Casework*, 58 (June 1977), 337–342.

SINGH, RAM NARESH. "Brief Interviews: Approaches, Techniques, and Effectiveness." *Social Casework*, 63 (December 1982), 599–606.

SIPORIN, MAX. "Current Social Work Perspectives on Clinical Practice." *Clinical Social Work Journal*, 13 (Fall 1985), 198–217.

———. "Marriage and Family Therapy in Social Work." *Social Casework*, 61 (January 1980), 11–21.

———. "Social Treatment: A New-Old Helping Method." *Social Work*, 15 (July 1970), 13–25.

———. "The Therapeutic Process in Clinical Social Work." *Social Work*, 28 (May–June 1983), 193–198.

SIRLES, ELIZABETH A. "Client-Counselor Agreement on Problem and Change." *Social Casework*, 63 (June 1982), 348–353.

SKOLNICK, ARLENE S., and JEROME H. SKOLNICK, eds. *Family in Transition*, 2d ed. Boston: Little, Brown, 1977.

SMALDINO, ANGELO. "The Importance of Hope in the Casework Relationship." *Social Casework*, 56 (July 1975), 328–333.

SMALL, LEONARD. *The Briefer Psychotherapies*. New York: Brunner/Mazel, 1971.

SMALLEY, RUTH E. "The Functional Approach to Casework Process." In Robert E. Roberts and Robert E. Nee, eds. *Theories of Social Casework*. Chicago: University of Chicago, 1970, 79–128.

SMITH, AUDREY D. "Egalitarian Marriage: Implications for Practice and Policy." *Social Casework*, 61 (May 1980), 288–295.

——— and WILLIAM J. REID. "Role Expectations and Attitudes in Dual-Earner Families." *Social Casework*, 67 (September 1986), 394–402.

SMITH, JOY R. POWLES. "Social Health Concepts for Family Practice." *Social Casework*, 63 (June 1982), 363–369.

SMITH, LARRY L. "Crisis Intervention in Practice." *Social Casework*, 60 (February 1979), 81–89.

———. "A Review of Crisis Intervention Theory." *Social Casework*, 59 (July 1978), 396–405.

SOBEY, FRANCINE. *The Non-Professional Revolution in Mental Health*. New York: Columbia University Press, 1970.

SOLOMON, MARION F. "Treatment of Narcissistic and Borderline Disorders in Marital Therapy: Suggestions Toward an Enhanced Therapeutic Approach." *Clinical Social Work Journal*, 13 (Summer 1985), 141–156.

SOSIN, MICHAEL R. "Delivering Services under Permanency Planning." *Social Service Review*, 61 (June 1987), 272–290.

SOSIN, MICHAEL, and SHARON CAULUM. "Advocacy: A Conceptualization for Social Work Practice." *Social Work*, 28 (January–February 1983), 12–17.

SPECHT, HARRY, and RIVA SPECHT. "Social Work Assessment: Route to Clienthood." *Social Casework*, 67 (November 1986), 525–532.

SPECK, ROSS V., and CAROLYN L. ATTNEAVE. "Social Network Intervention." In Clifford J. Sager and Helen Singer Kaplan, eds., *Progress in Group and Family Therapy*. New York: Brunner/Mazel, 1972, 416–439.

SPEER, DAVID C. "Family Systems: Morphostasis and

Morphogenesis, or 'Is Homeostasis Enough?'" *Family Process*, 9 (September 1970), 259–278.

SPIEGEL, JOHN P. "Conflicting Formal and Informal Roles in Newly Acculturated Families." In Gertrude Einstein, ed., *Learning to Apply New Concepts to Casework Practice*. New York: Family Service Association of America, 1968, 53–61.

———. "Some Cultural Aspects of Transference and Counter-Transference." In Jules Masserman, ed., *Individual and Familial Dynamics*. New York: Grune & Stratton, 1959, 60–182.

———. "The Resolution of Role Conflict Within the Family." In Norman W. Bell and Ezra F. Vogel, eds., *Modern Introduction to the Family*. New York: Free Press, 1968, 391–411.

———. "The Social Roles of Doctor and Patient in Psychoanalysis and Psychotherapy." *Psychiatry*, 17 (November 1954), 369–376.

SPITZ, RENE A. "Anaclitic Depression." *Psychoanalytic Study of the Child*, vol. 2. New York: International Universities Press, 1946, 313–342.

STAPLE, ROBERT. "Towards a Sociology of the Black Family: A Theoretical and Methodological Assessment." *Journal of Marriage and the Family*, 33 (February 1971), 119–135.

STAMM, ISABEL. "Ego Psychology in the Emerging Theoretical Base of Casework." In Alfred J. Kahn, ed., *Issues in American Social Work*. New York: Columbia University Press, 1959, 80–109.

STANTON, GRETA W. "Preventive Intervention with Stepfamilies." *Social Work*, 31 (May–June 1986), 201–206.

STARTZ, MORTON R., and CLAIRE W. EVANS. "Developmental Phases of Marriage and Marital Therapy." *Social Casework*, 62 (June 1981), 343–351.

STARTZ, MORTON R., and HELEN F. COHEN. "The Impact of Social Change on the Practitioner." *Social Casework*, 61 (September 1980), 400–406.

STEMPLER, BENJAMIN L. "Effects of Adversive Racism on White Social Work Students." *Social Casework*, 56 (October 1975), 460–467.

STIERLIN, HELM. "Countertransference in Family Therapy with Adolescents." In Max Sugar, ed., *The Adolescent in Group and Family Therapy*, New York: Brunner/Mazel, 1975, 161–177.

———. "Group Fantasies and Family Myths." *Family Process*, 12 (June 1973), 111–125.

——— et al. *The First Interview with the Family*. New York: Brunner/Mazel, 1980.

STILES, EVELYN, et al. "Hear It Like It Is." *Social Casework*, 53 (May 1972), 292–299.

STREAN, HERBERT. "The Extramarital Affair: A Psychoanalytic View." *Psychoanalytic Review*, 63 (Spring 1976), 101–113.

STREEPY, JOAN. "Direct-Service Providers and Burnout." *Social Casework*, 62 (June 1981), 352–361.

STUART, RICHARD B. *Helping Couples Change*. New York: Guilford Press, 1980.

STUDT, ELIOT. "An Outline for Study of Social Authority Factors in Casework." *Social Casework*, 35 (June 1954), 231–238.

———. "Worker-Client Authority Relationships in Social Work." *Social Work*, 4 (January 1959), 18–21.

SUESS, JAMES F. "Short-Term Psychotherapy with the Compulsive Personality and the Obsessive-Compulsive Neurotic." *American Journal of Psychiatry*, 129 (1972), 270–275.

SUNLEY, ROBERT. "Family Advocacy from Case to Cause." *Social Casework*, 51 (June 1970), 347–357.

SUPER, STACIA I. "Successful Transition: Therapeutic Interventions with the Transferred Client." *Clinical Social Work Journal*, 10 (Summer 1982), 113–122.

SWENSON, CAROL. "Social Networks, Mutual Aid, and the Life Model Practice." In Carel B. Germain, ed., *Social Work Practice*. New York: Columbia University Press, 1979, 213–238.

TAIBBI, ROBERT. "Handling Extramarital Affairs in Clinical Treatment." *Social Casework*, 64 (April 1983), 200–204.

TAINEY, PHYLLIS. *Adult Children of Alcoholics: Workshop Models for Family Life Education*. Milwaukee, Wisc.: Family Service America, 1988.

TAYLOR, JOHN W. "Social Casework and the Multimodel Treatment of Incest." *Social Casework*, 67 (October 1986), 451–459.

———. "Structured Conjoint Therapy for Spouse Abuse Cases." *Social Casework*, 65 (January 1984), 11–18.

TAYLOR, RONALD L. "Marital Therapy in the Treatment of Incest." *Social Casework*, 65 (April 1984), 195–202.

TAYLOR, SHIRLEY S., and NORMA SIEGEL. "Treating the Separation-Individuation Conflict." *Social Casework*, 59 (June 1978). 337–344.

TERMAN, LEWIS N. *Psychological Factors in Marital Happiness*. New York: McGraw-Hill, 1938.

THOMAS, EDWIN. "Selected Sociobehavioral Tech niques and Principles: An Approach to Interpersonal Helping." *Social Work,* 13 (January 1968), 12–26.

———. *The Sociobehavioral Approach and Application to Social Work.* New York: Council on Social Work Education, 1967.

THOMLISON, RAY J. "Something Works: Evidence from Practice Effectiveness Studies." *Social Work,* 29 (January–February) 1984, 51–56.

THRASHER, SHIRLEY, and GARY ANDERSON. "The West Indian Family: Treatment Challenges." *Social Casework,* 69 (March 1988), 171–176.

TITELMAN, PETER, ed., *The Therapist's Own Family: Toward the Differentiation of Self.* Northvale, N.J.: Jason Aronson, 1987.

TOSELAND, RONALD W. "Treatment Discontinuance." *Social Casework,* 68 (April 1987), 195–204.

TOWLE, CHARLOTTE. *Common Human Needs,* rev. ed. New York: National Association of Social Workers, 1957, 68–72.

———. "Factors in Treatment," *Proceedings of the National Conference of Social Work, 1936.* Chicago: University of Chicago Press, 1936, 179–191.

———. "Social Work: Cause and Function." In Helen H. Perlman, ed., *Helping: Charlotte Towle on Social Work and Social Casework.* Chicago: University of Chicago Press, 1969, 277–299.

TRUAX, CHARLES B., and ROBERT R. CARKUFF. *Toward Effective Counseling and Pyschotherapy: Training and Practice.* Chicago: Aldine, 1967.

——— and KEVIN MITCHELL. "Research on Certain Therapist Interpersonal Skills in Relation to Process and Outcome." In Allen E. Bergin and Sol L. Garfield, eds., *Handbook of Psychotherapy and Behavior Change: An Empirical Analysis.* New York: Wiley, 1971, 299–344.

TROESTER, JAMES D., and JOEL A. DARBY. "The Role of the Mini-Meal in Therapeutic Play Groups." *Social Casework,* 57 (February 1976), 97–103.

TURNER, FRANCIS J., ed. *Adult Psychopathology: A Social Work Perspective.* New York: Free Press, 1984.

———. "A Comparison of Procedures in the Treatment of Clients with Two Different Value Orientations." *Social Casework,* 45 (May 1964), 273–277.

———, ed. *Differential Diagnosis and Treatment in Social Work,* 3d ed. New York: Free Press, 1983.

———. "Ethnic Difference and Client Performance." *Social Service Review,* 44 (March 1970), 1–10.

———. "A Multitheory Perspective for Practice." In Turner, *Social Work Treatment,* 3d ed. New York: Free Press, 1986, 645–658.

———. "Social Work Treatment and Value Differences." Doctoral Dissertation, Columbia University School of Social Work, New York, 1963.

ULLMANN, ALICE. "Teaching Medical Students to Understand Stress in Illness." *Social Casework,* 57 (November 1976), 568–574.

VALLIANT, GEORGE. *Adaptation to Life.* New York: Little, Brown, 1977.

VAN LAWICK-GOODALL, JANE. *In the Shadow of Man.* Boston: Houghton Mifflin, 1971.

VESPER, SUE. "Casework Aimed at Supporting Marital Role Reversal." *Social Casework,* 43 (June 1962), 303–307.

VIGILANTE, FLORENCE WEXLER. "Use of Work in the Assessment and Intervention Process." *Social Casework,* 63 (May 1982), 296–300.

——— and MILDRED D. MALLICK. "Needs-Resource Evaluation in the Assessment Process." *Social Work,* 33 (March–April 1988), 101–104.

VINCENTIA, SISTER M., and SISTER ANN PATRICK CONRAD. "A Parish Neighborhood Model for Social Work Practice." *Social Casework,* 61 (September 1980), 423–432.

VINOKUR-KAPLAN, DIANE. "A National Survey of In-Service Training Experiences of Child Welfare Supervisors and Workers." *Social Service Review,* 61 (June 1987), 291–304.

VISHER, EMILY B., and JOHN S. VISHER. *Stepfamilies: A Guide to Working with Stepparents and Stepchildren.* New York: Brunner/Mazel, 1979.

VOGEL, EZRA F., and NORMAN W. BELL. "The Emotionally Disturbed Child as the Family Scapegoat." In Bell and Vogel, eds., *Modern Introduction to the Family.* New York: Free Press, 1968, 412–427.

VONTROSS, CLEMMONT. "Cultural Barriers in Counseling Relationships." *Journal of Counseling Psychology,* 18 (January 1971) 7–13.

WALD, ESTHER. *The Remarried Family: Challenge and Promise.* New York: Family Service Association of America, 1981.

WALKER, PHILIP W. "Premarital Counseling for the Developmentally Disabled." *Social Casework,* 58 (October 1977), 475–479.

WALLACE, MARQUIS EARL. "A Focal Conflict Model of Marital Disorders." *Social Casework,* 60 (July 1979), 423–429.

WALLER, WILLARD. *The Old Love and the New.* New York: Liveright, 1930.

WALSH, M. ELLEN. "Rural Social Work Practice: Clinical Quality." *Social Casework,* 62 (October 1981), 458–464.

WALSH, JOSEPH A. "Burnout and Values in the Social Service Profession." *Social Casework,* 68 (May 1987), 279–283.

WALZ, THOMAS H., and HARRY J. MACY. "The MSW and the MPA: Confrontation of Two Professions in Public Welfare." *Journal of Sociology and Social Welfare,* 5 (January 1978), 100–117.

WALZER, HANK. "Casework Treatment of the Depressed Parent." In Francis J. Turner, ed., *Differential Diagnosis and Treatment in Social Work,* 2d ed., New York: Free Press, 1976, 302–312.

WARMBROD, MARY. "Counseling Bereaved Children: Stages in the Process." *Social Casework,* 67 (June 1986), 351–358.

WARREN, CAROL. "Homosexuality and Stigma." In Judd Marmor, ed., *Homosexual Behavior.* New York: Basic Books, 1980, 123–141.

WASSERMAN, HENRY. "Some Thoughts About Teaching Social Casework Today." *Smith College Studies in Social Work,* 43 (February 1973), 124–125.

WATSON, ANDREW. "Reality Testing and Transference in Psychotherapy." *Smith College Studies in Social Work,* 36 (June 1966), 191–209.

WATZLAWICK, PAUL. *The Language of Change: Elements of Therapeutic Communication.* New York: Basic Books, 1978.

———, JANET BEAVEN, and DON D. JACKSON. *Pragmatics of Human Communication: A Study of Interactional Patterns, Pathologies and Paradoxes.* New York: Norton, 1967.

WEAVER, DONNA R. "Empowering Treatment Skills for Helping Black Families." *Social Casework,* 63 (February 1982), 100–105.

WEBB, NANCY BOYD. "Crisis Consultation: Preventive Implications." *Social Casework,* 62 (October 1981), 465–471.

———. "A Crisis Intervention Perspective on the Termination Process." *Clinical Social Work Journal,* 13 (Winter 1985), 329–340.

WECHTER, SHARON L. "Separation Difficulties Between Parents and Young Adults." *Social Casework,* 64 (February 1983), 97–104.

WEEKS, GERALD R., and LUCIANO L'ABATE. *Paradoxical Psychotherapy: Theory and Practice with Individuals, Couples, and Families.* New York: Brunner/Mazel, 1982.

WEGSCHEIDER, SHARON. *Another Chance: Hope and Health for the Alcoholic Family.* Palo Alto, Calif.: Science and Behavior Books, 1981.

WEICK, ANN. "The Philosophical Context of a Health Model of Social Work." *Social Casework,* 67 (November 1986), 551–559.

——— and LOREN POPE. "Knowing What's Best: A New Look at Self Determination." *Social Casework,* 69 (January 1988), 10–16.

WEIDMAN, ARTHUR. "Therapy with Violent Couples." *Social Casework,* 67 (April 1986), 211–218.

WEINGARTEN. "Strategic Planning for Divorce Mediation." *Social Work,* 31 (May–June 1986), 194–200.

WEISBERGER, ELEANOR B. "The Current Usefulness of Psychoanalytic Theory to Casework." *Smith College Studies in Social Work,* 37 (February 1967), 106–118.

WEISMAN, AVERY D. *On Dying and Denying: A Psychiatric Study of Terminality.* New York: Behavioral, 1972.

WEISMAN, IRVING. "Offender Status, Role Behavior and Treatment Considerations." *Social Casework,* 48 (July 1967), 422–425.

WEISSMAN, HAROLD H. *Overcoming Mismanagement in the Human Services.* San Francisco: Jossey Bass, 1973.

WEISSMAN, MYRNA M., and EUGENE S. PAYKEL. *The Depressed Woman.* Chicago: University of Chicago Press, 1974.

——— et al. "Treatment Effect on the Social Adjustment of Depressed Patients." *Archives of General Psychiatry,* 30 (June 1974), 771–778.

WEITZMAN, JACK. "Engaging the Severely Dysfunctional Family in Treatment: Basic Considerations." *Family Process,* 24 (December 1985), 473–485.

——— and KAREN DREEN. "Wife Beating: A View of the Marital Dyad." *Social Casework,* 63 (May 1982), 259–265.

WELLS, RICHARD A., and VINCENT J. GIANNETTI. "Individual Marital Therapy: A Critical Reappraisal." *Family Process,* 25 (March 1986), 42–65.

————— and ALAN E. DEZEN. "The Results of Family Therapy Revisited: The Nonbehavioral Methods." *Family Process,* 17 (September 1978), 251–274.

WERTHEIM, ELEANOR S. "Family Unit Therapy and the Science and Typology of Family Systems II." *Family Process,* 14 (September 1975), 285–309.

WETZEL, JANICE WOOD. *Clinical Handbook of Depression.* New York: Gardner Press, 1984.

—————. "Interventions with the Depressed Elderly in Institutions." *Social Casework,* 61 (April 1980), 234–239.

WHITAKER, CARL A., et al. "Countertransference in the Family Treatment of Schizophrenia." In Ivan Boszormenyi-Nagy and James L. Framo, eds., *Intensive Family Therapy.* New York: Harper & Row, 1965, 323–341.

WHITE, ROBERT W. *Ego and Reality and Pyschoanalytic Theory.* New York: International Universities Press, 1963.

WHITTAKER, JAMES K., and JAMES GARGARINO, eds. *Social Support Networks: Informal Helping in the Human Services.* Hawthorne, N.Y.: Aldine Publishing, 1983.

————— et al. "The Ecological Paradigm in Child, Youth, and Family Services: Implications for Policy and Practice." *Social Service Review,* 60 (December 1986), 483–503.

WICKENDEN, ELIZABETH. "A Perspective on Social Services." *Social Service Review,* 50 (December 1976), 570–585.

WIEDEMAN, GEORGE, ed. *Personality Development and Deviation: A Textbook for Social Work.* New York: International Universities Press, 1975.

WILLIAMS, JANET B. W. "DSM-III: A Comprehensive Approach to Diagnosis." *Social Work,* 26 (March 1981), 101–106.

WILSON, SUANA J. *Confidentiality in Social Work: Issues and Principles.* New York: Free Press, 1978.

WINNICOTT, DONALD W. *Collected Papers.* London: Tavistock, 1958.

—————. "Hate in Countertransference." *International Journal of Pyschoanalysis,* 30 (1949), 69–74.

—————. *Home Is Where We Start From.* New York: W. W. Norton, 1986.

—————. "Transitional Objects and Transitional Phenomena: A Study of the First Not-Me Possession." In Peter Buckley, ed., *Essential Papers on Object Relations.* New York: New York University Press, 1986.

WISEMAN, REVA S. "Crisis Theory and the Process of Divorce." *Social Casework,* 56 (April 1975), 205–212.

WITMER, HELEN LELAND. *Social Work.* New York: Rinehart, 1942.

WOLBERG, LEWIS. *Handbook of Short-Term Psychotherapy.* New York: Thieme-Stratton, 1980.

WOLINSKY, MARY ANN. "Marital Therapy with Older Couples." *Social Casework,* (October 1986), 475–483.

WOOD, KATHARINE M. "Casework Effectiveness: A New Look at the Research Evidence." *Social Work,* 23 (November 1978), 437–458.

—————. "The Contribution of Psychoanalysis and Ego Psychology to Social Casework." In Herbert S. Strean, ed., *Social Casework.* Metuchen, N.J.: Scarecrow Press, 1971.

WOODROOFE, KATHLEEN. *From Charity to Social Work in England and in the United States.* Toronto: University of Toronto Press, 1962.

WOODS, MARY E. "Childhood Phobia and Family Therapy: A Case Illustration." In Florence Lieberman, ed., *Clinical Social Workers as Psychotherapists.* New York: Gardner, 1982, 165–178.

—————. "The Implications of Psychosocial Practice for Clinical Social Work Education." In Louise S. Bandler, ed., *Education for Clinical Social Work Practice, Continuity and Change.* New York: Pergamon Press, 1983, 55–75.

—————. "Personality Disorders." In Francis J. Turner, ed., *Adult Psychopathology: A Social Work Perspective.* New York: The Free Press, 1984, 200–248.

WYNNE, LYMAN C., et al. "Pseudomutuality in the Family Relations of Schizophrenics." In Norman W. Bell and Ezra F. Vogel, eds., *A Modern Introduction to the Family.* New York: Free Press, 1968, 628–649.

—————. "Some Indications and Contraindications for Exploratory Family Therapy." In Ivan Boszormenyi-Nagy and James L. Framo, eds., *Intensive Family Therapy.* New York: Basic Books, 1965, 289–322.

YALOM, IRVING D. *The Theory and Practice of Group Psychotherapy.* New York: Basic Books, 1985.

YOUNG, LEONTINE R. *Wednesday's Children: A Study of Child Neglect and Abuse*. New York: McGraw-Hill, 1964.

YOUNG-EISENDRATH, PAULINE. "Ego Development: Inferring the Client's Frame of Reference." *Social Casework*, 63 (June 1982), 323–332.

ZANGER, ALLYN. "A Study of Factors Related to Clinical Empathy." *Smith College Studies in Social Work*, 38 (February 1968), 116–131.

ZBOROWSKI, MARK. "Cultural Components in Response to Pain." *Journal of Social Issues*, 8 (1952), 16–30.

ZENTNER, ERVIN, and MONNA ZENTNER. "The Psychomechanic, Nonchemical Management of Depression." *Social Casework*, 66 (May 1985), 275–286.

ZENTNER, MONNA. "The Paranoid Client." *Social Casework*, 61 (March 1980), 138–145.

ZIMBERG, SHELDON, et al., eds. *Practical Approaches to Alcoholism Psychotherapy*. New York: Plenum Press, 1978.

ZIMMERMAN, SHIRLEY L. "The Family: Building Block or Anachronism." *Social Casework*, 61 (April 1980), 195–204.

———. "Reassessing the Effect of Public Policy on Family Functioning." *Social Casework*, 59 (October 1978), 451–457.

ZUK, GERALD H., and DAVID RUBINSTEIN. "A Review of Concepts in the Study and Treatment of Families of Schizophrenics." In Ivan Boszormenyi-Nagy and James L. Framo, eds., *Intensive Family Therapy*. New York: Harper & Row, 1965, 1–25.

Index

Abreaction, differentiated from ventilation, 116
Acceptance, 25–26
  anxiety reduction and, 300
  in marriage counseling, 410–411
  sustainment and, 106–107
Ackerman, Nathan W., 308, 317, 319, 329, 330, 354
Acting out, corrective relationship and, 220
Adaptation, 29
Adaptive patterns (see Personality change)
Additions as crises, 427
Adolescent(s):
  anger at being required to see worker and, 202
  family therapy and, 338
  transference and, 359
Advice, refusal to give, 114
Advice giving:
  anxiety aroused by, 297
  risks in, 113–114
  (See also Direct influence)
Advocacy, 99, 170–171
  case, 170
  social action, 170–171
  (See also Environmental intervention)
Affect(s):
  control of, 33
  flat, 261
  (See also Feelings)
Affective preparation for initial interview, 231
Aging client, case illustration of, 65–69

AIDS, homosexual couples and, 393–394
Alexander, Ernestina, 217
Altruism as defense mechanism, 35
Anger/hatred:
  exploration-description-ventilation and, 116
  expression in joint interviews, 119–120
  id and, 32
  lack of understanding of others' feelings and, 126
  in worker, 131
Anthropology, interactive aspects of personality development and, 41–43
Anxiety:
  aroused by treatment process, 297–299
    preconscious material and, 298
    self-understanding and, 297 298
  choice of treatment procedure and, 296–302
    anxiety reduction and, 299–300
    balancing anxiety and movement and, 300–302
    observation of anxiety and, 296
    treatment process and, 297–299
    worker style and, 300
  coming for help and, 202
  as contraindication to family therapy, 341

Anxiety (Cont.):
  defense mechanisms and, 137
  directiveness and, 113
  in early interviews, person-situation reflection and, 290–291
  exploration-description-ventilation and, 118
  in fact-gathering process, 243
  helping client to bring into the open, 301
  motivation and, 274–275
  observation of, 296
  reassurance and, 107–108
  reduction of, 299–300
  seeking treatment and, 105–106
  sustainment and, 301
  unexpressed, 118
Anxiety attacks, case illustration of psychosocial approach with, 474–483
Aponte, Harry, 308
Appearance, health and, 241
Appel, Yetta, 181
Artificial networks, 165
Assertiveness, emphasis on, 4
Assessment, 171–172
  of client reactions to termination, 444–447
    client satisfaction and, 446
    conditions of endings and, 447
    current life circumstances and, 447
    experiences with loss and, 446–447
    intensity of relationship and, 444–446

Assessment: of client reactions to termination (*Cont.*):
social supports and, 447
in crisis intervention, 430–432
for marriage counseling, 375–377
special concerns in, 377–381
(*See also* Diagnosis; Diagnostic understanding)
Assumptions as communication problem, 212, 213
Auld, Frank, 492
Austin, Lucille N., 88, 92, 219
Autonomy, 32
Average expectations:
in diagnostic understanding, 250–252
for personality, in diagnostic understanding, 253–254
Avoidance:
as defense mechanism, 35–36
in marriages, 384
Awareness:
inwardly directed, 128–130
of personality characteristics, pattern-dynamic reflection and, 140
of worker, termination and, 443–444, 451–452

Bales, R. F., 396
Bateson, Gregory, 317, 324
Beck, Dorothy Fahs, 18, 197, 201, 490
Behavior modification, development of, 14
Bellak, Leopold, 33
Benedict, Ruth, 42
Bentley, Wilson, 251
Berkowitz, Sidney, 89
Bibring, Grete, 87, 88
Bipolar disorders, diagnostic understanding and, 261
Blacks:
single-parent households among, 364
(*See also* Sociocultural factors)
Boatman, Louise, 110, 195, 196
Boie, Maurine, 42
Boszormenyi-Nagy, Ivan, 319
Boundaries:
in families, 313–314, 349
family therapy and, 310–311, 365

Boundaries: in families (*Cont.*):
marital, 349
(*See also* Generational boundaries)
Bowen, Murray, 312, 313
Bowlby, John, 329
Bradley, Trudy, 181
Brief treatment, 434–440
characteristics and benefits of, 436–438
diagnostic understanding and, 267–268
extended treatment and, 438–440
in marriage counseling, 413–416
non-negotiable contracts in, 434, 438
psychosocial approach to, 434–435
selection of clients for, 435–436
special training needed for, 439
(*See also* Crisis intervention)
Burnout, 8, 210

Cabot, Richard, 230
Carkhuff, Robert R., 218
Case illustrations (*see* Clinical social work, examples of)
Case management, 490
Casework:
education for, 489, 490
effectiveness of, 17
empirical base of, 16–20
future of, 490
goals of, 490–491
historical background of, 11–14
limitations of, 148
recent developments in, 4–11
new practice trends and, 7–9
other disciplines and, 9–11
terminology and overlapping concepts and, 5–7
roots of marriage counseling in, 374–375
use of term, 5
(*See also* Clinical social work)
Casework treatment (*see* Treatment; Treatment objectives; Treatment procedures)
Caseworker(s):
acceptance conveyed by, 106–107
anxiety reduction and, 300

Caseworker(s) (*Cont.*):
agency policies and, 155–157
anticipatory preparation for termination by, 448
appearance of, 203
assisting client to express hidden material and, 129–130
attempts to persuade clients of particular points of view, 360–361
corrective relationship and, 219–221
demonstration of, 218–219
realistic, 204–208
sociocultural factors and, 42, 43
barriers to effective communication and, 213
burnout of, 8, 210
characteristics of, treatment outcome related to, 201
client's reactions to, person-situation reflection and, 131–133
conveying attitude of, in marriage counseling, 410–411
countertherapeutic reactions of, 208
countertransference and (*see* Countertransference)
direction of fact-gathering interview by, 239–240
encouragement conveyed by, 108
environmental intervention by, 149–151
in family therapy, initial interview for, 347
feedback regarding reactions of, therapeutic use of, 207
importance of knowledge of system, 158
inability to meet all of client's needs, 165
indications of sustainment from, 106
knowledge of non-social work agencies, 161–162
offensive feelings ventilated to by collateral, 152
partiality of, in marriage counseling, 420–421
participation in developing diagnostic understanding, 246–247

Caseworker(s) (*Cont.*):
  personal therapy for, 423
  reactions of:
    as diagnostic tool, 207–208
    in diagnostic understanding, 255
  realistic attitudes and responses of, 204–208
  recognition of family's need for attention, 307
  relationships with other professionals, 155, 161
  resigning, termination and, 450
  roles of:
    as aggressive intervener, 169–170
    as creator of resource, 166–167
    in environmental intervention, 166–171
    classification by, 99
    as interpreter of resource, 167, 170
    as locator of resource, 166
    as mediator, 167–170
    as provider of resource, 166
  self-awareness of, termination and, 443–444, 451–452
  skill of:
    for environmental intervention, 149
    treatment objectives and, 284–285
  style of communication, anxiety reduction and, 300
  tension between researchers and, 20
  therapeutic optimism of, 221
  training of, 156
  transference and (*see* Transference)
  untherapeutic reactions of, 204–207
  values of (*see* Values, of caseworker)
  (*See also* Client-worker communications; Client-worker relationship; Couple-worker relationship)
Chamberlain, Edna, 195
Change:
  family adaptation to, 308–310
  fear of, 299

Change: fear of (*Cont.*):
  resistance and, 361–362
  in personality (*see* Personality change)
Children:
  corrective relationship and, 220
  in dysfunctional triadic structures, 320–321
  environmental intervention and, 50
  family therapy and, 338
    transference and, 359
  overreliance on, by single parents, 362–363
  parentification of, 319
  reaching out to, 109
  school problems and, 234
  in stepfamilies, 368
  symptoms of, family therapy and, 362
  [*See also* Adolescent(s); Early life; Parent(s); Parent-child problems]
Clarification:
  in FSAA classification, 88–89
  in Hollis typology, 87–88
  personality change and, 92
Cleveland School of Social Work, 12
Client:
  acceptance of, 25–26, 106–107, 300
  assessment of (*see* Assessment; Diagnosis; Diagnostic understanding)
  attitudes of:
    toward agency, 203
    development of, 43–44
    toward mental health services, 5
    realistic, 202–204
    unrealistic, modifying, 53
    toward worker, 203
  for brief treatment, selection of, 435–436
  capacities of:
    diagnostic assessment of, 248
    in diagnostic understanding, 251
  characteristics of, treatment outcome related to, 201
  crisis-prone, 433–434
  current adaptive capacity of, 431

Client (*Cont.*):
  decision to terminate made by, 447
  encouraging to terminate, 452
  enlisting in cause, 170
  evaluation of own problems, in diagnostic understanding, 258
  feedback from, 212, 450–451
  increasing awareness of, 128–130
  involuntary, 202
    case illustration of psychosocial approach with, 468–474
    initial interview with, 232
    treatment objectives for, 274
  meaning of crisis to, 430–431
  as most important source of information, 236, 422
  motivation of (*see* Motivation)
  negation of worker's efforts by, 214–215
  over- and underprotection of, 169
  overidentification with, 162
  participation of:
    in developing diagnostic understanding, 246–247
    in environmental intervention, 149–151
    in treatment, 213–217
  preference for individual therapy, 341
  reactions to worker and treatment, person-situation reflection and, 131–133
  recall of early experiences by, 143–144
  safeguards against advice giving and, 113–114
  satisfaction of, termination and, 446
  self-determination in, 12, 13
  self-evaluation by, person-situation reflection and, 130–131
  self-reliance in, 127, 130
  termination and (*see* Termination)
  transference and (*see* Transference)
  treatment objectives and, 271
  use of term, 6

Client (*Cont.*):
(*See also* Client-worker communications; Client-worker relationship; Couple-worker relationship)
Client-centered treatment, development of, 14
Client-worker communications:
classification of, 94–97, 99–100
coding of, 181–192
problems in, 210–213
secondary directiveness in, 114–115
study of, 181
(*See also* Hollis typology, study of)
worker's goodwill and, 218
Client-worker relationship, 201–224
agency where worker is employed and, 157–159
agency where worker is not employed and, 159–160
bringing into discussion, 218–219
client participation and movement and, 213–217
communication problems and, 210–213
developmental understanding of, 144–145
disagreement on goals and, 215–216
emphasis placed on by various theories, 486
in family therapy, single-parent families and, 364
intensity of, termination and, 444–446
mutuality and, 223–224
person-situation reflection and, 131–133
realistic attitudes and responses and, 202–208
of client, 202–204
of worker, 204–208
sociocultural factors and, 203–204, 235–236
transference and countertransference in, 208–210
treatment dynamics and, 217–222
treatment outcome related to, 201

Client-worker relationship (*Cont.*):
worker burnout and, 210
(*See also* Couple-worker relationship)
Clinical diagnosis (*see* Assessment; Diagnosis; Diagnostic understanding)
Clinical social work, 5
diverse approaches to, 485–486
education for specialization in, 14–16
examples of, 61–83
anxiety attacks and, 474–483
early deprivation and, 76–83
inpatient treatment of psychosis and, 453–461
involuntary clients and, 468–474
marital crisis and, 62–65
problems of aging and, 65–69
public welfare case and, 72–76
terminal illness and, 461–468
three-generation "multiproblem" family and, 69–72
use of term, 5
(*See also* Casework)
Coding of client-worker communications, 181–192
Cognitive preparation for initial interview, 231
Cognitive theory, 14
Collateral(s):
attitudes of:
assessment of, 151
modifying, 162–163
confidentiality and, 151
direct influence with, 152
environmental intervention and, 162–166
expressive collaterals and, 163
family sessions on behalf of individual treatment and, 163–164
instrumental collaterals and, 162–163
joint client-worker intervention and, 150
network therapy and, 164–166
in fact-gathering process, 243

Collateral(s) (*Cont.*):
purposes of discussions with, 151
reflective discussion and, 153–154
sustainment with, 152
use of term, 6
ventilation by, 152
Collateral sources, use of term, 6
Collateral-worker communication, 98–99
Collis, John Stewart, 252
Columbia University (*see* New York School of Social Work)
Communication(s):
client-worker (*see* Client-worker communications; Couple-worker communication)
between collateral and worker, 98–99
in environmental intervention, 151–154
in families, 323–326, 349
double bind and, 324–325
family therapy and, 338
mystification and, 325–326, 349
faulty, 46
honest, in family therapy, 353–354
interaction patterns and, in diagnostic understanding, 256–257
in premarital therapy, 389
worker's style of, anxiety reduction and, 300
Communication theory, 9
Community Service Society of New York, 89
Competence, 34
Complementarity:
in interpersonal relationships, in diagnostic understanding, 255–256
in marriages, 313
Compton, Beulah Roberts, 213
Confidentiality in communication with collaterals, 151
Conscience, 39
Consequences, person-situation reflection and, 127–128
Consultation:
influence on treatment objectives, 284

Consultation (*Cont.*):
  psychiatric, value of, 263
Contention in carrying out family roles, 319
Contract, 217
  contribution to psychosocial approach, 8
  non-negotiable, in brief treatment, 434, 438
Controlled instability of families, 317–318
Cooper, Shirley, 15
Cooperation in carrying out family roles, 319
Corrective feedback, family processes and, 317
Corrective relationship, 219–221
  marriage as, 386, 418
  modifying balance of forces and, 53
  mutuality and, 224
  personality change and, 92
Countersustainment, 196–197
Countertransference, 209–210
  communication problems and, 210
  in marriage counseling, 420–423
  safeguards against, 423
Couple(s) (*see* Marriage; Marriage counseling; "Nontraditional" couples)
Couple-worker relationship, 418–423
  countertransference and, 420–423
  transference and, 418–420
Crises:
  anticipated and unanticipated, 427
  termination as, 448
Crisis intervention, 426–434
  assessment process and, 430–432
  categories of crises and, 427
  contribution to psychosocial approach, 7–8
  "crisis-prone" clients and, 433–434
  crisis state and, 427
  development of, 14
  generic stages and, 429–430
  individualized, 432–433
  outcomes of crisis and, 427–428

Crisis intervention (*Cont.*):
  preventive intervention and, 428–429
Cross-cultural relationships, 392–393
Culture (*see* Sociocultural factors)
Current life situations:
  helping client to deal with, personality change and, 92
  as source of problems, 46, 47

Dare, Christopher, 377
Davis, Inger P., 110, 195
Deduction during initial interview, 237
Defense mechanisms, 34–39
  altruism as, 35
  anxiety demonstrated by, 296
  avoidance as, 35–36
  classification of, 37–39
  denial as, 36–37
  devaluation as, 37
  in diagnostic understanding, 253
  displacement as, 36
  healthy versus pathological ends served by, 34–35
  humor as, 35
  intellectualization as, 36
  isolation as, 36
  in neuroses, 262
  pattern-dynamic reflection and, 137
  in personality disorders, 262
  primitive idealization as, 37
  projection as, 36
  projective identification as, 37
  rationalization as, 36
  reaction formation as, 36
  regression as, 37
  repression as, 35
  restrictive, as source of problems, 47, 48
  splitting as, 37
  sublimation as, 35
  suppression as, 35
Defensiveness as contraindication to family therapy, 341
de la Fontaine, Elise, 42
Delusions, 261
Denial:
  as defense mechanism, 36–37

Denial (*Cont.*):
  grief reactions and, 116–117
  of transference, 418–419
Depression:
  chronic, 428
  diagnostic understanding and, 261
  directiveness and, 113
Description, 96
  amount of, in client-worker communication, 191–192
  in collateral-worker communication, 99
  prior to sustainment, 108
  (*See also* Exploration-description-ventilation)
Detriangulation in family therapy, single-parent families and, 365
Devaluation as defense mechanism, 37
Developmental reflection, 97, 141–145, 288
  amount of, in client-worker communication, 192–195
  in brief treatment, 436
  choice as treatment procedure, 294–296
  motivation and, 294–295
  widespread use of, 295–296
  description-ventilation versus, 141–142
  in family therapy, 351
  movement into, 142–144
  relationship with worker and, 144–145
Dewey, John, 12
Diagnosis:
  in diagnostic understanding, 260–267
  hazards and misuse of, 265–267
  neuroses and personality disorders and, 262–263
  psychosis and, 261–262
  value of, 263–265
  in family therapy, 354–355
  treatment objectives and, intermediate, 281–283
  (*See also* Assessment; Diagnostic understanding)
Diagnostic and Statistical Manual of Mental Disorders (DSM-III; DSM-III-R), 10, 260

Diagnostic approach (*see* Psychoanalytic approach)
Diagnostic understanding, 246–
268
assessment process and, 247–
258
client's assessments in, 258
family systems theory, complementarity, and com-
munication in, 255–257
personality system in, 251–
255
requirements for effective
treatment and, 249
situation in, 250–251
symptoms in, 249–250
use of past in, 257–258
attempting to develop, 238–
239
brief treatment and, 267–268
central role in treatment, 246
choice of treatment procedures
and, 288–302
anxiety and guilt and, 296–
302
environmental change and,
289
interpersonal relationships,
internal change, and
person-situation reflec-
tion and, 289–294
pattern-dynamic and developmental reflection and,
294–296
person-situation reflection as
treatment procedure
and, 293–294
classification and, 258–267
clinical diagnosis and, 260–
267
medical, 259
of problem, 259–260
client-worker participation in,
246–247
psychosocial study differentiated from, 230
time factor and, 267–268
treatment objectives and, 271–
285
intermediate, 278–283
intervening variables and,
283–285
long-range, 272–274
motivation and, 274–276

Diagnostic understanding (*Cont.*):
resistance and, 276–278
worker's subjective reactions
as tool in, 207–208
Differential approach, 12–13
classifications in, 86–89
growth of theory and practice
within, 13–14
influence of, 13
(*See also* Psychoanalytic theory)
Differentiation:
family therapy and, 310–311
lack of, 349
in marriages, 385
Direct influence, 96, 110–115,
195
amount of, in client-worker
communication, 192, 193
client confidence and, 218–219
in collateral-worker communication, 99
with collaterals, 152
in crisis intervention, 432
degrees of directiveness in,
111–113
in family therapy, 350, 351
relationship to sustainment, 115
risks in advice giving and,
113–114
secondary directiveness and,
114–115
suspicion of, 110–111
sustainment and, 218–219
uses of, 111
Direct treatment, 11, 87, 95
with individual, 50–51
interacting sources of stress
and, ameliorating, 50–51
Displacement as defense mechanism, 36
Dissociations, trading of, family
therapy and, 328–329
Divorce:
aftermath of, 397–398
prevalence of, 305, 374
separate therapists and, 375
Divorce mediation, 388
Divorce therapy, 388
Dollard, John, 492
Double bind in families, 324–325
Drives, 32
regulation of, 33
Drug(s):
fact gathering about, 241

Drugs(s) (*Cont.*)
personal adjustment problems
and, 241
Drug therapy, 10
in schizophrenia, 261
DSM-III (see *Diagnostic and Statistical Manual of Mental Disorders*)
Dynamic reflection, 288
Dynamic understanding, 248

Early deprivation, case illustration of, 76–83
Early life:
fact gathering about, 241–242
history of, in diagnostic understanding, 257–258
personality development and,
39–40, 141
(*See also* Children; Developmental reflection)
Ecological approach, 14, 28–30
contributions of, 8, 9
Education:
for brief treatment, 439
for casework, 489, 490
for clinical social work specialization, 14–16
Ego, 32–39
balance of forces and, 51–52
modifying, 52–55
in diagnostic understanding,
252, 253
functions of, 33–34
(*See also* Defense mechanisms)
Ego-alien behavior, 136–137
Ego functioning:
differentiation and, 312
inadequate, as source of problems, 46–48
pattern-dynamic reflection
and, 139–140
strengthening through mutuality, 216–217
Ego ideal (*see* Superego)
Ego psychology, 32, 486
interactive aspects of personality development and, 41
(*See also* Ego functioning; Psychoanalytic theory)
Ego strength in diagnostic understanding, 253
Ego-syntonic behavior, 136–137

Ego-syntonic behavior (*Cont.*):
  personality disorders and, 140–
    141
Ehrenkranz, Shirley M., 110,
  119, 181, 195, 350, 351
Empathic preparation for initial
  interview, 231
Empathy, 26
  acceptance and, 107
Employee assistance programs, 8
Encouragement, sustainment
  and, 108
Enmeshed family systems, 349
  denial of homosexuality by, 395
Environment:
  assessment of deficits in, 147
  average expectable, in diagnos-
    tic understanding, 250–251
  interactions with, 40–46
    communication and, 46
    role theory and, 44–45
    social components in percep-
      tions and expectations
      and, 43–44
    sociological and anthropo-
      logical perspectives on,
      41–43
  personality development and,
    40
Environmental intervention, 48–
  50, 147–174, 288
  aggressive, 99, 169–170
  assessment of person-environ-
    ment gestalt and, 171–174
  choice as treatment procedure,
    289
  classification of, 98–100
    employing agency and, 98
    other social agencies and, 98
    type of communication used
      and, 98–99
    type of resource and, 98
    type of role and, 99
  by client versus worker, 149–
    151, 172
  communication types and,
    151–154
  complexity of, 97–98, 149
  concentrating on system most
    accessible to change and,
    49
  in family therapy, 351
  personality change and, 49–50,
    148

Environmental intervention
  (*Cont.*):
  resources for, 154–166
    individual collaterals as,
      162–166
    non-social work agency
      where worker is not em-
      ployed as, 161–162
    non-social work organization
      employing worker as,
      157–160
    social agency where worker
      is not employed as, 160–
      161
    worker's own agency as,
      154–157
  roles in, 166–171
  [See also Collateral(s)]
Environmental modification in
  Hollis typology, 87
Environmental treatment:
  use of term, 6
  [See also Collateral(s); Environ-
    mental intervention]
Erikson, Erik H., 31, 40
Existential approach, 14
Expectations:
  influence of role on, 44–45
  social components in, 43–44
Experiential therapy in Austin
  classification, 88
Explanations in crisis intervention, 432
Exploration, 96
  in collateral-worker communi-
    cation, 99
  empathy and, 218–219
  prior to sustainment, 108
  (See also Exploration-description-
    ventilation)
Exploration-description-
  ventilation, 115–120
  amount of, in client-worker
    communication, 194, 195
  anger and hatred and, 116
  anxiety and, 118
  contraindications to, 118–119
  developmental reflection ver-
    sus, 141–142
  in family therapy, 350
  grief reactions and, 116–117
  guilt feelings and, 117–118
  in joint interviews, 119–120
  relationship to sustainment, 117

Expressive collaterals, 163
External pressures, 28
  couples strained by, 384
External situations as crises, 427
Externalization (*see* Projection)
Extramarital relationships, 398–
  399
Extrareflection, 125, 194–195, 288

Family(ies):
  assessment of, 171–172, 354–
    356
    single-parent families and,
      362–364
  challenges to, 305–306
  controlled instability of, 317–
    318
  crises and, 431–432
  cutback in services to, 305
  dysfunctional:
    boundaries and, 311, 314–
      316
    family system and, 314, 316–
      317
  functional, boundaries and,
    311
  homeostasis of, 317–318
  influence on treatment objec-
    tives, 283–284
  normal functioning of, 355
  of origin:
    impact of, 328
    marital maladjustment and,
      384–386
    negative reaction to cross-
      cultural relationships,
      392
    single-parent families and,
      364
    transition from, 390
  relational styles of, 309–310
  resistant to family therapy,
    339–340
  roles in, 349
    irrational role assignments
      and, 349, 386–387
    scapegoat and, 349
    triangles and, 349
  single parents and, in family
    therapy, 362–366
  subsystems of, 314
  as system, 316–318
  "urban matriarchal," 309

Family(ies) (*Cont.*):
(*See also* Family therapy; Parent-child problems)
Family concepts, Russo family case and, 348–350
Family interviews:
on behalf of individual treatment, 163–164
problems associated with sustainment in, 110
understanding of others fostered by, 126, 128
Family projection process, 328
Family Service Association of America, casework classification of, 88–89
Family systems theory, diagnostic understanding and, 255–257
Family therapy, 305–330, 335–370
advantages of, 342–343
case illustration of, with three-generation "multi-problem" family, 69–72
change, stress, and family adaptation and, 308–310
communication and, 323–326
double bind and, 324–325
mystification and, 325–326
contraindications for, 340–342
contribution to psychosocial approach, 7
dangers of, 342, 353–354
development of, 306–308
diagnosis and goals in, 354–356
differentiation and boundaries and, 310–316
diversity in, 486
effectiveness of, 337
environmental intervention and, 50
family as system and, 316–318
homeostasis and, 317–318
family concepts and, Russo family case and, 348–350
family roles and, 318–323
myths and secrets and, 322–323
pseudomutuality and, 321–322
scapegoating and, 319–320
triangles and, 320–321

Family therapy (*Cont.*):
indications for, 337–340
typology for selecting families and, 337–339
individual therapy and, 339–340
influence of social sciences on, 42
initial interview and, 343–348
guidelines and ground rules for, 346–348
intake request and, Russo family case and, 335–337
modern, 308
psychosocial approach and, 326–330
person-in-situation and, 326–327
personality system and, 327–330
special emphases in, 351–354
resistance and, 360–362
Russo family case and, 335–337, 343–348, 350–351, 353–354, 356–358
single-parent families and, 362–366
social casework tradition and, 306–308
special emphases in, 351–354
stepfamilies and, 366–370
issues related to, 369–370
treatment considerations with, 368–369
testing feasibility of, 341
transference and countertransference in, 358–360
treatment procedures and techniques in, 350–351
Russo family case and, 350–351
(*See also* Marriage counseling)
Feedback, 30
from client, 450–451
importance of, 212
corrective, family processes and, 317
Feelings:
differentiating between intellectual processes and, 312–313
distinction between experiencing and expressing, 115
failure to express, 118

Feelings: failure to express (*Cont.*):
expression of a different emotion and, 118
increasing awareness of, 128–130
of others, lack of understanding about, 126
positive, anxiety aroused by, 299
about termination, eliciting and dealing with, 448–449
Flat affect, 261
Framo, James L., 316, 355, 375, 384, 388
Frank, Jerome D., 218
Freud, Anna, 31, 296
Freud, Sigmund, 31, 32, 40–41, 327
Freudian theory (*see* Psychoanalytic theory)
Friedman, Edwin H., 392, 393
Frustration, optimum, 218
Functionalism, 12
influence of, 13

Galaway, Burt, 213
Garrett, Annette, 222
Generalists, 5
Generational boundaries, 349
in family therapy, single-parent families and, 365
violation of, family therapy and, 338–339
Generic social work practitioners, 5
Geographical obstacles to family therapy, 340
Germain, Carel B., 9, 29, 149, 231, 451
Gestalt, 28
person-environment, assessment of, 171–174
Gitterman, Alex, 9, 231, 451
Glueck, Bernard, 12
Golan, Naomi, 427
Goldner, Virginia, 397
Grandparents:
as consultants, 365
in stepfamilies, 367–368
Grief:
chronic, 428
crisis intervention and, 426–427

Grief (*Cont.*):
exploration-description-ventilation and, 116–117
in family therapy, single-parent families and, 365
Group treatment, contribution to psychosocial approach, 8
Groves, Ernest, 12
Growth, termination as opportunity for, 449
Guilt:
aroused by treatment process, 297
constructive purposes served by, 117
divorce and, 363
excessive, 117–118
exploration description-ventilation and, 117–118
reassurance and, 107
Gurman, Alan S., 347

Haley, Jay, 323
Hallucinations, 261
Hamilton, Gordon, 9, 28, 307, 449
Hankins, Frank, 14
Hard-to-reach client, resistance and, 277
Hartman, Ann, 317, 318
Hartman, Heinz, 31
Hatred (*see* Anger/hatred)
Health in psychosocial study, 240–241
Healy, William, 12
Hellenbrand, Shirley, 181
Helping professions, 5
Hidden agenda, resistance and, 360
Hollis, Florence, 12–14, 16, 88, 90, 119, 195, 289, 290, 308, 375
on practice wisdom, 16 20
Hollis typology, 93–100
applications of:
to brief treatment, 436
to family therapy, 350
to marriage counseling, 424–425
client-worker communications in, 95–97
development of, 93–95
further studies based on, 195–197
sustainment and countersustainment and, 196–197

Hollis typology (*Cont.*):
need for further research on, 197
person-in-situation or environmental situations in, 97–100
preliminary study and, 93–94
reliability of, 492–493
study of, 180–197
coding for, 182–183
comparison with findings of other studies, 192–195
distribution of procedures and, 190–192
informal use of typology and, 183, 190
profile of casework process and, 195
Home visit, fact gathering during, 242
Homosexual couples, 309, 393–396
living together, 392
Hope, effect on motivation, 274
Horney, Karen, 14
Hospitals, social workers in, 158, 159
Hostility (*see* Anger/hatred)
Humor as defense mechanism, 35

Id, 32
balance of forces and, 51–52
modifying, 52–55
in diagnostic understanding, 252
Illness, physical and emotional, in psychosocial study, 240–241
Impulse control, 33
Indirect treatment method, 11, 87
Individuation, family therapy and, 329
Induction in family therapy, 359
Initial interview:
for family therapy:
guidelines and ground rules for, 346–348
Russo family case and, 343–348
psychosocial study and (*see* Psychosocial study)
Insight development in Hollis typology, 87

Insight therapy in Austin classification, 88
Insisting, 112
Instrumental collaterals, 162–163
Intellectualization as defense mechanism, 36
Intelligence in diagnostic understanding, 253
Interaction, 29
fact gathering about, 240
of family members, 316–318
family therapy and, 326–327
negative, 353–354
between individuals and their environments, 40–46
communication and, 46
role theory and, 44–45
social components in perceptions and expectations and, 43–44
sociological and anthropological perspectives on, 41–43
of personality components, in diagnostic understanding, 254–255
in premarital therapy, 389
among sources of distress, 46–48, 248
ameliorating, 48–51
of systems, 29–30
treatment of (*see* Environmental intervention)
Intergenerational transmission process, 328, 386
Internal pressure, 28
Internalization, family therapy and, 327
Interpersonal relations, satisfying, 32
Interpretation in psychosocial family therapy, 352–353
Intervention:
forceful, 112–113
use of term, 6
(*See also* specific types of intervention)
Interviews:
family:
on behalf of individual treatment, 163 164
problems associated with sustainment in, 110

Interviews: family (*Cont.*):
  understanding of others fostered by, 126, 128
  psychosocial study and (*see* Psychosocial study)
  (*See also* Joint interviews)
Intrareflection, 288, 299
Introjection, family therapy and, 327, 356
Involuntary client, 202
  case illustration of psychosocial approach with, 468–474
  initial interview with, 232
  treatment objectives for, 274
Irrational role assignment, 319
  in families, 349
  negatively affecting marriages, 386–387
Isolation as defense mechanism, 36

Jackson, Don D., 317, 323, 324
Jewish Family Service, 308
Joint interviews:
  as adjunct to individual treatment, 53
    illustration of, 54–55
  deciding whether to use, 236–237
  exploration-description-ventilation in, 119–120
  fact gathering in, 242
  understanding of others fostered by, 126
Jones, Mary Ann, 18, 201
Josselyn, Irene, 308
Judgment, 33

Kaplan, David M., 279
Kardiner, Abram, 42
Kenworthy, Marion, 12
Kniskern, David P., 347
Kohut, Heinz, 10, 32
Kris, Ernst, 31
Kubler-Ross, Elizabeth, 429

Laing, R. D., 325
Laird, Joan, 317, 318
Leader, Arthur, 308, 329
Levinson, Hilliard, 451

Licensure for social workers, 5
Life circumstances, termination and, 447
Life experiences, crises and, 431
Life model approach (*see* Ecological approach)
Life transitions:
  as anticipated crises, 427
  couples stressed by, 382–383
Lindemann, Erich, 426–427
Listening, therapeutic, in marriage counseling, 410–411
Loewenstein, Sophie Freud, 49, 379, 395
Loss:
  experiences with, termination and, 446–447
  in family therapy, single-parent families and, 365
  as unanticipated crises, 427
Lowenstein, Rudolph, 31
Lukton, Rosemary Creed, 429

McGoldrick, Monica, 392, 392, 393
Mahler, Margaret S., 31, 39, 329
Manic-depressive disorders, diagnostic understanding and, 261
Mann, James, 437
Marital boundaries in families, 349
Marriage:
  categories of relationships in, 382–389
    avoidance and, 384
    "calcified," 388
    chronically conflictual, 384
    dysfunctional family-of-origin relationships and, 384–386
    ending of marriage by mutual agreement and, 388–389
    extraordinary external pressures and, 384
    negative projections and role assignments and, 386–387
    with one spouse who wants to leave, 388
    one symptomatic partner and, 383

Marriage: categories of relationships in (*Cont.*):
    second marriages and, 387–388
    solid, committed with minor dysfunctions, 382
    stress of life cycle transitions and, 382–383
  complementarity in, 313
  as corrective relationship, 418
  dynamics of, 381
  extramarital relationships and, 398–399
  second, with special difficulties, 387–388
  self-differentiation and, 313
  "trial," 391
  women in, 396–398
  (*See also* "Nontraditional" couples)
Marriage counseling, 374–399
  assessment and general treatment considerations in, 375–377
    special assessment concerns and, 377–381
  case illustration of, 62–65
  concurrent individual sessions versus, 416–417
  contraindications to, 375
  extramarital relationships and, 398–399
  historical perspective on, 374–375
  treatment issues and techniques in, 404–425
    cautions regarding, 409–410
    couple versus concurrent individual sessions and, 416–417
    couple-worker relationship in, 418–423
    illustration of, 423–425, 404–409
    rapid assessment, brief treatment, and referral and, 413–416
    treatment steps and, 410–413
  typology of couple relationships and problems and, 381–398
    categories of relationships and, 382–389
    nontraditional couples and, 389–396

Marriage counseling: typology of couple relationships and problems and (*Cont.*):
women in couples and, 396–398
Mason, Edward A., 279
Mastery, 34
Maturity, classification of defenses on basis of, 37–38
Mead, Margaret, 42, 392
Mediation, 167–169, 170
Medical classification in diagnostic understanding, 259
Medical knowledge, contributions of, 10
Mental health services, attitudes toward, 5
Mental illness:
indications of, 241
(*See also* specific disorders)
Meyer, Carol, 20
"Midlife crises," extramarital relationships and, 398
Milieu work (*see* Environmental intervention)
Minuchin, Salvador, 313, 314, 320, 330
Montgomery, Mitzie I. R., 195, 196
Motivation:
choice of treatment procedure and, pattern-dynamic or developmental reflection as, 294–295
of client, participation in treatment and, 215
diagnostic assessment of, 248
in diagnostic understanding, 251
treatment objectives and, 274–276
factors affecting motivation and, 274–275
values and, 275–276
Moultroup, David, 330
Mudd, Emily, 308
Mullen, Edward J., 145, 181, 192, 194–196
Multigenerational families, single-parent, 364
Murray, Henry A., 9
Mutuality, 27, 213–217, 223–224
deciding on treatment duration and, 233
degree of informality and, 223–224

Mutuality (*Cont.*):
emphasis placed on by various theories, 486
in environmental intervention, 147–148
in family therapy, 361
resistance and, 277
sustainment and, 106
Mystification in families, 325–326, 349
Myths in families, 322–323
exposing and dispelling, 369

National Institute of Mental Health (NIMH) grant for research on Hollis typology, 180
Nelsen, Judith C., 276
Network therapy, 164–166
artificial networks and, 165
Neurosis, 263–264
diagnostic understanding and, 262–263
Freudian view of, 41, 327
treatment objectives for, 282–283
New York School of Social Work (now Columbia University), 12
coding of communications by student of, 181
typology study at, 94
NIMH (*see* National Institute of Mental Health)
"Nontraditional" couples, 389–396
cross-cultural, 392–393
homosexual, 309, 392–396
premarital relationships and, 389–390
unmarried and living together, 390–392
Nonverbal communication, 211
in assessment of family system, 323–324
Nonverbal sustainment, 109

Object constancy, 40
Object relations, 33
Observation:
as advantage of family therapy, 342

Observation (*Cont.*):
in diagnostic understanding, 255
fact gathering through, 240
during initial interview, 237
Obsessive-compulsive disorder, 263–264
advice seeking and, 114
transference and, 221
"Open door" approach:
in brief treatment, 438
termination and, 447
Opportunities in diagnostic understanding, 248, 250
Orcutt, Ben Avis, 181, 196
Organismic approach, 9
Overcontrol, 33
Overgeneralization, danger of, 17
Overidentification:
with client, 162
with family member, in family therapy, 360
Overstreet, H. A., 12

Palumbo, Joseph, 445
Paraprofessionals:
environmental intervention by, 149
relegation of crisis intervention to, 430
Parent(s):
fears and prejudices held by, 125–126
lack of understanding about normal reactions and, 125
single, 309
in family therapy, 362–366
stepfathers as, 367
stepmothers as, 367
[*See also* Family(ies), of origin]
Parent-child problems:
directiveness and, 111, 113
fact gathering about, 239
[*See also* Adolescent(s); Children]
Parental overprotection, personality development and, 40
Parental subsystem, 314
Parentification, 319
Parenting, personality development and, 40, 376
Parsons, T., 396

Pattern-dynamic reflection, 97, 124, 135–145
  amount of, in client-worker communication, 192–195
  in brief treatment, 436
  choice as treatment procedure, 294–296
    motivation and, 294–295
    widespread use of, 295–296
  concerning dynamic factors, 136–141
    ego defenses and, 137
    ego functioning and, 139–140
    personality disorders and, 140–141
    superego and, 138–139
  developmental understanding and, 141–145
    movement into developmental reflection and, 142–144
    reflection versus description-ventilation and, 141–142
    relationship with worker and, 144–145
  in family therapy, 351
Pennsylvania School of Social Work, 12, 13
  (See also Functionalism)
Perception(s):
  distortion of, in diagnostic understanding, 252
  social components in, 43–44
Perlman, Helen Harris, 13
Perls, Fritz, 196
Person-environment gestalt, assessment of, 171–174
Person-situation configuration, 27–28
  balance of forces in, 51–55
    modifying, 52–55
    understanding, 51–52
  family therapy and, 326–327
  interacting sources of stress in, ameliorating, 48–50
Person-situation disequilibrium, assessment of, 147
Person-situation reflection, 96–97, 124–133, 288
  amount of, in client-worker communication, 192, 195
  choice as treatment procedure, 289–294

Person-situation reflection: choice as treatment procedure (Cont.):
    anxiety in early interviews and, 290–291
    diagnostic understanding and, 293–294
    personality factors and, 291–292
    situational and ethnic factors and, 293
    thought processes and self-understanding and, 292–293
  in collateral-worker communication, 99
  decisions, consequences, and alternatives in, 127–128
  in family therapy, 350–351
  inwardly directed awareness in, 128–130
  other people, health, situation in, 124–127
  procedures used in, 124
  reactions to worker and treatment and, 131–133
  responses to situational provocations and stimuli in, 130
  self-evaluation in, 130–131
Personality, 31–40
  crises and, 431
  development of, 39–40
    parenting and, 376
  in diagnostic understanding, 251–255
    disentangling interactions and, 254–255
    tripartite personality structure and, 252–253
    variable expectations and, 253–254
  diverse approaches to, 486
  ego and (see Ego; Ego functioning)
  environmental modification and, 49–50
  fear of change in, anxiety aroused by, 299
  health and, 241
  id and (see Id)
  person-situation reflection and, 291–292
  psychosocial approach to, family therapy and, 327–330

Personality (Cont.):
  social functioning and, 31
  superego and (see Superego)
  as system, 30
  unmodifiable contributing factors in, 280
Personality change:
  clarification and, 92
  corrective relationship and, 92
  diverse approaches to, 91–93
  environmental intervention and, 148
  helping client to deal with current life situation and, 92
  more favorable life experiences and, 92
  positive reinforcement resulting from more effective functioning and, 92
  structural, 91–92
  treatment techniques and, 89–93
Personality disorders:
  avoidant, 264
  as contraindication for brief treatment, 435
  corrective relationship and, 220
  diagnostic understanding and, 262, 263
  need for support and, 218
  pattern-dynamic reflection and, 140–141
  treatment objectives for, 282–283
Pharis, David, 19
Physical closeness, caution against, in marriage counseling, 409–410
Pinkus, Helen, 192, 194
Pittman, Frank S., III, 315, 397, 416
Planned time-limited treatment (see Brief treatment)
Pleasure principle, 32
Polemis, Bernice, 217
Pollak, Otto, 251
Positive reinforcement from more effective functioning, personality change and, 92
Poverty, psychosocial approach and, 8–9
Power, use by worker, 169–170
Practice wisdom, 16
Precipitating factors, determining, 235
Preconscious material:
  anxiety aroused by, 298

Preconscious material (*Cont.*):
  pattern-dynamic reflection
    and, 135–141
    ego defenses and, 137
    ego functioning and, 139–
      140
    personality disorders and,
      140–141
    superego and, 138–139
Pregnancy, unwanted, 259
Premarital relationships, 389–390
Premarital therapy, areas empha-
  sized in, 389–390
Presenting problem, intermediate
  objectives and, 279
Press, 28
Pressure:
  external, 28
  internal, 28
Preto, Nydia Garcia, 392, 393
Prevention in crisis intervention,
  428–429
Primary process, 32
Primitive idealization as defense
  mechanism, 37
Privacy in family therapy, single-
  parent families and, 365
Private practice, 488
Problem(s):
  classification of, in diagnostic
    understanding, 259–260
  definition of, differences
    among theories in, 486
  emergence of, 273
  interacting sources of, 46–48
  locating, 233–235
  order of consideration of fac-
    tors in, 281
  point of intervention and tip-
    ping the balance and, 280–
    281
  point of maximum reverbera-
    tion and, 281
  presenting:
    family therapy and, 338
    intermediate objectives and,
      279
    unmodifiable contributing fac-
      tors and, 279–280
Problem-solving approach, development of, 13–14
Process recording, coding client-
  worker communication and,
  182

Professional ethics, 170
Progress during initial interview,
  237–238
Projection:
  as defense mechanism, 36
  in families, 328, 343, 356
  negatively affecting marriages,
    386–387
Projective identification as defense mechanism, 37
Pseudomutuality in families,
  321–322
Psychiatric consultation, value
  of, 263
Psychoanalysis, transference in,
  221–222
Psychoanalytic theory, 12, 13
  neurosis and, 41, 327
  of personality, 32–39
  psychosocial approach and,
    family therapy and, 327–
    330
Psychoeducational approach,
  contributions of, 10
Psychological support in Hollis
  typology, 87
Psychosis:
  case illustration of
    psychosocial approach in,
    453–461
  as contraindication to family
    therapy, 340
  as contraindication to ventila-
    tion, 119
  diagnostic understanding and,
    261–262
  treatment objectives for, 283
  (*See also* Schizophrenia)
Psychosocial approach, 86
  to brief treatment, 434–435
  clinical case examples of, 453–
    483
    anxiety attacks and, 474–483
    involuntary clients and, 468–
      474
    short-term inpatient treat-
      ment for psychosis and,
      453–461
    terminal illness and, 461–468
  defined, 5–6
  empirical basis of, 16–20
  family therapy and, 326–330
    person-in-situation and, 326–
      327

Psychosocial approach: family
    (*Cont.*):
    personality system and, 327–
      330
    special emphases in, 351–354
  interactive aspects of personal-
    ity development and, 41
  new practice trends in, 7–9
  origin of term, 14
  private practice and, 488
  sociocultural groups served by,
    487–488
  techniques of, 55
Psychosocial study, 230–243
  diagnostic understanding dif-
    ferentiated from, 230
  exploratory period and fact-
    gathering process in, 238–
    243
    additional sources of infor-
      mation in, 242–243
    early history and, 241–242
    physical and emotional ill-
      ness and, 240–241
  initial interview and, 231–238
    client-worker differences
      and, 235–236
    deciding on length of treat-
      ment and, 233
    deciding who is to be seen
      and, 236–237
    initial decisions and, 231–232
    observation and deduction
      and, 237
    precipitating factors and, 235
    problem identification and,
      233–235
    progress in, 237–238
Psychosomatic illness as
  contraindication to family
  therapy, 341
Psychotherapy, Austin's classification of, 88
Public welfare case, case illustration of, 72–76

Rank, Otto, 12, 426
  (*See also* Functionalism)
Rapaport, David, 31
Rapoport, Lydia, 427, 433
Rationalization as defense mech-
  anism, 36
Reaching out, sustainment and, 109

Reaction formation as defense mechanism, 36
Reality principle, 32
Reality testing, 33
Reassurance:
sustainment and, 107–108
(*See also* Sustainment)
Redefinition following crises, 428
Referral, 232
for marriage counseling, 414–415
at termination, 450
Reflection:
amount of, in client-worker communication, 191
in crisis intervention, 432–433
developmental, 97
dynamic, 288
extrareflection and, 125, 194–195, 288
pattern-dynamic (*see* Pattern-dynamic reflection)
person-situation (*see* Person-situation reflection)
Reflective discussion, with collaterals, 153–154
Reframing in marriage counseling, 411–412
Regression:
as defense mechanism, 37
prevention of, in crisis intervention, 432–433
Reid, William J., 17, 110, 145, 181, 192, 194, 436, 439
Reliability of coding client-worker communications, 182
Relinquishment following crises, 428
Repetitiveness:
of behavior, in diagnostic understanding, 255
of interaction patterns, in diagnostic understanding, 256
Repression as defense mechanism, 35
Research, 16–20
criticisms of quantitative model and, 19–20
on Hollis typology (*see* Hollis typology, study of)
intrusion on process by, 19
need for, 180, 485
single-case or single-subject design and, 18–19

Research (*Cont.*):
tension between researchers and caseworkers and, 20
weaknesses in, 17
Resistance:
disagreement with client's views as, 215
in family therapy, 360–362
forms of, 361–362
as manifestation of anxiety, 296
treatment objectives and, 276–278
Resolution of crises, 427–428
Resource(s):
developing knowledge of, 160–161
in environmental intervention, 154–166
non-social work agency where worker is not employed as, 161–162
non-social work organization employing worker as, 157–160
social agency where worker is not employed as, 160–161
worker's own social agency as, 154–157
type of, 98
in family therapy, single-parent families and, 365–366
understanding of, person-situation reflection and, 130
worker and (*see* Caseworker, roles of)
Reynolds, Bertha C., 13
Richmond, Mary, 11, 12, 13, 87, 230, 306–307
Ripple, Lilian, 217
Robins, Eli, 396
Robinson, Virginia P., 13
Rogers, Carl, 14, 196, 219
Role(s):
classification of environmental work by, 99
in family, 318–323, 349
cooperation and contention and, 319
irrational role assignment and, 319, 349, 386–387

Role(s): in family (*Cont.*):
myths and secrets and, 322–323
parentification and, 319
pseudomutuality and, 321–322
role flexibility and, 319
scapegoating and, 319–320, 349
triangles and, 320–321, 349
irrational assignment of, 319
of women:
in couples, 396–398
homosexual, 396
of worker (*see* caseworker, roles of)
Role flexibility in families, 319
Role reciprocity, dysfunctional, in families, 318–319
Role theory, 44–45

Saghir, Marcel T., 396
Sanville, Jean, 446
Satir, Virginia, 196, 213, 308, 323
Satisfaction with worker and treatment, termination and, 446
Scapegoating in families, 319–320, 349
Scherz, Frances, 308
Schizophrenia:
course of, 261–262
need for support and, 218
symptoms of, 261
School(s), social workers in, 158
School problems, locating, 234
Secondary process, 32–33
Secondary sustainment, 110
Secrets:
in families, 322–323
in marriage counseling, 416
Self-determination, 12, 13, 26–27
emphasis placed on by various theories, 486
Self-differentiation, assessment of, 312
Self-evaluation, person-situation reflection and, 130–131
Self-fulfilling prophecy, defenses and, 38
Self-image, corrective relationship and, 220, 221
Self-psychology, contributions of, 10
Self-realization, search for, 4

Self-understanding:
    anxiety aroused by, 297–298
    extrareflection and, 194–195
    person-situation reflection and,
        292–293
Separation, family therapy and, 329
Sexual dysfunction in marriages,
    383
Sexuality in premarital therapy,
    390
Sexuality problems in
    stepfamilies, 370
Shapiro, Barbara, 110
Sherman, Sanford N., 308, 340
Shyne, Ann W., 17, 145, 192
Sibling subsystem, 314
Simmons College School of So-
    cial Work, 12
Single-case studies, 18–19
Single-subject studies, 18–19
Siporin, Max, 19
Situation:
    diagnostic assessment of, 248
    in diagnostic understanding,
        250–251
    person-situation reflection and,
        124–127, 293
    (See also Current life situations,
        Person-situation configura-
        tion)
Situational intervention (see Envi-
    ronmental intervention)
Smith College School of Social
    Work, 12, 14
    coding of communications by
        student of, 181
    typology study at, 94
Social action advocacy, 170–171
Social agency:
    ability to meet client's needs, 249
    child welfare, 155–156
    classification of, 98
    client's attitude toward, 203
    influence on treatment objec-
        tives, 284
    non-social work:
        where worker is employed,
            as resource in environ-
            mental intervention,
            157–160
        where worker is not em-
            ployed, as resource in
            environmental interven-
            tion, 161–162

Social agency (Cont.):
    policies of, 155–157, 161
    pressure for change in, 158–159
    public welfare, 156
    relevance to duration of treat-
        ment, 437–438
    social action advocacy and,
        170–171
    where worker is not em-
        ployed, as resource in en-
        vironmental intervention,
        160–161
    worker's own, as resource in
        environmental interven-
        tion, 154–157
Social functioning:
    impact of small environmental
        changes on, 173
    personality and, 31
Social network, termination and,
    447
Social role, personality develop-
    ment and, 42
Social sciences, interactive as-
    pects of personality develop-
    ment and, 41–43
Social supports, termination and,
    447
Social work private practice, 488
Social workers:
    growth of family therapy and,
        308
    [See also Caseworker(s); Client-
        worker communications;
        Client-worker relationship;
        Couple-worker relation-
        ship]
Sociocultural factors:
    attitudes toward treatment re-
        lated to, 203
    brief treatment and, 439
    caseworker attitudes and, 42
    client-worker communication
        and, 211
    client-worker relationship and,
        235–236
    clinical diagnosis and, 266
    contributions of, 9–10
    cross-cultural relationships
        and, 392–393
    direct influence and, 111
    in marriage counseling, 422
    matching clients and workers
        on, lack of effect of, 490

Sociocultural factors (Cont.):
    motivation and, 275–276
    person-situation reflection and,
        293
    personality development and,
        42–43
    psychosocial approach and,
        487–488
    role expectations and, 45
    stereotypes and, 44
Sociology, interactive aspects of
    personality development
    and, 41–43
Speer, David C., 317
Spiegel, John P., 318
Spitz, René, 31
Splitting as defense mechanism,
    37
Spouse subsystem, 314
Stepfamilies in family therapy,
    366–370
    issues related to, 369–370
    treatment considerations with,
        368–369
Stereotypes:
    brief treatment and, 439
    as communication problem, 213
    as danger of using diagnostic
        categories, 265
    of male and female personality
        styles, 254
    racial, 44
Stress, 28
    on families, 308–310
    sources of, 308–309
    on worker, in family therapy,
        359–360
Sublimation as defense mecha-
    nism, 35
Substance abuse, fact gathering
    about, 241
Suggestion, 111–112
Sullivan, Harry Stack, 14
Superego, 39
    balance of forces and, 51–52
    modifying, 52–55
    in diagnostic understanding,
        252, 253
    pattern-dynamic reflection
        and, 138–139
Superego function, inadequate,
    as source of problems, 46–48
Support:
    anxiety reduction and, 300

Support (*Cont.*):
  familial, inadequate, family therapy and, 339
Support systems:
  crises and, 432
  in crisis intervention, 433
  in family therapy, single-parent families and, 365–366
  network therapy and, 164–166
  termination and, 447
Supportive methods:
  in Austin classification, 88
  in FSAA classification, 88, 89
  improvements in functioning and, 89–91
Suppression as defense mechanism, 35
Sustainment, 95–96, 105–110
  acceptance and, 106–107
  amount of, in client-worker communication, 192–195
  anxiety and, 105–106, 301
  with collaterals, 99, 152
  countersustainment and, 196–197
  direct influence and, 115, 218–219
  encouragement and, 108
  in family therapy, 350, 351
  indirect, 196–197
  nonverbal, 109
  reaching out and, 109
  reassurance and, 107–108
  relationship to ventilation, 117
  secondary, 110
Symptoms:
  in children, family therapy and, 362
  in diagnostic understanding, 249–250
  treatment of, 249–250
Synthetic-integrative functioning, 34
Systems theory, 28–30
  contributions of, 9
    to psychosocial approach, 8
  families and, 349
    family therapy and, 327
  organizational change and, 159

Taft, Jessie, 12
Task-centered treatment, 436
  development of, 14

Terminal illness, case illustration of psychosocial approach in, 461–468
Termination, 443–452
  assessment of client reactions to, 444–447
    client satisfaction and, 446
    conditions of endings and, 447
    current life circumstances and, 447
    experiences with loss and, 446–447
    intensity of relationship and, 444–446
    social supports and, 447
  encouraging, 452
  special features of, 443–444
  treatment process and, 448–451
    anticipatory preparation by worker and, 448
    client feedback and, 450–451
    eliciting and dealing with clients' feelings and, 448–449
    evaluation of progress and, 449
    opportunities for growth and, 449
    referral or transfer and, 450
    worker and, 451
  worker self-awareness and, 443–444, 451–452
Therapy:
  use of term, 6
  (*See also* Treatment; Treatment objectives; Treatment procedures)
Third-party reimbursement, licensure and, 5
Thought disorders, 261
Thought processes, 33–34
  person-situation reflection and, 292–293
Time, influence on treatment objectives, 284
Time-limited treatment, contribution to psychosocial approach, 7–8
Towle, Charlotte, 14
Trading of dissociations, family therapy and, 328–329
Transaction, 29
Transactional analysis, 14

Transfer at termination, 450
Transference, 208–209
  communication problems and, 210–211
  developmental understanding and, 144
  in family therapy, 343, 358–359
  handling, 209, 222
    psychosocial casework versus psychoanalysis and, 221–222
  in marriage counseling, 418–420
  nature of, diagnosis and, 221
  termination and, 445–446
  therapeutic use of, 221
Traux, Charles B., 218
Treatment:
  anxiety aroused by, 297–299
    preconscious material and, 298
    self-understanding and, 297–298
  assessment of requirements for, 249
  classifications of, 85–100
    by Austin, 88
    by Bibring, 87
    client-worker communications and, 95–97
    by Community Service Society of New York, 89
    developing typology and, 93–95
    by Family Service Association of America, 88–89
    by Hollis:
      early, 87–88
      (*See also* Hollis typology)
    person-in-situation or environmental interventions and, 97–100
    personality changes and, 89–93
    purpose of, 93
    representing growth, 87–89
  client's reaction to, person-situation reflection and, 131–133
  deciding on length of, 233
  direct, 11
  dynamics of, 94–95
    client-worker relationship in, 217–222

Treatment (*Cont.*):
in family therapy, single-parent
families and, 364–366
indirect, 11
internalized modifications resulting from, 55
in marriage counseling, 375–377
outcome of, client-worker relationship and, 201, 217–218
parsimony in, 125
of systems most accessible to
change, 49, 148, 258
termination and, 448–451
anticipatory preparation by
worker and, 448
client feedback and, 450–451
eliciting and dealing with
clients' feelings and,
448–449
evaluation of progress and,
449
opportunities for growth
and, 449
referral or transfer and, 450
worker self-awareness and,
450–451
transference in (*see* Transference)
uncovering of diagnosis in, 248
use of term, 6
Treatment objectives, 271–285
client's role in determining,
271
diagnostic understanding and,
271
intermediate, 278–283
clinical diagnosis and, 281–
283
presenting problem and, 279
systems considerations and,
279–281
intervening variables and, 283–
285
needs of other family members as, 283–284
peripheral factors as, 284–285
long-range, 272–274
emergence of additional
problems and, 273
scope of, 273
motivation and, 274–276
factors affecting, 274–275
values and, 275–276
resistance and, 276–278

Treatment planning:
mutuality in, 214–216
(*See also* Treatment objectives)
Treatment procedures:
choice of, 288–302
anxiety and guilt and, 296–
302
anxiety reduction and,
299–300
balancing anxiety and
movement and, 300–
302
observation of anxiety
and, 296
treatment process and,
297–299
worker style and, 300
environmental change and,
289
interpersonal relationships,
internal change, and
person-situation reflec-
tion and, 289–294
anxiety in early interviews
and, 290–291
diagnostic understanding
and, 293–294
personality factors and,
291–292
situational and ethnic factors and, 293
thought processes and
self-understanding
and, 292–293
pattern-dynamic and developmental reflection and,
294–296
motivation and, 294–295
widespread use of, 295–296
distribution of, 190–192
in family therapy, 350–351
with stepfamilies, 368–369
for fostering understanding of
others, 126–127
in marriage counseling, 409–
425
cautions regarding, 409–410
couple versus concurrent
individual sessions and,
416–417
couple-worker relationship
and, 418–423
extramarital relationships
and, 399

Treatment procedures: in marriage counseling (*Cont.*):
rapid assessment, brief treatment, and referral and,
413–416
steps in, 410–413
personality change and, 89–93
(*See also specific procedures*)
Triangles in families, 320–321, 349
Tripodi, Tony, 19
Turner, Francis J., 181, 196
Turner, Frank, 485

Ulrich, David N., 319
Undercontrol, 33
Underlining, 112
University of North Carolina
School of Social Work, 13
Unmarried couples living to-
gether, 390–392
"Urban matriarchal" family, 309
Urging, 112

Values:
of caseworker, 25–27
acceptance as, 25–26
concern for well-being of
individual as, 25
self-determination of client
as, 26–27
treatment objectives and,
276
of client, motivation and, 275–
276
Ventilation, 96
amount of, in client-worker
communication, 191–192
anxiety aroused by, 297
anxiety reduction by, 299–300
caution against, in marriage
counseling, 409
by collaterals, 99, 152
dangers of, 294
empathy and, 218–219
in family therapy, 351
modifying balance of forces
and, 53
prior to sustainment, 108
(*See also* Exploration-
description-ventilation)
Verdiani, Fil, 181
Vigilante, Florence Wexler, 29

Webb, Nancy Boyd, 445
Wegscheider, Sharon, 320
Weissman, Myrna M., 18
White, Robert W., 31
White, William A., 12
White House Conference on
    Child Welfare, 306
Women:
    aftermath of divorce and, 397–
        398

Women (*Cont.*):
    changing role of, 305
    in couples, 396–398
    in extramarital relationships, 398
    lesbian, 395–396
Woods, Mary E., 378
Worker [*see* Caseworker(s); Client-
        worker communications;
        Client-worker relationship;
        Couple-worker relationship]

Wynne, Lyman C., 321, 328, 329

Zimmer, Donna, case illustration
    of early deprivation and,
    76–83
Zimmerman, Shirley L., 306